Innovation and Sustainability in Digital Era

Pedro Fernandes da Anunciação
Cátia Susana Claro Chasqueira
Helder Miguel da Graça Alexandre (eds.)

Innovation and Sustainability in Digital Era

The Role of Economics and Business Strategies with Education Perspectives

PETER LANG
Berlin - Bruxelles - Chennai - Lausanne - New York - Oxford

Library of Congress Cataloging-in-Publication Data

Names: Anunciação, Pedro Fernandes, editor | Chasqueira, Cátia Susana Claro editor | Alexandre, Helder Miguel da Graça editor Title: Innovation and sustainability in digital era : the role of economics and business strategies with education perspectives / Pedro Fernandes da Anunciacao, Cátia Susana Claro Chasqueira, Helder Miguel da Graca Alexandre. Description: New York : Peter Lang, [2025] | Includes bibliographical references. | Summary: "Our book, Innovation and Sustainability in the Digital Era, comprises 39 chapters authored by 77 distinguished scholars and practitioners. It provides a comprehensive exploration of contemporary trends and innovations across the fields of economics, business, and education, offering valuable insights into the evolving dynamics of these disciplines in the digital age. Designed for researchers, students, and academics, this volume serves as a valuable resource for those seeking to deepen their understanding of current developments and challenges. With its diverse range of topics and interdisciplinary perspectives, we believe this book will be both intellectually stimulating and academically enriching for its readers"-- Provided by publisher. Identifiers: LCCN 2025015800 | ISBN 9783631935934 paperback | ISBN 9783631938454 ebk | ISBN 9783631938461 epub Subjects: LCSH: Economics | Management | Education Classification: LCC HB171.I55 2025 | DDC 330--dc23/eng/20250508 LC record available at https://lccn.loc.gov/2025015800

Bibliographic information published by the Deutsche Nationalbibliothek.
The German National Library lists this publication in the German National Bibliography; detailed bibliographic data is available on the Internet at http://dnb.d-nb.de.

ISBN 978-3-631-93593-4 (Print)
E-ISBN 978-3-631-93845-4 (E-PDF)
E-ISBN 978-3-631-93846-1 (EPUB)
DOI 10.3726/b22930

Published by Peter Lang GmbH, Berlin, Germany

info@peterlang.com - www.peterlang.com

This publication has been peer reviewed.

Foreword

Our book called "Innovation and Sustainability in Digital Era" consists of 39 chapters 77 authors have contributed to our book. This book contains trends and innovations in the field of economy and business. The target audience of this book is researchers, students and academics interested in business and economics. We think that it is a book in which you can find various topics and read with pleasure.

Table of Contents

List of Figures and Graphs

CHAPTER 26

CHAPTER 27

CHAPTER 30

CHAPTER 31

List of Tables

Transparency in Finances and their Control in Public Administration - Participatory Democracy and Its Effects on Educational Systems

Lothar Huschbeck, Torsten Huschbeck, Kerstin Knees

1. Introduction

Transparency in the financial sector is the accountability of political actors to their supervisory bodies. This is associated with fiscal information that should be available. According to an ideal model, the public administration would make information about allocated financial resources freely available to its citizens (Androniceanu, 2021). This would strengthen the sense of responsibility of government officials and, at the same time, make it easier for citizens to understand state action (Manaf & Harvey, 2022). Fiscal information on the budget is essential for third parties to understand the decision-making processes for financial expenditure. The budget in the public sector comprises the two dimensions of "budget" and "participation." The latter is also an essential element in the stabilisation of democracy, which is of particular importance against the background of increasing populism and authoritarian systems (Merkel & Lührmann, 2021). Based on the authors' interests, this article analyses the role of participatory democracy in shaping education systems. It emphasises its potential to promote civic engagement and the democratic values of citizens. This study focuses specifically on how such participatory mechanisms impact the education sector and provides an in-depth analysis through a systematic literature review. The study evaluates how participatory democracy contributes to educational outcomes, focusing on how it can enhance students' democratic skills and promote civic education.

2. Current state of dealt problems

While transparency is directly connected to increased democratisation and accountability of economic performance, different conceptualisations of transparency in the public sector could be distinguished (Erkkilä, 2020).

Definitions of transparency could be either normative or observational (Grimmelikhuijsen et al., 2017). Generally, transparency refers to the open provision of information to specific stakeholders. Grimmelikhuijsen et al. define transparency by these conditions as "the extent to which a public organisation permits external actors to monitor and assess its internal workings and performance". Enhancing transparency in the public sector is contingent upon implementing open government and open administration. Information and communication technologies, including Web 2.0 services, social media, and open data, offer numerous avenues for enhancing the transparency and accountability of public policies and administration (Gunawong, 2014). Digital approaches can also facilitate greater citizen involvement in opinion formation and decision-making processes and enable broader participation by civil society (Bass, 2010). Consequently, a more significant proportion of the population can be better informed about and engaged in government and public administration activities. Establishing new forms of transparency-based exchange between government and external actors facilitates closer cooperation. Information asymmetries will be reduced, and administrative action will be more efficient (Gupta & Mason, 2014). Furthermore, open government and administrative practices can improve data sets by raising awareness of the importance of high data quality in the public sector. The relevance of open government is underpinned by a diverse portfolio of issues and methods (Gil-Garcia et al., 2020). The probability of acceptance of political decisions is enhanced when a broad public is engaged in forming opinions, deliberations, and decision-making processes within the government. Furthermore, networking and feedback can facilitate improved dialogue between politics, administration, and civil society (Nissen, 2021). The reciprocal appreciation of all parties involved has the potential to engage civil society stakeholders. The implementation of open participation processes and interaction may facilitate the identification of solutions to social problems. In this manner, novel insights are unearthed and rendered more readily accessible to policymakers. Governments, businesses, and citizens can reuse and reengineer existing, freely available administrative data sets (Boje, 2021). This creates new business opportunities for growth and employment and new forms of collaboration among policymakers, government, civil society, and industry. These offer new funding opportunities, ways of doing business, and ways to save money. Open accountability helps control cash flows and prevent misused and wasted funds, thereby increasing the sense of responsibility of decision-makers (Boje, 2021). Information on measures, their current implementation status, and successes and failures can be obtained through open monitoring of government and administrative actions (Ingrams et al., 2020). A distinctive form of transparency is financial transparency in public administration, exemplified by the Participatory Budgeting [PB] approach. Developed in several Brazilian municipalities in the 1990s, PB has since been adopted in other countries worldwide (Brun-Martos & Lapsley, 2020). Initially, the primary objectives of the first PB programs were to combat corruption, reduce social injustice, and involve citizens in the political process. As transparency in public administration gained traction, a range of concepts with varying objectives and process designs emerged globally (Brun-Martos & Lapsley, 2020). One specific model that facilitates the transformation above by incorporating civic stakeholders into the political process is participatory democracy [PD]. The PD delineates a governance system wherein citizens can engage actively in decision-making processes instead of merely casting votes for representatives (Wampler & McNulty, 2011). It has been argued that the representative system does not meet the needs of citizens. In contrast, the PD emphasises direct participation from individuals in political decision-making, policy formation, and problem-solving at various levels of society (Wampler & McNulty, 2011). This can occur through public consultations, referendums, citizen assemblies, or community-driven initiatives. These mechanisms aim to increase civic engagement and ensure that decisions reflect the people's will more closely. Some models, such as the PD, empower citizens by devolving decision-making authority (Rogers, 2008). The advent of participatory elements in politics, notably in Brazil, is associated with the "participatory turn" (Bherer et al., 2016). This participatory turn constrains the diverse range of participatory practices developed by many organisations and groups across various sectors, including the educational system (Bherer et al., 2016).

The theoretical approach to the link between PD and education is provided by communicative action and the public sphere. Education is critical in fostering the skills necessary for effective participation in this democratic process (Vitale, 2006). This theory forms the link between democracy and participation, formed by the constitutional state, establishing the rights system as an institutionalised framework. The legitimacy of this system of law is contingent upon its genesis from a comprehensive and inclusive process of PD (Baxter, 2002). The constitutional state arises from and is constrained by the "communicative power" forged through citizens' public political discourse (Baxter, 2002). The fundamental assumption is that communicative action in a rational discourse enables citizens to reach mutual understanding and agreement. In summary, democratic legitimacy arises when decisions result from inclusive and reasoned public deliberation. This approach forms the basis of deliberative democracy, which shares much with PD. In this model, citizens engage in rational-critical debates in the public sphere (Olson, 2014). Conversely, in a participatory democracy, citizens must be well-informed and critical thinkers capable of deliberating (Vitale, 2006). Education facilitates the development of these skills by promoting critical thinking, civic engagement, and the capacity to engage in reasoned debate (Deakin Crick & Joldersma, 2006).

3. Methods

Since the introduction of PB in Porto Alegre, Brazil, a substantial body of academic literature has emerged examining its versatility. These studies employed disparate research methodologies and techniques. The scientific literature focuses on particular geographical regions, examines specific aspects, and is based on different scientific disciplines. Moreover, there is no consensus within the literature or among the authors regarding the criteria and characteristics that define PB. This is evidenced by diverse approaches to analysing and classifying citizen participation in the budget process. This study employs a systematic literature analysis on PD in education as its research design. The objective is to present a comprehensive overview of the current research on PD in municipal contexts. On the one hand, the findings of scientific studies on PD will be recorded. On the other hand, the literature review will identify research gaps, highlighting areas where knowledge about PD is lacking. The systematic literature review was conducted using Fink's review process. Fink describes a literature review as "[...] a systematic, explicit, and reproducible method for identifying, evaluating, and synthesising the existing body of completed and recorded work produced by researchers, scholars, and practitioners" (Fink, 2014). By this definition, the systematic and repeatable approach constitutes the fundamental criterion of a systematic literature review. It is a process that can be subdivided into six phases:

1. Formulating the research question
2. Selection of the database
3. Choice of search terms
4. Defining inclusion and exclusion criteria
5. Conducting the review
6. Presentation of the results

The literature selection is systematically structured by conducting a literature review per Fink's proposed method. This approach ensures that the existing research is represented thoroughly and unbiasedly. Fink's method underscores the significance of explicitly delineating the research questions or objectives, which subsequently inform the formulation of meticulous inclusion and exclusion criteria. Such criteria should encompass considerations such as the study's relevance to the research topic, the methodology's quality, the publication date, and whether the work has undergone peer review (Fink, 2014).

The process commences with a comprehensive search of academic databases, journals, and other scholarly resources utilising specific keywords and search terms to capture all pertinent studies. Fink's method emphasises the importance of documenting and justifying the search strategy, including the databases used and the rationale for choosing specific search terms, to enhance the review's reproducibility and transparency (Fink, 2014). Once potential studies have been identified, a rigorous evaluation of each source is undertaken, assessing methodological quality, theoretical frameworks, and the robustness of findings. This guarantees that only studies of the highest quality and relevance are included in the final review. Furthermore, Fink suggests cross-referencing the selected literature with other significant works to guarantee a comprehensive and balanced field representation (Fink, 2014). By following these steps, Fink's literature review method aims to minimise bias and enhance the validity and reliability of the review findings, providing a solid foundation for drawing meaningful conclusions from the existing body of research. The inclusion and exclusion criteria for the publications to be included in the literature review are defined by several factors. Firstly, the publications are selected based on the medium in which they were published and the language in which they were written. Secondly, the publications included in the literature review are selected based on their content. The working definition of PD is derived from the PD literature. The review includes both empirical-quantitative and empirical-qualitative studies. The review of existing literature also significantly contributes to identifying research gaps by providing an overview of the field of PD. In addition to the categorisation above of the inclusion criteria, a restriction based on publication date is applied. Only publications published between 2009 and 2024 are included in the literature review. The topic of education imposes another limitation. Only studies that include a relationship between PD and the effects of the education system are considered. The search was conducted using the pre-defined search terms and specified databases, combining the terms "PD*" and "education*" using the operator AND. The 'exact terms' were searched using each database's 'full text' search option (except Web of Science and Emerald Insight, which do not offer this search option). The two search terms were, therefore, placed in quotation marks. In addition, the search procedure was adapted to the databases' respective search options. Web of Science, Ebsco Host, SpringerLink, Emerald Insight, and Wiley Online Library are the databases used. The search terms are derived from the central research question and the underlying topic (Fink, 2014). According to these limitations, the inclusion and exclusion criteria of the database search are defined as follows (Table 1):

Table 1: Inclusion and exclusion criteria of the literature review

Inclusion criteria	**Type**
The article deals with participatory budgeting and its effect on the education system.	Content
The process examined and discussed in the publication corresponds to the criteria of the working definition of participatory budgeting.	Content, definition
Publication period 2009 to 2024	Publication date
"Peer-reviewed" articles in scientific journals and books	Publication medium
Empirical-qualitative, empirical-quantitative, conceptual/theoretical and review article	Research design
English and German	Publication language
Web of Science, Ebsco Host, Springerlink, Emerald Insight and Wiley Online Library	Database
Exclusion criteria	**Type**
Introductions, book reviews, working papers, commentary, conclusions, book series	Publication medium

4. Results

The results of the systematic database search could be distinguished according to the topic they were involved in. The distinguishing of the results was linked to four topics:

1. Teaching students to use democratic elements
2. Democratic Education
3. PD as an essential element to stabilise democracy
4. Student participation.

Most of the included studies relate to PD as a form of democratic education integrated into the school curriculum. The findings of the evaluated studies can be summarised as follows.

4.1 Teaching students to use democratic elements

Chanicka et al. analyse the potential for an inclusive approach to transform the Canadian educational system into a vehicle for fostering PD and responsible citizenship (2018). The article emphasises the importance of student engagement, critical thinking, and social justice in education. The authors argue for establishing a collaborative learning environment in which teachers and students engage in the co-construction of knowledge and in which traditional power dynamics within the classroom are challenged. Furthermore, the necessity of restructuring the curriculum to include inquiry-based learning that promotes social justice and critical literacy is discussed (Chanicka et al., 2018). This approach provides students with the tools to address real-world issues and develop global competencies. The article presents examples from Aldergrove Public School, where students engage with guiding questions around identity, culture, and social justice, fostering a deeper connection to their learning and encouraging social activism. Regarding the PD, the authors emphasise the significance of collaborations between students, faculty, and the community to establish an inclusive educational setting. The PD model fosters student autonomy and empowerment, with students actively engaged in decision-making. The comprehensive vision presented in the article postulates that education should serve as a means of liberation, equipping students with the competencies necessary to shape a more equitable and democratic society (Chanicka et al., 2018).

Jormfeldt analyses the relationship between Swedish upper secondary students' experiences of democracy in school and their future roles as democratic citizens (2023). The study compares the experiences of male and female students about school democracy and their intentions to vote. The principal findings are as follows: ambition is the most significant predictor of democratic attitudes and future civic engagement. Female students tend to demonstrate greater ambition in their schoolwork than males. However, there is no notable direct correlation between experiences of school democracy and future voting intentions. School democracy experiences influence students' views of democracy. It can be concluded that the results demonstrate a negative impact of experience on students' perceptions of democracy, which challenges the theory of PD (Jormfeldt, 2023).

4.2 Democratic Education

Sant analyses the theoretical review of how democratic education is conceptualised within educational scholarship (2019). The study discursively analyses 377 articles from peer-reviewed journals published between 2006 and 2017, identifying both supportive and critical views on democratic education. Six discourses in favour (liberal, deliberative, multiculturalist, participatory, critical, and agonistic) and two against (elitist and neoliberal) construct the meaning of democratic education. These discourses respond to differing assumptions about democracy and the relationship between education and politics. The review critiques elitist and neoliberal policies and promotes PD-making in education, highlighting the need for diverse pedagogies across the discourses (Sant, 2019).

Striano outlined the importance of "educating for democracy" increases for expanding post-democratic systems (2016). This focus on democratic education represents an emerging narrative that aligns with the concept of "democratic education" that evolved in the 20th century and is represented by several EU and UN projects. The ongoing debate surrounding these concepts is situated within a complex socio-political and economic landscape and an ongoing cultural discourse surrounding the meaning and value of democracy, particularly during periods of anxiety, disaffection, and distress. In this context, learning democratic skills about the PD has assumed a heightened relevance (Striano, 2016).

Lupien explores how PD mechanisms in Latin America - particularly in Venezuela, Ecuador, and Chile - affect women's learning and engagement in political life (2022). The research highlights that through participatory processes, women gain significant skills, such as public speaking and project planning. This contributes to their increased political efficacy and confidence in public participation. Despite these gains, the study identifies issues. Participatory mechanisms often overlook women's specific concerns, such as gender inequality, domestic violence, and wage disparities. The design of these mechanisms tends to assume a universal citizen, which limits the expression of gender-specific needs (Lupien, 2022).

Kurz and Zenke discuss the emergence and significance of laboratory schools for PD and education within the European educational landscape, particularly in the Erasmus+ project and LabSchoolsEurope (2023). Their chapter outlines four fundamental research principles that guide laboratory schools: Transdisciplinarity, Collaboration, Experimentation, and Transformativity. The participating laboratory schools prioritise democratic education, which fosters "compassionate citizenship" and encourages students to engage in community decision-making processes actively. This approach is vital in addressing the rise of anti-democratic movements and the challenges posed by individualistic learning trends and digitalisation. Overall, the chapter emphasises the potential of laboratory schools to bridge theory and practice, enhance democratic education, and respond to contemporary educational challenges through participatory research (Kurz & Zenke, 2023).

Pinnington and Schugurensky discuss the historical context and emerging empirical evidence regarding the educational impact of democracy and outline the relevance of PD in modern times (2010). Although influential thinkers like Aristotle, Rousseau, and J.S. Mills have acknowledged the educational benefits of participation, empirical research in this area still needs to be expanded. Research conducted in various locations, including Porto Alegre and Toronto, supports these findings, showing that participation leads to significant learning and changes in knowledge, skills, values, and attitudes. The overarching conclusion is that engaging in PD is an effective way for citizens to learn about democracy, enhancing their civic virtues and social capital. Moreover, participatory democracy fosters better governance and is a vital educational space for developing the competencies and values necessary for active citizenship. Practices such as participatory budgeting and workers' cooperatives often act as entry points into political life, promoting a more inclusive and horizontal political culture (Pinnington & Schugurensky, 2010).

4.3 Important elements to stabilise democracy

Leiviskä discusses the link between education and PD. The deliberative model is 'normal' and involves certain 'entry conditions' for democratic participation (2020). This introduces the idea of democracy as 'disruption' and the associated subjectification conception of education. Leiviskä contradicts the critique of deliberative democracy by demonstrating that deliberation's 'entry conditions' are linked to an essential normative function (Leiviskä, 2020). In conclusion, Leiviskä underlines the relevance of the link between democracy and education by arguing that the entry conditions are necessary for PD.

4.4 Student participation

García-Pérez and González-Lamas concluded that student participation is a significant topic in global educational discussions, though definitions and practical implications vary widely (2023). The authors analyse how educational policies in Western countries have understood student participation, focusing on the liberal model's influence on school democracy. The authors argue that this model is facing a crisis due to limitations in democratic processes within schools and the neoliberal emphasis on standardisation and individual achievement over democratic goals (García-Pérez & González-Lamas, 2023).

5. Discussion

The relationship between education and PD is increasingly relevant in contemporary scholarly discourse, particularly as global challenges necessitate a more engaged and informed citizenry. The reviewed articles illuminate how educational systems can be transformed into platforms that foster PD and responsible citizenship. The integration of participatory elements in school and the relevance of education for PD, with students as citizens in the future, are relevant. In summary, the educational system is relevant for schooling students in democratic skills linked to participation in democracy. The coexistence of diverse discourses, including liberal, deliberative, and critical, underscores the intricacy of implementing democratic education in disparate political and cultural settings. Democratic education and elitist and neoliberal critiques encompass these multiple discourses. These critiques posit that conventional educational policies are frequently inadequate for genuinely fostering democratic engagement, necessitating an investigation of diverse pedagogical approaches that can facilitate participatory practices (Sant, 2019). However, the relevance of empowering marginalised groups could highlight the significant role of PD (Lupien, 2022). By addressing structural inequalities, educational frameworks can ensure that all voices are heard and valued in democratic discourse. The current crisis of the liberal model has brought into sharp focus the importance of participatory skills in the education system. The findings indicate that the liberal model of democracy, which has historically influenced educational policies, is currently facing significant challenges (García-Pérez & González-Lamas, 2023). This crisis can be attributed to the inherent limitations of democratic processes within schools and the increasing dominance of neoliberal agendas prioritising standardisation and individual success over collective democratic goals. This perspective calls for a reassessment of how student participation is conceptualized and implemented within educational settings, advocating for policies that promote democratic engagement. Teaching students with democratic elements is linked with the construction of knowledge, where students actively participate in decision-making processes. This collaborative learning environment empowers students and promotes social justice, aligning with the broader objectives of participatory democracy (Chanicka et al., 2018). The case study by Chanicka et al. illustrates how students engage with critical issues such as identity and culture, enhancing their connection to democratic processes and encouraging social activism. Laboratory Schools are a model for teaching students relevant participatory skills. With that function, laboratory schools could be defined as vital spaces for participatory research and democratic education. These schools exemplify the principles of transdisciplinarity, collaboration, experimentation, and transformation, serving as experimental platforms for cultivating "compassionate citizenship" (Kurz & Zenke, 2023). By encouraging students to actively engage in their learning and decision-making processes, laboratory schools can address the rise of anti-democratic movements and adapt to contemporary educational challenges.

6. Conclusion

A notable limitation of the literature review method is the possibility of selection bias, whereby the researcher may unintentionally privilege studies that corroborate a specific hypothesis while overlooking those with contradictory or discrepant findings. This bias can compromise the comprehensiveness and objectivity of the review, leading to skewed conclusions. Furthermore, the effectiveness of the literature review is constrained by the quality, scope, and availability of existing research, which makes it challenging to draw meaningful insights on emerging topics or underexplored areas with limited published literature. In conclusion, the comprehensive study has demonstrated the multifaceted models and functions of participatory democracy in educational systems. The articles collectively argue for educational reforms that emphasise the importance of participatory democracy as a fundamental component of democratic education. Educational systems can equip learners with the requisite skills and values for active citizenship by fostering environments prioritising student engagement, critical thinking, and inclusivity. This transformative approach enhances the educational experience and contributes to developing a more equitable and participatory democratic society. While challenges remain concerning structural inequalities and the neoliberal agenda, there are promising pathways for integrating PD into educational practices. The ongoing evolution of educational policies will play a crucial role in shaping the future of democratic citizenship.

References

Androniceanu, A. (2021). Transparency in public administration as a challenge for a good democratic governance. *Administratie si Management Public* (36), 149–164. https://doi.org/10.24818/amp/2021.36-09

Bass, G.D., & Moulton, S. (2010). Bringing the Web 2.0 Revolution to the Government. In D. Lathrop & L. Ruma (Eds.), *Open Government* (S. 289-305). USA: O'Reilly Media, Inc. ISBN 9781449388805.

Baxter, H. (2002). Habermas's Discourse Theory of Law and Democracy. *Buffalo Law Review* (50), 205-340.

Bherer, L., Dufour, P., & Montambeault, F. (2016). The participatory democracy turn: an introduction. *Journal of Civil Societz, 12*(3), 225–230. https://doi.org/10.1080/1744868 9.2016.1216383

Boje, T. P. (2021). *Civility and Participatory Democracy The Importance of Civil Society and Active Citizenship*. UK: Edward Elgar Publishing. ISBN 9781789907773.

Brun-Martos, M. I., & Lapsley, I. (2020). Democracy, governmentality and transparency: participatory budgeting in action. In M.F. Sicilia & I. Steccolini, (Eds.), *Public Budgeting in Search for an Identity* (S. 102-118). UK: Routledge. ISBN 9781000329513.

Chanicka, J., Mahari de Silva, R., & Merkley, K. (2018). An inclusive design vision for Canada – schooling as a process for participatory democracy and responsible citizenship. *Intercultural Education 29*(5-6), 632–646. https://doi.org/10.1080/14675986.201 8.1508620

Deakin Crick, R.; & Joldersma, C. W. (2006). Habermas, lifelong learning and citizenship education. *Studies in Philosophy and Education 26*(2), 77–95. https://doi.org/10.1007/s 11217-006-9015-1

Erkkilä, T. (2020). Transparency in Public Administration. *Oxford Research Encyclopedia of Politics*. https://doi.org/10.1093/acrefore/9780190228637.013.1404

Fink, A. (2014). *Conducting research literature reviews: from the Internet to paper.* Los Angeles: Sage.

García-Pérez, D., & González-Lamas, J. (2023). Student participation: between the twilight of the liberal model of democracy and the rise of neoliberal policies. *Pedagogy, Culture & Society*, 1–21. https://doi.org/10.1080/14681 366.2023.2243318

Gil-Garcia, J. R., Gasco-Hernandez, M., & Pardo, T. A. (2020). Beyond Transparency, Participation, and Collaboration? A Reflection on the Dimensions of Open Government. *Public Performance & Management Review 43*(3), 483–502. https://doi.org/10.1 080/15309576.2020.1734726

Grimmelikhuijsen, S.G., Weske, U., Bouwman, R., & Tummers, L. (2017). Public Sector Transparency. In O. James, S. Jilke, & G. Van Ryzin (Eds.), *Experiments in Public Management Research. Challenges and Contributions* (S. 291-312). USA: Cambridge University Press.

Gunawong, P. (2014). Open Government and Social Media. *Social Science Computer Review 33*(5), 587–598. https://doi.org/10.1177/0894439314560685

Gupta, A., & Mason, M. A. (2014). Transparency Turn in Global Environmental Governance. In A. Gupta & M. Mason (Eds.), *Transparency in Global Environmental Governance: Critical Perspectives* (S. 3-38). USA: MIT Press.

Ingrams, A., Piotrowski, S., & Berliner, D. (2020). Learning from Our Mistakes: Public Management Reform and the Hope of Open Government. *Perspectives on Public Management and Governance* 3(4), 257–272. https://doi.org/10.1093/ppmgov/gvaa001

Jormfeldt, J. (2023). Experiences of school democracy connected to the role of the democratic citizen in the future: A comparison of Swedish male and female upper secondary school students. *JSSE - Journal of Social Science Education 22*(3), 2-25. https://doi.org/ 10.11576/jsse-5530

Kurz, B., & Zenke, Ch. T. (2023). *LabSchoolsEurope. Participatory research for democratic education*. Julius Klinkhardt.

Leiviskä, A. (2020). Disruptive or deliberative democracy? A review of Biesta's critique of deliberative models of democracy and democratic education. *Ethics and Education, 15*(4), 499–515. https://doi.org/10.1080/17449642.2020.1822611

Lupien, P. (2022). Participatory Democracy, Democratic Education, and Women. *Journal of Latin American Studies* 2022, *54*(4), 617–645. https://doi.org/10.1017/s0022216x22000 517

Manaf, H. A., Mohamed, A. M., & Harvey, W. S. (2022). Citizen Perceptions and Public Servant Accountability of Local Government Service Delivery in Malaysia. *International Journal of Public Administration, 46*(12), 1–10. https://doi.org/10.1080/0190069 2.2022.2025829

Merkel, W., & Lührmann, A. (2021). Resilience of democracies: responses to illiberal and authoritarian challenges. *Democratization, 28*(5), 869–884. https://doi.org/10.1080/135 10347.2021.1928081

Nissen, S. (2021). Political Participation: Inclusion of Citizens in Democratic Opinion-Forming and Decision-Making Processes. In W.L. Filho, A.M. Azul, L. Brandli, A. Lange Salvia, P. Gökçin Özuyar, & T. Wall (Eds.), *Encyclopedia of the UN Sustainable Development Goals* (S. 665-675). Springer. https://doi.org/10.1007/978-3-319-95960-3

Olson, K. (2014). Deliberative democracy. In B. Fultner (Eds.), *Jurgen Habermas Key Concepts* (S. 140-155). Routledge.

Pinnington, E., & Schugurensky, D. (2010). *Learning Citizenship by Practicing Democracy*. UK: Cambridge Scholars Publishing.

Rogers, K. (2008). *Participatory Democracy*. London: Palgrave Macmillan.

Sant, E. (2019). Democratic Education: A Theoretical Review (2006–2017). *Review of Educational Research* 2019, *89*(5), 655–696. https://doi. org/10.3102/0034654319862493

Striano, M. (2016). The challenge of democratic education for educational research. An overview. *Civitas educationis. Education, Politics, and Culture* 5(2), 29–45. https://doi. org/9788857542270

Vitale, D. (2006). Between deliberative and participatory democracy. *Philosophy & Social Criticism* 32(6), 739–766. https://doi.org/10.1177/0191453706064022

Wampler, B., & McNulty, S. L. (2011). *Does participatory governance matter?: exploring the nature and impact of participatory reforms*. Washington, D.C.: Woodrow Wilson International Center for Scholars.

Emotional Intelligence in the Intergenerational Entrepreneurship in Latvia

Yuliia Fedorova, Maija Zakrizevska-Belogrudova, Anna Pilková, Juraj Mikuš

1. Introduction

A brief review of entrepreneurial activity over the first 25 years of GEM (GEM, 2023b) suggests that the levels have increased overall, and that entrepreneurship has been consistently resilient during and after global crises. Entrepreneurship continues to be a powerful engine of economic growth and social well-being for many countries.

Intergenerational collaboration is an essential driver in sustainable entrepreneurship. Positive synergies in an intergenerational team can be achieved by understanding and effectively utilising the potential of each generation (Econ, 2021; Perez-Encinas et al., 2021). Ensuring mutual understanding between representatives of different generations and building effective communication in professional activities contributes to sustainable entrepreneurship and corresponds to the Sustainable Development Goals for 2015–2030 (United Nations, 2015).

EI is a critical soft skill that enhances mutual understanding and facilitates effectively bringing together diverse individuals to solve a common problem (Farelo & Gómez, 2021). EI in entrepreneurship increases team member engagement, facilitates the open exchange of entrepreneurial ideas and solutions, increases loyalty, and fosters trustworthy and credible relationships.

Promoting entrepreneurship is a central perspective for Latvia, as it is for many other European countries, especially given the negative effects on the economy due to the pandemic (GEM, 2023a). Intergenerational entrepreneurship is a driving factor in creating jobs and improving the quality of work and life of the Latvian people, too.

The rest of the research is structured as follows. Firstly, a literature review reflecting a) the current state and future directions of entrepreneurship research in Latvia and b) future directions of using EI in intergenerational entrepreneurship. Secondly, the methodological approach used to assess respondents and construct group profiles of EI is described. Thirdly, based on the survey results, generational profiles of EI are constructed, and recommendations for strengthening intergenerational collaboration in entrepreneurship in Latvia are developed. The chapter ends with a Conclusion of this paper's results and theoretical and practical contributions.

2. Literature review

2.1 Perspective of entrepreneurship development in Latvia

"In 2022, Latvia had 10 of its 13 Entrepreneurial Framework Conditions (EFCs) scored as at least sufficient, but by 2023 this had fallen to seven" (GEM, 2023b, p.149). Latvia's National Entrepreneurial Context Index (NECI, a score that shows the level of favourable conditions for business creation in the country, it summarizes 13 national EFCs, is extremely unstable (2019 - 4,9%, 2022 - 4,6%, 2021 - 5,0%, 2022 - 5,3%, 2023 - 5,0%). According to NECI, Latvia ranked 20th of the GEM economies in 2019 and 13th in 2023 (GEM, 2023b, p.149).

According to the GEM report (GEM, 2023b), more than 50 % of Latvian respondents aged 18–64 answered positively to the question "I have the knowledge, skills and experience to start my own business". However, less than 20 % plan to start a business in the next three years. Among men, the fear of failure in entrepreneurship is 10 % higher than among women. However, as in most countries, there are almost twice as many men as women among owners of established businesses (EBOs).

Generally, younger individuals are more likely to initiate new business ventures than older age groups. Over the past years, 37 of the 49 countries in the GEM APS have seen the overall Total Early-stage Entrepreneurial Activity rate (TEA) in the 18-34 age group exceed that in the 35-64 age group (GEM, 2023b). However, according to the GEM report, "there are seven economies in which younger people are more than twice as likely than older people to be starting new businesses (Romania, Lithuania, Slovakia, Latvia, Poland, Germany, and Canada). In these countries, people over 35 may be a hidden reservoir of entrepreneurial potential, and support activities aimed at them might boost the overall TEA rate". (GEM, 2023b, p.69)

In 2023, Latvia ranked seventh for social support for women's entrepreneurship (Lithuania 4th, Estonia 9th) and 39th, respectively, for relative access to resources (Lithuania 36th, Estonia 45th) (GEM, 2023b, p.125). The report noted that it is an "interesting phenomenon worthy of further research, given that for the majority of other economies, access to resources scored much higher than social support" (GEM, 2023b, p.149).

Therefore, utilising the potential of the older generation is an important and promising way to increase the level of entrepreneurship in Latvia. Research should also include gender differences, contributing to a more detailed study of how to involve more women in entrepreneurship.

2.2. Prospects for the development of intergenerational collaboration in entrepreneurship through EI

There are four generations (Baby Boomers (1947-1964), Generation X (1965-1980), Generation Y (1981-1995) and Generation Z (1996-Present) (Oblinger & Oblinger, 2005)) present in the Latvian labour market today. Each generation has different visions, attitudes, skills, and experiences. These differences in generational diversity can be beneficial in joint activities (Dietz & Fasbender, 2022; Yadav & Lenka, 2020; Rožman et al., 2020). EI creates additional potential for collaboration in intergenerational teams.

Generation Z is innovative yet flexible enough to tolerate different genders, races and religions. They multitask and are more focused on social media (Cho et al., 2018), often leading to a lack of social skills (Evrensel-İnanç et al., 2022). Baby boomers and Generation X are more likely to develop and maintain social relationships as a matter of habit and have higher levels of organisational commitment in the workplace.

Age diversity in collaborations can promote cohesion and benefit all participants. For example, the experience of older generations allows younger people to save energy and time. On the other hand, young people's motivation, openness, and tolerance increase the engagement of older generations (Bakker et al., 2014). Thus, an increased intergenerational collaboration enhances the socialisation of younger generations (Evrensel-İnanç et al., 2022) and prevents emotional burnout of older generations (Uzunbacak et al., 2022).

Older generations have more experience understanding market opportunities, more professional knowledge, and more reliable social contacts. However, they are also more aware of their own limitations and more sensitive to risk (GEM, 2023a).

Generally, young people have more desire and energy to organise entrepreneurship and can easily take responsibility, especially when they feel supported by more experienced adult mentors. Contrary, youth have fewer of the abovementioned resources of older generations. Still, they have more enthusiasm and faith in their abilities (members of Generation Z even tend to overestimate their capabilities (Evrensel-İnanç et al., 2022)). They are less sensitive to risk, as they do not yet have the obligation to support a family and pay the mortgage (GEM, 2023a). In addition, young people have better digital knowledge and can easily learn new technologies, including quickly applying the possibilities of artificial intelligence. These digital skills significantly increase competitiveness and chances of success if the right strategy is chosen under the guidance of senior mentors.

On intergenerational cooperation empathy (Ingram & Zou, 2008; Lee et al., 2018; Fasbender et al., 2020), self-determination, self-modelling, intergenerational reflection, and resilience (Nurhas et al., 2022; Labanauskaitė et al., 2021; Lojda et al., 2020; Perez-Encinas et al., 2021) help increase mutual understanding. EI has emerged as a crucial factor in understanding and navigating the complex web of human relationships, particularly in the context of intergenerational dynamics. The ability to perceive, understand, and manage emotions in oneself and others plays a pivotal role in fostering meaningful connections and facilitating effective communication across generations (Salovey & Mayer, 1990; Mayer et al., 2000). EI also serves as a bridge between generations, enabling individuals to empathise with and understand the experiences of those in different life stages. By fostering this ability, individuals can navigate the challenges and nuances of intergenerational relationships more effectively, leading to deeper connections, improved communication, and greater understanding and appreciation (Sneed & Chan, 2023). EI in entrepreneurship promotes a better understanding and utilisation of the differences in generational and cultural perspectives of the participants in collaboration. The EI assessment results in Ukraine and Slovakia revealed higher overall Self-Awareness, Self-Management and Relationship Management scores among Baby Boomers, presumably due to their professional experience. While older generation members show high levels of Self-Management, Generation Z showed high levels of empathy. Generation Z has an exceptionally high level of empathy in Slovakia, where they started to pay attention to developing social skills earlier than in Ukraine (Fedorova et al., 2024). Investigating EI profile characteristics allows us to form recommendations for team building in intergenerational entrepreneurship (Mikuš et al., 2023).

Numerous studies have highlighted the far-reaching benefits of EI in various domains, from academic and professional success to the quality of personal relationships (Ulutaş et al., 2021; Salovey & Mayer, 1990; Mayer et al., 2000; Harris et al., 2022). As individuals develop a greater awareness and understanding of their emotions and those of others, they are better equipped to resolve conflicts, engage in constructive dialogue, and forge lasting, meaningful connections across generations.

EI is increasingly recognised as critical in understanding and navigating intergenerational relationships. EI plays a vital role in enhancing social-emotional development by fostering meaningful connections and facilitating effective communication across generations, particularly in early childhood settings. Cultivating EI during formative years can profoundly impact individuals' ability to empathise and understand others, bridging gaps between diverse age groups. The research underscores the benefits of EI across various domains (Salovey & Mayer, 1990; Mayer et al., 2000; Ulutaş et al., 2021; Harris et al., 2022).

Typically, EI is defined as the capacity to recognise our emotions and those of others, motivate ourselves, and manage emotions in ourselves and others (Goleman, 1995). It is also characterised as the ability to sense emotions and use that awareness to enhance cognitive processes (Mayer & Salovey, 1997), incorporating essential human values that contribute to the quality of social and interpersonal relationships and overall life satisfaction (Bar-On, 2010). Given this foundation, several models have emerged to facilitate the development of EI. Among the prominent frameworks are Bar-On's non-cognitive theory of EI, Mayer and Salovey's theory of emotional and intellectual capacities, and Goleman's mixed approach to emotional competence. Collectively, these theories enrich our understanding of how EI can be nurtured to benefit interpersonal interactions across generations.

The latest version of D. Goleman's EI model, consisting of four components (self-awareness, self-management, social awareness, and relationship management) (Wolff, 2005), is the most acceptable in entrepreneurship. Our research is based on this four-component model of EI.

Researchers typically categorise groups of questionnaires for measuring EI based on three primary EI models: the ability-based model, the trait-based model, and the mixed approach model (Bru-Luna et al., 2021; Sweis et al., 2022). The best-known psychometric tests for determining the level of EI are the Mayer-Salovey-Caruso Emotional Intelligence Test (MSCEIT, MSCEIT 2.0); EQ-i, based on Goleman's work and Bar-On's measurements; ECI 2.0; EQ 360 2.0 Schutte Self Report-Inventory (SSRI), Wong and Law's Emotional Intelligence Scale (WLEIS), and Trait Emotional Intelligence Questionnaire (TEIQue) (Ackley, 2016, Bru-Luna et al., 2021). The mentioned questionnaires allow to determine the level of EI without considering the professional field of activity. There are only a few questionnaires that allow to determine EI in the field of management, among them the QEPro test, specifically designed for French managers (Haag & Jilinskaya-Pandey, 2023) and Emotionally Intelligent Leadership for Students (Shankman et al., 2020). Thus, we found a lack of research in the interdisciplinary field of Emotional Research in Entrepreneurship.

Therefore, we conclude that EI knowledge must be practically applied in entrepreneurship and that further research in intergenerational entrepreneurship and collaboration is relevant and needed.

The aim of this paper is to study the components of EI in intergenerational entrepreneurship (Self-Awareness (SA), Self-Management (SM), Social Awareness (SocA), and Relationship Management (RM)) and to provide recommendations for intergenerational collaboration in entrepreneurship in Latvia. This approach contributes to developing Latvia's potential for sustainable entrepreneurship.

3. Research Methodology

The study investigates differences in the group profiles of EI in entrepreneurship of Latvian residents. It involves the voluntary participation of representatives of four generations: Generation Z, Generation Y, Generation X, and the Baby Boomers Generation. The age and gender of the respondents are taken into account.

The data for this study were obtained solely by the use of questionnaires, and the research objectives are formulated as follows:

1. To postulate the profiles of EI in entrepreneurship across Generation Z, Generation Y, Generation X and Baby Boomers Generation in Latvia in 2024.

2. To identify the most potent components of EI of Generation Z, Generation Y, Generation X and Baby Boomers Generation in Latvia in 2024.
3. To identify the influence of gender on the profile of EI in entrepreneurship among respondents in Latvia.
4. To formulate recommendations for intergenerational collaboration in the entrepreneurial sector in Latvia.

3.1. Sample Selection and Data Collection

The study employs a non-probability sampling method to examine the perspectives of different generational cohorts. 124 respondents are included, comprising 14 representatives from Generation Z, 63 from Generation Y, 39 from Generation X, and 8 Baby Boomers. The gender distribution among the overall respondents is 67% female and 33% male. The survey was conducted using Google Docs in English.

The selection of participants is done through a combination of strategies, including (a) sending an invitation to complete the survey to publicly accessible email addresses and (b) implementing a snowball sampling technique, where respondents were identified based on recommendations from others (Nadányiová et al., 2020). The study's approach aligns with the National Youth Policy's objectives, which aim to highlight each youth's potential and celebrate diversity and differences (Abdullah et al., 2018).

Existing literature suggests that generational cohort theory has gained significant importance in consumer marketing, as today's consumers are increasingly interested in sustainable food choices (Kamenidou et al., 2020) as important component of sustainable entrepreneurship. The diverse perspectives of the five Greek generational cohorts, including the Silent Generation, Baby Boomers, Generation X, Generation Y, and Generation Z, have been the subject of recent investigations (Kamenidou et al., 2020).

3.2. Method.

The 4EI Model is used for measuring EI in entrepreneurship. The 4EI model has four components (Self-Awareness (SA), Self-Management (SM), Social Awareness (SocA), and Relationship Management (RM)), containing the 19 most important entrepreneurship competencies (Mikuš et al., 2022). According to this model, a specially developed measuring tool in entrepreneurship and business is the "Emotional Intelligence in Business" questionnaire. A total of 158 individuals participated in the psychometric validation of the test. Demonstrative and confirmatory analyses were conducted using MS Excel, SPSS, STATISTICA, FACTOR, and R-Studio software (Lutsenko et al., 2021).

The "Emotional Intelligence in Business" questionnaire includes statements reflecting the level of development of 19 competencies of an entrepreneur, grouped into four components (SA, SM, SocA, and RM). The questionnaire contains 40 statements. Each statement is evaluated on a five-point Likert scale ranging from 0 (never) to 4 (always). The responses are analysed to calculate the self-awareness, self-management, social awareness and relationship management on a 10-point scale (low level *(LL ϵ (0–3))*, average level *3 –7))*, high level *(HL ϵ (7–10)))*.

Based on the results of the survey, individual profiles of EI in the business of the respondents are constructed in two ways: 1) quantitatively in the form of a formula, 2) graphically in the form of an EI diagram, where the area of a quadrant represents the level of development of each component.

To further analyze the collected data, both F-tests and t-tests were conducted to assess the statistical significance of differences among the different populations within the sample. These tests were crucial for identifying statistically significant variations and differences in emotional intelligence components across diverse groups defined by gender and age. The F-tests were applied to compare the variances across multiple groups, while t-tests were used to compare the means between two groups. This statistical approach ensures an evaluation of the underlying patterns and differences in emotional intelligence components across various segments of the sample, facilitating a deeper understanding of how these components manifest in different entrepreneurial contexts.

4. Findings and Discussion

The survey conducted in 2024 in Latvia using the "Emotional Intelligence in Business" questionnaire resulted in 124 profiles of EI in business of respondents of generations Z, Y, X, and Baby Boomers. **Hata! Başvuru kaynağı bulunamadı.**1 presents the group profiles of EI for each generation present in the labour market in Latvia.

Table 1. The average value of 4 EI components of respondents in Latvia

Generation	SA	SM	SocA	RM
Generation Z	7,68	6,34	7,41	6,23
Generation Y	8,09	7,21	8,02	7,52
Generation X	8,20	7,26	7,99	7,71
Baby Boomers	8,13	7,94	8,38	8,00

Thus, the profiles of EI in the business of representatives of different generations of Latvia are as follows:

EI Generation Z {$7{,}68^{SA}$; $6{,}34^{SM}$; $7{,}41^{SocA}$; $6{,}23^{RM}$}, in general {$\mathbf{HL}^{SA}$; AL^{SM}; $\mathbf{HL}^{SocA}$; AL^{RM}}
EI Generation Y {$8{,}09^{SA}$; $7{,}21^{SM}$; $8{,}02^{SocA}$; $7{,}52^{RM}$}, in general {$\mathbf{HL}^{SA}$; $\mathbf{HL}^{SM}$; $\mathbf{HL}^{SocA}$; $\mathbf{HL}^{RM}$}
EI Generation X {$8{,}20^{SA}$; $7{,}26^{SM}$; $7{,}99^{SocA}$; $7{,}71^{RM}$}, in general {$\mathbf{HL}^{SA}$; $\mathbf{HL}^{SM}$; $\mathbf{HL}^{SocA}$; $\mathbf{HL}^{RM}$}
EI Baby Boomers {$8{,}13^{SA}$; $7{,}94^{SM}$; $8{,}38^{SocA}$; $8{,}00^{RM}$}, in general {$\mathbf{HL}^{SA}$; $\mathbf{HL}^{SM}$; $\mathbf{HL}^{SocA}$; $\mathbf{HL}^{RM}$}
where AL – average level (3–7); HL – high level (≥ 7).

The results shown in **Hata! Başvuru kaynağı bulunamadı.**1 demonstrate an average level of Self-Management (SM) and Relationship Management (RM) in Generation Z and the high level of all four components of the EI for the other older generations (SA, SM, SocA, and RM). Figure 1 shows a general tendency to increase EI in business with age, especially its components such as Self-Management (SM) and Relationship Management (RM). There is no apparent difference between the composition of EI of Generation X and Generation Y; they are at a high level. However, the large difference between Baby Boomers and Generation Z indicates the potential of Baby Boomers in intergenerational collaboration. This means that the involvement of seniors (Baby Boomers) in teams initiated by young people (Generation Z) could promote synergy in intergenerational collaboration and lead to sustainable entrepreneurship in Latvia.

Analyses of variance and t-tests for EI components of youth (Y) and seniors (S) are shown in **Hata! Başvuru kaynağı bulunamadı.**2.

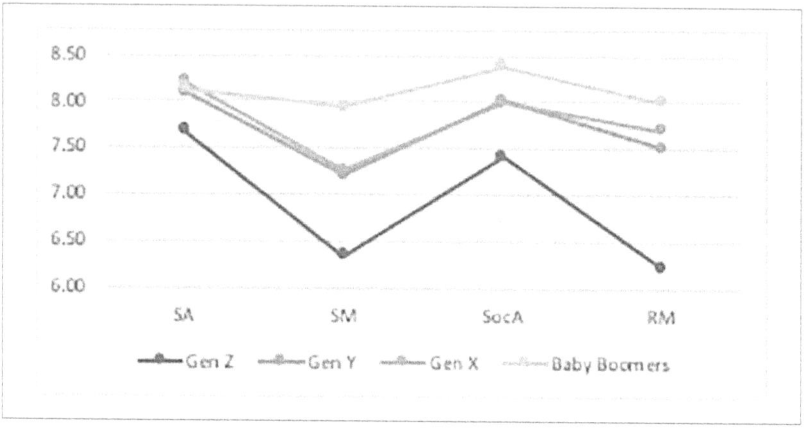

Fig.1 EI in entrepreneurship of different generations in Latvia

Table 2. Analyses of variance and t-tests

	SA_Y	*SA_S*	*SM_Y*	*SM_S*	*SocA_Y*	*SocA_S*	*RM_Y*	*RM_S*
F-Test Two-Sample for Variances								
Mean	7.846	8.171	7.051	7.379	7.731	8.064	6.885	7.864
Variance	0.963	0.749	1.448	1.332	1.544	1.317	1.559	1.928
Observations	39	35	39	35	39	35	39	35
df	38	34	38	34	38	34	38	34
F	1.285		1.087		1.172		0.809	
P(F<=f) one-tail	0.231		0.405		0.321		0.261	
F Critical one-tail	1.753		1.753		1.753		0.576	
t-Test			**Two-Sample Assuming Equal Variances**					
Mean	7.846	8.171	7.051	7.379	7.731	8.064	6.885	7.864
Variance	0.963	0.749	1.448	1.332	1.544	1.317	1.559	1.928
Observations	39	35	39	35	39	35	39	35
Pooled Variance	0.862		1.393		1.437		1.733	
Hypothesised Mean Difference	0		0		0		0	
df	72		72		72		72	

Table 2. *Continued*

	SA_Y	*SA_S*	*SM_Y*	*SM_S*	*SocA_Y*	*SocA_S*	*RM_Y*	*RM_S*
t Stat	-1.505		-1.191		-1.195		-3.196	
P(T<=t) one-tail	0.068		0.119		0.118		0.001	
t Critical one-tail	1.666		1.666		1.666		1.666	
P(T<=t) two-tail	0.137		0.238		0.236		0.002	
t Critical two-tail	1.993		1.993		1.993		1.993	

Note: Y - youth (<35), S – seniors (>50).

The F-tests were conducted to compare the variances among the different age groups in all four components of EI. The results indicated no significant differences in variances, allowing for the use of t-tests assuming equal variances across the groups. Subsequent t-tests on SA, SM, and SocA did not reveal any statistically significant differences, suggesting that these EI components are consistently developed across both younger and older generations. However, a notable exception was observed in RM, where the t-test showed a statistically significant higher mean score among seniors compared to younger respondents. This significant difference underscores the seniors' stronger capabilities in relationship management, highlighting their critical role in enhancing intergenerational collaboration within business contexts.

Given the importance of research on women entrepreneurship in Latvia, we also conducted a gender analysis of EI in business (**Hata! Başvuru kaynağı bulunamadı.**3).

Table 3. Gender analysis of EI in entrepreneurship in different age groups

	SA	SM	SocA	RM
Generation Z				
Male	7,55	5,75	6,90	5,55
Female	7,75	6,67	7,69	6,61
Generation Y				
Male	7,46	7,28	7,42	7,22
Female	8,33	7,17	8,22	7,59

Table 3. *Continued*

	SA	SM	SocA	RM
Generation X				
Male	7,63	7,00	7,78	7,93
Female	8,50	7,41	8,16	7,55
Baby Boomers				
Male	8,00	7,63	7,88	7,63
Female	8,17	8,04	8,54	8,13

All components of EI for females are higher in the Baby Boomer and Generation Z generations. In males, only the components of Self-Management in Generation Y and Relationship Management in Generation X were higher. These indicators may also suggest that there is a hidden potential for Latvian women's involvement in entrepreneurship. This confirms the suggestion made in the GEM report (GEM, 2023b, p.149) that women in Latvia need increased access to resources in entrepreneurship. Analyses of variance and t-tests for gender differences are shown in **Hata! Başvuru kaynağı bulunamadı.**4.

Table 4. Analyses of variance and t-tests

	SA_F	*SA_M*	*SM_F*	*SM_M*	*SocA_F*	*SocA_M*	*RM_F*	*RM_M*
F-Test Two-Sample for Variances								
Mean	8.307	7.622	7.244	7.030	8.181	7.524	7.512	7.360
Variance	0.735	1.375	1.279	1.657	1.057	1.778	1.951	2.172
Observations	83	41	83	41	83	41	83	41
df	82	40	82	40	82	40	82	40
F	0.535		0.772		0.595		0.898	
P(F<=f) one-tail	0.009		0.161		0.024		0.335	
F Critical one-tail	0.649		0.649		0.649		0.649	

Table 4. *Continued*

t-Test								
	Two-Sample Assuming Unequal Variances		Two-Sample Assuming Equal Variances		Two-Sample Assuming Equal Variances		Two-Sample Assuming Equal Variances	
Mean	8.307	7.622	7.244	7.030	8.181	7.524	7.512	7.360
Variance	0.735	1.375	1.279	1.657	1.057	1.778	1.951	2.172
Observations	83	41	83	41	83	41	83	41
Pooled Variance			1.403				2.024	
Hypothesised Mean Difference	0		0		0		0	
df	62		122		64		122	
t Stat	3.328		0.944		2.771		0.561	
P(T<=t) one-tail	0.001		0.173		0.004		0.288	
t Critical one-tail	1.670		1.657		1.669		1.657	
P(T<=t) two-tail	0.001		0.347		0.007		0.576	
t Critical two-tail	1.999		1.980		1.998		1.980	

F-tests assessing variances between genders in EI components revealed equal variances in SM and RM, with unequal variances in SA and SocA. Subsequent t-tests revealed no significant differences in SM and RM between genders, indicating similar levels of these competencies among males and females. However, significant differences were observed in SA and SocA, where females demonstrated higher levels than their male counterparts. These findings are particularly significant in the context of fostering intergenerational collaboration within businesses. The enhanced SA and SocA exhibited by women can contribute greatly to team dynamics and leadership, complementing the strengths brought by different generations.

5. Conclusion

This study extends the geographical scope of research on intergenerational entrepreneurship in European countries. It complements the research on EI in intergenerational entrepreneurship conducted in recent years in Slovakia and Ukraine (Fedorova et al., 2024). It confirms the feasibility of involving the adult generation in intergenerational collaboration for sustainable entrepreneurship.

The results of research on the composition of EI in entrepreneurship in Latvia show a high level of EI components of older generations and women in entrepreneurship, which once again supports the assumption made in the GEM report about the latent potential of older generations and women in entrepreneurship in Latvia.

This study's practical contribution is its recommendation to strengthen the involvement particularly between Generation Z (under 27) and Baby Boomers (over 60 years old) in entrepreneurship in Latvia which can significantly enhance intergenerational collaboration.

Developing recommendations for building intergenerational teams in entrepreneurship based on EI profiles is a future step for research. Further research should also expand the coverage of respondents with entrepreneurial experience. This will clarify the bottlenecks of intergenerational collaboration in Latvian entrepreneurship.

Funding

This work was funded by the EU NextGenerationEU through the Recovery and Resilience Plan for Slovakia under the project No. 09I03-03-V01-00055; and the Slovak Research and Development Agency under Grant APVV-19-0581.

Author contributions

Conceptualisation, AP and YF; methodology, AP, YF; formal analysis, JM; investigation, MZ-B; data curation, YF, JM, MZ-B; writing—original draft preparation, JM, JR, MZ-B; writing—review and editing, AP, MZ-B; All authors have read and agreed to the published version and have contributed significantly throughout this research in all its phases.

Disclosure statement

The authors declare no conflict of interest. The funders had no role in the design of the study; in the collection, analyses, or interpretation of data; in the writing of the manuscript, or in the decision to publish the results.

References

Abdullah, A., Ismail, M. M., & Albani, A. (2018). At-Risk Generation Z: Values, Talents and Challenges. *In International Journal of Asian Social Science*, 8 (7) https://doi.org/10.18488/journal.1.2018.87.373.378

Ackley, D. (2016). Emotional intelligence: A practical review of models, measures, and applications. *Consulting Psychology Journal: Practice and Research*, 68(4), 269–286. https://doi.org/10.1037/cpb0000070

Bar-On, R. (2010), "Emotional intelligence: An integral part of positive psychology", *South African Journal of Psychology*, 40, 54-62.

Bru-Luna, L.M.; Martí-Vilar, M.; Merino-Soto, C. & Cervera-Santiago, J.L (2021). Emotional Intelligence Measures: *A Systematic Review. Healthcare*, 9, 1696. https://doi.org/10.3390 healthcare9121696

Cho, M. et al. (2018), "Generation Z's sustainable volunteering: *Motivations, attitudes and job performance*", *Sustainability*, 10, 1-16. https://doi.org/10.3390/su10051400

Dietz, L., & Fasbender, U. (2022). Age-diverse workplace friendship: A systematic literature review and recommendations for future research. *Work, Aging and Retirement*, 8(2), 163–197. https://doi.org/10.1093/workar/waab028

Ekoh, P. C. (2021). Anxiety, isolation and diminishing resources: The impact of COVID-19 pandemic on residential care home facilities for older people in south-east Nigeria. *Working with Older People*, 25(4), 273–282. https://doi.org/10.1108/WWOP-01-2021-0001

Evrensel-İnanç, E., Aydoğmuş, C., Metin-Camgöz, S., & Özdilek, E. (2022). For generation Z: What is the underlying reason between emotional intelligence and depression relationship? *Sosyoekonomi*, 30(53), 27-48. https://doi.org/10.17233/sosyoekonomi.2022.03.02

Farelo, R. & Gómez, F. (2021). Hacia la construcción de un modelo de Liderazgo Intergeneracional. *Re- vista Internacional de Organizaciones*, (25–26), 127–150. https://doi.org/10.17345/rio25-26.127-150

Fedorova, Y., Mikuš, J., Pilková, A., Holienka, M., Korniush, H. (2024). Emotional Intelligence in Business: Intergenerational Study. In: Auer, M.E., Cukierman, U.R., Vendrell Vidal, E., Tovar Caro, E. (eds) *Towards a Hybrid, Flexible and Socially Engaged Higher Education. ICL* 2024., vol 1. Springer, Cham.

GEM (Global Entrepreneurship Monitor) (2023a). Global Entrepreneurship Monitor 2022/2023 *Global Report: Adapting to a "New Normal"*. London: GEM https://gemconsortium.org/file/open?fileId=51147

GEM (Global Entrepreneurship Monitor) (2023b). Global Entrepreneurship Monitor *2023/2024 Global Report: 25 Years and Growing*. London: GEM. https://www.gemconsortium.org/report/global-entrepreneurship-monitor-gem-20232024-global-report-25-years-and-growing

Goleman, D. (1995). *Emotional intelligence*. Bantam Books.

Haag, C., Bellinghausen, L. & Jilinskaya-Pandey, M. QEPro: An ability measure of emotional intelligence for managers in a French cultural environment. *Curr Psychol* 42, 4080–4 02 (2023). https://doi.org/10.1007 s12144-021-01715-6

Harris, V. W., Anderson, J., & Visconti, B. (2022). Social emotional ability development (SEAD): An integrated model of practical emotion-based competencies. *Motivation and Emotion,* 46 (2) https://doi.org/10.1007/s11031-021-09922-1

Yadav, S., & Lenka, U. (2020). Workforce diversity: From a literature review to future research agenda. *Journal of Indian Business Research*, 12, 577–603. https://doi.org/10.1108/JIBR-08-2019-0243

Kamenidou, I., Stavrianea, A., & Bara, E.-Z. (2020). Generational Differences toward Organic Food Behavior: Insights from Five Generational Cohorts. *Sustainability,* 12(6) https://doi.org/10.3390/su12062299

Lutsenko, O., Fedorova, Yu., & Tsokota, V. R. (2021). Emotional intelligence as a general personality self-regulation resource – design of a new test "Emotional Intelligence in Business". *In Proceedings on Problems of personal resources in educational and professional activities, FOP Brovin O.V., Kharkiv, Ukraine* (pp. 51–55). http://dspace.univer.kharkov.ua/handle/123456789/16260

Mayer, J. D., Salovey, P., & Caruso, D. R. (2000). Models of Emotional Intelligence. In Cambridge University Press eBooks. https://doi.org/10.1017/cbo9780511807947.019

Mayer, J.D. & P. Salovey (1997, "What is emotional intelligence?", in: P. Salovey & D. Sluyter (eds.), *Emotional development and emotional intelligence: Implications for educators* (3- 31), New York: Basic Books

Mikuš, J., Pilková, A., Fedorova, Y., & Btytan, Y. (2022). Model for the emotional intelligence's develop- ment in entrepreneurship. *In The Poprad*

Economic and Management Forum 2022 (pp. 402–409). VERBUM. https://www.pemf-conference.com/publishing/

Mikuš, J., Pilková, A., Holienka, M., Fedorova, Y. (2023), Emotional Intelligence in the Development of Entrepreneurial Competence. In: Auer, M.E., Pachatz, W., Rüütmann, T. (eds) *Learning in the Age of Digital and Green Transition. ICL 2022. Lecture Notes in Networks and Systems*, vol 634. Springer, Cham. https://doi.org/10.1007/978-3-031-26190-9_11

Nadányiová, M., Gajanová, Ľ., & Majerová, J. (2020). Green Marketing as a Part of the Socially Responsible Brand's Communication from the Aspect of Generational Stratification. *Sustainability*, 12(7) https://doi.org/10.3390/su12177118

Oblinger, D. & J. Oblinger (2005), "Is it age or IT: First steps toward understanding the Net generation", in: D. Oblinger & J. Oblinger (eds), *Educating the Net Generation* (20-27), Washington: EDUCASE

Perez-Encinas, A., Bueno, Y., Santos, B., & Nieto-Mejia, C. (2021). Are there differences and comple- mentarities between senior and young entrepreneurs? An intergenerational perspective. *Sustainability*, 13(9), Article 5202. https://doi.org/10.3390/su13095202

Rožman, M., Treven, S., & Čančer, V. (2020). The impact of promoting intergenerational synergy on the work engagement of older employees in Sloveni. *Journal of East European Management Studies*, 25, 9–34. https://doi.org/10.5771/0949-6181-2020-1-9

Salovey, P., & Mayer, J. D. (1990). Emotional Intelligence. *Imagination Cognition and Personality*, 9 (N°) https://doi.org/10.2190/dugg-p24e-52wk-6cdg

Shankman ML, Allen SJ, Miguel R. (2015). Emotionally intelligent leadership for students: Inventory, 2nd ed. San Francisco, CA: Jossey-Bass. https://books.google.sk/books?hl=en&lr=&id=9b5gA_z-cMoC&oi=fnd&pg=PR9&dq=info:qQVJkwCCKmEJ:scholar.google.com&ots=ue1LlgyHns&sig=muUOMLPvrf9jj3_FxEAiKfAopew&redir_esc=y#v=onepage&q&f=false

Sneed, R., & Chan, A. C. Y. (2023). The Implications of Intergenerational Relationships for Minority Aging: a Review of Recent Literature [Review of The Implications of Intergenerational Relationships for Minority Aging: a Review of Recent Literature]. *Current Epidemiology Reports*. https://doi.org/10.1007/s40471-023-00319-x

Sweis, R., S. Aldaod, N. Alsayyed & L.Sukkari (2022). Self vs. Other Raters' Assessment of Emotional Intelligence in Private and Public Hospitals: *A Comparative Study. Administrative Sciences* 12: 194. https://doi.org/10.3390 admsci1204019

Ulutaş, İ., Engin, K., & Polat, E. B. (2021). Strategies to Develop Emotional Intelligence in Early Childhood. *IntechOpen eBooks. IntechOpen.* https://doi.org/10.5772/intechopen.98229

United Nations. (2015). General assembly resolution A/RES/70/1. Transforming our world: The 2030 agenda for sustainable development. *Seventieth United Nations General Assembly*, 25 September 2015, New York. https://en.unesco.org/sustainabledevelopmentgoals

Wolff, S. (2005). *Emotional Competence Inventory: Technical manual.* Boston, MA, The Hay Grop.

Rewarding Taxes and the Health Impact Factor: Insights from the Theory of the Cycle of Money

Constantinos Challoumis

1. Introduction

This chapter explores the money cycle dynamics with and without the consideration of health as an impactful factor. Based on this, it considers that this health impact factor facilitates uncontrolled transactions, thus strengthening the economic vitality to support the investments and consumer spending. Through this analysis, what has been emphasized, more than anything else, is the role of health-not just as a sector itself but as a driver of economic processes. Our methodology uses the Quantification of Everything (Q.E.) approach to analyze these effects, drawing conclusions on the pivotal role of health in economic sustainability. This chapter conducts a comparative analysis in the cycle of money, with and without health-related factors of impact. The study depicts two scenarios, one considering the health impact factor, and the other without this factor, thus highlighting its contribution to economic dynamics. By applying the Quantification of Everything methodology, this paper derives a number of far-reaching implications for the contribution of health to economic sustainability and growth. This, therefore, impact factor would really influence the inter-relationship between public administration and the private sector in the use of redistributed revenues from taxation, especially for health purposes. The results highlight how important health investments are as a driver of economic activity and point to influences on public policy and responses by the private sector. This chapter extends the discussion on health economics by showing how health-related policies and expenditures can act as a strong mechanism for economic stabilization and growth.

2. Literature review

This chapter explains the significant role that contracts and agreements play in ascertaining the profit or loss that should be accrued to a party entering into controlled transactions. It provides a reason for referencing changes in those contracts, thereby highlighting why periodic inspections by the tax authorities are necessary. This is not only to ensure that the contracts are followed but also to enable comparability analyses, which are required under the arm's length principle. Periodic inspections are essential for companies involved in controlled transactions, as these inspections help in the correct determination of cost sharing among tested parties. The main goal of such companies is to ensure that taxation issues regarding their activities are resolved and that their operational policies fall within the arm's length principle. Therefore, it is important that these companies structure their agreements in such a way as to maximize their profits in jurisdictions with lower tax rates and increase cost allocations in higher-tax-rate countries (Challoumis, 2018, 2019, 2024e, 2024a, 2024b, 2024c, 2024d, 2021, 2022, 2023d, 2023e, 2023b, 2023f, 2023c, 2023a; Challoumis & Eriotis, 2024). Further, it is important to emphasize that the operations of firms involved in controlled transactions, as well as the field inspections conducted by the tax authorities, are all framed under the concept of proportional adjustments. This approach becomes imperative since, under comparative conditions, comparable data for uncontrolled transactions is frequently not available, which inevitably forces companies to proportionally adjust their data. The principle of proportionate adjustments means that when companies acting as tested parties realize huge deviations in profits or losses from those realized in uncontrolled transactions, they have to use the proportion analogy. This way, they are able to adjust their data to bring about a fairer comparison. Such adjustments are quite important in maintaining compliance with regulatory requirements and ensuring equity in tax assessments. The production of goods or services generates profits and costs for the companies.

$$u = s(zf + \tilde{z}d) \tag{1}$$

$$z = |\tilde{z} - 1| \tag{2}$$

The symbol u is about the impact factor of the comparability analysis which has any method to the s. The symbol z is a coefficient which takes values between 0 and 1. What value could receive is determined by the influence of the method (using the best method rule) to the s. The symbol of f is about the cost which comes up from the production of goods, and the symbol of d

is about the cost which comes from the distribution of the goods. According to equations from (1) to (2) is plausible to determine the following equations:

$$u_c = zf + \tilde{z}d \quad (3)$$
$$\mathrm{b} = (\mathrm{p} - u_c)^* j_1 \quad (4)$$

The symbol of b in the prior equation is about the amount of taxes that should pay the companies of controlled transactions in the application of the arm's length principle. The u_c is the amount of tax obligations that can avoid through the allocations of profits and losses. Moreover, j_1 is a coefficient for the rate of taxes. Then, the equation (4) shows the case of the arm's length principle. In the case of fixed length principle:

$$\nu = \mathrm{p}^* j_2 \quad (5)$$

The symbol of v in the previous equation shows the taxes that should pay the enterprises of controlled transactions in the application of the fixed length principle. Then, j_2 is a coefficient for the rate of taxes in the case of fixed length principle.

$$\nu \geq b \quad (6)$$

In transfer pricing, the taxation of companies engaged in controlled transactions typically adheres to the arm's length principle, where taxes are calculated based on comparable transactions between independent entities. However, when applying the fixed length principle, these companies often face a tax burden that is equal to or greater than that imposed under the arm's length principle. The fixed length principle provides a structured approach, enabling companies to address challenges arising from the allocation of profits and losses. This principle is particularly effective in managing discrepancies and ensuring that profit allocation reflects economic activity realistically, thereby stabilizing global tax revenues (Aleksei Matveevic Rumiantsev, 1983; Boughton, 1994; Canh & Thanh, 2020; Engels, 1844; Gilpin & Gilpin, 2001; Harris, 2020; IMF, 1994, 2021; Keynes, 1936; Lenin, 1916; Marx, 1867; OECD, 2021; Papageorgiou, 2012; Richardson, 1964; Rikhardsson et al., 2021; Stiglitz, 2002; World Bank, 2003; World Bank Group, 2024b, 2024a). Tax authorities use the fixed length principle as a tool to reduce the negative impact of transfer pricing on tax revenue worldwide. It helps in recovering the tax loss that would have otherwise been lost because of mismatched profit shifting in various tax jurisdictions. The following diagram will show the procedural framework that companies follow in their profit and loss allocations, including the steps for proportional data adjustments, and the application of the fixed length principle. The methodology which followed stands on the Q.E. method.

3. Methodology

The tax revenues reflect potential savings for the companies had they not been subjected to taxation. The management of these savings can vary from case to case. In return, the benefits to the companies can be administered either way, that is, they can be saved or taxed. In fact, the Theory of the Cycle of Money shows that, similar to taxes, saving might strengthen or weaken an economy. To understand such process properly, it would be important to differentiate savings not returned (or savings that have escaped) and returned savings (or enforcement savings). Let the following equations define clearly the difference:

$$\alpha = \alpha_s + \alpha_t \tag{7}$$

$$x_m = m - a \tag{8}$$

$$\mathrm{m} = \mu + \alpha_p \tag{9}$$

$$\mu = \sum_{\iota=0}^{n} \mu_\iota \tag{10}$$

$$\alpha_p = \sum_{j=0}^{m} \alpha_{pj} \tag{11}$$

$$c_m = \frac{dx_m}{da} \tag{12}$$

$$c_\alpha = \frac{dx_m}{dm} \tag{13}$$

$$c_y = c_m + c_\alpha \tag{14}$$

The variable of α is symbolized the case of the escaped savings. This means that savings which are not return back to the economy, or come back after long term period. The variable of α_s symbolizes the case that there are escaped savings which come from transfer pricing activities. The variable of α_t is symbolizes the case that there are escaped savings not from transfer pricing activities but from any other commercial activity. For instance α_t could refer to the commercial activities which come from the uncontrolled transactions. The variable of m symbolizes the financial liquidity in an economy. The variable of μ symbolizes the consumption in an economy. The variable of α_p symbolizes the enforcement savings, which come from the citizens and from small and medium sized enterprises. The variable of x_m symbolizes the condition of financial liquidity in an economy. The variable of c_m symbolizes the velocity of financial liquidity increases or decreases. The variable of c_α symbolizes the velocity of escaped savings. Therefore, the variable of c_y symbolizes the term of the cycle of money. Thereupon, the cycle of money shows the level of dynamic of an economy, and its robustness.

The Theory of the Cycle of Money outlines several key principles that explain the dynamics of financial liquidity within an economy:

1. Role of Citizens and SMEs: Citizens along with small and medium-sized enterprises (SMEs) often end up substituting for the services and property provided by companies that choose to save rather than invest or consume proportionally within the economy. This substitution typically occurs when these companies are involved in controlled transactions, making them primary contributors to escaped savings.
2. Impact of Escaped Savings: Escaped savings, primarily accumulated by companies engaged in controlled transactions such as transfer pricing, are a significant factor in diminishing the economic dynamism. These savings do not re-enter the market, leading to a scarcity of financial liquidity which hampers economic growth.
3. Substitution and Added Value: In cases where it is not feasible for citizens and SMEs to offer comparable added value to products and services, substitution does not occur. This is often the case with specialized sectors like manufacturing and research. In such scenarios, tax policy should treat these transactions as uncontrolled, regardless of their involvement in controlled transactions, applying principles like the fixed length principle to ensure fair taxation.

4. Enforcement Savings and Economic Dynamism: Enforcement savings, generated from the investments and consumption by citizens and SMEs, are crucial for maintaining a high economic dynamic. These savings are actively circulated within the economy, promoting robustness and growth.
5. Velocity of Financial Liquidity and Escaped Savings: The velocity of financial liquidity indicates how quickly an economy's robustness is either strengthening or weakening. Similarly, the velocity of escaped savings measures the rapidity with which non-returned savings are lost from the market due to lack of investment or consumption.
6. Overall Economic Condition: The cycle of money serves as an indicator of the overall economic condition, reflecting the effectiveness of the tax system and the economy's general dynamism. A high indicator suggests a robust economy with substantial financial liquidity, while a low indicator points to economic frailty.
7. Definition of Controlled and Uncontrolled Transactions: Within the context of the cycle of money, controlled transactions include not only traditional transfer pricing scenarios but also any manipulation of profits and losses to evade taxes. Conversely, uncontrolled transactions encompass ordinary commercial activities by citizens, SMEs, factories, research centers, and others that cannot be easily substituted by companies engaged in controlled transactions.
8. Application of the Fixed Length Principle: While the fixed length principle addresses issues related to the cycle of money, its application should not be overly restrictive. The theory of the cycle of money transcends the scope of transfer pricing, advocating for a tax system that lowers taxes on uncontrolled transactions and raises them on controlled transactions, aligning with the financial liquidity of citizens and SMEs.

This framework illustrates how the management of savings and their re-integration into the market, either through enforcement or escape—impacts overall economic health and liquidity.

4. Results

For the purposes of the mathematical approach of the cycle of money:

$$\alpha_p = \alpha_r + \alpha_n * h_n + \alpha_m * h_m \tag{15}$$

$$\alpha_r \geq \alpha_n * h_n \geq \alpha_m * h_m \tag{16}$$

In the prior two equations used some impact factors, which are the a_p, α_r, α_n, h_n, α_m and the h_m. The variable α_r symbolizes the impact factor of the rest rewarding taxes. The symbol of α_n is the impact factor of the health and any technical knowledge. The symbol of α_m is about the impact factor of health anything relevant and supporting of this issue. The symbol of h_n, and of the h_m, are the coefficients of the health and the health impact factor accordingly.

Table: Compiling coefficients

Factors	Values(/)	Values'(/)
α_s	0.6	0.6
α_t	0.7	0.7
μ	0.9	0.9
α_r	0.4	0.4
α_n*h_n	0.3	0.3
α_m*h_m	0.2	-

The generator of this procedure used the coefficients which appeared on the previous table. Therefrom, the factors have an upper limit of 1, and a lower limit 0, but s and $\tilde{s}$ are plausible to receive values greater than one as their mathematical structure allow this.

As the framework above has demonstrated, it becomes evident that the condition of the health sector plays a major role in the flow of money. An economy burdened with structural burdens relative to healthcare exhibits lower economic vitality. Taxes meant to facilitate healthcare are, therefore, supportive taxes that provide a means to economic security. Any shortcomings in healthcare delivery at whatever level thus have a negative impact on the strength of an economy.

5. Conclusions

Healthcare supports the private sector and strengthens the economy as expected. The impact of healthcare catalyzes economic growth. A healthy workforce provides a backbone for market stability and increases the

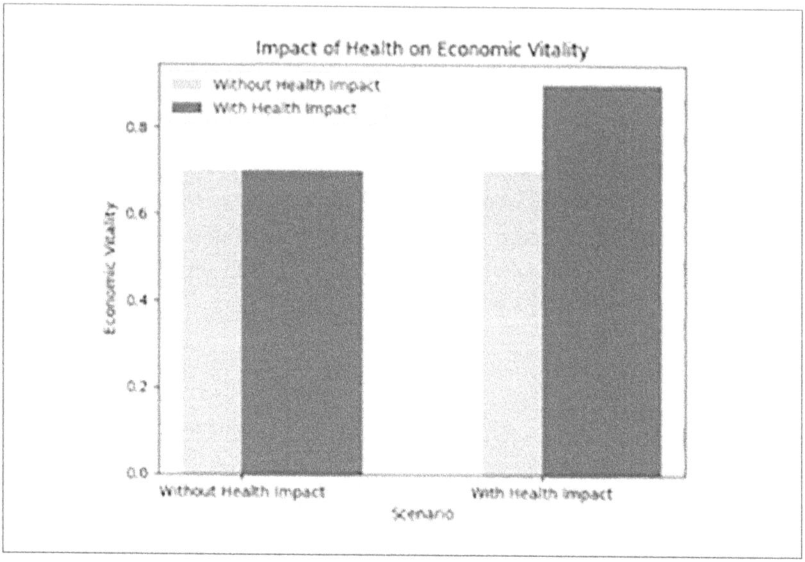

Figure 1: Comparison of cycle of money with all rewarding taxes and without the impact factor of the health (see Appendix)

economic momentum of any setting. Therefore, the health care system significantly contributes to market growth. The taxes levied towards healthcare are beneficial to the economy as they are one of the few taxes which actively contributes to its increase.

Appendix

A Python program for assessing health impacts in the Theory of the Cycle of Money:

```
scenarios = [‘Without Health Impact’, ‘With Health Impact’]
economic_vitality_without = [0.7, 0.7] # Assuming a baseline
economic vitality
economic_vitality_with = [0.7, 0.9] # Enhanced economic vitality
with health impact
x = range(len(scenarios)) # X-axis positions
fig, ax = plt.subplots()
ax.bar(x, economic_vitality_without, width=0.4, label=’Without
Health Impact’, align=’center’, color=’lightblue’)
```

```
ax.bar(x, economic_vitality_with, width=0.4, label='With Health
Impact', align='edge', color='green')
ax.set_xlabel('Scenario')
ax.set_ylabel('Economic Vitality')
ax.set_title('Impact of Health on Economic Vitality')
ax.set_xticks(x)
ax.set_xticklabels(scenarios)
ax.legend()
plt.show()
```

References

Aleksei Matveevic Rumiantsev. (1983). Political Economy. PROGRESS Guides to the Social Sciences.

Boughton, J. M. (1994). The IMF and the Latin American Debt Crisis: Seven Common Criticisms. IMF Policy Discussion Papers. https://www.elibrary.imf.org/view/journals/003/1994/023/article-A001-en.xml

Canh, N. P., & Thanh, S. D. (2020). Financial development and the shadow economy: A multi-dimensional analysis. Economic Analysis and Policy, 67(2020), 37–54.

Challoumis, C. (2018). Methods of Controlled Transactions and the Behavior of Companies According to the Public and Tax Policy. Economics, 6(1), 33–43. https://doi.org/10.2478/eoik-2018-0003

Challoumis, C. (2019). The R.B.Q. (Rational, Behavioral and Quantified) Model. Ekonomika, 98(1), 6–18. https://doi.org/10.15388/ekon.2019.1.1

Challoumis, C. (2021). Index of the cycle of money -the case of Bulgaria. Economic Alternatives, 27(2), 225–234. https://www.unwe.bg/doi/eajournal/2021.2/EA.2021.2.04.pdf

Challoumis, C. (2022). Conditions of the CM (Cycle of Money). In Social and Economic Studies within the Framework of Emerging Global Developments, Volume -1, V. Kaya (pp. 13–24). https://doi.org/10.3726/b19907

Challoumis, C. (2023a). A comparison of the velocities of minimum escaped savings and financial liquidity. In Social and Economic Studies within the Framework of Emerging Global Developments, Volume - 4, V. Kaya (pp. 41–56). https://doi.org/10.3726/b21202

Challoumis, C. (2023b). FROM SAVINGS TO ESCAPE AND ENFORCEMENT SAVINGS. Cogito, XV(4), 206–216.

Challoumis, C. (2023c). Impact Factor of Liability of Tax System According to the Theory of Cycle of Money. In Social and Economic Studies within the Framework of Emerging Global Developments Volume 3, V. Kaya (Vol. 3, pp. 31–42). https://doi.org/10.3726/b20968

Challoumis, C. (2023d). Index of the cycle of money: The case of Costa Rica. Sapienza, 4(3), 1–11. https://journals.sapienzaeditorial.com/index.php/SIJIS

Challoumis, C. (2023e). Risk on the tax system of the E.U. from 2016 to 2022. Economics, 11(2).

Challoumis, C. (2023f). Utility of Cycle of Money without the Escaping Savings (Protection of the Economy). In Social and Economic Studies within the Framework of Emerging Global Developments Volume 2, V. Kaya (pp. 53–64). https://doi.org/10.3726/b20509

Challoumis, C. (2024a). A historical analysis of the banking system and its impact on Greek economy. Edelweiss Applied Science and Technology, 8(6), 1598–1617. https://learning-gate.com/index.php/2576-8484/article/view/2282/892

Challoumis, C. (2024b). Approach on Arm's Length Principle and Fix Length Principle Mathematical Representations. In Innovations and Contemporary Trends in Business & Economics (pp. 25–44). Peter Lang.

Challoumis, C. (2024c). From Economics to Economic Engineering (The Cycle of Money): The case of Romania. Cogito, XVII(2), 161–170.

Challoumis, C. (2024d). Impact factor of liability using the Sensitivity Method. In Social and Economic Studies within the Framework of Emerging Global Developments.

Challoumis, C. (2024e). Rewarding taxes on the cycle of money. In Social and Economic Studies within the Framework of Emerging Global Developments (Vol. 5).

Challoumis, C., & Eriotis, N. (2024). The Historical View of Banking System in Greece During the Financial Crisis. Journal of Ecohumanism, 5(8), . 991 – 1011. https://ecohumanism.co.uk/joe/ecohumanism/article/view/4776

Engels, F. (1844). The Condition of the Working Class in England. Otto Wigand.

Gilpin, R., & Gilpin, J. M. (2001). Global Political Economy. PRINCETON UNIVERSITY PRESS PRINCETON AND OXFORD.

Harris, J. (2020). Economic Policy Responses to the COVID-19 Pandemic. Journal of Economic Perspectives, 34(4), 35–60.

IMF. (1994). World Economic Outlook. DC: International Monetary Fund. https://www.imf.org/en/Publications/WEO/Issues/2016/12/31/World-Economic-Outlook-May-1994-A-Survey-by-the-Staff-of-the-International-Monetary-Fund-5

IMF. (2021). Fiscal Policies to Support the COVID-19 Recovery. International Monetary Fund.

Keynes, J. M. (1936). The General Theory of Employment, Interest, and Money. Harcourt Brace.

Lenin, V. I. (1916). Imperialism, the Highest Stage of Capitalism. The Marx-Engels-Lenin Institute.

Marx, K. (1867). Das Kapital: Critique of Political Economy. Verlag von Otto Meissner.

OECD. (2021). Economic Outlook for Greece. Organisation for Economic Co-operation and Development.

Papageorgiou, A. (2012). Fiscal policy reforms in general equilibrium: The case of Greece. North-Holland, 34(2), 504–522.

Richardson, G. B. (1964). Economic Theory. Routledge Taylor&Francis Croup.

Rikhardsson, P., Rohde, C., & Christensen, L. (2021). Management controls and crisis: evidence from the banking sector. Accounting, Auditing & Accountability Journal. https://research-api.cbs.dk/ws/portalfiles/portal/72293372/rikhardsson_et_al_management_controls_acceptedversion.pdf

Stiglitz, J. E. (2002). Globalization and Its Discontents. NY: W.W. Norton & Company.

World Bank. (2003). *World Development Report 2003: Sustainable Development in a Dynamic World*. DC: World Bank. https://openknowledge.worldbank.org/handle/10986/5985

World Bank Group. (2024a). *Open Data*. World Bank Open Data. https://data.worldbank.org

World Bank Group. (2024b). *World Development Indicators: Structure of value added*. World Bank Data.

Digital Transformation of Tax Authority and Accounting Professionals

Bruna Costa, Humberto Nuno Rito Ribeiro, Amélia Cristina Ferreira da Silva, Albertina Paula Monteiro

1. Introduction

The use of new technologies in accounting has provided unprecedented opportunities to improve accounting practices, enabling tasks to be performed more quickly, efficiently, and accurately (Andrade et al., 2020; Aleixo, 2024). In Portugal, the digitalization of processes promoted by the Tax Authority (AT) has enhanced transparency and fiscal oversight, intending to combat tax fraud and evasion more effectively (Warner et al., 2015; Tamanaha, 2020). In addition to facilitating compliance with tax obligations and reducing fraud, digitalization also presents significant opportunities for the accounting profession (Sari et al., 2019).

In today's dynamic and complex environment, driven by technological advancements, tax administrations worldwide recognize the need for efficient, transparent, and fair tax auditing and control measures. The Committee on Fiscal Affairs (CFA) of the Organization for Economic Co-operation and Development (OECD) has highlighted the importance of implementing effective tools to carry out tax audits and addressing the ongoing challenges of tax evasion and fraud.

Technological advancements expand governments' access to information, strengthening their ability to mitigate tax evasion (Alm, 2021; Kitsios et al., 2023). Recent studies, including those by Warner et al. (2015), Hashimzade et al. (2015), and Hemberg et al. (2016) demonstrate that artificial intelligence (AI) can effectively predict and detect potential cases of tax evasion. However, adapting to this new digital context poses considerable challenges for both accounting professionals and their clients. The complexity of the tax system and the requirements for continuous updates can complicate the adaptation process for professionals, while some clients' resistance to digital environments can create barriers to the full implementation of digital practices.

Additionally, concerns related to data privacy and the use of personal information within the tax system arise as areas of concern for professionals and taxpayers alike (García & Cuello, 2017).

Tamanaha (2020) highlights that technology in tax administration is a key strategy to manage complex and volatile income sources in the digital economy. Digital systems enhance tax authorities' ability to monitor electronic transactions and boost compliance, addressing areas prone to tax evasion. Similarly, the OECD (2015) sees digitalization as a unique opportunity for tax authorities to handle large data volumes effectively. However, Scarcella (2019) cautions that tax management relies on aligning administrative processes with technology to avoid compromised efforts. While governments use these tools to track transactions, corporations can also exploit them to obscure income and shift profits to low-tax jurisdictions through strategies like transfer pricing (Alm, 2021).

Despite these challenges, digital taxation enhances regulatory quality and corruption control. García and Cuello (2017) argue that digitalization significantly reduces evasion by equipping authorities with advanced tools to monitor transactions and ensure compliance. The Finance Portal, enabling taxpayers to submit invoices digitally, exemplifies how technology simplifies reporting while fighting evasion (Melo, 2018). Additionally, the Portuguese Tax and Customs Authority (2022) has implemented digital measures like creating risk profiles to detect and prevent false invoices, a frequent evasion tactic, and uses the VAT Information Exchange System (VIES) to enhance cross-border transparency.

Further, the Portuguese Tax Authority (2023) employs initiatives like pre-filled tax returns, expanded online services, and VIES to improve compliance, transparency, and anti-fraud measures. Mosteanu and Faccia (2020) argue that AI, coupled with other technologies, can reduce human error in tax administration. This AI-driven oversight transforms tax operations by enhancing fraud detection, personalizing taxpayer services, and optimizing processes (Melnychenko et al., 2020).

The digital era has transformed accounting, necessitating rapid adaptation to new tools. Automation of accounting tasks requires professionals to master digital skills for managing complex data environments (Dias, 2012; Taib et al., 2023). Firms increasingly value accountants who can leverage digital tools for data analysis and reporting (Laar et al., 2020). This shift demands a broad knowledge of ICT, with Leitner-Hanetseder et al. (2021) noting these skills enhance accountants' efficiency and decision-making.

Historically seen as record-keepers, accountants now assume strategic roles in analysis and consulting (Pereira et al., 2017). Mastery of digital tools boosts their organizational value and opens new responsibilities (Dias, 2012; Newman & Westrup, 2005). Arango-Morales et al. (2020) define digital competence as a mix of knowledge, skills, and attitudes essential for technology use, enabling ongoing learning.

Given this demand, accountants must continuously update technical skills. Silva (2021) emphasizes the need to validate and interpret automated data to maximize the benefits of digitalization. Emerging technologies like AI, IoT, and blockchain demand technological skills for competitiveness (Khan et al., 2021; Bakarich & O'Brien, 2021). The profession embraces digital transformation for greater efficiency, client communication, and data quality (CPA Australia, 2019).

Gaibazzi et al. (2021) and Kruskopf et al. (2020) identify essential digital skills in data management, computing, and digital leadership. These skills help accountants handle large datasets, make strategic decisions, and maintain human interaction in an increasingly digital profession. Digitalization expands accountants' roles from data processing to decision-making and business strategy (Due et al., 2018), reshaping public perceptions of the profession.

Digital processes improve transparency, accuracy, and efficiency, but also challenge accountants to remain relevant in an AI-driven world (Silveira et al., 2018). Advanced tools enable higher-quality insights, supporting strategy and new business models (Cavelius et al., 2020). Three phases mark accounting's tech evolution: IT adoption, ERP systems, and current AI and big data advances, which shift accountants from repetitive tasks to strategic roles (Duong & Fledsberg, 2019; Fernandez & Aman, 2018). Digital transformation positions accountants as strategic advisors, essential for navigating complex financial landscapes (Morales & Lambert, 2013; Smith, 2018).

Digitalization supports remote work through online tools, fostering job satisfaction, work-life balance, and autonomy (Coenen & Kok, 2014; EconStor, 2020; Baert et al., 2020). This shift allows accountants to focus on high-value tasks like strategic analysis and advisory, enhancing their role in helping organizations meet future challenges.

In Portugal, the digitalization of the relationship between taxpayers and the Tax Authority (AT) has significantly evolved since the early 21st century. Electronic invoicing (Francisco, 2019; Silva, 2019) and Standardized Audit Files for Tax Purposes (Rolo, 2021) were two leading accelerators of this process. Later, the Lucky Invoice encouraged citizens to request invoices for personal expenses, further reinforcing fiscal transparency and participation. AT has also developed a Customer Relationship Management (CRM) system to improve taxpayer interaction with public administration services (Bala & Ponduri, 2014). Thus, AT launched the E-balcão, a platform facilitating online communication that allows taxpayers to access information and services remotely, improving service quality (Pereira, 2019).

These digital initiatives align with the government's SIMPLEX program, which seeks to modernize and simplify public administration by focusing on accessibility and reducing bureaucratic burdens (Lopes and Rodrigues, 2010). Simultaneously, the Finance Portal, an essential tool within this digital ecosystem, has become increasingly crucial for accounting professionals and citizens. This platform allows users to fulfill tax obligations conveniently and accurately, providing services that streamline various procedures, from document submission to payment deadlines (Santos, 2023). Through these numerous innovations, Portugal's Tax Authority has implemented systems that automate tax data collection and analysis, enhancing transparency and strengthening its capacity to monitor compliance.

In this context, this study focuses on capturing accountants' perceptions of the impact of the digital transformation promoted by the AT on accounting practices. Specifically, it examines how this digital transformation contributes to preventing fraud and tax evasion, how it influences the relationship between accountants and their clients, and how it fosters the digitalization of accounting itself. To address these questions, a qualitative, exploratory study was conducted, based on semi-structured interviews with seven accounting professionals, providing an in-depth analysis of the implications of digitalization on their daily practices.

2. Methodology

This study adopts a qualitative methodology, gathering descriptive data through direct interactions with participants. Qualitative research is particularly suited to exploring complex social issues, providing deep insights into individual perceptions, behaviors, and experiences. Its open-ended, flexible approach is essential for examining complex topics, such as digital transformation's impact on accounting practices, enabling the researcher to assess how accountants perceive the effects of the Tax Authority's (AT) digital initiatives on their work and client relationships.

Focusing on participants' perspectives, qualitative research offers a comprehensive view of the phenomena under study. This methodology aligns with the study's goals of exploring how digitalization influences fraud prevention, client relationships, and overall transformation in accounting. Through narrative data collection, it allows for an in-depth examination of these themes, revealing complexities in professional adaptation to digital tools.

Semi-structured interviews are the primary data collection method, selected for their balance between structure and flexibility. With a predefined set of open-ended questions, this approach allows exploration of specific topics while giving participants freedom to add new points or elaborate. This structure ensures comprehensive coverage of digital transformation aspects and captures participants' experiences in their own words, yielding insights often missed in more rigid formats.

The sample includes seven accounting professionals, selected to offer diverse perspectives on AT's digital initiatives. The sample features varied experience levels and digital tool familiarity, providing balanced views from seasoned and newer professionals. Each participant contributed unique insights into digitalization's effects on work practices, client relationships, and perceived challenges, allowing the study to capture a broad understanding of digital transformation's impact on accounting.

Data collection involved individual interviews, with prior information provided about the study's purpose, confidentiality, and voluntary participation. Informed consent was obtained to ensure participants understood that their responses would be anonymous and used solely for research. The one-on-one setting encouraged open discussions without external influence.

The semi-structured interview guide covered key study themes, addressing participants' backgrounds, AT's digitalization initiatives, and their impacts. Topics included digitalization's advantages and disadvantages, digital tools' role in fraud prevention, changes in client interactions, and essential digital skills. These questions prompted detailed responses, revealing digital transformation's practical and conceptual implications.

Each interview lasted approximately 45 minutes and was audio-recorded, with consent, for accurate transcription and analysis. Verbatim transcripts preserved the depth of responses, and were reviewed multiple times to ensure accuracy and support reliability.

A thematic analysis approach was applied, a standard method for identifying, analyzing, and reporting data patterns. This approach allowed systematic categorization into themes, facilitating the interpretation of complex narratives. Thematic analysis is particularly suited to this study, enabling a thorough examination of themes like efficiency, fraud prevention, client relationships, and skill adaptation.

Thematic coding was used to organize data into meaningful categories. Initial coding highlighted relevant themes, such as challenges with AT's systems, benefits of digital tools, and the changing client-accountant relationship. Themes were refined through an iterative process to accurately represent participants' views.

The analysis focused on identifying both commonalities and divergences among responses. Consensus areas highlighted shared views, like digital tools' positive impact on fraud prevention, while differing responses revealed unique perspectives, such as adaptation levels based on experience. This dual approach provides a well-rounded view of digital transformation's influence on accounting.

To ensure validity and reliability, member checking allowed participants to review transcripts and provide feedback, verifying statement accuracy. Peer debriefing was conducted with colleagues experienced in qualitative methods to offer feedback on coding and thematic analysis, helping reduce researcher bias. Reliability was further supported by consistent interview protocols and core questions across participants, ensuring comparability and robust analysis. All data was securely stored, with transcripts reviewed multiple times for reliable interpretation.

The profile of the participants is described in Table 1:

Table 1 – Participant's profile

Participant Code	Age	Gender	Academic Training	Profession	Years of experience
A1	26	Male	Accountancy degree; Postgraduate Auditing	Certified Accountant	3
B1	50	Male	Degree in Economics	Certified Accountant	23
C1	49	Female	Degree in Economics	Certified Accountant	21
D1	51	Female	Degree in Economics	Accounting Consultant	27
E1	23	Female	Accounting degree	Accounting Technician	2
F1	53	Female	Degree in Accounting and Management	Certified Accountant	31
G1	34	Female	Accounting Technician Vocational Course	Accounting Assistant	13

Source: Own elaboration

Informed consent was obtained prior to each interview, and participants were fully briefed on the study's aims, their rights, and the measures taken to ensure data protection.

3. Results Presentation and Discussion

The interviews, conducted in April 2024 (six in-person and one online), each lasting around 45 minutes, revealed how Portuguese accounting professionals view the Tax Authority's (AT) digital transformation initiatives. Their technological profile reveals how equipped these professionals are to handle AT's digital tools. It shows a wide use of digital tools like CRM, SAGE, Primavera, CentralGest, SAP, Excel, PHC, Toconline, and Olisoft. This diversity reflects the range of software needed in modern accounting, underscoring the importance of digital skills in managing complex tax tasks (Dias, 2012; Laar et al., 2020).

Codes representing key themes were developed to analyze interview data, aligning with the study's main objectives: examining AT's digital transformation's impact on fraud prevention, accountant-client relationships, and further digitalization.

1. **TechSkills:** Focuses on required tech skills due to AT's digital initiatives, referencing CRM, SAGE, and Microsoft 365, and highlighting adaptability and digital literacy needs. This theme supports the study's goal of analyzing the impact of digital tools on accounting skills.
2. **PortalUse:** Captures the Finance Portal's role in tax digitalization, including VAT filings and tax document access. It also notes limitations, such as system overloads and fragmented information, relevant to examining AT's digital measures' impact on daily practices.
3. **FraudPrev:** Covers the influence of AT's digitalization on fraud prevention, including tools like electronic invoicing and data cross-referencing for enhanced transparency and compliance. This aligns with the study's goal of assessing digital tools' role in fraud prevention.
4. **BureauPriv:** Addresses the complexity and privacy concerns within AT's digital systems, discussing how bureaucracy and privacy issues (e.g., with E-invoice) affect compliance. This theme supports analyzing challenges in digital tax transformation.
5. **ClientRel:** Examines the effect of digitalization on accountant-client relationships, noting improved information-sharing and some client resistance to digital methods. This aligns with the study's objective of exploring digitalization's influence on client interactions.
6. **DataCrossRef:** Focuses on data cross-referencing as a tool for fraud detection and digitalization, referencing data integration between AT and banking systems and proposed expansions with Social Security. This supports the study's objective of evaluating digitalization's role in regulatory improvements.
7. **DigImpact:** Encompasses broader impacts of AT's digitalization on accounting roles, identity, and strategic functions, aligning with the study's objective to understand digital initiatives' effects on accounting practices and the profession's future.

Participants emphasized essential skills like proficiency in Microsoft 365 (especially Excel), adaptability, and familiarity with accounting software, essential for using AT's digital tools effectively. These skills echo Gaibazzi et al. (2021) and Kruskopf et al. (2020), who argue that digital competence in data management and computing is now critical for accountants.

The Finance Portal was highlighted as central to AT's digital ecosystem for tasks such as tax filing and document consultation, supporting daily workflows and aligning with Santos (2023). However, limitations were noted. A1 mentioned fragmented data complicating access, suggesting that better centralized information could improve efficiency. D1 also pointed out system overload during peak filing times, echoing Silva (2019) on the need for system improvements to enhance digital tax measures.

A primary study goal is to assess how AT's digitalization supports fraud prevention. Interviewees agreed that mechanisms like electronic invoicing and data cross-referencing with banks have strengthened fraud detection. B1 noted that E-invoice allows real-time transaction tracking, aligning with Alm (2021) on transparency improving compliance.

Some limitations in fraud detection remain, as noted by A1 and C1, who pointed to challenges in detecting fraud in areas lacking digital trails, such as misuse of per diems. This gap aligns with Mosteanu and Faccia (2020) on the limitations of digital systems in certain fraud cases. The findings suggest that while effective, AT's digital tools may require enhancements, like advanced data analytics, for improved fraud detection.

Digital processes have also impacted accountant-client relationships. Interviewees observed improved information-sharing as clients are encouraged to submit documents digitally, though some still prefer paper. This shift mirrors Due et al. (2018) on digital efficiency but also the adaptation challenges. A1 noted client resistance, which can hinder digital adoption, a barrier identified by Rasid et al. (2019). Greater client education may be needed to overcome these challenges.

F1 noted that digital transparency may cause discomfort for clients used to privacy, aligning with Laar et al. (2020) on managing transparency sensitively. Overall, these dynamics highlight the complexities digitalization brings to accountant-client interactions, meeting the study's objective of examining these professional changes.

A critical component of AT's digital strategy is data cross-referencing, recognized as essential for promoting further digitalization. A1 stressed cross-checking AT data with income declarations, which aids systematic verification, supporting Warner et al. (2015) on integrated data systems' role in fiscal transparency. Cross-referencing with banking systems also helps reduce tax evasion by verifying transaction data, as D1 noted. Scarcella (2019) similarly emphasizes the value of integrating financial data for detecting irregularities.

Interviewees suggested expanding data-sharing to include Social Security, which would help detect discrepancies between income and assets, supporting Tamanaha (2020) on comprehensive data sharing's benefits for fraud detection and digitalization. These insights align with the study's goal of evaluating how AT's initiatives promote digitalization in accounting.

Findings indicate that AT's digital transformation has significantly impacted Portuguese accounting practices, fulfilling the study's objectives. First, tools like E-invoice and bank data cross-referencing have strengthened fraud prevention, supporting Alm (2021) and Scarcella (2019) on digital tools' compliance role. Second, digital processes have reshaped accountant-client relationships, improving efficiency but requiring adaptation by both parties, as Due et al. (2018) and Rasid et al. (2019) discuss. Finally, data cross-referencing supports broader digitalization, integrating financial and tax data to enhance compliance, in line with Warner et al. (2015) and Tamanaha (2020).

4. Conclusion

The Tax Authority (AT)'s digitalization efforts have advanced tax management, fraud prevention, and modernized accounting practices in Portugal. This study captures Portuguese accountants' views on how these digital changes have impacted their routines, client relations, and adaptation to new standards. Findings show that digitalization boosts efficiency and transparency, enabling accountants to work with greater accuracy and control. Yet, challenges persist, including system complexity, client resistance to digital transitions, and privacy concerns.

A key contribution of the study is its focus on fraud prevention. AT's digital tools, like electronic invoicing and data cross-referencing with banking information, enhance transparency and compliance monitoring, aligning with studies linking digitalization to improved fiscal oversight (Alm, 2021; Scarcella, 2019). However, certain fraud types remain undetected, suggesting the need for ongoing improvements, possibly via advanced analytics and expanded data integration.

Digitalization's effect on accountant-client relationships also emerged as a critical theme. While digital tools ease communication and information sharing, some clients struggle with adapting to new methods. Confirming findings by Rasid et al. (2019), client resistance can hinder transformation. The study recommends greater client education to facilitate smoother digital transitions and build trust in these systems.

Data cross-referencing is highlighted as essential for promoting further digitalization in accounting. It allows AT to verify financial data comprehensively, reinforcing tax reporting accuracy and accountability. Expanding data-sharing to entities like Social Security could strengthen these outcomes, aligning with Warner et al. (2015) and Tamanaha (2020) on the value of integrated data systems for effective tax administration.

In conclusion, while AT's digital initiatives provide significant benefits in fraud prevention, client interactions, and digital adaptation, ongoing improvements are essential. Addressing system limitations, enhancing usability, and supporting client adaptation will amplify these initiatives' impact. This research enriches the literature on digital tax transformation, offering insights for policymakers on refining digital tools to strengthen relationships between the tax system and accounting professionals, ultimately fostering a more effective and trusted tax environment in Portugal.

AKNOWLEDGMENT: This work was financially supported by the research unit on Governance, Competitiveness and Public Policy (UIDB/04058/2020) + (UIDP/04058/2020), funded by national funds through FCT - Fundação para a Ciência e a Tecnologia.

References

Aleixo, M. M. (2024). Impacts of Technological Innovation on Accounting Practices and Accountants' Competences.

Alm, J. (2021). Tax evasion, technology, and inequality. *Economics of Governance,* 22(4), 321-343.

Andrade, C. B. H., & Mehlecke, Q. T. C. (2020). Technological innovations and digital accounting: A case study on the acceptance of digital accounting in the process of generating accounting information in an accounting office in Vale do Paranhana/RS. *Electronic Journal of Accounting Sciences*, *9*(1), 93-122.

Arango-Morales, A. J., Delgado-Cruz, A., & Tamayo-Salcedo, A. L. (2020). Digital competence of tourism students: Explanatory power of professional training. European Journal of Investigation in Health, Psychology and Education, 10(1), 310-326.

Augusto, R. P. D., Braga, T., & Kruklis, A. G. (2018). The evolution of accounting. Brazilian Journal of Business Management, 9(23), 17.

Baert, S., Lippens, L., Moens, E., Sterkens, P., & Weytjens, J. (2020): The COVID-19 Crisis and Telework: A Research Survey on Experiences, Expectations and Hopes.

Bakarich, K. M., & O'Brien, P. E. (2021). The robots are coming... but aren't here yet: The use of artificial intelligence technologies in the public accounting profession. Journal of Emerging Technologies in Accounting, 18(1), 27-43.

Bala, E. S., & S. B., P. (2014). Role of Information Technology in Effective Implementation of Customer Relationship Management. Journal of Marketing & Communication, 50-55.

Cavelius, F., Endenich, C, Zicari, A. (2020): Back to basics or ready for take-off? The tensions on the role of management controllers in the digital age, Comptabilité, Contrôle, Audit, 26(2): 87-121.

Coenen, M., & Kok, R. A. (2014). Workplace flexibility and new product development performance: The role of telework and flexible work schedules. *European management journal*, *32*(4), 564-576.

CPA Australia. (2019). CPA Australia's my firm. My future. CPA Australia.

Dias, B. S. M. M. (2012). New information and communication technologies in accounting and their contribution to decision-making (Doctoral Thesis, University of Beira Interior (Portugal)).

Due, B., Traerup, J., Hennelund M. & Christensen H. (2018). Digital transformation: Impact of new technologies on the accounting industry.

Duong, D. C. T., & Fledsberg, K. (2019). Digitalisation of the Accounting Industry: The influence of digitalisation on the accountants' role and their self-understanding. An exploratory study based on 13 Norwegian accounting firms (Master's thesis, Universitetet i Agder; University of Agder).

Endenich, C., Lachmann, M., Schachel, H., & Zajkowska, J. (2022). The relationship between management control systems and innovativeness in start-ups: Evidence for product, business model, and ambidextrous innovation. *Journal of Accounting & Organisational Change, 19*(5), 706-734

Fernandez, D., & Aman, A. (2018). Impacts of Robotic Process Automation on Global Accounting Services. Asian Journal of Accounting and Governance, 9, 123-132.

Francisco, T. M. M. (2019). The impact of the use of information and communication on the practice of the certified accountant profession: the perception of certified accountants in the district of Leiria (Master's thesis in Management Control). Polytechnic Institute of Leiria - School of Technology and Management, Leiria.

Gaibazzi, M. F., Berizzo, M. L., & Trottini, A. M. (2021). Demand for digital competences in Public Accountants. A view from Higher Education. SaberEs, 13(1), 7390

García, A. M. D., & Cuello, R. O. (2017). The Immediate Supply of Information in value added tax. IDP. Revista de Internet, Derecho y Política, (25), 83-93.

Hashimzade N, Myles GD, Page F, Rablen MD (2015) The use of agent-based modelling to investigate tax compliance. Economics of Governance 16 (2): 143-164.

Hemberg, E, Rosen J, Warner G, Wigesinghe G, O'Reilly U-M (2016) Detecting tax evasion: A co-evolutionary approach. Artificial Intelligence and Law 24 (2): 149-182.

International Accounting Education Standards Board (2018). Accounting Education Insights - ICT Skills Development: The Digital Age and Opportunities for Accountants.

Khan, N., Khan, S., Tan, B. C., & Loon, C. (2021). Driving digital competency model towards IR 4.0 in Malaysia. Journal of Physics: Conference Series (Vol. 1793, No. 1, p. 012049).

Kitsios, E., Jalles, J. T., & Verdier, G. (2023). Tax evasion from cross-border fraud: does digitalisation make a difference? *Applied Economics Letters, 30*(10), 1400-1406.

Kruskopf, S., Lobbas, C., Meinander, H., Söderling, K., Martikainen, M. & Lehner, O., (2020). Digital Accounting and the Human Factor: Theory and Practice. *ACRN Journal of Finance and Risk Perspectives.* 9(1). 78-89.

Laar, E., Van., Deursen, A. J., Van Dijk, J. A., & De Haan, J. (2020). Measuring the levels of 21st-century digital skills among professionals working within the creative industries: A performance-based approach. Poetics, 81, 101434.

Leitner-Hanetseder, S., Lehner, O. M., Eisl, C., & Forstenlechner, C. (2021). A profession in transition: actors, tasks and roles in AI-based accounting. Journal of Applied Accounting Research, 22(3), 539-556. https://doi.org/10.1108/JAAR-10-2020-0201

Lopes, A., & Rodrigues, C. (2010). The Modernisation of Public Administration requires a Bureaucratic Revolution. Lusíada. Economy and Business

Marr, B. (2018). The Digital transformation of accounting and finance-artificial intelligence, robots and chatbots. *Retrieved on May, 5*, 2020

Melnychenko, S., Volosovych, S., & Baraniuk, Y. (2020). Dominant ideas of financial technologies in digital banking. *Baltic journal of Economic studies*, *6*(1), 92-99.

Melo, C. (2018). E-fatura - AT's digital reform. Implications for tax revenue growth. Master's dissertation, Instituto Superior de Gestão, Lisbon.

Morales, J., & Lambert, C. (2013). Dirty work and the construction of identity. An ethnographic study of management accounting practices. Accounting, Organisations and Society, 38(3), 228- 244.

Mosteanu, N. R., & Faccia, A. (2020). Digital systems and new challenges of financial management-FinTech, XBRL, blockchain and cryptocurrencies. *Quality-Access to Success*, *21*(174), 159-166.

Newman, M., & Westrup, C. (2005). Making ERPs work: Accountants and the introduction of ERP systems. European Journal of Information Systems, 14(3), 258-272. https://doi.org/10.1057/palgrave.ejis.3000539

OECD (2015), Addressing the Tax Challenges of the Digital Economy, Action 1 - 2015 Final Report, OECD Publishing, Paris.

Pereira, M. J., & da Silva, B. M. (2017). The acceptance of information technology by the accounting area. *Sistemas & Gestão*, *12*, 516-524.

Pereira, M. V. (2019). *Administrative Modernisation: a general perspective in the area of taxation* (Master's thesis).

Rolo, I. S. (2021). *The SAF-T (PT) Accounting file*. Coimbra Polytechnic Institute, Coimbra Higher Institute of Accounting and Administration.

Santos, R. J. S. (2023). Digital evolution in accounting and the Tax Authority.

Sari, N. Z. M., Afifah, N. N., Susanto, A., & Sueb, M. (2019). Quality accounting information systems with 3 important factors in BUMN Bandung Indonesia. Advances in Social Science, Education and Humanities Research, 343(1), 93-96. https://doi.org/10.2991/icas-19.2019.20

Silva, C. D. S. D. (2021). *The transition to digital accounting: a case study at Conceito Norte-Consultadoria de Gestão, Lda* (Doctoral dissertation).

Silva, D. A. A. (2019). *Tax fraud and "E-Fatura" in Portugal* (Master's thesis). Faculty of Economics, University of Porto.

Silveira, F. A., Cardoso, A. A., & Costa, E. S. (2018). Blockchain and accounting in the digital age: challenges or opportunities? *Annals of Applied Social Sciences Seminar*, *6*(6).

Smith, S. S. (2018). Digitisation and financial reporting-how technology innovation may drive the shift toward continuous accounting. Accounting and Finance Research, 7(3), 240-250.

Taib, A., Awang, Y., Shuhidan, S. M., Zakaria, Z. N. Z., Sulistyowati, S., & Ifada, L. M. (2023). Digitalisation of the accounting profession: An assessment of digital competencies in a Malaysian comprehensive university. *Asian Journal Of University Education*, *19*(2), 365-380.

Tamanaha, R. T. (2020). Taxation and the digital economy: analysing the tax treatment of cloud computing income (PhD Thesis, University of São Paulo).

Tax and Customs Authority (2022). Report on combating tax and customs fraud and evasion 2022. Ministry of Finance.

Warner G, Wijesiinghe S, Marques U, Badar O, Rosen J, Hemberg E, O'Reilly U-M (2015) Modelling tax evasion with genetic algorithms. Economics of Governance 16 (2): 165-178.

Warren Jr, J.D., Moffitt, K.C., Byrnes, P. (2015). How Big Data Will Change Accounting, Accounting Horizons, 29(2): 397-407.

Mental Accounting as an Alternative Approach to Financial-Literacy Education Programs

Amélia Cristina Ferreira da Silva, Anabela Martins da Silva,
Ione Aparecida Silva Cruz, Humberto Nuno Rito Ribeiro

1. Introduction

Individual financial imbalance refers to a situation where an individual has insufficient financial resources and income to cover their debts and expenses. This can stem from different factors, such as overspending, job loss, unexpected expenses, or poor financial planning. Often, these factors are exacerbated by specific socio-cultural contexts. In addition to causing financial stress, and inability to meet financial obligations, it also causes general instability for the individual and households. Thus, the financial education of families is a problem that causes worldwide concern due to the growing financial risks (Loomis, 2018), having already impacted the release of funding by the World Bank for developing countries (Xu & Zia, 2012). To reduce these risks, the OECD - Organization for Economic Cooperation and Development, or OCDE - Organisation de Coopération et de Développement Économiques, through INFE - International Financial Education Network, suggests creating national public policies, known worldwide by the acronym ENEF - National Strategy for Financial Education. Some countries have already adopted this strategy, such as the United States, Portugal and Brazil, but several are still adopting or regulating it. According to OCDE (2015), a broad group of countries is linking the development of their national strategies for financial education to fighting households and individuals' over-indebtedness. The financial imbalance of households and individuals is a social problem in many countries. People with financial imbalances live in a condition of economic distress that they cannot quit. Financial imbalance can be described as a condition in which there is a continual imbalance between obligations and assets and an incapacity to accomplish the agreements regularly (d'Alessio & Iezzi, 2013).

The literature has extensively studied the efficacy of financial education programs (Austrian et al., 2020; Hewett et al., 2017; Jones et al., 2019; Lucey & Henning, 2021; Riitsalu, 2018; Sims et al., 2020). The absence or insufficiency of financial knowledge in families, or the simple inability to apply this knowledge in everyday decisions, tends to have more negative consequences, the more unfavourable the starting socioeconomic condition of the individual, thus creating a cycle of poverty challenging to break (Atkinson, & Messy, 2012). However, although financial literacy is essential, it is not enough (Fernandes, Lynch, & Netemeyer, 2014). The simple transmission of economic and financial knowledge has been criticized due to its limited impact on individual behaviour. This debate puts into confrontation the traditional economic approach (homo economicus) and the behavioural economics approach (irrational decisions).

The theory of mental accounting warns about the environment's effect on individual economic decisions. Moreover, it advocates that a nudge can redesign the personal decision process, in its favour. Nudging refers to using subtle changes to the environment or decision-making process to encourage people to make choices that are in their best interest, i.e., individual can change their financial behavior through the proposition of a choice's architecture that helps individuals and families make more rational decisions. By using nudging techniques to encourage people to allocate their money more effectively, individuals can improve their overall financial well-being.

This research aims to measure and understand factors associated with financial imbalance. We performed a multiple regression with independent variables based on the traditional economic approach. We then added four news dimensions: Receiving, Saving, Donating, and Spending - RSDS, a financial education program inspired by mental accounting approach.

After this introduction, we presented the theoretical framework that focuses on mental accounting theory principles and RSDS as an alternative approach for redesigning individual financial decision behaviour. In chapter 3, we will explain the methodology used in the study, and chapter 4 addresses the results and discuss the model obtained. Finally, we will draw conclusions from the results, as well as some suggestions for further research.

2. Theoretical framework

2.1. Mental accounting theory

The basis of the study of mental accounting is in the work entitled A Behavioural Model of rational Choice, when Hebert Simon discusses bounded rationality in the decision-making process (Simon, 1955). However, the history of mental accounting is strongly associated with the research developed by Richard Thaler, especially in the field of microeconomics. He criticized Expected Utility Theory and presented Transaction Utility Theory (Rabin & Thaler, 2001; Thaler, 1980, 1999, 2008, 2017), highlighting psychological aspects that impact most people's behavioural attitudes. He argues that misapprehension in decision-making is the rule rather than the exception because the human mind's capacity to formulate and solve complex problems is tiny (Thaler, 1980).

Five years later, Thaler published his new theory of consumer behaviour, the transaction utility theory, in opposition to the standard economic theory, the expected utility theory (Thaler, 2008). Mental Accounting is conceptualized as the set of cognitive operations used by individuals and families as a function of the need to organize, evaluate, and track the control of financial activities (Thaler, 1999).

Throughout the research on mental accounting, Thaler and Sunstein (2008) started looking for solutions that would help individuals make the best decision, hence raising the expression Nudge. In other words, Nudge is any aspect of the architecture of choice that predictably changes people's behaviour without prohibiting any options or significantly altering their economic incentives. An intervention must be easy and cheap to avoid for it to be considered a mere Nudge. Moreover, Nudges are not impositions. For instance, arranging fruit at eye level is regarded as a Nudge, but banning junk food is not. Choice architecture is the proposition of alternatives that mirrors a good understanding of human behaviour, intending to encourage humans to make the best choice, also known as "good architecture" (Thaler & Sunstein, 2008). The authors who defend it propose that by using it, individuals can improve their decisions regarding health, money, happiness, and others. The "good" choice architecture helps people improve their ability to map and select options that can enhance their well-being.

2.2. RSDS model

The RSDS heuristic (Receiving, Saving, Giving, and Spending) is a financial education tool that aims to assist individuals in decisions involving according to four principles:

Receive and give thanks first: people must reflect and act in a way they can receive before spending. What they can and should do and how they will help, such as avoiding instalment payments and prioritizing cash payments.

Save for dreams to come true: people should be encouraged to save to make dreams come true. If saving is associated with something negative, like losing your job or getting sick, people will be discouraged because they unconsciously fear something terrible will happen.

Donate time and money: The goal of encouraging giving as a pillar for family financial sustainability stems from the idea that people who donate are happier. They also start to have different experiences that lead them to feelings of satisfaction more significant than those produced by financial spending for themselves. That is, they leave their often unnoticeable "selfishness" to go in search of attitudes and actions that benefit society as a whole

Spend consciously and avoid debt: aims to raise awareness that spending should be pleasurable, yes, but that, as a rule, it should be done intentionally, in a balanced way, and that it comes to fulfil its intended purpose, which is to increase well-being somehow, meet a need, and bring more comfort. Individuals seeking to buy in cash, and if they do not have the immediate resources, they seek to wait until they have them.

2.3. Financial imbalance

Financial imbalance is strongly linked to indebtedness, i.e., compromising one's ability to pay. This condition is being increasingly common in recent years, as excessive leverage and debt levels are leading to more unbalanced economies (vid. e.g. Ribeiro et al., 2012, Ribeiro & Pereira, 2022). The main cause that leads to this imbalance is the disordered desires in the face of scarce resources, that is, the lack of a project that encourages one to focus on what one wants more than the needs often created by the market. In modern societies, individuals are strongly stimulated to buy impulsively by paying with a credit card, thus generating short-term indebtedness and poor financial management. Despite personal reasons, many external factors can lead individuals to situations of financial imbalance, namely political, economic, social, and cultural factors.

In the table below, we present a summary of the constructs mentioned in the literature.

Table 1: Construct associated with individual financial imbalance.

Constructs	Author
Self-confidence	(Banco Central do Brasil, 2015)
Stress caused by debts	(Bylander & Res, 2021)
Personality traits	(Hamid & Loke, 2021)
Moral lessons associated with credit	(Bylander & Res, 2021)
Consumption Profile	(Amagir et al., 2020)
Risk Profile	(Thaler, 1980)
Financial Literacy	(Atkinson, & Messy, 2012; Banco Central do Brasil, 2015; Dituri et al., 2019)
Financial Knowledge	(Brugiavini et al., 2020); (Fernandes, Lynch, & Netemeyer, 2014)
Financial Imbalance	(d'Alessio & Iezzi, 2013; Cruz, Silva & Silva, 2021b)

The table above lists the concepts we retained from the literature review on financial imbalance.

3. Methodology

3.1. Data collection and participant's profile

To participate in the study, respondents must accomplish the following conditions:

To Work at State University of Feira de Santana – UEFS, in Brazil.

To have been through over-indebtedness

To have attended at least two of the three workshops of the financial education program based on RSDS, run at the State University of Feira de Santana.

The final database consisted of fifty participants: 72% female; 70% are between 31 and 50 years old; 78%have religion; 54% have up to 3 family members; and 92% complete college degrees.

By the time of data collection, may of 2019, the current exchange rate Euro (EUR) to Brazil Real (BRL) was approximately 1EUR = 4,39 BRL.

Compared with Brazilians' average monthly income, the respondents are well above because the average is up to 2 minimum wages (IBGE, 2010). According to this survey, only 15% receive up to 2 minimum wages. Regarding family income, 51% of respondents have a family income between 4 to 10 minimum wages; 10% have family incomes between 10 and 20 minimum wages, and only 3% have incomes over 20 minimum wages. When asked about the variation in wealth, 50% agree that it hasn't changed significantly, 24% consider that it has decreased a lot or somewhat, and 26% assume it has increased a little or a lot.

3.2. Factor Analysis

A factor analysis was developed for each dimension (factor), setting the number of factors to one in each procedure. For this purpose, only the items (the questions) with a variance greater than 0.1 were considered, thus excluding six items. Curiously, all excluded items due to a variance less than 0.1 belong to the financial knowledge group, thus inferring that financial knowledge often has little influence on financial decisions.

In the table below, we describe the ten factors (Dimensions) and the corresponding items (the questions):

Table 2: Dimensions resulting from factor analyses

Factor		Item	MIN	MAX	AVG	SD	VAR
Self-confidence	1.1	I am satisfied with my current financial situation	1	5	1,84	,79	,63
	1.2	I trust my retirement planning	1	5	1,98	,91	,84
	1.3	Generally, I feel able to manage my finances on my own	1	5	3,50	,93	,87
	1.4	I prefer to live for the present and let the future run by itself	1	5	2,22	,93	,87
Consumerist Profile	2.1	I admire people who exhibit their money, like expensive clothes and luxury cars	1	5	2,50	1,18	1,40
	2.2.	Money is there to be spent	1	5	3,00	,83	,69
Risk Tolerance	3.1	I am willing to risk some of my money when I save or invest	2	5	3,43	,87	,75
	3.2	I have a lot of debts these days	1	5	3,49	1,28	1,63
	4.1	In most cases, the responsibility for the financial decisions with some importance in the monthly expenses is mine	1	5	3,67	1,15	1,33

Table 2: *Continued*

Factor		Item	MIN	MAX	AVG	SD	VAR
Level of financial literacy	4.2	Are there people under eighteen in your household who own or have owned a piggy bank or something similar for savings?	0	1	,57	,50	,25
	4.3	Do you have a family budget at home? (Previously, you decide, for example, what part of the income goes to general expenses, mortgage/loan payment, savings or donation)	0	2	,90	,74	,54
Level of financial knowledge	5.1	A higher-return investment is likely to have a higher risk	0	1	,93	,26	,07
	5.2	In a country where inflation is high, prices do not change as much over time	0	1	,40	,49	,24
	5.3	A person should invest in different alternatives to reduce risks (e.g. savings, stocks, real estate, etc.)	0	1	,58	,50	,25
	5.4	Whenever someone pays the minimum amount on their credit card bill, they are subject to interest on the remaining balance	0	1	,92	,27	,08
	5.5	An excellent way to control monthly expenses is to make a budget	1	1	1,00	,00	,00
	5.6	Imagine three friends who have won a lottery ticket for $1500 (one thousand five hundred dollars). How much does each one get if they decide to split the money equally?	0	1	,98	,14	,02
	5.7	Now, imagine that one of the friends has received the money and stored it in his safe at home. Considering that inflation is 5% per year, after one year, he will be able to buy: ...	0	1	,88	,33	,11
	5.8	Suppose you borrow $100 from a friend and, after a week, pay back $100. How much interest are you paying?	0	1	,92	,27	,08
	5.9	Suppose you put $100 into a savings account that yields 2% per year. You do not make any other deposits or withdraw money from this account. How much would you have in this account at the end of the first year, including interest?	0	1	,94	,24	,06
	5.10	if you do not make any deposits or withdrawals in the period, and if the interest is integrated into the principal, what would the balance be five years from now?	0	1	,46	,50	,25

Table 2: *Continued*

Factor		Item	MIN	MAX	AVG	SD	VAR
Attitude towards receiving	6.1	My expenses have never been higher than my income	1	5	2,18	1,04	1,09
	6.2	Regarding covering monthly expenses.... [If I lost my primary source of income today, would I be able to cover all expenses, without taking out a loan, for: ...	1	5	2,17	1,27	1,61
Attitude towards savings	7.1	Regarding savings, in the last 12 months...	0	3	,62	,80	,63
	7.2	I withdrew money from savings in the last 12 months	1	5	3,49	1,43	2,05
	7.3	I cut expenses in the last 12 months	1	5	3,48	1,28	1,64
Attitude towards Donation	8.1	I believe that giving produces happiness	1	5	3,78	,89	,79
	8.2	I donate because I want to contribute to a better world	1	5	3,76	,85	,72
	8.3	I donate for religious reasons	1	5	2,90	1,10	1,22
	8.4	I am satisfied with my life	1	4	3,19	,84	,71
	8.5	Do you practice any religion?	0	1	,80	,41	,17
	8.6	Regarding donations, in the last 12 months	0	4	1,22	1,26	1,59
	8.7	Are you registered in the "Nota Premiada" Bahia Campaign?	0	1	,50	,51	,26
	8.8	Are you aware that you can participate in a monthly state government lottery and allow an institution to benefit from it?	0	1	,58	,50	,25
	8.9	If your donation can be deducted from the amount due in your Individual Income Tax - IRPF, you: ...	-1	2	,70	,93	,87
Attitude towards Expenditure	9.1	Regarding financing... [The percentage of income paid monthly for home financing is].	0	3	,79	1,01	1,03
	9.2	Regarding financing... [The percentage of income paid monthly for car/motorcycle financing is].	0	4	,91	1,25	1,57
	9.3	Regarding financing... [The percentage of income paid each month for financing other debts is (e.g., credit cards, store carnets, loans)]	0	6	3,05	1,90	3,63

Table 2: *Continued*

Financial imbalance	10.1	I took out a new loan to pay other debts in the last 12 months	1	5	3,04	1,40	1,96
	10.2	I have used an overdraft in the last 12 months.	1	5	2,80	1,64	2,69
	10.3	I have paid the minimum on my card bill for the last 12 months.	1	5	2,20	1,44	2,08
	10.4	I have overdue or failed to pay some bills in the last 12 months	1	5	2,92	1,53	2,33

3.3. Traditional Research model

Our dependent variable is called "financial imbalance". Analyzing the data descriptively, we find that, when comparing the financial imbalance of the participants with the national sample, we find that the subjects in our sample are generally more balanced since it presents indebtedness indexes that suppose to be much lower, as revealed in table 3.

Table 3: Participants' financial imbalance vs national sample

	Servers	National Sample
Variables	**Agree/strongly agree**	**Agree/strongly agree**
I took out a loan cheaper than my debt, in the last 12 months	32%	7%
I have used an overdraft in the last 12 months.	20%	3%
I have paid the minimum on my card bill for the last 12 months.	20%	5%
I have overdue or failed to pay some bills in the last 12 months	40%	19%

Source: Research data (2019) and Banco Central do Brasil (2017)

When we compare the financial unbalance variables with the national average we notice that the participating servers present worrying situations in all items, because, in order to pay the bills or cover expenses, they took out loans, used overdraft checks, paid the minimum on their credit cards, and delayed or stopped paying some bills, the last item being the one that presents the most worrying value, 40% compared to the national average of only 19%.

Research Hypotheses: the traditional model

Decision-making capacity and financial imbalance

Our first hypothesis is that individuals' perception of their decision-making capacity may influence their financial decisions and behaviors. When comparing the participants' *self-confidence* in personal financial management with the national sample, we find that our sample is in a generally less favorable position, as shown in table 4:

Table 4: Participants employees' self-confidence vs national sample

	Servers	National Sample
Variables	Agree/strongly agree	Agree/strongly agree
I trust my retirement planning	6%	36%
I am satisfied with my current financial situation	2%	32%
I prefer to live for the present and let the future take care of itself	12%	33%
Generally speaking, I feel able to manage my personal finances on my own	62%	60%

*Inverted variables
Source: Survey data (2019); Banco Central do Brasil, (2017); OECD, 2013)

It is interesting that when comparing the data from the public servants with the national sample, a very big difference is noticed in all answers, the main difference being the confidence in retirement planning, where the public servants answer that they trust in 6%, while the national sample trusts in 36%, here it reveals the optimism of the Brazilian people, because, although the public servants have job stability, they are conservative when giving their opinion about the future.

As for satisfaction with their current financial situation, only 2% are satisfied and 86% report that they are not satisfied. The data also shows the concern with the future, since only 12% report living for the present without worrying about the future.

Of the responses, the one that is closest to the national average is the ability to manage personal finances alone, with a difference of only two percentage points, because, the majority agree at 62% and 60%, servers and national sample respectively, that they are able alone to manage finances. Thus, we formulate our first hypothesis:

H1: The lower the subject's **self-confidence** in his ability to manage personal finances, the greater his financial imbalance.

Consumerist Profile and financial imbalance

Consumerist Profile is, naturally, a variable that influences the way individuals manage their personal finances and, consequently, their financial imbalance. When we compare the participants' Consumerist Profile with the national sample, we find that our sample is generally less permeable to consumer behavior, as shown in table 5:

Table 5: Participants servers' Consumerist Profile vs national sample

	Servers	National Sample
Variables	**Agree/strongly agree**	**Agree/strongly agree**
I admire people who have possessions, like expensive clothes and luxury cars	16%	27%
Money is there to be spent	28%	43%

Source: Survey data (2019); Banco Central do Brasil, (2017); OECD (2013)

Admiring people who own expensive goods or clothes is not predominant to the respondents, as only 16%, agreed that they had this kind of feeling. In addition, only 28% of respondents agreed that "money is there to be spent", compared to the national average of 43%.

Thus, our second hypothesis is formulated in the following terms:

H2: The greater the subject's **Consumerist Profile**, the greater his or her financial imbalance

Risk tolerance and financial imbalance

The attitude towards risk, here called risk profile, is another factor that influences the management of individual finances. When comparing the risk profile of the participants, with the national sample, we find that the subjects in our sample are generally more tolerant to risk, as shown in table 6:

Table 6: Participants servers' risk profile vs national sample

	Servers	National Sample
Variables	Agree/strongly agree	Agree/strongly agree
I am willing to risk some of my money when I save or invest	56%	14%
I have too much debt these days	59%	24%

*Inverted variables
Source: survey data (2019)/(Banco Central do Brasil, 2017; OECD, 2013)

In relation to the national sample, it can be seen that the participants' aversion to risk is lower, since 56% are willing to risk part of their money on investments, compared to only 14% of the national average. In relation to debts, it can be seen that twice as many servant respondents are more indebted compared to the national sample, corresponding to 59%, while the participants of the national sample, 24% agree that they have many debts.

Thus, our third hypothesis is formulated in the following terms:

H3: The higher an individual's **risk tolerance** in personal finance, the greater his/her financial imbalance

Financial Literacy and Financial Imbalance

The level of financial literacy reflects the conscious behavior of the individual in terms of his personal finances, and it is expected that this level of financial literacy influences his financial balance. Indeed, one can regard financial literacy as key for a more balanced status, both at institutional and individual level (Ribeiro, 2024). When we compare the participants with the national sample, we find that the level of financial literacy of the subjects in our sample is generally higher than the national average, as shown in table 7:

When asked about financial decisions, 67% of respondents report that they are responsible, presenting a higher percentage compared to the national sample, where respondents are responsible for 43.4%. Of the respondents, the majority at 69.4%, claim to own the family budget. When compared

Table 7: Participants servers' attitude vs national sample

	Servers	National Sample
Variables	Agree/strongly agree	Agree/strongly agree
In most cases the responsibility for the financial decisions with some importance in the monthly expenses is mine	67,0%	43,4%
In your household are there people under the age of eighteen who own or have owned a piggy bank or something similar for savings?	57,1%	31,8%
Do you have a family budget at home? (Previously you decide, for example, what part of the income will go to general expenses, mortgage/loan payment, savings or donation)	69,4%	44,0%

Source: survey data (2019) / (Banco Central do Brasil, 2017; OECD, 2013)

to the national sample (Banco Central do Brasil, 2017) only 44% have one. Evidencing that the servers have a greater concern with the control that the sample of the Brazilian population surveyed.

Of the respondents who have children and young people at home, 57.1% have the habit of saving money, which reflects that there is a concern to educate children financially. This result was higher than the national sample, where only 31.8% of people under 18 have the habit of saving.

Thus, the fourth hypothesis is formulated in the following terms:

H4: The lower the subject's ***level of financial literacy***, the higher their financial imbalance.

Level of financial knowledge and financial balance

Financial literacy is being the focus of a wide range of literature, from financial advice and literacy, financial capability and satisfaction, inclusion and risk tolerance (vid. e.g. Çera et al. 2020a, 2020b, 2021), up to topics concerning ways to improve financial capability through improvement of financial literacy (Çera et al. 2020a). Financial knowledge translates into the technical knowledge that allows the individual to equate a financial problem and solve it rationally using technical and scientific concepts that can be acquired/transmitted through training in a classroom or similar context. As for the questions about financial knowledge, the results show that most of them have a good level of financial knowledge, since the level of correct answers for most questions was from 90% onwards, highlighting that the questions about credit cards and budgets were answered 100% correctly by the participants.

In questions that involve some mathematical skill, such as compound interest, there was a percentage of 46% of those who answered correctly, showing that less than half know the methodology that involves compound interest. Regarding the payment without interest that 66.7%, got it right, but still, 33.3% do not know the correct calculation. When compared to the results of a similar survey applied to a national sample of 2,002 participants (Banco Central do Brasil, 2017). When compared to the results of a similar survey applied to a national sample of 2,002 participants, it can be seen that the results of this survey mostly exceed the level of correct answers, especially for the question involving compound interest.

Table 8: Rate - Knowledge Variables

Variables	Correct answers	%
Risk Return	45	90,00%
Notions of inflation	47	94,00%
Investment Diversification	45	90,00%
Card Interest	50	100,00%
Budgeting	50	100,00%
Division	50	100,00%
Notions of inflation	43	86,00%
Interest-free payment	33	66,70%
Savings interest	47	94,00%
Compound Interest	23	46,00%

Source: survey data (2019).

It is evident that the public servants' respondents of this research have a higher level of knowledge in relation to the respondents of the national sample, getting on average 86.67% of the total of the questions, while the respondents of the national sample, had on average 76.51% of correct answers, with a positive difference of 10.16 percentage points, corresponding to a financial knowledge.

Thus, the fifth hypothesis is formulated in the following terms:

H5: The lower the subject's **level of financial knowledge**, the higher their financial imbalance

Traditional model on the financial imbalance of the individual

In view of the above, the proposed research model, based on traditional argumentation, takes the following configuration:

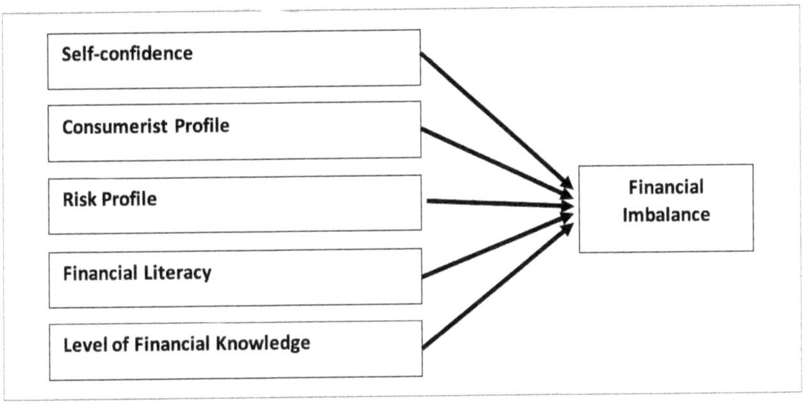

Figure 1. Financial Imbalance Variables

3.4. Research Model with RSDS dimensions

As argued in the previous chapter, the problem of the financial balance of families is not exhausted in the rationality principle of the decision maker, present in the Utility Theory. In fact, the limited reach of public policies that have sought to combat the phenomena of social exclusion for financial reasons, in general, have led policy makers to question their founding principles, particularly those that refer to the Classical and Neoclassical inspiration of Finance. For example, experience has shown that equipping the individual with a higher level of financial knowledge is no guarantee of better personal financial decisions, thus anticipating that the decision process is influenced by factors beyond rational control.

The behavioral finance approach, where the Mental Accounting theory is included, has highlighted the importance of a set of cognitive operations used by individuals and families and behavior patterns that violate the fungibility principle. Within this perspective, the most effective way to induce the individual to make decisions and adopt financial behaviors more in line with his rational interests, would be to reprogram his mental architecture. The most direct path to this change would be the creation of a "trigger" (*Nudge* theory), which allows the individual to neutralize the cognitive biases that lead him to irrational decisions. The RSDS model intends to be this "trigger", that is, it proposes to restructure the mental architecture of individuals, reorienting them in their individual financial choices and behavior with the ultimate goal of leading them to situations of greater financial equilibrium.

Next, the characterization of our sample will be presented, in each of the RSDS variables, before they attended the RSDS training.

Wheel - Receiving and financial imbalance

The level of attitude towards receipt reveals that in relation to income lower than expenses, the servers have a relatively low percentage of 18% compared to the national sample, which corresponds to 50%. table 9:

Table 9: Comparison of the attitude towards receiving with the national sample

	Servers	National Sample
Variables	**Agree/strongly agree**	**Agree/strongly agree**
My expenses have never been higher than my income	18%	50,0%
Regarding covering monthly expenses.... [If I lost my main source of income today, I would be able to cover all expenses.	14%	13,1%

Source: research data (2019) / (Banco Central do Brasil, 2017)

When asked about the coverage of monthly expenses, the results reveal that the response of the employees and the national sample were very close, between 14% of the employees and 13.1% of the national sample, that is, a very small percentage would be able to cover the monthly expenses if they lost their main source of income.

From these data the sixth hypothesis is formulated in the following terms:

H6: The lower the ***receiving attitude of*** the subject, the higher his financial imbalance.

RSDS - Savings and financial unbalance

The level of attitude towards savings are relatively low, which translates the much lower behavior in relation to the financial behavior that the national average presents, as revealed in table 10:

Table 10: Comparison of the attitude towards savings with the national sample

	Servers	National Sample
Variables	Agree/strongly agree	Agree/strongly agree
Regarding savings, in the last 12 months saved up to 10%	10%	53%
I withdrew money from savings in the last 12 months	26%	12%
I cut expenses, in the last 12 months	66%	35%

Source: research data (2019)/(Banco Central do Brasil, 2017)

When questioned, only 10% of the employees saved, compared to the national sample, in which 53% saved in the last 12 months. And as for withdrawals from savings, 26% of the servers took out, twice the percentage of the national sample, showing a greater lack of control over the budget, which can be explained by the need to cut expenses, representing 66%, almost twice the value of the national sample that cut expenses by 35%.

From these data the seventh hypothesis is formulated in the following terms:

H7: The lower the subject's **saving attitude**, the greater his or her financial imbalance.

Wheel - Giving and the financial imbalance

The level of attitude towards donation shows a behavior attentive to the need to donate, as revealed by table 11:

Table 11: Comparison of the attitude towards donation with the national sample

Variables	Servers Agree/strongly agree	National Sample Agree/strongly agree
I believe that giving produces happiness	74%	n. d.
I donate because I want to contribute to a better world	72%	n.a.
I donate for religious reasons	28%	n.a.
I am satisfied with my life	40%	n.a.
Do you practice any religion?	78%	n.a.
Regarding donation, in the last 12 months I have not donated anything	46%	n.a.
Are you registered in the "Nota Premiada" Bahia Campaign?	50%	n.a.
Are you aware that you can participate in a monthly state government lottery and also benefit an institution of your choice to receive benefits?	58%	n.a.
If your donation can be deducted from the amount due in your Individual Income Tax - IRPF, you: ...	46%	n.a.

n.a. - Not available
Source: Survey data (2019)

When asked about donation, 74% believe that donating produces happiness and 72% donate because they want to contribute to a better world, although 46% claim not to have donated anything.

From these data the eighth hypothesis is formulated in the following terms:

H8: The lower the subject's **giving attitude**, the greater his or her financial imbalance

Spending and the financial balance

The level of attitude towards spending by public servants translates the biased behavior towards purchases through indebtedness, especially of long term goods, well above the national average data. This behavior is explained by the ease with which public servants can obtain credit, unlike other workers, as revealed in table 12:

Table 12: Comparison of attitude towards spending with the national sample

	Servers	National Sample
Variables	**Agree/strongly agree**	**Agree/strongly agree**
Regarding financing... [The percentage of income paid monthly for home financing is up to 31-40	66%	34%
Regarding financing... [The percentage of income paid monthly for car/motorcycle financing is 11 to 20%.	62%	15%
Regarding financing... [The percentage of income paid each month for financing other debts is (e.g., credit cards, store carnets, loans)], more than 50%	20%	18%

Source: research data (2019)/(Banco Central do Brasil, 2017)

When questioned about financing their own homes, 66% totally agree that they finance from 31 to 40%, against 34% of the national average. As for mobile goods such as cars and motorcycles, most agree (62%) that they have financed goods, while the national average, most disagree with these values.

As for financing consumer goods, 20% of the employees agree that they finance 50% of their income monthly, a percentage that is very close to the national average, which corresponds to 18%.

From these data the ninth hypothesis is formulated in the following terms:

H9: The higher the subject's **spending attitude**, the greater his or her financial imbalance

Proposed model with the inclusion of the Wheel

This is the proposed model with the inclusion of the components of the RSDS Wheel, with emphasis on the financial activities of receiving, saving, giving, and spending:

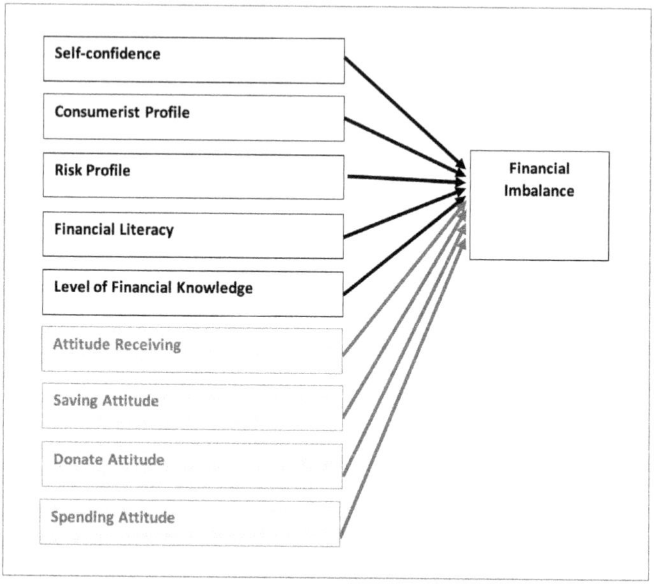

Figure 2: Financial Imbalance and attitudes RSDS variables

4. Results and discuss

Of the factors created, the following are significantly, positively and moderately correlated with financial imbalance: Consumerist Profile (32.1%), risk tolerance (47.5%) and level of financial knowledge (30.1%). Since they are positive, a higher assessment of these domains is associated with greater financial imbalance. Already significantly, but negatively correlated, is the attitude towards receiving (54.8%) and, being negative, higher values of the attitude towards receiving are associated with lower financial imbalance.

Table 13: Pearson Correlation of Financial Imbalance

		Self-confidence	Consumerist Profile	Risk Tolerance	Financial Literacy Level	Level of financial knowledge	Attitude towards receiving	Attitude towards savings	Attitude towards donation	Attitude towards spending
Financial Imbalance	R	,082	**,321***	**,475****	,006	**,301***	**-,548****	-,089	,251	,031
	p	,577	**,026**	**,001**	,974	**,037**	**,000**	,561	,101	,863

*: significant for 95% confidence
**: significant for 99% confidence

Considering that the objective of this study is to assess whether the attitude towards receiving, the attitude towards saving, the attitude towards giving and the attitude towards spending enhance the remaining factors in the financial balance, a Multiple Linear Regression with *backward* method was applied, initially taking the factors self-confidence, consumption profile, risk tolerance, level of financial literacy and level of financial knowledge as possible predictors of financial balance. The following valid models were obtained:

Table 14. Financial Imbalance Assessment Model without the Wheel components

Model 1: R = 0.645 R^2_{aju} =0.304 p=0.011 Error=0.79099		
Predictor variables	**B**	**P**
Constant	,020	,897
Self-confidence	,275	,216
Consumerist Profile	,207	,166
Risk Tolerance	,540	,003**
Financial Literacy Level	-,118	,487
Level of Financial Knowledge	,312	,042*
Model 2: R = 0.637 R^2_{aju} =0.317 p=0.006 Error=0.78359		
Predictor variables	**B**	**P**
Constant	,002	,990
Self-confidence	,194	,297
Consumerist Profile	,186	,199
Risk Tolerance	,522	,003**
Level of Financial Knowledge	,317	,037*
Model 3: R = 0.617 R^2_{aju} =0.314 p=0.003 Error=0.78543		
Predictor variables	**B**	**P**
Constant	-,037	,796
Consumerist Profile	,181	,210
Risk Tolerance	,483	,005**
Level of Financial Knowledge	,307	,042*
Model 4: R = 0.587 R^2_{aju} =0.299 p=0.002 Error=0.79416		
Predictor variables	**B**	**P**
Constant	-,051	,728
Risk Tolerance	,489	,004**
Level of Financial Knowledge	,310	,042*

*: significant for 95% confidence
**: significant for 99% confidence

Model 1 has an explanatory power of 30.4% and an associated forecast error of 0.79099. Model 2 has an explanatory power of 31.7% with an associated error of 0.78358, in model 3 these values are, respectively, 31.4% and 0.78543 and in the last Model 29.9% and 0.79416.

Thus, the best Model (significant, with higher explanatory power and lower error) is model 2, even though only risk tolerance and level of financial knowledge are significant predictors. Thus:

$$DESE\ F = 0.002 + 0.194{*}AC + 0.186{*}CP + 0.522{*}TR + 0.317{*}NCF$$

where,

DESE F: financial balance
AC: self-confidence
CP: Consumerist Profile
TR: risk tolerance
NCF: level of financial knowledge.

Introducing now in this Model the RSDS variables: attitude towards receiving, attitude towards saving, attitude towards giving and attitude towards spending, and applying again the Multiple Linear Regression with enter method for the variables identified in the above model and backward method for new variables, the model was obtained:

Table 15: Financial Imbalance Assessment Model with the components of RSDS

Model R = 0.787 R^2_{aju} =0.440 p=0.015 Error=0.86061		
Predictor variables	**B**	**P**
Constant	-,079	,655
Self-confidence	,234	,260
Consumer Appetite	**,084**	**,686**
Risk Tolerance	**,642**	**,016***
Level of Financial Knowledge	**,289**	**,137**
Attitude towards receiving	**-,459**	**,059**
Attitude towards savings	,004	,983
Attitude towards donation	-,165	,563
Attitude towards spending	-,103	,671

Thus, the model obtained is:

$$EF = -0.079 + 0.234*AC + 0.084*CP + 0.642*TR + 0.289*NCF - 0.459*AR + 0.004*AP - 0.165*AD - 0.103*AG$$

where,

EF: financial equilibrium
AC: self-confidence
CP: Consumerist Profile
TR: risk tolerance
NCF: level of financial knowledge
AR: attitude towards receiving
AP: attitude towards saving
AD: attitude towards donation
AG: attitude towards spending

The new model obtained continues to be significant and has an explanatory capacity for the variation in the financial balance of 44.0% and an error associated with the estimate of 0.86061. Now, although in this model the level of financial knowledge is no longer a significant predictor and the error increases by about 0.077, the value increases by 12.3% the ability to explain the variation in the financial balance at the expense of the predictor variables considered in the model. It can then be concluded that the RSDS variables enhance the prediction of financial balance at the expense of the variables included in the initial model.

The purpose of this paper was to explain the financial imbalance. In order to find a model that best explained financial imbalance, a factor analysis was developed, with the groups previously defined in 10 factors: (1) self-confidence; (2) Consumerist Profile; (3) risk tolerance; (4) level of financial literacy; (5) level of financial knowledge, (6) attitude towards receiving; (7) attitude towards saving; (8) attitude towards giving; (9) attitude towards spending and (10) financial imbalance. Each factor contains the corresponding items, where the mean, standard deviation and variance were calculated, and the items with variance lower than 0.10 were discarded.

After calculating the Pearson correlation between the independent variables and Financial Imbalance, the results were analyzed by applying a Multiple Linear Regression with the backward method, obtaining 4 valid models to explain the financial imbalance, with model 2 achieving the best correlation result, presenting $\mathbf{R^2_{aju}=0.317}$. being the most significant correlation of the three valid models. By introducing in this same model the behavioural variables of the RSDS model (attitude towards receiving, attitude towards saving, attitude towards giving and attitude towards spending), applying again the Multiple Linear Regression with the enter method for the variables identified in the model above and the new variables, we obtained the model where the correlation level was $\mathbf{R^2_{aju}=0.440}$, continuing to be significant and increasing the correlation between the variables, thus deducing that the variables of the RSDS model are relevant in the analysis of the financial imbalance. In this context, the results stimulate research on the effectiveness of the RSDS Wheel as a tool to combat individual financial imbalance.

Nevertheless, only four variables proved to be significant, as evidenced by the table below:

Table 16: Summary of results

	Correlation with financial imbalance	Result
H1: The lower the subject's **self-confidence** in his ability to manage personal finances, the greater his financial imbalance	Not significant	H1 not confirmed
H2: The greater the subject's **Consumerist Profile**, the greater his or her financial imbalance	Positively	H2 confirmed
H3: The **higher** an individual's **risk tolerance** in personal finance, the greater his/her financial imbalance	Positively	H3 confirmed
H4: The lower the subject's **level of financial literacy**, the higher their financial imbalance.	Not significant	H4 not confirmed
H5: The **lower** the subject's **level of financial knowledge**, the higher their financial imbalance	Positively	H5 not confirmed
H6: The **lower the receiving attitude of** the subject, the higher his financial imbalance.	Negatively	H6 confirmed

Table 16: *Continued*

	Correlation with financial imbalance	Result
H7: The lower the subject's **saving attitude**, the greater his or her financial imbalance.	Not significant	H7 not confirmed
H8: The lower the subject's **giving attitude**, the greater his or her financial imbalance	Not significant	H8 not confirmed
H9: The higher the subject's **spending attitude**, the greater his or her financial imbalance	Not significant	H1 not confirmed

When we look at the RSDS variable that was significantly related to financial imbalance - receiving attitude, we see that its concept is very close to the classical concept of the relationship between income and expenses, that is, the individual is able to secure enough income to cover his expenses. In this sense, the RSDS model does not seem to add anything new to what is already studied and known by classical economic and social theories. In fact, the model that results from the analysis can be represented in the figure below:

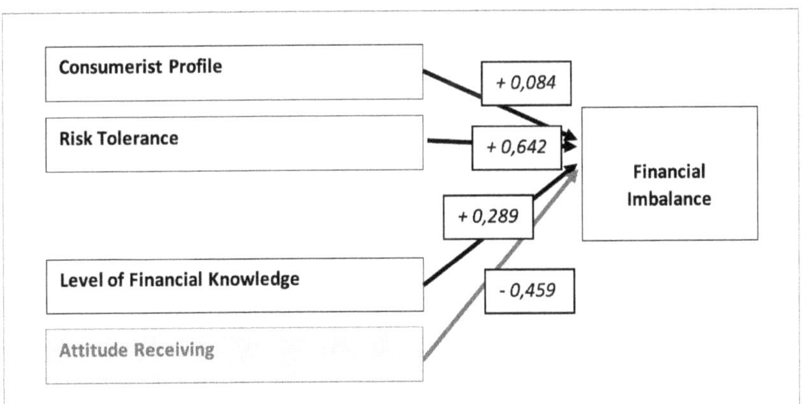

Figure 3. Final Financial Imbalance Model and RSDS attitudes

The model represented in figure 3, although it includes a component created from the model, maintains the paradigm of the classical theory. In fact, all the variables that explain financial imbalance in the model have been explored by the classical theories that explain the behaviour of economic agents. In view of the results obtained, it will be important to develop further studies on the RSDS model before investing in it as an instrument to combat Financial Imbalance.

5. Conclusions

From the various theoretical frameworks consulted and from studies by international organizations, the constructs that make up the model proposed to explain the financial imbalance were extracted. The initial model proposed 7 hypotheses, however, after statistical analysis and theoretical discussion, we were left with only 3 confirmed hypotheses:

H2: The greater the subject's **Consumerist Profile**, the greater his or her financial imbalance
H3: The **higher** an individual's **risk tolerance** in personal finance, the greater his/her financial imbalance
H6: The **lower the receiving attitude of** the subject, the higher his financial imbalance.

Overall, the results motivate further research on RSDS as a nudge, that is, as a "trigger" to leverage the redefinition of the financial choice architecture of individuals and families leading them to make more rational financial decisions, but do not allow for conclusions on its effectiveness. Additional, more robust studies will be needed for RSDS's effectiveness to be scientifically evaluated. Despite the effectiveness of such could not be observed, the authors believe that the inclusion of RSDS dimensions on research models may be a driver of an improved financial condition for individuals and households.

The main limitations of the study refer to the small sample size, because, larger samples would enable more in-depth analysis. Moreover, the instrument used to measure the variables under study is not validated, although it has been tested in previous studies.

For future investigations, it is recommended a case-control research design, using, applying validated scales. Thus, the model could be tested before and after the implementation of the RSDS program in a given population, to measure its impact on financial imbalance.

ACKNOWLEDGMENT: This work was financially supported by the research unit on Governance, Competitiveness and Public Policy (UIDB/04058/2020) + (UIDP/04058/2020), funded by national funds through FCT - Fundação para a Ciência e a Tecnologia.

References

Amagir, A., Groot, W., van den Brink, H. M., & Wilschut, A. (2020). Financial literacy of high school students in the Netherlands: knowledge, attitudes, self-efficacy, and behavior. *International Review of Economics Education, 34*. https://doi.org/10.1016/j.iree.2020.100185

Atkinson, A., & Messy, F. A. (2012). Measuring financial literacy: Results of the OECD/International Network on Financial Education (INFE) pilot study.

Austrian, K., Soler-Hampejsek, E., Behrman, J. R., Digitale, J., Jackson Hachonda, N., Bweupe, M., & Hewett, P. C. (2020). The impact of the Adolescent Girls Empowerment Program (AGEP) on short and long term social, economic, education and fertility outcomes: A cluster randomized controlled trial in Zambia. *BMC Public Health, 20*(1). https://doi.org/10.1186/s12889-020-08468-0

Aversion, L., & Quo, S. (1999). *Mental accounting. 5*(1991), 1–2.

Banco Central do Brasil. (2015). *Série Cidadania Financeira*. 1–39.

Banco Central do Brasil. (2017). *Série Cidadania Financeira: Estudos em Educação, Proteção e Inclusão* (5a.).

Brugiavini, A., Cavapozzi, D., Padula, M., & Pettinicchi, Y. (2020). On the effect of financial education on financial literacy: Evidence from a sample of college students. *Journal of Pension Economics and Finance, 19*(3), 344–352. https://doi.org/10.1017/S1474747218000276

Bylander, M., & Res, P. (2021). 'If You Fall, Stand Up Again': The Moral Nature of Financial Literacy in the Global South. *Development and Change, 52*(1), 26–53. https://doi.org/10.1111/dech.12627

Çera, G., Khan, K. A., Mlouk, A., & Brabenec, T. (2020b). Improving financial capability: the mediating role of financial behaviour. Economic Research-Ekonomska Istraživanja, 1–18.

Çera, G., Khan, K. A., Rowland, Z., Ribeiro, H. (2021). Financial Advice, Literacy, Inclusion and Risk Tolerance: The Moderating Effect of Uncertainty Avoidance. E&M Economics and Management, 24(4), 105–123.

Çera, G.; Khan, K.; Belas, J.; Ribeiro, H. (2020a). The role of financial capability and culture on financial satisfaction, Economic Papers, The Economic Society of Australia, 39(4), 389-406

Cruz, Ione; Silva, Anabela; Silva, A. (2021a). O papel da educação financeira na contabilidade mental das famílias: O caso do projeto de extensão da Universidade Estadual de Feira de Santana - UEFS. In F. I. de C. y R. Públicas (Ed.), *Libro de actas del Congreso CUICIID 2021* (1a., p. 1162).

Cruz, Ione; Silva, Anabela; Silva, A. (2021b). The impact of financial education on families: Financial education program for public servants. In *International Congress on 21st Century Literacies (ICCL2021) Livro de Atas* (Issue July, p. 481).

d'Alessio, G., & Iezzi, S. (2013). Household over-indebtedness: definition and measurement with Italian data. *Bank of Italy Occasional Paper*, (149).

Dituri, P., Davidson, A., & Marley-Payne, J. (2019). Combining Financial Education With Mathematics Coursework: Findings From a Pilot Study. *Journal of Financial Counseling and Planning*, *30*(2), 313–322. https://doi.org/10.1891/1052-3073.30.2.313

Fernandes, D., Lynch Jr, J. G., & Netemeyer, R. G. (2014). Financial literacy, financial education, and downstream financial behaviors. *Management science*, *60*(8), 1861-1883.

Hamid, F. S., & Loke, Y. J. (2021). Financial literacy, money management skill and credit card repayments. *International Journal of Consumer Studies*, *45*(2), 235–247. https://doi.org/10.1111/ijcs.12614

Hewett, P. C., Austrian, K., Soler-Hampejsek, E., Behrman, J. R., Bozzani, F., & Jackson-Hachonda, N. A. (2017). Cluster randomized evaluation of Adolescent Girls Empowerment Programme (AGEP): Study protocol. *BMC Public Health*, *17*(1). https://doi.org/10.1186/s12889-017-4280-1

IBGE. (2010). *Cidades*.

IBGE. (2019). Orçamentos Familiares 2017-2018. In *IBGE*.

Jones, C., Fouty, J. R., Lucas, R. B., & Frye, M. A. (2019). Integrating individual student advising into financial education to optimize financial literacy in veterinary students. *Journal of Veterinary Medical Education*, *46*(12), 562–572. https://doi.org/10.3138/jvme.1117-156r1

Kahneman, D., & Tversky, A. (1979). Prospect Theory: An Analysis of Decision under Risk. *Econometrica*, *47*(2), 263–292. https://doi.org/10.2307/1914185

Loomis, J. M. (2018). Rescaling and reframing poverty: Financial coaching and the pedagogical spaces of financial inclusion in Boston, Massachusetts. *Geoforum*, *95*, 143-152.

Lucey, T. A., & Henning, M. B. (2021). Toward critically compassionate financial literacy: How elementary preservice teachers view the standards. *Theory and Research in Social Education*, *49*(1), 107–136. https://doi.org/10.1080/00933104.2020.1859422

OCDE (2015). National strategies for financial education. OECD/INFE policy handbook.

OECD. (2013). *OECD/INFE toolkit to measure financial literacy and inclusion.*

Rabin, M., & Thaler, R. H. (2001). Anomalies - Risk Aversion. *Journal of Economic Perspectives*, *15*(1), 219–232.

Ribeiro, H. (2024). Benefits from improving low financial literacy through the lens of artificial intelligence. International Scientific Research and Innovation Congress,12, 923-932.

Ribeiro, H., Pereira, B. (2022), The role of debt and monetary policy on the mitigation of economic crises, Economic and Social Development Book of Proceedings, International Scientific Conference, 78, 48-49.

Ribeiro, H.; Vaicekauskas, T.; Lakštutienė, A. (2012). The Effect of Public Debt and Other Determinants on the Economic Growth of Selected European Countries. Economics and Management Journal, 17(3): 914-921.

Riitsalu, L. (2018). Goals, commitment and peer effects as tools for improving the behavioural outcomes of financial education. *Citizenship, Social and Economics Education*, *17*(3), 188–209. https://doi.org/10.1177/2047173418812045

Schulman, M. (1988). *RSDS da Fortuna*. Grupo Editorial Summus.

Simon, H. A. (1955). A Behavioral Model of Rational Choice. *The Quarterly Journal of Economics*, *69*(1), 99–118.

Sims, T., Raposo, S., Bailenson, J. N., & Carstensen, L. L. (2020). The future is now: Age-progressed images motivate community college students to prepare for their financial futures. *Journal of Experimental Psychology: Applied*, *26*(4), 593–603. https://doi.org/10.1037/xap0000275

Thaler, R. H. (1980). Toward a positive theory of consumer choice. *Journal of Economic Behavior & Organization*, *1*, 39–60. https://doi.org/10.1016/0167-2681(80)90051-7

Thaler, R. H. (1999). Mental Accounting Matters. *Behavioral Decision Making*, *206*, 183–206.

Thaler, R. H. (2008). Mental Accounting and Consumer Choice. *Marketing Science*, *27*(1), 15–25. https://doi.org/10.1287/mksc.1070.0330

Thaler, R. H. (2017). *Comportamento Inadequado: a construção da economia comportamental*. Actual.

Thaler, R. H., & Sunstein, C. R. (2008). *Nudge* (1a.). Academia do Livro.

Tiburi, M. (2007). A vida poderia ser diferente. *Revista Vida Simples*, *Ano 5*, n., 52–53.

Xu, L., & Zia, B. (2012). Financial literacy around the world: an overview of the evidence with practical suggestions for the way forward. *World Bank Policy Research Working Paper*, (6107).

The Importance of Governance for Religious Charities

Augusto Simões, Humberto Nuno Rito Ribeiro

1. Introduction

Religious charities have shown themselves to have an enormous capacity to respond effectively to social emergencies and to support citizens in situations of greater vulnerability. The importance of their assistance activities and the lack of capacity of the State to resolve many of the social problems that affect contemporary society, has sparked interest in the study and adoption of governance practices and principles, as a way of optimising performance, protecting the interests of stakeholders and contributing to the sustainability of these institutions.

Given the public nature of religious charities and the scarcity of resources with which they operate, the issue of trust becomes very important, since those who support them seek to ensure that the resources invested have been and are being used honestly and efficiently. Therefore, their success depends on their ability to demonstrate accountability and transparency, which, in turn, strengthens trust (Connolly & Hyndman, 2013b; Cordery & Morgan, 2013). There should be public concern about whether the resources entrusted to them are being used appropriately, effectively and efficiently, and charities should therefore be required to disclose and clarify how they have exercised their responsibilities (Vinten, 1997). Grey Matter Research (2008) concluded in their study that it is necessary to value donors' perceptions and expectations in order to maintain the continued support of charities, and that charities must be prudent in their spending and transparent with the donations they receive, so accountability and prudence are necessary components for maintaining donor support. Charities must adapt to the current situation of greater and better accountability and be seen as an example of good governance practices, since they are not self-sufficient; their survival depends on raising donations and other resources, and it is desirable that they develop (Vinten, 1997). It is important for charities to demonstrate the effective presence of control mechanisms and common governance practices, which keep managers at an acceptable level of discretionary action and increase the degree to which resources are allocated to the mission (Blevins, Eckardt & Ragozzino, 2018). However, despite the recognized importance of charities in social support, governance structures in the sector are often neglected, which leads to weak accountability and governance, weak financial management and internal controls, and a lack of necessary transparency (Newton, 2015).

There will be greater motivation to support the development of religious charities if their activities and the competence with which they are carried out are known, and if those who allocate resources are concerned with their use and maximizing the satisfaction of the needs they aim to meet. Good governance practices are seen as a way of improving management and aim to create value for society, the long-term vision of social activities, improved performance and access to donations and contributions.

The topic becomes interesting, since it examines how the adoption of governance practices and principles by Misericórdias can influence their financial performance and fundraising, seeking to provide insights into the effectiveness of certain governance practices and principles in mobilizing resources, essential to fulfilling objectives and achieving the mission.

2. Literature Review

The Social Economy, the Non-Profit Sector or Third Sector, has become relevant in Europe, providing services that the public and private sectors cannot meet (Chaves & Monzón, 2001). The term "Third Sector" is the most common, especially in Europe, and includes entities in the non-profit sector and the Social Economy, which are not profit-making and focus on meeting the needs of the community. However, in order to maintain their financial sustainability, these entities can generate surpluses, as long as these profits are applied to achieve their main objectives (vid. e.g. Ben-Ner & Jones, 1995; Hallock, 2002; Hopt, 2010; Simões & Ribeiro, 2022a,b,c, 2023, 2024a,b).

Social Economy entities play a fundamental role in responding to local social problems and are increasingly recognized for their vital economic and social roles, increasingly acting in areas that the State cannot meet. Despite the growth in the number of these entities over the last decades, their management and governance models have not kept up with this evolution. These entities are private and autonomous, do not distribute profits and generally depend heavily on human and financial resources. Portugal is considered one of the first countries in Europe to have specific legislation for the Social Economy sector, defining it as the set of economic and social activities that aim to pursue the general interest of society, either directly or through the pursuit of the interests of its members, users and beneficiaries, carried out, among others, by the Misericórdias.

The Misericórdias are among the oldest Social Economy entities in Portugal (Andrade & Franco, 2007), with a focus on social assistance and the practice of the Catholic religion. The Misericórdias emerged in a period of economic prosperity, went through a period of economic uncertainty and evolved into comprehensive institutions over the centuries, contributing significantly to charity and the social well-being of the most vulnerable. In 2023, there were 388 active Misericórdias in Portugal ("Who We Are in Misericórdias", 2024), which provide, in addition to Catholic worship, a variety of services, while maintaining a commitment to the principles of solidarity and human dignity. With the Discoveries, Misericórdias also reached Brazil, Japan, India and other regions of the world (Union of Portuguese Misericórdias). Misericórdias play a fundamental role in filling the gaps left by the public and private sectors in the provision of social services and in responding to the needs of the community. Misericórdias' main mission is to improve the quality of life of the population, especially those most in need, playing an important economic and social role in social cohesion. Their importance arouses interest in the study and adoption of governance practices and principles, as a way of optimizing their performance, protecting the interests of stakeholders and contributing to their sustainability. The adoption of good governance practices aims to increase the value of these institutions and facilitate access to resources, contributing to their sustainability.

Governance in religious charities is significantly related to donation behaviour, affecting transparency, effectiveness, and donor trust. Poor governance quality can lead to a decrease in donation values, as donors consider governance aspects in their decisions (Lacruz, Nossa, Guedes & Lemos, 2021). Yasmin, Haniffa and Hudaib (2014), in their study on accountability reported by religious charities, concluded that the accountability of these institutions is generally basic, focusing on descriptive information rather than more complete information based on value judgments, due to the high levels of trust among donors, which results in a lower demand for detailed information on accountability. In turn, Muslih, Panjaitan, Hotang and Delfira (2022) in their study on good institutional governance based on religion, concluded that transparency, accountability, independence and equity are crucial principles of good governance to maintain trust and effective management of the church and that the church should encourage the participation of the congregation in governance processes, in order to increase accountability and collective decision-making. They also concluded that these institutions do not have a governance structure and that their governance practices are influenced by religious teachings, which shape church operations and interactions with the community. Rossini and Silva (2018), in their study on the analysis of good practices in a religious institution, concluded that, despite the lack of specific knowledge of governance principles, the religious institutions analyzed had already adopted many of the governance practices in their management, as well as identified possible areas for improvement, such as strategic planning and raising financial resources.

There are several studies that establish a strong link between institutional performance and governance practices and principles (vid. e.g. Gregg, 2001; Hilmer, 1998; Kiel & Nicholson, 2002). There is also evidence that improved governance is correlated with economic growth and development. In turn, Zainon, Atan, Ahmad & Wah (2012) and Bellante, Berardi, Machold, Nissi & Rea (2018) highlight the existence of positive relationships between financial performance and governance variables. Good governance practices allow charities to have easier access to resources, reduce capital costs, improve stakeholder reputation and institutional performance (Claessens, Djankor, Fan & Lang, 2002). Governance practices affect financial management by promoting accountability, transparency and responsible management of resources, and in turn, governance practices that promote transparency and accountability can increase the trust of stakeholders, including donors and partners, by demonstrating that resources are being managed effectively and responsibly, attracting financial support and other resources (Bellante et al., 2018). Governance practices are essential to ensure the trust of the public, donors and all other stakeholders, as well as to ensure the appropriate use of resources and the effective delivery of services. It is therefore important to define clear principles, procedures and relationships, to be accountable to all stakeholders and to seek efficiency and effectiveness in the management of these institutions. By implementing sound governance practices, charities can foster the trust of donors, beneficiaries and the wider community, demonstrating a commitment to effectiveness, ethics and positive impact. Trust is essential for these institutions to obtain the resources they need to achieve their objectives, and trust depends on the quantity and quality of disclosures (the first step towards accountability) and transparency (the basis of all forms of accountability) in the efficiency with which resources are used to achieve objectives and fulfil the mission. Governance practices are considered as resource management mechanisms that help ensure the effective and efficient allocation of resources available to charities (Elmagrhi, Ntim, Malagila, Fosu & Tunyi, 2018). Governance practices play a crucial role in helping charities make their donors want to give more money to the mission they aim to serve (Blevins, Eckardt & Ragozzino, 2018), positively influencing charitable missions. It is also important that governance practices are aligned with the relevant principles and recommendations of governance codes, as a way to ensure that the charity is operating according to recognized standards of accountability, transparency and effectiveness, which can strengthen its credibility, social impact and stakeholder trust. Governance codes provide guidance on best governance practices that charities should follow, which is why the Portuguese Institute of Corporate Governance (IPCG) published the Governance Code for Third Sector Entities (CGETS) in 2014, with the aim of proposing a set of guidelines, principles and recommendations that aim to promote the modernization and professionalization of governance models for Third Sector institutions, so that they can continue to innovate in responding to social problems.

Because charities rely on external resources to fund their activities and accomplish their mission, governance practices must be geared toward ensuring that these institutions maintain and optimize their relationships with donors, and how they manage these dependencies without compromising their ability to survive and thrive is important (Pfeffer & Salancik, 1978). Governance practices that encourage innovation and flexibility can help these institutions respond quickly to new opportunities and challenges, thereby ensuring continued access to resources (Bellante et al, 2018).

Governance is essential to ensuring that religious charities operate effectively, ethically, and responsibly, fostering community trust and engagement, and ensuring sustainability. Effective governance promotes transparency in the operations and financial management of religious charities, ensuring that resources are used responsibly and that community members have confidence in leadership, as well as helping to identify and develop leaders within the institution itself. Proper governance not only allows for improved management of financial and human resources, which is essential for its sustainability, but also for regular assessment of the institution's practices and results, which allows for identifying areas for improvement and implementing changes that can increase the institution's effectiveness and relevance. Governance should be aligned with the values and mission of the religious charity, ensuring that all actions and decisions are in line with the institution's fundamental principles, and should provide for the involvement and participation of its members, strengthening social cohesion and a sense of belonging, in addition to allowing its members' voices to be heard in decision-making (Yasmin, Haniffa & Hudaib, 2014).

3. Methodology

Multiple Linear Regression was used to analyse how governance practices and principles adopted by the Misericórdias influence the receipt of donations.

The proportion of donations obtained in relation to the total amounts received was used as a proxy for the dependent variable (performance), and the following independent variables were used: the existence of time limits applicable to the exercise of the position of senior manager in office at the Misericórdia; the use of key indicators in monitoring/evaluating the performance of the Misericórdia's activity; the use of the website and/or social networks for the purpose of presenting the Misericórdia and for the purpose of publicising the activities carried out by the Misericórdia; the publication of the social impact report and the annual report on the Misericórdia's website/webpage; the description of the Misericórdia's strategic stance; the number of senior management members with executive functions paid at the Misericórdia; the degree of autonomy of the senior manager in office at the Misericórdia, in relation to the understanding and use of information technologies; and the method of selecting the senior manager in office at the Misericórdia; which reflect governance practices and are related to the guidelines, principles and recommendations set out in the Governance Code for Third Sector Entities.

Initially, a verification of the assumptions necessary for the application of the linear regression model was carried out. In order to adequately represent the dependent variable through the use of independent variables, the Ordinary Least Squares method was used.

The empirical data were obtained through the National Institute of Statistics (INE), with the collaboration of the António Sérgio Cooperative for the Social Economy (CASES), through a survey launched between June and September 2019, among members of the senior management of Social Economy entities. The survey had as its reference period the year 2018 and its target population comprised Social Economy (SE) entities active in 2018, headquartered in Portugal. The results of this survey were released on November 27, 2019 and were grouped by large families, including the Misericórdias, and focused essentially on the analysis of the management practices of Social Economy entities. Because the highest response rate was precisely from the Misericórdias (76.7%), this sample can be classified as quite rich.

4. Results

The model presented an R of 0.54, indicating a moderate correlation between the explanatory variables and the dependent variable. The R^2 was 0.291, suggesting that approximately 29.1% of the variation in the proportion of donations can be explained by the variables included in the model. The adjusted R^2 was slightly lower (0.26), suggesting that, when adjusting for the number of predictors, the model still maintains a significant explanation (Table 1).

The overall significance of the model was confirmed by the F statistic of 8.65 and a p-value of <0.001, indicating that, collectively, the independent variables included in the model contribute significantly to explaining the proportion of donations obtained by the Misericórdias.

When examining the coefficients of the variables in Table 1, the variables "Existence of limits on the exercise of the position of the top manager in office", "Use of key indicators to monitor activity performance", "Purpose of using the website and social networks to present the entity", "Purpose of using the website and social networks to publicize the activities carried out" and "Disclosure of the report and accounts on the website", do not present statistically significant values, with p-values well above the significance level

($p<0.05$) and all of them present negative values, suggesting that they are not associated with the proportion of donations received.

However, the variable “Description of the strategic stance” stood out as a positive factor. The “maintenance” stance, in relation to the “growth” stance, presented a coefficient of 31.72 ($p=0.04$), indicating that the Misericórdias that adopt a maintenance strategy, rather than growth, tend to obtain a greater value of donations. This result suggests that donors prefer to support Misericórdias that focus on stability and sustainability, rather than expansion or social innovation. Another significant finding of this model was that, regarding the method of selecting the top manager in office, the coefficient related to the “recruitment process” presented an extremely high value of 478.73 ($P=0.001$). This result suggests that, when the top manager is selected through a formal recruitment process, rather than being appointed by the entity, there is a very strong and positive association with the proportion of donations received, which may reflect greater trust from donors in leaders who are chosen more carefully and based on the merit of the candidates, and may be seen as a commitment to professionalization, namely, of those who lead these institutions. The IPCG’s Code of Governance for Third Sector Entities establishes that the top management role must be held by a professional and must be exercised, preferably, exclusively and remunerated.

On the other hand, the variables “Disclosure of the social impact report on the website”, “Number of senior management members with paid executive functions”, and “Degree of autonomy of the senior manager in functions regarding the understanding and use of information technologies”, did not show a statistically significant relationship with the percentage of donations obtained, suggesting that these factors may not directly influence the decision of donors to support the Misericórdias.

Although the various variables investigated did not individually show statistical significance, the regression model suggests that certain governance strategies and practices may play a key role in obtaining donations by Misericórdias. Specifically, the adoption of strategies focused on maintenance, rather than diversification, expansion, or innovation, appears to be positively associated with obtaining donations. In times of uncertainty, the preference for strategies that seek to maintain solid and sustainable operations may have a strong impact on those who wish to ensure that their donations are used effectively and efficiently. Furthermore, the process of selecting top management, particularly when carried out through formal and careful recruitment, has been shown to be an extremely significant factor in obtaining donations. The strong association between an organized recruitment process and a higher percentage of donations received indicates that donors value leaders who are chosen based on the desired skills, experiences, and personal characteristics (such as knowledge of the non-profit sector, leadership skills, and social sensitivity), and who go through a rigorous selection process, which can be seen as a commitment to adopting good governance practices and efficiently managing the resources obtained. Institutions that invest in fair and open selection processes, and that demonstrate a commitment to integrity and accountability, are likely to find greater receptivity among those seeking to make impactful and responsible donations.

Table 1 - Results of the linear regression model for donations (as a % of total amounts received)

Donations (as % of the total amounts received)				
Predictor	**Estimated Coefficient**	**Standard Error**	**t-value**	**p-value**
Intercept	14.34	6.74	0.21	0.83
Existence of limits on the term of office for top management functions:				
yes – no	-12.16	1.86	-0.65	0.51
Use of key indicators to monitor the performance of activities undertaken:				
yes – no	-0.45	1.20	-0.38	0.70
Purpose of using the website and social media for presenting the organization:				
yes – no	-0.60	1.20	-0.50	0.62
Purpose of using the website and social media for publicizing activities undertaken:				
yes – no	-0.85	1.13	-0.76	0.45
Disclosure of the social impact report on the website:				
yes – no	11.11	6.30	0.18	0.86
Description of strategic posture:				
development – growth	30.49	1.76	17.34	0.08

Table 1 - *Continued*

Donations (as % of the total amounts received)				
Predictor	**Estimated Coefficient**	**Standard Error**	**t-value**	**p-value**
maintenance - growth	31.72	1.51	21.02	0.04
survival - growth	26.64	2.11	12.60	0.21
Number of top management members with paid executive roles:	0.03	0.44	0.08	0.94
Degree of autonomy of top management regarding the understanding and use of IT:				
very autonomous – moderately autonomous	-12.58	1.16	10.83	0.28
not autonomous – moderately autonomous	-19.92	2.69	-0.74	0.46
slightly autonomous – moderately autonomous	15.09	1.86	0.81	0.42
fully autonomous – moderately autonomous	-13.86	1.20	11.52	0.25
Disclosure of the financial statements on the website:				
yes – no	-10.03	1.17	0.861	0.39
Selection method for top management:				
elected by social bodies – appointed by the organization	22.24	6.18	0.36	0.72
other – appointed by the organization	21.96	10.62	0.21	0.84
recruitment process – appointed by the organization	478.73	7.41	64.58	<0.001

5. Conclusions

The main mission of the Misericórdias is not only to practice Catholic worship, but also to improve the quality of life of the population, especially those most in need, playing an important economic and social role in social cohesion, acting in areas that the State is unable to serve, which awakens interest in the study and adoption of governance practices and principles, as a way of optimizing their performance, protecting the interests of stakeholders and contributing to their sustainability.

Governance in religious charities is significantly related to donation behaviour, affecting transparency, effectiveness and donor trust. Governance practices are essential to ensure the trust of the public, donors and all other stakeholders, as well as to ensure the appropriate use of resources and the effective provision of services, and trust is essential for these institutions to obtain the resources necessary to achieve their objectives. Trust depends on the quantity and quality of disclosures and transparency in the efficiency with which resources are used to achieve objectives and accomplish their socio-economic mission.

Because charities depend on external resources to finance their activities and realise, satisfactorily, at least, their mission, governance practices should be geared towards ensuring that these institutions maintain and optimize their relationships with donors (Pfeffer & Salancik, 1978), as well as encouraging innovation and flexibility as a way to respond quickly to new opportunities and challenges, thus ensuring continued access to resources (Bellante et al, 2018).

The regression model indicates that governance principles and practices that promote transparency, stability and strategic sustainability, and meritocracy in leadership, are key to maximizing resource acquisition in Misericórdias. The statistical significance of the variables related to strategic posture and the way in which the top leader was selected suggests that, for Misericórdias, the combination of a maintenance strategy with rigorous governance practices, such as the way in which leaders are selected, are sensitive areas that must be managed with due care to ensure the financial sustainability of Misericórdias.

These results offer valuable insights into the governance of Misericórdias, indicating that stability, transparency, and meritocracy are not only desirable values, but essential components for the financial performance of these institutions, and for strengthening their relationship of trust with donors and other stakeholders as well, while increasing their possibilities of attracting higher levels of resources to accomplish their socio-religious goals, which have notorious impacts on the broader socio-economic environment.

ACKNOWLEDGMENT: This work was financially supported by the research unit on Governance, Competitiveness and Public Policy (UIDB/04058/2020) + (UIDP/04058/2020), funded by national funds through FCT - Fundação para a Ciência e a Tecnologia.

References

Andrade, A., & Franco, R. C. (2007). Economia Do Conhecimento E Organizações Sem Fins Lucrativos. Retrieved from http://www.spi.pt/coleccao_economiadoconhecimento/documentos/manuais_PDF/Manual_VIII.pdf

Bellante, G., Berardi, L., Machold, S., Nissi, E., & Rea, M.A. (2018). Accountability, governance and performance in UK charities. *Int. J. Business Performance Management, 19*(1), 55-74.

Ben-Ner, A., & Jones, D. (1995). Employee Participation, Ownership, and Productivity: A Theoretical Framework. *Industrial Relations, 34*(4), 532-554.

Blevins, D.P., Eckardt, R., & Ragozzino, R. (2018). *Understanding the link between governance and performance in charities*. Paper presented at the 78th Annual Meeting of the Academy of Management, Chicago, USA.

Chaves, R. & Monzón, J. (2001). Economía social y setor no lucrativo: actualidad científica y perspectivas. *Revista de Economía Pública, Social y Cooperativa, CIRIEC-España, 37*, 7-33.

Claessens, S., Djankor, S., Fan, J.P., & Lang, L.H. (2002). Disentangling the incentive and entrenchment effects of large shareholders. *Journal of Finance, 57*(6), pp. 741-2771.

Connolly, C., & Hyndman, N. (2013b). Charity accountability in the UK: Through the eyes of the donor. *Qualitative Research in Accounting & Management Journal, 10*(3/4), 259-278.

Cordery, C., & Morgan, G. (2013). Special Issue on Charity Accounting, Reporting and Regulation. *International Society for Third-Sector Research, 24*, 757-759.

Elmagrhi, M.H., Ntim, C.G., Malagila, J., Fosu, S., & Tunyi, A.A. (2018). Trustee Board Diversity, Governance Mechanisms, Capital Structure and Performance in UK Charities. *Corporate Governance: The International Journal of Business in Society.*

Gregg, S. (2001). *The Art of Corporate Governance: A Return to First Principles*. Centre for Independent Studies, St Leonards, NSW.

Grey Matter Research. (2008). Where'd my money go? Americans' Perceptions of the Financial Efficiency of Non-profit Organizations. Retrieved from http://greymatterresearch.com/

Hallock, K.F. (2002). Managerial pay and governance in American nonprofits. *Industrial Relations, 41*(3), 377-406.

Hilmer, F.G. (1998). *Strictly Boardroom: Improving Governance to Enhance Company Performance*. 2nd edn, Information Australia, Melbourne.

Hopt, K.J. (2010). The board of nonprofit organizations: some corporate governance thoughts from Europe. In K. J. Hopt, T. von Hippel. Eds. *Comparative Corporate Governance of Non-Profit Organizations*. Cambridge University Press, Cambridge 2010.

Instituto Nacional de Estatística. Inquérito ao Setor da Economia Social 2018. Retrieved from https://www.cases.pt/inquerito-ao-setor-da-economia-social-ises/

Instituto Português de Corporate Governance. (2014). Código de Governo de Entidades do Terceiro Setor. Retrieved from https://cgov.pt/images/ficheiros/2018/codigo_de_governo_de_entidades_do_terceiro_sector.pdf

Kiel, G., & Nicholson, G. (2002). Real world governance: driving business success through effective corporate governance. *Mt Eliza Business Review, 5*(1), 17-28.

Lacruz, A.J., Nossa, V., Guedes, T.A., & Lemos, K.R. (2021). Efeito das dimensões de governação no recebimento de doações vinculadas às ONGs ambientais no Brasil. *ASAA Journal, 14*(1), 198–216.

Muslih, M.M., Panjaitan, I., Hotang, K.B., & Delfira, A. (2022). Religion-Based Organizational Good Governance. *American Research Journal of Humanities & Social Science (ARJHSS), 5*(1), 01-10

Newton, A.N. (2015). Executive compensation, organizational performance, and governance quality in the absence of owners. *Journal of Corporate Finance, 30*, 195-222.

Pfeffer, J.; Salancik, G. R. (1978). The external control of organizations: A resource dependence perspective. New York: Harper & Row.

Rossi, A.M., & Silva, A.A. (2022). Corporate Governance: Analysis of Good Practices in a Religious Institution. *Revista Científica Hermes, 20*, 202-227.

Simões, A. & Ribeiro, H. (2022a). Governance in Charities: The Case of the Portuguese Misericórdias. 78th International Scientific Conference on Economic and Social Development, University of Aveiro, 39-51.

Simões, A. & Ribeiro, H. (2022b). The Importance of the Charities in the scope of The Social Economy in Portugal. 90th International Scientific Conference on Economic and Social Development, Zagreb, Croatia, 29-30.

Simões, A. & Ribeiro, H. (2022c). Governance in Charities: The Case of the Portuguese Misericórdias. In A. Oliveira (Ed.), Ciências Sociais Aplicadas: Estado, organizações e desenvolvimento regional (vol. 3), Atena Editora, Ponta Grossa, Brasil, 200-217

Simões, A. & Ribeiro, H. (2023). The role of misericordias in the scope of the importance of charities for the third sector. 20th International Conference on Corporate Social Responsibility, Madrid, Spain, 64-65.

Simões, A. & Ribeiro, H. (2024a). Governance and Performance in Misericórdias. 119th International Scientific Conference on Economic and Social Development, Lisbon, Portugal.

Simões, A. & Ribeiro, H. (2024b). The role of misericordias in the context of the importance of social solidarity institutions for the third sector. In D.Crowther and Seifi, S. (Ed.), Society and Sustainability: Developments in Corporate Governance and Responsability, Vol.24, Emerald Publishing Limited, Leeds, UK, 233-251.

União das Misericórdias (2024). Quem Somos nas Misericórdias 2024. Lisboa, União das Misericórdias.

Vinten, G. (1997). Corporate Governance in a Charity. *Corporate Governance, Oxford*, *5*(1), 24-28.

Yasmin, S., Haniffa, R., & Hudaib, M. (2014). Communicated Accountability by Faith-Based Charity Organisations. *Journal of Business Ethics, 122*, 103-123.

Zainon, S., Atan, R., Ahmad, R.A.R., & Wah, Y.B. (2012). Associations between organizational specific-attributes and the extent of disclosure in charity annual returns. *International Journal of Mathematical Models and Methods in Applied Sciences, 6*, 482-489.

The Impact of ESG Practices between Opportunities, Risks and Corporate Sustainability

Ubaldo Comite, Alba M. Gallo, Maria Carmela Serluca

1. Introduction

The literature analysis, which was conducted on databases such as Scopus and Wos through the selection of articles by targeted keywords, aims to explore how the adoption of ESG practices influences not only the financial performance of companies, but also their reputation and sustainability oriented in the long run.

The research question that prompted our study is:

What are the impacts of ESG practices? Are they always positive?

This contribution aims to outline both the positive and negative (or rather limited) impacts that emerge from the study of academic and sectoral sources, to be able to guide future strategic interventions and policy decisions.

The dynamics through which ESG practices can be a source of competitive advantage or, conversely, sources of risk and conflict will also be explored. It will also be highlighted how the operational context of the company itself plays an impactful role in terms of operational results.

The objective of this study is to analyze how ESG practices can lead to business success and to analyze the critical factors that might limit the expected effectiveness. Other aspects of governance such as board diversity, the importance of transparency and communication without which stakeholder trust cannot be built will also be studied.

This paper aims to explore the role of digitization and emerging technologies in enhancing the adoption and effectiveness of ESG practices. It also looks at how geographical and cultural variations can influence the effectiveness of ESG practices, emphasizing the importance of contextualizing and adapting business strategies to local markets to maximize benefits and reduce risks.

This study aims, therefore, to contribute to the academic and practical debate on the impacts of ESG practices by suggesting possible future directions for sustainable business policy research and development.

2. Methodology

The methodology adopted for this research was designed to analyze in detail the impacts of environmental, social and governance (ESG) practices on corporate performance, reputation and long-term sustainability and to do so, we adopted an approach based on literature review.

2.1 Research process

The research was divided into different phases, the first step was the selection of sources up to the processing and interpretation of the results.

The selected papers were searched in the Scopus and Web of Science (WoS) databases, chosen for their relevance and broad coverage of academic literature.

Keywords such as "ESG practices", "sustainability", "corporate performance" and "governance" were analyzed and subsequently, a screening was carried out aimed at identifying the most significant articles, narrowing the field to studies published between 2018 and 2024.

This step was fundamental for our analysis to be updated and representative of the most recent trends in the field of ESG practices.

After this initial selection, a more in-depth analysis of the articles' contents was carried out, and each contribution was assessed based on its relevance to the research questions and also to the methodology and originality of the results.

MySLR software was used to organize and classify the collected data, which allowed to summarize the results in visual representations such as time graphs and word clouds that were useful to identify the areas of analysis and to highlight any discrepancies in the results emerging from the literature.

2.2 Analytical approach

The data analysis was based on a qualitative approach, aimed at understanding the complexity and variability of the impacts of ESG practices in different business and geographical contexts. It was studied how they can generate competitive advantages and how they can expose companies to risks and challenges.

An important element was the comparative analysis between business sectors, which highlighted differences in the adoption and results of ESG practices, for example, resource-intensive sectors, such as energy and industrial, were analyzed, and more controversial sectors, such as tobacco and alcohol, whose comparison allowed the identification of common trends.

The role of emerging technologies, such as artificial intelligence, blockchain and big data analytics, in improving the adoption and effectiveness of ESG practices was also explored, as these technologies facilitate the monitoring and reporting of ESG performance, and provide opportunities for innovation that can contribute to risk reduction and the creation of added value for companies.

2.3 Reflections on limitations

Although reserved for the methodology, it has some limitations that could influence the results, such as the choice to focus exclusively on Scopus and WoS may have excluded relevant sources present in other databases and the variability of geographical and cultural contexts represents a challenge in the generalization of the results.

Finally, the bias in the literature towards the positive aspects of ESG practices may have influenced the peer analysis hence the need for further studies to balance this perspective.

In conclusion, this methodological approach aims to provide a deep and nuanced understanding of the impacts of ESG practices serving as a basis for future research by academic scholars.

3. Literature analysis

The literature analysis was conducted on two databases which are Scopus and Wos. The first interesting aspect that emerged from the search for articles is the time factor.

In fact, as can be seen from Figure 1, it is from 2022 that this topic began to be the subject of interest for the scientific community, reaching a notable peak in 2023.

The Figure 2, the word cloud aligns perfectly, which provides a visual representation of the core areas of our analysis (i.e. the impact of ESG practices, the benefits and risks, the need for contextualized and transparent strategies) and reinforces the message of the contribution, namely the importance of considering the complexity and variability of the impacts of ESG practices.

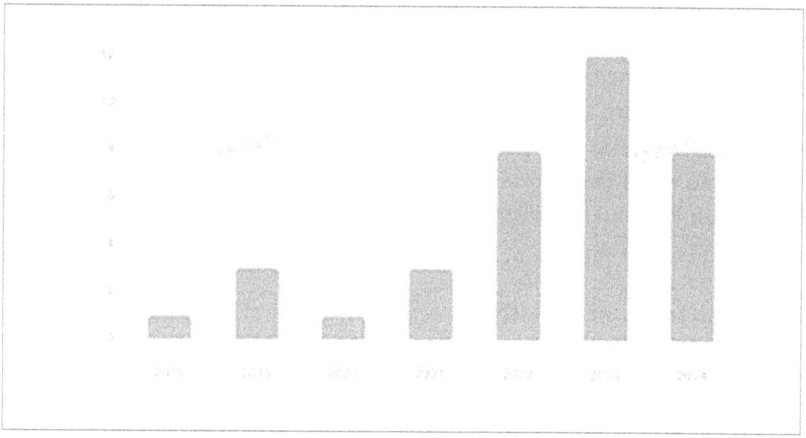

Fig. 1: Publications over time
Source: own elaboration on MySLR.

Fig. 2: word cloud
Source: own elaboration

From the literature review, there appears to be a kind of discrepancy in that there are articles that purely highlight the positive impacts of ESG practices and others that focus on the negative aspects.

Regarding the positive impacts of ESG practices, it can be seen that they have become a growing point of interest in sustainability discussions and also an evaluation criterion for certain aspects such as resilience and corporate growth potential.

The literature review emphasises how targeted commitment to sustainability practices can bring significant tangible benefits, both in terms of cost reduction and improved reputation and market value for the company.

Indeed, the integration of sustainability practices can have a direct and measurable impact on the market value of companies by substantially shaping the perception and market value of a company (Tamayo-Torres, Gutierrez-Gutierrez, and Ruiz-Moreno,2019).

These findings also emerge from company analyses carried out on different sectors (even controversial ones such as alcohol and tobacco) and indeed it emerges how ethical and responsible management in these areas can reduce financial costs and improve economic sustainability (The study by Hmaittane, Bouslah and M'Zali,2019).

This focus on ethics extends to the role of auditors, especially in times of crisis as they play a key role in managing risks related to ESG issues. In such cases, effective management of these risks is extremely relevant, as it can protect and even enhance corporate reputation in less tranquil times (Asante-Appiah and Lambert, 2023).

An important object of analysis emerging from the literature is diversity in boards of directors as it can positively influence governance and corporate performance, in fact, it is inferred that a greater presence of women on boards is associated with both a reduction in ESG controversies and an improvement in corporate performance leading to a not insignificant competitive advantage (Issa and Hanaysha, 2023).

In addition to gender diversity, transparency in corporate operations is equally critical for long-term success; in fact, ESG disclosure has proven beneficial as it has been found that greater transparency can substantially improve corporate value (Grishunin et al., 2023).

Risk reduction is an additional benefit of a sound ESG strategy, especially when environmental and social aspects are considered as they particularly contribute to the reduction of idiosyncratic business risk, facilitating investment decisions that are both more informed and safer (Sciarelli et al., 2024).

All these elements also pave the way for more effective controversy management strategies in fact, a strong commitment to the social pillar of ESG practices is correlated with superior company performance, positively influencing workplace culture and further motivating staff; by appropriately handling ESG controversies, companies not only mitigate risks but can turn them into growth opportunities, effective controversy management can improve performance and attract investment (Ahmad et al., 2023).

Finally, the ability to turn controversies into opportunities for improvement plays a relevant role the soundness of governance structures, as well as ESG strategies are also important in mitigating the negative impacts of controversies, turning them into opportunities for reputation enhancement; such frameworks can be decisive and determinants of long-term oriented success (Elamer and Boulhaga 2024).

On the other side of the coin, however, studies emerge that instead reveal how the effectiveness of such practices can vary significantly, sometimes with not so positive and sometimes even counterproductive results.

Indeed, our literature review reveals several scenarios in which ESG practices not only failed to generate the hoped-for benefits, but also presented challenges, limitations and negative impacts on financial performance as well as corporate reputation and sustainability.

A questionable aspect emerges in the context of corporate social responsibility reports where contrary to expectations, ESG practices have not shown a positive impact on companies' financial performance, and this may not have significant improvements in returns on assets (ROA) or equity (ROE) (Sachin N. and Rajesh R., 2022).

It turns out that voluntary disclosure of corporate social responsibility reports often lacks transparency (especially on controversial issues), which can reduce public trust and the effectiveness of the reports themselves as accountability tools (Sethi S.P. et al., 2016).

These aspects consequently impact the work of financial analysts, who are faced with increases in margins of error due to ESG controversies that can affect their work by increasing forecast errors and affecting investor confidence (Schiemann F. et al., 2022).

Similarly, companies with serious ESG controversies tend to underperform against market benchmarks (De Franco C., 2020) and this dynamic is also clearly manifested in the case of so-called 'sin stocks', creating an environment where companies try to mitigate negative perceptions through ESG initiatives, without real sustainable change (Cayón E. ; Gutierrez J.C., 2021).

At the same time, there is evidence that negative ESG performance directly affects companies' financial costs, in particular environmental controversies tend to increase the cost of equity (COE), eroding the financial value of companies (La Rosa F.; Bernini F.,2022).

These complex phenomena vary by geographical region, highlighting the importance of cultural context in the perception of ESG practices (de Vincentiis, P, 2023; Ford, JM et al., 2022)

emphasizing the urgency of greater transparency and oversight, especially to combat phenomena such as greenwashing, the increase of which (particularly in the technology sector) requires greater transparency and oversight to prevent unsupported sustainability claims from negatively affecting stakeholder trust and market integrity (Horobet A. et al., 2024).

In the banking sector, ESG controversies are a relevant factor for performance and reputation assessment, significantly influencing ESG scores and public perception (Staroverova M., 2022; DasGupta R.; Roy A., 2023).

Finally, it also emerged that social media influence s the perception of shareholders on ESG reputation, highlighting the importance of effective management of digital communications (Nicolas et al., 2024).

4. Implications

In this study, therefore, through an in-depth literature review, it was analyzed how environmental, social and governance (ESG) practices have a significant impact on the financial performance, reputation and sustainability of companies.

It was enlightening to understand how such practices, even if taking on different roles, can generate competitive advantages without excluding that they can expose companies to risk situations.

This duality of ESG practices is a gap to be studied further as it is something that can be problematic especially for decision-makers who must carefully balance short-term impacts with long-term oriented strategies.

The debate on ESG practices is further complex due to different interpretations and applications in various contexts. Indeed, there are cases where the effective integration of ESG policies has proven to decrease corporate risk and increase market value, but in other contexts, these practices have not significantly improved financial performance or have been counterproductive, negatively affecting both financial performance and public perception of companies.

This variability implies the need for targeted and more transparent strategies that can, on the one hand, optimize positive effects and, on the other hand, minimize the risks of negative outcomes.

Regulatory dynamics in the implementation of ESG practices play a relevant role, in fact, each region has specific peculiarities in terms of stakeholder expectations, environmental and social regulations, and cultural sensitivity.

All these factors have an impact on the perception and effectiveness of ESG practices, for example, in emerging markets, priority is given to social issues, such as improving working conditions and access to resources, while in developed countries the focus is mainly on practices related to transparency.

Companies should aim to develop flexible strategies that consider what characterizes local markets, while ensuring compliance with international standards. From this, the need for a multivariate approach emerges, as a uniform one could be counterproductive and ineffective, negatively impacting stakeholder trust.

On the other hand, technological innovation presents itself as a relevant opportunity in order to improve both the adoption and the effectiveness of ESG practices.

In this context, some advanced tools such as artificial intelligence, big data analytics and blockchain technologies can support companies in monitoring and reporting their performance more accurately, including those related to ESG (for example, real-time data analytics can help identify and promptly manage disputes, while blockchain can improve the transparency and traceability of supply chains.

The adoption of emerging technologies not only helps reduce the risks associated with ESG practices but can also create new growth opportunities. However, it is essential that companies carefully evaluate technology investments, ensuring that they are aligned with sustainability objectives and do not generate further complexity or inefficiencies.

A characterizing element for the success of ESG practices is represented by corporate leadership, in fact, leaders must promote a corporate culture based on values such as social and environmental responsibility, while ensuring that these principles are integrated into everyday strategies and operations.

Board diversity, for example, has been associated with a greater ability to address ESG challenges and improved overall corporate performance.

A clear and transparent policy approach can help companies mitigate risks and turn them into growth opportunities, and this is where governance plays an important role in ESG controversies.

Stakeholder communication is also an essential tool as it helps build trust and legitimacy, especially in an environment where expectations, in terms of sustainability, are constantly increasing.

5. Conclusions and future research

Future research directions should therefore be oriented towards how companies could implement ESG practices more effectively and efficiently, analyzing how they can transform ESG challenges into opportunities for growth and development.

A promising area is that which draws on integrated models that mix ESG practices with sector-specific innovations, for example, within energy-intensive sectors, technologies such as carbon capture systems could be inserted into operational processes as an integral part of ESG strategies. Similarly, companies could use artificial intelligence platforms to monitor ESG performance and to develop forecasting models aimed at predicting different business aspects.

In this context, digitalization plays an important role to enable more dynamic and accurate ESG reporting that includes the improvement of reporting processes and the possibility of creating universal standards for the assessment of ESG impact, reducing the discrepancies that exist between different sectors in different markets.

Another important area draws on the evolution of sustainability regulations, in fact, T

the introduction of increasingly stringent requirements by regulatory bodies, both nationally and internationally, lays the foundation for research that examines how companies can comply and use regulations as a real strategic element, for example in this area, state incentive programs for ESG projects could become catalysts for business innovation.

In this perspective, future research could study how to balance the costs of regulatory compliance with the benefits, oriented in the long term.

Another area of great importance is that which draws on the role of cultural differences in the perception and application of ESG practices, in fact, it would be necessary to investigate how ESG priorities vary according to different socioeconomic contexts and also local expectations.

This type of analysis would allow companies to adapt ESG strategies to meet the needs of stakeholders even in diversified markets, while at the same time ensuring an approach that respects global standards.

Finally, a neglected but relevant area is the development of managerial skills needed to lead the implementation of ESG practices, in fact, training and education should be seen as indispensable tools of future ESG strategies, promoting a cultural change within organizations.

In this context, future research could therefore focus on the study of skills and development programs useful for building corporate leadership that is able to address ESG challenges effectively and efficiently.

To conclude, the future of research on ESG practices must go beyond the analysis of direct impacts and must build a framework that considers technological innovation, regulatory adaptation, cultural differences and the development of managerial skills. In this way, companies can optimize the benefits of ESG practices and foster the adoption of new standards for long-term oriented corporate sustainability.

References

Ahmad, R. A. R., Samsuddin, M. E., Azmi, N. A., & Abdullah, N. (2023). Is Environmental, Social and Governance (ESG) Disclosure Value Enhancing? Evidence from Top 100 Companies. *Asia-Pacific Management Accounting Journal.*https://doi.org/0

Asante-Appiah, B., & Lambert, T. A. (2023). The role of the external auditor in managing environmental, social, and governance (ESG) reputation risk. *Review of Accounting Studies.* https://doi.org/10.1007/s11142-022-09706-z

Cayón, E., & Gutierrez, J. C. (2021). Sin stocks and ESG scores: Does the nature of your business really matter? *Journal of International Studies.* https://doi.org/10.14254/2071-8330.2021/14-3/7

Elamer, A. A., & Boulhaga, M. (2024). ESG controversies and corporate performance: The moderating effect of governance mechanisms and ESG practices. *Corporate Social Responsibility and Environmental Management.* https://doi.org/10.1002/csr.2749

Grishunin, S., Naumova, E., Burova, E., Suloeva, S., & Nekrasova, T. (2022). The impact of sustainability disclosures on value of companies following digital transformation strategies. *International Journal of Technology*.https://doi.org/10.14716/ijtech.v13i7.6194

Hmaittane, A., Bouslah, K., & M'Zali, B. (2019). Does corporate social responsibility affect the cost of equity in controversial industry sectors? *Review of Accounting and Finance*. https://doi.org/10.1108/RAF-09-2018-0184

Horobet, A., Smedoiu-Popoviciu, A., Oprescu, R., Belascu, L., & Pentescu, A. (2024). Seeing through the haze: greenwashing and the cost of capital in technology firms. *Environment, Development and Sustainability*.https://doi.org/10.1007/s10668-024-04817-w

Issa, A., & Hanaysha, J. R. (2023). Breaking the glass ceiling for a sustainable future: The power of women on corporate boards in reducing ESG controversies. *International Journal of Accounting and Information Management*. https://doi.org/10.1108/IJAIM-03-2023-0053

La Rosa, F., & Bernini, F. (2022). ESG controversies and the cost of equity capital of European listed companies: The moderating effects of ESG performance and market securities regulation. *International Journal of Accounting and Information Management*. https://doi.org/10.1108/IJAIM-03-2022-0047

Nicolas, M. L. D., Desroziers, A., Caccioli, F., & Aste, T. (2024). ESG reputation risk matters: An event study based on social media data. *Finance Research Letters*. https://doi.org/10.1016/j.frl.2023.104712

Sachin, N., & Rajesh, R. (2022). An empirical study of supply chain sustainability with financial performance of Indian firms. *Environment, Development and Sustainability*. https://doi.org/10.1007/s10668-021-01717-1

Sciarelli, M., Landi, G., Turriziani, L., & Prisco, A. (2024). Does corporate sustainability mitigate firm risk? An empirical analysis on S&P 500 controversial companies. *Social Responsibility Journal*. https://doi.org/10.1108/SRJ-09-2021-0388

Sethi, S. P., Martell, T. F., & Demir, M. (2016). Building corporate reputation through corporate social responsibility (CSR) reports: The case of extractive industries. *Corporate Reputation Review*. https://doi.org/10.1057/s41299-016-0004-1

The Role of Healthcare Management in the Application of Nudging for Public Health Promotion

Ubaldo Comite, Eveny Ciurleo, Alba M. Gallo

1. Introduction

Health management today faces increasingly complex challenges in promoting healthy choices to citizens. In this context, the concept of nudging is gaining more and more attention as it is seen as the gentle but effective nudge that can influence individuals' choices without restricting their freedom of choice.

One of the fundamental pillars of nudging is the use of psychological theories through which decisions are guided; among these, the theory of anticipated regret plays an important role since people have a tendency to make decisions that reduce the likelihood of experiencing future regret.

This principle can be used, for example, to encourage healthy choices such as vaccination or participation in screening programmes by suggesting the possible consequences of not acting. Another nudging startegy is the framing effect, as the way in which information is presented can have an influence on the outcome of the choice. In health management, in fact, presenting the benefits of a healthy lifestyle or the negative consequences of harmful habits in a positive or negative context can make a big difference in the choice of the adoption of the compro-ducts; thus, it is evident that the framing effect can contribute to making choices that promote well-being more attractive. Kahneman and Tversky's 'prospect theory', for example, which highlights how people assess risk and gain in a non-linear way, can be very useful in the healthcare context in order to understand patients' risk perceptions and optimise interventions that minimise perceived losses and maximise gains. Furthermore, ambiguity aversion may direct people to avoid choices with high uncertainty, preferring known risks.

This paper aims to explore how nudging strategies, based on these and other psychological theories, can be effectively applied in healthcare management to incentivise healthy behaviour, increase treatment adherence and improve healthcare resource management.

The aim is to demonstrate how a scientifically based approach that respects individual freedoms can help improve health outcomes and promote a healthier society.

To achieve this goal, after a careful review of the literature through databases such as Scopus and Wos, an analysis of data from an ISTAT questionnaire on the behaviour of Italians will be carried out to find a match between the literature and the econometric analysis. Health management implications will then be formulated.

2. Literature analysis

Nudging fits seamlessly into healthcare management as a low-cost approach that tends to achieve significant results through behavioural change inducing nudges. This method has proven to be particularly effective in that it respects the freedom of choice of individuals, improving health system outcomes and consequently, public health.

Furthermore, 'health management' and 'nudging' are a perfect combo in public health and health systems management, as together they can achieve the goal of improving public health outcomes through innovative and sustainable strategies that tend to positively change the behaviour of individuals within society.

From the literature review, it emerges specifically that the very concept of 'nudging' has the potential to influence people's dietary and lifestyle decisions (Ensaff, 2021). This observation points to the need for better information management to ensure consumer knowledge of nudges and awareness of their current implementation, encouraging their use for health-related behaviour (Junghans et al., 2015).

By changing the attractiveness of available options and designing environments that facilitate healthier choices, it is possible to steer or rather 'push' people towards behaviour that is healthier and more sustainable (List & Samek, 2015). These methods researched in the literature have extremely relevant implications for public health and also for the environment, as they can lead to the promotion of a lifestyle that brings considerable benefits to both the individual and society as a whole (Hansen et al., 2016).

In the field of behavioural economics, the 'framing effect' represents an important cognitive bias that fits well in the context of nudging (Gong et al., 2013). Indeed, the way information is presented can influence a person's decision, with relevant implications for the promotion of preventive behaviour.

In addition to the above, much research has been able to show that low-cost, non-invasive 'nudges' can be very effective in promoting the selection of specific foods without limiting consumers' overall choices (Wilson et al., 2017). Also in order to incentivise the purchase of healthy foods, the use of the bundling strategy can be important; this strategy, which consists of combining different products in predefined packages reducing the cognitive load associated with purchase, can support healthier food choices (Carroll et al., 2018).

In addition to the nudging methods examined, it is relevant to consider the role of risk attitudes. Depending on the relevant health contexts, attitudes to risk may vary, but risk aversion remains a predominant tendency (Arrieta et al., 2017). A highly connected aspect is regret aversion, which plays a central role in motivating people to avoid decisions that might lead to future regrets (Van Der Swaluw et al., 2018).

Furthermore, ambiguity aversion appears to be a key factor in health management decisions. Strong ambiguity aversion emerged as the strongest predictor of therapeutic inertia, followed by low uncertainty tolerance (Saposnik et al., 2017). An example of this principle is time-based lotteries that exploit anticipated regret can motivate overweight people to go to the gym regularly. Incorporating principles of behavioural economics into clinical decision support modules is an innovative step towards improving adherence to health monitoring guidelines.

Finally, to improve the effectiveness of long-term interventions, more complex strategies involving both patients and providers are deemed necessary. In general, it is believed that more complex strategies involving patients and providers are needed to improve and maintain the outcomes of interventions in the long term (Shapiro et al., 2020). The concept of 'nudging' and choice architecture offer a promising approach to positively influence health-related behaviour. Although the application of these concepts presents challenges, their potential to improve public health and individual well-being is significant (Zullig et al., 2018).

In the context of healthcare management, behavioural economics, in this case nudging strategies in particular, represent a tool aimed at improving therapeutic compliance and directing towards healthier behaviours, complementing traditional healthcare policies. It emerges from the literature that these types of approaches are very effective in health behaviour management, especially in patients with chronic diseases such as diabetes (Benartzi et al., 2017).

Clearly, the effectiveness of this strategy depends very much on how it is implemented and the individual characteristics of the patients, e.g. gamification interventions aimed at support or competition rather than collaboration have proven to be more successful (Patel et al., 2021). Therefore, with this evidence, the need to tailor interventions to maximise effectiveness and adherence is emphasised, and a good means of enhancing the use of gamification by making better use of behavioural economics principles is the use of smart tools and apps (Cotton & Patel, 2019).

A practical example of success brought by this strategy is represented by an experiment conducted through the use of an app (Carrot Rewards) whose rewards-focused approach was shown to be effective in increasing physical activity, especially among physically inactive individuals, demonstrating the potential of such interventions (Mitchell et al., 2018).

Thus, the combined use of mobile technologies and SBIRT (Screening, Brief Intervention, and Referral to Treatment) can be an effective and also educational strategy for patients (Yin et al., 2020). User-centred applications, supported by basic behavioural science, offer important insights into incorporating personalisation through user choice, thereby improving the potential effectiveness of digital health interventions (Graham et al., 2021).

The design of these applications takes into account users' preferences and needs, enabling them to make personalised choices, which could increase engagement and improve the overall effectiveness of digital health interventions. Reminders, feedback and planning reminders consistently improve the self-management of chronic diseases and are among the least controversial types of nudges generally recommended for health policy makers (Möllenkamp et al., 2019).

In the field of healthcare management, a synergy between 'nudging', public health policies and effective resource management is important to ensure an overall improvement in patients' quality of life and to reduce overall healthcare costs.

3. Methodology and results

The methodology of the paper, provide for an econometric analysis that follows and supports the literature review.As reported in the introductory section, metadata obtained from the most recent ISTAT questionnaire on the behaviour of Italians was used to carry out this analysis. The estimated equation for the Health Behaviour Index (Health_Index) is as follows. The Regression equation for the Healthy Behaviour Index:

$$Y = \beta_0 + \beta_1 * X_1 + \beta_2 * X_2 + \beta_3 * X_3 + \beta_4 * X_4 + \beta_5 * X_5 + \varepsilon \quad (1)$$

Where:

- Y: Healthy Behaviour Index
- β_0: Constant (intercept)
- β_1, β_2, β_3, β_4, β_5: Coefficients of independent variables
- X_1: Age (ages)
- X_2: is a binary variable (gender: 1 = woman, 0 = man)
- X_3: represents the level of education (istrmi)
- X_4: represents household income (redprmi)
- X_5: represents the geographical breakdown of Italy (ripmf)
- ε: Error term (represents the part of the variability not explained by the model)

This form makes it possible to clearly visualise the effect of each independent variable on the Health Behaviour Index (Y), represented as the sum of the coefficients multiplied by the variables plus the error term.

Table 1: Numerical Regression Results

Variable	Coefficient	t-statistics
Average age (etami)	0.0628***	(56.88)
Gender (sex)	0.157***	(19.05)
Average education (istrmi)	0.00190***	(6.15)
Per-capita income (redprmi)	0.00929***	(4.29)
Family per-capita income (ripmf)	0.0557***	(18.03)
Constant (_cons)	0.821***	(42.65)

Note: t statistics in parentheses. *$p < 0.05$, **$p < 0.01$, ***$p < 0.001$.
Source: own elaboration

- Age, $\beta1 = 0.0628$, $p < 0.01$): Age appears to have a positive and statistically significant effect on the Healthy Behaviour Index, whereby as age increases, people tend to adopt more healthy behaviours.
- Gender (sex, $\beta2 = 0.1574$, $p < 0.01$): Sex has a positive effect on the Healthy Behaviour Index and the results show that women tend to score higher than men on healthy behaviours.
- Level of education (istrmi, $\beta3 = 0.0019$, $p < 0.01$): Education has a positive, albeit small, effect on the Healthy Behaviour Index; thus, greater adoption of healthy behaviours is associated with high levels of education.
- Main household income (redprmi, $\beta4 = 0.0093$, $p < 0.01$): Household income has a positive effect on the adoption of healthy behaviours, in fact, households with a higher income level tend to score higher on the Healthy Behaviour Index.
- Geographical distribution (ripmf, $\beta5 = 0.0557$, $p < 0.01$): There are significant geographical differences in health behaviour, with people in Northern Italy tending to follow more health behaviour than those in the South and Islands.

4. Results and implications

The regression results showed that age, education level, income and geographical distribution can have a significant influence on the adoption of healthy behaviour.

For healthcare managers, this implies the need to design 'nudging' policies that target different demographic and geographic groups.

For example, as also suggested in the literature by Ensaff (2021), it is essential to structure choice environments that can have a positive influence on the population's dietary and physical activity decisions, especially in those contexts where the adoption of healthy behaviour is at a lower level.

The presence of significant geographical differences (as indicated by the variable 'ripmf') in healthy behaviour, on the other hand, implies that health management should consider entirely different territorial interventions, in fact, regions in Northern Italy show greater involvement in healthy behaviour than the South and Islands which is consistent with the need for localised interventions, as also argued in the literature by List & Samek (2015), who specify when it is important to tailor nudging strategies to regional contexts in order to achieve better public health outcomes.

The positive sex effect, in which women tend to adopt healthier behaviours than men, implies that health interventions could be more effective if designed with a specific focus on raising men's health awareness.

The level of education has a positive impact on health behaviour, indicating that more education leads to a greater understanding of the benefits of healthy choices. In the context of health management, this implies that health education and awareness campaigns should be considered an integral part of health interventions.

The positive effect of income on healthy behaviour, on the other hand, suggests that economic barriers are a real barrier to the adoption of healthy lifestyles. Health systems should, therefore, work with the well-established goal of reducing these barriers, e.g. by offering incentives for purchasing healthy food or low-cost physical activity services.

The heterogeneity in health habits observed across age groups, education levels and geographical settings suggests that health management should adopt personalised interventions, rather than generic strategies, and this is supported by the research of Patel et al. (2021), which shows that personalised interventions, such as gamification for diabetic patients, can lead to more significant results than standardised interventions.

In this perspective, health systems should exploit technologies such as mobile applications to tailor public health programmes to the specific needs of individual patients. Finally, socio-demographic variables such as age, gender, education and income influence the adoption of healthy behaviours and this supports the idea of using nudging as a health management tool, to create targeted incentives, such as 'commitment devices' or rewards for healthy choices, to improve adherence to healthy behaviours among more vulnerable or less likely groups.

Healthcare management can improve the effectiveness of prevention strategies through the use of digital technologies to monitor and incentivise healthy behaviours, such as mobile applications with reminders, feedback and planning can be powerful tools to support chronic disease self-management and increase treatment adherence.

5. Directions for future research

Directions for future research on the topic of nudging applied to the healthcare sector should focus on the integration of advanced digital technologies, such as artificial intelligence and machine learning, with the ultimate goal of being able to optimize and even personalize interventions.

All these technologies allow us to develop solutions that take into account individual characteristics, personal preferences and the social contexts in which citizens find themselves as recipients of healthcare policies.

It would be appropriate to increase the studies that evaluate the sustainability of behavioral changes that are induced by long-term oriented nudging interventions, analyzing their change between different demographic and geographical groups.

One area of research instead concerns the deepening of the role of cultural and social factors in ensuring the effectiveness of nudging strategies, for example, the evident disparities between Northern and Southern Italy that are highlighted by the results of this research highlight the need to design specific interventions for each reality, addressing the challenges that each context presents.

Furthermore, the ethical aspects related to the application of nudging should be addressed, ensuring that interventions are oriented towards respecting individual autonomy and are transparent in their objectives.

Collaboration between behavioral economics, public health sciences and data analysis can increase the development of innovative low-cost strategies that are also capable of promoting healthier and more sustainable lifestyles.

Another line of research could draw on the development and implementation of digital tools, such as mobile applications and online platforms, with the ultimate goal of ensuring treatment adherence and promoting self-management of chronic diseases.

Studies on the effectiveness of interventions based on gamification, rewards and personalized notifications could optimize the impact of health policies on groups resistant to change.

Finally, it would be appropriate to reduce economic barriers and improve equity in access to health services and resources, thus contributing to a more inclusive and sustainable public health through the potential of nudging.

6. Conclusions

The regression results therefore confirmed the need for a tailored approach in health management aimed at promoting healthy behaviour in the population.

The application of the principles of nudging and choice architecture must be carefully tailored to the demographic and socio-economic characteristics of the population in order to maximise the effectiveness of interventions; indeed, regional disparities in health behaviours highlight the importance of context-specific interventions.

The differences between Northern and Southern Italy, for example, call for health policies tailored to address the specific cultural and economic challenges of each region.

Digital technologies, particularly mobile applications, can be a vehicle for implementing nudging interventions, as they guarantee personalisation and easy access.

At the same time, the use of systems such as gamification and automatic reminders provides a way to improve self-management of chronic diseases and increase adherence to prescribed treatments.

Finally, ensuring equal access to various facilities through economic incentives for healthy behaviour, such as subsidies for purchasing healthy food or participating in physical activity programmes, proves essential to reduce economic barriers.

It is essential that health systems adopt an integrated strategy that combines the use of nudging, health education and the reduction of economic barriers to create environments of choice that make healthy and sustainable decision-making by the population accessible and therefore feasible. The promotion of more equitable public health and the adoption of healthy behaviours must therefore become priority objectives to ensure an improvement in the general well-being of society.

References

Arrieta, A., García-Prado, A., González, P., & Pinto-Prades, J. L. (2017). Risk attitudes in medical decisions for others: An experimental approach. *Health Economics (United Kingdom).*

Benartzi, S., Beshears, J., Milkman, K. L., Sunstein, C. R., Thaler, R. H., Shankar, M., Tucker-Ray, W., Congdon, W. J., & Galing, S. (2017). Should governments invest more in nudging? *Psychological Science.*

Carroll, K. A., Samek, A., & Zepeda, L. (2018). Food bundling as a health nudge: Investigating consumer fruit and vegetable selection using behavioral economics. *Journal of Public Health (United Kingdom).*

Cotton, V., & Patel, M. S. (2019). Gamification use and design in popular health and fitness mobile applications. *American Journal of Health Promotion.*

Ensaff, H. (2021). A nudge in the right direction: The role of food choice architecture in changing populations' diets. *Proceedings of the Nutrition Society.*

Gong, J., Zhang, Y., Yang, Z., Huang, Y., Feng, J., & Zhang, W. (2013). The framing effect in medical decision-making: A review of the literature. *Psychology, Health and Medicine.*

Graham, A. K., Munson, S. A., Reddy, M., Neubert, S. W., Green, E. A., Chang, A., Spring, B., Mohr, D. C., & Wildes, J. E. (2021). Integrating user-centred design and behavioral science to design a mobile intervention for obesity and binge eating: Mixed methods analysis. *Health Psychology.*

Hansen, P. G., Skov, L. R., & Skov, K. L. (2016). Making healthy choices easier: Regulation versus nudging. *Annual Review of Public Health.*

Junghans, A. F., Cheung, T. T., & De Ridder, D. D. (2015). Under consumers' scrutiny - An investigation into consumers' attitudes and concerns about nudging in the realm of health behaviour. *BMC Public Health.*

List, J. A., & Samek, A. S. (2015). The behavioralist as nutritionist: Leveraging behavioral economics to improve child food choice and consumption. *Journal of Health Economics.*

Mitchell, M., White, L., Lau, E., Leahey, T., Adams, M. A., & Faulkner, G. (2018). Evaluating the carrot rewards app, a population-level incentive-based intervention promoting step counts across two Canadian provinces: Quasi-experimental study. *JMIR mHealth and uHealth.*

Möllenkamp, M., Zeppernick, M., & Schreyögg, J. (2019). The effectiveness of nudges in improving the self-management of patients with chronic diseases: A systematic literature review. *Health Policy.*

Nahum-Shani, I., Rabbi, M., Yap, J., Philyaw-Kotov, M. L., Klasnja, P., Bonar, E. E., Cunningham, R. M., Murphy, S. A., & Walton, M. A. (2021). Translating strategies for promoting engagement in mobile health: A proof-of-concept microrandomized trial. *Health Psychology*.

Patel, M. S., Small, D. S., Harrison, J. D., Hilbert, V., Fortunato, M. P., Oon, A. L., Rareshide, C. A. L., & Volpp, K. G. (2021). Effect of behaviorally designed gamification with social incentives on lifestyle modification among adults with uncontrolled diabetes: A randomized clinical trial. *JAMA Network Open*.

Saposnik, G., Sempere, A. P., Prefasi, D., Selchen, D., Ruff, C. C., Maurino, J., & Tobler, P. N. (2017). Decision-making in multiple sclerosis: The role of aversion to ambiguity for therapeutic inertia among neurologists (DIScUTIR MS). *Frontiers in Neurology*.

Shapiro, M. F., Shu, S. B., Goldstein, N. J., Victor, R. G., Fox, C. R., Tseng, C.-H., Vangala, S., Mogler, B. K., Reed, S. B., Villa, E., & Escarce, J. J. (2020). Impact of a patient-centered behavioral economics intervention on hypertension control in a highly disadvantaged population: A randomized trial. *Journal of General Internal Medicine*.

Van Der Swaluw, K., Lambooij, M. S., Mathijssen, J. J. P., Schipper, M., Zeelenberg, M., Berkhout, S., Polder, J. J., & Prast, H. M. (2018). Commitment lotteries promote physical activity among overweight adults: A cluster randomized trial. *Annals of Behavioral Medicine*.

Wilson, N. L. W., Just, D. R., Swigert, J., & Wansink, B. (2017). Food pantry selection solutions: A randomized controlled trial in client-choice food pantries to nudge clients to targeted foods. *Journal of Public Health (United Kingdom)*.

Yin, Z., Lesser, J., Paiva, K. A., Zapata, J. Jr., Moreno-Vasquez, A., Grigsby, T. J., Ryan-Pettes, S. R., Parra-Medina, D., Estrada, V., Li, S., & Wang, J. (2020). Using mobile health tools to engage rural underserved individuals in a diabetes education programme in South Texas: Feasibility study. *JMIR mHealth and uHealth*.

Zullig, L. L., Blalock, D. V., Dougherty, S., Henderson, R., Ha, C. C., Oakes, M. M., & Bosworth, H. B. (2018). The new landscape of medication adherence improvement: Where population health science meets precision medicine. *Patient Preference and Adherence*.

A Comparative Analysis of Risk Management Practices

Nida Turegun

1. Introduction

In the ever evolving and increasingly interconnected global business landscape, organizations must navigate a myriad of risks and uncertainties to achieve sustainable growth, maintain a competitive edge, and ensure long-term resilience. The growing complexity of business environments, coupled with the unpredictability of external factors such as technological advancements, geopolitical events, and natural disasters necessitates the development and implementation of comprehensive risk management frameworks align with a company's strategic goals and unique risk profile (Margherita et al, 2023).

The importance of risk management cannot be overstated, as failure to identify and manage risks effectively can result in significant financial losses, reputational damage, and even bankruptcy (Lodhia, & Mitchell, 2022). Despite the criticality of risk management, there is no one-size-fits-all approach suitable for all organizations (Giannakis & Louis, 2016;). Each company faces a distinct set of risks that require tailored risk management strategies (Peljhan & Marc., 2021). Consequently, it is essential to examine the risk management practices of industry leaders to glean insights into the best practices and strategies adaptable to individual company needs (Oliva et al.,2019).

The motivation behind this chapter is to address the increasing significance of risk management in today's globalized and competitive market environment. By examining the risk management practices of successful multinational corporations operating in different industries, this research offers valuable insights for other companies seeking to enhance their risk management strategies.

The uniqueness of this study arises from its comparative assessment of risk management methodologies used by Toyota Motor Corporation (TMC), General Electric (GE), and Goldman Sachs (GS), three global corporations operating in various industries. This comparison gives a more thorough understanding of risk management tactics across numerous sectors, as well as how these techniques are tailored to each company's specific business models and needs. This study provides light on the connection between risk management and various aspects of company management by studying annual reports, SEC filings, and other relevant documents, giving significant insights for firms wishing to better their risk management frameworks.

2. Review of Risk Management Practices

The effective management of risk is critical to the success of any organization, regardless of its industry. However, the way risk is managed can vary significantly from one sector to another due to differences in the nature and prevalence of potential threats. This disparity in risk management practices across industries presents a complex and intricate issue, thus motivating this chapter. Prior research underscores the significance of tailoring risk management strategies to cater to an organization's unique industry, business model, and risk profile (Tarasova et al., 2017; Naseem et al., 2020). Such studies provide a theoretical basis for our exploration of industry-specific risk management strategies at TMC, GE, and GS. Furthermore, extant literature illuminates the merits of fostering a robust risk management culture characterized by openness, communication, and accountability (Braumann et al., 2020; Saeidi et al., 2021). These cultural dimensions play a pivotal role in our analysis of the risk management practices at TMC, GE, and GS. The proactive identification and mitigation of threats, combined with a comprehensive perspective of internal and external risks, is also a consistent theme in the literature (Babu et al., 2021; Taherdoost, 2021). These insights offer a theoretical lens through which we scrutinize the proactive and comprehensive risk management approaches of TMC, GE, and GS. The central research question is: How do risk management practices vary among industries, and what can be gleaned from these variances and commonalities? In essence, this chapter aims to bridge the gap in the literature on cross-industry comparisons of risk management practices. It strives to offer practical insights of value to organizations across diverse sectors. By applying existing theories and methodologies in a unique cross-industry context, this study endeavor to contribute to academic discourse and inform practical applications in risk management.

The subsequent section delves into risk management practices and strategies employed by multinational corporations, with a focus on three specific organizations: TMC, GE, and GS.

2.1. Goldman Sachs

GS is an international investment banking, securities, and investment management company based in New York City. The organization places considerable importance on risk management throughout all levels and maintains a specialized risk management department with over 800 employees (GS, 2020a). The firm's risk management policies undergo regular review and updates to ensure continued effectiveness amidst evolving market conditions (Mashiach, 2021). GS also employs advanced risk models and analytics as part of its risk management practices (Nenovski et al., 2017). Utilizing various quantitative models, such as value-at-risk (VaR) models, stress testing, and scenario analysis, the firm can identify potential risks and formulate mitigation strategies (GS, 2021a).

GS also emphasizes diversification in its risk management approach. Operating across diverse asset classes and geographies allows the firm to distribute risk and reduce vulnerability to specific markets or sectors (GS, 2019). Actively managing its asset portfolio, GS ensures it remains well-diversified and in line with its risk appetite. Alongside these factors, GS fosters a risk management culture promoting transparency and accountability. The company regularly discloses its risk management practices, providing detailed information on risk exposure and mitigation tactics to investors and regulators. This transparency bolsters trust in the firm's risk management practices and reinforces its reputation as a reliable financial institution (GS, 2017; 2018).

GS's risk management practices are supported by solid internal controls and governance structures. A dedicated risk management committee oversees the risk management framework's execution, and senior executives are tasked with managing risks within their respective business units (GS, 2021b). The firm also emphasizes a strong compliance culture, focusing on meeting regulatory requirements and upholding ethical standards.

2.2. Toyota Motor Corporation

TMC, a Japanese multinational automaker, has successfully integrated risk management techniques into its worldwide financial operations (TMC, 2023). TMC's use of a holistic risk management framework covering diverse risk mitigation measures has been a major contributor to its effectiveness in controlling financial risks. Addressing foreign exchange risk is a critical component of TMC's risk management approach. TMC is very vulnerable to currency rate swings because to its activities in various countries and exposure to a variety of foreign currencies. To manage this risk, TMC implements measures such as currency hedging, netting, and optimization to reduce the impact of currency changes on its financial performance (TMC, 2022a).

The emphasis on supply chain risk is another critical component of TMC's risk management approach. TMC relies on a complicated network of global suppliers as a global car manufacturer. TMC has introduced measures such as supplier risk assessment, supplier diversity, and inventory management to mitigate supply chain disruption risks (TMC, 2022b). TMC is able to maintain a stable and robust supply chain that can survive different interruptions thanks to these measures (Ivanov and Ivanov, 2018). TMC also stresses internal controls and risk management governance, with a specialized risk management committee supervising the application of the risk management framework and guaranteeing adequate risk identification, evaluation, and management. This group is made up of top executives from various business units and roles, as well as independent specialists who offer objective opinion and assistance (Toyoda, 2023b).

2.3. General Electric

GE is a worldwide company with interests in a variety of areas, including aviation, energy, healthcare, and finance (GE, 2023). Due to exposure to foreign currency swings, particularly the Japanese yen, the company faced significant financial risk in the late 1990s. To address this risk, GE designed an all-encompassing risk management plan that incorporates financial tools such as futures, options, and swaps.

The establishment of a centralized risk management team responsible for supervising and handling the corporation's financial risks was vital to the success of GE's risk management initiative (GE, 2018). Another key aspect was the company's focus on diversification, both in terms of business operations and financial instruments. GE maintained several subsidiaries operating in diverse sectors and regions, enabling the distribution of its financial risk across various markets. Additionally, the firm employed a range of financial tools to manage risk, allowing for adaptability in response to fluctuating market conditions and risk reduction at minimal expense (GE, 2023b).

3. Methodology

This research employs a qualitative research methodology, relying on an analysis of existing literature on risk management approaches as well as a review of annual reports, SEC filings, and other relevant documents. The approach facilitates an in-depth evaluation of risk management practices in three global companies: TMC, GE, and GS. This method enables the identification of common themes and differences in their risk management strategies, providing valuable insights into effective risk management practices.

Data was collected from various sources to conduct a comprehensive investigation of risk management techniques, strategies, and organizational factors at TMC, GE, and GS. Among the sources utilized were annual reports, SEC filings, and other relevant documents. The annual reports and SEC filings provided information on the organizations' risk management structures, strategies, and policies, as well as financial performance and risk exposure. To gather annual reports, the investor relations sections of each company's official website were visited, where they publicly disclose their financial information, including annual reports from previous years. Electronic Data Gathering, Analysis, and Retrieval (EDGAR) system of the U.S. Securities and Exchange Commission used to retrieve SEC filings, such as 10-K and 20-F reports. From the websites of the firms or reliable news sources, other relevant documents were collected, including presentations, white papers, and press announcements. After the data had been gathered, a content analysis was done to systematically categorize and look at the advantages, difficulties, and risk management techniques for TMC, GE, and GS. A system for classifying risk management approaches, tactics, advantages, and challenges was initially created. This framework was based on the tools and techniques used by the companies and the respective benefits and challenges of each approach. Once the coding process was finalized, the coded data was analyzed to identify patterns, trends, and differences in risk management practices, strategies, benefits, and challenges among the three companies. This research entailed comparing the codes allocated to each firm and synthesizing the data to draw conclusions and insights regarding the success of various risk management systems and the issues that each company faced. A comprehensive content analysis of the collected data gave useful insights into TMC, GE, and GS risk management procedures, strategies, and organizational variables.

4. Results

Figure 1 presents consolidated risk management practices overview. Examining TMC, GE, and GS annual reports demonstrates that all three corporations have robust risk management systems in place. The annual report of TMC stresses its risk management approach, which focuses on detecting and reducing operational risks to assure product safety and quality. TMC's risk management system includes, among other things, risk assessments, internal audits, and safety and quality management systems. In addition, the corporation acknowledges growing risks such as cybersecurity threats and climate change and takes steps to minimize them. GE's annual report emphasizes the importance of risk management in attaining its strategic goals. To control risks and stimulate development, the company's risk management strategy incorporates diversity and innovation. To ensure the efficacy of its risk management framework, GE also implements extensive risk management procedures such as risk assessments, risk mitigation strategies, and scenario analysis. The company's commitment to compliance and regulatory risk management is highlighted in GS' annual report. Compliance with laws, regulations, and internal policies, as well as the adoption of rigorous risk management procedures and controls, are all part of GS' risk management practices. The organization also emphasizes the significance of risk culture, risk governance, and risk transparency in risk management.

TMC, GE, and GS's SEC filings give more insight into their risk management processes. TMC's SEC filings include information on the company's risk management activities, including as risk management policies, procedures, and frameworks. Specific risks like as supply chain interruptions, legislation changes, and reputational challenges are also investigated. TMC makes information about its risk-mitigation strategies, such as its quality and safety management systems and business continuity plans, available to the public. GE's SEC filings outline the company's risk management methods, including how it detects, assesses, and mitigates risks. GE describes their risk management strategy, which includes enterprise, compliance, and operational risk management components. GE discusses the specific risks it faces, including as market-related hazards, cyber threats, and geopolitical challenges, as well as data on its risk-reduction initiatives. GS discloses its risk management strategies, including procedures for identifying and managing risks across its businesses, in SEC filings. Market, credit, and operational risk

Figure 1. Consolidated Risk Management Practices Overview

management are all part of the company's risk management system. In addition to adhering to compliance rules and adopting internal control measures, GS discusses its attempts to mitigate certain risks, such as regulatory, legal, and reputation-related risks.

A review of TMC, GE, and GS's relevant resources, such as their corporate governance principles and risk management standards, provides a better understanding of their risk management processes. TMC's corporate governance records highlight its risk management focus, which aims to prevent issues from arising. Risk evaluations, monitoring, and reporting processes are part of the company's risk management standards, which emphasize the significance of a risk-conscious culture. TMC's risk management policies demonstrate the company's dedication to compliance and safe technology use. The risk management approach, which is incorporated into the company's overall business plan, is highlighted in GE's corporate governance papers. The organization's risk management practices include a rigorous risk identification process that includes identifying new threats, as well as a risk mitigation plan that promotes variety and innovation. GE's risk management principles highlight the company's dedication to ethical behavior, compliance, and stakeholder involvement. The company's risk management plan, which is based on a thorough risk management framework, is described in GS's corporate governance rules. Risk management methods include a thorough risk identification process that includes identifying and assessing dangers across the company's activities, as well as risk mitigation plan that integrates different risk management techniques and strategies. GS's risk management principles highlight the company's dedication to compliance, transparency, and stakeholder participation.

Figure 2 provides a comprehensive summary of the risk management tools and techniques employed by three large corporations: TMC, GE, and GS. Each business has its own risk management plan that focuses on several elements to ensure long-term success. TMC's risk management approach, which primarily targets operational risks, is built on the Toyota Production System, a lean manufacturing technique that focuses on waste reduction and continuous improvement. This strategy fosters an improvement culture by enabling employees at all levels to discover and reduce waste and inefficiencies in their operations. TMC also use a variety of tools and techniques to achieve its objectives, including Hoshin Kanri, FMEA, and Kaizen. TMC's approach

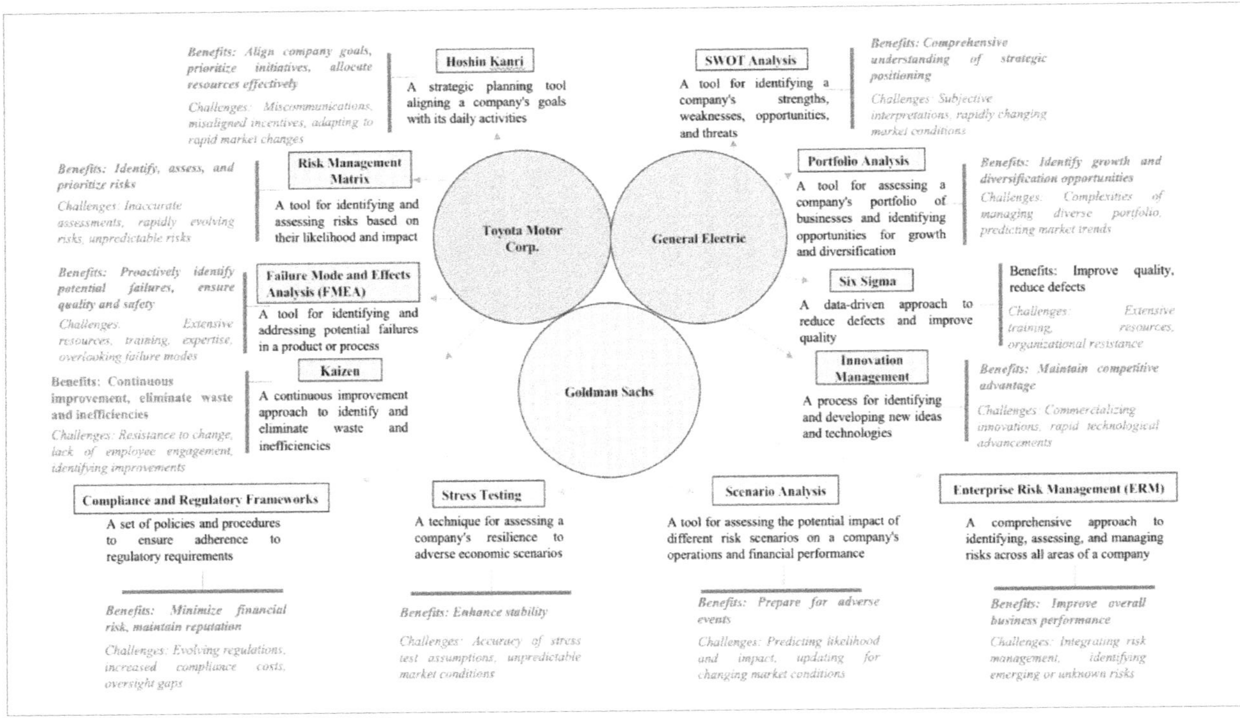

Figure 2. Overview of the Risk Management Tools

is focused on providing high-quality, low-cost goods while emphasizing client happiness.

The Hoshin Kanri tool is a strategic planning strategy that matches a company's goals with its day-to-day operations. The advantages of Hoshin Kanri include goal alignment, initiative prioritization, and optimal resource allocation. Miscommunications between management levels, mismatched incentives leading to resource allocation disputes, and difficulty responding to quickly changing market conditions are some of Hoshin Kanri's issues. The Risk Management Matrix tool assists in the identification and evaluation of hazards based on their likelihood and effect. The Risk Management Matrix provides benefits such as detecting, analyzing, and prioritizing risks, allowing businesses to understand possible hazards and establish appropriate risk mitigation solutions. The Risk Management Matrix faces challenges such as erroneous assessments, quickly developing hazards, and unforeseen risks, which necessitate ongoing examination and update of risk management techniques. To maintain quality and safety, the Failure Mode, and Effects Analysis (FMEA) tool proactively identifies probable product or process problems. FMEA benefits include proactive failure detection and quality and safety assurance. Identifying probable failure modes, analyzing their impact, and devising suitable mitigation methods are all part of this methodical process. FMEA problems, on the other hand, include the requirement for substantial resources, training, and experience for effective implementation, as well as the danger of missing failure modes. The Kaizen method assists in the identification and elimination of waste and inefficiency. Kaizen advantages include continual improvement and the elimination of waste and inefficiencies, as well as involving employees at all levels in finding and implementing improvements to increase efficiency and quality. However, hurdles to Kaizen include reluctance to change, a lack of staff involvement, and difficulty finding areas for improvement (Ikeda, 2020).

GE, on the other hand, emphasizes variety and innovation in their risk management strategy. GE's strategy is around continuous improvement. The firm has a history of developing new products and services in a variety of areas, including aviation, healthcare, and energy. To attain its objectives, GE additionally employs tools and techniques such as Six Sigma and innovation management. GE's strategy focuses on delivering new goods and services that address its customers' evolving demands.

The SWOT Analysis tool aids in the identification of a company's strengths, weaknesses, opportunities, and threats. SWOT analysis provides a complete knowledge of strategic positioning, helping businesses to identify areas where they have a competitive advantage and areas where they need to improve. However, the limitations of SWOT analysis include subjective interpretations and frequently changing market conditions, which means that firms must constantly analyze and update their SWOT analysis to remain relevant. The Portfolio Analysis tool evaluates a company's portfolio of businesses and uncovers growth and diversification opportunities. Benefits of portfolio analysis include identifying growth and diversification opportunities, helping companies understand the performance of various businesses in their portfolio, and pinpointing areas for investment to enhance performance. Nevertheless, challenges of portfolio analysis encompass the complexities of managing a diverse portfolio and forecasting market trends. Six Sigma, a data-driven approach, reduces defects and boosts quality. Benefits of Six Sigma include improved quality and reduced defects. However, challenges of Six Sigma include the extensive training and resources necessary for effective implementation and organizational resistance to change. The Innovation Management process identifies and develops new ideas and technologies to maintain a competitive advantage. Benefits of innovation management include sustaining a competitive advantage by identifying areas for new technologies or product development, creating appropriate solutions, and commercializing them. However, challenges of innovation management include commercializing innovations and rapid technological advancements, implying that companies must continuously evaluate and update their innovation strategies to stay competitive.

GS's strategy revolves around delivering exceptional client service and effectively managing risks. The company offers various financial services to its clients, including investment banking, securities, and asset management. GS utilizes tools and techniques such as compliance and regulatory frameworks, stress testing, and scenario analysis to achieve its objectives. These tools and techniques enable the company to manage risks effectively and provide customized financial solutions to its clients. GS's strategy concentrates on offering exceptional client service while effectively managing risks.

The Compliance and Regulatory Frameworks tool guarantees that regulatory standards are met to reduce financial risk and keep a good reputation.

The advantages of compliance and regulatory frameworks include reduced financial risk and reputation preservation. However, compliance and regulatory framework concerns include shifting rules and rising compliance expenses. To be compliant with new legislation, businesses must constantly update their compliance frameworks. To promote stability, the Stress Testing approach assesses a company's adaptability to bad economic conditions. The benefits of stress testing include increased stability by simulating negative economic scenarios and measuring their impact on the company's financial performance, as well as developing appropriate mitigation strategies. The limitations of stress testing, however, are the correctness of stress test assumptions and the unpredictability of market situations. To prepare for unfavorable occurrences, the Scenario Analysis tool assesses the possible consequences of various risk scenarios on a company's operations and financial performance. The advantages of scenario analysis include planning for unfavorable occurrences by constructing scenarios based on numerous risk variables and estimating their possible influence on the financial performance of the firm. However, the challenges of scenario analysis include projecting likelihood and impact as well as adjusting to changing market conditions. The Enterprise Risk Management (ERM) strategy detects, analyses, and manages risks across all aspects of a firm to improve overall business performance. ERM benefits include increased overall corporate performance and the identification and mitigation of emerging or undiscovered hazards. However, challenges of ERM include integrating risk management into all aspects of the company's operations and identifying/addressing emerging or unknown risks. Companies need to continuously evaluate and update their ERM framework to ensure its effectiveness.

5. Conclusion

The chapter emphasizes the significance of collaboration and communication among many stakeholders, including as management, employees, regulators, and investors. Companies may foster a common awareness of risk and assist the development of successful risk management strategies that are consistent with the company's goals and objectives by fostering an open and transparent culture. As businesses grow and face new problems, such as the ongoing effects of climate change, geopolitical upheavals, and technology breakthroughs, it is critical for organizations to review their risk management procedures and adapt to the changing environment. Companies may manage possible dangers and capitalize on new possibilities by remaining educated about emerging risks and trends, eventually driving innovation and development. Furthermore, businesses should think about adding environmental, social, and governance considerations into their risk management procedures. Companies may better connect their strategies with public expectations and long-term sustainability goals by including these elements into their risk assessment and decision-making processes. This technique not only reduces risk but also improves a company's reputation and brand value.

In addition, the chapter emphasizes the need of developing a risk-aware culture inside a business. Businesses may become more adaptive and stronger by integrating employees at all levels in risk management activities and creating a communal awareness of risk. This entails investing in staff education and development, as well as establishing clear accountability and responsibility lines for risk management duties. The findings also suggest that the relevance of technology in risk management will continue to expand. To increase their risk management capabilities, businesses should embrace digital transformation and invest in sophisticated analytics, artificial intelligence, and machine learning technology. Organizations may make better-informed decisions, enhance processes, and efficiently minimize risks by leveraging data-driven insights.

The chapter highlights that firms need to regularly update risk management frameworks, benchmark against industry leaders, and invest in advanced models, technology, and employee skills to adapt to evolving risks. Effective risk management not only strengthens individual firms but also contributes to global economic stability by preventing financial losses and crises. On a policy level, governments and regulators should emphasize strong risk management practices across industries, consider industry-specific regulations, and promote sharing of best practices to foster continuous improvement.

References

Babu, H., Bhardwaj, P., & Agrawal, A. K. (2021). Modelling the supply chain risk variables using ISM: a case study on Indian manufacturing SMEs. Journal of Modelling in Management, 16(1), 215-239.

Braumann, E. C., Grabner, I., & Posch, A. (2020). Tone from the top in risk management: A complementarity perspective on how control systems influence risk awareness. Accounting, Organizations and Society, 84, 101128.

GE. (2018). Risk Management: A Centralized Approach. Retrieved from https://www.ge.com/reports/risk-management-centralized-approach/ ↩

GE. (2023). Investor Conference. Cincinnati, Ohio. Retrieved from https://www.ge.com/sites/default/files/2023-ge-investor-conference-presentation.pdf

GE. (2023b). Notice of Annual Meeting and Proxy Statement. Retrieved from https://www.ge.com/sites/default/files/ge_proxy2023.pdf

Giannakis, M., & Louis, M. (2016). A Multi-agent Based System with Big Data Processing for Enhanced Supply Chain Agility. *Journal of Enterprise Information Management, 29*(5), 706-727.

GS. (2017). Building a Diverse and Inclusive Workplace. Retrieved from https://www.goldmansachs.com/citizenship/10000-women/news-and-events/building-a-diverse-and-inclusive-workplace.html

GS. (2018). Risk Management: Our Principles and Approach. Retrieved from https://www.goldmansachs.com/what-we-do/risk-management/principles-and-approach.html

GS. (2019). 2019 Annual Report: Our Commitment to Risk Management. Retrieved from https://www.goldmansachs.com/investor-relations/financials/current/annual-reports/2019-annual-report/our-commitment-to-risk-management/index.html

GS. (2020a). Our Approach to Risk Management. Retrieved from https://www.goldmansachs.com/what-we-do/risk-management/our-approach.html

GS. (2021a). Risk Management. https://www.goldmansachs.com/what-we-do/investing-and-lending/risk-management/

GS. (2021b). Risk Management Policies. https://www.goldmansachs.com/what-we-do/investing-and-lending/risk-management/risk-management-policies.html

Ikeda, N. (2020). Toyota Becomes Stronger - The Hidden Power of Kaizen. Retrieved from https://toyotatimes.jp/en/report/financial_results_2021/100.html

Ivanov, D., & Ivanov, D. (2018). New Drivers for Supply Chain Structural Dynamics and Resilience: Sustainability, Industry 4.0, Self-adaptation. *Structural Dynamics and Resilience in Supply Chain Risk Management*, *265*, 293-313.

Lodhia, S., & Mitchell, N.A. (2022). Corporate Social Responsibility Disclosures and Reputation Risk Management Post the Banking Royal Commission: A Study of the Big Four Banks. *Qualitative Research in Accounting & Management*, *19*(2), 162-185.

Margherita, A., Nasiri, M., & Papadopoulos, T. (2023). The application of digital technologies in company responses to COVID-19: An integrative framework. *Technology Analysis & Strategic Management*, *35*(8), 979-992

Mashiach, D. (2021). Goldman Sachs Investment Report. Retrieved from https://ecommons.luc.edu/cgi/viewcontent.cgi?article=1259&context=ures

Naseem, T., Shahzad, F., Asim, G. A., Rehman, I. U., & Nawaz, F. (2020). Corporate social responsibility engagement and firm performance in Asia Pacific: The role of enterprise risk management. Corporate Social Responsibility and Environmental Management, 27(2), 501-513.

Nenovski, T., Jolevska, E.D., & Trpovska, S. (2017). How Investment Banking Influenced the Appearance of the World Economic Crises-The Cases of Lehman Brothers and Goldman Sachs. *Journal of Sustainable Development*, 7(17), 50-70.

Oliva, F.L., Couto, M.H.G., Santos, R.F., & Bresciani, S. (2019). The Integration between Knowledge Management and Dynamic Capabilities in Agile Organizations. *Management Decision*, *57*(8), 1960-1979.

Peljhan, D., & Marc, M. (2021). Risk management and strategy alignment: influence on new product development performance. *Technology Analysis & Strategic Management*, 1-13.

Saeidi, P., Saeidi, S. P., Gutierrez, L., Streimikiene, D., Alrasheedi, M., Saeidi, S. P., & Mardani, A. (2021). The influence of enterprise risk management on firm performance with the moderating effect of intellectual capital dimensions. Economic Research-Ekonomska Istraživanja, 34(1), 122-151.

Taherdoost, H. (2021). A review on risk management in information systems: Risk policy, control and fraud detection. Electronics, 10(24), 3065.

Tarasova, E. V., Nikulina, E. N., & Moskvicheva, N. V. (2017). Analysis of risk assessment methods of innovative projects. Revista Espacios, 38(49).

TMC. (2022a). Integrated Report 2022. Retrieved from https://global.toyota/pages/global_toyota/ir/library/annual/2022_001_integrated_en.pdf

TMC. (2022b). Risk Management Strategies. Retrieved from https://global.toyota/en/sustainability/risk_management/strategies/ ↩

TMC. (2023). Overview. Retrieved from https://global.toyota/en/company/?_gl=1*1aivi23*_ga*MjQyNzg2MDU5LjE2ODMwMjQ5MDU.*_ga_FW87SM9FNZ*MTY4MzAyNDkwNC4xLjEuMTY4MzAyNTU1Ny4yMy4wLjA.&_ga=2.31116351.1011644629.1683024907-242786059.1683024905

Toyoda, A. (2023). President's Message: Continuous Improvement and Innovation in Risk Management. Retrieved from https://global.toyota/en/company/messages_from_executives/risk_management/ ↩

Quality Assurance Assessment. Critical Success Factor for Digital Financial Markets Trust

Cláudia Ramião, Francisco José Videira Cachatra,
Pedro Fernandes da Anunciação

1. Introduction

In an increasingly digital age, where applications and information systems and technologies play a key role in people's daily lives, software quality is emerging as a crucial foundation for ensuring user satisfaction, trust and loyalty (Maxim & Kessentini, 2016).

The dependence on online services has been intensifying year after year, so ensuring excellence in software delivery is increasingly an imperative. Banks have found in digital options a way to be closer to their customers and create customer needs regarding access and use of financial services. The most used digital mobile platform in Portugal is an excellent example, as it was created to facilitate bank transfers and payments without having to go to the banks' counters or access internet banking. Currently, this solution has become a vital tool in the daily lives of the Portuguese, offering a user-friendly interface and practical features that simplify financial transactions. This solution allows the execution of financial operations by associating the customer's mobile phone number to his bank card, thus allowing payments, transfers, or send, receive and ask for money, among other features, with QR Code or Near Field Communication (NFC).

However, its growing popularity also entails a greater responsibility in terms of maintaining quality, preventing failures and ensuring the security of users' data. Being a banking application, there are also some fears and fears on the part of users who do not master the software, especially due to access through the mobile phone and the dispensation of some information necessary for the execution of more traditional operations (such as IBAN). In addition, within the scope of software quality, there are other aspects also relevant, such as performance, reliability, usability, security and accessibility, which together form the user's perception about a digital product or service.

2. Quality and life cycle of software development

Although traditionally, the software development life cycle (SDLC) encompasses phases of Requirements/Specification, Design, Development/Implementation, Verification/Testing, Maintenance and Support (Boyle, 2015), software development companies, especially those operating in environments with multiple concurrent projects, have adapted the methodologies to improve project management, allowing them to use their resources more efficiently (Christine Xiaoyi DAI, 2004). In a study done by Cooper, K., Reitsma, R. & Duan, X. (2017), where 1,023 professionals were surveyed in information technologies, it is found that development methodologies are divided into three major groups: traditional methodologies, agile methodologies and iterative methodologies. As examples of these methodologies, we have the methodology *Waterfall*, as being traditional methodology, SCRUM, Extreme Programming, Lean, Dynamic Systems Development Method (LDSDM) and Feature-driven development (FDD), as agile methodology and the RUP methodology, as iterative methodology. This study also indicates that 38.6% of the total professionals use Agile methodologies, 19.5% use iterative methodologies, 13% use traditional methodologies and finally 28.8% do not use any methodology in software development.

There are several differences between agile methodologies and traditional methodologies, the main difference being the planning. In traditional methodologies, planning is done in detail before the start of development. In contrast, in agile methodologies, planning is iterative and incremental, developing and adjusting itself throughout the project progress. According to Alistair Cockburn (2001), agile methodologies focus primarily on solving a specific problem within a fixed budget and time frame. In contrast, in traditional methodologies, specifications take precedence over time and cost. All details are defined in advance, with the time and cost necessary to achieve these specifications being a consequence of this initial planning. In technical terms, the two types of approach differ in how they deal with issues of time, cost, specifications and quality.

However, in any of the methodologies, software quality is a critical factor. Quality, besides being a factor of advantage in the market, is necessary and indispensable condition for it to be possible to compete successfully (Andrade, 2015).

Software quality can be defined as compliance with explicitly stated functional and performance requirements, clearly documented development standards, and the implicit features that are expected of all software developed by professionals (Roger S. Pressman, 1994). But also as the set of software attributes that must be satisfied so that the software meets the user's needs (whether it is an end-user, who develops the software or an organization) (Andrade, 2015).

A software can be understood as a program, a procedure, documentation or data of the operations of a computer (Galin, 2004), or, more generally, as a set of all the programs that enable from the operation of the system and its management at the lowest level, to the performance of the most varied tasks such as drawing up graphs, accounting of any company, the organization of personal agenda and all kinds of educational games and programs (Sousa, 2003).

In quality assessment, testing plays a central role. Software testing is a critical activity in software quality assurance. It is the verification of the conditions that must be fulfilled by the implemented code. According to Roger S. Pressman (1994) there are two types of testing: functional tests and structural tests. Functional tests or black-box tests are a typology of tests that focus on the functional requirements of the software. Another type of tests is structural or white box tests, which have as characteristics the fact that they are performed in advance in the test process. White box test uses a design control structure to derive test cases, that is, a software quality tester can derive the test cases that ensure that all independent paths within a module have been exercised at least once or that they exercise all logical decisions for false or true values (Molinari, 2003).

The Quality Assurance software activities are related to the following points (Molinari, 2003):

- Software testing - how to manage risk and ensure compliance with the requirements defined for the product throughout design, coding and documentation.
- Quality Control - set of processes and methods used to monitor the work and requirements involved in a given project.
- Software Configuration Management - integrates the identification, tracking and control of changes in the elements of the software or even the system itself.

Another important element in evaluating the quality of software refers to specifications and standards. A specification corresponds to the definition of the quality attributes of a product in isolation, while a standard defines the quality attributes, but of a class of products (Coelho, 1986).

There are several types of standards, including: international, national, industry, organizational and design (Coelho, 1986). As an example of the importance of standards in guiding software development we can indicate one of the leading organizations in the field of software engineering, which supports a large number of projects from a set of relevant standards, as, for example, IEEE 829/1983 - Software Testing Documentation, IEEE 1008/1987 - Software Unit Test, IEEE 1012/1986 - Software Verification & Validation Plan, IEEE 730/1998 - Software Quality Assurance Plan, or IEEE 1228/1994 - Software Security Plans.

One last point that should be stressed is the cost of quality. We know that quality is important, but there are costs associated with. There is no doubt that quality has a price, but lack of quality also has a price - not only for users who will have to live with a software with errors, but also for the software organization that created it and in addition will have to do its maintenance. The quality costs can have three different natures: costs associated with prevention, evaluation and failures (Roger S. Pressman, 1994).

3. Objectives and methodologies

The specific objective of this study was to evaluate the impact of software quality and its influence on the user experience but taking as reference the *Quality Assurance* (QA) professionals. The study was conducted in two phases. Knowing the quality requirements of the entity that manages the digital financial services platform, it was decided, in the first phase of the study, to identify the life cycle phases with impact on the QA of the digital services provided. This phase aimed to understand the existing life cycle and its relevance in quality assurance of applications that are placed on the platform. For this, a focus group was created with the most experienced quality assurance professionals, from which were identified the main phases corresponding to the software development life cycle for the digital services platform, having reflected on its relevance in the QA of services provided.

The second phase corresponded to the completion of a questionnaire to testers, elements with the function of QA, to verify the respective perception of the quality of the solutions that certify from the perspective of the digital service provider. In this context, the main parameters included in the questionnaire focused on the following dimensions: QA experience, platform knowledge, quality, usability, safety and user satisfaction with the software platform.

4. Analysis and results discussion

Regarding the first phase of the study, it was noticeable through the focus group that the certification process of the software produced involves several essential steps. Each plays a crucial role in ensuring that the software developed meets business requirements and is safe for end users, namely:

- Identification of the business need - The process begins with the identification of a business need, usually proposed by several stakeholders, such as banks, which may be related to the introduction of new functionalities, improvements to existing services or adaptations to regulatory requirements.
- Definition of objectives - definition of the specific goals that are desired to achieve and what should be delivered to customers, aligning them with the expectations of stakeholders.
- Business Requirements Creation - detail the main idea, project objectives and deadline, ensuring that all involved understand the vision and purpose of the project.
- Distribution of work for the Technical Teams - requirements are presented to the technical teams, identifying the areas that will be impacted by the new development, to identify, plan, develop and implement the necessary changes.
- Order Management - updating the associated documentation in the project management tool), to facilitate monitoring, coordination and communication between the various teams involved.
- Software Development - development of the software, based on the requirements and structured management thereof, being subsequently tested internally to ensure compliance with specified requirements.
- Certification in a non-productive environment - After development, the software is transferred to a certification team, which performs tests in a

non-productive environment, validating the expected functioning and compliance with all technical and safety requirements.
- Migration to Pre-Production Environment - After certification, the software is migrated to the Pre-Production environment for final testing. This environment serves as a final validation point before the solution is implemented in production.
- Evolution to Production Environment - the software is migrated to the production environment after the tests in Pre-production are successful. At this stage, the software becomes available to all end-users. If any problem is detected in production, an Incident is opened, which can evolve into a preventive improvement, thus starting a new cycle of correction and improvement.

As reiterated by the focus group, they consider that this detailed cycle ensures that each new feature or update is carefully planned, developed and tested before being made available to end users, ensuring the quality and safety of services.

In the second phase of the study, 16 professionals in the area of QA were interviewed with the objective of identifying and evaluating, in a more the perception of quality relative to the solutions that certify in the perspective of the digital service provider in the previously referenced dimensions. The results were as follows:

- In total, 16 professionals were interviewed, and it was found that most already have solid knowledge in software testing. The analysis of the results showed that the QA team is made up mostly of experienced professionals with more than two years of experience in the area. This is a positive indication of the maturity of the QA team, suggesting that there is an ability to perform rigorous testing and identify problems effectively. The results also show that most of the respondents (62.5%) have direct experience with the testing of platform functionalities, being evident the knowledge of the QA process and ensuring that the tests are performed by professionals familiar with the application. However, it was also found that 37.5% of the respondents did not test any functionality which, despite training for the exercise of functions, may eventually compromise the requirement of tests due to lack of knowledge and experience in the specific case study.

- The results show that there are three features that stand out in the opinion of QA professionals, as being those that return more anomalies when their certification. We talk about the generation of cards, payments (through QR Code or mobile phone number) and authorized payments. All these features recorded a value of more than 50% of the answers. Other features such as "use ATM", the fourth feature that presents more anomalies (40%), or the features of "send money" and "split account" and "be supportive" with 20% each, or even "ask for money", with 10% of the answers, are indicators that also deserve particular attention from the QA.
- As users of the platform, in the user-client perspective, it was found that 87.5% already found some anomaly when using the application. This result is significant and indicates that most QA have already been faced with problems or failures while using the platform. Only 12.5% of respondents report not having found any anomaly.
- Regarding usability, 93.7% of respondents said they consider the application easy to use. This result demonstrates a strong trust among testers in the usability of the platform, considering the solution as intuitive and easy to navigate. In this sense, they consider that the use of the platform can be carried out effectively and without great difficulties. Only 6.3% said that they do not consider the application easy for the user. Although this is a minority, the answer may highlight specific aspects of usability that still need to be improved.
- The results also show that the platform interface is widely well evaluated by testers (93.7%), and only 6.3% of the sample rate the interface as "medium".
- It is found that 93.7% answered that they consider the navigation in the intuitive application. Intuitive navigation is a key indicator for user attraction. Only 6.3% said they did not consider intuitive navigation, mentioned it could be confusing or unclear for some users.
- All respondents answered that they consider the use of the platform practical. This unanimity suggests that it meets the expectations of users in practical terms regarding their needs.
- This finding is reinforced when 56.3% of respondents consider that the platform meets all users' needs. This majority indicates that more than half of testers consider the application to be comprehensive and

effective, offering the necessary functionalities for users to carry out their operations satisfactorily. Already 43.7% of respondents stated that the application does not meet all users' needs. This percentage indicates that a substantial part of the testers identifies gaps or areas for improvement in the software platform.

- Regarding security, 87.5% of respondents consider the application safe. Most indicate strong confidence among testers in the ability to protect users' data and provide a secure experience. The perception of security is fundamental for any financial application, and these results suggest that, in most cases, the necessary standards are met to ensure protection against threats and vulnerabilities. Only 12.5% of respondents do not consider it safe. Although it is a minority, the fact that some testers express concerns about safety is significant. This may indicate the existence of specific areas where the platform could be improved to enhance security or where communication about security measures could be clearer and more effective.
- The results of the questionnaire also show a division between testers who have already found safety problems and those who did not. This result suggests that although the platform's security is solid in many aspects, there are areas where flaws or vulnerabilities may arise, requiring continuous attention and improvement. The presence of security problems in 50% of reported cases is a clear sign that the application needs a continuous and rigorous review of its security measures. Implementing corrective actions based on testers' feedback is essential to strengthen user protection and ensure continued trust.
- The majority of respondents (56.3%) consider that users' satisfaction with the platform's user experience is positive and 37.5% consider that users' satisfaction is very positive. Only 6.25% think users may feel unsatisfied.
- As regards the protection of personal data, 62.5% consider that users' level of security is good and 25% even consider that users are very good. Only 12.5% who consider that the degree of security of users in relation to the application is not satisfied or even dissatisfied.
- Regarding the reliability of the platform, 93.75% answered that there is a positive assessment. However, 6.25% do not.

- Regarding the recommendation for the use of the platform, although some dimensions lack improvements, which should be specifically understood in view of the deviation from the majority results obtained, it is the belief of respondents that the platform should be recommended. This feedback obtained from the platform's QA provider is relevant, as it will convey more security and confidence to current and future users.

5. Conclusion

The results of the testers' answers allow to confirm the relevance of the software quality is an essential element both to ensure user satisfaction and to ensure that the system is reliable and efficient. QA professionals, when performing rigorous testing, focus on application reliability, usability and performance, ensuring that errors and failures are minimized before final implementation.

The main conclusions that result from this study are:

- The quality of the software is directly proportional to the reliability and stability of the application. This ensures that users can complete transactions with confidence, without fear of errors that could compromise their financial operations.
- Security is one of the fundamental pillars for any financial application/form due to the sensitive nature of the operations that users perform. Well-built software protects users' data and prevents fraud, providing a sense of security and confidence.
- The quality of the software must ensure that all features offered work as expected. Bugs or features that do not perform properly and may cause frustration, such as transactions that are not completed or notifications that are not received compromises the usability of the application and trust.
- The quality of the software also covers the design and usability of the user interface, should favor a pleasant, intuitive user experience, improving satisfaction and service adoption.
- The introduction of new features and updates must be made from strict quality criteria, should proceed smoothly and without interruptions.

Also, most QA respondents guarantee that, as testers, users' perception of the platform characterizes it as easy to use, quick to execute, simple to understand and safe in financial transactions.

In short, the quality of the software is a determining factor for the user experience. High quality software provides a positive user experience, characterized by reliability, security, efficiency and usability. This study reaffirms the importance of an integrated and careful approach to software quality management, which is the key to developing digital solutions that are reliable, secure and appreciated by users. Thus, companies that want to thrive in the digital environment must continuously invest in software quality practices, ensuring that the user experience remains at the heart of all their development strategies.

References

Alistair Cockburn, L. W. (2001). The Costs and Benefits of Pair Programming. *Extreme Programming Examined, G. Succi and M. Marchesi (eds.).*

Andrade, M. (2015). Quality of software. Rio de Janeiro: 1ºEdição. (In Portuguese)

Aitken, A., & Ilango, V. (2013, January). A comparative analysis of traditional software engineering and agile software development. In *2013 46th Hawaii International Conference on System Sciences* (pp. 4751-4760). IEEE.

Boyde, J. (2014). A Down-To-Earth Guide To SDLC Project Management: Getting your *system/software development life cycle project successfully across the line using PMBOK adaptively*. Joshua Boyde. 49-51, 2nd Edition.

Christine Xiaoyi DAI, W. W. (2004). An exploration of project management office features and their relationship to project performance. International Journal of Project, 523–532.

Coelho, H. (1986). Notions and Concepts, Information Technologies, 35-40, Lisboa, 1st edition. *(In Portuguese)*

Cooper, K., Reitsma, R. & Duan, X. (2017). Forrester Data Global Business Technographics® Developer Survey, 2017: Overview - A Business Technographics Presentation, Forrester. Retrieved of: https://www.forrester.com/report/forrester-data-global-business-technographics-developer-survey-2017-overview/RES139851, Accessed at: 7 November 2024

Galin, D. (2004). Software quality assurance: from theory to implementation. Pearson education.

Maxim, B. R., & Kessentini, M. (2016). An introduction to modern software quality assurance. In *Software quality assurance* (pp. 19-46). Morgan Kaufmann.

Marks, A. (2012). Information Systems Development Methodolgies in Developing Higher Education. Creative Education.

Mendes, E. (2005, November). A systematic review of Web engineering research. In 2005 International Symposium on Empirical Software Engineering, 2005, IEEE.

Molinari, L. (2003). Software testing. São Paulo, 1ª Edição. (In Portuguese)

Offutt, J. (2002). Quality Attributes of Web Software Applications. IEEE Software, April 19th.

Mendes, A. M. (2023). *MB WAY reaches 5 million users.* Executive. Retrieved of: https://executivedigest.sapo.pt/noticias/mb-way-atinge-marca-dos-5-milhoes-de-utilizadores-em-portugal/, Accessed at: 2 December 2024 *(In Portuguese)*

Roger S. Pressman, B. R. (1994). Software Engineering. A Professional Approach. 9th edition. *(In Portuguese)*

Scholte, T., Balzarotti, D., & Kirda, E. (2012). Have things changed now? An empirical study on input validation vulnerabilities in web applications. Computers & Security, *31*(3), 344-356.

Snyder, C. S. (2014). A guide to the project management body of knowledge: PMBOK (®) guide. Project Management Institute: Newtown Square, *PA, USA*, 128-129.

Sousa, S. (2003). Information Technologies - What are they? What are they for? Lisbon: 4th. edition. *(In Portuguese)*

Sullivan, K. (2011). Protecting Users: The Importance of Defending Public Sites.

Project Management Practices Optimization in Information Systems and Technologies Services

Mariana dos Santos Miranda, Francisco Joaquim Madeira Esteves,
Pedro Fernandes da Anunciação

1. Introduction

Currently, because of market instability and constant changes in the different environments, project management is an activity under pressure regarding budgets and deadlines, making them increasingly limited and increasing the scarcity of allocated resources. Most companies currently work or develop their activities from projects. The specificity and requirement associated with project management results from the need to reach the final objectives and the constraints of costs and deadlines that may condition the deliverables (IPMA, 2015) (PMI, 2017). This is why the management associated with projects is so relevant. Management is based on a set of relevant dimensions, which must be considered and prepared, such as the planning, organization, direction and control of resources (Kerzner, 2009); the processes, methods, skills, experience and knowledge (APM, 2012); the tools, techniques and stakeholders various benefits (IPMA, 2015); the requirements, the determination of clear objectives, the negotiation of resources time, quality and costs, the conceptualization of plans and management of stakeholder expectations, that enable organizations to carry out projects with the necessary efficiency (PMI, 2017). With efficient and effective project management, organizations can align their business objectives with the project results, becoming more competitive in the market in which they are inserted and improving their adaptation to situations resulting from market instability (PMI, 2017).

Companies can currently use frameworks and methodologies of Project Management relevant for the adoption in their management. PMBOK, for example, is a standard for project management developed by the PMI, which is considered the largest international reference for project management (Obrutsky & Erturk 2017). Proposes a project life cycle is composed of a series of phases that the project runs through from its beginning to its completion, such as the start of the project, organization and preparation, work execution and the closure of the project (PMI, 2017).

However, methodologies have evolved over time as they establish the functions of a project, and the specific activities associated with the development of projects (Bērziša & Grabis, 2009). Thus, this evolution has gone from traditional methodologies, as sequential design processes applied in software development, where each step of the sequence must be completed and approved before proceeding to the next step (Singhto & Denwattana, 2016). The Waterfall methodology, created by Royce (1970) is an example. Focused on timely determination of requirements, extensive documentation and the requirement for formal approvals and reviews at each stage of the process (Palmquist, Lapham, Miller, Chick, & Ozkaya, 2013). Agile methodologies were created to improve the software development process and mitigate the problems of using traditional methodologies (Jerom et al., 2020), as the rigidity and extensive documentation (Ríos & Pedreira-Souto, 2019) or the weak flexibility and some rigidity in responding to changes and new requirements during the process (Kumar & Bhatia, 2014). Agile methodologies are an adaptive and incremental approach to fast and efficient software development (Singhto & Denwattana, 2016). As examples we have the Scrum that presents an adaptive, iterative, fast, flexible and effective structure, developed with the objective of providing a significant value quickly and continuously throughout a project (Sutherland, 2012) (SCRUMstudy, 2016). Emerges from the need to manage rapidly changing project requirements (Lei et al., 2017). It is a simple and useful methodology for multidisciplinary teams to achieve excellent quality results (Usman, et al. 2014).

Another dimension that has been gaining significant relevance, and which will be the subject of a more detailed analysis in the first phase of the study carried out, is the governance (da Anunciação, Gonçalves & Martins, 2023) (de Oliveira, & Anunciação, 2019). A project must present a governance structure, which should be to contemplate the various dimensions associated with the project in question. In the field of Information Systems and Technologies (ITS), governance should be reflected in two areas of intervention: in the strategic domain, related for example to planning and service strategy, conditions of change, innovation, among others; operational domain, related to Service Level Agreement management, major incidents, orders, project planning and modifications, among others.

2. Methodology

The present research work was developed in three phases. In the first one we tried to identify the existing governance structure associated with the project. In the second phase, the current situation (As-Is) regarding project management practices specifically related to the chosen case study was surveyed and characterized. And in the third and last phase, we tried to identify the improvement lines with a view to an objective or desired situation (To-Be) that can be expressive of an improvement in practices and methodologies adopted in view of future evolution.

Given the objectives, a qualitative methodology was chosen to explore and understand the meaning that individuals or groups attribute to a social or human problem (Creswell, 2009). In this context, for the collection of information, documentary analysis was used, since there was necessary information to the study that have documentary support (Bardin, 2011). Interviews were also conducted with project managers and line managers to obtain the necessary information regarding existing project management practices, seeking to facilitate expression, increase authenticity and depth (Quivy e Campenhoudt, 2005). Regarding the treatment of interviews, content analysis was used to (Bardin, 2011). The case study concerns a company providing ITS services that develops projects in a multinational electric energy company.

3. Analysis of results

Focusing again the study carried out, it is reinforced that this study aimed to optimize the project management practices developed by a consultant in IS services in a multinational energy company. The initial premise of approximation concerns the analysis of project management practices in a service delivery, developed as a project, identifying current vulnerabilities, for subsequent elaboration of improvement proposals. The organizational domains covered in the service provision are finance and management (accounting, taxation, wealth, treasury), logistics (purchasing, procurement, inventory management), decision-making (business intelligence) and human resources (time management and activities).

Regarding the first phase of the study, it was possible that the project has a governance team associated with the project. The Strategic Governance is composed of the following corporate bodies:

- Management Committee, which, every 2 years, carries out an evaluation of the organizational, technical and financial aspects; presents and validates the contractual adaptations, if necessary; and resolves conflicts that have not been dealt with by the Contract Committee.
- Contract Management Committee, which, on a monthly basis, performs an analysis of the indicators for monitoring and verifying the compliance of the service; the activities panel (service levels and financial report); the action plans and progress identified; it studies proposals for amendments to the contract that have a financial impact on it; and proceeds to the treatment of conflicts that have not been resolved by the Steering Committee.
- Innovation Cross-Sectional Committee, which annually identifies and defines the proposed innovation and how this innovation can be used; and values and identifies sources of financial gains for the project.

As regards the Operational Governance, it is part of the following committees:

- Operational management committee, which every two months, carries out a balance sheet of the last month for each application and presentation of the dysfunctions in terms of organization; monitors risks; presents the table of charges and plans consumed and validate the billing elements of the month-1; checks the action plans and progress identified; presents the matrix of competences and the updated list of stakeholders; presents the business plan by application and overall for the next six months; prepares the Contract Management Committees; and resolves conflicts that have not been dealt with by the Operational Committee.
- IS Safety Committee, which annually reviews the security issues since the previous committee; and identifies future regulatory standards as

well as checks identified action plans. In addition, it carries out a risk analysis twice a year, verifying the progress of previously defined action plans; updating the risk monitoring table (addition, closure, change); and defining, assigning and scheduling related action plans.

In addition to the governance committees, it is also worth mentioning, within the operational management, the Operational Committee which monitors twice a month the performance of the service in the application and the progress of the versions and the difficulties encountered in the application; prepares the operational management committee; and resolves conflicts that have not been dealt with by the operational monitoring.

Regarding the second phase of the study, we proceeded to the characterization of the management of the existing project (As-Is). The scope of current project management comprises the provision of service by the ITS company to the customer, which consists in maintaining the operational condition, implementing evolutions and building or implementing new applications (projects) in the technical and functional SAP.

In the maintenance of the operational condition, corrective maintenance is carried out, which consists of the analysis and subsequent treatment of errors reported by the customer; preventive, which consists of analysis and estimation (budgeting), related to the prevention of errors; adaptive, which consists of an analysis and an estimate (budgeting), which comes from the sequence of some changes applied, which cause an adjustment of existing functionalities; and applicative, which consists of an analysis and an estimate (budgeting) of applications that are characterized as application evolutions.

In addition to maintenance, management and monitoring of applications is also carried out, through the monitoring of application performance and incidents.

The service provided is based on a monthly rate. Each iteration, lasting one month, constitutes a mini project with precise pre-established objectives. The results of an iteration are objectively evaluated through a systematic analysis of its results (documentation, produced versions, volume of activity carried out, etc.).

Each iteration is part of a cycle, which consists of the following activities: definition, identification of the unitary tasks and detailed schedule of the iteration; execution, achievement of objectives and daily management;

and evaluation, evaluation of the results of the iteration, Comparison with defined goals, definition of the goals for the next iteration and adjustment of the overall strategy.

The project manager draws up a workload plan with four perspectives: weekly (where low uncertainty is expected), monthly, quarterly and long-term. The latter are approximate projections designed to anticipate fluctuations in team size through capacity planning.

The objectives of an iteration are defined based on the activity planned for the period, for each of the activities, and constitute the starting point of the planning process of the project team's activity. Then, objectives related to the project as a whole are added: reports, human resources, tools, etc. These different objectives are ranked, mainly according to the risks associated with them.

The results are associated with the different activities carried out: production of new versions, number of incidents treated, volume of capitalized elements, etc. These elements allow to evaluate the progress of the iteration and identify the degree of fulfillment of the objectives. This is an important phase for the continuous improvement of the project and for the preparation of the following iterations.

The results of these evaluations form the basis of reports prepared by the project team, which are presented to the client at service management meetings and made available in real time through a collaboration portal, namely activity report, Activity volume, team performance, and monitoring indicators.

As far as the development management methodology used by the project team is concerned, it is based on the waterfall model. This model is used for the treatment of anomalies and for the development of evolution requests.

Project management uses the SAP Solution Manager SOP module, which was developed to measure, for the management of support tickets and incidents. More specifically, this module is used for the creation, monitoring and management of support tickets, as well as for tracking the status of each ticket and ensuring that they are resolved within the established deadline.

In addition, this module is also used for transport orders to transport objects from one SAP system to another, so as to ensure that changes made in a system are reflected in other systems such as test and production systems.

Project management uses an Excel file to manage the service level indicators. This file is composed of a set of spreadsheets, which contain several formulas to calculate the indicators and some macros to automate the process.

After the completion of the Excel document with the service level indicators, Power BI is used to produce reports that allow you to evaluate the service levels.

The third phase of the study focused on the TO-BE of the Project Management Model. Given the analysis of the current situation, and based on the identification of inefficiencies and potential improvements in operational efficiency and productivity, the project management intends to introduce some proposals for improvement in some areas of action:

- Replace the use of the SAP Solution Manager SOP module for managing support tickets and incidents, since this is designed to measure, which means that there are associated development costs, and in addition there is the issue of maintenance, that it is also necessary to maintain;
- Significantly reduce requirements analysis and planning by implementing shorter development cycles. In addition, at the end of each cycle, it is expected that an assessment of progress and important feedback will be provided, which will define priorities for the next development cycle. This way, it will be possible to create a new version of the solution with each iteration, which can be distributed to a wide range of stakeholders. So, each version will be installed in production, which means that results can be generated immediately.
- Replace the use of Excel to manage the indicators of service levels, due to the complexity and performance of the file, since this is a file contains many developments tailored to obtain the necessary settings, as the use of various querys and macros. This motivation also stems from the fact that the file is heavy and extensive, due to the large volume of data, and the process is prone to errors, since the update of the data is done manually, being subject to human failures, compromising the accuracy of the indicators.
- Additionally, the project management would like to include the process of creating service level indicators and producing service level reports in the same solution, so that there is collaboration and sharing between all stakeholders in the process.

4. Conclusions

Project management practices represent a major challenge and are crucial for the success of projects in information systems. Continuous improvement in project management and the proper use of support techniques and tools are essential and crucial for an efficient and effective management of organizations.

To differentiate itself competitively from its competitors, the IS consulting company recognizes the importance of implementing good project management practices to ensure success, particularly in relation to scope, time and cost.

With this project, we sought to highlight the importance of optimizing project management practices within a service delivery, related to the SAP management system, of an energy sector customer. In this sense, the current practices of project management (AS-IS) and the desired project management practices (TO-BE) were analyzed. With this analysis it was possible to propose improvement solutions, based on the identified gaps.

One of the recommended solutions is the adoption of Agile as a development management methodology. This approach will reduce the impact that exists in the development of solutions, when the customer requests modification after the development phase and during the test phase. In addition, this methodology will reduce the duration of development of applications and their final cost, there is an increase in the efficiency of this process. Since this methodology is characterized by several deliveries to the customer, it allows to obtain constant feedback from the same throughout the development cycle. In this way, it will be possible to ensure that what is being implemented corresponds to the expectations and needs of the client, increasing their level of satisfaction.

6. References

APM-Association for Project Management. (2012). *APM Body of Knowledge* (6th ed.). APM Publishing.

Bardin, L. (2011). Content analysis, 70 Publishing. *(In Portuguese)*

Bērziša, S., & Grabis, J. (2010). An approach for implementation of project management information systems. *Information Systems Development: Towards a Service Provision Society*, 423-431.

da Anunciação, P. F., Gonçalves, F. M., & Martins, F. A. C. (2023). The Importance of Information Systems Governance: The Case of the Cement Industry. Social and Economic Studies within the Framework of Emerging Global Developments Volume 3, 207.

de Oliveira, A., & Anunciação, P. F. (2019). Information Systems Governance: The Case of the Largest Companies in Portugal. In Global Information Diffusion and Management in Contemporary Society (pp. 260-286). IGI Global. *Development* (423–431). Springer US. https://doi.org/10.1007/b137171_44

Creswell, J. W. (2009). *Research Design: Qualitativa, Quantitative and Mixed Methods Approaches* (3ª ed.). Sage.

IPMA. (2015). *Individual Competence Baseline for Project, Programme and Portfolio Management* (4th ed.). International Project Management Association.

Jerom, A., Sp, R., & Scholar, P. G. (2020). A survey on comparative analysis of agile software development methodologies. Journal of Software Engineering and Applications, 5(1), 36-48. *Methodologies*. Journal of Software Engineering and Applications.

Kerzner, H. (2009). *Project Management: A Systems Approach to Planning, Scheduling, and Controlling*. Wiley.

Kumar, G., & Bhatia, P. K. (2014). *Comparative Analysis of Software Engineering Models from Traditional to Modern Methodologies*. In International Conference on Advanced Computing and Communication Technologies (pp. 73-78). IEEE. https://doi.org/10.1109/ACCT.2014.73

Lei, H., Ganjeizadeh, F., Jayachandran, P. K., & Ozcan, P. (2017). *A Statistical Analysis of the Effects of Scrum and Kanban on Software Development Projects*. Robotics and Computer-Integrated Manufacturing, 43, 59-67. https://doi.org/10.1016/j.rcim.2016.08.005

Obrutsky, S., & Erturk, E. (2017). The agile transition in Software Development Companies: the most common barriers and how to overcome them. Business and Management Research, 6(4), 40-53.

Palmquist, M. S., Lapham, M. A., Miller, S., Chick, T., & Ozkaya, I. (2013). *Parallel Worlds: Agile and Waterfall Differences and Similarities*. SEI, Carnegie Mellon University.

PMI-Project Management Institute. (2017). *A Guide to the Project Management Body of Knowledge* (PMBOK® GUIDE) (6th ed.). Pennsylvania: Project Management Institute, Inc.

Quivy, R. & Campenhoudt, L.V. (2005) *Manual de Investigação em Ciências Sociais* (4ª ed.). Gradiva.

Ríos, J. M., & Pedreira-Souto, N. (2019). *Approach of Agile Methodologies in the Development of Web-Based Software*. Information, 10(10), 314. https://doi.org/10.3390/info10100314

Royce, W. W. (1970). *Managing the Development of Large Software Systems*. In IEEE WESCON (pp. 1-9). The Institute of Electrical and Electronics Engineers.

SCRUMstudy. (2016). *A Guide to the Scrum Body of Knowledge* (SBOK Guide) (3rd ed.). Arizona, USA: VMEdu, Inc.

Singhto, W., & Denwattana, N. (2016). *An Experience in Blending the Traditional and Agile Methodologies to Assist in a Small Software Development Project*. In 2016 13th International Joint Conference on Computer Science and Software Engineering (JCSSE) (pp. 1-6). IEEE. https://doi.org/10.1109/JCSSE.2016.7748914

Sutherland, J. (2012). *The Scrum Papers: Nut, Bolts, and Origins of an Agile Framework*. Scrum Inc.

Usman, M., Soomro, T. & Brohi, M. (2014). *Embedding Project Management Into XP, SCRUM and RUP*. European Scientific Journal.

Impact of new Technologies on the Population Warning Information Systems

José Luís Riço Bucho de Matos, Francisco Joaquim Madeira Esteves, Pedro Fernandes da Anunciação

1. Introduction

Territories and societies are often subject to extreme manifestations of natural phenomena (Allen & Melgar, 2019) (Giri & Islam, 2021). The need for technical and scientific study of these phenomena, such as their type, origin, causes, frequency, magnitude or intensity, is aimed at seeking answers to potential and actual effects concerning society or regions (UNISDR, 2015). It is within this need for protection that science seeks to study, in a multidisciplinary way the causes, vulnerabilities, or exposure to them (Mileti & Sorensen, 1990). But, consequently, science must also continue the study and development of new methodologies, processes and technologies more appropriate to emerging risks, allowing a better adaptation of the management of responses to natural events, with a degree of effectiveness proportional to the complexity of the situations that occurred (UNISDR, 2015). It is a permanent challenge of resilience (World Bank, 2010).

With the increasing incidence of extreme weather events and other emergencies, effective communication of warnings and alerts has become essential to ensure the well-being of populations (Jensen, 2014).

Warning and alert systems are solutions of strategic importance to support and manage the risk of populations and civil society in general, in preventive or emergency cases, instantiated by the imbalance of natural elements, directly or indirectly caused by human action (Reuter & Kaufhold, 2018) (Sorensen, 2000). Especially considering the anticipatory function (Early Warning Systems) (Šakić Trogrlić, et al. 2022) (Meléndez-Landaverde & Sempere-Torres, 2022) (UNISDR, 2006) or reactive, it is generally assumed that Information Systems and Technologies (IST) can play a major role in the streamlining and operationalization of responses to needs arising from civil protection (Silva & Costa, 2019). New IT, such as mobile, APP or social networks have played a major role in warning and alert systems (Lara Tan, et al. 2017) (Meléndez-Landaverde & Sempere-Torres, 2023) (Mirbabaie, Amojo & Stieglitz, 2021) (Montarnal, et al. 2017) (Paul, et al. 2021) (Reuter, et al. 2017).

However, these systems need to be thought, designed and architected (Turoff, et al. 2004), because they must be people-focused and serve the people. For this reason, it is essential that the population has access to accurate information, effective means of relief and timely responses (Dallo & Marti, 2021) and, in this sense, IST are a crucial means in the implementation of organizational strategies, constituting these as key information service providers in the operational and tactical corporate domains (Anunciação & Esteves, 2021). The IST to support prevention should be focused on three axes: people, as the core elements of actions and strategies developed and actors of a scenario that it is important to understand and to which it is important to react; the processes, as integrated transversal rationalization, standardization and optimization capabilities; and, information, as critical assets for decision support and the realization of value.

The range of available technologies can significantly improve warning and alert systems (Appleby-Arnold, et al. 2019) (Auclair, et al. 2019) (Colombelli, et al. 2020). And in this context social networks can have a significant impact (Gao, Barbier & Goolsby, 2011). Technology is a enabler of operational efficiency and effectiveness, inducing transformation and innovation. It is in a scenario involving several stakeholders (civil protection, firefighters or police) that the interoperability of IST assumes a crucial relevance as it conditions the dissemination of alert information, conditioning a faster and more coordinated response, as well as greater accuracy in the prediction and monitoring of risk events. It is in the intersection and aggregation of the different components that IS assumes a multidimensional role determining in warning and alert systems, ensuring foundational dimensions such as:

- Connectivity - by providing effective communication between the different agents using technological infrastructures based on scalability, availability, resilience and responsiveness.
- Integration - by ensuring the functional and informational integration between different infrastructure, application and management solutions.
- Interoperability - by making possible the technical operationalization of the interaction between different solutions in the heterogeneity of existing systems.

- Information Management - by ensuring the security, availability, integrity and completeness of data and information necessary to support all constituent processes.

There are several challenges that face civil protection requiring improved responses in increasingly unpredictable contexts and with extreme effects or consequences. In this sense, the development of integrated warning and alert systems becomes critical, since the "window of opportunity" for prevention appears to be increasingly narrow. The development of an integrated warning and alert system is a key strategy to improve the efficiency and effectiveness of civil protection actions and should address the following critical success factors (CSF):

- Centralization and unification of information - a system that allows the consolidation in a single platform of all information related to emergencies, facilitating communication between different agencies and ensuring that warnings are consistent.
- Extension of the alerts' reach - the integration of different communication channels should allow a greater reach both in relation to the number of people and the geographical area covered.
- Improved accuracy and timeliness of warnings - the adoption and incorporation of disruptive technologies, such as artificial intelligence (AI), "streaming" or Internet of Things platforms, should facilitate real-time risk monitoring and issuing alerts, ensuring faster response.

These transformation challenges presuppose sensitivity and focus for the adoption and management of a set of dimensions, structural and structuring, which are also critical in a digital transformation project in the field of IST, namely:

- Governance - identification of the responsibilities of governance and governance of STI as well as of the different "stakeholders" along the value chain, ensuring a unity in the coordination of resources (human, technological, equipment, procedural and informational) (Ahrens & Rudolph, 2006) (Anunciação, Kuchta & Guégués, 2024).
- Architecture/Urbanism - design and implementation of the different levels of IST architecture and ensuring integration and interoperability

of the various systems (urban planning) in order to support the operation of the meta-system in terms of processes, applications, data/information/knowledge, technology and services (Anunciação &Zorrinho, 2006).

- Knowledge and learning - capitalizing on the volume and diversity of data, capturing them from multiple sources, transforming and loading them into a single or articulated infrastructure (data warehouse, data lake, data lakehouse, etc.), analyzing their patterns, trends or insights through the use of multidimensional models, data mining or machine and deep learning, and enabling the respective intuitive and clear visualization in delayed or real time, in order to support decision making.
- Service - implementation and operation of an integrated service to support the internal users of ITS and target users (people and entities) of the system, assisting in the resolution of technical-functional problems and providing accurate and timely information.
- Security - implementation of an information security policy at the physical and logical level, and operationalization of procedures and solutions that include identity and access management, data protection, intrusion detection, vulnerability management, the defense of the perimeters of the networks involved, the analysis of logs, etc., and the activation of a disaster recovery plan in case of disruption of the system.

2. Objectives and methodology

The present research work had as main objective the development of a study for a future digital transformation in civil protection in Portugal, taking as reference one of the main municipalities of the country. To this end, through the participation of several stakeholders' experts, a study was developed in three phases. In the first one we characterized the current situation of the Civil Protection Alert and Prevention Systems (AS-IS). In the second, some innovative and potentially disruptive IST were identified in the area of civil protection considering existing practices. In the third phase, a digital transformation framework is presented, with a matrix of evaluation of potential and opportunity for a future decision. Regarding the size of the potential, dimensions such as value creation, technological maturity and degree of disruption were considered. Regarding the opportunity, variables such as level of investment, interoperability and mastery of new technologies were considered.

A qualitative methodological approach was adopted, and a focus group was created to. The focus group was made up of national and international experts from Portugal and Spain, namely, the National Head of Risk Prevention and Management National Authority for Emergency and Civil Protection National Authority for Emergency and Civil Protection (Portugal), the Coordinator of 112 in Madrid (Spain), four experts from the Municipal Civil Protection Service of Lisbon (Portugal), two experts from the Regional Civil Protection and Fire Service of the Azores (Portuguese Autonomous Region) and Emergency, Prevention and Civil Protection Coordinator of the Government of Navarra (Autonomous Region of the Government of Navarra in Spain). This approach was understood as the most appropriate to understand and interpret the associated social reality (Stake, 2012) and obtain valuable insights resulting from the wealth of perceptions and experiences of the experts involved. Having as reference the case study (Stake, 2012) (Yin, 2018) the experts, national and international, were stimulated to the reflection of the various proposed points, having been asked to classify the potential and opportunity inherent in the identified technologies through a Likert scale of 5 levels (1 - Non-existent, 2 - Weak, 3 - Improvement, 4 - Transformational, 5 - Disruptive).

3. Analysis of the results

Regarding the first phase of the study, it was possible to assess that the current state of the IST of Warnings and Civil Protection Alert in Portugal currently has a set of limitations, namely:

- Non-integrated IST - software that does not communicate with each other; duplicate or inaccessible information; storage and processing limitations; inability to integrate new technological tools; maintenance of legacy systems expensive and in some cases impossible to perform.
- Limitations in the availability of information - manual treatment of information; inefficient processes and subject to human errors; slow

and time-consuming information provision; low productivity; and limitations in functional agility.
- Limited remote access - limitations on remote access; limited or no mobile channels; difficulty of working for decentralized or remote teams.
- No secure security protocols - no robust security protocols; vulnerability to attacks; risk of data loss.

Regarding the second phase of the study, disruptive and more potential IT that could change the status quo of warning and alert systems to the population were identified. The main technologies referenced were the following:

- Social media and Streaming Platforms (SM/SP) - The dissemination of warnings and alerts through social networks is a powerful approach and increasingly used, given the wide adoption of these platforms and their ability to reach large audiences quickly and effectively. (Potential - T; Opportunity - T)
- Internet of Things (IoT) - The dissemination of warnings and alerts through IoT enabled devices offer an advanced and efficient approach to communicate critical information during emergencies, allowing real-time data exchange and automated responses. (Potential - T; Opportunity - I)
- Artificial Intelligence/Machine learning (AI/ML) - The dissemination of warnings and alerts through artificial intelligence can be a powerful approach to provide critical information and alert people about impending emergencies. (Potential - D; Opportunity - T)
- Augmented Reality (AR) - The dissemination of warnings and alerts through augmented reality can be an innovative and effective approach, especially in situations where the visualization of contextualized information and interactivity are crucial. (Potential - I; Opportunity - W)
- Avatar (AVT) - The dissemination of warnings and alerts through avatars is an innovative approach that uses interactive visual representations to communicate critical information on various digital platforms, such as websites, mobile applications, social networks and virtual/augmented reality devices, providing engaging and personalized alerts. (Potential - I; Opportunity - W)

- Drones (DRN) - The dissemination of warnings and alerts through drones can be an innovative and effective approach, especially in hard-to-reach areas or during emergencies where mobility is limited. (Potential - D; Opportunity - T)
- Geographic Information System (GIS) - Geolocation systems integration allows alerts to be directed to specific areas that are at risk, avoiding unnecessary information overload for people outside these areas. In addition, alerts can be customized according to the type of risk, adjusting communication for different scenarios such as forest fires, floods or landslides. (Potential - T; Opportunity - T)
- Low Orbit Satellite Networks (LEO) - Low-orbit satellite networks, such as SpaceX's Starlink constellation, have the potential to provide fast and reliable global communications, including the dissemination of warnings and alerts in real time to remote areas without other type of coverage. (Potential - D; Opportunity - D)
- 5G communication technology (5GT) - The dissemination of warnings and alerts through cellular broadcasting across different generations of mobile technology can be extremely effective in reaching many people in emergency-affected areas. (Potential - T; Opportunity - T)
- Blockchain for Data Security (BCH)- Blockchain technology may be employed to ensure the security and integrity of civil protection data. With immutable and transparent records, it will be possible to trace the origin and authenticity of information, preventing fraud and false alarms and ensuring that critical data is available when needed. (Potential - D; Opportunity - T)

To facilitate future decision-making, a matrix was developed in the third phase, which reflects the potential and opportunity of each technology, as can be seen in table 1.

4. Conclusion and future research

The inclusion of new IST requires awareness-raising among decision makers and investment capacity, to ensure adequate warning and alert systems in the future. Any of the technologies considered should always consider their integration and articulation with existing IST, respecting solutions, standards

Table 1. Potential and opportunity of each technology

Potencial	Disruptive				AI/ML DRN BCH	LEO
	Transforma-tional			IoT	SM/SP GIS 5GT	
	Improvement		AR AVT			
	Weaker					
	Non-existent					
		Non-existent	Weaker	Improve-ment	Transfor-mational	Disruptive
		Opportunity				

and processes to ensure overall operability, efficiency and effectiveness. Here are some examples:

- Artificial intelligence - can be used to improve the accuracy and speed of alerts by analyzing large volumes of real-time data (e.g., meteorological, seismic or hydrological data and forest fires) and predicting disasters more effectively. Using AI to create more sophisticated predictive systems, capable of sending early warnings and customizing notifications based on the type of risk and users' geographical location.
- Internet of Things (IoT) - can connect environmental sensors (such as water level, temperature, atmospheric pressure, smoke, mass movement, earthquakes and tsunamis) directly to warning systems, automating the sending of messages when risk parameters are detected. There is significant potential in the development and implementation of IoT sensor networks in urban and rural areas, with the aim of monitoring risks in real time and increasing the efficiency of automatic alerts.
- The development of multi-channel platforms that combine different technologies, such as SMS, social networks, radio, television, sirens and mobile applications, could ensure that alerts reach all groups of the population regardless of the channel used. It is important to study ways of integrating these platforms and hybrid systems that work

even offline, for example, using satellite technology in areas where conventional infrastructure fails, such as natural or technological disasters.

- Geolocation - need to send personalized alerts, according to the exact location of affected people, can avoid unnecessary alarms and ensure that only those who are in a certain risk area receive notifications, whether they are regular residents, tourists or passing people. Studying ways to optimize these systems, using GPS data, cellular networks and satellites is relevant to send segmented alerts with the lowest possible margin of error.

It is important to note that as systems become more complex people are sensitized, motivated and trained for their use ensuring that everyone knows how to respond to an alert and understand the importance of following the instructions issued (Fischer-Preßler, Bonaretti & Fischbach, 2021).

As alert systems become more digital and connected, they also become vulnerable to cyber-attacks, which can compromise the issuance of critical alerts. It is essential to strengthen security measures, making them more advanced to protect IST against hackers and develop security protocols that ensure the integrity of data and the reliability of alerts.

Civil protection warning and alert systems have played a vital role in disaster prevention. Although they face several limitations, such as lack of integration, limited reach or vulnerability to infrastructure failures, it is important to evolve towards the integration of new IST, which integrate emerging and disruptive technologies, as AI, IoT and analytics to make existing systems more robust and create more efficient, inclusive and resilient warning systems.

References

Ahrens, J., & Rudolph, P. M. (2006). The importance of governance in risk reduction and disaster management. Journal of Contingencies and Crisis Management, 14(4), 207-220.

Allen R.M. & Melgar D. (2019), "Earthquake Early Warning: Advances, Scientific Challenges, and Societal Needs", Annu Rev Earth Planet Sci 47 (2019), 361–388, doi: 10.1146/annurev-earth-053018-060457

Appleby-Arnold, S., Brockdorff, N., Fallou, L., & Bossu, R. (2019). Truth, trust, and civic duty: Cultural factors in citizens' perceptions of mobile phone apps and social media in disasters. Journal of Contingencies and Crisis Management, 27(4), 293–305. https://doi.org/10.1111/1468-5973.12282

Auclair, S., Boulahya, F., Birregah, B., Quique, R., Ouaret, R., & Soulier, E. (2019). SURICATENat: Innovative citizen centered platform for Twitter based natural disaster monitoring. 6th International Conference on Information and Communication Technologies for Disaster Management, ICT-DM 2019. https://doi.org/10.1109/ICT-DM47966.2019.9032950

Colombelli, S., Carotenuto, F., Elia, L., & Zollo, A. (2020). Design and implementation of a mobile device app for network-based earthquake early warning systems (EEWSs): Application to the PRESTo EEWS in southern Italy. Natural Hazards and Earth System Sciences, 20(4), 921–931. https://doi.org/10.5194/NHESS-20-921-2020

da Anunciação, P. F. & Zorrinho, C. (2006). Organizational Urbanism - How Managing Technological Shock in Companies, Lisbon, Sílabo Publishing (In Portuguese)

da Anunciação, P. F., & Esteves, F. M. (2021). Challenges to business models in the digital transformation context. In Research Anthology on Digital Transformation, Organizational Change, and the Impact of Remote Work (pp. 116-129). IGI Global.

da Anunciação, P.F., Kuchta, D. & Guégués, C.C.F. (2024). Organizational urbanism, digital transformation and smart cities: The case of civil protection of a Portuguese city, In Veysel, K., Innovations and Contemporary Trends in Business & Economics, 2024, 185–194.

Dallo, I., & Marti, M. (2021). Why should I use a multi-hazard app? Assessing the public's information needs and app feature preferences in a participatory process. International Journal of Disaster Risk Reduction, 57, 102197. https://doi.org/10.1016/J.IJDRR.2021.102197

Fischer-Preßler, D., Bonaretti, D., & Fischbach, K. (2021). A Protection-Motivation Perspective to Explain Intention to Use and Continue to Use Mobile Warning Systems. Business and Information Systems Engineering. https://doi.org/10.1007/S12599-021-00704-0

Gao, H., Barbier, G., & Goolsby, R. (2011). Harnessing the crowdsourcing power of social media for disaster relief. IEEE Intelligent Systems, 26(3), 10-14.

Giri, R. K., & Islam, T. (2021). Advances in Early Warning Systems for Disaster Risk Reduction: An Overview. Natural Hazards Review, 22(2), 1-13.

Horstmann, A. C., Winter, S., Rösner, L., & Krämer, N. C. (2018). S.O.S. on my phone: An analysis of motives and incentives for participation in smartphone-based volunteering. Journal of Contingencies and Crisis Management, 26(1), 193–199. https://doi.org/10.1111/1468-5973.12174

Jensen, J. R. (2014). Remote Sensing of the Environment: An Earth Resource Perspective Second Edition. In Pearson Education (Vol. 1). https://www.pearson.com/en-us/subjectcatalog/p/remote-sensing-of-the-environment-an-earth-resourceperspective/P200000006978/9780131889507

Lara Tan, M., Prasanna, R., Stock, K., Hudson-Doyle, E., Leonard, G., & Johnston, D. (2017). Mobile applications in crisis informatics literature: A systematic review. International Journal of Disaster Risk Reduction, 24, 297–311. https://doi.org/10.1016/j.ijdrr.2017.06.009

Meléndez-Landaverde, E. R., & Sempere-Torres, D. (2022). Design and evaluation of a community and impact-based site-specific early warning system (SS-EWS): The SS-EWS framework. Journal of Flood Risk Management, e12860. https://doi.org/10.1111/JFR3.12860

Meléndez-Landaverde, E. R., & Sempere-Torres, D. (2023). A user experience evaluation of a mobile application for disseminating site-specific impact-based flood warnings: The A4alerts app. Journal of Flood Risk Management, e12951. https://doi.org/10.1111/JFR3.12951

Mileti, D. S., & Sorensen, J. H. (1990). Communication of Emergency Public Warnings: A Social Science Perspective and State-of-the-Art Assessment. Federal Emergency Management Agency.

Mirbabaie, M., Amojo, I., & Stieglitz, S. (2021). Affording twitter in emergency situations: The occurrence of rumor sense-making. Journal of Database Management, 32(2). https://doi.org/10.4018/JDM.2021040104

Montarnal, A., Halse, S., Tapia, A., Truptil, S., & Benaben, F. (2017). Automated emergence of a crisis situation model in crisis response based on tweets. IFIP Advances in Information and Communication Technology, 506, 658–665. https://doi.org/10.1007/978-3-319-65151- 4_58/FIGURES/3

Paul, J. D., Bee, E., & Budimir, M. (2021). Mobile phone technologies for disaster risk reduction. Climate Risk Management, 32, 100296. https://doi.org/10.1016/J.CRM.2021.100296

Reuter, C., & Kaufhold, M. A. (2018). Fifteen years of social media in emergencies: A retrospective review and future directions for crisis Informatics. Journal of Contingencies and Crisis Management, 26(1), 41–57. https://doi.org/10.1111/1468-5973.12196

Reuter, C., Kaufhold, M. A., Spielhofer, T., & Hahne, A. S. (2017). Social Media in Emergencies: A Representative Study on Citizen's Perception in Germany. Proceedings of the ACM on Human-Computer Interaction, 1(CSCW), 1–19. https://doi.org/10.1145/3134725

Šakić Trogrlić, R., van den Homberg, M., Budimir, M., McQuistan, C., Sneddon, A., & Golding, B. (2022). Early warning systems and their role in disaster risk reduction. In *Towards the "perfect" weather warning: bridging disciplinary gaps through partnership and communication* (pp. 11-46). Cham: Springer International Publishing.

Silva, F. L., & Costa, M. S. (2019). Tecnologias de Informação e Comunicação na Proteção Civil: Integração de Alertas Precoce e Inteligência Artificial. Revista Brasileira de Gestão de Riscos, 18(3), 57-75.

Sorensen, J. H. (2000). Hazard warning systems: Review of 20 years of progress*. *Natural Hazards Review, 1(2), 119–125.

Turoff, M., Chumer, M., Van de Walle, B., & Yao, X. (2004). The Design of a Dynamic Emergency Response Management Information System (DERMIS). Journal of Information Technology Theory and Application, 5(4), 1-35.

UNISDR – United Nations Office for Disaster Risk Reduction. (2015). Global Assessment Report on Disaster Risk Reduction. United Nations.

UNISDR. (2006). Developing Early Warning Systems: A Checklist. Third International Conference on Early Warning, March, 1–13. https://www.undrr.org/publication/developingearly-warning-systems-checklist-third-international-conference-early-warning

UNISDR. (2015). Sendai framework for disaster risk reduction 2015-2030. United Nations Office for Disaster Risk Reduction Publications, 30(3). https://www.undrr.org/publication/sendai-framework- disaster-risk-reduction-2015-2030.

World Bank. (2010). Building Resilient Communities: Risk Management and Response to Natural Disasters through Social Protection*. The World Bank.

Establishing Enterprise Architecture Practice in Public Administration. Brief Analysis of Implementation Models

Hélder Miguel da Graça Alexandre, Pedro Fernandes da Anunciação, Francisco Joaquim Madeira Esteves

1. Introduction

In recent years, the demand for Enterprise Architecture (EA) in public administration has significantly increased. The integration EA in public administration has become critical for addressing complex governance challenges, improving service delivery, and ensuring efficiency. Public administration entities face growing demands for transparency, interoperability, and citizen-centric services while managing constrained resources. EA provides a structured approach to align strategy, processes, and technology across organizations.

Public entities often grapple with the challenges of managing and integrating disparate processes, systems, and data sources, which can result in inefficiency, redundancy, and a lack of alignment with strategic goals. As organizations increasingly recognize the value of EA as a strategic asset, there is a pressing need for a structured approach to implementing the EA function effectively. The adoption of EA enables government institutions to build a holistic architecture that supports the integration of business processes, technology framework and strategic goals, creating an adaptable and robust enterprise structure. According to (Adegboyega Ojo, 2012) state that the implementation of Government Enterprise Architecture (GEA) practices largely depends on the high-level support, together with a high involvement at a business unit level.

Another typical challenge faced by public administration is the siloed nature of operations and systems. Different departments often employ distinct processes and technologies, hindering seamless data sharing and communication. Furthermore, regulatory requirements and public accountability increase the complexity of managing public services. These issues necessitate a comprehensive Enterprise Architecture framework that can facilitate standardization, interoperability, and alignment of IT investments with the broader goals of the organization.

The aim of this article is to present an analysis of roadmap or implementation models for establishing an Enterprise Architecture capability focused on public administration entities. This analysis will address the unique challenges faced by governmental entities, evaluating different structured approaches to develop and implement robust EA practices.

The structure of the article is as follows:

- The first section will review the existing literature on EA in public administration, followed by an exploration of various roadmap and implementation models derived from academic studies and papers from reference institutions.
- The second section will synthesize these findings
- The third section will considerations and implications for future research.

2. Literature Review

In this section we will review the existing literature on EA in public administration, followed by an exploration of various roadmap and implementation models.

Enterprise Architecture in Public Administration

Enterprise Architecture (EA) has become increasingly important for public administration organizations to improve efficiency, coordinate digital transformation efforts, and deliver better digital services to citizens. Several key themes emerge from the literature regarding EA implementation in government:

- Importance and Benefits - EA is recognized as a critical factor for whole-of-government capability and digital transformation (Adegboyega Ojo, 2012). It helps public agencies address business, data, infrastructure, and information systems in a coordinated manner. Implementing EA in government is considered very important for improving the efficiency of electronic-based services (Puspitaningrum, 2021).

- Challenges - Despite its importance, implementing EA in government faces several challenges:
  - The documentation process is often time-consuming, error-prone, and requires collecting quality data (Puspitaningrum, 2021).
  - There is limited understanding of what makes EA practice effective in a government enterprise context (Adegboyega Ojo, 2012).
  - Many governments struggle with developing and sustaining EA capabilities across agencies (Dave Hornford S. S., 2018).
- Key Success Factors - Research has identified several factors critical for successful EA implementation in government:
  - Management commitment and support is crucial (Adegboyega Ojo, 2012). This includes having strong political and senior leadership backing for EA initiatives (Dave Hornford S. S., 2018).
  - Participation of business units is another critical factor (Adegboyega Ojo, 2012). EA efforts need to involve stakeholders across different government agencies and departments (Dave Hornford S. S., 2018).
  - Perceived usefulness of EA efforts influences both management commitment and business unit participation (Adegboyega Ojo, 2012). Demonstrating tangible benefits is important for sustaining support.
  - Effective governance structures play a role in EA maturity. This includes having clear decision rights and accountability for EA-related activities (Dave Hornford S. S., 2018).
  - Adequate resources and skills are necessary. Many governments struggle with attracting and retaining personnel with the right mix of EA and public sector expertise (Pavel Hrab, 2022).
- Outcomes and Benefits - When successfully implemented, EA in public administration can lead to (Dave Hornford S. S., 2018):
  - Improved coordination and interoperability across government.
  - More efficient and citizen-centric digital services.
  - Better alignment of IT investments with government priorities.
  - Reduced duplication of systems and data.

However, realizing these benefits requires sustained effort and commitment over many years.

Roadmap and Implementation Models for Enterprise Architecture

This section describes several roadmap and implementation models for EA capability, identifying the steps and activities for each model analysed.

Roadmap for Enterprise Architecture: The cornerstone for the evolution of Information Systems (Esteves, Anunciação & Graça Alexandre, 2024)

The paper presents a roadmap for implementing enterprise architecture (EA) and information systems (IS) architecture to support organizational strategy, governance, and agility in the digital economy.

Steps:

1. Drawing of the EA Function
   · Define the purpose and scope of the EA function.
   · Map current capabilities and identify future needs.
   · Propose an organisational structure tailored to EA.
2. Engagement Model
   · Identify and engage stakeholders.
   · Establish mechanisms for collaboration and communication.
   · Create frameworks for stakeholder involvement.
3. Governance Model
   · Define decision-making structures and policies.
   · Implement standards for compliance and quality assurance.
   · Monitor and adjust governance processes regularly.
4. Definition of the EA Framework
   · Select or customise an EA framework, such as TOGAF or IndEA.
   · Define principles, standards, and guidelines for architecture.
   · Document all processes and methodologies.
5. Operationalisation Programme
   · Develop a phased implementation plan.
   · Train teams and build technical capacity.
   · Introduce continuous improvement processes.

The TOGAF® Leader's Guide to Establishing and Evolving an EA Capability (Dave Hornford, 2022)

The paper presents a guide for establishing and evolving an Enterprise Architecture (EA) Capability that aligns to the requirements and expectations of an enterprise, based on the TOGAF framework.

Steps:
1. Establish Context
2. Develop EA Capability
3. Governance Structure
4. Realising the EA Capability

World-Class Enterprise Architecture (Group, 2010)

This paper provides guidance on how organizations can develop a world-class enterprise architecture function using a modular, iterative, and incremental approach.

Steps:
1. Set Strategic Vision
   · Define clear goals for achieving EA excellence.
   · Align EA objectives with organisational strategy and vision.
2. Develop Governance Framework
   · Implement decision-making structures and governance policies.
   · Monitor the adherence to and effectiveness of governance mechanisms.
3. Implement Best Practices
   · Apply modular and agile methodologies for architecture development.
   · Adopt tools and techniques that enhance integration and collaboration.
4. Measure and Adapt
   · Use KPIs to assess the impact and success of EA initiatives.
   · Continuously refine processes to address changing needs.

India Enterprise Architecture Framework (Technology, 2018)

The paper presents the India Enterprise Architecture (IndEA) framework, which is a comprehensive and convenient framework for developing Enterprise Architectures by governments to enable a boundary-less flow of information across the government and facilitate the delivery of integrated services to citizens, businesses, and employees.

Steps:
1. Assessment
   · Conduct a baseline evaluation of current architectural maturity.
   · Identify specific requirements of the public sector entity.

2. Design Reference Models
   · Create modular reference models for data, applications, technology, and integration.
   · Emphasise reuse of components across departments.
3. Establish Governance
   · Set up centralised governance for overseeing architectural standards.
   · Define policies for compliance and interoperability.
4. Implementation
   · Tailor the framework to specific organisational needs.
   · Manage legacy system integration and transformation.

Agile Enterprise Architecture (Gampfer, 2019)

("Investigation on the Future of Enterprise Architecture in Dynamic Environments")

The paper aims to describe a future-proof approach for practicing enterprise architecture in increasingly dynamic environments.

Steps:

1. Promote Decentralised Competence
   · Delegate responsibilities to ensure flexibility in EA initiatives.
   · Train teams to adopt architectural thinking.
2. Adopt Agile Methodologies
   · Integrate agile principles into architectural processes.
   · Promote lightweight governance and decentralised decision-making.
3. Develop Adaptive Content
   · Design modular architectures with interoperability as a priority.
   · Extend the scope to include emerging technologies and practices.
4. Leverage Modern Tools
   · Use automated tools for architecture documentation and analysis.
   · Enable collaboration through advanced platforms.

Starting an EA Capability in the Government Sector (Dave Hornford, 2018)

The paper provides a comprehensive guide for government organizations on establishing and operating an enterprise architecture capability to support strategy, portfolio, project, and solution delivery. This paper is a guide from The Open Group.

Steps:

1. Initiation
   · Identify an EA leader and form a core team.
   · Establish the initial purpose and scope of EA efforts.
2. Strategic Alignment
   · Align EA initiatives with organisational objectives.
   · Prioritise focus areas and define key deliverables.
3. Implementation Guidance
   · Tailor the EA capability to address government-specific challenges.
   · Manage change through proactive engagement with stakeholders.
4. Sustain and Evolve
   · Establish mechanisms for continuous monitoring and feedback.
   · Refine and adapt the EA capability to meet evolving needs.

TOGAF® 10: EA Capability and Governance
(from TOGAF 10: Enterprise Architecture Capability and Governance)

TOGAF 10, states that "Establishing a sustainable architecture practice within an organization can be achieved by adhering to the same approach that is used to establish any other capability — such as a Business Process Management (BPM) capability — within an organization. The ADM is an ideal method to be used to architect and govern the implementation of such a capability. Applying the ADM with the specific Architecture Vision to establish an architecture practice within the organization would achieve this objective."

Steps:

1. Phase A: Architecture Vision
   · Define the scope, vision, and objectives of the EA capability.
   · Secure commitment from stakeholders.
2. Phase B: Business Architecture
   · Design organisational structures and governance for the EA function.
   · Identify key processes and stakeholder interactions.
3. Phase C: Information Systems Architecture
   · Develop data and application architectures to support EA activities.
4. Phase D: Technology Architecture
   · Establish the technical environment for EA tools and processes.
5. Phases E to H: Opportunities, Migration, Governance, and Change Management

- Plan and implement the EA capability iteratively.
- Manage requirements and ensure alignment with organisational goals.

Czech GEA Implementation (Hrabě, 2013)
("The Proposal of Czech Government Enterprise Architecture Implementation")

The paper proposes a specific implementation process for a Government Enterprise Architecture (GEA) framework in the Czech Republic, including defining the phases, deliverables, and components of the Czech GEA to support the transformation and reform of public administration.

Steps:

1. Creating the Initial Model of Federated Architectures
   - Identify areas of responsibility for architecture at different levels of government.
2. Developing a Thesaurus of Terms in Public Administration
   - Define and standardise terms to ensure clarity and consistency across GEA efforts.
3. Creating a Methodology for the Lifecycle Management of GEA
   - Develop processes to manage the creation, update, and use of GEA throughout its lifecycle.
4. Creating a Model for Assessing the Maturity of Public Administration Organisations
   - Define a framework for evaluating how well organisations are prepared to implement and sustain GEA.
5. Creating a Concept for Applying Knowledge of Architecture in Managing Transformational Change
   - Develop strategies for using architectural knowledge to guide organisational and IT technology changes.
6. Establishing Key Institutions
   - Create governing bodies such as the Higher State Architect and the State Architectural Council to oversee GEA.
7. Beginning the Implementation of GEA Content in Pilot Architectural Engagements
   - Apply the developed GEA framework to initial, controlled use cases within selected entities.

8. Applying GEA in the Reform of a Pilot Department or Agency
   · Leverage GEA to drive transformation in a specific department or agency.
9. Generalising Pilot Experience and Formulating Binding "Architectural Principles for the Czech Republic"
   · Use learnings from pilot projects to establish national principles for architectural practices.
10. Expanding the Voluntary Use of Czech GEA
    · Encourage broader adoption of GEA across public administration on a voluntary basis.
11. Announcing Czech GEA as a Binding Methodology
    · Establish GEA as mandatory through legal and procedural mechanisms, with phased duties.
12. Creating Standardised Packages of Czech GEA Reference Models and Governance Processes
    · Provide templates and resources to guide implementation at various levels of government.
13. Creating Templates for Different Levels and Sectors
    · Develop tailored templates for public administration, local governments, and public services.
14. Rolling Out the Deployment and Usage of Czech GEA
    · Scale the implementation of GEA across all levels of government, public administration, and services.

Building an Enterprise Architecture Practice: Tools, Tips, Best Practices, Ready-to-Use Insights (Berg, 2016)
This book provides practical advice, tools, and models to help organizations develop and implement a successful enterprise architecture practice.

Steps
1. Assess the organization's current state and readiness for enterprise architecture
2. Define the enterprise architecture vision, goals, and scope
3. Establish the enterprise architecture function and team
4. Develop the enterprise architecture framework, methods, and tools

5. Implement the enterprise architecture practice and integrate it into the organization
6. Continuously improve and evolve the enterprise architecture practice

3. Findings

In this section findings are synthesized.

Phased Approach
The literature suggests a phased approach to implementing Enterprise Architecture (EA) in public administration. Several papers propose multi-stage roadmaps for EA adoption and maturation.

Initial Preparation
The first phase typically involves creating the initial framework and governance structures. This includes (Hrabě, 2013):

- Developing an EA framework tailored to the country's context.
- Establishing governance rules and implementation roadmaps.
- Creating initial models of federated architectures across government levels.
- Developing a thesaurus of public administration terms.

Pilot Implementation
The next phase often involves pilot projects to test and refine the EA approach:

- Implementing EA content in initial pilot architectural engagements 5
- Applying EA in the reform of a pilot department or agency 6
- Generalizing pilot experiences to formulate binding "Architectural Principles" 7

Voluntary Adoption
Many roadmaps include a period of voluntary adoption before mandating EA use:

- Expanding EA use for public administration transformation on a voluntary basis 8
- This allows agencies to experiment with EA and build support organically.

Official Establishment
After the voluntary period, roadmaps typically call for officially establishing EA as a mandatory approach:

- Announcing EA as a binding methodology with phased implementation of duties provided by law (Hrabě, 2013).

Widespread Rollout
The final phase involves rolling out EA across all levels of government:

- Creating standardized EA packages and governance processes for various government levels.
- Developing templates for different sectors of public administration and local government.
- Deploying EA across various levels of government, public administration, and public services.

Key Components of Implementation
Successful implementation models emphasize developing several key components (Hrabě, 2013):

- Methodology: Creating lifecycle management methodologies for EA in public administration.
- Maturity Model: Developing models to assess organizational EA maturity.
- Knowledge Management: Establishing knowledge management systems and portals.
- Tools: Providing EA modeling and registration tools, especially for smaller offices.
- Reference Models: Creating national reference models and databases.

- Training and Certification: Developing curricula, certification exams, and accreditation processes.

Timeframe
The Czech Republic case study suggests that implementing EA in government is a long-term process, spanning multiple years 23. The roadmap presented includes stages from 2014 to 2021 and beyond, indicating that full implementation and maturation of EA practices can take 7+ years (Dave Hornford S. S., 2018).

Flexibility and Iteration
Implementation models stress the need for flexibility and iteration. The Czech approach, for example, involved "continuously evolving" prerequisites for EA over several years. This allows for adjusting the approach based on lessons learned during implementation (Dave Hornford S. S., 2018).

4. Considerations

The Role of Top Management Commitment in GEA Implementation
In government organizations, top management commitment is one of the main ingredients for the successful implementation of EA. The binding to high-listed officials tells widely the level importance in perceptions that borne. By allocating resources, establishing priorities, and supporting the EA initiatives, senior leaders are essential in ensuring that the implementation process has the attention and funding it needs to succeed. For example, when there is a CIO invested in EA values, the development of coherent policies that support the integration of multiple systems and processes of the organization becomes possible.

Top management commitment can be demonstrated in various forms like sponsoring EA initiative, working together in the governance, providing high-level strategic input, promoting sharing of knowledge and driving for constant improvement. Furthermore, dedicated leadership can help address traditional obstacles like limited funding, lack of trained resources, and siloed IT environments. Numerous studies have found that organizations with strong top management support are likely to achieve higher levels of EA maturity and receive the intended benefits from their EA initiatives.

Similarly, leadership buy-in goes beyond simple verbal support to concrete activities such as embedding EA goals into organizational performance measures and accountability systems. When EA objectives are scoped with the organization's strategy, top management can commit to embedding EA into the organization's decision-making process. The role of IT also helps creating a more agile and responsive organization, capable of adjusting in case of changing external conditions and new technologies appearing.

To summarize, top management commitment is the wind that drives EA initiatives, keeping them on course, up to date, and effective.

Public Administration Entities Participation in GEA

Another important factor that contributes to successfully implementing EA is responsible and engaged government departments. IT systems and processes that EA integrates and optimizes are used by government departments. This also ensures that EA as a framework is not imposed from the top down, focusing on technology and IT solutions without a ground-level understanding, so real issues across the organization are prioritized. However, such an engagement process helps government departments feel the sense of ownership and accountability, which is critical for EA practices to thrive in the long run.

IT and business units can work together to create more realistic EA goals and objectives. By involving business units in the EA process, government departments and agencies can also gain a deeper understanding of their organizational culture and dynamics, leading to more effective EA practices — one of the main barriers for an aligned enterprise architecture. It strives for a unified and comprehensive architecture that aligns IT capabilities with business needs, ultimately leading to improved overall organizational performance.

A government agency focused on ensuring public safety, for instance, may involve its operational units in the EA process to make sure the resulting framework meets their unique needs, such as real-time access to data, multi-agency communication, and resource allocation. This allows the agency to build an IT infrastructure capable of better supporting its mission-critical functions in a dynamic environment.

In addition, developing a cohesive culture between IT and business units can promote communication, trust, and understanding and can help to break down the silo mentality that characterizes so many government entities.

Comprehensive Roadmap for Effective EA Implementation

A well-defined roadmap is vital for the meaningful deployment of enterprise architecture in public sector institutions. An EA roadmap provides a high-level overview of major milestones, key deliverables, and timelines for the enterprise architecture initiatives. It offers a straightforward, actionable bridge from the strategic goals of the organization to specific, actionable and measurable EA work. It should cover aspects like IT resource utilization, project portfolio, stakeholder engagement, etc.

Project portfolio management is another key piece to the EA roadmap. It is about identifying, prioritization, and management of EA projects so they align with the organization's strategic objectives and delivery of expected value. Project portfolio management is the process of managing a portfolio of projects. EA also acts as a final authority to prevent the fragments and silos in organization essentially guides and acts like a framework to direct architecting and overcome the pitfalls that otherwise end up in fragmented / siloed executing projects and their initiatives.

Stakeholder involvement is critical to EA getting put into action too. By engaging with stakeholders early on, organizations can create a common understanding of EA goals, value, and obstacles, promoting a collaborative environment for addressing challenges and making decisions. Establishing communication and feedback loops can ensure that the concerns of stakeholders are being addressed and their input is taken into consideration during the EA process.

A case in point is that of the Australian Government's Digital Transformation Agency (DTA): the DTA has created a whole-of-agency EA Roadmap to guide its digital transformation initiatives. The roadmap details high-level initiatives, priorities, and timelines, while also stressing on the need for stakeholder engagement, resource optimization, and project portfolio management. This systematic approach has allowed the DTA to make great strides toward improving its IT systems efficiency, interoperability, and service delivery.

Finally, all things considered, a well-structured Roadmap is a necessity to ensure a smooth and successful adoption of EA in governmental bodies. This approach ensures that EA initiatives are aligned with the organizational strategy, managed in a systematic manner, and become operationally embedded throughout the organization, which ultimately results in higher levels of organizational performance and service delivery.

Implementation Approaches

Successful EA implementation in government often involves (Dave Hornford S. S., 2018):

- Developing a national EA framework tailored to the country's context, while leveraging international standards like TOGAF.
- Creating reference models and shared services to promote reuse across agencies.
- Establishing a central EA authority to coordinate efforts, often situated in a ministry like the Ministry of Interior.
- Phased implementation starting with pilot projects before wider rollout.
- Legal and policy backing to mandate EA adoption across government agencies.
- Developing EA skills and knowledge through training programs and communities of practice.

5. Conclusion

Addressing the various challenges that come with implementing EA in government organizations is no small feat; however, these challenges can be mitigated through careful planning, stakeholder involvement, and a stepwise approach to implementation. The successful examples in territories like Czech Republic, Canada or Australia unlock valuable lessons and insights for other actors in the context of their EA endeavours.

In summary, with a focus on the key factors for successful EA implementation and by learning from best practices, government organizations can leverage the full potential of EA to improve service delivery, enhance their operational efficiency, and achieve strategic objectives.

References

Adegboyega Ojo, T. J. (2012). Improving Government Enterprise Architecture Practice--Maturity Factor Analysis. *Hawaii International Conference on System Sciences*. IEEE.

Banaeianjahromi, N. (2018). Where enterprise architecture development fails a multiple case study of governmental organizations. *Research Challenges in Information Science*.

Berg, M. (2016). *Building an Enterprise Architecture Practice.* Springer.

Carrillo, J., Cabrera, A., Román, C., Abad, M., & Jaramillo, D. (n.d.). Roadmap for the implementation of an enterprise architecture framework oriented to institutions of higher education in Ecuador. *2010 2nd International Conference on Software Technology and Engineering.* IEEE.

Dave Hornford, S. S. (2018). *The Open Group Guide - Starting an Enterprise Architecture Capability in the Government Sector.* The Open Group.

Dave Hornford, T. H. (2022). *The TOGAF ® Leader's Guide to Establishing and Evolving an EA Capability.* The Open Group.

Esteves, F. J. M., Anunciação, P. F. & Graça Alexandre, H. M. (2024). Roadmap for Enterprise Architecture. The cornerstone for the evolution of Information Systems. In M. B. Cemil Senel, *Innovations and Contemporary Trends in Business & Economics* (pp. 194-205). Peter Lang.

Frank Lin, H. D. (2010). The Value of Implementing Enterprise Architecture in Organizations. *Journal of International Technology and Information Management.*

Gampfer, F. (2019). Investigation on the Future of Enterprise Architecture in Dynamic Environments.

Group, T. O. (2010). *World-Class Enterprise Architecture.* The Open Group.

Hjort-Madsen, K. (2006). Enterprise Architecture Implementation and Management: A Case Study on Interoperability. *Proceedings of the 39th Annual Hawaii International Conference on System Sciences (HICSS'06).* IEEE.

Hrabě, P. (2013). The Proposal of Czech Government Enterprise Architecture Implementation. *CONFENIS, At Prague, Volume 2013.*

Iacob, M., Jonkers, H., Quartel, D., Franken, H., & Van den Berg, H. (2012). *Delivering Enterprise Architecture with TOGAF® and ARCHIMATE®.* BIZZdesign.

ISO/IEC/IEEE. (2011). *ISO/IEC/IEEE 42010:2011(en) - Software, systems and enterprise — Architecture description.* Retrieved from Sítio web do ISO/IEC/IEEE: https://www.iso.org/obp/ui/#iso:std:iso-iec-ieee:42010:ed-1:v1:en

Lankhorst, M., & et Al. (2017). *Enterprise Architecture at Work, Modelling, Communication and Analysis.* Springer.

Marijn Janssen, G. K. (2006). A Complex Adaptive System Perspective of Enterprise Architecture in Electronic Government. *Proceedings of the 39th Annual Hawaii International Conference on System Sciences (HICSS'06).* IEEE.

Nihayah Afarini, D. H. (2023). The Proposed Implementation of Enterprise Architecture in E-Government Development and Services. *International Journal Software Engineering and Computer Science*, 219-229.

Pavel Hrab, T. Š. (2022). *Czech Government Enterprise Architecture A Case Study by: Ministry of the Interior of the Czech Republic.* The Open Group.

Pessi, K., Magoulas, T., & Hugoson, M.-Å. (2011). Enterprise Architecture Principles and their impact on the Management of IT Investments. *Electronic Journal of Information Systems Evaluation.*

Puspitaningrum, A. C. (2021). Literature Review: Elements and Criteria Methodology of Enterprise Architecture for E-Government. *Jurnal Sistemasi sistem informasi.*

Robertson, D., Ross, J. W., & Weill, P. (2006). *Enterprise architecture as strategy: Creating a foundation for business execution.* Harvard Business Review Press.

Saha, P. (2009). *Advances in Government Enterprise Architecture.* IGI Global.

Seogjun Lee, S. W. (2016). Transformational and Transactional Factors for the Successful Implementation of Enterprise Architecture in Public Sector.

Sukaina Al Nasrawi, M. I. (2013). An enterprise architecture mapping approach for realizing e-government. *International Conference on Communications and Information Technology.* IEEE.

Svyatoslav, K. (2018). *The Practice of Enterprise Architecture: A Modern Approach to Business and It Alignment.*

Technology, M. o. (2018). *IndEA Framework.* Ministry of Electronics & Information Technology.

Digital Transformation in the Bakery Industry

Pedro Fernandes da Anunciação, Cátia Susana Claro Chasqueira, Fernando Miguel do Couto Gonçalves, Antonio Juan Briones Peñalver

1. Introduction

An information society is one in which the main activity of society is centered on the production and consumption of information. At the same time, information is considered the most important resource, new information and communication technologies become foundational technologies and the information environment refers to everything that is the object of the generation or consumption of information (social, economic, ecological, etc.). In the information age, the intellectual level of society depends on the production of new knowledge and the adoption of technologies that enhance it.

The Fourth Industrial Revolution represents a global technological shift that radically changes modes of production, interaction, and life in society. Unlike previous revolutions, which involved mechanization and automation, the Fourth Industrial Revolution is based on the integration of new digital technologies, artificial intelligence, the Internet of Things, and other technological innovations. This is an era where physical, digital, and biological systems are becoming inseparable, opening new horizons for humanity (Schwab, 2016).

The development of artificial intelligence, the Internet of Things, robotics, blockchain, and other innovations not only alters production processes but also creates new business models. This challenges companies to use these technologies correctly to improve competitiveness and efficiency. Knowledge is becoming an important asset, as it now determines success and competitiveness in a rapidly changing world.

Some figures about Industry 4.0 (I4.0) illustrate its impact on the economy. I4.0 was valued at 159.56 billion dollars in 2024 and is expected to grow from 188.89 billion dollars in 2025 to 728.51 billion dollars by 2033, with a CAGR of 18.38% during the forecast period (2025-2033) (Straits Research, 2024).

According to McKinsey (2024), the economic impact of implementing generative AI products across various sectors could range from 2.6 to 4.4 trillion dollars per year.

By incorporating strong security, privacy, and ethics into AI systems, organizations not only protect their assets but also create a foundation of trust that drives innovation, increases customer loyalty, and opens new opportunities for sustainable growth. Robotics and automation in production are among the main trends of recent years. Companies have started using collaborative robots (cobots).

All of this has geopolitical and economic impacts. Accenture (2023) believes that the accelerated adoption of digital technologies, such as generative AI, combined with regulatory complexity, will revolutionize how we manage cyber risk. In this rapidly changing environment, it is essential that business leaders include cybersecurity within the framework of their digital transformation initiatives.

This evolution highlights the critical and evolving role of cybersecurity in Industry 4.0, emphasizing the importance of proactive and holistic strategies in managing cyber risk to ensure modern production elements are protected and resilient. On the other hand, it also requires leaders who are heralds of change, driving innovation and ensuring that their teams are aligned with the new technological paradigm (Schellenberg, n.d.).

From the integration of advanced AI technologies that are revolutionizing operational efficiency and expanding their impact beyond production, to the critical role of cybersecurity in protecting interconnected industrial systems, the landscape of Industry 4.0 is evolving rapidly. The emergence of interconnected manufacturing ecosystems underscores the shift towards more flexible and holistic manufacturing operations, where technology not only enhances productivity but also harmonizes various elements of the manufacturing process.

Furthermore, the rise of smart manufacturing encapsulates the growing trend of interconnectivity, demonstrating how integrated technologies can deliver unprecedented efficiencies across multiple operations. Finally, the transformation in leadership reflects the need for a new generation of visionary leaders who can navigate the complexities of this digital age, foster innovation, and align teams with the new technological paradigms.

These trends will not only shape the immediate future of the manufacturing industry, but will also lay the foundation for continuous innovation and progress.

The concept of Industry 4.0 represents the introduction of cyber-physical systems into industrial processes. Industry 4.0 encompasses a concept that describes the transition to intelligent, automated, and interconnected production systems that use advanced digital technologies to increase production efficiency and flexibility. At its core, there are four principles:

- Human-machine interoperability, which offers the possibility of direct contact through the Internet;
- Information transparency and the ability of systems to create a virtual replica of the physical world;
- Technical assistance of machines to humans to aggregate large amounts of data and perform tasks that are unsafe for humans;
- The ability of systems to make decisions independently and autonomously. The term articulates an understanding of the ongoing changes and is, therefore, conceptual. It provides a foundation for a series of political initiatives produced and supported by the government and businesses to advance the R&D program and, consequently, appears to be institutional.

Framing the current challenges of industry involves considering the introduction of cyber-physical systems into manufacturing processes, their networking, real-time communication between them, self-adjustment, and learning.

2. New Technologies and Industry 4.0

At the heart of Industry 4.0 are several key technological areas that shape its structure and development.

- *Artificial Intelligence and Machine Learning* – Artificial Intelligence (AI) relies on algorithms to provide problem-solving skills, decision-making capabilities, and perform human-like tasks (Santhi & Muthuswamy, 2022). The application of AI in Industry 4.0 has demonstrated significant potential in predictive maintenance, predictive analytics, inventory management, computer vision, industrial robotics, and supply chain management (Muthuswamy & Shunmugesh, 2022).

- *Cyber-Physical Systems (CPS)* – Cyber-Physical Systems (CPS) integrate computational processes with physical objects (da Anunciação, et al., 2022; de Lemos Dinis, Esteves, & da Anunciação, 2021). These systems can interact with the environment and with one another in real time, enabling automatic control, monitoring, and analysis. CPS play a critical role in Industry 4.0 by enabling more flexible and adaptable production systems.
- *Edge, Fog, and Cloud Computing* – The massive amount of data generated by the Industrial Internet of Things (IIoT) is driving the adoption of edge, fog, and cloud computing capabilities in Industry 4.0. Customized hardware and software solutions, such as connected clouds, distributed clouds, distributed computing and storage, hybrid computing, low-code development platforms, microservices, mobile computing, and multi-access edge computing, are shaping this Industry 4.0 trend. Cloud computing offers the ability to store and process data on remote servers.
- *Network and Connectivity* – A range of technological advancements, such as edge-cloud, gigabit Ethernet, time-sensitive networks, low-power wide-area networks (LPWAN), 5G, machine-to-machine (M2M) communication, real-time deterministic Ethernet, time-sensitive networks (TSN), ubiquitous radio access, unified IoT frameworks, and zero-touch networks, is driving factories to adopt IIoT and transform into Industry 4.0 facilities. These technologies are continuously improving machine-to-machine and human-to-machine communication as well as data transfer.
- *Robotics and Automation* – Automation and robotics go hand in hand, as their goal is to work independently and efficiently in industries to boost productivity. By connecting robots to a centralized computer system, their actions can be monitored, enabling them to complete tasks without human intervention (Javaid, Haleem, Singh, 2021). Modern robots can perform tasks requiring high precision and operate in environments that are hazardous to humans. Collaborative robots (cobots) interact with humans to complement their abilities and provide

greater flexibility in manufacturing processes. Automation and robotics can enhance production performance and reduce labor costs.

- *Internet of Things (IoT)* – The Internet of Things combines real-time data, machine intelligence, and human skills, resulting in faster, more efficient, and cost-effective manufacturing processes (Cooper & James, 2009). The interoperability and unified structure of IoT are essential for the seamless implementation of Industry 4.0 systems. Smaller and more affordable IoT sensors will enable the connection of more physical objects, making the system operate efficiently, intelligently, and securely (Devarshi Shah, Wang, & Peter, 2020).
- *Big Data* – Big Data refers to the large variety and volume of data arriving at high speed. However, other authors add additional "V's" such as Liao et al. (2014) or Gandomi and Haider (2015). Since raw data holds no inherent value until its potential is unlocked, various analyses are conducted in the industry, primarily categorized as descriptive, inquisitive, operational, prescriptive, and proactive (Bihani & Patil, 2014). This analysis helps large organizations focus on and support customers, target products, and optimize pricing offers in the service market, preventing inefficiencies after decision-making (Raja Santhi & Muthuswamy, 2022).
- *Additive Manufacturing* – Additive manufacturing is an advanced technology that enables the creation of new products, business models, and supply chains. Additive manufacturing (AM) involves the printing of solid three-dimensional objects by layering materials on top of each other using CAD models (Muthuswamy, 2022). The technologies that enable the "3D printing" of physical objects fall under the term "additive manufacturing." Unique products can be manufactured without the usual redundancies, offering a significant advantage.
- *Cybersecurity, Transparency, and Privacy* – The flow of information due to connectivity in Industry 4.0 raises concerns about security, transparency, and privacy. As production methods become more personalized and customizable, data management practices inside and outside the factory floor will significantly impact a company's attractiveness. The transmission and processing of sensitive industrial data must be secure to prevent cyberattacks on critical industrial facilities. Ethical and digital privacy, privacy-enhancing technologies,

self-adaptive security, zero-trust security, end-to-end communication security, DevSecOps, and blockchain are some of the new developments in this domain. Emphasizing cybersecurity must be balanced with transparency and privacy.

- *Digital Twins* – Digital twins are virtual replicas of physical objects, processes, or systems. These models enable real-time simulation and prediction of behavior, helping to optimize production processes and improve management. Digital twin technology creates virtual models of industrial assets by combining dynamic sensor data with real-time visualizations. Digital twins provide valuable insights into all stages of the manufacturing process.

3. Objectives and Methodology

In today's competitive landscape, digital transformation and the implementation of advanced technologies have become essential for companies seeking to remain relevant, efficient, and profitable. To achieve this, it is necessary to plan, manage, and control the entire change project. The case study presented focuses on a digital transformation project developed by a team of Information Systems and Technology professionals, centering on the bakery and pastry sector. This sector is traditionally characterized by manual processes and a reliance on human expertise. The adoption of integrated management systems and Smart Factory technologies presents an opportunity to overcome classic challenges, such as product quality variations, waste, and the inability to respond to constant shifts in consumer patterns.

The case aims to describe the implementation of an organizational and technological transformation project in a company engaged in daily bakery and pastry production, with the goal of modernizing its processes, increasing overall efficiency, and improving competitiveness in the market. The definition of the As Is and To Be stages was crucial to identifying the main points of intervention and creating a clear vision for the company's future. The transformation strategy was designed around four fundamental pillars:

1. Technology and Automation – Leveraging advanced technologies to automate processes and enhance operational efficiency.

2. Integration and Digitalization – Establishing seamless connectivity and digitizing workflows for streamlined operations.
3. Investment in Training and Organizational Culture – Empowering employees and fostering a culture of innovation and adaptability.
4. Continuous Improvement – Implementing iterative processes to ensure ongoing optimization and adaptation to market demands.

4. Case Study – Smart Factory in the Bakery Sector

In the analysis of the company's current situation, several structural and operational issues were identified that significantly limited its efficiency, quality, and market competitiveness. Regarding to operational processes, production was predominantly manual, with tasks such as mixing, shaping, and monitoring the baking process relying almost entirely on human intervention. This approach led to considerable variations in product quality, with products frequently leaving production with inconsistent weights, sizes, or baking levels. The lack of automation, combined with the use of basic and non-integrated equipment, constrained productivity and increased dependence on operator expertise, creating a vulnerable environment prone to errors and inefficiencies. Furthermore, the absence of optimized processes resulted in excessively long production times, limiting the company's ability to effectively respond to market demands.

Another critical issue identified was the inventory and logistics management. Raw materials and finished products were manually managed, lacking technological tools that could enable rigorous control. This limitation often resulted in stockouts, which compromised the ability to fulfill orders, or in overstocking, leading to additional costs and waste of perishable materials. The absence of mechanisms to anticipate demand further hindered the alignment of production levels with market realities, exacerbating inefficiencies and waste.

Additional structural challenges amplified the difficulties faced by the company. A key obstacle was the lack of integrated processes. Financial, sales, and production information was recorded in distinct systems, with no integration between them. This fragmentation hindered the ability to obtain a comprehensive view of the business, delayed performance analyses, and impaired strategic decision-making. Finally, the absence of standardized production processes led to inconsistencies in product quality. Variations in texture, flavor, and appearance undermined the consistency expected by consumers, ultimately affecting customer loyalty.

In summary, the company's current state was marked by a strong reliance on manual processes, lack of integration between different areas, and low overall efficiency. These factors significantly constrained both production capacity and the quality and predictability of products. Such structural challenges highlighted the urgent need for a comprehensive transformation, focused on technological modernization, process integration, and automation. These initiatives aimed to enhance operational performance and ensure the company's competitiveness in the market.

Based on the problems identified in the analysis of the current situation, a future vision for the company was outlined, aligned with the principles of Industry 4.0 and best practices of operational excellence. The main objective of the desired situation is to transform the company's operation, making it more efficient, integrated, and competitive. Regarding operational processes, the plan includes replacing manual methods with advanced automation technologies. Equipment such as smart ovens and automatic molding systems will be implemented to ensure product consistency and improve overall production efficiency. Additionally, IoT sensors will be installed to monitor real-time critical parameters such as temperature, humidity, and fermentation time, ensuring a consistent quality standard across all produced batches.

In the area of inventory and logistics management, the need to adopt an ERP (Enterprise Resource Planning) system was identified, allowing integration across all company departments. This system will include specific modules for inventory management, production planning, and logistics, enabling strict and real-time control. The use of machine learning algorithms will enable the prediction of consumption patterns, adjusting production to market needs efficiently and reducing waste. Raw materials management will be optimized based on historical data and sales projections, minimizing excesses and ensuring greater sustainability.

In the financial and commercial management aspect, all company information – financial, sales, and production – will be consolidated into a single system, which will facilitate real-time analysis and strategic decision-making. At the same time, the company will expand its digital presence through an e-commerce platform integrated directly with production and logistics systems. This approach will allow for greater product customization, fast deliveries, and a differentiated customer experience, which will strengthen the brand's competitiveness.

Regarding quality and competitiveness, the focus will be on standardization. New technologies will ensure product consistency, eliminating variations in texture, taste, and appearance, regardless of human intervention. Additionally, the capacity for customization will be significantly expanded, enabling the company to fulfill custom orders and respond quickly to demand spikes. Another key pillar will be sustainability: the adoption of practices that reduce energy consumption and minimize waste will align with modern environmental requirements and consumer expectations for more responsible operations.

In summary, the desired situation represents a qualitative and strategic leap for the company, modernizing all aspects of the operation and positioning it as a reference in efficiency, innovation, and sustainability in the bakery and pastry sector. This future not only guarantees greater customer satisfaction but also strengthens the company's profitability and its ability to adapt to an ever-evolving market.

To ensure a successful transformation, a phased implementation plan was developed, allowing for a structured transition from the current situation ("As-Is") to the desired situation ("To-Be"). The project was divided into five main phases, each with specific objectives, timelines, and expected outcomes, promoting an efficient and integrated approach.

With the transition from the "As-Is" to the "To-Be" state, the bakery and pastry company expects to achieve a series of strategic and operational benefits that will boost its competitiveness in the market. Among the anticipated gains, operational efficiency stands out, with a significant reduction in production time and an increase in production capacity. Automation and process integration will eliminate operational bottlenecks, optimizing workflow and reducing the dependency on manual interventions.

Another crucial benefit is the consistent quality of the products. The standardization ensured by the technology will prevent variations in texture, taste, and appearance, which will result in greater customer satisfaction and loyalty. As a result, the company will be better positioned to meet the quality standards required by the market. Additionally, there will be a reduction in costs, with significant savings derived from the elimination of waste and the better utilization of resources, including raw materials, energy, and labor.

The transformation will also enhance the company's competitiveness. The ability to respond to new markets will open growth opportunities, especially with the expansion into e-commerce and the use of data to predict consumption patterns. Finally, alignment with good sustainability practices, such as optimizing energy consumption and minimizing waste, will strengthen the company's image as a responsible organization committed to environmental obligations.

The strategy for this transformation was designed based on four fundamental pillars. The first is technology and automation, with the acquisition of advanced equipment and systems that eliminate the bottlenecks identified in operational processes. Replacing outdated machines and adopting IoT sensors will not only ensure efficiency but also enable real-time monitoring, allowing for immediate adjustments.

The second pillar is integration and digitalization, which aims to unify the company's management through digital platforms such as ERP. This will link all areas – from production to finance and sales – offering a comprehensive view and enabling strategic decisions based on accurate and up-to-date data.

The third essential element is investment in training and organizational culture. Adapting to new tools and processes will require significant effort in employee training, ensuring that they are prepared to operate with the new systems and contribute to the success of the transformation. At the same time, creating an innovation culture will be crucial to sustain the changes and promote adherence to the introduced practices.

Finally, the fourth pillar is continuous improvement, ensuring that the results achieved are monitored and that operations are constantly adjusted to maximize gains. The company will adopt performance indicators and implement regular cycles of analysis and optimization.

This structured set of strategies aims to deeply transform the company's operations, elevating it to a new level of efficiency, quality, and competitiveness, with sustainable long-term benefits.

The first phase of the project, lasting 1 to 2 months, was dedicated to diagnosis and strategic planning. This phase involved a detailed survey of current processes and identification of technological and operational needs. Additionally, the requirements for the systems to be implemented, such as ERP and IoT sensors, were defined, along with a detailed timeline and investment plan. The primary return from this phase was qualitative, providing clarity in the strategic vision and alignment of the teams, while minimizing future costs related to possible execution deviations.

The second phase, lasting 4 to 6 months, focused on the implementation of an ERP system that allowed for the integration of all company areas. This system included modules for inventory management, production planning, and financial integration. Additionally, training sessions were conducted to empower the teams in using the new tool. The return from this phase included stricter control of processes and a 15% reduction in raw material waste, as well as a 30% increase in inventory management efficiency.

The third phase (still in implementation), with an estimated duration of 3 to 4 months, focused on the acquisition and installation of automation equipment. This step included the replacement of manual processes with automated machines, such as smart ovens and automatic molding systems, as well as the installation of IoT sensors for real-time monitoring of critical parameters like temperature and fermentation time. The impacts of this phase are becoming visible in the standardization of product quality and reduction of inconsistencies. In quantitative terms, it is expected that by the end of the implementation, a 20% increase in productivity and a 10% reduction in production failure-related costs will be achieved.

The fourth phase, lasting 3 to 4 months, will focus on the company's digital expansion, with the creation of an e-commerce platform integrated with the ERP system. This solution will allow for the customization of orders, optimization of deliveries, and a differentiated customer experience. The expected return includes a 25% increase in sales and a significant expansion of the customer base.

Finally, the fifth phase will be dedicated to process optimization and continuous improvement, starting in month 12 and continuing thereafter. During this phase, the results of all previous phases will be monitored, and adjustments will be made to maximize efficiency. This ongoing process will ensure the consolidation of the company as a reference in quality and sustainability within the sector.

With this implementation plan, the company expects to achieve a 35% increase in profitability, reduce waste by 25%, and expand its market presence, positioning itself as a modern, efficient company aligned with the trends of Industry 4.0.

5. Conclusion

The digital transformation project for the bakery and pastry company demonstrates that applying Industry 4.0 technologies and best practices offers a clear path for modernization and enhanced competitiveness in the sector. By implementing an integrated ERP system, automating processes, digitalizing inventory management, and introducing new technologies such as IoT sensors and smart ovens, the company establishes a solid foundation for a more efficient, agile operation with greater control over its processes.

With automation, production standardization, and the elimination of manual processes, the company will ensure product quality consistency, increase productivity, and reduce waste. Investing in employee training and fostering an organizational culture of innovation are also critical for the successful adaptation of staff to the changes, maximizing the return on the technologies implemented.

Continuous improvement and regular monitoring of results will ensure that the company maintains its success trajectory, adjusting processes and strategies as needed to stay aligned with market trends and consumer expectations.

By doing so, the company is expected to not only become more efficient and competitive but also position itself as a leader in quality, innovation, and sustainability within the bakery and pastry sector. This transformation will generate long-term benefits for both the organization and its customers, reinforcing its ability to adapt in a rapidly evolving market.

Ultimately, the transformation lays the groundwork for sustainable growth, helping the company to deliver greater value to stakeholders while maintaining a forward-thinking approach to operational excellence and market leadership. The integration of advanced technologies and digital tools will empower the company to respond effectively to future challenges, strengthen its position in the marketplace, and ensure continued success in the ever-changing business landscape.

References

Accenturte (2021). How aligning security and the business creates cyber resilience - State of Cybersecurity Resilience 2021. Retrieved of: https://www.accenture.com/content/dam/accenture/final/a-com-migration/pdf/pdf-165/accenture-state-of-cybersecurity-2021.pdf, Available at: 27 November 2024

Bauer, H., Patel, M., & Veira, J. (2014). The Internet of Things: Sizing up the opportunity. Retrieved from: McKinsey at http://www.mckinsey.com/insights/high_tech_telecoms_internet/the_internet_of_things_sizing_up_the_opportunity

Bihani, P., & Patil, S. T. (2014). A comparative study of data analysis techniques. International journal of emerging trends & technology in computer science, 3(2), 95-101.

Cooper, J., & James, A. (2009). Challenges for database management in the internet of things. IETE Technical Review, 26(5), 320-329. https://doi.org/10.4103/0256-4602.55275)

da Anunciação, P. F., de Lemos Dinis, V. M., Peñalver, A. J. B., & Esteves, F. J. M. (2022). Functional Safety as a critical success factor to industry 4.0. Procedia Computer Science, 204, 45-53.

de Lemos Dinis, V. M., Esteves, F. J. M., & da Anunciação, P. F. (2021). Charting a Path for Industry 4.0. An Industry and University Experience. In *Perspectives and Trends in Education and Technology: Selected Papers from ICITED 2021* (pp. 229-239). Singapore: Springer Singapore.

Gandomi, A., & Haider, M. (2015). Beyond the hype: Big data concepts, methods, and analytics. International journal of information management, 35(2), 137-144. https://doi.org/10.1016/j.ijinfomgt.2014.10.007

Javaid, M., Haleem, A., Singh, R. P., & Suman, R. (2021). Substantial capabilities of robotics in enhancing industry 4.0 implementation. Cognitive Robotics, 1, 58-75.

Liao, Z., Yin, Q., Huang, Y., & Sheng, L. (2015). Management and application of mobile big data. International Journal of Embedded Systems, 7(1), 63-70. https://doi.org/10.1504/IJES.2015.066143]

Mckinsey (2024). Technology Trends. Outlook 2024, Mckinsey Digital, Mckinsey Company. Retrieved of: https://www.mckinsey.com/~/media/mckinsey/business%20functions/mckinsey%20digital/our%20insights/the%20top%20trends%20in%20tech%202024/mckinsey-technology-trends-outlook-2024.pdf?trk=public_post_comment-text, Available at: 14 November 2024

Muthuswamy, P. (2022). Influence of powder characteristics on properties of parts manufactured by metal additive manufacturing. Lasers in Manufacturing and Materials Processing, 9(3), 312-337

Raja Santhi, A., & Muthuswamy, P. (2022). Pandemic, war, natural calamities, and sustainability: Industry 4.0 technologies to overcome traditional and contemporary supply chain challenges. Logistics, 6(4), 81.

Schellenberg, L. (w.d.). Deep Tech Talk With Lucas Schellenberg, Retrieved of: https://hiec.com/deep-tech-talk-with-lucas-schellenberg/, Available at: 29 November 2024

Schwab, K. (2024). 8. The Fourth Industrial Revolution-What It Means and How to Respond. In Handbook of Research on Strategic Leadership in the Fourth Industrial Revolution (Vol. 29). Edward Elgar Publishing.

Shah, D., Wang, J., & He, Q. P. (2020). Feature engineering in big data analytics for IoT-enabled smart manufacturing–Comparison between deep learning and statistical learning. Computers & Chemical Engineering, 141, 106970. https://doi.org/10.1016/j.compchemeng.2020.106970

Ownership structure variations and artificial intelligence risk management disclosure in listed ICT firms in Africa

Israel Seriki Akinadewo, Oluyinka Isaiah Oluwagbade, Jeremiah Oreoluwa Akinadewo, Temitayo Oluwatimilehin Abe, Omobolade Stephen Ogundele, Ifeoluwa Mary Adebiyi

1. Introduction

In contemporary discourse, considerable scholarly attention has been devoted to cyber-physical systems (CPS). This technological domain, representing the forefront of digital systems evolution, is recognized for its capacity to enhance operational efficiency through the seamless integration of computational components with physical capabilities and human interfaces (Albitar et al., 2022; Castro et al., 2023) In this new evolution, Castro et al. (2023) emphasized that CPS represent a pivotal field of study and innovation, merging computing, communication, and control within physical systems. This integration, therefore, has the potential to significantly transform diverse sectors like transportation, healthcare, energy, and manufacturing, among others (Castro et al., 2023). Their argument suggests that by improving the functionality, efficiency, and reliability of intricate systems, CPS holds promise for tackling societal issues and propelling technological progress forward. Javaid et al. (2023) provided context by stating that artificial intelligence (AI) encompasses a broader scope, consolidating cyber-physical characteristics.

Artificial intelligence (AI) and cyber-physical systems (CPS) are deeply interconnected, synergizing to elevate the capabilities of modern technology [Alowaidi et al., 2023; Javaid et al., 2023). AI furnishes the cognitive prowess to analyze copious CPS-generated data, empowering systems to dynamically adapt to evolving circumstances. CPS, in turn, furnish the physical infrastructure for AI algorithms, melding computational and physical processes across sectors like manufacturing, transportation, healthcare, and smart cities (Javaid et al., 2023). This fusion presents transformative opportunities for efficiency optimization, reliability enhancement, and tackling multifaceted challenges across industries (Joshi & Masih, 2023; Song et al., 2023).

The recent proliferation of internet-mediated activities has emerged as a significant cybersecurity imperative (Jha & Kumar., 2021). The operational paradigms and virtual manifestations inherent to cyber-physical systems (CPS), coupled with the advancements in Internet of Things (IoT) and AI technologies, engender intricate interplays that present formidable challenges for seamless integration within contemporary industrial frameworks (Goyal et al., 2023). In recent years, meanwhile, there has been a significant increase in the utilization of artificial intelligence (AI) technologies worldwide, especially within the Information and Communication Technology (ICT) sector in Africa, the focus of this study. This rapid expansion of AI implementation, which (Kiemde & Kora, 2020) noted is accelerating swiftly across the African continent, has led to substantial transformations across various industries, resulting in the reconfiguration of business models and operational frameworks. However, despite its advantages, the widespread adoption of AI has introduced new complexities and challenges, particularly concerning risk management and disclosure protocols.

Within this swiftly evolving technological landscape, an essential inquiry emerges concerning the impact of ownership structure on the disclosure practices of AI risk management, specifically within the sphere of listed ICT firms in Africa. It is crucial to comprehend the degree to which variations in ownership structure like - board ownership, CEO ownership, foreign ownership, contestable ownership influence the communication of AI-related risks, as this information is vital for stakeholders, including investors, regulators, and policymakers, given its direct implications for decision-making processes and risk evaluation strategies.

This study aims to elucidate the relationship between ownership structure and AI risk management disclosure, thereby contributing to the broader conversation surrounding corporate governance, technological advancements, and strategies for risk mitigation, particularly within emerging markets.

2. Literature Review and Hypotheses Development

2.1 Ownership Structure and Artificial Intelligence Risk Management Disclosure

Ownership structure, defined as the allocation of ownership rights among shareholders, has been a central theme in corporate governance research

(Lazarides, 2020). Researchers have scrutinized its influence on diverse organizational results such as financial performance, strategic decision-making, and risk management protocols (Ambarwati & Haryono, 2022; Nazir & Asad, 2023). Nevertheless, the surge in AI technologies has spurred a shift in scholarly focus towards investigating how ownership structure shapes firms' strategies for addressing AI-related risks and their disclosure methods.

Studies have explored how ownership concentration, the identity of dominant shareholders, and institutional ownership influence firms' perspectives on disclosing AI risk management (Albitar et al., 2022; Pijoh et al., 2023). For instance, Liang et al. (2021) argued that firms characterized by greater ownership concentration tend to disclose less information concerning AI-related risks, potentially attributed to diminished pressure for transparency from dispersed shareholders. Conversely, these authors hypothesized that firms boasting a more heterogeneous shareholder base may encounter heightened scrutiny, consequently leading to more comprehensive disclosure regarding strategies for managing AI risks (Bhimavarapu et al., 2022; Liang et al. 2021)

Scholars such as Sanders (2021) have highlighted that firms controlled by technology-focused investors or venture capital firms could prioritize transparency in AI risk management, recognizing the importance of maintaining trust and credibility in innovation-driven industries. Conversely, companies affiliated with established industrial conglomerates often adopt conservative disclosure practices, possibly as a safeguard for proprietary AI innovations or to manage reputational risks. Hence, institutional ownership, which involves the ownership of shares by financial institutions and other significant investors, plays a crucial role in influencing firms' strategies for disclosing AI risk management (Sanders, 2021).

2.2 Board Ownership and Artificial Intelligence Risk Management Disclosure

According to Wang and Yen (2023), board members with significant ownership stakes in the firm are more likely to advocate for comprehensive disclosure of AI-related risks and mitigation strategies. High levels of board ownership align the interests of directors with those of shareholders, leading to a greater emphasis on transparency and accountability in managing technological risks. Furthermore, board ownership can enhance firms' resilience to AI-related risks by facilitating more robust oversight and strategic guidance. This position is more solidified with the argument of Pijoh et al. (2023) which indicates that boards with substantial ownership stakes are better positioned to understand the implications of AI technologies for the firm's operations and reputation, thereby fostering proactive risk management practices and disclosure transparency. Regarding this, and whilst there is still dearth of articles on the link between the variables, we still hypothesize that firms with higher levels of board ownership will demonstrate greater transparency in disclosing AI risk management practices.

H_{01}: Board ownership has a positive significant influence on AI risk management disclosure

2.3 CEO Ownership and Artificial Intelligence Risk Management Disclosure

Studies by Bonareri et al. (2023) suggest that CEOs with substantial ownership stakes are more likely to prioritize transparency in disclosing AI-related risks and mitigation strategies. High levels of CEO ownership align personal interests with those of shareholders, fostering a culture of accountability and proactive risk management. Moreover, CEO ownership can signal commitment and confidence in the firm's technological strategies, influencing disclosure practices. Similarly, Zhao et al. (2023) opined that CEOs with significant ownership stakes are more inclined to communicate AI risk management efforts to stakeholders, viewing transparency as a strategic imperative to enhance corporate reputation and investor confidence. Based on this, we hypothesize that firms with higher levels of CEO ownership will exhibit greater transparency in disclosing AI risk management practices.

H_{02}: CEO ownership has a positive significant relationship with AI risk management disclosure

2.4 Foreign Ownership and Artificial Intelligence Risk Management Disclosure

Foreign ownership, denoting the proportion of a firm's shares held by investors from abroad, is a crucial aspect of corporate governance that reflects global investment patterns and cross-border capital flows (Safitri et al., 2023). For instance, studies by Kurniasari and Achyani (2022) suggested that firms with higher levels of foreign ownership would exhibit better transparency in AI-related risks and mitigation strategies' disclosure. Foreign investors frequently introduce varied viewpoints and stringent governance criteria, compelling firms to embrace proactive disclosure measures to allure and maintain international investments (Kurniasari & Achyani, 2022). Furthermore, foreign ownership can serve as a catalyst for technology-driven innovation and risk management (Nakonechna & Petryk, 2022). Therefore, companies with foreign ownership are inclined to give priority to transparent disclosure to showcase their dedication to technological progress and adherence to regulatory standards in global markets. Based on this, we hypothesize that firms with higher levels of foreign ownership will demonstrate greater transparency in disclosing AI risk management practices.

H_{03}: There is a significant positive nexus between foreign ownership and AI risk management disclosure

2.5 Contestable Ownership and Artificial Intelligence Risk Management Disclosure

On contestable ownership, Bhimavarapu et al. (2022) argued that firms with more contestable ownership structures tilt more in the direction of transparent disclosure on AI-related risks and mitigation strategies. The presence of diverse and vigilant stakeholders fosters a culture of accountability and transparency, prompting firms to adopt more proactive disclosure practices to address the concerns and interests of various ownership groups. In addition, Zouari and Dhifi (2022) indicates that firms with contestable ownership structures are more likely to engage in rigorous risk assessment processes and prioritize disclosure transparency to maintain stakeholder trust and reputation. Furtherance to this argument, contestable ownership can enhance firms' resilience to AI-related risks by fostering robust governance mechanisms and strategic oversight. We, therefore, hypothesize thus:

H_{04}: Contestable has a positive significant nexus with AI risk management disclosure

2.6 Firm Size

Firm size, typically measured by factors such as total assets, revenue, or market capitalization, plays a significant role in shaping disclosure practices and governance dynamics (Zhang & Sharon, 2023). Larger firms often face greater scrutiny from stakeholders and regulatory authorities, leading to higher transparency expectations and more extensive disclosure (Zhang & Sharon, 2023).. Therefore, the size of the firm will have a controlling effect on the disclosure patterns of in the angle of AI risk management disclosure.

2.7 Leverage

Leverage, representing the extent of a firm's debt financing relative to its equity, influences firms' risk management strategies and disclosure practices. Highly leveraged firms may face additional pressures to disclose AI-related risks to reassure creditors and investors about their ability to manage technological uncertainties (Wang & Yen, 2023). Thus, firms with higher leverage ratios may prioritize disclosure to mitigate concerns about financial stability and creditworthiness (Wang & Yen, 2023)..

The originality of this study, however, comes from the gap identified in the structure of business ownership as the explanatory variable in understanding the impact on AI risk management disclosure. The insufficiency of study on this topic is noticed from the number of articles coming from the African continent, the area of focus. For instance, Albitar et al. (2023) focused on ownership concentration and Covid-19 disclosure, Almiani et al. (2022) examined efficient data balancing cyber physical system on quality of service, Bhimavarapu et al. (2022) investigated ownership concentration and transparency disclosures of banks in India, this current study aims in the direction of Ai risk management disclosures within the African ICT firms. In addition, this study adopted twelve African countries, covering Western Africa, Southern Africa, and Eastern Africa, unlike that of (Bonareri et al., 2023) which focused on East Africa, using only CEO Ownership as against several proxy of ownership structure of this current study, along with integrated reporting as controlled variable. Furthermore, Munisi (2023) which focused on Sub-Sahara Africa only used data from eleven (11) countries, excluding South Africa, one of the major economic hub of the continent, which this current study considered. The research of Munisi (2023) also covered 2005-2009, while the current study covered 2012-2022. Consequent to these identified gaps, this current study aims to contribute to the body knowledge in how diverse ownership variables could minimize and avoid the potential AI risk through transparency in disclosures.

Theoretical Framework

This study is underpinned by two theories: Theory of Mind AI and Agency Theory.

Theory of Mind Artificial Intelligence (AI)

The philosophy of mind has long ceased to be the exclusive domain of human philosophers (Quiros et al., 2021) To Quiros et al. (2021), this became increasingly noticeable with the advent of technological advancement. For this purpose, the creation of hybrid intelligence was of existential essence. These scholars Quiros et al. (2021) argued that the creation of hybrid intelligence, which is the combination of human thinking with the AI modeled intelligence. Therefore, there exists the possibility of translating consciousness problem into a sort of problem of intelligence, with the intent of creating a machine that could think like human (Quiros et al., 2021), which Winfield (2018) similarly argued on the predictive model of self and others through the machine as created by the philosophers and psychologists. Thus, AI has dramatically changed the world as it was understood (Cuzzolin et al. 2020) Furtherance to this premix, the theory of mind conceptualized on the strength of judging the trustworthiness of others correctly (Williams et al., 2022). Thus, it is deduced that behavioural patter of man through ownership structure could be effectively replicated in decision making through AI for risk management disclosure.

Agency Theory

The diverse and contrasting interests of managers (agents) of firms, and the owners (principals), elicited the agency theory proposition. Whilst contributing to the works of the pioneering authors of agency theory, El Kouiri (2023) examined how self-interests' decision brought conflicts between the principals and agents of firms. It is, therefore of vital importance that principals exhibit managing actions for the purpose of managing agency cost (El Kouiri, 2023). For the interest of the firm's growth, it is expedient for the introduction of the most appropriate way to resolve the near continuous emergence of the conflicts. Based on this, Flayyih and Khiari (2023) argued that issues like poor governance mechanism could jeopardise the needed conciliatory activities between these stakeholders. It is against these theoretical review that this study believes there is a connecting link between theory of mind AI and agency theory as regards the relationship between the two main variables. Thus, both theories underpin this study. This interconnectivity is shown in Figure 1.

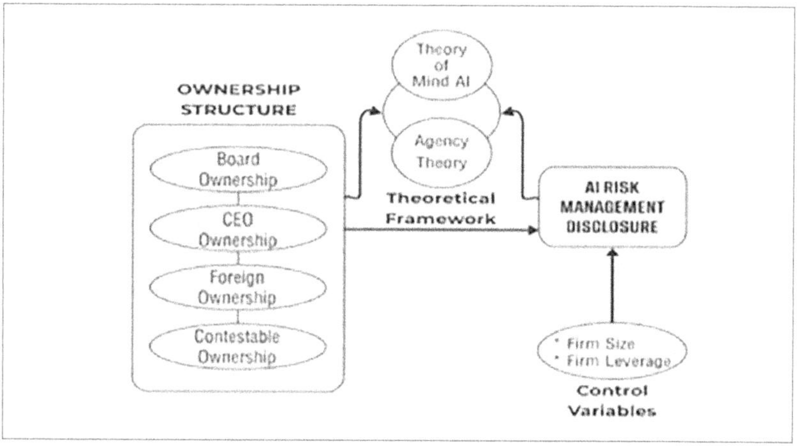

Figure 1: Conceptual/Theoretical Framework
Source: Authors' Conceptual/Theoretical Framework (2024)

3. METHODOLOGY

The study used secondary data. Population of the study consists of 33 companies from Bostwana (1), Ghana (2), Kenya (5), Malawi (2), Namibia (1), Nigeria (4), Rwanda (1), South Africa (11), Tanzania (1), Uganda (2), Zambia (1), and Zimbabwe (2), covering 12 years (2012-2022), with census sampling technique adopted for the sample size, which equals to the population. Some of the firms did not have the financial for the complete years, hence, pooled data regression utilized for the analysis of data. Stata through the MachameRatios DataPc was used for the Pooled multiple regression analysis. Meanwhile, the number of observations was 274 as shown in Table 1.

Table 1: List of the Africa Firms for Data Generations and Observations

Details	Country	Years covered	Observations
Botswana Tel	Botswana	2016-2022	7
Digicut Advertising	Ghana	2018-2022	5
MTN Ghana	Ghana	2018-2022	5
Longhorn Kenya	Kenya	2012-2022	11
Nation Media Group	Kenya	2012-2022	11
Safaricom	Kenya	2012-2022	11
Scangroup	Kenya	2012-2022	11
Standard Group	Kenya	2012-2022	11
Airtel Malawi Plc	Malawi	2020-2022	3
Telekom Networks	Malawi	2012-2022	11
Mobile Telecom.	Namibia	2021-2022	2
Afromedia	Nigeria	2021-2022	11
Briclinks Africa Plc	Nigeria	2020-2022	3
Daar Comm.	Nigeria	2012-2022	11
MTN Nigeria	Nigeria	2018-2022	5
MTN Rwandacell	Rwanda	2021-2022	2
African Media	South Africa	2012-2022	11
Blue Label Tel	South Africa	2012-2022	11
Caxton & Ctp Publishers	South Africa	2012-2022	11
E Media Holdings	South Africa	2014-2022	9
Huge Group	South Africa	2012-2022	11
MTN Group	South Africa	2012-2022	11
Multichoice Group	South Africa	2019-2022	4
Naspers	South Africa	2012-2022	11
Telemasters Holdings	South Africa	2012-2022	11
Telkom	South Africa	2012-2022	11
Vodacom Group	South Africa	2012-2022	11
Vodacom Tanzania	Tanzania	2017-2022	6
MTN Uganda	Uganda	2021-2022	2
New Vision Printing	Uganda	2012-2022	11
Airtel Zambia	Zambia	2012-2022	11
Econet Wireless	Zimbabwe	2012-2022	11
Zimbabwe Newspaper	Zimbabwe	2022	1
Total Observations			**274**

Source: Authors' Computation (2024)

Model Specification

The study adapted the model of [16] establishing the relationship between ownership and disclosure:

$$\text{Disclosure Index}ij = \beta_{1j} + \sum p\, \beta p X p i j + \sum r \beta Z r i j + e i j$$

The following model specification is proposed as a multiple regression to assess the impact of ownership structure on AI risk management disclosure:

$$\text{AIRMD}i = \beta_0 + \beta_1 \text{BO}i + i\beta_2 \text{CO}i + \beta_3 \text{FO}i + \beta_4 \text{CONO}i + \beta_5 \text{FS}i + \beta_6 \text{LEV}i + \epsilon i$$

Dependent Variable: AI Risk Management Disclosure (AIRMD): This variable represents the level of Technological risk disclosure by the listed ICT firms.

Independent Variables: Board Ownership (BO): The proportion of shares owned by the board members, with the following sub-components: CEO Ownership (CO): The proportion of shares owned by the CEO; Foreign Ownership (FO): The proportion of shares owned by foreign investors; Contestable Ownership (CONO): The proportion of shares that are potentially contestable or held by investors likely to challenge management decisions.

Control Variables: Firm Size (FS): Measured by the total assets or market capitalization of the firm, and Leverage (LEV): The ratio of total debt to total assets.

4. Findings and Discussions

4.1 Descriptive Statistics

In Table 2, firm size, measured in USD, had a mean of 1,254,703 and a standard deviation of 2,670,251. Firm leverage had a mean of 0.5629, indicating that, on average, firms have a leverage ratio slightly above 50%, which is in line with the descriptive statistics of (Munisi, 2023).. The ownership variables show varying levels of ownership stakes, board ownership at 3,220.311 USD, CEO ownership at 1,435.162 USD, foreign ownership at 0.0473 USD, and contestable ownership at 73,219.38 USD. Technological risk, measured by the ratio of software assets to total assets, had a mean of 0.0531, which aligns with study of Pijoh et al. (2023) on risk disclosure. Meanwhile, these findings are consistent with the work of (Munisi, 2023).

Table 2: Descriptive Analysis

Variable	Obs	Mean	Std. Dev.	Min	Max
Technological Risk	273	0.0531	0.5885	0	9.7217
Board Ownership	264	3,220.311	9,490.789	0	79,695.5
CEO Ownership	262	1,435.162	4,068.062	0	24,461.84
Foreign Ownership	250	0.0473	0.1780	0	1
Contestable Ownership	235	73,219.38	268,976.8	0	2,174,220
Firm Size	274	1,254,703	2,670,251	0	14,900,000
Firm Leverage	273	0.5629	0.4879	0.089	3.955

Source: Authors' Computation (2024)

4.2 Correlation Analysis

In Table 3, there is a positive correlation between firm size and technological risk (0.3606), indicating larger firms tend to have higher technological risk, which corresponds fundamentally to the study of (Munisi, 2023).. The correlation between board ownership and CEO ownership is strong (0. 8748), suggesting firms with significant board investors also have substantial CEO ownership, which aligns with the study of (Safitri et al., 2023). Meanwhile, the results were shown in US Dollars in view of the diverse reporting currencies of the selected geographical areas (countries) used for the sample size.

Table 3: Correlation Analysis

	Firm Size	Firm Lev	Board Owner	CEO Owner	Foreign Owner	Contest. Owner	Tech Risk
Firm Size	1.0000						
Firm Lev	-0.0163	1.0000					
Board Owner	-0.0922	0.464	1.0000				
CEO Owner	-0.0601	0.0535	0.8748	1.0000			
Foreign Owner	0.0540	-0.0159	0.3430	0.2305	1.0000		
Con Owner	0.0160	-0.0035	0.1465	0.0824	0.5172	1.0000	
Tech Risk	0.3606	-0.0333	0.0461	-0.0067	-0.0836	-0.0419	1.0000

Source: Authors' Computation (2024)

4.3 Regression Analysis

Table 4 shows the influence of ownership structures and control variables on AI risk management disclosure, measured as technological risk. The model has an R-squared value of 0.3169, indicating that about 31.69% of the variation in technological risk is explained by the model.

Table 4: Regression Analysis

Technological risk	Coefficient	Std. Error	T	P>|t|	[95% Conf.	Interval)
Board Members Shares USD	9.69e-07	3.49e-07	2.78	0.006	2.81e-07	1.66e-06
CEO shares USD	-1.34e-06	7.96e-07	-1.68	0.094	2.91e-06	2.32e-07
Foreign Parent Ownership USD	-.0122497	.0213594	-0.57	0.567	-.0543657	.0298663
Contestable Ownership USD	2.03e-08	3.17e-08	0.64	0.521	-4.21e-08	8.28e-08
Firm size	4.55e-09	6.13e-10	7.42	0.000	3.34e-09	5.76e-09
Firm Leverage	.0058872	.0023927	2.46	0.015	.0011692	.0106051

Source: Authors' Computation (2024)

5. DISCUSSION, CONCLUSION AND RECOMMENDATIONS

5.1 Discussion of Findings

The study concludes that ownership structures have varied impacts on AI risk management disclosure among listed ICT firms in Africa. Board ownership significantly enhances disclosure practices, as board members with substantial shares are more likely to promote transparency in AI risk management due to their involvement in governance and strategic decision-making. This agrees substantially with the study of (Munisi 2023; Pijoh et al., 2023; Song 2021 & Zouari & Dhifi, 2022) but at variance with the assertions of (Gupta & Symss, 2023) that asserted that board size and ownership are insignificant to risk disclosure. In contrast, institutional investors may prioritize financial performance over detailed disclosures or lack engagement in day-to-day governance, which contradicts the study of (Kamaruzaman et al., 2019). Foreign ownership does not significantly impact AI risk management disclosure, likely due to differing expectations and regulatory environments, but this is at variance with the study of (Munisi, 2023). Interestingly, higher CEO ownership might reduce AI risk management disclosure, as CEOs with substantial ownership stakes may prefer to control and limit disclosed information to protect proprietary strategies or due to conflicts of interest. This aligns with the study of Gupta and Symss (2023). Contestable ownership also does not significantly impact AI risk management disclosure; as activist investors may focus on short-term gains rather than comprehensive risk disclosures.

The findings highlight the importance of considering ownership dynamics in regulatory and corporate governance frameworks to improve AI risk management transparency. Regulators and policymakers should recognize the varying impacts of different ownership structures and implement measures encouraging better disclosure practices. This could include mandatory AI risk management disclosure requirements, encouraging active engagement by institutional and foreign investors, and balancing CEO incentives to ensure transparency. Enhancing board ownership and strengthening the role of independent directors can also promote more robust disclosure practices, helping to build investor confidence, improve corporate governance, and ensure firms are better prepared to manage AI-related risks.

5.2 Conclusion and Recommendations

To enhance transparency and governance in listed ICT firms in Africa, several measures are recommended based on the analysis of ownership structures and AI risk management disclosure. To begin with, increasing board ownership through stock options and incentives can align board members' interests with the firm, promoting comprehensive disclosure. Conversely, the study found a negative relationship between CEO ownership and disclosure, suggesting a need to balance CEO incentives to maintain transparency. Furthermore, strengthening the role of independent directors and committees can further ensure effective oversight. Institutional investors, while not significantly impacting disclosure in the study, can still enhance transparency through active engagement and supportive voting policies. Leveraging foreign ownership to adopt international best practices can improve local disclosure standards. Firms should also ensure transparency in changes of large ownership blocks and engage with activist investors to align with long-term transparency goals. Regulatory bodies should implement mandatory AI risk management disclosure frameworks, regularly updating requirements to keep pace with technological advancements. Finally, firms should strengthen internal risk management practices, conduct comprehensive AI risk assessments, and provide ongoing training for management and board members. These steps will enhance AI risk management disclosures, fostering better transparency, investor confidence, and corporate governance.

References

Albitar, K., Elmarzouky, M., & Hussainey, K. (2022). Ownership concentration and Covid-19 disclosure: the mediating role of corporate leverage. *International Journal of Accounting & Information Management, 30*(3), 339-351. https://doi.org/10.1108/ijaim-10-2021-0202

Almiani, M., Razaque, A., Alotaibi, B., Alotaibi, M., Amanzholova, S., & Alotaibi, A. (2022). An Efficient Data-Balancing Cyber-Physical System Paradigm for Quality-of-Service (QoS) Provision over Fog Computing. *Applied Sciences, 12*(1), 246-260. https://doi.org/10.3390/app12010246

Alowaidi, M., Sharma, S., Alenizi, A., & Bhardwaj, S. (2023). Integrating artificial intelligence in cyber security for cyber-physical systems. *Electronic Research Archive, 31*(4), 1876-1896. https://doi.org/10.3934/era.2023097

Ambarwati, S., & Haryono, S. (2022). Ownership structure and corporate restructuring: Does it have an impact? *International Journal of Economics, Business and Accounting Research (IJEBAR), 5*(14), 581-593. https://doi.org/10.29040/ijebar.v5i4.3830

Bhimavarapu, V., Rastogi, S., & Kanoujiya, J. (2022). Ownership concentration and its influence on transparency and disclosures of banks in India. *Corporate Governance: The International Journal of Business in Society, 23*(1), 18-42. https://doi.org/10.1108/cg-05-2021-0169

Bonareri, T., Cheboi, D., & Ronald, D. (2023). Effect of CEO ownership power and integrated reporting among listed firms in East Africa. *Journal of Economics, Finance and Management Studies, 6*(4), 1414-1429. https://doi.org/10.47191/jefms/v6-i4-03

Castro, D., Sales, A., Farias, N., Medeiros, R., Silva, V., & Junior, V. (2023). Monitoring and controlling industrial cyber-physical systems with Digital Twin and Augmented Reality. 2023 *IEEE International Conference on Consumer Electronics (ICCE), 1*(1), 1-17. https://doi.org/10.1109/ICCE56470.2023.10043445

Cuzzolin, F., Morelli, A., Cirstea, B., & Sahakian, B. J. (2020). Knowing me, knowing you: theory of mind in AI. Psychological Medicine, 50, 1057-1061. https://doi.org/10.1017/S0033291720000835

El Kouiri, K. (2023). Exploring the development of agency theory: review of theory. Ibn Khaldoun Journal for Studies and Researches, 3(10, 365-380. https://doi.org/10.56989/benkj.v3i10.698

Flayyih, H. H., & Khiari, W. (2023). An empirical study to detect agency problems in listed corporations: the emerging market study [special issue]. Journal of Governance & Regulation, 12(1), 208-218. https://doi.org/10.22495/jgrv12i12i1siart1

Goyal, S., Rajawat, A., Solanki, R., Zaaba, M., & Long, Z. (2023). Integrating AI with cyber security for Smart industry 4.0 Application. *2023 International Conference on Inventive Computation Technologies (ICICT)*, 1223-1232. https://doi.org/10.1109/ICICT57646.2023.10134374

Gupta, R., & Symss, J. (2023). Does Corporate Governance Impact Risk Disclosure? An Empirical Analysis in the Indian Context. *Indian Journal of Corporate Governance*, *16*(1), 9-27.

Javaid, M., Haleem, A., Singh, R. P., & Suman, R. (2023). An integrated outlook of Cyber–Physical Systems for Industry 4.0: Topical practices, architecture, and applications. *Green Technologies and Sustainability*, *1*(1), 1–17. https://doi.org/10.1016/j.grets.2022.100001

Jha, S., & Kumar, S. (2021). Cybersecurity in the age of the internet of things: An assessment of the users privacy and data security. *Expert Clouds and Applications*, 209, 49-56. https://doi.org/10.1007/978-981-16-2126-0_5

Joshi, A. & Masih, J. (2023). Enhancing employee efficiency and performance in Industry 5.0 Organizations through artificial intelligence integration. *European Economic Letters (EEL)*, *13*(4), 1-15. https://doi.org/10.52783/eel.v13i4.589

Kamaruzaman, S. A., Ali, M. M., & Ghani, E. K. (2019). Ownership structure, corporate risk disclosure and firm value: a Malaysian perspective. *International Journal Managerial and Financial Accounting*, *11*(2), 113-131.

Kiemde, S., & Kora, A. (2020). The Challenges Facing the Development of AI in Africa. *2020 IEEE International Conference on Advent Trends in Multidisciplinary Research and Innovation (ICATMRI)*, 1-6. https://doi.org/10.1109/ICATMRI51801.2020.9398454

Kurniasari, P., & Achyani, F. (2022). Analysis of factors affecting risk management disclosure. *International Journal of Scientific and Research Publications (IJSRP)*, *12*(7), 575-585. https://doi.org/10.29322/ijsrp.12.07.2022.p12763

Lazarides, T. (2020). Minority Shareholders: Useful Idiots, Free Riders or the Achilles Heel of the Corporate Idea? *Theoretical Economics Letters*, 10(3), 488-499. https://doi.org/10.4236/tel.2020.103031

Liang, S., Jiang, Y., Yu, J., & Xu, W. (2021). Large shareholders' tunneling and stock price crash risk. *China Journal of Accounting Studies*, *9*(4), 469 - 489. https://doi.org/10.1080/21697213.2022.2082717

Munisi, G. (2023). Ownership structure and information disclosure in Sub-Saharan African countries. *African Journal of Applied Research*, *9*(1), 51-77. https://doi.org/10.26437/ajar.v9i1.521

Nakonechna, T., & Petryk, T. (2022). Risk management of foreign goods supply chain. *Eastern Europe: economy, business and management*. https://doi.org/10.32782/easterneurope.34-20

Nazir, W., & Asad, H. (2023). Ownership Concentration, Firm Risk taking and Performance: Evidence from Developing Economy of Pakistan. *Pakistan Journal of Humanities and Social Sciences*, *11*(2), 2679-2701. https://doi.org/10.52131/pjhss.2023.1102.0566

Pijoh, D., Pratama, B., Pramono, H., & Hapsari, I. (2023). Does Institutional Ownership Moderate the Relationship Between the Board of Directors and Risk Disclosure? *Jurnal Akademi Akuntansi*, *5*(4), 547-564. https://doi.org/10.22219/jaa.v5i4.23071

Quiros, J. L. G., & de Vera, D. D. P. (2021). Theory of mind: from artificial intelligence to hybrid intelligence. *Techno Review, International Technology, Science and Society Review*, *9*(2), 103-119. https://doi.org/10.37467/gka-revtechno.v9.2816

Safitri, E., Hady, H., & Nalurita, F. (2023). The Effect of Foreign Ownership and Asset Management on Capital Structure in the Manufacturing Sector Listed on the Indonesia Stock Exchange (Idx). *International Journal of Social Science and Human Research*, *6*(6), 3311-3318. https://doi.org/10.47191/ijsshr/v6-i6-13

Sanders, T. (2021). Testing the black box: Institutional investors, Risk disclosure, and ethical AI. *Philosophy & Technology*, *34*(1), 105 - 109. https://doi.org/10.1007/s13347-020-00409-4

Song, J. (2021). Research on the relationship between the ownership structure and business performance of listed Companies. *International Journal of Frontiers in Sociology*, *3*(12), 14-20. https://doi.org/10.25236/IJFS.2021.031203

Song, J., Xie, X., & Ma, L. (2023). SIEGE: A Semantics-Guided Safety Enhancement Framework for AI-Enabled Cyber-Physical Systems. *IEEE Transactions on Software Engineering*, *49*(8), 4058-4080. https://doi.org/10.1109/TSE.2023.3282981

Wang, T., & Yen, J. (2023). Does AI bring value to firms? Value relevance of AI disclosures. *Die Unternehmung*, 77(2), 134-161. https://doi.org/10.5771/0042-059x-2023-2-134

Williams, J., Fiore, S. M., & Jentsch, F. (2022). Supporting artificial social intelligence with theory of mind. Frontier Artificial Intelligence, *5*(750763), 1-12. https://doi.org/10.3389/frai.2022.750763

Winfield, A. F. T. (2018). Experiments in artificial theory of mind: from safety to story-telling. Hypothesis and Theory, *5*(75), 1-13. https://doi.org/10.3389/frobt.2018.00075

Zhang, Y., & Sharon, C. (2023). The Influence of Firm Size and Institutional Environment on ESG Disclosure - Evidence from Listed Companies in China. *International Journal of Academic Research in Economics and Management Sciences, 12*(2), 130-142. https://doi.org/10.6007/ijarems/v12-i2/16284

Zhao, Y., Elahi, E., Khalid, Z., Sun, X., & Sun, F. (2023). Environmental, Social and Governance Performance: Analysis of CEO Power and Corporate Risk. *Sustainability, 15*(2), 1-18. (2023). https://doi.org/10.3390/su15021471

Zouari, G., & Dhifi, K. (2022) The impact of ownership structure on integrated reporting in European firms. *Corporate Communications: An International Journal, 27*(3), 527-542. https://doi.org/10.1108/ccij-05-2021-0057

Developing a Multidimensional Child Well-Being Index for Uzbekistan: An Empirical Analysis

Dildora Karimova, Diydor Berdiklichev, Dostonbek Djalilov

1. Introduction

Child poverty and well-being are inherently multidimensional concepts that extend beyond mere economic parameters to include material, social, physical, and mental aspects of a child's life (Biggeri & Cuesta, 2020; Domínguez-Serrano & Moral-Espín, 2022). Recognizing this complexity, this study is grounded in the principles of the UN Convention on the Rights of the Child, which underscores a comprehensive set of rights and obligations aimed at ensuring the holistic well-being of children (UNICEF, 2004). These principles mandate that governments enforce and protect the rights and freedoms of children, providing a robust framework for assessing child well-being.

Traditional measures of child well-being often rely primarily on family income as an indicator (World Bank, 2017). However, this narrow focus fails to capture the full range of factors that influence a child's quality of life (UNICEF, 2007). To address this gap, our study takes a broader approach by developing the Child Well-Being Index (CWI) for Uzbekistan. This index assesses children's well-being across multiple dimensions, including material well-being, housing, educational opportunities, health, family and peer relationships, behaviours and risks, and children's subjective perceptions of their well-being (Alkire & Foster, 2011). The methodology used in this study is based on the UNICEF and Alkire-Foster frameworks, which are respected for their flexibility and comprehensiveness in assessing multidimensional poverty and well-being (Alkire et al., 2015). Using data from a sociological survey of 2,000 households with children, we developed the CWI to provide a detailed and nuanced picture of child well-being in Uzbekistan. The index consists of seven sub-indices derived from 30 indicators, covering both objective indicators and subjective assessments to provide a holistic assessment.

2. Theoretical Framework and Empirical Studies

2.1 Conceptual Distinctions: Child Poverty vs. Child Well-Being

Recent studies, such as Zwal (2022), highlight the severe deprivation impacting child well-being in Nigeria and emphasize the need for restructuring social policies and service delivery to children. The impact of housing insecurity on child health and well-being is also explored in a systematic review, revealing that forced moves, temporary accommodation, and overcrowding adversely affect children's health (Hock et al., 2023). Additionally, research in South African rural communities examines the emotional well-being of elementary students and critiques deficiencies in government strategies aimed at poverty alleviation (Okoye & Mensah, 2021).

The OECD defines poverty as the ratio of the number of people (in a given age group) whose income falls below the poverty line, which is taken as half the median household income of the total population. This definition primarily focuses on income and conceptualizes poverty as a relative measure (OECD, 2019).

Child well-being also takes into account positive dimensions such as educational achievement, social relationships, and access to cultural and recreational activities (Bradshaw, Hoelscher, & Richardson, 2007). Recent research explores the multidimensional nature of child poverty and well-being, such as the Integrated Child Poverty Framework, which brings together the capabilities, human rights, and basic needs approaches to better understand these dynamics (Biggeri & Cuesta, 2020). In Vietnam, research shows how high household wealth can positively impact all dimensions of child well-being (Ngo et al., 2023).

2.2 Evolution of Indicators: From Negative to Positive

Historically, the assessment of child well-being was heavily focused on negative indicators such as poverty, mortality, malnutrition, and disease prevalence. These metrics were prioritized because they were easily quantifiable and directly aligned with immediate survival needs (UNICEF, 2007; Land, Lamb, & Mustillo, 2001). Early measures of child welfare concentrated on these negative outcomes to identify and address urgent health and safety concerns for children, reflecting a reactive approach to child well-being that was prevalent in public health and policy discussions.

Empirical studies have shown the benefits of incorporating positive indicators in evaluating child well-being. For example, a study conducted by the International Society for Child Indicators found that countries with a balanced approach to well-being measurement tend to have higher overall child satisfaction and development outcomes. Additionally, case studies from countries like Canada and Australia illustrate how positive indicators have informed successful policy innovations aimed at fostering healthy and supportive environments for children (ISCI, 2015).

2.3 Multidimensional Indices and Methodologies

The assessment of child well-being requires a comprehensive approach that goes beyond traditional economic measures. Multidimensional indices have been developed to capture the complex and interconnected aspects of children's lives, providing a more holistic view of their well-being. Unlike single-dimensional measures that focus solely on income or health, multidimensional indices incorporate a variety of dimensions that reflect the diverse experiences and needs of children (Land, Lamb, & Mustillo, 2001; Shoh-Jakhon, K. (2023).

Recent studies have continued to explore multidimensional child well-being across various contexts. For example, Hoang et al. (2023) investigated the roles of household welfare and early childbearing on child well-being in Vietnam, employing multidimensional methods for a comprehensive analysis. In another study, the Russian Child Well-Being Index (CWBI) focuses on both objective and subjective well-being indicators, emphasizing subjective well-being evaluation (Archakova & Garifulina, 2021).

Five dimensions of well-being are often emphasized: physical health, income and wealth, social relationships, absence of depression, and work and leisure time. This structure is highlighted in the Gallup-Healthways Well-Being Index (Gallup & Healthways, 2014). Another study in Central America explores the socioeconomic factors determining multidimensional child poverty groups, focusing on rural areas, indigenous children, young mothers, and low education levels (Guillén-Fernández, 2024).

Furthermore, the development of data dashboards has been seen as a promising approach for presenting a comprehensive view of young people's well-being by categorizing indicators across different domains (Anderson et al., 2023). The independent influence of relationship quality between parents and between parents and children on childhood outcomes has also been examined in a South Korean context, showing significant relationships with child well-being (Jarvis et al., 2020).

Several studies have explored various approaches to measuring multidimensional child well-being in different countries. Researchers such as Dijkstra (2009), Heshmati et al. (2008), and Richardson and Ali (2014) have examined different methodologies and their implications, highlighting the flexibility and applicability of the Alkire-Foster method in diverse contexts. This method is particularly noted for its ability to account for multiple dimensions relevant to children's lives, offering a comprehensive assessment beyond conventional economic indicators. By adjusting thresholds and weights according to local conditions, the Alkire-Foster method allows for a nuanced understanding of community and household needs, thus addressing specific issues that affect children's well-being.

The resulting Child Well-Being Index (CWI) for Uzbekistan serves as a valuable tool for identifying areas for policy intervention and improving the overall quality of life for children. It underscores the importance of integrating both objective and subjective measures to provide a holistic view that informs effective policy interventions. By contributing to the global discourse on child well-being, the application of the Alkire-Foster method in Uzbekistan demonstrates its potential to address regional and national challenges.

3. Methodology

This study employs a multidimensional approach to assess child well-being in Uzbekistan, drawing on methodologies from UNICEF and the Alkire-Foster framework for calculating integral indices. The study's aim is to create a comprehensive Child Well-Being Index (CWI) that reflects the diverse aspects of children's lives across the country. The methodology was implemented as follows:

3.1. Selection of Components and Indicators

We selected seven components and 30 indicators based on several principles. First, we considered the principles of the Convention on the Rights of the Child, which was ratified by the Republic of Uzbekistan in 1992, reflecting the country's commitment to child well-being in all spheres of life. Second, we incorporated international experiences in assessing multidimensional child well-being (see Annex 1). Third, we utilized available national statistics and microdata from the 2022 Multiple Indicator Cluster Survey (MICS), household budget surveys (HBS), and the International Program for the Assessment of Student Achievement (PISA), among others. The Child Well-Being Index was formed using data from interviews conducted with 2,000 households with children. The selection of components, including Material Well-being, Housing Conditions, Educational Opportunities, Health and Safety, Family and Peer Relations, Behavior and Risk, and Subjective Well-Being, was guided by their relevance to the socio-economic context of Uzbekistan and their importance in capturing the multidimensional nature of child well-being.

3.2. Determination of Threshold Values and Weights

Experts determined the threshold values and weights for each of the seven components and 30 indicators. We then created a matrix of achievements with a binary structure, assigning a value of 1 for achievements and 0 for the absence of achievements. For instance, consider the following hypothetical example (See table 1).

Table 1. Determination of Threshold Values

	Indicator 1	Indicator 2	Indicator 3
Household 1	34	3.2	1200
Household 2	25	3.5	2300
Household 3	20	1.7	2200
Household 4	37	2.6	1600
Household 5	40	4.0	2400
Household 6	19	2.2	2100

Source: Developed by authors.

The threshold values for each indicator were set as follows: Indicator 1 - 30, Indicator 2 - 3, Indicator 3 - 2000.

3.3. Weighting of Indicators

The indicators were equally weighted within the index, with each component receiving a weight of 1/3 in this example. Applying these weights to the achievement matrix gives the following weighted achievement matrix (See table 2).

Table 2. Weighting of Indicators

	Indicator 1	Indicator 2	Indicator 3	Achievement Share
Household 1	1/3	1/3	0	2/3
Household 2	0	1/3	1/3	2/3
Household 3	0	0	1/3	1/3
Household 4	1/3	0	0	1/3
Household 5	1/3	1/3	1/3	1
Household 6	0	0	1/3	1/3

Source: Developed by authors.

The total proportion of achievement within households was then calculated by summing all indicators of the weighted achievement matrix.

3.4. Setting the Well-Being Threshold

The threshold level for well-being was set at two-thirds (2/3), and we determined the percentage of children (H) categorized as well-off (See table 3).

Table 3. Setting the Well-Being Threshold

	Indicator 1	Indicator 2	Indicator 3	Achievement Share	Well-being
Household 1	1/3	1/3	0	2/3	1
Household 2	0	1/3	1/3	2/3	1
Household 3	0	0	1/3	1/3	0
Household 4	1/3	0	0	1/3	0
Household 5	1/3	1/3	1/3	1	1
Household 6	0	0	1/3	1/3	0

Source: Developed by authors.

In this example, 50% of the children (H = 1/2) are classified within the advantaged category.

Step 5: Determining the Intensity of Well-Being

The well-being intensity coefficient (A) reflects the depth of well-being and is calculated as follows:

$$A = \frac{\frac{2}{3} + \frac{2}{3} + 1}{3} = \frac{7}{9} \quad (1)$$

Step 6: Calculating the Child Well-Being Index (CWI)
The Child Well-Being Index is calculated by multiplying the Child Headcount Ratio (H) by the Well-Being Intensity Coefficient (A):

$$CWI = H \times A = \frac{1}{2} \times \frac{7}{9} = \frac{7}{18} \quad (2)$$

Using this methodology, the Uzbekistan Child Well-Being Index (UCWI) has been calculated to provide a comprehensive assessment of child well-being across the country. This integral index encompasses a broad spectrum of factors that are pertinent to child well-being, ensuring a multidimensional approach to understanding children's lives. Seven key components have been selected to capture the various dimensions of well-being: Material Well-being (MW), Housing Conditions (HC), Educational Opportunities (EO), Health and Safety (HS), Family and Peer Relations (FPR), Behavior and Risk (BR), and Subjective Well-Being (SW). Each of these components is disaggregated into specific indicators, totaling 30, which have been carefully selected to reflect the diverse aspects of children's well-being. The indicators are weighted to ensure a fair allocation of importance across the respective components, as detailed in Appendix 1. This weighting distribution is designed to provide an equitable evaluation of each aspect of well-being, aligning with international standards and best practices in child welfare assessment. By incorporating these components and indicators, the UCWI offers a nuanced and robust measurement of child well-being, guiding targeted interventions and informing policy development aimed at improving the quality of life for children in Uzbekistan.

4. Results

The Child Well-Being Index (CWI) for Uzbekistan provides a thorough assessment of children's well-being across the country and its respective regions, looking closely at seven key dimensions: material circumstances, living conditions, educational opportunities, health and safety, family and peer relationships, behavioral risks, and children's subjective assessments of their well-being. The index operates on a continuum from 0 to 1, where a score of 0 represents the minimum level of well-being and a score of 1 represents the optimal level of well-being. The overall integrated CWI for Uzbekistan is fixed at 0.440, reflecting the spectrum of well-being across different components. Each component is assigned the following scores: Material Well-Being (MW) - 0.361, Housing Conditions (HC) - 0.364, Educational Opportunities (EO) - 0.291, Health and Safety (HS) - 0.898, Family and Peer Relationships (FPR) - 0.559, Behavioural Risks (BR) - 0.588 and Subjective Well-Being (SW) - 0.647.

The results show marked inequalities between the components of child well-being. The lowest scores are recorded in Educational Opportunities, Material Well-Being and Housing Conditions, indicating significant barriers to children's development and implying the need for targeted interventions. A score of 0.291 for Educational Opportunities indicates limited access to quality education, highlighting the need to improve educational infrastructure and resources to improve learning outcomes. Material well-being and housing conditions, with scores of 0.361 and 0.364 respectively, highlight the economic adversities faced by households, including insufficient income and inadequate living conditions. Addressing these challenges requires comprehensive socio-economic policies aimed at raising living standards and expanding financial assistance to families. In contrast, the Health and Safety component achieves the highest score of 0.898, suggesting effective access to health and safety protocols for children. The relatively high score of 0.647 for Subjective Well-being indicates that children generally assess their well-being positively, despite the objective challenges they face.

Regional analysis using Sturges' formula groups Uzbekistan's regions into five categories based on their child well-being index scores. Group 1, which includes Navoi Province and Tashkent City, shows the highest indicators of child well-being due to better access to resources and services. Group 2 comprises Samarkand, Khorezm, Fergana, and Andijan Provinces, reflecting above-average well-being scores. Group 3 includes Jizzak and Tashkent regions with average scores, while Group 4, consisting of Bukhara, Namangan, and Surkhandarya regions, shows below-average scores. Group 5, encompassing Kashkadarya and Syrdarya oblasts and the Republic of Karakalpakstan, records the lowest index scores, indicating severe challenges that require focused policy interventions to address deficits in resources and services.

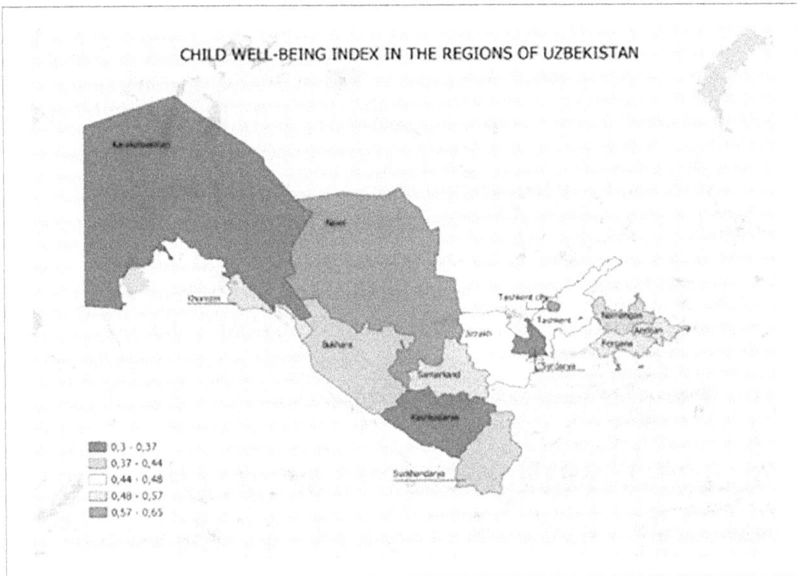

Figure 1. Child well-being index in the regions of Uzbekistan
Source: Developed by authors.

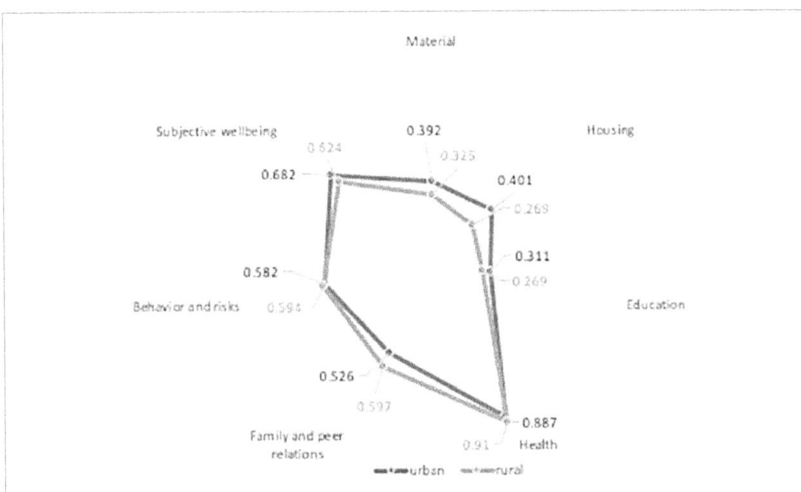

Figure 2. Child well-being index: urban vs. rural area
Source: Developed by authors.

The Composite Well-being Index (CWI) indicates that the aggregate well-being of children residing in urban environments (0.454) surpasses that of their rural counterparts (0.447) by a marginal margin. Although this disparity does not achieve statistical significance at the integral level, it is evident that variances are present within specific components of well-being. In urban locales, children benefit from superior material conditions, enhanced housing situations, and improved educational opportunities, attributable to superior access to infrastructure and resources. In contrast, children living in rural regions often enjoy more robust familial and peer relationships, diminished behavioral risks, and a more favorable subjective evaluation of their own well-being, which likely arises from the cohesion of their communities and the presence of supportive social frameworks.

5. Discussion and Policy Implications

The examination of the Child Well-Being Index (CWI) for Uzbekistan, which categorizes regions based on an aggregate index, sub-indices, and specific metrics, indicates considerable regional inequalities in child well-being. The regions positioned at 12th, 13th, and 14th places, specifically the Republic of Karakalpakstan, Syrdarya Province, and Kashkadarya Province, are recognized as being at substantial risk. These areas encounter a variety of disadvantages that adversely affect their standings on the index. Kashkadarya Province, which occupies the 14th rank, confronts severe obstacles associated with material hardships, substandard housing conditions, and restricted educational opportunities. These elements collectively jeopardize the well-being and developmental trajectory of children within the region. To effectively tackle the risk factors impacting children's well-being in Kashkadarya Province, it is imperative to formulate a comprehensive regional initiative aimed at alleviating these challenges. This initiative ought to incorporate targeted strategies to augment family income, bolster social protections for economically disadvantaged households, and ameliorate housing conditions. The expansion of educational opportunities is vital, as it has a direct bearing on the future prospects and overall well-being of children. Furthermore, health initiatives concentrated on maternal and child health should be prioritized to guarantee that essential health requirements are fulfilled. Fortifying the family unit through community-based support programs can further enhance the resilience of families, thereby fostering a nurturing environment for children to flourish.

6. Conclusion

In world practice, child well-being is comprehensively monitored across several parameters, with the main ones being material well-being, health, education, and behavioral risks. The United Nations Children's Fund (UNICEF), together with other international organizations, conducts periodic monitoring of child well-being. Based on the results of comparing the living conditions of children in different countries, WHO and UNICEF have ranked the Global Child Prosperity Index among 180 countries. This ranking is based on the parameters of the Sustainable Development Goal targets, such as poverty level, child and maternal mortality, child immunization, and environmental conditions. According to this ranking, children and adolescents have the most favorable living conditions and the greatest chances to prosper in Northern Europe, South Korea, and Japan. Uzbekistan is ranked 71st out of 180 countries and is correlated with countries that have a satisfactory assessment of the situation of children. The Child Well-Being Index developed by the authors, with a value of 0.440, is characterized as an average level of child well-being, which confirms the results of the Global Child Prosperity Index.

Acknowledgements

This publication has been produced within the framework of the Grant «Development of Child Wellbeing Index in Uzbekistan» (REP-1/11 10.08.2022), funded under the MUNIS Project, supported by the World Bank and the Government of the Republic of Uzbekistan. The statements do not necessarily reflect the official position of the World Bank and the Government of the Republic of Uzbekistan.

References

Alkire, S., & Foster, J. E. (2011). Counting and multidimensional poverty measurement. Journal of Public Economics, 95(7-8), 476-487. https://doi.org/10.1016/j.jpubeco.2010.11.006

Alkire, S., Foster, J., Seth, S., Santos, M. E., Roche, J. M., & Ballon, P. (2015). Multidimensional poverty measurement and analysis. Oxford University Press. https://doi.org/10.1093/acprof/9780198748597.001.0001

Archakova, T., & Garifulina, E. S. (2021). Review of contributions to the Russian Child Well-Being Index: Focus on subjective well-being indicators. Psychology in Russia: State of the Art, 14(3), 200-216. https://doi.org/10.11621/pir.2021.0313

Anderson, N. W., Russ, S. A., Eisenberg, D., & Halfon, N. (2023). Dashboards as mechanisms for community empowerment: Developing a prototype for child and adolescent well-being in California. Journal of Public Health Management and Practice, 29(4), 314-323. https://doi.org/10.1097/PHH.0000000000001746

Biggeri, M., & Cuesta, J. (2020). An integrated framework for child poverty and well-being measurement: Reconciling theories. Child Indicators Research, 13(4), 1107-1130. https://doi.org/10.1007/S12187-020-09774-0

Dijkstra, T. (2009). Measurement of well-being and quality of life in the European Union. Social Indicators Research, 91(3), 371-387. https://doi.org/10.1007/s11205-008-9301-2

Domínguez-Serrano, M., & Moral-Espín, L. (2022). The capability approach and child well-being: A systematic literature review. Child Indicators Research, 15(4), 1249-1275. https://doi.org/10.1007/s12187-022-09953-1

Gallup Inc., & Healthways Inc. (2014). State of global well-being. Results of the Gallup-Healthways Global well-being index.

Guillén-Fernández, Y. B. (2024). Socioeconomic factors determining multidimensional child poverty groups in Central America: A measurement proposal from the well-being approach using a comprehensive set of children's rights. Child Indicators Research, 17(4), 985-1004. https://doi.org/10.1007/s12187-024-10148-z

Hoang, H. T., Ngo, P. T. X., Nguyen, L. T., Le, Y. T. B., Tran, C. K., & Le, P. T. (2023). Child well-being in Vietnam: The roles of household welfare and early childbearing. Journal of Social Economics Research, 10(4), 355-371. https://doi.org/10.18488/35.v10i4.3556

Heshmati, A., Bajalan, C. S., & Tausch, A. (2008). Measurement and analysis of child well-being in middle and high-income countries. European Journal of Comparative Economics, 5(2), 187-249. https://doi.org/10.2139/ssrn.1078897

Hock, E., Blank, L., Fairbrother, H., Clowes, M., Castelblanco Cuevas, D., Booth, A., & Goyder, E. (2023). Exploring the impact of housing insecurity on the health and well-being of children and young people: A systematic review. Health and Social Care Delivery Research, 11(12). https://doi.org/10.3310/twwl4501

International Society for Child Indicators (ISCI). (2015). Measuring and Monitoring Child Well-being: Beyond Survival. ISCI.

Jarvis, J. A., Gibby, A., Dufur, M. J., & Pribesh, S. L. (2020). Family structure and child well-being in a non-western context: The role of parent–child relations and parental conflict in South Korea. Population Research and Policy Review, 39(2), 263-289. https://doi.org/10.1007/s11113-020-09586-8Land, K. C., Lamb, V. L., Meadows, S. O., & Taylor, A. (2007). Measuring trends in child wellbeing: An evidence-based approach. Social Indicators Research, 80, 105–132.

Shoh-Jakhon, K. (2023). Theoretical and Methodological Aspects of Intensive Economic Growth in Ensuring Sustainable Economic Development. Social and Economic Studies within the Framework of Emerging Global Developments, 3, 283.

Ngo, T. X. B., Le, T. B. Y., Le, T. P., Tran, K. C., & Nguyen, T. L. (2023). The role of household welfare on child well-being in Vietnam. Research Review International Journal of Multidisciplinary, 8(2). https://doi.org/10.31305/rrijm.2023.v08.n02.011

OECD. (2019). Poverty rate (indicator), August 17. https://doi.org/10.1787/0fe1315d-en

Okoye, F., & Mensah, P. A. (2021). Child poverty and food scheme in rural South African schools: The prospects and limits towards improving the emotional well-being of the elementary school students. International Journal of Scientific Research and Management, 9(8), EL-2021. https://doi.org/10.18535/ijsrm/v9i08.el02

Richardson, D., & Ali, N. (2014). An Evaluation of International Surveys of Children. OECD Social Employment and Migration Working Papers, No. 146, OECD Publishing.

UNICEF. (2004). State of the World's Children 2005 – Children Under Threat. New York: UNICEF.

UNICEF. (2007). Child Poverty in Perspective: An Overview of Child Well-being in Rich Countries. Innocenti Report Card 7. UNICEF Innocenti Research Centre, Florence.

World Bank. (2017). Monitoring Global Poverty: Report of the Commission on Global Poverty. Washington, DC: World Bank. https://openknowledge.worldbank.org/handle/10986/25141

Zwal, U. I. (2022). The implication of child poverty to the economy of Nigeria. International Journal of Business and Finance Research, 8(2), 92-101. https://doi.org/10.56201/ijbfr.v8.no2.2022.pg92.101

Appendix 1. Dimensions, components, indicators and wellbeing cut-offs

	Dimensions	Components	Indicators	Wellbeing cut off	Weight
Child Wellbeing Index	Material Well-being 1/7	Absolute income poverty	Per capita income of the household	Above the minimum consumption expenditure	1/28
		Households without job	Number of employed household members	>0	1/28
		Reported deprivation	Educational resources (computer, table, text-books, uniform, sport-wear&-shoes, school bag, table lamp)	At least 6	1/28
			Number of books (non-textbooks)	At least 10	1/28
	Housing Conditions 1/7	Overcrowd-ing	Number of people per bedroom	1 room per person	1/35
		Housing problems	Quality of the ceiling, floor, wall and windows of the house	No leakage or damage of ceiling, floor, wall or windows of the house	1/35
			Separate room for kids for studying	Exists	1/35
			Shower/bath	Existence of shower or bath inside the house	1/35
			Type of the toilet	Flushing toilet or ventilated pit latrine	1/35
	Educational opportuni-ties 1/7	Family education	Number of household members who has higher education degree	At least 1	1/49
		Knowledge	Math	Getting 4 out of 5 correct	1/49
			Reading	Reads without difficulties	1/49
			Russian	Reads without difficulties	1/49
			English	Reads without difficulties	1/49
		Attendance	Attendance to school	Never missed the class last month	1/49
			Kindergarten	The child goes the kindergarten	1/49
	Health and safety 1/7	Immuniza-tion	Vaccine against Measles, Mumps, & Rubella	The child is vaccinated against all of them	1/28
		Infant mor-tality	Infant mortality	There was no infant mortality case in the house	1/28
		Low birth weight	Low birth weight	There was no low birth weight (birth weight<2.5kg) case in the house	1/28
		Death from accident, injuries or suicide	Accident, sickness or suicide death among children	There was no accident, sickness related death or suicide among children	1/28

Appendix 1. *Continued*

Dimensions	Components	Indicators	Wellbeing cut off	Weight
Family and peer relations 1/7	Family structure	Family structure (nuclear family)	The child is in nuclear family (both parents exist)	1/21
	Family relations	Family relations	Both parents spends at least 6 days with their kid for eating together and talking to them, the kid thinks parents are ready to help anytime, the kid does not argue with parents often, the kid thinks both parents pay enough attention and the kid believes s/he can discuss her/his problems with parents T19>=6, T20>=6, T21>=6, T22>=6, T24=1, T25=2, T26=1, T27=1, T28=1	1/21
	Peer relations	Relationship among schoolmates and at the neighborhood	The child has the person outside the family as a friend whom s/he can get help from T29=1& T30=1& T31=1& T32=1& T31=2	1/21
Behavior and risks 1/7	Health behaviors	The child eats breakfast every day, eats fruit every day, eats meat every day, exercises everyday	The child eats breakfast every day (A28), eats fruit every day (A29), eats meat every day (A30), exercises at least 3 times a week (T34) A28=1& A29=1& A30=3& A34>=3	1/21
	Risk behaviors	Smoking, alcohol and HIV knowledge	Does not smoke, does not drink, and knows about the HIV T35A=1& T35B=1& T35C1	1/21
	Violence	Fighting, bullying, domestic violence	Does not fight, no bullying and no domestic violence T36=2& T37=2& T38=2& T40=2	1/21
Subjective well-being 1/7	Life satisfaction scale	Cantril ladder	Life satisfaction 8 or more T45>=8	1/28
	School-life satisfaction	Attitude to school	Likes the school	1/28
	Personal wellbeing	Personal questions about health, stranger, lonely, happy in family, happy in friendship, happy in neighborhood	T41=1& T46=2& T47=2& T48=1& T49=1& T50=1	1/28
	Subjective poverty	Subjective poverty	Both the child and parents think they are middle income or rich family T51=1 OR T51=2	1/28

Knowledge Management Sustainability in European University Alliances: The KreativEU Perspective

Margarita Bogdanova, Evelina Parashkevova,
Marusya Smokova, Mariela Stoyanova

1. Introduction

With the launch of the European Universities Initiative in 2019, universities, as key participants in the innovation process, were given the opportunity to unite in strategic alliances. This encouraged them to work toward overcoming their differences and developing common solutions to harmonize their management systems. In the long term, they involve developing a comprehensive strategy for sustainable management to achieve the alliance's objectives, generally aimed at improving the quality of joint education and research, fostering innovation, and enhancing staff competencies. Achieving these goals necessitates creation of a shared system for sustainable knowledge management (KM).

The paper reviews the literature on KM in the context of university alliances and presents a case study of the KreativeEU alliance, with which the authors are familiar. The authors propose a model for the KM process in university alliance and highlight potential risks associated with the expected network dynamics of the alliance.

Given the interdisciplinary nature of knowledge, as well as the different goals of its management, the paper focuses specifically on challenges related to collaborative learning within a network. Addressing these challenges requires thorough preliminary analysis and planning of KM processes. Such efforts help reduce uncertainty, enhance transparency and trust among partners, and foster an environment conducive to the sustainable development of the alliance.

2. Literature Review: Locating the research in current academic debates

Knowledge management in networks is a field that explores how organizations and their partners create, share, store, and utilize knowledge to achieve common goals (Tang et al., 2020). It is crucial in contexts such as university alliances, international consortia, and industrial partnerships, where participants are often geographically dispersed and culturally diverse, yet united in their aim to grow and innovate through knowledge (Lam et al., 2021) (Asiedu et al., 2022).

Among the key challenges facing such complex partnerships are: 1) Variations in university cultures and procedures, which hinder standardization, obstruct knowledge sharing, and reduce synergy among partners (Al-Kurdi et al., 2018); 2) Ambiguous or fragmented leadership structures, which complicate decision-making processes and cause delays (Gunn, A., 2020); 3) Disparities in knowledge management technologies within the alliances, making the integration of shared data for collaborative research challenging (Vaio et al., 2021); Overlooking informal learning opportunities within the network (Dabbagh & Kitsantas, 2012). Going beyond operational influencing factors, other researchers focus on the lack of a clear strategic vision, limited stakeholder participation (Camarinha-Matos & Boucher, 2012) or lack of coordination between partners (Rensimer & Brooks, 2024) regarding the effective allocation of resources and information, which leads to duplication of efforts and lower results.

European policy recognizes the positive role of alliances in higher education by encouraging the creation and development of European University Alliances. (European Commission, 2020). The initiative is defined as paving the way for the future of higher education in the European Union. The prospects for these forms of cooperation are in removing administrative barriers between Member States, developing sustainable and funding mechanisms and building a new framework for the governance of higher education in the EU (Charret, A., Chankseliani, M., 2022), expanding the agenda and scope of interventions (Vukasovic & Stensaker, 2018). This in turn can have a beneficial impact on KM between the organizations participating in an alliance. Learning and innovation are key reasons why many universities decide to enter into alliances (Maassen et al., 2023). This also raises questions such as how university alliances can organize and use their work and activities in ways that facilitate knowledge transfer, learning and innovation within the partnership.

3. Research Methodology

The specificity of the chosen topic and its limited development in both theory and practice prompted the authors to adopt a research approach known as bricolage theory.

Bricolage is a pragmatic approach to innovation research that relies on interdisciplinary qualitative methodologies and can be applied to a wide range of phenomena (Mäkelä, 2023). This approach has previously been utilized in the study of university alliances (Charret, A., Chankseliani, M., 2022).

The concept of European university alliances (EUAs) is relatively new and knowledge about their management processes is still limited. The application of the bricolage method provides an appropriate framework for capturing the interdisciplinary nature of KM within this novel and previously unexplored educational structure.

The authors' perspective has been developed specifically within such an environment, combining the case study method with the conceptual design approach to present a model for the knowledge management process in a university network. The case of one of the newly established EU alliances – the KreativEU Alliance – is described. Based on the specific characteristics of the participating universities and the goals of the alliance, a model of the knowledge management process is developed, and some potential risks associated with the expected network dynamics of the alliance are identified.

The model, created using academic bricolage as a methodologically innovative approach, is critically analyzed through the lens of the participants' accumulated understanding to date. It is considered a foundational step toward developing a comprehensive knowledge management system for the consortium.

4. Description of the KreativEU alliance

The KreativEU alliance is among the 64 consortia in Europe that have received financial support from the European Commission (EC) to build their EUAs. The KreativEU alliance aims at establishing a fully European University that puts the creative potential derived from Europe's cultural heritage at the heart of its teaching, research, and knowledge transfer activities. The consortium is unique of its kind, delivering a competitive and attractive European education and research system with students, scholars, and society at large, collaborating within different cultures, languages, across borders, and disciplines (IPT, February 2024, p. 6).

The KreativEU alliance includes internal and external collaborative innovation networks composed of 100 actors in total. The internal network of the KreativEU alliance is made up of 11 participating HEIs (a.k.a. 'the pioneers') originating from 10 Member States and 1 associated country geographically spread in all 4 European regions (Figure 1). The external network of the alliance includes 89 associated partners (a.k.a. 'the associates') that contributed to the development of the consortium, varying from HEIs, local, regional, and national public bodies, non-governmental organizations, foundations, small and medium-sized enterprises, and student associations. The large number and variety of 'the associates' will make it challenging for 'the pioneers' to involve them in alliance life and engage them to contribute to alliance activities.

Figure 1. Geographical composition of the KreativEU alliance
Source: Authors' calculation

Recently, research on EUAs formation (Lambrechts, Cavallaro, & Lepori, 2024, p. 1241) has found that the majority of EUAs are principally formed between similar HEIs with pre-existing ties created through long-standing cooperation. The KreativEU alliance is formed based on a mix of mechanisms: attribute-based homophily (relative similarity in some of the attributes), resource-based heterophily (partners with complementary capabilities and assets), and pre-existence of trust-based ties between the partners.

Looking at the composition of the KreativEU alliance in terms of the age and size of the constituent entities, the consortium embraces primarily middle-sized (91%) HEIs located in historical cities. The number of enrolled students in 2023 for almost all partners ranges between 2,500 and 10,000, being closer to the lower boundary of the class interval. Only one of the partners is large, with slightly more than 10,000 enrolled students. The alliance is composed only of public HEIs and is dominated by the mature HEIs (55%) over the old (27%), middle-aged (9%), and young universities (9%). Three of the members are among the oldest universities in Europe.

Cultural characteristics affect the relationship between the partners (Pinheiro R. , Gänzle, Klenk, & Trondal, 2023, p. 214), knowledge management, and the persistence of university alliances (Maassen et al, p. 959). The KreativEU alliance is composed of countries that originate from 5 cultural groups and is dominated by the Slavic and Roman cultural groups (Figure 2).

Although the alliance is highly specialized and has a strong subject orientation on cultural heritage, in terms of the disciplinary scope of the educational activities of the partners (Figure 2), most of the members (73%) are broad HEIs, which deliver programmes in the range between 5 and 7 fields of study.

Previous collaborations, knowledge of each other, and exciting trust among the members of the alliance are recognized as distinguishing features that might create strong ties between the partners and allow for new knowledge to be created through inter-cohesion (Maassen, Stensaker, & Ross, 2023, p. 958) (Pinheiro R. , Gänzle, Klenk, & Trondal, 2023). A survey conducted among the KreativEU members shows that all partners have entered the consortium cooperating with almost one other partner. Although there was no exhaustive collaboration between all partners at the stage of entering the alliance, shared vision and specific subject orientation on cultural heritage triggered active collaboration in education, research, and mobilities in 2022-2024. Joint work and implementation of Erasmus projects, co-ordination of blended intensive programmes, co-authorship of various research materials, co-organization of scientific events, student and staff exchange are among the activities the partners did together to build trust and mutual respect.

Organizational coordination is among the key dimensions impacting university alliances (Maassen, Stensaker, & Ross, 2023, p. 958). To ensure

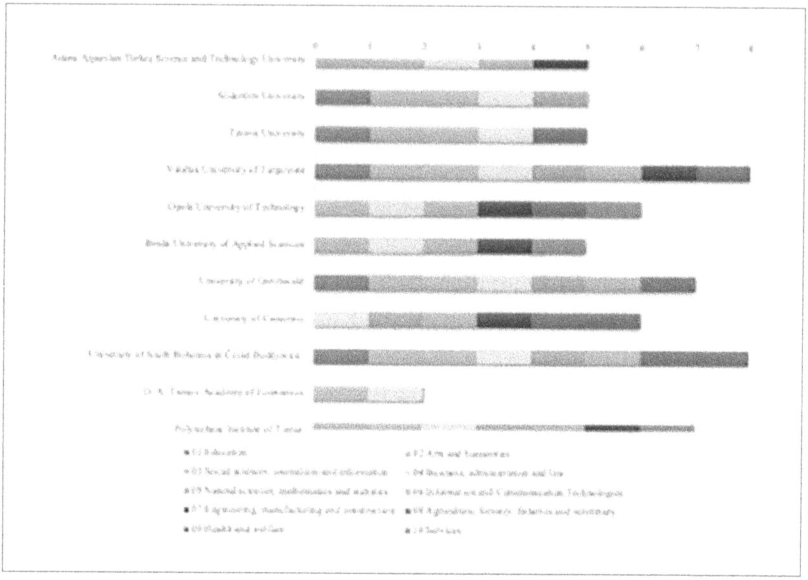

Figure 2. Number of fields of study of the participating HEIs in the KreativEU alliance
Source: KreativEU database; Authors' calculation

transparency and inclusiveness in decision-making and KM, the KreativEU alliance is intended to function as a three-level governance system (Figure 3). The first level, 'Network governance', is focused on the general management of the consortium as a whole and representation in EU governing bodies and international or European organizations. The second level, 'Project governance', highlights the management of the project, its supervision, and control. The last third level, 'Activity governance,' is focused on project activities. It encompasses the supervision and coordination of all functional, non-governance work package teams that are responsible for completing project deliverables and expected results.

The existence and type of practice for solving conflicts between the consortium members is a mechanism for securing the persistence of the alliance (Maassen, Stensaker, & Ross, 2023, p. 958) and KM. Although in defining the status of the members of the governing bodies of the KreativEU alliance, the descriptors 'voting' and 'non-voting' are used, prior experience and collaboration on project proposal writing, implementation of project

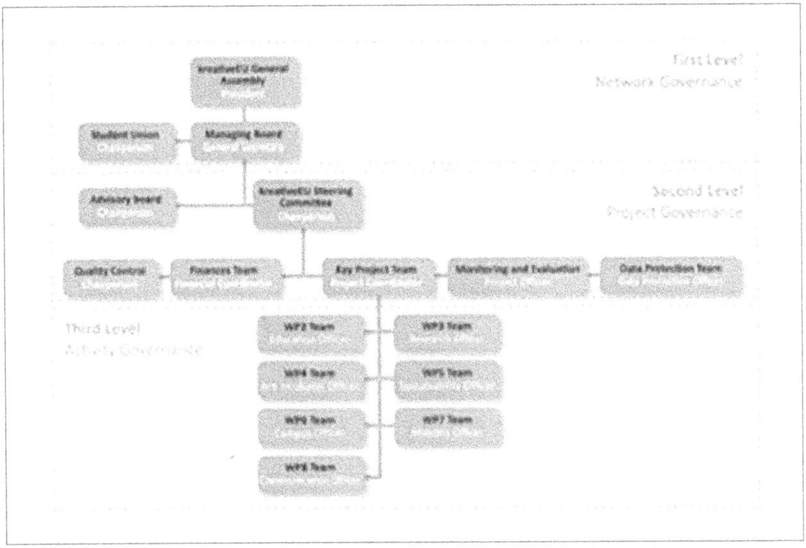

Figure 3. Governance of the KreativEU alliance
Source: (IPT, February 2024, p. 33)

activities, and competing of project deliverables indicate a preference of the partners towards the consensus-oriented mechanism. All work packages have coordinators, but they do not play a managerial role, and all partners are collectively involved in the work package implementation. Consensus-oriented conflict resolution mechanism takes more time to reach a decision, but it could strengthen the cultural bond and trust between the consortium members (Maassen, Stensaker, & Ross, 2023, p. 459).

Although the KreativEU alliance has all the necessary prerequisites to be successful and persist over time, the lifespan of the consortium and its potential to deliver new knowledge will also depend on the type of knowledge the alliance possesses and the way the knowledge within the alliance is shared.

5. Knowledge Management Process in a University Network – Conceptual Model

The proposed knowledge management process model has been designed taking into account the specifics of the relationships in the KreativEU alliance and its strategic objectives. The alliance is built upon a foundation of trust-based relationships among the partners, which initially stem from informal connections. Over time, these informal ties evolve, gain stability, and are gradually complemented by formal relationships, often shaped by collaborative opportunities arising from public policies in the European educational space.

The general understanding of the participating universities in KreativEU is that the synchronization of workflows between participants in a formal network is a continuous process, which aims to ensure effective and efficient, sustainable functioning over time. Challenges in network cooperation in KM are related to building strong connections between the individual stages, extracting lessons learned from each university participating in the network and integrating them into a shared knowledge management system.

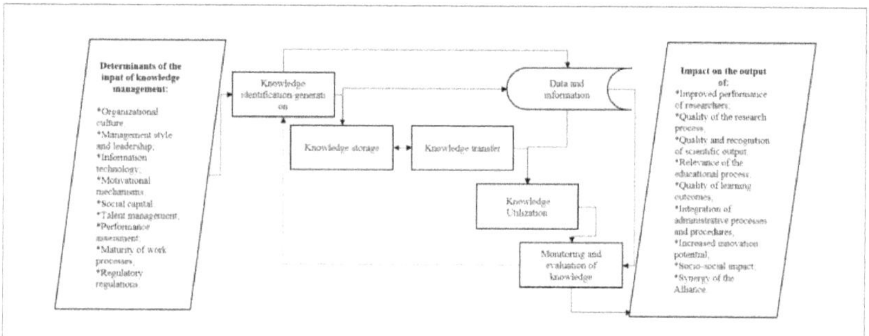

Figure 4. Model of a knowledge management process in a university network
Source: Authors' elaboration

In the model (Figure 4), five basic sub-processes of KM are distinguished: generation, storage, transfer, utiltsation and evaluation. These stages are also identified within the framework of KreativEU, without clear boundaries being set between them, since the flows of knowledge are continuous. The generation of new knowledge is often provoked by environmental determinants, such as competition, new user requirements, technological progress, regulatory changes, public policies, etc. (Maassen et al, 2023).

In established knowledge management practices, the effectiveness of sub-processes depends on factors such as organizational culture, leadership style, technological infrastructure, motivation mechanisms for staff, investments in social capital, talent management, performance assessment, process maturity, and regulatory frameworks. While not exhaustive, these determinants are critical in creating an adaptable knowledge management system for the universities in the alliance.

The expected outcomes of such a system align with the vision for KreativEU's sustainable operation in areas such as education, research, social engagement, innovation, and synergy.

A key step in knowledge identification is determining knowledge needs, inventorying available knowledge, and creating a knowledge map for the alliance. This is a challenge due to the heterogeneity of the network, comprising universities of varying scale and academic focus. Developing a knowledge map that integrates both explicit and tacit knowledge (Nonaka & Takeuchi, 1995) is a strategic priority for the Alliance.

Knowledge storage must be organized for accessibility based on hierarchical authority levels. Additionally, scientific knowledge should be legally protected from the outset. Therefore, defining access rights and methods is crucial for mid-level management within the Alliance.

Knowledge sharing is vital (Jiang & Li, 2009), particularly in organizations with diverse cultural identities and experiences, such as KreativEU. Identifying tools to enhance internal knowledge exchange and transfer to external stakeholders is a strategic priority for educational institutions. The alliance's success will largely depend on the value it delivers to students, researchers, and partners.

The application of knowledge within the consortium forms the basis of the Alliance's competitive advantage. A shared understanding of how to apply accumulated knowledge is key to effective cooperation. Furthermore, the use of knowledge by external stakeholders aligns with both the alliance's objectives and EEA development policies. Therefore, establishing a common mechanism for applying existing and new knowledge within the consortium is essential.

Knowledge assessment should be a permanent process, as the dynamics and scale imply a turbo-fluid variability of its boundaries. The pursuit of a continuous process of KM should be embedded in the agenda of KreativEU, which would ensure synergy and reduce the risk to the alliance's initiatives.

As the university network matures, the knowledge management system should function to support researchers and administrative staff with minimal administrative burden. This is possible if the overall organizational structure of the alliance is designed to ensure KM, both at the strategic level and in individual functional areas.

6. Findings and Discussion

Knowledge and creativity are core values of KreativEU, reflected in its name and strategic goals of generating, sharing, and transferring knowledge. Given its focus on cultural heritage, the alliance aims to engage stakeholders and drive positive transformation at local, regional, and global levels.

The alliance's goals align with its strategic intentions for sustainable knowledge management, as outlined in official documents.

Operationally, the contract includes activities for joint research in interdisciplinary teams. Digital platforms will facilitate knowledge transfer, with plans for a shared digital repository, security measures, interoperability standards, knowledge-sharing events, common platforms, and curriculum integration.

Several additional suggestions could further support the sub-processes and improve outcomes.

1) Active stakeholder input (internal and external). Mechanisms for such communication are foreseen in the work packages, but it is important that they are carried out in the context of a bricolage approach, with stakeholders bringing their prior knowledge and interpreting it in a new constellation. (Matthews, 2019).

2) An agile approach to building structures and operational models can be applied incrementally, with artifacts developed, tested, and implemented after reaching consensus. Success in document development during the alliance's preparatory phase shows both capacity differences and a willingness to overcome them.

3) Creating a supportive environment for informal learning, informal contacts and creation of learning communities; supporting accessibility to knowledge, through mentoring, for example, of representatives of associated partners, etc.

In methodological terms, the theory of bricolage is a useful ad-hoc tool for discussing knowledge management processes in the alliance. The presented model is the first step of a longer process of detailing the five basic sub-processes and ensuring the conditions for their optimal implementation.

7. Conclusion

This paper presents a case study of one of the newly established university alliances – KreativEU alliance. A conceptual model has been developed that describes a knowledge management process and the five related sub-processes. Some of the likely risks associated with the expected network dynamics of the alliance have been highlighted. Since the alliance is in the process of being launched, and there are no real results to be critically assessed, an ad-hoc assessment of the attitudes towards the implementation of knowledge management processes has been made. The analysis shows a high degree of strategic readiness, demonstrated in the contract and in the preliminary agreement in the consortium. With a view to improving the knowledge management process, proposals have been made that concern the role of the active contribution of stakeholders - internal and external, the application of an agile approach in building different structures and operational models, and the mastery of informal learning processes, which can have a complementary effect on the overall knowledge management process in the alliance.

The authors argue that alliance building faces many challenges to collaborative learning. Overcoming these barriers requires a sustainable model of KM, creating an environment for more efficient generation and sharing of new knowledge.

The model, created using academic bricolage as a methodologically innovative approach, is critically analyzed through the lens of the participants' accumulated understanding to date. It is considered a foundational step toward developing a comprehensive knowledge management system for the consortium.

Funding: This research was supported by Project № КП-06-Н65/10 of 12.12.2022 "Formal and informal innovation networks", funded by The National Science Fund at the Bulgarian Ministry of Education and Science

References

Al-Kurdi, O., El-Haddadeh, R., & Eldabi, T. (2018). Knowledge sharing in higher educationinstitutions: a systematic review. *Journal of Enterprise Information Management, Vol. 31 Issue: 2*, 226-246. doi:DOI:10.1108/JEIM-09-2017-0129

Asiedu, N., Abah , M., & Dei, D. (2022). Understanding knowledge management strategies in institutions of higher learning and the corporate world: A systematic review. *Cogent Business & Management 9:1.* doi:https://doi.org/10.1080/23311975.2022.2108218

Camarinha-Matos , L., & Boucher, X. (2012). Sustainable collaborative networks – case studies. *Production Planning & Control: The Management of Operations*, 237-239. doi:DOI: 10.1080/09537287.2011.627653

Campisi, B., Elmo, G. C., Fusillo, F., & Lanzafame, V. (2024). European University Alliances and Good Quality Assurance Practice. *Innovation, Quality and Sustainability for a Resilient Circular Economy. AISME 2022. Circular Economy and Sustainability* (pp. 357–364). Springer, Cham. doi:https://doi.org/10.1007/978-3-031-55206-9_45

Charret, A., Chankseliani, M. (2022). The process of building European university alliances: a rhizomatic analysis of the European Universities Initiative. *Higher Education, 1-24.*

Craciun, D., Kaiser, F., Kottmann, A., & Van der Meulen, B. (2023). *Research for CULT Committee –The European Universities Initiative, first lessons, main challenges and perspectives.* Brussels: Policy Department for Structural and Cohesion Policies.

Dabbagh, N. & Kitsantas, A. (2012). Personal Learning environment, social media, and self-regulated learning: A natural formula for connecting formal and informal learning. . *The Internet and Higher Education, 15(1)*, 3-8.

European Commission. (2020). *European Universities Initiative factsheet.* Retrieved from https://education.ec.europa.eu/

Gunn, A. (2020). The European Universities Initiative: A Study of Alliance Formation in Higher Education. In A. D. Curaj, *European Higher Education Area: Challenges for a New Decade.* Cham: Springer. doi:https://doi.org/10.1007/978-3-030-56316-5_2

IPT. (February 2024). *KreativEU – Knowledge & Creativity European University.* IPT.

Jiang, X., & Li, Y. (2009). An empirical investigation of knowledge management and innovative performance: The case of alliances. *Research Policy, 38*(2), 358-368. doi:https://doi.org/10.1016/j.respol.2008.11.002

Kaur, V. (2019). *Knowledge- based dynamic capabilities the road ahead in gaining.* Springer Nature Switzerland AG. doi:doi.org/10.1007/978-3-030-21649-8

Kianto, A., Ritala, P., Vanhala, M., & Hussinki, H. (2018). Critical perspectives on accounting reflections on the criteria for the sound measurement of intellectual capital : A knowledge-based perspective. Critical Perspectives on Accounting. *Critical Perspectives on Accounting.* doi:doi.org/10.1016/j.cpa.2018.05.002

Lam, L., Nguyen, P., Le, N., & Tran, K. (2021). The Relation among Organizational Culture, Knowledge Management, and Innovation Capability. *Open Innov. Technol Mark. Complex 7, 66.* doi:https://doi.org/10.3390/joitmc7010066

Lambrechts, A., Cavallaro, M., & Lepori, B. (2024). The European Universities initiative: between status hierarchies and inclusion. *Higher Education, 88*, 1227–1247.

Lehmann, L. (2019). The controversy surrounding the idea of a European supranational university. In M. &. Roos (Ed.), *The Informal Construction of Europe* (pp. 75-91). Routledge.

Maassen, P., Stensaker, B., & Ross, A. (2023). The European university alliances - an examination of organizational potentials and perils. *Higher Education 86:9*, 53–968. doi:https://doi.org/10.1007/s10734-022-00951-4

Mäkelä, M. (2023). Designing the Process of Academic Recognition – Implementing "Bricolage" As A Methodological Tool to Analyze A Development Process in The Ulysseus European University Alliance. *European Journal of Education Studies, 11(1).* doi:http://dx.doi.org/10.46827/ejes.v11i1.5143

Matthews, A. (2019). Design as a Discipline for Postdigital Learning and Teaching: Bricolage and Actor-Network Theory. *Postdigital Science Education 1*, 413–426. doi:10.1007/s42438-019-00036-z

Nonaka, I., & Takeuchi, H. (1995). *The knowledge-creating company.* New York: Oxford University Press.

Pinheiro, R., Gänzle, S., Klenk, T., & Trondal, J. (2023). Unpacking strategic alliances in European higher education. *Tertiary Education and Management*, 213–228. doi:https://doi.org/10.1007/s11233-024-09133-6

Rensimer, L., & Brooks, R. (2024). he European Universities Initiative: further stratification in the pursuit of European cooperation? *Compare: A Journal of Comparative and International Education*, 1-19. doi:https://doi.org/10.1080/03057925.2024.2307551

Serger, S., Malmberg , A., & Benner, M. (2021). *Renewing Higher Education: Academic Leadership in Times of Transformation.* Lund, Sweden: Media-Tryck, Lund University.

Tamirat, S., Amentie, C. (2023). Advances in knowledge-based dynamic capabilities: A systematic review of foundations and determinants in recent literature. *Cogent Business & Management, 10(3)*. doi:doi.org/10.1080/23311975.2023.2257866

Tang , H., Ma, Z., Xiao, J., & Xiao, L. (2020). Toward a more Efficient Knowledge Network in Innovation Ecosystems: A Simulated Study on Knowledge Management. *Sustainability, 12, 6328*. doi:doi:10.3390/su12166328

Vaio, A., Palladino, R., Pezzi, A., & Kalisc, D. (2021). The role of digital innovation in knowledge management systems: A systematic literature review. *Journal of Business Research, Volume 123*, 220-231. doi:https://doi.org/10.1016/j.jbusres.2020.09.042

Vukasovic, M., & Stensaker, B. (2018). University alliances in the Europe of knowledge: Positions, agendas and practices in policy processes. *European Educational Research Journal, 17(3)*, 349–364.

Wang, H., Lu, W., Söderlund, J., & Chen, K. (2018). The Interplay Between Formal and Informal Institutions in Projects: A Social Network Analysis. , 49(4), 20-35. *Project Management Journal, 49*(4), 20-35. doi:https://doi.org/10.1177/8756972818781629

On the Future of Long-Term Care in the Context of Increasing Life Expectancy of European Citizens

Nikolay Ninov

1. Introduction

Within the European Union (EU), there is not yet a unified definition of long-term care. Still, the European Commission sees it as "a cross-cutting policy issue that brings together a range of services for people dependent on help with basic activities of daily living for an extended period of time" (European Commission, 2008). The concept of "basic activities of daily living" covers the self-manipulations that a person has to carry out daily, such as bathing, dressing, eating, getting around, etc. In this respect, long-term care intends to ensure that the person who is unable to fully self-care, over a long period, can maintain the best possible quality of life, with the greatest possible degree of independence, autonomy, participation, personal satisfaction and dignity. Appropriate long-term care is therefore based on respect for values, preferences and individual needs. Their essential characteristics are that: - care can be home-based, community-based or institutionally provided; - it is defined as formal and informal, depending on the entity that provides it; - it can be seen as an unavoidable side-effect of other (more stereotypical) social risks, such as old age, illness and disability; - it belongs to the field of both the health system and the medico-social sector because it is designed to meet both health and social needs; - the range of services that should be provided is extremely broad.

The ageing population in the EU is a key determinant of one of the most important social systems for Europe's elderly citizens - that of long-term care, especially as regards its future public costs. The combination of the ageing process as a result of the demographic transition - resulting from the retirement of the large 'baby boom' post-war generation (born between 1946 and 1964) on the one hand, the declining fertility rate on the other, and the projected increase in life expectancy on the third hand, hint at a serious problem ahead (Ninov, 2024). This problem has specific dimensions and is related to the significant increase in the number of European citizens who will need, respectively consume, long-term care. Moreover, it has been scientifically proven that the range of physical and/or mental disabilities increases dramatically with age (especially when it comes to those in the higher age groups, "80+"), resulting in the majority of cases in the emergence of long-term care dependency (European Commission's Directorate-General for Economic and Financial Affairs, 2021). In support of the above, we apply an expert forecast by the European Commission, according to which "the number of people in the EU in need of long-term care is projected to rise from 30.8 million in 2019 to 38.1 million in 2050" (European Commission, 2024).

It is the latter that set the aim of this study and provoked the idea of investigating the increase in life expectancy of European citizens (subject), and the impact it will have on the long-term care systems of EU Member States (object). The thesis of the study is that the projected increase in life expectancy in the EU generates challenges that require political commitment, significant investment and wide-ranging interventions by European institutions and national long-term care delivery systems.

2. Literature Review and Development Hypothesis

In the modern world, the concept of "old age" is now identified with a much longer period than in previous generations, due to the increased life expectancy of individuals (Hoffmann & Nachtmann, 2010). According to Hoffmann & Nachtmann, viewed as a stage of human life, old age continues to lengthen reaching even values of 40 years or more, making advanced age a new dimension of ageing. In addition to this, it should be stressed that people aged 80 and over represent the fastest-growing population group in Europe.

It is undeniably true that the average life expectancy in the first half of the 19th century was extremely low, ranging between 20 and 50 years (Olshansky et al., 2024). A century later, the progress made, especially in terms of public health, and in particular the advances in medicine, has resulted in a significant change in life expectancy values. While the latter had been increasing "on average by 1 year every one or two centuries over the previous 2000 years", in the twentieth century, it accelerated to "3 years of added life per decade", a process that has been termed "radical life extension" (Olshansky et al., 2024). The variable rate of improvement has been attributed to causes such as geography, economic development and time factors (Riley, 2005).

In 1990, an American team of researchers put forward the scientific hypothesis that humanity was approaching the upper limit of life expectancy, the so-called "limited life expectancy hypothesis" concerning longevity, since the effect of the above advances resulting from improvements in public health and medical care was by then largely already a fact, leaving biological ageing as the major risk factor for disease and death (Olshansky et al., 1990). In this regard, they project that the rate of improvement in life expectancy will slow in the 21st century and, for national populations, will probably not exceed approximately 85 years (88 years for women and 82 years for men) unless an intervention against biological ageing is discovered, tested for safety and efficacy, and widely disseminated.

Inevitably, accurately predicting future trends in life expectancy is key to shaping the socio-economic and especially health policies of EU Member States. Accelerated ageing of the European population is already occurring and the absolute number of people reaching older age continues to grow rapidly. There is no doubt that population ageing will have a significant structural impact on European economies. The gradual reaching of retirement age of the large "baby boom" post-war generation born between 1946 and 1964 will inevitably have an impact on European Union policies, with the pension and long-term care systems expected to be most seriously affected by the accelerated ageing of the European population. The vulnerability of both systems logically and directly corresponds to the expected critical increase in costs. While tackling them in the pension system involves building on the reform to link the retirement age more closely to the continuing rise in life expectancy in the years ahead, in the long-term care system it is crucial to strike the right balance between extending the scope of long-term care (thus responding to the increased needs of the European population) and ensuring the sustainability of public finances (without which, all intentions will remain unrealised).

In this line of thought, August Österle considers that since the beginning of this century, the problem of improving the adequacy of social protection for long-term care (in all forms of care, including - home care, community care and residential care) has become a central issue - an object of social and health policy (Österle, 2024). He argues that the challenges are common across the globe and that international organisations are increasingly recognising long-term care as a distinctive social risk, as evidenced by the fact that several EU countries, as early as the 1990s, began to establish more comprehensive long-term care systems, while in many countries these do not even exist.

It is the institutional commitment of the European Commission that underpins the production of in-depth analyses and projections of the future costs of ageing, based on up-to-date population projections from Eurostat. The European Commission accepts that population ageing is a key determinant of future public spending on long-term care (European Commission, 2021). On the one hand, it is the result of the demographic transition due to the ageing of the baby boom cohorts and, on the other hand, the increase in life expectancy and the decrease in fertility. It is predicted that due to the increasing number of old and especially very old people, there is likely to be an increase in the number of people who will need and receive long-term care. It is scientifically proven that the prevalence of physical or mental disability increases with age (especially in the very old age groups, 80+) and in many cases can lead to dependency. Moreover, in a study, a team of authors (Spillman & Lubitz, 2000) has shown that, as a consequence of an increase in the proportion of older people, the consequences for health care costs can be serious, as people in older age groups use health care services more than younger people.

An important prerequisite for meeting the growing number of elderly people in need of long-term care of the required quality and volume is the provision of the necessary human resources. According to a group of authors (Midje et al., 2024), overcoming the impending challenge could be addressed through a "significant increase in services and workforce". This is supported by a study by the OECD (OECD, 2024), which argues that it is important to assess "the impact of policy reforms aimed at improving affordability for users, as well as those that address the implications of better targeting of spending, promoting healthy ageing and improving productivity". In the same direction is the research of a team of academics (Jensen et al., 2024) who, by examining recent policy efforts and reforms in the field of long-term care in selected European countries, aim to understand the direction in which long-term care policy is moving and to show the measures that are required to be taken in preparation for future increases in demand for care, in the context of an ageing population and increasing life expectancy of European citizens.

A promising approach, with high potential for achieving these goals and for the effective management of the ageing population in long-term care in Europe, is the application of reliable integrated technology solutions (Kaufmann, 2024). The importance of the latter lies not only in improving the safety and communication of older people but also in their key role in improving access to health and social services. Furthermore, technological innovations could improve the quality of long-term care by streamlining operations and staff tasks, helping health professionals to spend more time with patients and in the performance of their job responsibilities. In other words, the introduction of new technologies in long-term care is considered promising, with the possibility of implementing a range of functionalities, as long as their purchase and implementation are beneficial to institutions, providers and users (Kaldy, 2024).

3. Research Methodology

This study aims to draw attention to the increasing impact of the rising life expectancy of European citizens on long-term care and the resulting challenges for the national long-term care systems of EU Member States. In this context, several strategic and foresight documents from the European Commission, the European Statistical Office, the OECD and others on life expectancy in the EU and its impact on long-term care have been studied in detail. In the framework of this publication, a systematic search of specialised publications on the topic was carried out in 5 electronic databases (Web of Science, Scopus /Elsevier/, EBSCOhost, BASE and Google Scholar) using the following key concepts - long-term care, life expectancy, formal and informal care. Descriptive and thematic analyses were performed based on hits, available statistics, and estimates. The latter aims to outline the key issues, and the types of evidence and, on this basis, arguments are made about options for addressing them.

4. Findings and Discussion

4.1. "Life expectancy" as a key demographic change affecting the European population

According to Eurostat, the statistical office of the European Commission, life expectancy at birth in the EU in 2023 is 81.5 years, which is 0.2 years higher than the same level in the pre-pandemic (COVID-19) year 2019 of 81.3 years (European Commission, 2023) (see Figure 1).

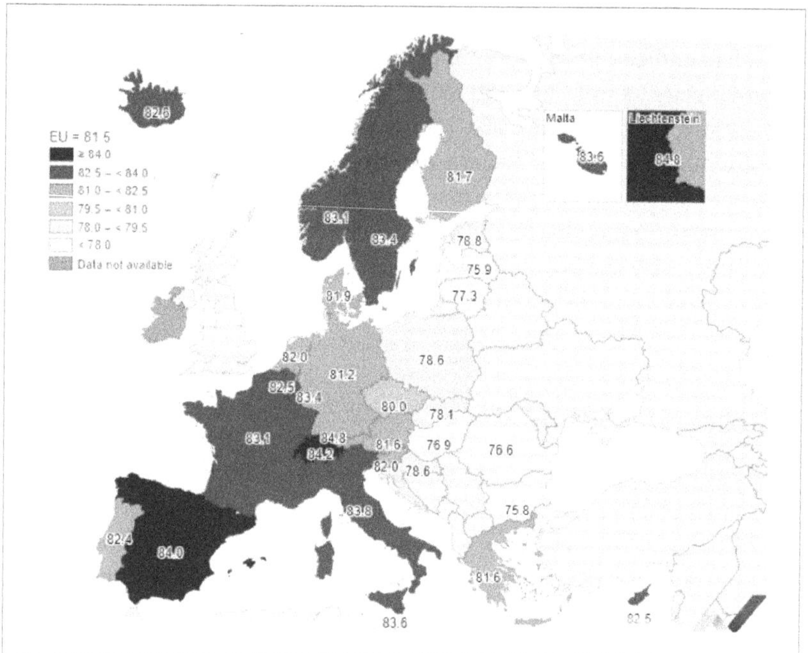

Figure 1. Life expectancy at birth, 2023 (years), according to Eurostat projections
Source: (Eurostat, 2024)

A more detailed look at the statistical information (Eurostat, 2024) allows us to draw the following conclusions and trends for 2023:

- in a total of 15 countries, the "life expectancy" indicator exceeds its EU average;
- Spain (84.0), Italy (83.8) and Malta (83.6) have the highest life expectancy;
- the lowest life expectancy rates are recorded in Bulgaria (75.8), Latvia (75.9) and Romania (76.6);
- 18 EU countries (including Belgium, Bulgaria, Cyprus, Czech Republic, Denmark, France, Hungary, Italy, Latvia, Lithuania, Luxembourg,

Malta, Poland, Portugal, Romania, Slovakia, Slovenia, Sweden) show an increase in life expectancy in 2023 compared to the pre-pandemic 2019[1] level, 6 countries (including Austria, Germany, Greece, Estonia, the Netherlands, Finland) show a decrease, and 2 countries (Croatia and Spain) remain unchanged;

- Romania reports the largest increase in life expectancy of +1.0 years, followed by Lithuania with +0.8 years and the Member States Bulgaria, Czech Republic, Luxembourg and Malta with an increase of +0.7 years. At the other pole are the countries Austria and Finland, which report the largest decreases of -0.4 years, followed by Estonia and the Netherlands with -0.2 years.

And if the trends towards the end of 2023 suggest unequivocally the direction of the process, namely - an increase in life expectancy, in this case, the task of accurately forecasting the future effects of life expectancy of the citizens of the EU Member States is of strategic importance for all social systems (including pension, health, social assistance, social services, long-term care, etc.). The fact that the European population is ageing at an accelerated rate is irrefutable, and the absolute number of people reaching older age continues to rise steadily. Evidence for the latter statement is provided by Eurostat's population statistics (see Figure 2), according to which the projected age composition of the EU population with a horizon of 2100 will undergo a major change.

The projected data shows that the group of European citizens aged "85+" is becoming the fastest-growing age group in the community. Statistics for 2022 found that people aged 85 or over account for 2.9% of the EU population. The share of this age group is projected to double by 2050 and almost triple by 2100, reaching approximately 10% of the total European population. In the long term, the projected increase in the EU dependency ratio will be mainly determined by the growing number of older Europeans. Between 2022 and 2100, the ratio of people aged "85+" to the working-age population

---

1 Note: COVID-19 has caused a sudden and temporary reduction in life expectancy in the EU. The pandemic is responsible for 1.2 million additional deaths in 2020-2021. As a result, the average life expectancy at birth dropped from 81.3 years in 2019 to 80.1 years in 2021. The decline is sharper for men than for women (European Commission, 2023; Ninova & Ninov, 2023).

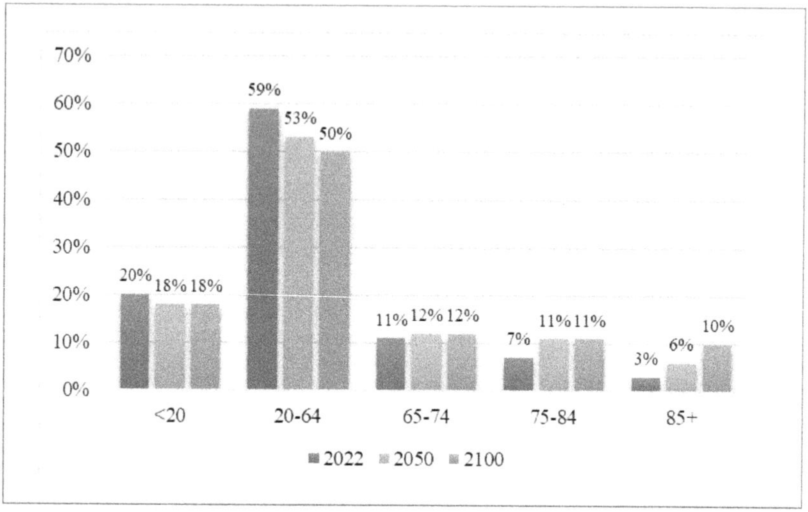

Figure 2. Population shares in the EU, by age group, 2022-2100 (%)
Source: author's design based on (Pinkus & Ruer, 2024)

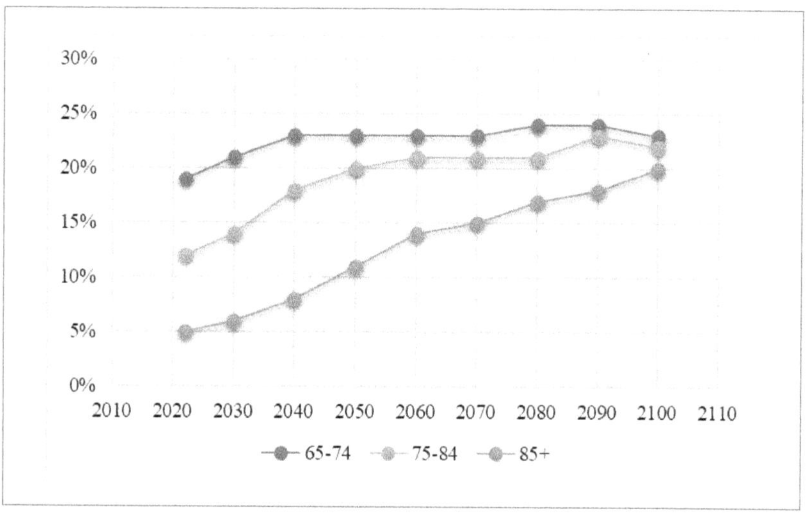

Figure 3. Decomposition of the old-age dependency ratio 2022-2010 (%)
Source: author's design based on (Pinkus & Ruer, 2024)

is projected to increase from 5% to 19.7%, i.e. by almost 15%. This projected increase significantly outpaces similar developments in the populations of Member States in the "65-74" and "75-84" age groups.

Figure 3. illustrates the imminent significant transformation of proportions from "younger" to "older" retirees. By 2100, each of the "65+", "65-74", "75-84" and "85+" age categories will account for approximately 1/3 of all seniors, which is clearly in stark contrast to the currently dominant "65-74" age category.

In the context of what has been said so far, it is important to answer the question: what will be the challenges for the national long-term care systems of the EU Member States as a result of the demographic outlook thus outlined?

4.2. Potential challenges for national long-term care systems of EU Member States

National long-term care systems are distinguished by their design, the degree of maturity and development they have reached, and not least by the traditions of providing the same, reflecting the specificities and strategic visions of the individual countries within the EU. The very fact that there is still no unified definition of long-term care at EU level suggests that there are differences in understanding of long-term care, behind which lie "differences in the duration of care, the service users covered and the often difficult-to-define boundary between medical (health) and non-medical (social) services offered" (Council of Ministers of the Republic of Bulgaria, 2014) reflecting precisely the specificities referred to.

Notwithstanding these facts, the challenges facing the national long-term care systems of the EU Member States are similar and the more important ones will be briefly presented without attempting to rank them in terms of importance and urgency to address.

The projected number of citizens in the EU who will need long-term care, as already highlighted, will increase from 30.8 million (in 2019) to 38.1 million (in 2050), i.e. a tangible increase of 7.3 million people (or 23.7%) is expected (European Commission, 2021). The expected increase, combined with parallel demographic developments and emerging adverse trends in terms of changing family patterns, higher labour market participation by women, etc., will invariably have the effect of undermining the sustainability of the traditional operating models of long-term care that rely heavily on informal caregivers (usually relatives, kin and others, who are mostly women).

The next challenge, which is directly related to what has been written above, would presumably be to attract and train professionals to practise the professional delivery of long-term care. In this case, the process in question is not just about intervening in national labour markets - to create new jobs. It will also require: legislating for this type of work (which is notoriously unattractive, especially for young people); tackling key issues relating to working conditions and, in particular, low wages, which sabotage efforts to attract and, above all, retain formal care workers. On the other hand, good working conditions in the long-term care sector are not only necessary to attract and retain workers but also serve to promote gender equality and show due respect for their efforts. EU Member States should commit themselves to developing appropriate programmes and to facilitating training in long-term care professions in educational institutions. This could be done by subsidising specialised education and paying scholarships to trainees in key specialities. In addition, specialised training programmes could be targeted specifically at people currently at risk of redundancy, offering them a viable alternative.

As has already been made clear, European long-term care systems are set to reflect the growing demand for services that is forecast for the next half-century. The latter, moreover, also means higher costs, which are directly related to securing sufficient financial resources for the provision of (mostly formal) long-term care, which is largely financed by the public sector. In other words, an increase in the cost of long-term care will inevitably have a significant impact on the public finances of the Community countries. Along these lines, social spending on long-term care is projected to grow from 1.7% to 2.5% of GDP between 2019 and 2050 (making it the fastest-growing social expenditure). Variations between countries - within the EU - are expected to be sensitive, as significant structural weaknesses are reported that need to be addressed urgently, which will require additional investment (European Commission, 2021).

The challenge of securing the necessary investment for long-term care purposes in the EU is emerging as a crucial one, as this needs to be secured for new care facilities, appropriate equipment and new jobs. Preliminary estimates suggest that investment in long-term care could create an additional 13.6 million jobs in the EU by 2030 alone (European Commission, 2021).

Further to the challenge outlined above, it should be noted that to date, not all long-term care needs have been met and addressed. This is a fact mainly due to the absence of long-term care services and lack of information awareness (both at the national and local level), partial and limited coverage for them under the social protection system to help cover the costs of this type of care, and to improve their currently unsatisfactory quality. Official EU documents confirm that in 2019, only around 1/4 of European citizens with severe difficulties in terms of needing personal care or support in household activities received it (European Commission, 2024). To this fact, it can be added that the unequal socio-economic situation of a significant number of European citizens living in poor and especially - rural areas, are also considered a barrier to access quality long-term care.

A future challenge could also be defined as the case of all informal carers in the EU. They are often affected by difficulties ranging from insufficient access to support measures to an inability to combine long-term care with paid employment. It is an undeniable fact that the majority of formal and informal long-term care is provided by and for women, which underlines the importance of gender in this case (almost 90% of formal long-term care is provided by women) (European Commission, 2022). In this line of thought, it is considered that the responsibility for long-term care distances women much more than men from the labour market. In support of this assertion, 7.7 million women in the EU are not working due to unpaid care work (European Commission, 2022).

Last but not least, we should point to a challenge that should not be underestimated and should be high on the European policy agenda - improving the health of older people by promoting healthy ageing. Only in this way will it be possible to curb, or at least slow down, the rate of demand for long-term care. Also, "European funds should support research into the treatment of cognitive diseases causing dementia, which is expected to be a significant factor in future long-term care needs" (Pinkus & Ruer, 2024).

As a final challenge, we should inevitably point to the key step of integrating artificial intelligence into the long-term care environment. The inevitability is dictated by the rapid rise of information and communication technologies (ICT), big data and artificial intelligence (AI), the foundation of the concept of "Society 5.0" (seen as a strategy for the socio-economic and cultural development of modern society that is based on the use of digital technologies that have the potential of social innovation, aiming to eliminate existing disparities and satisfy a range of needs). It is thanks to them that smart healthcare systems have emerged, "including the integration of healthcare systems with capital, the introduction of healthcare systems into long-term care institutions, and the integration of measurement data for care or exposure" (Wang & Hsu, 2023). The approbation of an integrated intelligent long-term care service management system focuses on building a personalized care service system for the elderly that covers a range of aspects such as their health, nutrition, diet, and health education. On the other hand, "The Wearable Internet of Things Care System primarily supports the development of portable physiological signal detection devices and electronic fences." (Wang & Hsu, 2023). Given the growing importance of those above, another need arises, driven by the societal and ethical implications of the introduction and expansion of AI (Lukkien et al., 2023; Ninova, Artificial Intelligence and Insurance: A Bibliometric Analysis, 2024). Smart technologies used in long-term care for the elderly will inevitably also necessitate the introduction of strict regulation and public regulation, both at the European and national levels.

5. Conclusion

As has already been made clear, the effect of the demographic projections of increased life expectancy for European citizens coming true will be multifold in terms of their impact on national long-term care systems and hence automatically on any European economy. It should be stressed that the response to this already anticipated effect while following a pan-European approach, will be individual and relevant to each EU Member State. The reason for this is that the level of maturity of the systems mentioned is not the same everywhere, taking into account the fact that some European countries are still "catching up" in their development with the "leaders", trying to "shorten the distance between them". The latter is reflected in existing differences in the parametric indicators of care, including duration, scope, coverage and, above all, the approach to financing them. Notwithstanding the catching-up role (determined by weaker economic opportunities, sluggish legislative changes in the social sphere and generally delayed reforms of social protection systems), national long-term care systems in the EU (both leaders and catchers) will inevitably face the serious challenges outlined. At the heart of successfully tackling these, it is crucial to strike the right balance between expanding the scope of long-term care (thus meeting the increased needs of the European population, ensuring its affordability), ensuring the sustainability of public finances (without which, all intentions will remain unrealised) and maintaining a standard of high-quality service provision. While issues related to formal long-term care are finding institutional answers much more quickly, issues related to informal care remain largely underestimated and half-resolved, opening up new ground for future research.

References

Council of Ministers of the Republic of Bulgaria. (2014). *National strategy for long-term care*. Retrieved from https://www.strategy.bg/StrategicDocuments/View.aspx?lang=bg-BG&Id=882

European Commission. (2008). *Employment, Social Affairs & Inclusion: Social protection & social inclusion*. Retrieved from European Union: ec.europa.eu/employment_social/spsi/joint_reports_en.htm

European Commission. (2021). *Economy and Finance: The 2021 Ageing Report: Economic and Budgetary Projections for the EU Member States (2019-2070)*. Retrieved from EU: https://economy-finance.ec.europa.eu/publications/2021-ageing-report-economic-and-budgetary-projections-eu-member-states-2019-2070_en

European Commission. (2022). *EUROPEAN CARE STRATEGY: FOR CARERS AND CARE RECEIVERS*. Retrieved from EU: https://ec.europa.eu/commission/presscorner/api/files/attachment/873459/CareStrategy.pdf

European Commission. (2023). The impact of demographic change – in a changing environment.

European Commission. (2024). *Employment, Social Affairs & Inclusion: Long-term care*. Retrieved from EU: https://ec.europa.eu/social/main.jsp?langId=en&catId=792

European Commission's Directorate-General for Economic and Financial Affairs. (2021, May). *The 2021 Ageing Report*. Retrieved from European Union: https://economy-finance.ec.europa.eu/document/download/58bcd316-a404-4e2a-8b29-49d8159dc89a_en?filename=ip148_en.pdf p.139

Eurostat. (2024). *Eurostat: EU life expectancy estimated at 81.5 years in 2023.* Retrieved from European Union: https://ec.europa.eu/eurostat/web/products-eurostat-news/w/ddn-20240503-2

Hoffmann, E., & Nachtmann, J. (2010). Old Age, the Need of Long-term Care and Healthy Life Expectancy. От G. Doblhammer, & R. Scholz, *Ageing, Care Need and Quality of Life.* VS Verlag für Sozialwissenschaften. https://doi.org/10.1007/978-3-531-92335-2_9

Jensen, S. E., Pinkus, D., & Ruer, N. (2024). *LONG-TERM CARE POLICIES IN PRACTICE: A EUROPEAN PERSPECTIVE.* Retrieved from https://www.bruegel.org/sites/default/files/2024-12/WP%20Full%20Paper_DavidandNina.pdf

Kaldy, J. (2024). *Top High-Tech Trends in Long Term Care*. Retrieved from American Health Care Association/National Center for Assisted Living: https://www.providermagazine.com/Issues/2024/Summer/Pages/Top-High-Tech-Trends-in-Long-Term-Care.aspx

Kaufmann, L. (2024). *Embracing Health Tech in Long-Term Care: A Strategic Approach to Future-Proofing Patient Care*. Retrieved from Smartlinx, LLC.: https://www.smartlinx.com/resources/blog/embracing-health-tech-in-long-term-care-a-strategic-approach-to-future-proofing-patient-care

Lukkien, D. R., Nap, H. H., Buimer, H. P., Peine, A., Boon, W. P., Ket, J. C., . . . Moors, E. H. (2023). Toward responsible artificial intelligence in long-term care: a scoping review on practical approaches. *The Gerontologist, 63*(1), 155-168.

Midje, H. H., Nyborg, V. N., Nordsteien, A., Øvergård, K. I., Brembo, E. A., & Torp, S. (2024). Antecedents and outcomes of work engagement among nursing staff in long-term care facilities—A systematic review. *Journal of Advanced Nursing, 80*(1), 42-59. https://doi.org/10.1111/jan.15804

Ninov, N. (2024). RETIREMENT AGE TRENDS IN THE CONTEXT OF RISING LIFE EXPECTANCY IN THE EU. *MARKET AND NON-MARKET SYSTEMIC CHALLENGES FOR INSURANCE AND REINSURANCE - THEORY, PRACTICE, PROBLEMS AND SOLUTIONS.* Svishtov: Academic Publishing House Tsenov. Retrieved from https://www.researchgate.net/publication/385244666_TENDENCII_VV_VZRASTTA_ZA_PENSIONIRANE_V_KONTEKSTA_NA_POVISAVASATA_SE_PRODLZITELNOST_NA_ZIVOTA_V_ES

Ninova, V. (2024). Artificial Intelligence and Insurance: A Bibliometric Analysis. In P. Chodnicka-Jaworska, & S. Bayrakdar, *Current Dynamics in Business and Economics: Theoretical Approaches and Empirical Discoveries* (pp. 115-141). Berlin - Bruxelles - Chennai - Lausanne - New York - Oxford: Peter Lang Verlag. https://doi.org/10.3726/b22541

Ninova, V., & Ninov, N. (2023). The Effect of the COVID-19 Pandemic on the Health Insurance Market in Bulgaria: Empirical Analysis of Market Concentration. *Optimizing Energy Efficiency During a Global Energy Crisis*, 165-177. https://doi.org/10.4018/979-8-3693-0400-6.ch011

OECD. (29 October 2024 r.). *Is Care Affordable for Older People?* (OECD Publishing) https://doi.org/10.1787/450ea778-en

Olshansky, S. J., Carnes, B. A., & Cassel, C. (1990). In search of Methuselah: estimating the upper limits to human longevity. *Science, 250*(4981), 634-640. https://doi.org/10.1126/science.2237414

Olshansky, S., Willcox, B., Demetrius, L., & Beltrán-Sánchez, H. (2024). Implausibility of radical life extension in humans in the twenty-first century. *Nat Aging*. https://doi.org/10.1038/s43587-024-00702-3

Österle, A. (2024). Chapter 12: Long-term care. От M. Powell, T. I. Agartan, & D. Béland, *Research Handbook on Health Care Policy* (стр. 191–207). Edward Elgar Publishing. https://doi.org/10.4337/9781800887565.00016

Pinkus, D., & Ruer, N. (2024). *Beyond retirement: a closer look at the very old.* Retrieved from BRUEGEL: https://www.bruegel.org/system/files/2024-06/beyond-retirement%3A-a-closer-look-at-the-very-old-9924_3.pdf

Riley, J. C. (2005). Estimates of regional and global life expectancy, 1800–2001. *Population and development review, 31*(3), 537-543. https://doi.org/10.1111/j.1728-4457.2005.00083.x

Spillman, B. C., & Lubitz, J. (2000). The Effect of Longevity on Spending for Acute and Long-Term Care. *The New England Journal of Medicine, 342*(19), 1409-1415. https://doi.org/10.1056/NEJM200005113421906

Wang, W. -H., & Hsu, W. -S. (2023). Integrating Artificial Intelligence and Wearable IoT System in Long-Term Care Environments. *Sensors, 23*(13), 5913. https://doi.org/10.3390/s23135913

Climate Policy Uncertainty and Sustainability Performance: The Role of Gender Diversity

Farah Hamila, Ouidad Yousfi

1. Introduction

Over the past five decades, the entire climate structure has witnessed major changes, as shown through the rising consistency, strength and impact of extreme natural incidents related to climate change (Li et al., 2021a). A report released by the United Nations Framework Convention on Climate Change (UNFCCC) on September 13, 2022, highlighted that the past seven years have been the hottest on record. In this vein, from 1960 to 2020, the U.S. experienced experienced a temperature increase of approximately 1.4°C and was ranked as the second-largest pollution emitter in the world with 4.7 billion metric tons in 2020. These alarming developments, which reflect the growing threat of climate change, have prompted governments to develop and implement environmental regulations and policies aimed at encouraging responsible corporate practices, directing capital toward sustainable initiatives, and supporting the transition to a low-carbon and resilient economy (Huang et lei., 2021). However, the effort to achieve policy synergy may escalate overall policy uncertainty when conflicts of climate resolutions, originating from divergent attitudes toward climate changes, exist among political forces.

From 2010 to 2015, climate policy uncertainty (CPU fluctuations remained relatively constant (see figure 1). However a notable increase was observed following the Paris Agreement declaration in 2015. This rise in uncertainty was further amplified by the announcement of the United States' withdrawal from the Paris Agreement by President Trump in 2017. This trend continued, peaking significantly during the UN Climate Action Summit in 2019. The highest spike was observed during the 26th UN Climate Change Conference in 2021. Consequently, Climate policies have become a politically divisive issue in the U.S and source of major concern all over the world.

The existing literature largely assumes that environmental protection programs are distinctly formulated, harmonious, and predictable (Fu et al.,

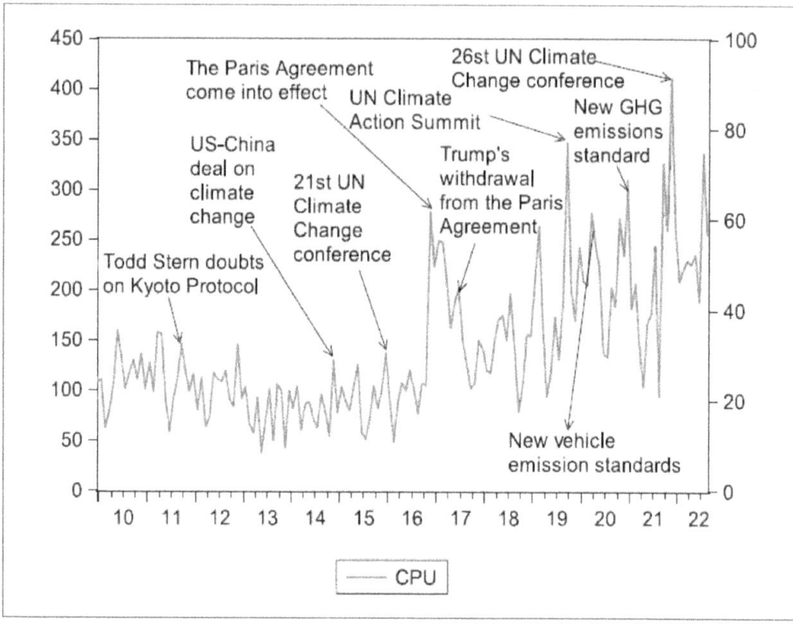

Figure 1: The trend of climate policy uncertainty (CPU)
Source: Gavriilidis, 2021

2020), overlooking the instability of environmental policies and their impact on sustainable funding (Ren et al., 2022). The current research reviews the studies on the uncertainty of surrounding environmental initiatives and their impact on sustainable investment. Understanding these dynamics is essential for developing effective strategies to navigate the complexities of sustainable finance amid policy uncertainty.

While firm-level determinants of ESG performance are well documented, increasing attention is being paid to macroeconomic factors. Recent studies, including those by (Niu and Zhou., 2022) and (Zhao et al., 2021), underscore the significant role of political uncertainty in shaping firms' ESG practices. Within this framework, climate policy uncertainty—defined as the unpredictability of future government actions related to climate change, such as carbon pricing, renewable energy incentives, and emissions targets—emerges as a critical concern. This uncertainty complicates decision-making and long-term investments in sustainability for firms, investors, and policymakers.

Despite awareness of its importance, the specific effects of climate policy uncertainty on ESG performance remain unclear. Therefore, examining how climate policy uncertainty affects ESG practices is essential for developing effective strategies that support firms in improving their sustainability efforts.

In this context, climate policy has emerged as a new external threat to enterprise operations, exerting an increasing influence on both financial and non-financial the ambiguity it introduces often creates hesitation among decision-makers, potentially constraining firms' commitment to ESG-related investments.

This highlighted a crucial exploration inquiry on how really does climate policy uncertainty affect ESG performance?

It's well documented that that strong ESG performance signifies robust financial and sustainable capabilities for businesses (Chen et al., 2023). Coupled with the notion of sustainable development and policy guidance from supervising authorities, investors consider ESG performance as an important factor in investment opinions. Nevertheless, the increasing uncertainty surrounding policies requires robust corporate governance to effectively analyse the relationship between sustainable performance such this uncertainty (Ahsan et al., 2021). In this context, several studies emphasize the important role of gender diversity on executive boards in enhancing strategic decision-making and reinforcing governance effectiveness (Al-Najjar and Salama., 2022; Alkhawaja et al., 2023; Atif et al., 2020). Women tend to evaluate risks with a broader perspective, integrating emotional intelligence with strategic analysis, resulting in more nuanced responses to uncertainty (Makrychoriti and Pyrgiotakis., 2022; Perrin and Weill., 2023). It is therefore interesting to explore how female leaders shape environmental responsibility strategies, especially in the contat of climate policy unpredictability.

Addressing women effects on CPU would bring two main contributions to the growing literature on the association between CPU and environmental, social, and governance (ESG) performance.

First, the existing literature on CPU-ESG association is still in its early stages, and the findings are inconclusive. By investigating the CPU index created by Gavriilidis (2021), this study identifies that CPU could positively affect corporate ESG practices: companies are likely to increase their focus on ESG initiatives to mitigate risks and enhance therefore stability amid political uncertainty.

Second, to the best of our knowledge, there is a lack of research on the gender-specific influence among executives on the correlation between climate policy uncertainty as well as corporate ESG performance. Despite the positive direct impact of female executives on ESG performance, their role as a moderator on CPU-ESG performance association is not yet fully explored.

The subsequent sections of this chapter are structured as follows:

> Section 2 reviews studies on how CPU could shape ESG performance, while section 3 discusses the influence of gender diversity among executives on ESG performance. Section 4 focuses on the moderating role of female executives on CPU-ESG performance association. Conclusion are presented in Section 5.

2. CPU and ESG performance

A careful review of the former literature identifies a nascent but expanding body of research dedicated to address the issue of CPU and sustainability (ESG) practices. Moreover, the association between climate policy uncertainty and corporate ESG performance is built on two contrary points of view as it is grounded on two fundamental theories: the real option theory and the growth option theory.

On the one hand, previous literature argues that adding complexity can lead enterprises to alter their strategies (Lowendahl et Revang, 1998). In this environment, (Blyth et al., 2007 and Li et al., 2022) believe that without stable climate programs, companies facing high uncertainty will be reluctant to invest assets in sustainable practices. with the real options theory (Dixit et Pindyck., 1994), which suggest that enterprises facing high uncertainty, are less inclined to make long-term investments, including sustainable investments.

In fact, this theory proposes a trade-off between immediate and postponed investments allowing companies to gather further information to decrease uncertainty (Cooper et Priestley, 2011). The main idea behind the "wait-and-see" approach is simple: Firms retain significant flexibility in deciding whether, when, and how to invest, including the strategic priority of sustainability-related investments. Supporting this notion, former studies in the investment under uncertainty literature (Kanagaretnam et al., 2022; Kim et Kung, 2017; Strobel et al., 2018; Xu, 2020) show that companies tend to retrench investment or indeed divest under risk pressure until more details is known to make further informed opinions. The reason is that investing in sustainable programs by firms is a long-term process, and once problems arise, it could lead to the loss of all original investments (Gao et Zhang, 2023). This perspective is supported by recent research in psychology and sociology (Hu et al, 2023). While companies are generally inclined to follow their peers and competitors in green investments to maintain competitiveness, policy rumors tend to decrease the likelihood of mimicry. Without clear policy guidance, companies face diminished incentives to invest, making it difficult for them to claim a first-mover advantage. As a result, an increasing uncertainty can cause anxiety and pessimism, which can reduce the confidence of directors and investors, particularly when they lack a clear understanding of risk factors and their potential impact on social responsibility and environmental outcomes (Ren et al., 2022; Sendstad and Chronopoulos., 2020).

On the other hand, although CPU has a dark side, it has also a positive side. In this vein, Vural and Yavas (2020) state that enterprises need to be well prepared to survive in an unpredictable setting, and explored the function of social capital in times of high policy uncertainty. According to this, an indispensable view assumes that higher climate policy uncertainty favors sustainable investment. This is in line with the growth options theory which considers that under uncertain conditions, ESG performance can help firms make a good financial character and strengthen market competitiveness run (Kulatilaka and Perotti, 1998). This view argues that delaying investment in socially responsible practices is illogical if the cost of waiting is very high. Waiting may limit a firm's development opportunities, thereby resulting in high waiting costs. Conversely, the risk mitigation thesis supports this point of view, suggesting that investing in ESG initiatives is a proactive strategy to mitigate adverse reactions to negative events. It provides companies with "moral capital," enabling them to navigate climate policy uncertainty and maintain business operations during extreme conditions (Ongsakul et al., 2020). Consistent with this perspective, (Lopez et al., 2017) used collective data for 250 European , found that climate policy uncertainty encourages firms to increase their investments in environmental protection. Additionally, (Zhang et al., 2022) demonsrate that, during periods of increased uncertainty, Chinese firms engage in ESG activities as a strategic signal to stakeholders. Such engagement serves to enhance corporate reputation and fosters more favorable stakeholder perceptions (Qiu et al., 2022). In conclusion, society well-accepts engagement in ESG actions during difficult times.

Based on this analysis, firms can efficiently manage risks associated with climate policy uncertainty by prioritizing ESG commitment.

2. Executives gender diversity (EGD) and ESG performance

There is a growing consensus that gender significantly influences executives' values, perspectives, and decision-making processes, particularly regarding ESG issues (Shahab et al., 2020; Nguyen et al., 2021). Research shows that women generally exhibit a higher preference for risk aversion than men (Croson and Gneezy, 2009), a tendency associated ithaf awareness of climate change risks and a proactive approach to their mitigation (Altunbas et al., 2022). The upper echelons theory further reinforces this perspective by emphasizing the significant influence of executives' values characteristics, and cognitive frameworks on organizational outcomes and ESG-related strategic decisions (Hambrick and Mason., 1984; Hambrick;, 2007; Legrand et al., 2019). Furthermore, several studies indicate that female leaders are more likely to prioritize social and environmental considerations, demonstrating greater concern for community well-being and sensitivity to fairness (Adams et al., 2011; Beji et al., 2021; Khemakhem et al., 2023; Gilligan and Attanucci., 1988; Eagly and Carli., 2007).

The unique characteristics of female executives have been extensively analyzed through various theoretical frameworks that underscore their potential to influence corporate ESG practices. From the perspective of stakeholder theory, female leaders are often more inclined to advocate for ESG initiatives due to their emphasis on stakeholder well-being and sustainable practices (Alkhawaja et al., 2023; Wasiuzzaman and Subramaniam, 2023). Furthermore, Agency theory suggest that female executives often exhibit greater commitment, a more democratic leadership style, and reduced self-serving behavior, which collectively enhance accountability and transparency in sustainability. Legitimacy theory highlights the crucial role of female executives in enhancing ESG transparency. Their sensitivity to socially responsible practices, aligns with stakeholder interests, enabling firms to meet social and environmental expectations (Hussain et al., 2018; Arayssi et al., 2020; Nicolò et al., 2022). Moreover, their intellectual and interpersonal skills support the integration of sustainability considerations into corporate strategy, contributing to more legitimate and impactful ESG outcomes (Jizi, 2017). Further supporting this notion, studies by (McGuinness et al., 2017 and Disli et al., 2022) show that female directors positively influence CSR performance. This aligns with earlier findings by (Pareek et al., and Bear et al,. 2010), which highlighted women's sensitivity to environmental issues and their tendency to minimize negative impacts, such as pollution. Recent findings by (Meng and Zhu., 2023), indicate indicate a strong association between female managers in China and improved ESG outcomes. However, research focusing on the Nordic market reveals a more nuanced view: while female CEOs tend to support environmental initiatives, their impact on social performance is marginal, with limited improvements in environmental and governance dimensions (Yahya, 2023). Additionally, (Shahbaz et al., 2020) noted that female board members positively affect environmental and governance aspects of CSR in the energy sector, (Walls et al., 2012) associated increased female representation on boards to reduced environmental concerns, whereas (Glass et al., 2016) found no significant impact of female directors on environmental practices.

Collectively, these findings highlight the complex relationship between gender diversity on corporate boards and ESG outcomes. Drawing on the existing literature, which emphasizes the unique values and characteristics that women bring to leadership roles, female executives could effectively and positively contribute to ESG performance.

3. Executives gender diversity as a moderator variable

When climate policy uncertainty increases, scholars assert that an efficient governance mechanism is necessary to enhance ESG performance and mitigate the impact of such uncertainty (Aprisma and Sudaryati, 2020). This necessity is underscored by (May et al., 2021), who highlight notable differences in perspectives on environmental issues between male and female suggesting that gender diversity—especially at the executive level—is crucial, as men and women often differ in work principles, risk aversion, and decision-making approaches (Ye et al., 2019). Such diversity can strengthen governance strategies and effectively address climate-related challenges. For instance, Gull et al. (2023) highlight how female executives, through their stakeholder-oriented approach, ensure environmentally friendly operations even in times of heightened uncertainty. Makrychoriti and Pyrgiotakis (2022) further support this view by demonstrating that women in executive roles positively mediate the relationship between CPU and increased ESG performance, suggesting that gender diversity enhances corporate resilience to policy fluctuations. Additionally, Benlemlih and Vural Yavaş (2024) underscore the ability of women on boards to reduce firms' CO2 emissions during periods of high uncertainty, further emphasizing their critical role in promoting sustainability under uncertain conditions. These findings align with resource dependence theory (Pfeffer and Salancik, 1978), which suggest that gender-diverse boards provide access to valuable resources and communication channels that help firms navigate external uncertainties. From this perspective, women's contributions to ESG performance are amplified as their expertise and networks facilitate the flow of information, making firms better equipped to respond to unpredictable policy shifts. Similarly, stakeholder theory supports this view, as female executives often advocate for stronger ESG practices during times of uncertainty (Alkhawaja et al., 2023; Wasiuzzaman and Subramaniam, 2023). Enhanced communication with stakeholders, as noted by Mirza et al. (2020) and Qureshi et al. (2020), helps reduce information asymmetry, which can lead to more effective investment decisions in the face of climate-related risks.

However, contrasting perspectives argue that female executives may exhibit higher risk aversion, particularly in uncertain environments, which can adversely affect sustainable investment decisions. This behavior aligns with the 'wait and see' approach, where firms perceive long-term investments as excessively risky. Consequently, female executives may prioritize stability over ambitious sustainability initiatives, particularly in high-risk contexts, resulting in a decline in sustainable investment levels. Perrin and Weill (2024) reinforce this view, observing that while uncertainty typically drives corporate investment, this trend is less pronounced under female leadership. Their findings suggest that the cautious investment strategies adopted by female executives may stem from a greater risk aversion compared to their male counterparts, potentially limiting participation in long-term sustainability projects perceived as riskier. In addition, Caby et al. (2022) analyzed 836 companies across 16 developed nations and found no significant correlation between gender diversity in top management and corporate commitments to climate change management. This implies that gender diversity alone may not enhance sustainability initiatives. Similarly, Tichenor et al. (2022) concluded that female leadership does not significantly bolster sustainable engagement, especially in high-uncertainty environments. Their research highlights that the influence of female executives on corporate social responsibility may depend on specific contextual factors and does not always lead to stronger sustainability outcomes.

Overall, while female executives tend to promote sustainability, their risk aversion during periods of policy uncertainty may dominate, resulting in more conservative strategies that reduce ESG investment initiatives.

4. Conclusion

Climate change has consistently been recognized as one of the most significant threats to enterprises in the coming decades (WEF, 2020, 2021). Consequently, U.S. firms may increasingly face uncertainty stemming from climate related risks. Examining the relationship between climate policy uncertainty (CPU) and ESG performance, reveals that firms tend to strengthen their commitment to sustainable practices in response to high CPU, focusing on reducing environmental degradation and optimizing resource efficiency. This strategic response prioritizes environmental and social initiatives over traditional governance practices.

The positive relationship between policy uncertainty and sustainable investment aligns with empirical findings. Bai et al. (2023), found that climate policy uncertainty significantly stimulates green investments in Chinese industrial firms, whereas (Ilyas et al., 2022) report positive effects across all ESG dimensions in U.S. companies.

In this context, reinforcing ESG strategies offers an effective response to climate policy uncertainty, enhancing companies' adaptability and long-term resilience. These strategies confer a sustained competitive advatange (Galbreath., 2012), improve their ability to anticipate and manage policy risks (Kim and Li., 2021), and attract long-term-oriented investors who are less sensitive to policy ambiguity and market volatility (Ellili., 2022). By prioritizing ESG, companies are better are better positioned to address environmental and social challenges (He et al., 2023; Khalfaoui et al., 2024).

firms with high environmental standards are perceived as less vulnerable to environmental risks, which increases their appeal to sustainability-focused investors. Investments in social factors—such as employee welfare, community engagement, and ethical supply chains—enhance productivity and foster customer loyalty, thereby increasing investment and stakeholder trust (Beji et al., 2021). Given the significant role of climate change as a source of uncertainty, firms are reinforcing their environmental and social responsibilities, not only to mitigate risks but also to align with stakeholder expectations and improve their impact.

During periods of high climate policy uncertainty, companies are likely to boost sustainable investments to enhance value and prepare for future regulatory shifts (Ongsakul et al., 2023). According to mitigation theory suggests that ESG investments act as "moral capital," enabling firms to navigate challenges and uncertainties. Strong ESG performance enhances corporate investment by improving reputation, reducing risk, bolstering financial performance, driving innovation, and aligning with stakeholder and investor expectations, supporting both immediate and long-term growth and sustainability.

Perrin and Weill (2024) observed that while uncertainty generally drives corporate investment, this effect is by under female leadership, which often involves more cautious investment strategies and a greater focus on risk aversion compared to male counterparts. Consequently, female executives may prioritize stability over long-term sustainability initiatives, often perceived as riskier investments. The literature suggests that while female leadership can enhance governance and ethical standards, existing corporate dynamics may constrain their capacity to pursue bold sustainability actions under climate policy uncertainty.

Analyzing the moderating effect of executive gender diversity sheds light on the urgent need to increase female representation in executive positions. It also highlights the importance of of institutional mechanisms that promote women's active participation in ESG-related decision-making, especially in addressing CPU. Numerous studies indicate that a weaker moderating effect may stem from the underrepresentation of women in leadership roles (Beji et al., 2021; Caby et al., 2022; Khemakhem et al., 2023), which constraint the ability of diverse leadership teams to drive meaningful changes in ESG practices.

References

Ahsan, T., Mirza, S. S., Al-Gamrh, B., Bin-Feng, C., & Rao, Z. (2020). How to deal with policy uncertainty to attain sustainable growth: the role of corporate governance. *Corporate Governance*, *21*(1), 7891. https://doi.org/10.1108/cg-04-2020-0121

Alkhawaja, A., Hu, F., Johl, S., & Nadarajah, S. (2023). Board gender diversity, quotas, and ESG disclosure: Global evidence. *International Review Of Financial Analysis*, *90*, 102823. https://doi.org/10.1016/j.irfa.2023.102823

Al-Najjar, B., & Salama, A. (2022). Mind the gap: Are female directors and executives more sensitive to the environment in high-tech us firms? *Technological Forecasting and Social Change*, *184*, 122024. https://doi.org/10.1016/j.techfore.2022.122024

Altunbas, Y., Gambacorta, L., Reghezza, A., & Velliscig, G. (2022). Does gender diversity in the workplace mitigate climate change? *Journal Of Corporate Finance*, *77*, 102303. https://doi.org/10.1016/j.jcorpfin.2022.102303

Arayssi, M., Jizi, M., & Tabaja, H. H. (2019). The impact of board composition on the level of ESG disclosures in GCC countries. *Sustainability Accounting Management and Policy Journal*, *11*(1), 137161. https://doi.org/10.1108/sampj-05-2018-0136

Atif, M., Alam, M. S., & Hossain, M. (2020). Firm sustainable investment: Are female directors greener? *Business Strategy and The Environment*, *29*(8), 34493469. https://doi.org/10.1002/bse.2588

Bai, D., Du, L., Xu, Y., & Abbas, S. (2023). Climate policy uncertainty and corporate green innovation: Evidence from Chinese A-share listed industrial corporations. *Energy Economics*, *127*, 107020. https://doi.org/10.1016/j.eneco.2023.107020

Beji, R., Yousfi, O., Loukil, N., & Omri, A. (2021). Board Diversity and Corporate Social Responsibility: Empirical Evidence from France. *Journal Of Business Ethics*, *173*(1), 133155. https://doi.org/10.1007/s10551-020-04522-4

Benlemlih, M., & Yavaş, Ç. V. (2023). Economic Policy Uncertainty and Climate Change: Evidence from CO2 Emission. *Journal Of Business Ethics*, *191*(3), 415441. https://doi.org/10.1007/s10551-023-05389-x

Blyth, W., Bradley, R., Bunn, D., Clarke, C., Wilson, T., & Yang, M. (2007). Investment risks under uncertain climate change policy. *Energy Policy*, *35*(11), 57665773. https://doi.org/10.1016/j.enpol.2007.05.030

Caby, J., Coron, C., & Ziane, Y. (2022a). The Effect of Top Management Team Gender Diversity on Climate Change Management: An International Study. *Sustainability, 14*(2), 1032. https://doi.org/10.3390/su14021032

Caby, J., Coron, C., & Ziane, Y. (2022b). The Effect of Top Management Team Gender Diversity on Climate Change Management: An International Study. *Sustainability, 14*(2), 1032. https://doi.org/10.3390/su14021032

Chen, K., Erzurumlu, Y. O., Gozgor, G., Lau, C. K. M., & Turkkan, M. (2024). The Impact of Economic Uncertainty on Corporate ESG Performance: Global Evidence. *Research In International Business and Finance*, *72*, 102533. https://doi.org/10.1016/j.ribaf.2024.102533

Chen, S., Song, Y., & Gao, P. (2023). Environmental, social, and governance (ESG) performance and financial outcomes: Analyzing the impact of ESG on financial performance. *Journal Of Environmental Management*, *345*, 118829. https://doi.org/10.1016/j.jenvman.2023.118829

Cooper, I., & Priestley, R. (2011). Real investment and risk dynamics. *Journal Of Financial Economics*, *101*(1), 182205. https://doi.org/10.1016/j.jfineco.2011.02.002

Croson, R., & Gneezy, U. (2009). Gender Differences in Preferences. *Journal Of Economic Literature*, *47*(2), 448474. https://doi.org/10.1257/jel.47.2.448

Disli, M., Yilmaz, M. K., & Mohamed, F. F. M. (2022). Board characteristics and sustainability performance: empirical evidence from emerging markets. *Sustainability Accounting Management and Policy Journal*, *13*(4), 929952. https://doi.org/10.1108/sampj-09-2020-0313

Dixit, R. K., & Pindyck, R. S. (1994). Investment under Uncertainty. Dans *Princeton University Press eBooks*. https://doi.org/10.1515/9781400830176

Eagly, A. H., & Carli, L. L. (2008). Through the labyrinth: the truth about how women become leaders. *Choice Reviews Online*, *45*(12), 456881. https://doi.org/10.5860/choice.45-6881

Ellili, N. O. D. (2022). Impact of environmental, social and governance disclosure on dividend policy: What is the role of corporate governance ? Evidence from an emerging market. *Corporate Social Responsibility and Environmental Management*, *29*(5), 13961413. https://doi.org/10.1002/csr.2277

Fu, L., Sun, Z., Zha, L., Liu, F., He, L., Sun, X., & Jing, X. (2019). Environmental awareness and pro-environmental behavior within China's road freight transportation industry: Moderating role of perceived policy effectiveness. *Journal Of Cleaner Production*, *252*, 119796. https://doi.org/10.1016/j.jclepro.2019.119796

Galbreath, J. (2012). Are boards on board? A model of corporate board influence on sustainability performance. *Journal Of Management & Organization*, *18*(4), 445460. https://doi.org/10.5172/jmo.2012.18.4.445

Gao, J., & Zhang, L. (2023). Climate Policy Uncertainty and Corporate Investment: Evidence From the U.S. Tourism and Hospitality Sector. *Journal Of Travel Research*, *63*(2), 517530. https://doi.org/10.1177/00472875221149319

Gavriilidis, K. (2021). Measuring climate policy uncertainty. *SSRN Electronic Journal*. https://doi.org/10.2139/ssrn.3847388

Gilligan, C., & Attanucci, J. (1988). Two Moral Orientations: Gender Differences and Similarities. *Merrill-palmer Quarterly*, *34*(3), 223237. https://eric.ed.gov/?id=EJ373883

Glass, C., Cook, A., & Ingersoll, A. R. (2015). Do Women Leaders Promote Sustainability? Analyzing the Effect of Corporate Governance Composition on Environmental Performance. *Business Strategy and The Environment*, *25*(7), 495511. https://doi.org/10.1002/bse.1879

Gull, A. A., Atif, M., & Hussain, N. (2022). Board gender composition and waste management: Cross-country evidence. *The British Accounting Review*, *55*(1), 101097. https://doi.org/10.1016/j.bar.2022.101097

Hambrick, D. C., & Mason, P. A. (1984). Upper Echelons: The Organization as a Reflection of Its Top Managers. *Academy Of Management Review*, *9*(2), 193206. https://doi.org/10.5465/amr.1984.4277628

Harjoto, M. A., & Wang, Y. (2024). Economic policy uncertainty and environmental, social and governance (ESG) disclosure: the moderating effects of board network centrality and political connections. *Corporate Governance*. https://doi.org/10.1108/cg-08-2023-0349

He, X., Jing, Q., & Chen, H. (2023). The impact of environmental tax laws on heavy-polluting enterprise ESG performance: A stakeholder behavior perspective. *Journal Of Environmental Management*, *344*, 118578. https://doi.org/10.1016/j.jenvman.2023.118578

Hu, Y., Bai, W., Farrukh, M., & Koo, C. K. (2023). How does environmental policy uncertainty influence corporate green investments? *Technological Forecasting and Social Change*, *189*, 122330. https://doi.org/10.1016/j.techfore.2023.122330

Huang, H., & Ye, Y. (2021). Rethinking capital structure decision and corporate social responsibility in response to COVID-19. *Accounting And Finance*, *61*(3), 47574788. https://doi.org/10.1111/acfi.12740

Ilyas, M., Mian, R. U., & Suleman, M. T. (2022). Economic policy uncertainty and firm propensity to invest in corporate social responsibility. *Management Decision*, *60*(12), 32323254. https://doi.org/10.1108/md-06-2021-0746

Jizi, M. (2017). The Influence of Board Composition on Sustainable Development Disclosure. *Business Strategy and The Environment*, *26*(5), 640655. https://doi.org/10.1002/bse.1943

Kanagaretnam, K., Lobo, G., & Zhang, L. (2022). Relationship Between Climate Risk and Physical and Organizational Capital. *Management International Review*, *62*(2), 245283. https://doi.org/10.1007/s11575-022-00467-0

Khalfaoui, R., Goodell, J. W., Mefteh-Wali, S., Chishti, M. Z., & Gozgor, G. (2024). Impact of climate risk shocks on global food and agricultural markets: A multiscale and tail connectedness analysis. *International Review Of Financial Analysis*, *93*, 103206. https://doi.org/10.1016/j.irfa.2024.103206

Khemakhem, H., Arroyo, P., & Montecinos, J. (2023). Gender diversity on board committees and ESG disclosure: evidence from Canada. *Journal Of Management & Governance*, *27*(4), 13971422. https://doi.org/10.1007/s10997-022-09658-1

Kim, H., & Kung, H. (2016). The Asset Redeployability Channel: How uncertainty affects corporate investment. *Review Of Financial Studies*, *30*(1), 245280. https://doi.org/10.1093/rfs/hhv076

Kim, S., & Li, Z. (2021). Understanding the Impact of ESG Practices in Corporate Finance. *Sustainability*, *13*(7), 3746. https://doi.org/10.3390/su13073746

Kulatilaka, N., & Perotti, E. C. (1998). Strategic growth options. *Management Science*, *44*(8), 10211031. https://doi.org/10.1287/mnsc.44.8.1021

Li, H., Wang, X., Zhao, X., & Qi, Y. (2021). Understanding systemic risk induced by climate change. *Advances In Climate Change Research*, *12*(3), 384394. https://doi.org/10.1016/j.accre.2021.05.006

Li, J., Fang, L., Chen, S., & Mao, H. (2022). Can low-carbon pilot policy improve atmospheric environmental performance in China? A quasi-natural experiment approach. *Environmental Impact Assessment Review*, *96*, 106807. https://doi.org/10.1016/j.eiar.2022.106807

Lopez, J. M. R., Sakhel, A., & Busch, T. (2016). Corporate investments and environmental regulation: The role of regulatory uncertainty, regulation-induced uncertainty, and investment history. *European Management Journal*, *35*(1), 91101. https://doi.org/10.1016/j.emj.2016.06.004

Løwendahl, B., & Revang, Ø. (1998). Challenges to existing strategy theory in a postindustrial society. *Strategic Management Journal*, *19*(8), 755773. https://doi.org/10.1002/(sici)1097-0266(199808)19:8

May, A. M., McGarvey, M. G., Gustafson, C. R., & Mieno, T. (2020). Gender, environmental issues and policy: An examination of the views of male and female economists. *Ecological Economics*, *182*, 106877. https://doi.org/10.1016/j.ecolecon.2020.106877

McGuinness, P. B., Vieito, J. P., & Wang, M. (2019). Proactive government intervention, board gender balance, and stakeholder engagement in China and Europe. *Asia Pacific Journal of Management*, *37*(3), 719762. https://doi.org/10.1007/s10490-018-9611-y

Mirza, N., Umar, M., Horobet, A., & Boubaker, S. (2024). Effects of climate change and technological capex on credit risk cycles in the European Union. *Technological Forecasting and Social Change*, *204*, 123448. https://doi.org/10.1016/j.techfore.2024.123448

Nicolò, G., Sannino, G., & De Iorio, S. (2021). Gender diversity and online intellectual capital disclosure: Evidence from Italian-listed firms. *Journal Of Public Affairs*, *22*(4). https://doi.org/10.1002/pa.2706

Ongsakul, V., Papangkorn, S., & Jiraporn, P. (2023a). Estimating the effect of climate change exposure on firm value using climate policy uncertainty: A text-based approach. *Journal Of Behavioral and Experimental Finance*, *40*, 100842. https://doi.org/10.1016/j.jbef.2023.100842

Ongsakul, V., Papangkorn, S., & Jiraporn, P. (2023b). Estimating the effect of climate change exposure on firm value using climate policy uncertainty: A text-based approach. *Journal Of Behavioral and Experimental Finance*, *40*, 100842. https://doi.org/10.1016/j.jbef.2023.100842

Perrin, C., & Weill, L. (2023). Girls will be girls. The gendered effect of economic policy uncertainty on corporate investment. *Applied Economics*, *56*(9), 9971011. https://doi.org/10.1080/00036846.2023.2174935

Pfeffer, J., & Salancik, G. R. (2011). External Control of Organizations: Resource Dependence Perspective. Dans *Routledge eBooks* (p. 267271). https://doi.org/10.4324/9781315701967-54

Qiu, Y., Li, Q., Wang, T., Yin, L., Chen, W., & Liu, H. (2022). Optimal planning of Cross-regional hydrogen energy storage systems considering the uncertainty. *Applied Energy*, *326*, 119973. https://doi.org/10.1016/j.apenergy.2022.119973

Qureshi, M. A., Kirkerud, S., Theresa, K., & Ahsan, T. (2019). The impact of sustainability (environmental, social, and governance) disclosure and board diversity on firm value: The moderating role of industry sensitivity. *Business Strategy and The Environment*, *29*(3), 11991214. https://doi.org/10.1002/bse.2427

Ren, X., Qin, J., & Dong, K. (2022). How Does Climate Policy Uncertainty Affect Excessive Corporate Debt? The Case of China. *Journal Of Environmental Assessment Policy and Management*, *24*(02). https://doi.org/10.1142/s1464333222500259

Ren, X., Zhang, X., Yan, C., & Gozgor, G. (2022). Climate policy uncertainty and firm-level total factor productivity: Evidence from China. *Energy Economics*, *113*, 106209. https://doi.org/10.1016/j.eneco.2022.106209

Sendstad, L. H., & Chronopoulos, M. (2019). Sequential investment in renewable energy technologies under policy uncertainty. *Energy Policy*, *137*, 111152. https://doi.org/10.1016/j.enpol.2019.111152

Shahab, Y., Gull, A. A., Rind, A. A., Sarang, A. A. A., & Ahsan, T. (2022). Do corporate governance mechanisms curb the anti-environmental behavior of firms worldwide? An illustration through waste management. *Journal Of Environmental Management*, *310*, 114707. https://doi.org/10.1016/j.jenvman.2022.114707

Shahbaz, M., Karaman, A. S., Kilic, M., & Uyar, A. (2020). Board attributes, CSR engagement, and corporate performance: What is the nexus in the energy sector ? *Energy Policy*, *143*, 111582. https://doi.org/10.1016/j.enpol.2020.111582

Strobel, J., Salyer, K. D., & Lee, G. S. (2018). Uncertainty, agency costs and investment behavior in the Euro area and in the USA. *Journal Of Asian Business And Economic Studies*, *25*(1), 122143. https://doi.org/10.1108/jabes-04-2018-0007

Sudaryati, R. A. E. (2020). Environmental Uncertainty and Firm Performance: The Moderating Role of Corporate Governance. *Journal Akuntansi*, *24*(2), 187. https://doi.org/10.24912/ja.v24i2.690

Tichenor, J., Green, A., West, J., & Croom, R. (2022). Moving beyond the business case for female leaders: A longitudinal panel study of the impact of female leadership on corporate social responsibility. *Business And Society Review*, *127*(3), 639661. https://doi.org/10.1111/basr.12287

Vural-Yavaş, Ç. (2020). Corporate risk-taking in developed countries: The influence of economic policy uncertainty and macroeconomic conditions. *Journal Of Multinational Financial Management*, *54*, 100616. https://doi.org/10.1016/j.mulfin.2020.100616

Walls, J. L., Berrone, P., & Phan, P. H. (2011). Corporate governance and environmental performance: is there really a link ? *Strategic Management Journal*, *33*(8), 885913. https://doi.org/10.1002/smj.1952

Wasiuzzaman, S., & Subramaniam, V. (2023). Board gender diversity and environmental, social and governance (ESG) disclosure: Is it different for developed and developing nations ? *Corporate Social Responsibility and Environmental Management*, *30*(5), 21452165. https://doi.org/10.1002/csr.2475

Xu, Z. (2019). Economic policy uncertainty, cost of capital, and corporate innovation. *Journal Of Banking & Finance*, *111*, 105698. https://doi.org/10.1016/j.jbankfin.2019.105698

Yahya, H. (2023). Female leadership and ESG performance of firms: Nordic evidence. *Corporate Governance*. https://doi.org/10.1108/cg-03-2023-0129

Zhang, C., Gao, L., Wang, W., Hao, D., & Wang, Q. (2022). ESG ratings, monetary policy uncertainty, and bond issuance premium. *Environmental Science And Pollution Research*, *31*(7), 1007110085. https://doi.org/10.1007/s11356-022-24719-6

Social Innovations as an Object of Research in Finance Theory

Olga Andreeva, Venelin Terziev

1. Introduction

The issues of meeting the social needs of citizens are in the field of view of various institutions, and state regulation is decisive here. In this regard, the development of theoretical concepts that analyze the role of these institutions and seek optimal solutions for determining social and personal responsibility, and duties of the state, business, and citizens themselves, which is implemented through appropriate proportions of redistribution of created value, including through financial relations, is of interest. In our opinion, for the most effective solution to social problems of society, one should turn to the theory of social innovations, which includes finding the most promising directions for financial regulation, since the financial aspect of the problem often becomes decisive in the implementation of social policy.

2. Social innovations as an object of research in finance theory

Social innovations are the object of scientific interest of a fairly large number of authors, however, the points of application of such interest are mainly limited to the sociological or philosophical context. From an economic point of view, social innovations are considered mainly within the framework of such a scientific field of research as "Economics and Management of the National Economy", for example, within the framework of labor economics or innovation management, while the financial aspects of social innovations are practically outside the field of interest of both domestic and foreign authors, which causes the separation of financial science from the existing practice of financing social innovations.

In general, at present, the features of the formation and use of financial resources in the sphere of social innovations have not been sufficiently studied from a theoretical standpoint, the methodological aspects of constructing their financial mechanism have not been covered, and its model that meets modern challenges in the economy and social sphere has not been formed. There are practically no works studying state and market methods of regulating the financial mechanism of social innovations. The instruments for financing social innovations, implemented, among other things, within the framework of new formats of cooperation between the state, business, and non-profit organizations, need to be systematized and assessed. Of course, the fruitfulness of the above-mentioned scientific developments largely depends on the clarity of understanding and defining the essential features of social innovations, the prerequisites for their emergence, and specific characteristics.

To form a holistic view of the essence of social innovation, it is advisable to consider the origin and interpretation of this term from the point of view of etymology.

Everything that is connected with the life and relationships of people in society is identified with the social. Social (from Latin socialis) means public, connected with the life and relationships of people in society. Social is generated by the conditions of social life, a certain environment, and a system, which indicates not only the social development of a person but also his orientation to social values, norms, and rules of the environment of life in which a person lives and realizes himself as an individual. This concept is not scientific but only supplements the characteristics, and definition of the content of such concepts as "social state", "social system" and others.

The concept of "innovation" (from the Latin innovatio) is no less multifaceted, denoting the introduction of any innovations into practice. Representing a complex organizational and economic mechanism, innovations include scientific and intellectual potential, thereby ensuring the possibility of their implementation at all stages of the reproduction process. Of course, the most important aspect of this mechanism is the attraction and reasonable use of financial resources. According to the authors, in a broad sense, innovations should be considered new technologies, types of goods and services, new organizational and technical solutions in the production, financial, social, and other spheres. The term "innovation" first appeared in the works of the famous economist I. Schumpeter proposed a theory of economic development, which designated a "new concept of resources" as the basis of this theory (Abernathy and Clark, 1985). The scientist believed that the implementation of this concept involves the discovery and development of new markets for the sale of goods, new sources of raw materials for its production, and an effective reorganization of the market and enterprise, which gave the concept of "innovation" a broader meaning in contrast to "innovation". The scientist also identified the term "social value", which denoted the conscious need of society (Shumpeter, 2008).

In the theory of creative destruction, which he developed later, it was noted that the vector of social development should be directed toward an economic system in which social value occupies a central place. It is in the space around "social value" that the field of social innovation and social entrepreneurship is formed and developed, where the main focus is on income that will bring social benefit, and not just individual value (McNeill, 2012) while transforming and improving socio-economic systems that are unable to satisfy the primary needs of society.

A significant contribution to the development and understanding of I. Schumpeter's theory of innovation was made by S. Kuznets, who singled out the social aspect as the most important component of innovative development. The scientist believed that social innovations, together with technological ones, determine each economic era, calling this the term "epochal innovations". He outlined the role of social innovations, which consists of maximizing the usefulness of technological innovations, and proved that social innovations can be created not only at the macro level but also, most importantly, at the micro level, forming standards of behavior of economic agents that serve as the basis for the process of forming social innovations (Kuznets, 1955).

One of the founders of modern theoretical sociology, American scientist T. Parsons believed that social innovations should be considered new forms of building human activity in society as a whole or within certain subsystems, for example, the economic subsystem of society (Parsons, 1966).

J. Mulgan, S. Tucker, R. Ali, and B. Sanders, based on the fact that "innovations" are new ideas that work, consider the concept of "social innovations" as new ideas aimed at achieving social goals, giving this term potentially broad boundaries without reflecting the essential characteristics that distinguish social innovations from innovations in general.

Later, scientists proposed a narrower interpretation of this concept, defining "social innovations" as innovative activities and services motivated by the need to meet social needs, implemented mainly by organizations whose main goals are social (Mulgan et al. 2007). This interpretation allows us to specify the concept of "social innovation" and reflects its main difference from "business innovation", which is motivated in its activities, as a rule, by profit maximization (Solovyeva, 2019).

At the same time, one should not agree with the authors on this point, since some business innovations, despite the fact that their initial goal is to make a profit and increase competitiveness, ultimately lead to the development of new social services and the creation of public goods, which is especially evident in modern conditions, characterized by active technologization of all spheres of public life. In this case, social innovations should be considered as a result of the actions of economic agents, which include politicians, intellectuals, businessmen, public representatives, etc., and the values created by them - as factors that set the vectors of the development of social innovations. According to J. Phils, social innovations, like any new and useful solution, are aimed at society as a whole, namely, the satisfaction and development of social needs or problems (Phills et al., 2008a). However, in our opinion, in this definition, the presentation of the requirement of usefulness is not entirely correct, since the effect of the introduction of social innovations is unpredictable and may not always be positive or is of a short-term nature, and then can bring negative effects (Popov and Omonov, 2016).

The Italian scientist E. Manzini believes that social innovations are changes that occur as a result of the process of transformation of existing assets (social capital, historical heritage, available advanced technologies), the vector of which is the achievement of important social goals in a new way (Manzini, 2014). In the context of this definition, social innovations are a natural component of social life and, like any other innovations, contain elements of novelty and contribute to the improvement of any processes, social innovations may not be completely new, but must necessarily be aimed at increasing the efficiency of these processes (Social innovations in the urban context, 2016a). The scientist, considering social innovations, divided them into two groups:

- arising "from below" - initiated, relying mainly on their resources, by local communities or associations of people who implement and manage the new solutions and ideas they have found;
- social innovations initiated "from above" – when the state, state organizations, and high-level government institutions record the existence of a

> problem and identify the public resources needed to solve it, orienting local initiatives toward further solving social problems by activating the identified resources and establishing interactions and relationships between the initiators.

Often, social innovations "from below" and "from above" are transformed and combined into "hybrid" ones under the influence of the increasing complexity of interactions between participants in the social innovation process (Manzini, 2014).

In domestic scientific literature, "social innovations" are considered one of the functional types in the general model of innovations, together with technological, organizational and managerial information, and other types of innovations. Thus, according to Polyakova E.V., social innovations are the transformation of social resources of economic systems following the civilizational trajectory of development, which are a necessary prerequisite for the successful implementation of technical and technological innovations (Polyakova, 2009).

Ivanovsky B.G. defines social innovations as "new solutions (products, services, models, markets, processes, etc.), simultaneously satisfying a social need with the greatest effects in contrast to existing solutions and leading to new or improved opportunities and relationships, more efficient use of assets and resources" (Ivanovskiy, 2020).

An increasing number of domestic researchers, under the influence of those significant transformation processes occurring in socio-economic systems in recent years, consider the concept of social innovations by analogy with the interpretations of foreign authors, focusing on their capabilities in the social sphere.

Popov E.V., Omonov Zh.K. understand social innovations as new ideas, opportunities, and actions in the social space that increase the possibilities of using resources to solve economic, social, cultural, and environmental problems. At the same time, the authors emphasize that social space should be understood as a multi-faceted and interconnected system of social processes, as well as social relations, positions, and practices. Consequently, based on the above, the essence of social innovations consists in expanding the possibility of using various resources to solve existing problems in public life, the main ones of which are social, and improving its quality (Popov and Omonov, 2016b).

Panteleeva T.S. considers social innovations as a result of scientific development, organization, and application of something new that satisfies the needs of a person and society and at the same time causes social changes (Panteleeva, 2003).

A.V. Negorzhina, N.V. Lazareva define social innovations as "new ideas, strategies, technologies that contribute to the solution of socially significant problems that cause social changes in society" (Negorozhina and Lazareva, 2016c). According to Romashchenko T.D. and Kisova E.V., social innovations act as "a set of qualitative changes in the areas of formation, development, and implementation of human and social capital with the aim of increasing the level of personal and public well-being" (Romashtenko and Kisova, 2020a).

Thus, at present, there are quite a large number of different views on the definition of social innovation, the content of which depends, among other things, on the breadth of the research conducted by the authors, the field of scientific knowledge, the goals and objectives set. At the same time, in our opinion, almost all existing points of view can be grouped within the framework of three theoretical and methodological approaches. Thus, within the framework of the first approach, it is possible to combine opinions that define social innovation as new ideas, solutions, technologies, etc., that is, considered by the authors as a result of creative, intellectual, and scientific research activities. In our opinion, this is a rather "narrow" vision of social innovation, since it is limited only to the initial stages of their life cycle.

3. Conclusion

A broader approach to understanding social innovations is demonstrated by their interpretations in the context of transformation processes that transform established structures, connections, and relationships. Often, within the framework of such a process approach, a certain line is drawn between social and technological innovations, however, a significant drawback of such positions is that they can lead to a substitution of cause-and-effect relationships for the implementation of social innovations. Within the framework of the third approach, social innovations are defined as new forms of influence on the social space as a whole or its specific structural components, i.e. the emphasis in such definitions is not on the essence of social innovations as such, but on the assessment of the results of their dissemination.

Thus, the following interpretation of the concept is proposed: social innovations are new ideas, solutions, and technologies, the implementation process of which allows to level out transformational changes caused by market and state failures, and to more effectively satisfy public needs as a result of qualitative transformations of existing socio-economic systems due to full financial support. The financial component is highlighted within the framework of the study conducted by the authors and suggests further study of issues of financial support for social innovations, including the principles and sources of their financing in the context of various entities (commercial enterprises, non-profit organizations, the state, citizens), forms, methods, instruments of the mechanism of financial support for social innovations, the interpenetration of financial, social and innovation policies, etc.

References

Abernathy, W.J., & Clark, K.B. (1985). Innovation: mapping the winds of creative destruction // *Research Policy*. 1985. N 1 (14). pp. 3-22.

Shumpeter, Y.A. (2008). Theory of Economic Development. *Moscow: Direct-Media Publishing*, 2008. pp. 277-350.

McNeill, J. (2012). Through Schumpeter: Public Policy, Social Innovation and Social Entrepreneurship // *The International Journal of Sustainability Policy and Practice*. 2012. N 1 (8). P. 81-94.

Kuznets, S. (1955). Economic Growth and Income Inequality // *The American Economic Review*. 1955. Vol. XLV. pp. 2-28.

Parsons, T. (1966). The Concept of Society: The Components and Their Interrelations // *T. Parsons. Societies: Evolutionary and Comparative Perspectives. Englewood Cliffs (N. J.): Prentice-Hall*, 1966. pp. 5-29.

Mulgan, G., Tucker, S., Ali, R., & Sanders, B. (2007). Social Innovation: What It Is, Why It Matters and How It Can Be Accelerated, 2007, ISBN 1-905551-03-7 / 978-1-905551-03-3,

Solovyeva, T. S. (2019). Support of social innovations as a vector of regional social policy / T. S. Solovyeva // Strategy and tactics of implementation of socio-economic reforms: regional aspect: *Proceedings of the VIII international scientific-practical conference, Vologda, December 12-14, 2018. – Vologda: Vologda Scientific Center of the Russian Academy of Sciences*, 2019. pp. 338-343.

Phills Jr., J. A., Deiglmeier, K., & Miller, D. T. (2008a). Rediscovering Social Innovation. *Stanford Social Innovation Review*, 6(4), 34–43. https://doi.org/10.48558/GBJY-GJ47.

Popov, E.V., & Omonov, Zh.K. (2016). The essence and typology of social innovations // *Innovations*. 2016. N°1 (207). pp. 53-58.

Manzini, E. (2014). Making things happen: Social innovation and design // *Design issues*. 2014. N 1. Vol. 30. pp. 57-66.

Social innovations in the urban context. (2016a) / Ed. by T. Brandsen, S. Cattacin, A. Evers, A. Zimmer. – Cham; Heidelberg; New York; Dordrecht; London: *Springer*, 2016. 313 p., DOI 10.1007/978-3-319-21551-8.

Polyakova, E.V. (2009). The essence and classification of social innovations // *Actual issues of economic sciences*. 2009. N°5-2 [Electronic resource] / Access mode: https://cyberleninka.ru/article/n/suschnost-i-klassifikatsiya-sotsialnyh-innovatsiy (Retrieved 03 October 2024).

Ivanovskiy, B.G. (2020). Social innovation as a factor in achieving sustainable socio-economic development // *Economic and social problems of Russia*. 2020. N° 1(41). pp. 104-126, DOI 10.31249/espr/2020.01.05.

Popov, E.V., & Omonov, Zh.K. (2016b). The essence and typology of social innovations // *Innovations*. 2016. N°1 (207) [Electronic resource] / Access mode: https://cyberleninka.ru/article/n/suschnost-i-tipologiya-sotsialnyh-innovatsiy (Retrieved 03 October 2024).

Panteleeva, T. S. (2003). Features of innovations in the field of social work // *Domestic journal of social work*. 2003. N° 2. pp. 24-29.

Negorozhina, A.V., & Lazareva, N.V. (2016c). Management of social innovations // *Humanitarian foundations of social progress: Russia and modern times: collection of articles of the International scientific and practical conference*. 2016. pp. 291-295.

Romashtenko, T.D., & Kisova, A.E. (2020a). Social innovations: content, subject forms and classification // *Proceedings of Voronezh State University. Series: Economics and Management*. 2020. N° 3. pp. 25-33. https://doi.org/10.17308/econ.2020.3/3102.

Effective Application of UAVs in Modern Livestock Agriculture

Marin Marinov, Marin Georgiev

1. Introduction

In addition to distortions, the quality of an image is also affected by the illumination and contrast in the acquired images. One widely used method to improve the quality of images is by increasing the contrast. Since these methods redistribute the brightness levels in a given dynamic range, their application to color images is associated with some peculiarities.

This paper explores three contrast enhancement algorithms. One is expanding the brightness dynamic range throughout the image. In the second case, the histogram of the image is used, and the goal of the processing is to achieve a more uniform histogram. The third algorithm is adaptive, where the uniform histogram algorithm is applied to individual regions of the image rather than the entire image.

Understanding the histogram of an image is a critical factor when working with images. The histogram shows whether the exposure of the image is correct, whether the light is hard or soft, and what changes need to be made to get a better image. Familiarity with its characteristics can enhance a user's skills in computer image processing.

Ideally, histograms of high-quality images should exhibit an even distribution, with the majority of pixels falling within the mid-levels region of brightness.

2. The histogram as a mean for analysis and correction of images

The histogram of gradient levels represents the frequency of occurrence of these levels in an image, forming a discrete function. It is easy to create an algorithm to obtain the histogram of an image. In an array with a dimension corresponding to the number of brightness levels (in practice, they rarely exceed 256), which is pre-zeroed, the number of pixels with the corresponding level is recorded. This is accomplished by reading the pixels from the image matrix and incrementing the array element that corresponds to the gradient level of each pixel by one.

The formation of the transfer function is based on analyzing the distribution histogram. It is possible to create a linear transfer function that has a non-zero slope for the portion of the histogram containing a non-zero number of elements or exceeds a certain critical minimum value. The histogram equalization algorithm for the resulting image is of particular interest (Bezryadin, 2003; Gu et al., 2013; Terziev and Petrova, 2019; 2019a).

The distribution change is derived by solving the equation:

$$\sum_{n=0}^{k} Pr\left\{g_n\right\} = \sum_{m=0}^{f} H_F\left\{g_m\right\}, \tag{1}$$

where represents the frequency of occurrence of brightness levels g_n in the converted image, and denotes the distribution of brightness levels $g_м$ of the input image.

An approximate solution in continuous form can be derived from the following equation:

$$\int_{f\ min}^{f} p_g\left(g\right)\cdot dg = \int_{f\ min}^{f} p_f\left(f\right)\cdot df, \tag{2}$$

where $p_g(g)$ represents the desired probability distribution of levels g of the resulting image, and $p_f(f)$ denotes the probability distribution of levels f of the input image.

For the case when the goal is to obtain a uniform histogram, the following dependence is used:

$$p_g\left(g\right) = \frac{1}{g_{max} - g_{min}} \tag{3}$$

Within the range of histogram equalization, the following relationship is obtained:

$$g = (g_{max} - g_{min}) \cdot P_f(f) + g_{min}, \tag{4}$$

Where:

$$P_f\left(f\right) = \int_{f\ min}^{f} p_f\left(f\right)\cdot df\ ; \tag{5}$$

A resultant histogram with a non-uniform distribution, such as exponential, Rayleigh, or power 2/3, can be generated (Petrova and Petrov, 2022).

When modifying the color characteristics for each color, independent adjustment functions can be employed. However, it is desirable that these adjustments ensure white balance across different brightness levels. This is accomplished through transformations that yield identical resultant histograms (Alanezi et al., 2022a; Stewart et al., 2021; Petrova and Petrov, 2023).

In automatic exposure mode, most cameras utilize a centered histogram, where the light intensity range of the photographed subject influences the distribution of peaks in image histogram. Images with an abundance of shadows are referred to as "low luminance", while "high luminance" images tend to emphasize bright elements. Commonly used cameras employ complex algorithms that attempt to mitigate limitations and estimate the optimal brightness level for an image. As a result, this approach frequently produces images with moderate brightness (Petrova and Petrov, 2023, Petrova and Petrov, 2022).

The histogram can also be used to describe the degree of contrast in the image. It enables clear and comprehensive evaluation of the contrast. Contrast quantifies the differences in brightness between the light and dark areas of an image. When histograms are narrow, the pixel intensities cluster around certain levels, and the rest are either not occupied or there are very few pixels with such levels indicating low contrast, resulting in a "dull" image lacking detail (see Figure 1). Wide histograms represent scenes with high contrast, characterized by two maxima located at the extreme ends of the intensity level scale (Saygılı and Özmen, 2022b; Matkovic et al., 2005; Petrova et al., 2021a). Furthermore, the histogram provides insights into the dynamic range of intensities present in the image.

A study was made of the three methods of contrast enhancement when applied to a color image. Figure 1 depicts the source image, captured by one of the authors at the University of Thrace's farm in the village of Sarnitsa, with dimensions of 1600x1200 pixels.

Figure 2 shows the resulting image when expanding the dynamic range. While the image quality has improved, variations in quality are observed across different areas of the image. Notably, this image exhibits enhanced details in the branches and grass, surpassing those present in the source image.

Figure 1: Source image

Figure 2: Contrast enhancement by linear dynamic range expansion

Figure 3: Contrast enhancement by histogram equalization

Figure 3 displays the image after contrast enhancement through histogram equalization. Enhanced sharpness is evident in the details of the branches and grass at the bottom of the image. However, the grass in front of the cow lacks detail and exhibits reflections. The obtained results indicate that there is no definitive answer regarding which of the two methods yields a superior image. This finding reinforces the importance of the operator possessing the necessary knowledge and experience to make informed decisions when selecting appropriate processing methods.

Figure 4 displays the resulting image obtained using adaptive histogram scaling for 8x8 pixel regions.

a) uniform distribution   b) Rayleigh distribution

Figure 4: Contrast enhancement by adaptive fitting the histogram to a desired distribution for 8x8 pixel regions

In Figure 4 a) the histogram is scaled to a uniform distribution. The resulting image exhibits better quality compared to those obtained through the linear expansion method and the histogram equalization method. In Figure 4 b) the histogram is reduced to a Rayleigh distribution. The resulting image demonstrates comparable quality to that achieved with a uniform distribution, but there are some differences in color shades. When employing the adaptive method with 8x8 pixel regions, processed images are without significant variations in quality across different regions of the image.

Figure 5 shows the resulting image using adaptive histogram scaling for 32x32 pixel regions.

In Figure 5 a) the histogram is scaled to a uniform distribution, and in Figure 5 b) to a Rayleigh distribution. Again, the quality of the resulting images is better compared to those obtained through the linear expansion method and the histogram equalization method. Furthermore, they

a) uniform distribution b) Rayleigh distribution

Figure 5: Enhancing contrast by adaptive fitting the histogram to a desired distribution for 32x32 pixel regions

Source: authors

demonstrate relatively consistent quality across different regions of the image. When comparing them with the use of 8x8 pixel regions reveals that in certain areas, the natural appearance of colors deteriorates when using 32x32 pixel regions. However, this effect is less pronounced in the displayed figures due to their reduced size (25% of the original). Research conducted using area sizes of 64x64 pixels indicates a significant amplification of this effect. The obtained results emphasize the importance of the operator selecting the appropriate size of the areas for processing when employing the adaptive histogram equalization method.

Figure 6 displays the brightness distribution histograms of the images from Figure 1 to Figure 5.

From Figure 6, it is evident that, the histogram of the source image does not contain brightness levels below 65. The histograms of images processed using the dynamic range extension algorithm and the uniform histogram exhibit significant fluctuations. Furthermore, these histograms contain values corresponding to low brightness levels, thus accounting for the presence of dark areas in the corresponding images.

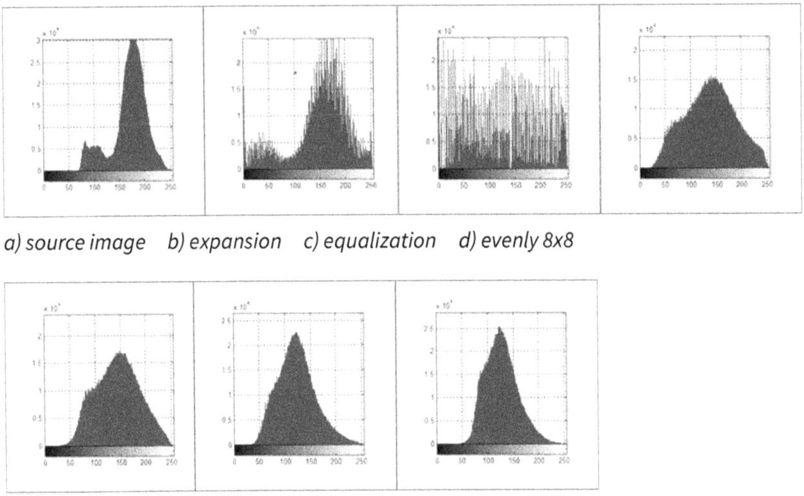

a) source image   b) expansion   c) equalization   d) evenly 8x8

e) Relay 8x8   f) uniformly 32x32   g) Relay 32x32

Figure 6: Histograms of the source and processed images
Source: authors

In the case of the adaptive method, the histogram does not exhibit such fluctuations and lacks values corresponding to very low brightness levels. This accounts for the absence of dark areas in the resulting images. The histograms with a uniform distribution appear wider, whereas histograms with a Rayleigh distribution exhibit higher concentration around the mean brightness (Terziev and Arabska, 2016; Kanev et al., 2017; Terziev, 2020; Terziev and Kanev, 2020a; Terziev and Solovev, 2020b; Solovev et al., 2020c; Kyriakopoulos et al., 2020d; Terziev and Solovev, 2020e; Dolganova et al., 2020f; Terziev, 2021b; Solovev et al., 2021c; Terziev and Solovev, 2022c; Vovchenko et al., 2023a; Albekov et al., 2023b; Terziev, 2023c; Terziev and Solovev, 2023d; Vovchenko et al., 2022d).

3. Conclusion

Appropriate selection of computer image processing methods is crucial in achieving the desired objectives in image processing. This paper study a method for image processing that is theoretically grounded and practically implemented in the Matlab environment. Multiple image processing algorithms may be required to achieve the desired result, considering factors such as illuminance, chrominance, brightness, and contrast. Histogram analysis can facilitate these processes.

Acknowledgement

The research leading to these results has received funding from the Bulgarian Ministry of education and science under the National science program Intelligent Animal Husbandry, grant agreement N° **Д01-62/18.03.2021.**

References

Bezryadin, S.N. (2003). Osnovnoy nedostatok sensorov sovremennah tsifrovah kamer. 05.11.2003.

Gu K., Zhai G., et.al. (2013). Subjective and objective quality assessment for images with contrast change, Proc. IEEE Int. Conf. on Image Processing, Melbourne, VIC, Australia, Sep. 2013. pp. 383–387.

Terziev, V., & Petrova, T., (2019). Analysis and evaluation of effectiveness of the use of unmanned aircrafts for environment monitoring, Proceedings of ADVED 2019- 5th International Conference on Advances in Education and Social Sciences, 21-23 October 2019- Istanbul, Turkey, pp. 419-425, ISBN: 978-605-82433-7-8.

Terziev, V., & Petrova, T., (2019a). Analysis of the methods for registration of images received from the information systems of non-motorized aircrafts, Proceedings of ADVED 2019- 5th International Conference on Advances in Education and Social Sciences, 21-23 October 2019- Istanbul, Turkey, pp. 485-492, ISBN: 978-605-82433-7-8.

Petrova, T., & Petrov, Zh. (2022). Linear Images Coprocessing in Environmental Monitoring. In Proceedings of the 23rd International Conference on Computer Systems and Technologies (CompSysTech '22). Association for Computing Machinery, New York, NY, USA, pp. 91–94. https://doi.org/10.1145/3546118.3546144.

Alanezi, M.A., Salami, A.F., Sha'aban, Y.A.; Bouchekara, H.R.E.H.; Shahriar, M.S.; Khodja, M. & Smail, M.K. (2022a). UBER: UAV-Based Energy-Efficient Reconfigurable Routing Scheme for Smart Wireless Livestock Sensor Network. Sensors 2022, 22, 6158. https://doi.org/10.3390/s22166158.

Stewart, A., Faraj, F., You, H., Plante, J., Lim, M., Kasa, K., Beauchamp, A., Webster, A., Martin-Boyd, L., Wong, K., Braun, A., & Macdonald, A. J. (2021). A modular system for behaviour analytics from airborne full-motion video, Proc. SPIE 11746, Artificial Intelligence and Machine Learning for Multi-Domain Operations Applications III, 117460I (12 April 2021); https://doi.org/10.1117/12.2584816.

Petrova, T., & Petrov, Zh. (2023), Contrast Enhancing by Applying Histogram Analysis in Image Processing, 2023, 22nd International Symposium INFOTEH-JAHORINA (INFOTEH), East Sarajevo, Bosnia and Herzegovina, 2023, pp. 1-4, doi 10.1109/INFOTEH57020.2023.10094055.

Saygılı, Z., & Özmen, G. (2022b). İnsansız Hava Araçlarında Gömülü Sistem Üzerinden Derin Öğrenme ile Nesne Tespiti, Avrupa Bilim ve Teknoloji Dergisi, No. 34, pp. 292-298, Mar. 2022, doi:10.31590/ejosat.1081713.

Matkovic, K. et al. (2005). Global Contrast Factor – a New Approach to Image Contrast, Computational Aesthetics, 2005, pp. 159-168.

Petrova, T., Petkova-Georgieva, St., & Petrov, Zh. (2021a). Improving the environmental monitoring process through the application of unmanned aerial vehicles, Journal of Environmental Protection and Ecology, Vol. 22, No 3 (2021), pp. 1144-1150, ISSN 1311-5065.

Terziev, V., & Arabska E. (2016). Sustainable rural development through organic production and community-supported agriculture in Bulgaria, Bulgarian Journal of Agricultural science (BJAS) 22, 2016, N 4, ISSN 1310-0351, pp.527-535.

Kanev, D., Toncheva, S., Terziev, V., & Narleva, K. (2017). Specific aspects of motivation of seafarers. 18 Annual General Assembly of the International Association of Maritime Universities Global perspectives in MET: Towards Sustainable, Green and Integrated Maritime Transport , Varna, 1, 2017, ISBN 978-954-8991-96-4, pp.392-400.

Terziev, V. (2020). Provision of Integrated Employment and Social Assistance Services in Bulgaria. In: Solovev, D. (eds) Smart Technologies and Innovations in Design for Control of Technological Processes and Objects: Economy and Production. FarEastCon 2018. Smart Innovation, Systems and Technologies, vol 138. Springer, Cham, pp. 24-39, (Print) ISBN978-3-030-15576-6, (Online) ISBN978-3-030-15577-3, https://doi.org/10.1007/978-3-030-15577-3_3.

Terziev, V., & Kanev, D. (2020a). Modern Developments in Behavioral Economics. In: Solovev, D. (eds) Smart Technologies and Innovations in Design for Control of Technological Processes and Objects: Economy and Production. FarEastCon 2018. Smart Innovation, Systems and Technologies, vol 138. Springer, Cham, pp. 10-23, Print ISBN 978-3-030-15576-6, Online ISBN978-3-030-15577-3. https://doi.org/10.1007/978-3-030-15577-3_2.

Terziev, V., & Solovev, D.B. (2020b). The Education of Cadets and Psychological Aspect of the Reasons for Their Drop-Out of the National Military University. In: Solovev, D.B., Savaley, V.V., Bekker, A.T., Petukhov, V.I. (eds) Proceeding of the International Science and Technology Conference "FarEastCon 2019". Smart Innovation, Systems and Technologies, vol 172. Springer, Singapore, pp 1013–1023, Print ISBN 978-981-15-2243-7, Online ISBN 978-981-15-2244-4 https://doi.org/10.1007/978-981-15-2244-4_98.

Solovev, D.B., Kuzora, S.S., Kyriakopoulos, G.L., & Terziev, V.K (2020c). Algorithmic Approach to the Assessment of Innovation. In: Solovev, D.B., Savaley, V.V., Bekker, A.T., Petukhov, V.I. (eds) Proceeding of the International Science and Technology Conference "FarEastCon 2019". Smart Innovation, Systems and Technologies, vol 172. Springer, Singapore, pp. 31-50, (Online) ISBN978-981-15-2244-4, (Print) ISBN ISBN978-981-15-2243-7 (Online). https://doi.org/10.1007/978-981-15-2244-4_2.

Kyriakopoulos, G.L., Solovev, D.B., Kuzora, S.S., & Terziev, V.K. (2020d). Exploring Research Methods and Dynamic Systems Toward Economic Development: An Overview. In: Solovev, D.B., Savaley, V.V., Bekker, A.T., Petukhov, V.I. (eds) Proceeding of the International Science and Technology Conference "FarEastCon 2019". Smart Innovation, Systems and Technologies, vol 172. Springer, Singapore, pp. 1-29, (Online) ISBN978-981-15-2244-4, (Print) ISBNOnline ISBN978-981-15-2243-7. https://doi.org/10.1007/978-981-15-2244-4_1.

Terziev, V., & Solovev, D.B. (2020e). Psychological Characteristics of Cadets from the Military Schools as Subjects of Educational Activity. In: Solovev, D.B., Savaley, V.V., Bekker, A.T., Petukhov, V.I. (eds) Proceeding of the International Science and Technology Conference "FarEastCon 2019". Smart Innovation, Systems and Technologies, vol 172. Springer, Singapore, pp 1025–1038, Print ISBN978-981-15-2243-7, Online ISBN978-981-15-2244-4, https://doi.org/10.1007/978-981-15-2244-4_99.

Dolganova, Y., Istomina, N., Zaborovskaya, A., & Terziev, V. (2020f). State financial resources as a tool for managing sustainable development of territories, E3S Web Conf., 208 (2020) 08015, (eISSN: 2267-1242), DOI: https://doi.org/10.1051/e3sconf/202020808015.

Terziev, V. (2021b). Management control as an effective instrument in implementation of the social program. 30th Eurasia Business and Economics Society Conference, Eurasian Business and Economics Perspectives, Eurasian Studies in Business and Economics 17, 2021, pp. 87-100, ISSN 2364-5067, ISSN 2364-5075 (electronic), ISBN 978-3-030-65146-6, ISBN 978-3-030-65147-3 (eBook), https://doi.org/10.1007/978-3-030-65147-3.

Solovev, D.B., Kuzora, S.S., & Terziev, V. (2021c). Simulation-Based Methodical Approach to Applying Managerial Decisions in Innovation. In: Solovev, D.B., Savaley, V.V., Bekker, A.T., Petukhov, V.I. (eds) Proceeding of the International Science and Technology Conference "FarEastCon 2020". Smart Innovation, Systems and Technologies, vol 227. Springer, Singapore, pp.1-11, Online ISBN978-981-16-0953-4, Print ISBN978-981-16-0952-7. https://doi.org/10.1007/978-981-16-0953-4_1.

Terziev, V., & Solovev, D.B. (2022c). Analysis of the Management of Sector "Security" as Part of the Strategic Management of Bulgaria. In: Solovev, D.B., Savaley, V.V., Bekker, A.T., Petukhov, V.I. (eds) Proceeding of the International Science and Technology Conference "FarEastCon 2021". Smart Innovation, Systems and Technologies, vol 275. Springer, Singapore, pp.95-111, Online ISBN 978-981-16-8829-4, Print ISBN 978-981-16-8828-7. https://doi.org/10.1007/978-981-16-8829-4_9.

Vovchenko, N.G., Andreeva, O.V., Dmitrieva, V.D., Kaptsova, V.S., & Terziev, V.K. (2023a). Technological, Economic, and Social Changes: The Role of End-to-End Technologies. In: Makarenko, E.N., Vovchenko, N.G., Tishchenko, E.N. (eds) Technological Trends in the AI Economy. Smart Innovation, Systems and Technologies, vol 625. Springer, Singapore, (pp. 13-20, Print ISBN978-981-19-7410-6, Online ISBN978-981-19-7411-3), https://doi.org/10.1007/978-981-19-7411-3_2 .

Albekov, A.U., Parkhomenko, T.V., Polubotko, A.A., & Terziev, V.K. (2023b), New Trends in the Sustainable Development of Logistics Systems During the Impact of COVID-19, Climate-Smart Innovation, pp. 319-328 (2023), https://doi.org/10.1142/9789811264252_0020.

Terziev, V. K. (2023c). Innovation Development of Industrial Business Organizations. In M. Okur Dinçsoy & H. Can (Eds.), Optimizing Energy Efficiency During a Global Energy Crisis (pp. 282-306). IGI Global. https://doi.org/10.4018/979-8-3693-0400-6.ch016.

Terziev, V., Solovev, D.B. (2023d). Development of the education system in Bulgaria in a period of economic transformations, AIP Conf. Proc. 2910,

020064 (2023), (Online ISSN 1551-7616, Print ISSN 0094-243X), https://doi.org/10.1063/5.0167861.

Vovchenko, N.G., Andreeva, O.V., Dmitrieva, V.D., Galazova, S.S., Terziev, V.K. (2022d). Modelling of Economic Clusters in the Russian Regions in the Context of Formation of the Industry 4.0. In: Trifonov, P.V., Charaeva, M.V. (eds) Strategies and Trends in Organizational and Project Management. DITEM 2021. Lecture Notes in Networks and Systems, vol 380. Springer, Cham. https://doi.org/10.1007/978-3-030-94245-8_91.

Social Transformations and Changes in the Educational Process

Venelin Terziev, Marin Georgiev, Simeon Simeonov

1. Introduction

Preparation and educational standards in the various stages of the educational process are undergoing development. Public development and the ongoing social transformations in societies require a rethinking of the main educational paradigms, technologies and tools

At this stage, the main form of implementing the educational process in Bulgaria (as well as in most countries) is the classroom-based form of training. The lesson is the main organizational form for this realization and represents a unity between the activity of the teacher and that of the students in the individual classes, where a specific topic from the curriculum (program) is developed for a specific learning time. The lesson is a logically complete element of the educational process. It shows the complex interaction between the goal, content, methods and means of education.

Labor markets place ever higher and more diverse demands on the workforce, which must be prepared for successful implementation in the primary labor market. In the modern school, different in nature and nature innovative approaches are being sought to improve the class-lesson format. These are: interactive lessons, using virtual reality technology, using AI in education, blended learning, 3D printing, use the design thinking process, project-based learning, inquiry-based learning, puzzle, cloud computing learning, flipped classroom, peer learning, peer feedback, crossover teaching, personalized learning, and more.

All this gives certain results, but cannot meet the entire set of requirements that appear so quickly due to the particular dynamism of the processes. Various results of research, studies and analyzes give a clear picture of insufficient preparation of all countries involved in this process.

If in the preparatory and initial course of study from the first to the fourth grade the changes that are made give sufficiently good results, then in the subsequent stages they are rather unsatisfactory. Changes in this process should be made after a thorough and in-depth analysis, because the results are available at a later stage.

The middle course of study from the fifth to the seventh grade, as well as the upper course of study - from the eighth to the twelfth grade, need changes that the class-lesson form cannot provide, and even its improvement will not be able to cover the new requirements that have arisen.

The long-known technology of social programming is a good opportunity that will allow the changes to be effective in a short enough time.

2. State of education in Bulgaria

Evaluating the educational process is a difficult and difficult task in its essence and characteristics, which by its nature has a number of conditionalities. They all need to be accounted for, noted and presented. In Bulgaria, various systems for evaluation and analysis of this process are applied, which have certain shortcomings and can be defined and accounted for even with a cursory analysis. The view from the outside gives certain reasons for greater objectivity, but also a reasonable assumption of a lack of detailed knowledge of the internal environment.

The interpretation of Lyuba Yordanova's results from the Bulgarian educational portal "Together in an Hour" is interesting (2024).

More than half of Bulgarian students lack the skills for personal and professional fulfillment in the modern world. It hurts our society and our economy.

Half of the Bulgarian students do not have skills such as analytical and critical thinking, making logical connections, reading with understanding, making sense of events, arguing, and solving everyday problems. Bulgaria is among the countries with the greatest educational inequalities in the world – the achievements of students depend on the financial status of their parents, the place where they live, on the type of school they attend.

We hear these conclusions every three years since 2001 when the results of the International Student Assessment Program of the Organization for Economic Co-operation and Development (OECD) - PISA - were released. Thus, for 22 years, Bulgaria has been ignoring the clear signs that its education system is not working and wasting generation after generation of students.

The results of the PISA 2022 study, which came out today, are even more alarming and one of the lowest since Bulgaria participated in the OECD program. The share of functionally illiterate 15-year-old students in the areas of reading literacy and mathematics already exceeds 50%. When in three years these students enter the labor market, they will not be able to realize themselves in the highly competitive environment in which the rules of new technologies dictate. They will not be able to compete with their peers from the EU - Bulgaria is in last place among the countries in the union in mathematics and second to last in reading literacy and natural sciences (before Cyprus). And the students from the countries that occupy the top places in the entire PISA ranking - the East Asian countries, Estonia, Switzerland, Canada, the Netherlands, Ireland, etc., are whole school years ahead of the Bulgarian 15-year-olds in their skills (2024).

2.1 Half of Bulgarian students are functionally illiterate

These results do not only affect the students and their future realization. They also affect the society in which we live and which in a few years will wait in vain for active citizens with the desire and skills to change the environment around them for the better. They also affect our economy, which suffers from a lack of quality human resources (Diagram 1) (2024).

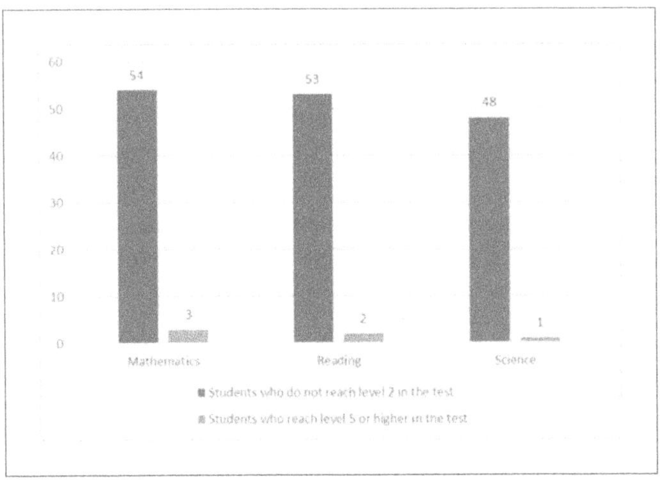

Graph 1. A worryingly high percentage of Bulgarian students are below basic level 2 in all directions of PISA 2022

Source: zaednovchas.bg, (2024)

2.2. What PISA tells us

PISA is not a test that measures what students have learned from their theoretical study material or after solving a certain number of problems of a similar type. PISA is a complex tool that assesses how well the Bulgarian education system has prepared young people to apply what they learn at school in their lives. PISA tasks are linked to everyday cases in which students have to apply key 21st-century skills. Therefore, the PISA is much more indicative of how well students are prepared for life than the Bulgarian national external assessments and matriculation exams, which mainly measure concepts learned by heart.

This year, the results of Bulgarian students are worrying in all three areas of study - reading literacy, mathematics, and natural sciences. 53% of 15-year-olds have not reached the PISA baseline reading literacy skills, making them functionally illiterate. In mathematics, the corresponding share is 54%, and in natural sciences – 48%. If we add the lessons that drop out of school before the 9th grade, when PISA is conducted, the share of functionally illiterate Bulgarian citizens jumps even more.

Bulgaria also has a very small proportion of students who reach the highest levels of skills - only 2% in reading literacy, 3% in mathematics and 1% in natural sciences. In 2022, the results of even the best-performing Bulgarian youth are decreasing - which shows that when an educational system is not effective, it affects all students.

Bulgaria's results have been bad since we participated in the research, but this year the decline is particularly serious. PISA shows that today's 15-year-olds are one academic year behind 15-year-olds in 2012. This can be explained by the lack of positive changes in two of the most important factors for student success - the quality of teaching and curricula that in today's highly technological world do nothing to help students (2024).

3. Social programming as an opportunity for change

The modern treatment of the term "programming" defines it as a general principle of management, on the basis of which the subject carries out his actions with certain means in the direction of the goals, according to the dynamic changes of his surrounding environment. In other words, on the specific content, structure and dynamics of the goal, the actions to achieve it are influenced by the challenges of the environment in which the system functions, by the degree of their knowledge and the dependence of the subject, his value orientation, priorities, opportunities, with available, the chosen forms and methods to achieve the desired result. This, more than ever, determines the need for alternative solutions and choosing the optimal option, contributing to management by results.

In the modern social, economic and political space, the phenomenon called social programming has gained popularity. To clarify its essence and significance for the theory and practice of management in the public sector, we refer to the etymology of the term "programming", the roots of which have ancient Greek origins ("pro" - in advance, before and "gram" - write, denote). From here and its manifestation is in the noun "program", which means "prescription", "announcement", "plan of work, activity... main tasks and goals of a political party, public organization, public actor and others... short an exposition of the content... of a subject of study...".

In its development, the concept of "programming" in its classical form became established in mathematics as a set of methods for creating an algorithm for the operation of an electronic computing machine... a complete computational process that aims to optimize a certain mathematical expression under given mathematical conditions. Applicable in its varieties of linear programming (a method of finding the maximum or minimum of a linear constraint function in the presence of linear constraint conditions) and nonlinear programming (a set of mathematical methods for determining the largest and smallest value of nonlinear functions in the presence of restrictive conditions), in the modern world of information technology this concept is key to the computer field (identified with coding). Moreover, in its broad interpretation, the term "programming" is associated with a range of actions in written form expressing prediction, foreshadowing, warning, declaring, proclaiming, prescribing, commanding.

In this set of meanings of the term "programming", the common thing is that it expresses a certain side of human activity, namely the pre-planning of future actions and activities, indicating their limitations. It is this country that is distinguished by a public character, the manifestation of which is the need, on the one hand, to make a decision, and on the other hand, to prepare a program expressing a certain prescription, a public announcement. In this sense, programming is a process of developing programs, understood as a specific model for purposeful activity to achieve a given goal of social, economic and political development in a period of active social transformations.

The modern treatment of the term "programming" defines it as a general principle of management, on the basis of which the subject carries out his actions with certain means in the direction of the goals, according to the dynamic changes of his surrounding environment. In other words, on the specific content, structure and dynamics of the goal, the actions to achieve it are influenced by the challenges of the environment in which the system functions, by the degree of their knowledge and the dependence of the subject, his value orientation, priorities, opportunities, with available, the chosen forms and methods to achieve the desired result. This, more than ever, determines the need for alternative solutions and choosing the optimal option, contributing to management by results. On this basis, the so-called program-target approach of management arises, which is manifested in the "Planning-Programming-Budgeting-System" (PPBS).

Originating in the mid-1960s in the United States as a system of planning, programming, and budgeting, the program-objective approach to management was first applied in the US military. Based on the idea of accelerating the processes of revealing the potential in a system with preset goals, the program-target approach quickly entered in the late 1960s and early 1970s and in civil life (initially in non-material, but in consequence also in the material sphere). This is why PPBS is seen as a progress in budgeting and a management ‚miracle'. In confirmation of this are the words of the then President of the United States Johnson, according to which: This system must ensure the execution of new tasks faster, better and cheaper, through more and better information, an opportunity must be generated for better decisions... Our decision-making process must be at the same level as that related to armaments and defense. To put it briefly and plainly, we must replace our donkey carts with trucks and our old cannons with new missiles.

What makes the approach unique for application is precisely the integration of its three main components - goals, programs, program-goal structure. And if the goals are connected with the mission (strategy) and hence the need for "unity of goals within an organization and the provision of a basis for the distribution of organizational resources", therefore also revealing the organizational potential, then the programs are the concretization of the ways, according to which the resources should be used for the realization of the goals. For this purpose, each program contains certain tasks, distributed over time and assigned to the respective contractors. From here, each of the PPBS components expresses certain management phases. Thus, planning defines long-term goals by stating what is firmly intended to be done. Programming is associated with the analysis and evaluation of the ways and possibilities for the realization of the goals (design and selection of alternative programs) in accordance with the "cost-effect (benefit)" analysis and the application of quantitative management methods. In other words, a program is a plan with definite terms (dates), thus indicating the time when what is firmly intended to be done will be done. Budgeting (financing) is associated with the selection of the most profitable and most effective programs and their inclusion in the budget for financing and implementation. And since the budget is nothing but a program of estimated prices, it gives an idea of how much money is needed and when it should be provided to ensure that what is firmly and at the right time intended to be done can be done. done

Through the systemic approach, the mentioned management phases are integrated into a single system on an interconnected basis and in a certain relationship and dependence with funding. This is the reason why one of the most authoritative specialists in the field of program management - Charles Hitch (former president of the University of California and former assistant secretary of defense of the USA) defines PPBS as "program funding" based on the principles characteristic of modern management practice. Of primary importance are the principles of:

- long-term goals and expected final results;
- prioritization and sequencing of activities and gradation of resources in the conditions of their limitation;
- complexity when studying any problem - considering each issue or separate field of activity as a system. From here is the treatment of each;
- system as a constituent part of one of a higher order and subordinating the goals and tasks of individual subsystems to the general goal of the system;
- multivariate decisions, ways and means of reaching a given goal, which requires the development of alternative decisions for action;

- evaluation and comparison of the effectiveness of individual alternatives on the basis of objective criteria and with the help of system analysis and its tools (modeling, economic-mathematical methods of research and value analysis, value-efficiency or value-utility, the method of operational research, machine and game imitation, etc.);
- continuity of planning or implementation of the so-called continuous planning horizon and making necessary adjustments to plans and programs in the process of their implementation;
- combining the program-target approach in management with financing of the programs in accordance with the degree of achievement of the goals.

From here, the basis for the functioning of PPBS are the application of the economic approach to each activity- object of management, management based on the system approach and analysis, financing on a program-target basis, which by their nature are three fundamental theoretical-methodological positions. This is what defines PPBS as a management concept with specific goals and objectives. The most important of them are:

- specification of national goals;
- coordination of activities at different levels with these goals;
- analysis and value assessment of possible action alternatives;
- increasing the role and effectiveness of control through financing.

It is the coordination of the activity of the management apparatus and its direction for the realization of the predetermined goals, which is the content of the programming. The value assessment of possible alternatives and their analysis, as well as increasing the role, importance and effectiveness of control, is related to the provision of funds, financing, which is also the most essential element of the system. On this basis, the positive characteristics of PPBS are also derived, the expression of which is in:

- the ability to coordinate planning and preparation for budgeting;
- the application of the continuous planning horizon method, on the basis of which the subordination and centralization of the decision-making process becomes possible;

- conducting a multi-year analysis, which allows to evaluate the advantages and disadvantages of each possible solution (global and rational), and from here the choice of the alternative adequate to the goals;
- the economic justification of the decisions taken from chap. of the usefulness and expediency of expenses;
- the commitment of the implementation of the decisions made to their financing, which is an expression of the simultaneous economization and efficient use of resources.

It is noteworthy that the PPBS presents the budget as a statement of basic policy that sets out the resources required to fulfill the ultimate management objectives. At the same time, the system considers activities as an intermediate stage of transforming resources into services and utility of each program. And this, by its very nature, is an expression of the "cost-effect" dependence, which is the basis of management by results.

Of course, PPBS is not without its weaknesses. Given that some of the goals and tasks have a specific nature, the opinion of the specialists is "that the great difficulty and the main weakness of the overall system consists in the general and generally recognized culturally specific values such as peace, freedom, security, justice, education and health care it is difficult to formulate such sub-goals that can serve as effective operational instruments of current policy".

Hence, programming is an important element in goal-oriented systems, a particular variety of which organizational systems are. By its very nature, the organizational system is such a system, the purpose of which is to coordinate the actions of goal-oriented parts, such as social groups and individuals, and goal orientation (means and objects of activity) with the global goal, namely obtaining a certain result (main end product).

In other words, programming in a certain image and manner connects the purposeful part of the organizational system with the means and objects of activity. In this way, a hierarchy arises in the organizational system, a distribution of power-distributive and executive functions between the subjects of the program.

The strong interrelationship between organizational system forms and programming should be taken into account. The "hard" (conditionally called "administrative-command") organizational system, as a rule, determines the corresponding forms of programming and the types of programs of the type of directive plan. The "soft" ("liberal-democratic") system defines only the general orientations and recommendations for reaching them. In practice, however, we can also encounter different symbioses between "hard" and "soft" systems in the diverse combinations of programming.

This is one side of the relationship between organizational system forms and programming. The other side is not to be neglected, where the manifestation is in the opposite impact of the form of programming and its product-programs on the organizational system. A program developed and fixed in a certain way can determine a certain form of the system (Terziev et al., 2017; Terziev, 2017a; Terziev et al., 2020; Terziev, 2021; 2021a; 2019; 2020a; Terziev and Georgiev, 2024a).

4. Conclusion

Unsatisfactory results in the educational process have their subsequent manifestations, such as a lack of sufficient skills and habits, an inability to meet certain minimum requirements for preparation in the higher education system, as well as the presence of sufficient work skills to realize the labor market. This objectively raises questions about the need for changes in the entire educational process, as well as in specific educational technologies. The improvement of the existing educational technologies only partially succeeds in responding to the ever-present new requirements, as well as to the dynamically changing environment.

The classroom system fails to satisfy the new requirements of the environment or the change happens too slowly, which leads to a set of crisis situations.

Social programming is a good opportunity that has its history and implementation. Social programming in much more detail can read and establish the requirements, plan the process, as an opportunity, and control its implementation. Of course, the preparation for this undertaking requires certain and targeted efforts in order to have some confidence in a good result. Some of the educational systems of countries in Asia much earlier and faster reconfigured their systems in a different way, which can be borrowed and tested, according to the internal environment.

The ongoing processes of social transformations in societies are an objective fact, which should be studied in the necessary comprehensiveness, and societies prepared for the upcoming changes.

References

https://zaednovchas.bg/rezultatite-ot-pisa-znak-koyto-balgaria-veche-22-godi-ni-ne-vizhda/, (2024), Retrieved 26 October 2024.

Terziev, V., Kanev, D., & Madanski, V. (2017). Social programming as an alternative in front of small business or small business a challenge to social programming. // Proceedings of ADVED 2017- 3rd International Conference on Advances in Education and Social Sciences 9-11 October 2017- Istanbul, Turkey, 2017, ISBN: 978-605-82433-0-9, pp.711-718.

Terziev, V. (2017a). Social entrepreneurship as an opportunity to model an active social program. // Proceedings of SOCIOINT 2017- 4th International Conference on Education, Social Sciences and Humanities 10-12 July 2017- Dubai, UAE, 2017, ISBN: 978-605-82433-1-6, pp.654-660.

Terziev, V., Georgiev, M., & Solovev, D. (2020). Management control in implementation of the social program. // Proceedings of INTCESS 2020- 7th International Conference on Education and Social Sciences 20-22 January, 2020 - DUBAI (UAE), International Organization Center of Academic Research, Istanbul, Turkey, 2020, pp. 870-879, ISBN: 978-605-82433-8-5.

Terziev, V. (2021). Management control as an effective instrument in implementation of the social program. // 30th Eurasia Business and Economics Society Conference, Eurasian Business and Economics Perspectives, Eurasian Studies in Business and Economics 17, 2021, pp. 87-100, ISSN 2364-5067, ISSN 2364-5075 (electronic), ISBN 978-3-030-65146-6, ISBN 978-3-030-65147-3 (eBook), https://doi.org/10.1007/978-3-030-65147-3.

Terziev, V. (2021a). Management control as an effective instrument in implementation of the social program. // 30th Eurasia Business and Economics Society Conference, Eurasian Business and Economics Perspectives, Eurasian Studies in Business and Economics 17, 2021, pp. 87-100, ISSN 2364-5067, ISSN 2364-5075 (electronic), ISBN 978-3-030-65146-6, ISBN 978-3-030-65147-3 (eBook), https://doi.org/10.1007/978-3-030-65147-3.

Terziev, V. (2019). The role and place of social programming in public governance. // Proceedings of SOCIOINT 2019- 6th International Conference on Education, Social Sciences and Humanities 24-26 June 2019- Istanbul, Turkey, International Organization Center of Academic Research, Istanbul, Turkey, 2019, pp. 354-362, ISBN: 978-605-82433-6-1.

Terziev, V. (2020a). Social programming in the context of social economy development in Bulgaria. // 51st International Scientific Conference on

Economic and Social Development (Rabat, 26-27 March 2020), Economic and Social Development, 2020, pp. 387-396, ISSN 1849-7535.

Terziev, V., & Georgiev, M. (2024a). Social transformations and social programming. // 112th International Scientific Conference on Economic and Social Development – "Creating a unified foundation for Sustainable Development: Interdisciplinarity in Research and Education" – Varazdin, 4-5 June, 2024, Economic and Social Development (Book of Proceedings), Cakovec, Croatia, 2024, pp.251-256, ISSN 1849-7535.

Processes in Changing Social Systems

Venelin Terziev, Marin Georgiev

1. Introduction

The setting of objectives and the planning of process activities in management, and hence strategic management in times of crisis, are complex and multifaceted. In accordance with the definitions of "crisis", in the broadest sense, crisis management is of strategic importance, since it is always about saving and surviving people, territories, objects, etc. Crisis management corresponds to the principles of general management, on the other hand, it is quite complex, which stems from the rapidly and dynamically changing environment - both national and international. This is most often and clearly observed in crisis circumstances that affect a huge part of the population of a country, region, continent, or even the entire world. Crises are diverse in both scale and nature, and their management is related to this. Different options for developing strategies in crises are considered, depending on whether they concern an administrative region, a country, a group of countries, or the whole world.

Overcoming crises, as well as eliminating their consequences, represent a particular challenge. Managing processes in such complex and unpredictable situations requires the readiness of leaders from different countries. Social systems are subject to specific stresses, and this even calls into question their existence as such. These processes are extremely interesting from a scientific and research point of view. Their analysis, research, and modeling will create conditions for an appropriate strategy for their management.

2. Social systems and their social mission

Social systems have their own characteristics and cannot exist by themselves. Despite the fact that there are different definitions and different interpretations in the scientific and popular literature, they form the social attitudes of individuals (people) in the environment. States can be seen as social systems, even the world can be seen as one such social system.

A welfare state is a form of government in which the state (or a well-developed network of welfare institutions) protects and promotes the economic and social well-being of its citizens, based on the principles of equal opportunity, fair distribution of wealth, and public responsibility for citizens who do not can benefit from the minimum conditions for a good life (2024a).

There are significant differences in the form and development of the welfare state in different countries and regions (Béland et al., 2021a). All welfare states involve some degree of public-private partnership, where the administration and implementation of at least some welfare programs are carried out by private organizations (Béland & Morgan, 2021b). Welfare state services are also provided at different territorial levels of government (Béland & Morgan, 2021b).

Early features of the welfare state, such as public pensions and social security, developed in the 1880s in industrializing Western countries (Béland et al., 2021a; Skocpol, 1995; Koehler–Derrick & Lee, 2023a). The First World War, the Great Depression, and the Second World War have been characterized as important events that initiated the expansion of the welfare state (Koehler–Derrick & Lee, 2023a; O'Hara, ed. Welfare state). The most comprehensive forms of the welfare state were developed after the Second World War (Béland et al., 2021a). The German term sozialstaat ("social state") has been used since 1870 to describe state support programs developed by German sozialpolitiker ("social politicians") and implemented as part of Otto von Bismarck's conservative reforms (Fay, 1950).

The literal English equivalent of "welfare state" has not taken root in English-speaking countries (Smith, 1901). During World War II, however, Anglican Archbishop William Temple, author of Christianity and the Social Order (1942), popularized the concept using the phrase "welfare state" (Gough, 1989). Bishop Temple's use of the term "welfare state" is linked to Benjamin Disraeli's 1845 novel The Sibyl, or the Two Nations (in other words, Rich and Poor), where he wrote: "Government has but one duty, and it is to provide for the social well-being of the PEOPLE" (Disraeli, 2024b). At the time he wrote The Sibyl, Disraeli (later Prime Minister) belonged to Young England, a conservative group of young Tories who disagreed with the Whigs' handling of the living conditions of the industrial poor. Members of Young England sought to enlist the support of the privileged classes to help the less fortunate and to recognize the dignity of labor that they believed characterized England during the feudal Middle Ages (Alexander).

Social systems work in an organization with certain rules. These rules are created to meet the specific needs of the individuals who participate in a given social system. The development of social systems leads to a distortion of the set of existing rules, which becomes unacceptable for individuals. This is one of the prerequisites for changing social systems or their destruction. The period of transformation of one social system into another is usually accompanied by cataclysms that societies experience.

Historians talk about cyclical changes in social systems. There is only a certain accuracy in this statement. However, it must be emphasized that the changes that occur in social systems are caused by certain circumstances and factors that affect the system itself. Turbulence preceding certain transformations in the social system is a signal that a period of systemic change will soon begin.

Signals of change in social systems are a large set of events and actions that occur in a certain sequence. These can be frequent regional military conflicts and tension in certain communities, creating discomfort in the coexistence of a certain group of people and many others.

All the elements of a state of tension in existing social systems are present. The internal and external environments operate in a series of defective processes. This not only creates a sense of failure in their existence but also foreshadows many transformations to come. The rules created for the normal functioning of these social systems have exhausted their essence and must be replaced by other rules that satisfy the existence of new social systems.

Even a cursory review of the behavior of the leaders of existing social societies clearly shows that a dramatic change is coming, in which all participants will be subjected to certain stresses, even strains, during this period of active transformations.

The changes that individuals participating in these new public social systems will have to accept may be intolerable for some, unacceptable for others, and objectively physically impossible for others to survive this transformation.

They seek the creation of new social systems, which will define new rules of interaction in them, which will also form new types of social relations. Undoubtedly, newly formed social leaders will play a key role in these transformations.

The process of active and overwhelming influence of public leaders is historically known. The dominant influence of strong public leaders was also evident after the end of the two world wars. Their decisions affect both large and small social systems. The rules for the functioning of transformed social systems are established and partly shaped by new social leaders of the historical moment.

The inevitability of such a process is almost impossible to predict with absolute accuracy, but considering that such processes take approximately several years, we can say that we are already in a stage of active social transformation.

The lack of research in this direction and the possibility of planning and forecasting these processes is puzzling. Even if we assume that some of it is done under the guise of protecting national security, the deepening of research in this direction should happen quite quickly and with the possibility of participation of researchers with high expertise in various fields.

3. Formation of new social centers

Ongoing geopolitical changes also imply changes in social systems. Many analysts predict dramatic changes in social relations that will lead to the formation of new spheres of influence. Whether this will happen and, above all, when it will happen, is a question from the point of view of the specific strategic analysis. Despite the impossibility of analyzing multidirectional information in this direction with a certain accuracy, it is possible to conclude with a high degree of objectivity about several main centers of influence. These centers have the economic, financial, military, political, and cultural potential to influence social systems. They have such a great power of influence that they can even model them. To a certain extent, this gives us an objective possibility of predictability, but on the other hand, it also predicts uncertainty in the direction of development of these processes.

4. The role of socially dominant leaders in the emergence of crises

The fear of ongoing realities turns out to be unexaggerated not only in our realities but also in our coexistence. Confusion from conflicting and ambiguous messages leaves us insecure as human beings with clear and coherent logical thinking, which further fuels our fears. Although we are used to the half-hearted and even sometimes lyrical political messages in the political market in Bulgaria and Europe, lately we feel a growing concern from more balanced and diplomatic political leaders. Their personal and political prudence has put us in the very unattractive position of having to wait for something for a long time, and this is against the background of public knowledge of their wanderings in search of certain solutions for which they are completely unprepared.

Personal and collective living in a political system has exhausted its meaning both for those who consume it and for those who observe it from the outside. The inability to preserve herself and respond to the changing world is a clear response to the fact that she is seeking her new and completely different transformation. These periods of transformation are usually accompanied by difficult and painful transitional states that are accompanied by many and varied conflicts. No matter how simplistic all this sounds, it has a secure and strong logical, and not only, basis - we should not underestimate our historical memory in this direction, which would prove these statements of ours with a high degree of relativity.

The question immediately arises, how and what happens to the political reality? The next question is not at all useless - what is happening to ourselves? And if the answer to the second question is relatively simpler, then the answer to the first is much more complex, both materially and procedurally. Ultimately, we will have to go through periods of active transformation of our entire social system to one degree or another, which will involve a change in political patterns of existence. If the social system is understood as the totality of relationships, then this will be practically more justifiable and more realistic.

The failures, ups, and downs of existing political realities are numerous and have their essential differences. Comparing and explaining them is important as it can be of some use as we move forward and also explain the new processes that are taking place. These processes will bring elements that we know well and even read and explain well, but also elements that will surprise us and be new with their high sensitivity.

A new political reality will try to preserve some of its elements, which it will successfully carry over into future periods. This is, of course, quite uncertain, even unlikely, because these elements exist in a unified relationship with all others, and even if some of them survive in one form or another, they will have different relationships with others that now exist.

If we are of the position that the defects in these political realities have already passed the possibility of being corrected or limited in the sense of the accumulated grievances of the people, then their destruction will occur in an avalanche. The consequences of the inadequate political reality will be felt with different strengths and to different degrees. This is quite real since they will be at different distances from the source of these processes. These influences will have a range of fluctuations that will be misunderstood by those involved because they are new and unpredictable in nature and consequences.

Organic examples of these processes in a certain concreteness as signals of what is happening can be found even now. We have developed a certain sensitive tolerance to various processes because we do not know them and do not have enough time to study them.

All of this is happening against the backdrop of multiple emerging signals from various places. Their power is enhanced by the abilities of those who create them and those who transmit them. Of course, those with the best set of active elements are the best and fastest at creating and transmitting such signals. Their creators are in the process of fighting not for survival, but for dominance. This process will form groups that will try to create new dependencies that will define a new social reality. Defining areas of influence will also lead to the social prominence of those who claim certain leadership in that environment. More important will be how the new socially dominant leaders will define or create a system of social relations that will determine the creation of new social systems. Political realities or systems will be the consequences of new social relations. The upheavals in the newly formed social systems will last very briefly from a historical point of view, and the point of view of the participants in them - very long.

These processes are extremely complex and ultimately unpredictable. Even if we have information and sufficient data about their progress, the impact force of certain elements cannot be accurately and faithfully determined and measured, which will lead to frequent and unpredictable changes. The fact that the social system is changing under the pressure of many social defects is visible and felt by almost everyone to a certain and varying degree. Much more interesting is how we will manage to get through this long and rather unpredictable difficult period, which we can clearly define as a process. It is unlikely that we will have the kind of readiness that would put us in a sufficiently advantageous position for everything to proceed to some degree of acceptability for all involved. Anxiety grows with the constant multi-directionality of signals and with the succession of emerging social defects in the system.

We know that a system - whatever it is - must have a certain efficiency, which is also associated with a certain financial value. It is difficult to predict whether those who are trying to become leading elements in the creation of a new social system have the knowledge and willingness to accept the existing dependencies. This system of social efficiency also creates problems in its existence. The problems that can be identified are behavioral. As unacceptable as all this may sound, all too often the behavior patterns of a particular person have so altered a particular social system that it continues to exist long enough without interest in any effective relationships. Certain behavioral elements may once again significantly affect the already started process and bring it to a certain stage where the new realities will have a different meaning.

The easiest way would be to wait and see what happens in the end. But will we have such an opportunity and will we, as direct participants, be able to evaluate this process? It is best to make some effort to ensure some readiness for all of this. Even if we understand and appreciate that the signals we will create and transmit will be relatively weak in strength, perhaps we should consider that they will be much stronger if there is significant content that is a reaction to these ongoing processes.

5. Dysfunctions of social systems

Social systems function according to certain rules and have their internal dependencies. Their main purpose is to serve the needs of the individuals participating in these social systems. The tension in social systems creates an objective danger to their existence. This leads to significant discrepancies between the expectations and needs of participants in social systems and their objective reality. All this may be the consequence of new expectations or new needs arising as a result of the social development of the systems, but may also be the result of internal tensions arising within the systems themselves. These stresses can be classified in different ways and according to different criteria, but this is beyond the scope of this analysis. Rather, what is important is that the tensions in social systems that arise or are created by crises lead to change. These changes can be desired or undesired. They will ensure the continued existence or transformation of the social system. The impossibility of maintaining their functioning in this way is more than obvious. Attempts to preserve them in this form will continue, but this will hardly be possible. The elites of the societies have set new demands that must be realized in some kind of social development, which will lead to serious transformations and changes in the social systems.

There are objective prerequisites for significant changes in social systems. New paradigms and new social demands are being proclaimed, multiple crises of different natures are occurring, and leading social leaders are creating expectations for change through their behavior.

Social leaders in their communication in the social environment use the whole range of means to impose their emergent desires. They do not always directly correspond to the wishes and expectations of the participants in a given system. The environment in the social system becomes unstable, and this further leads to the creation of future expectations of change.

Objective scientific and research approaches provide only a small part of the answers to managing change in social systems and can even be misleading and incorrect in some cases.

Social systems begin to obey the managerial views and specific decisions of social leaders who have a dominant influence. Historical hindsight provides some answers to these new expectations. They are not always related to the logic and correctness of the subsequent decisions, but rather to the objectification in some reality of the strategic decisions of dominant social leaders. Dominant social leaders begin to create social systems according to new rules and new requirements. If this is objectively possible, they try to transform them, or rather adapt them to their views, requirements, and intentions. In other extreme situations, they try to destroy and recreate them. This version of the existence of social systems is most critical from the point of view of the individuals participating in them, but sometimes also the most pragmatic from the point of view of the dominant social leaders. Naturally, in the course of transformations or the creation of new social systems, various environmental factors will have a significant or uncertain influence. They will be carriers of both progressive and regressive ideas. Support for both will change and take on different meanings over time. It would be illusory to claim that the sustainability of newly created or transformed systems will become an acceptable state for all participants. The emergence of new demands and new conditions will subject them to trials such as they have not experienced at any other time in their human existence. Objectively, most participants in social systems will try to adapt to the new social conditions, but a significant number will not be able to do so. Here it is perhaps correct to divide them into two groups - those who fully or partially disagree with the imposed new social rules, and those who, due to their social nature, will be unsuitable for the new social conditions. However, this group of individuals will be noticeably small to sustain the forward movement of social systems. Rather, change will only register the emergence of such fluctuations, and new social systems will try to extinguish or ignore their existence.

Social systems are under a number of strains and the current form of existence shows signs of collapse. The study of impact processes is becoming increasingly complex and challenging, and their management is subject to counterintuitive influences. This suggests a great variety and different influences that lead to similar changes in different directions.

It cannot be denied that various societies are undergoing changes that will change both the nature of existing social systems and the rules by which they operate. The known research methods give only partial answers about their future state.

The challenges are related to the speed of future scientific research, as well as the complex use of different approaches to provide accurate and truthful information and reach correct conclusions.

6. Conclusion

Processes of successive crises lead to the deepening of imbalances in social systems. The different scales and intensity of the impacts on them subject them to a series of cyclical tests. Determining the scale of changes occurring at the macro- and micro-level is difficult, and the consequences are almost unpredictable. A standard set of methods and approaches proves insufficient to define and characterize all of this. The main factor is the speed of the processes and the lack of effective time for accurate and objective analysis.

This places us, as participants in the transformation of social systems, in front of a set of challenges and tests of our suitability to be able to accept and successfully adapt to the changes that are coming. Studying these processes requires a full-scale effort and diverse experience. This is also necessary from the point of view of forecasting and planning transformation processes and effective solutions for getting out of the critical state in which social systems are (Terziev & Georgiev, 2023b; 2023c; Terziev, 2024c).

References

https://www.britannica.com/money/topic/welfare-state, (2024a). Retrieved November 6, 2024.

Béland, D., Morgan, K.J., Obinger, H., & Pierson, C. (2021a). Introduction, The Oxford Handbook of the Welfare State, Oxford University Press, pp. 1–20, 2021, doi:10.1093/oxfordhb/9780198828389.013.1, ISBN 978-0-19-882838-9.

Béland, D., & Morgan, K.J. (2021b). Governance, The Oxford Handbook of the Welfare State, Oxford University Press, pp. 172–187, 2021, doi:10.1093/oxfordhb/9780198828389.013.10, ISBN 978-0-19-882838-9.

Skocpol, T. (1995). Protecting Soldiers and Mothers, Belknap Press, 1995, ISBN 9780674717664, https://www.hup.harvard.edu/books/9780674717664, Retrieved November 6, 2024.

Koehler–Derrick, G., & Lee, M.M. (2023a). War and Welfare in Colonial Algeria. International Organization. 77 (2): 263–293, 2023. doi:10.1017/S0020818322000376. ISSN 0020-8183. S2CID 256724058.

O'Hara, P.A., ed. Welfare state. Encyclopedia of Political Economy. Routledge. p. 1247. ISBN 978-0-415-24187-8.

Fay, S.B. (1950). Bismarck's Welfare State. Current History. XVIII (101): 1–7, 1950. doi:10.1525/curh.1950.18.101.

Smith, M. (1901). Four German Jurists. IV. Political Science Quarterly. 16 (4): 641–679, 1901.

Gough, I. (1989). The Welfare State, The New Palgrave Social Economics, New York: W.W. Norton, pp. 276–281, 1989.

Disraeli, B. (2024b). Chapter 14. Sybil. Vol. Book 4, https://www.gutenberg.org/files/3760/3760-h/3760-h.htm, Retrieved November 6, 2024.

Alexander. M. Medievalism. pp. XXIV–XXV, 62, 93.

Terziev, V., & Georgiev, M. (2023b). Challenges to active social policies in Bulgaria, gabriell-e-lit, Sofia, Bulgaria, 2023, 356 p., ISBN: 978-619-7705-20-1.

Terziev, V., & Georgiev, M. (2023c). The Labor Market Policies and Social Development in Bulgaria. Optimizing Energy Efficiency During a Global Energy Crisis, 2023, DOI: 10.4018/979-8-3693-0400-6, aISBN13: 9798369304006, EISBN13: 9798369304013.

Terziev, V. (2024c). Global transformations and formation of new social systems. Revista Gestão e Secretariado (GeSec), São Paulo, SP, v. 15, n. 1, 2024, p. 1109-1127, ISSN 2178-9010.

Cultural Transformations as Part of Social Transformations

Venelin Terziev, Marin Georgiev, Simeon Simeonov

1. Introduction

Historians, with some degree of authoritative academic conviction, argue that history always moves forward. There is a certain timidity in their current announcements, coupled with an involuntary sense that history may repeat itself in one form or another. If we answer at least some of the questions asked, or at least think deeply and impartially about them, it can protect us from those repetitions that we would not like.

It would be important to examine the ongoing modern processes that require rapid and timely changes in social systems. If in the recent past, there were certain signs of ongoing changes that could be studied and analyzed, now changes happen suddenly and quickly. The emergence of new social leaders creates the conditions through their behavior, ideas, interests, and even a set of irrational views to transform the existing social systems. The influence of the new social leaders can be presented as sensitive and in many cases decisive for the ongoing transformations. It is necessary to identify a new criterion apparatus that is objective and quick enough to give us true and accurate information. The reliability of this venture is quite difficult to accomplish.

Social processes during severe crises are accompanied by a high rate of development. Their detailed and systematic description and subsequent analysis are practically impossible. Finding specific research approaches is imperative in these situations. Of particular importance is the study of the behavior patterns of dominant social leaders. Here, any researcher will face two sets of problems. The first is related to obtaining sufficiently accurate and reliable information, which is obtained using statistical methods of analysis, as well as sociological methods. This will create a particular difficulty in using them. The existence of such information and data is difficult to collect, but even if it is possible somewhere, it will be filtered especially by the relevant state security services. The second group of problems will arise in the assessment of the development of the behavioral model of the respective individual who has acquired the role of a socially significant and dominant leader. The knowledge and characteristics of his personality will undergo various transformations during his reign, namely, these characteristics will not be public enough and the information we will get will be from the media or other public sources.

Overcoming both sets of difficulties in certain situations may prove insurmountable, and using similar approaches to conducting research may prove impossible.

No matter what research situation we find ourselves in, it is necessary to look for opportunities to study the influence of socially dominant leaders on social processes.

Similar and analogous examples from a historical point of view can be set forth quite a lot. Even if we conditionally accept the two world wars as such severe crises, the actions of the leaders who participated in these processes cannot always be explained logically and do not carry their own economic, political, and other arguments. Conditionally, these are also social processes that have changed their direction and speed as a result of socially dominant leaders. An important clarification should be made here, namely that they happened too slowly, according to modern social processes. The factors of the external and internal environment have changed both in their essential characteristics and their quantitative dimensions. Some researchers would pay special attention to the study of environmental factors that undoubtedly have and will continue to influence current social processes. Another question is how much they influence the decisions and behavior of the new socially dominant leaders. This can be established too late and only at the end of a certain stage of a given social process.

Socially dominant leaders who are empowered to make decisions and have sufficient resources (political, economic, financial, etc.) tend to make decisions of an operational nature in crisis situations, sometimes these decisions exclude consideration of the environment, and rather, they are influenced by motives other than political and economic logic. Usually, when a crisis occurs, the instruments of power focus on a small group of people who follow and must bear the burden of decision-making in an extreme situation.

With a quick analysis of the social processes currently taking place in the world, one can make a relatively correct conclusion that they are primarily controlled by new socially dominant leaders. The use of the term "new socially dominant leaders" has a relative meaning, since the individuals we now define as such may have been leaders of states, corporations, unions, etc. in previous periods, but only now have they acquired such importance.

Undoubtedly, modern social processes are due to active changes in recent decades in political, economic, military and financial aspects. The results of all this will be seen most clearly in the imposition of new social rules in new social systems. The inevitability of imposing new regulatory functions in the structure of new social systems is almost obvious. Resistance to change is also evident. Evolutionary social processes currently dominate revolutionary social processes. Perhaps a proviso should be made that these social processes are inevitably linked to local military conflicts, financial crises or political instability of individual regions, but not to the continental or worldwide presence of social discomfort. The imposition or possibility of establishing a new social system with new rules cannot but be accompanied by certain negative actions and consequences.

Unfortunately, the scientific community will study, analyze and predict all this too late. The utility of such an undertaking at a later stage in time will have its value, but it will be much less than if it happened now.

The importance of such actions and research in this direction is of particular importance both for each individual and for different communities. Even if these studies represent little progress at this stage, they should find their place as an element in the preparation of our societies for new interactions in a new social environment.

Understanding that everything should be left at the current level of preparedness could be catastrophic for any of our societies. Moreover, there is good reason to believe that some leaders of smaller communities or those who will not play a dominant role will prove too unprepared, even ill-suited, for the new social situation.

2. Identity and cultural transformations

Identity is a general term used in the social sciences to describe one's understanding of oneself as a distinct entity. Although the term is general, it can be said that it most refers to psychology and sociology and especially to social psychology.

Psychological identity nurtures an individual's sense of self-wholeness. It helps him feel a sense of identity, permanence, perspective, and continuity. Identity is what makes an individual a whole self, distinct from others yet connected to them. Individually, identity implies a realistically developed self-concept related to the mastery of the environment at various levels and the social recognition of the individual in society. The different dimensions of identity imply the sense of unity of different ego-states and the sense of belonging to a given community. Since the individual does not exist independently, he constructs his identity through his belonging to different groups.

Identity is the set of qualities, beliefs, personality traits, appearance, and/or expressions that characterize a person or a group (Compare Collins Dictionary of Sociology, quoted in Covington, 2008; Schwartz et al., 2011a; Herman, 2011b; Franco-Zamudio, Dorton, 2014).

Identity emerges during childhood as children start to comprehend their self-concept, and it remains a consistent aspect throughout different stages of life. Identity is shaped by social and cultural factors and how others perceive and acknowledge one's characteristics (Schmeck et al., 2013). The etymology of the term "identity" from the Latin noun identitas emphasizes an individual's mental image of themselves and their "sameness with others" (The term identity comes from the Latin noun Definition, 2023a). Identity encompasses various aspects such as occupational, religious, national, ethnic or racial, gender, educational, generational, and political identities, among others.

Identity serves multiple functions, acting as a "self-regulatory structure" that provides meaning, direction, and a sense of self-control. It fosters internal harmony and serves as a behavioral compass, enabling individuals to orient themselves towards the future and establish long-term goals (Schwartz et al., 2006). As an active process, it profoundly influences an individual's capacity to adapt to life events and achieve a state of well-being (Laliberte-Rudman, 2002a; Unruh, 2004). However, identity originates from traits or attributes that individuals may have little or no control over, such as their family background or ethnicity (Identity: Definition, 2023b).

In sociology, emphasis is placed by sociologists on collective identity, in which an individual's identity is strongly associated with role-behavior or the collection of group memberships that define them (Burke, 2020). According to Peter Burke, "Identities tell us who we are and they announce to others who we are." (Burke, 2020). Identities subsequently guide behavior, leading "fathers" to behave like "fathers" and "nurses" to act like "nurses" (Burke, 2020).

In psychology, the term "identity" is most commonly used to describe personal identity, or the distinctive qualities or traits that make an individual unique (Cheek, 1989; Identity, 2024a). Identities are strongly associated with self-concept, self-image (one's mental model of oneself), self-esteem, and individuality (Weinreich, 1986; Leary & Tangney, 2003a). Individuals' identities are situated, but also contextual, situationally adaptive and changing. Despite their fluid character, identities often feel as if they are stable ubiquitous categories defining an individual, because of their grounding in the sense of personal identity (the sense of being a continuous and persistent self) (Kurzwelly, 2019).

Erik Erikson (1902–94) became one of the earliest psychologists to take an explicit interest in identity. An essential feature of Erikson's theory of psychosocial development was the idea of the ego identity (often referred to as the self), which is described as an individual's personal sense of continuity (APA Dictionary of Psychology, 2024b). He suggested that people can attain this feeling throughout their lives as they develop and is meant to be an ongoing process (Erikson, 1968). The ego-identity consists of two main features: one's personal characteristics and development, and the culmination of social and cultural factors and roles that impact one's identity. In Erikson's theory, he describes eight distinct stages across the lifespan that are each characterized by a conflict between the inner, personal world and the outer, social world of an individual. Erikson identified the conflict of identity as occurring primarily during adolescence and described potential outcomes that depend on how one deals with this conflict (Weinreich & Saunderson, 2002b). Those who do not manage a resynthesis of childhood identifications are seen as being in a state of 'identity diffusion' whereas those who retain their given identities unquestioned have "foreclosed" identities (Weinreich & Saunderson, 2003b). On some readings of Erikson, the development of a strong ego identity, along with the proper integration into a stable society and culture, lead to a stronger sense of identity in general. Accordingly, a deficiency in either of these factors may increase the chance of an identity crisis or confusion (Cote & Levine, 2002c).

The "Neo-Eriksonian" identity status paradigm emerged in 1966, driven largely by the work of James Marcia (Marcia, 1966). This model focuses on the concepts of exploration and commitment. The central idea is that an individual's sense of identity is determined in large part by the degrees to which a person has made certain explorations and the extent to which they have commitments to those explorations or a particular identity (Schwartz, 2001). A person may display either relative weakness or strength in terms of both exploration and commitments. When assigned categories, there were four possible results: identity diffusion, identity foreclosure, identity moratorium, and identity achievement. Diffusion is when a person avoids or refuses both exploration and making a commitment. Foreclosure occurs when a person does make a commitment to a particular identity but neglected to explore other options. Identity moratorium is when a person avoids or postpones making a commitment but is still actively exploring their options and different identities. Lastly, identity achievement is when a person has both explored many possibilities and has committed to their identity (Marcia et al., 2012).

Although the self is distinct from identity, the literature of self-psychology can offer some insight into how identity is maintained (Cote & Levine, 2002c). From the vantage point of self-psychology, there are two areas of interest: the processes by which a self is formed (the "I"), and the actual content of the schemata which compose the self-concept (the "Me"). In the latter field, theorists have shown interest in relating the self-concept to self-esteem, the differences between complex and simple ways of organizing self-knowledge, and the links between those organizing principles and the processing of information (Cote & Levine, 2002c).

Weinreich's identity variant similarly includes the categories of identity diffusion, foreclosure and crisis, but with a somewhat different emphasis. Here, with respect to identity diffusion for example, an optimal level is interpreted as the norm, as it is unrealistic to expect an individual to resolve all their conflicted identifications with others; the refore wc should be alert to individuals with levels which are much higher or lower than the norm – highly diffused individuals are classified as diffused, and those with low levels as foreclosed or defensive (Weinreich & Saunderson, 2003b). Weinreich applies the identity variant in a framework which also allows for the transition from one to another by way of biographical experiences and resolution of conflicted identifications situated in various contexts – for example, an adolescent going through family break-up may be in one state, whereas later in a stable marriage with a secure professional role may be in another. Hence, though there is continuity, there is also development and change (Weinreich & Saunderson, 2003b).

Laing's definition of identity closely follows Erikson's, in emphasising the past, present and future components of the experienced self. He also develops the concept of the "metaperspective of self", i.e. the self's perception of the other's view of self, which has been found to be extremely important in clinical contexts such as anorexia nervosa (Weinreich, & Saunderson, 2002b). Harré also conceptualises components of self/identity – the "person" (the unique being I am to myself and others) along with aspects of self (including a totality of attributes including beliefs about one's characteristics including life history), and the personal characteristics displayed to others.

2.1. Cultural identity and cultural transformations

Svetlana Kuyumdzhieva makes interesting generalizations about the concept of cultural identity and presents it as follows: Cultural identity can be formulated in hundreds of different ways. It is usually associated with belonging to a certain nation, group, race, religion... However, national and cultural identity nowadays are concepts that do not easily find their boundaries. Today, a person builds his cultural identity thanks to his social experience and the individual choices he makes and has to make constantly. Cultural identity is a concept with an almost unlimited capacity to define possibilities. Perhaps this is exactly what makes it an extremely convenient occasion for many different artists to gather in one place (Kuyumdzhieva, 2007).

The ongoing cultural transformations that are part of our social experience are the result of the so-called diffusion processes that have taken place to one degree or another throughout our human existence. The dominant influences were of the greatest importance in this process, and from there, the consequences were of the greatest consequence. In every society, there are established regulatory mechanisms that encourage some and limit other influences.

Visits to the cinema, library, theater, and various television programs are things that are a donor of cultural influence and they enable the penetration of knowledge about different cultures in the local communities. The National Statistical Institute of Bulgaria made similar observations until 2016, disclosing statistical data in this direction, which well and clearly define the groups of different users and their characteristics (Table 1-2).

Table 1: Persons according to cinema visits by sex, age, education, employment status and place of residence

	2016										
	Total	1-3 times in the last 12 the month		4-6 times in the last 12 the month		7-12 times in the last 12 the month		More than 12 times in the last 12 months		They did not visit during the last 12 months	
	number	number	%	number	%	number	%	number	%	number	%
Total	3863951	949901	24.6	323609	8.4	133419	3.5	55582	1.4	2401441	62.31
By age: 25-34 years	931504	286450	30.8	137437	14.8	68088	7.3	27324	2.9	412204	44.3
By age: 35-54 years	1983473	548052	27.7	168646	8.5	58573	3	21414	1.1	1186788	59.8
By age: 55-64 years	948974	115399	12.2	17526	1.8	6758	0.7	6843	0.7	802448	84.6
By education: Primary and lower education	620834	39217	6.3	2834	0.5	793	0.1	618	0.1	577371	93
Education: Secondary education	2108203	480975	22.8	142957	6.8	47504	2.3	17047	0.8	1419720	67.3
By education: Higher education	1134914	429709	37.9	177817	15.7	85121	7.5	37916	3.3	404350	35.6

Source: National Statistical Institute, Bulgaria

Table 2: Persons by number of books read and by gender, age, education, employment status and place of residence

	2016						
	Total	Less than 5 books in recent 12 months		5-10 books in the last 12 the month		More than 10 books in recent 12 months	
	number	number	%	number	%	number	%
Total	2057433	1072432	52.1	569546	27.7	415455	20.2
By age: 25-34 years	490375	249189	50.8	138643	28.3	102543	20.9
By age: 35-54 years	1086119	564408	52	307218	28.3	214492	19.7
By age: 55-64 years	480939	258834	53.8	123684	25.7	98421	20.5
By education: Primary and	61609	43015	69.8	13986	22.7	4607	7.5
lower education	1002345	672882	67.1	211933	21.1	117530	11.7
Education: Secondary	993479	356534	35.9	343627	34.6	293318	29.5
By employment status: Employed	1577462	796495	50.5	446981	28.3	333986	21.2
By employment status: Unemployed	190325	115735	60.8	44678	23.5	29912	15.7
By place of residence: In the cities	1773285	883772	49.8	512218	28.9	377295	21.3
By place of residence: In the villages	284148	188660	66.4	57328	20.2	38160	13.4

Source: National Statistical Institute, Bulgaria

On the one hand, the interest is determined by the attitudes of the generality, and on the other hand, by the variety of the offered product. Different groups that define their interests in a certain way can be differentiated and the consequences of this traced.

The existence of such a culture of exchange of knowledge and information is accepted as normal in modern societies, as various scientific and research organizations periodically ascertain the changes in the ongoing processes.

Far different is the impact, which is a consequence of processes and phenomena that are not predictable and give a clear reflection on the cultural identity of a certain community.

For Bulgaria, those that are caused by the influence of the external environment and those that take place in the internal environment can be established.

A significant contribution to the changes of this process is the presence of an active migration process in both directions, as well as the establishment of permanently or temporarily living people who have other cultures, habits,

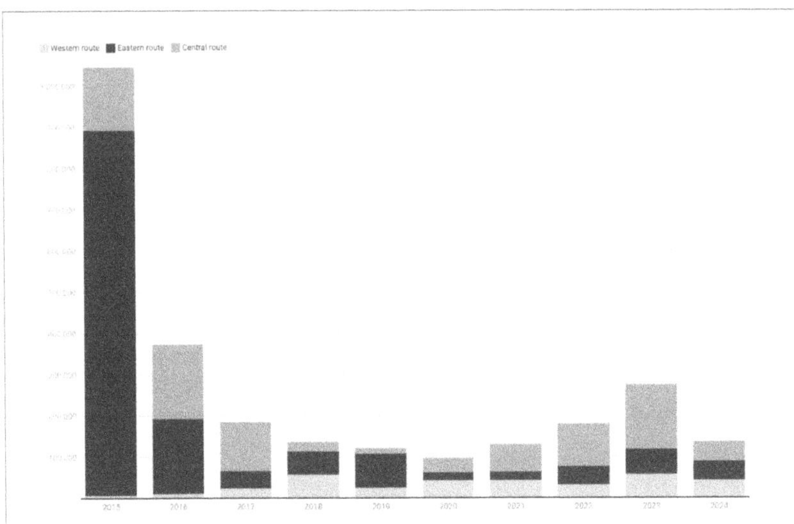

Graph 1: Yearly irregular arrivals (2015-2024). Migration flows: Eastern, Central and Western routes. Western route refers to Western Mediterranean and Western African routes (September 2024)

Source: Frontex and Spanish Ministry of Interior

traditions, and in the most general sense of this interpretation - another way of life. This significantly changes the cultural traditions of the local communities and puts them to certain tests, which are related to a change in their overall way of life and existence.

It can be said without exaggeration that these processes of cultural transformations take place relatively slowly, but their consequences are more stable and long-lasting in terms of time.

The data for Europe are disturbing and lead to drastic changes in some of the European societies. Empowered governing bodies try to create regulatory mechanisms, taking into account the humanitarian nature of these actions. Unfortunately, these processes are chaotic, unpredictable, and quite intensive. All of this creates additional stress on social systems that are constantly being tested (Diagram 1-3).

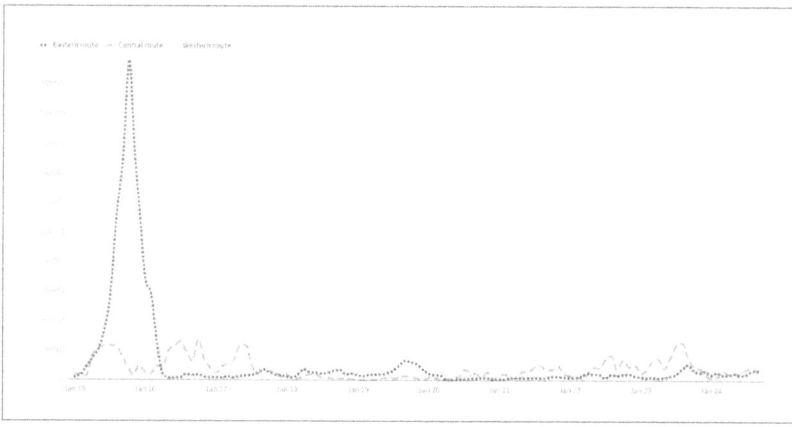

Graph 2: Monthly irregular arrivals (2015-2024). Migration flows: Eastern, Central and Western routes. Western route refers to Western Mediterranean and Western African routes (September 2024)

Source: Frontex and Spanish Ministry of Interior

3. Conclusion

Processes of successive crises lead to the deepening of imbalances in social systems. The different scales and intensity of the impacts on them subject them to a series of cyclical tests. Determining the scale of changes occurring

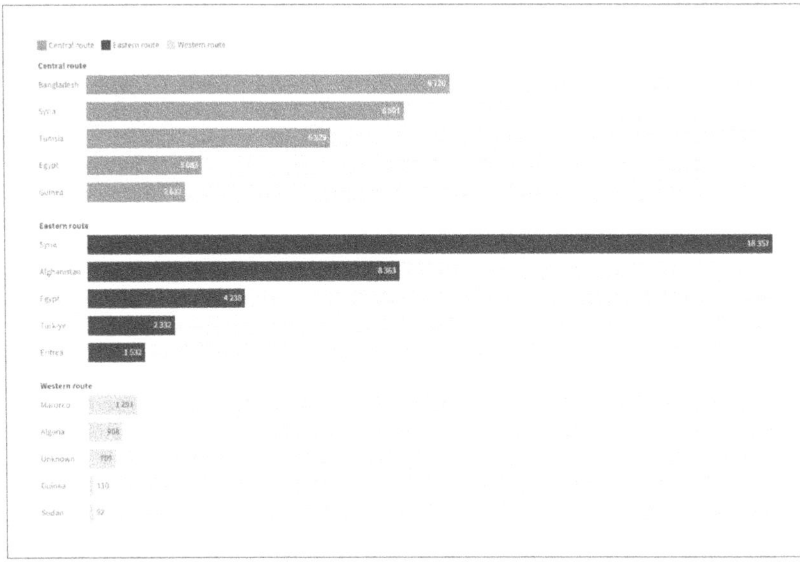

Graph 3: Top nationalities per route (2024). Western route arrivals exclude arrivals to Canary Islands (September 2024)

Source: Frontex

at the macro- and micro-level is difficult, and the consequences are almost unpredictable. A standard set of methods and approaches proves insufficient to define and characterize all of this. The main factor is the speed of the processes and the lack of effective time for accurate and objective analysis. This places us, as participants in the transformation of social systems, in front of a set of challenges and tests of our suitability to be able to accept and successfully adapt to the changes that are coming. Studying these processes requires a full-scale effort and diverse experience. This is also necessary from the point of view of forecasting and planning transformation processes and effective solutions for getting out of the critical state in which social systems are (Terziev, 2024c).

References

Compare Collins Dictionary of Sociology, quoted in Covington, Peter (2008). "Culture and Identity". Success in Sociology. Dublin: Folens Limited. p. 12. ISBN 9781850082606.

Schwartz, S.J., Luyckx, K., Vignoles, V.L., eds. (2011a). Handbook of Identity Theory and Research. New York, NY: Springer New York. doi:10.1007/978-1-4419-7988-9. ISBN 978-1-4419-7987-2.

Herman, W. E. (2011b). Identity Formation. Encyclopedia of Child Behavior and Development. Boston, MA: Springer US. pp. 779–781. doi:10.1007/978-0-387-79061-9_1443. ISBN 978-0-387-77579-1.

Franco-Zamudio, J., Dorton, H. (2014). Collective Identity. Encyclopedia of Critical Psychology. New York, NY: Springer New York. pp. 256–259. doi:10.1007/978-1-4614-5583-7_381. ISBN 978-1-4614-5582-0.

Schmeck, K., Schlüter-Müller, S., Foelsch, P. A, & Doering, S. (2013). The role of identity in the DSM-5 classification of personality disorders. Child and Adolescent Psychiatry and Mental Health. 7 (1): 27. doi:10.1186/1753-2000-7-27. ISSN 1753-2000.

The term identity comes from the Latin noun Definition. (2023a). Law Insider. Retrieved May 30, 2023.

Schwartz, S.J., Montgomery, M.J., & Briones, E. (2006). The Role of Identity in Acculturation among Immigrant People: Theoretical Propositions, Empirical Questions, and Applied Recommendations. Human Development. 49 (1): 1–30. doi:10.1159/000090300. ISSN 0018-716X.

Laliberte-Rudman, D. (2002a). Linking Occupation and Identity: Lessons Learned Through Qualitative Exploration. Journal of Occupational Science, 9(1), 12–19. https://doi.org/10.1080/14427591.2002.9686489.

Unruh, A.M. (2004). Reflections on: "So… What Do You Do?" Occupation and the Construction of Identity. Canadian Journal of Occupational Therapy. 2004;71(5):290-295. doi:10.1177/000841740407100508.

Identity: Definition, (2023b). Types, & Examples. The Berkeley Well-Being Institute. Retrieved June 21, 2023.

Burke, P. (2020). Identity. In: Kivisto P, ed. The Cambridge Handbook of Social Theory. Cambridge University Press; 2020:63-78.

Cheek, J.M. (1989). Identity Orientations and Self-Interpretation. In: Buss, D.M., Cantor, N. (eds) Personality Psychology. Springer, New York, NY. https://doi.org/10.1007/978-1-4684-0634-4_21.

Identity. (2024a). dictionary.apa.org. Retrieved November 5, 2024.

Weinreich, P. (1986). "14: The operationalisation of identity theory in racial and ethnic relations". In Rex, John; Mason, David (eds.). Theories of Race and Ethnic Relations. Comparative Ethnic and Race Relations. Cambridge: Cambridge University Press (published 1988). pp. 299ff. ISBN 9780521369398.

Leary & Tangney, (2003a). 2003.

Kurzwelly, J. (2019). Being German, Paraguayan and Germanino: Exploring the Relation Between Social and Personal Identity. Identity, 19(2), 144–156. https://doi.org/10.1080/15283488.2019.1604348.

APA Dictionary of Psychology. (2024b). dictionary.apa.org. Retrieved November 5, 2024.

Erikson, E.H. (1968). Identity: Youth and Crisis. W. W. Norton & Company. ISBN 978-0-393-31144-0.

Weinreich, P., & Saunderson, W. (Eds.). (2002b). Analysing Identity: Cross-Cultural, Societal and Clinical Contexts (1st ed.). Routledge. https://doi.org/10.4324/9780203988800.

Weinreich & Saunderson, (2003b). 2003.

Cote & Levine, (2002c). 2002.

Marcia, J.E. (1966). Development and validation of ego-identity status. Journal of Personality and Social Psychology, 3(5), 551–558. https://doi.org/10.1037/h0023281.

Schwartz, S. J. (2001). The Evolution of Eriksonian and, Neo-Eriksonian Identity Theory and Research: A Review and Integration. Identity, 1(1), 7–58. https://doi.org/10.1207/S1532706XSCHWARTZ.

Marcia, J.E., Waterman, A.S., Matteson, D.R., Archer, S.L., & Orlofsky, J.L. (2012). Ego Identity: A Handbook for Psychosocial Research. Springer Science & Business Media. ISBN 978-1-4613-8330-7.

Kuyumdzhieva, S. (2007). Cultural Identity, Culture - Issue 29 (2733), 2007.

Terziev, V. (2024c). Global transformations and formation of new social systems. Revista Gestão e Secretariado (GeSec), São Paulo, SP, v. 15, n. 1, 2024, p. 1109-1127, ISSN 2178-9010.

General Bibliometric Analysis of Studies on the Concept of Digital Marketing Strategy with VOSviewer

Hamit Can, Meltem Okur Dinçsoy, Venelin Terziev

1. Introduction

Radical changes have begun to occur with the full integration of technology into social and institutional life. Many issues that we can evaluate within certain conventional patterns and standards have been forced to develop with the combination of technology and the internet. Institutions that do not integrate digital marketing applications that combine traditional marketing methods with the possibilities of technology into their own structures and do not use digital marketing in their interactions with consumers, it is very difficult to compete with their competitors in today's information, communication and technology age. Digital marketing applications, which provide the opportunity to "meet" the consumer in a much shorter time, at very low costs and within an instant interaction, can also be considered as an area where creativity and innovation are 'consumed' very quickly. For this reason, digital marketing strategies, which require the implementation of constantly renewed and creative works, by taking into account the personality traits and behavioral patterns of the target audience, reveal the necessity of creating a 'composition' that will use all the multimedia features provided by the new media.

Although the word revolution is used quite haphazardly today, if a revolution is to be mentioned in the field of technology or the digital world, it should be said that the Internet is the leading actor of this revolution. The Internet, which can also be considered as the most important invention of the last century, has become the trigger of many innovations and changes by increasing its usage area and speed every passing day, especially since the beginning of the 21st century. This new revolutionary process, which can be gathered under the title of new media and communication technologies and in which the Internet is at the center, has started a period that completely revised the entire system after the transition from traditional methods to modern methods in the marketing world. Digital marketing is an approach that can be seen as adding a "virtual" component to traditional marketing methods, and offers many advantages to businesses with its own differences. This new method has also transformed the communication processes with the target audience. In general, it can be defined as a method carried out with digital connections and where all marketing activities are carried out in a digital environment. Digital marketing can be explained as the application of traditional marketing methods on digital platforms, but it offers much greater advantages when compared to traditional methods. First of all, digital marketing, which provides serious economic savings, enables growth with features such as instant interaction with the target audience, constant updating, innovation and rapid adaptation.

In recent decades, ICT (Information and Communication Technologies) has seen a significant development and has an increasing impact on economic and social activities in the world (Okur Dinçsoy, 2008). ICT has also played an important role in economic growth for developed and developing countries (Okur Dinçsoy, 2009). Countries in East Asia, one of the most important geographical regions based on ICT, have been quite dynamic in recent years. Turkey has a great potential as a rapidly developing country and a growing ICT market for foreign market players in the near future; however, it needs to create its own strong and effective world-class companies to use ICT as a better development tool (Okur Dinçsoy, 2010). When the ICT and economic development of Japan and South Korea are compared and the lessons to be learned for Turkey are examined, it is seen that Japan, South Korea and Turkey started with their historical telecommunications history. These countries show similarities in the development of the telecommunications sector throughout history, including the privatization of the sector. However, a significant difference has emerged due to the use of technologies in these countries and the production of new technologies by companies worldwide. ICT developments have strong relationships with the socio-economic development of these countries. Therefore, the study focuses on (i) economic development indicators, (ii) ICT indicators and (iii) Principal Component Analysis. The aim of the findings is to find applicable policies for Türkiye (Okur Dinçsoy, 2009).

It should not be overlooked that studies on digital marketing strategies can also create an impact in different areas. For example, renewable energy production and consumption have a triggering effect on the components related to the energy sector (Korkmaz and Can, 2018; Dinçsoy and Can, 2023). In this context, the use of digital marketing strategies in the energy sector can increase efficiency in this area. The increase in efficiency in the use of technologies such as digitalization, artificial intelligence, etc. in various fields can also create positive effects in different areas (Can et al., 2020). Possible economic development can also affect property rights and government integrity and economic freedom, which are thought to be related in the long term (Dinçsoy et al., 2024).

In this study, it is aimed to create a resource from which studies on digital marketing strategies can be used in detail.

2. Literature Review

As a result of the literature review, there are various widely used digital marketing strategies that enable businesses to reach their target audience in a short time (Gibson, 2018). Social media platforms, which have become quite popular in recent years, where short videos with more visual content are shared, are constantly emerging with new features and applications (Gretzel, 2019). Since entrepreneurs want to introduce their products to consumers quickly and impressively, social media platforms are the most effective marketing channel for them.

With IoT (Internet of Things) technology, businesses can enhance their operational efficiency, conserve time and resources, continuously track and store collected data, and respond swiftly through an ongoing monitoring system (OECD, 2018). Digital marketing is an umbrella term for all types of online marketing, including search engine optimization, email marketing, content marketing, and social media marketing. Digital marketing is an adaptable, technology-enabled process by which companies work with their customers and partners to create, communicate, deliver, and sustain shared value for all stakeholders. Research on digital marketing shows that companies that use internet marketing capabilities will benefit from reduced information uncertainty and increased capacity to develop international networking capabilities. In addition, the use of digital marketing tools provides a business with the opportunity to increase market share and enhance competitiveness (Kotane et al., 2019; Kannan and Li, 2017).

Traditional marketing is losing its effectiveness in today's world. Advancements in technology have not only transformed people's lifestyles but also their buying and consumption behaviors. As a result, standing out and capturing attention has become increasingly challenging for businesses. Companies that recognize this shift have started to focus on reaching their target audiences more quickly through digital channels, shifting a significant portion of their advertising budgets to these platforms. In some cases, rather than targeting broad audiences, it may prove more efficient to identify the right audience and engage with them directly. With its greater ability to measure results compared to traditional methods, digital marketing has become a primary focus for many companies. Digital marketing offers two key benefits: it allows for precise targeting, and it enables the measurement of performance and goal achievement. As a result, the importance of digital marketing continues to grow for businesses every day (Royle and Laing, 2014).

Digital marketing is no longer limited to channels that require an internet connection, it goes far beyond. Digital technologies redefine the perspective of communication with their unique features such as interactivity, measurability, customer engagement, customization, accessibility and managing large informative resources. Businesses resort to digital marketing communication because it allows them to provide real-time, personalized services and content to customers. Interactive and targeted communication with customers through digital channels is at the core of digital marketing communication (Dahiya and Gayatri, 2018).

Leung and Mo (2019) selected the ideal digital marketing tool among the digital marketing tools they determined in their study using the Fuzzy AHP method. The alternative digital marketing tools determined in the Fuzzy AHP method are as follows; social media marketing, influencer marketing, e-mail marketing, search engine optimization and pay-per-click advertising. The criteria determined in the study are; 4 criteria were determined as business fundamentals, customer demographics, business acquisition performance and online viewing.

In the study conducted by Zare and Vılys (2019), digital marketing strategies were determined for pharmaceutical companies. In the study, 5 criteria were determined and evaluations were carried out by experts. In the study, the social media usage of companies was analyzed using AHP and TOPSIS methods and it was revealed which channel companies should use and to what extent. In the study by Ashtıanı and Davıdavıčıenė (2019), the problem of choosing digital marketing tools for a company was addressed. Evaluations were made with 5 alternatives and 10 main criteria determined by experts in the field of marketing. In the study, the weights were determined with the AHP method and the ideal digital marketing tool was selected among the alternatives with the TOPSIS method.

Can and Terziev (2016) concluded that with the emergence of the Information Society, developments in information and communication technologies have had significant effects on national economies. He concluded that today, it is difficult to talk about the concept of development in a society without technological developments, and in this context, it is very important to examine how technological developments affect the economic dimension in particular. He also concluded that it reduces the economic impact of physical distances, the costs of accessing information, and the costs of establishing new small businesses, making businesses more efficient and competitive.

In the Akbiyik and Can (2023) study, it was examined which applications were implemented using information technologies in order to respond to the needs of the local people in a shorter and faster time thanks to the digital transformation applications implemented by local governments.

3. Method

This section of the study includes the purpose of the research, the analyses and findings.

3.1. Purpose of the Research

As a result of the bibliometric analysis conducted on the concept of digital marketing strategies as a result of quantitative data and numerical measurement indicators, aims to present the studies on the concept to the attention of researchers with a holistic perspective.

3.2. Data and Analysis

Different bibliometric analysis tools are used in the literature. In this study, the VOSviewer program was preferred due to its strong functional aspects. It is considered to be an important program that provides convenience to researchers in order to discover the evolutions, relationships and new concepts in the literature. In addition, it allows for in-depth analysis of data sets due to the visualization, mapping and multi-dimensional analysis opportunities it provides. The Web of Science database was used in the current study. The selection of the Web of Science database for various analyses including bibliometric analyses is an important factor in terms of the reliability of the research. The Web of Science database has advanced search indicators for advanced data analysis and uses various control mechanisms. It covers qualified and reliable studies in terms of publication ethics. In addition, it provides access to a comprehensive data collection from different disciplines. On 11.10.2024, 193 results were reached in the search made by selecting "all fields" in Web of Science with the keyword "digital marketing strategy". By year, 147 articles from different disciplines, the oldest being 2011 and the newest being 2024, 37 Proceeding Papers, 8 Review Article, 7 Early Access, 3 Book Chapter, 1 Data Paper, 1 Editorial Material, and 1 Meeting Abstract were accessed. In terms of disciplines, the majority of the studies were seen in the fields of Business (46), Managment (36), Computer Science Information Systems (21), Environmental Studies (14), Environmental Sciences (13), Green Sustainable Science Technology (13), Hospitality Leisure Sport Tourism (13), Social Science Interdisciplinary (12), Computer Science Interdisciplinary Applications (5), Computer Science Theory Methods (5), Information Science Library Science (5) and Operation Research Mangment Science (5). Business Finance (4), Computer Science Software Engineering (4), Engineering Industrial (4), Computer Science Hardware Architecture (3), Engineering Electrical Electronic (3), Health Care Sciences Services (3). The accessed data was examined through author-citation-journal, country-institution and keyword analyzes. The contents indexed in Web of Science were taken as the criterion as the database.

4. Conclusion

In this study, the summary of the studies conducted on the concept of digital marketing strategy is presented. It is thought that the results obtained will lead to studies on the same and similar subjects. It is very important to understand the possible effects of digital marketing strategies and the building blocks underlying the implementation of digital marketing strategies in the development of strategies. The quantitative table that will be presented to those interested in the subject by a series of statistics obtained as a result of this bibliometric analysis clearly shows the points that need to be emphasized.

The general summary of the results obtained can be presented as follows:

The unit of analysis is the bibliometric data of different types of works scanned in the Web of Science database and published between 2011 and 2024. When the distribution of 193 documents published on digital marketing strategy by publication years is examined, it is seen that the highest density was in 2023 (38 documents), 2024 (34 documents), 2020 (32 documents) and 2021 (32 documents); Jose Ramon Saura (7 documents), Damianos Sakas (7 documents), Nikolaos Giannakopoulos (5 documents) were the names that produced the most documents; The publication types were mostly article (147), Proceeding Paper (37), Review Article (8) and Early Access (7); In terms of research areas, it was determined that studies were published in the fields of Business (46), Managment (36), Computer Science Information Systems (21), Environmental Studies (14), Environmental Sciences (13), Green Sustainable Science Technology (13); when the distribution of publications by country was examined, it was determined that the leadership was with publishers from the Spain (20), USA (20), China 19 and England (17); the studies were mostly published in English (175), Spanish (13) and Portugese (4); the majority of publications were scanned in the Emerging Sources Citation Index (ESCI) (80), Social Sciences Citation Index (SSCI) (55) and Science Citation Index Expanded (SCI-EXPANDED) (40) indexes. When we look at the most common ones are digital marketing with 81 repetitions, Social Media 21 with 21 repetitions, Marketing with 15 repetitions, Digital Marketing Strategy with 14 repetitions, and Big Data with 9 repetitions. The strongest expressions in terms of total link strength were digital marketing, big data, and social media.

In an environment where artificial intelligence is on the rise and humanity feeds on the data it produces on the internet, studies on the spread of artificial intelligence and digital marketing strategies are also valuable. The effectiveness and effects of existing social awareness strategies are among the issues that need to be examined. The importance of training in this direction is great in the development of digital marketing strategies. With technological developments, virtual learning can be shown as a learning style that facilitates access to information for people with different learning and perception styles in terms of education quality and information accessibility. The trend towards Massive Open Online Course systems facilitates access to information (Can and Terziev, 2017), and can contribute to the development of strategic marketing strategies.

The critical limitations of the study are the inclusion of studies listed in the WOS Core Collection in the scope of the analysis, the exclusion of databases such as TÜBİTAK Ulakbim and YÖK Thesis Archive in Turkey, and Scopus and Pubmed in the international arena, and other sources that are not in online circulation.

References

Akbiyik, S. & Can, H. (2023). Structural and Qualitative Defects in Adaptation to Digital Transformation in Local Governments. In M. Okur Dinçsoy & H. Can (Eds.), Optimizing Energy Efficiency During a Global Energy Crisis (pp. 327-340). IGI Global. https://doi.org/10.4018/979-8-3693-0400-6.ch018.

Ashtiani, N. S., & Davidavičienė, V. (2019, April). Planning Of Digital Marketing Strategy Formation. In 22nd Conference for Young Researchers "Economics and Management".

Can, H., Minkovska, D., & Stoyanova, L. (2020, October). Estimation of Energy Performance Classes of Concrete Structures with Artificial Intelligence Models. In 2020 III International Conference on High Technology for Sustainable Development (HiTech) (pp. 1-3). IEEE. DOI: 10.1109/HiTech51434.2020.9364003.

Can, H., & Terziev, V. (2016). The relationship economic growth and information technologies. Retrieved from SSRN: https://ssrn.com/abstract=3383899 or http://dx.doi.org/10.2139/ssrn.3383899

Can, H., & Terziev, V. (2017). Massive Open Online Courses: Motivation and Success of Learners. Available at SSRN 3143988. http://dx.doi.org/10.2139/ssrn.3143988.

Dahiya, R. ve Gayatri. (2018). A Research Paper on Digital Marketing Communication and Consumer Buying Decision Process: An Empirical Study in the Indian Passenger Car Market. Journal Of Global Marketing, Vol. 31(2), 73-95.

Okur Dincsoy, M. (2008). A Statistical Analysis of ICT Developments and Regional GDP per capita Convergence in Major East Asian Countries. 岡山大学大学院社会文化科学研究科紀要, 26(1), 125-143.

Okur Dincsoy, M. (2009). Can ICT Economically Catalyze a Regional GDP Per Capita Convergence ?– A Case Study of Major East Asian Countries–. 北東アジア経済研究, 7(1), 45-64.

Okur Dincsoy, M. (2009). A comparative Study of Japan and the ROK on ICT and Economic Development: Lessons for Turkey. 岡山大学大学院社会文化科学研究科紀要, 28, 123-141.

Okur Dincsoy, M. (2010). ICT Experience in East Asia and Modelling for Turkey. ProQuest LLC.

Okur Dinçsoy, M. & Can, H. (2023). The Relationship of Renewable Energy Generation, Renewable Energy Consumption, and Economic Growth: The Case of Türkiye.

Okur Dinçsoy, M. & H. Can (Eds.). (2023). Optimizing Energy Efficiency During a Global Energy Crisis (pp. 65-74). IGI Global. https://doi.org/10.4018/979-8-3693-0400-6.ch005

Okur Dinçsoy, Meltem. and Can, Hamit and Dinçsoy, Enver Erdinç and Terziev, Venelin, The Impact of Property Rights and Government Integrity on the Economic Freedom: The Case of the European Region, the BRICS Countries, and the USA (February 16, 2024). Available at SSRN: https://ssrn.com/abstract=4905470.

Gibson, C. (2018). The most effective digital marketing strategies & approaches: a review of literature. International Journal of Scientific and Research Publications, 8(2), 12-16.

Gretzel, U. (2019). The role of social media in creating and addressing overtourism: issues, realities and solutions. R. Dodds ve R. Butler (Ed.) Overtourism içinde (62-75 ss.). Berlin: De Gruyter. https://doi.org/10.1515/9783110607369-005.

Kannan, P. ve Li, H. (2017). Digital Marketing: A Famework, Review And Research Agenda, International Journal of Research in Marketing, 34, 22-45.

Korkmaz, Ö., & Can, H. (2018, December). Yenilenebilir Enerji, Fosil Enerji ve Ekonomik Büyüme İlişkisi: Rusya, Çin ve ABD Örneği. In İzmir International Congress on Economics and Administrative Sciences (IZCEAS)

(No. 2018, pp. 2953-2966). İzmir International Congress on Economics and Administrative Sciences (IZCEAS).

Kotane, I., Znotina, D. ve Hushko, S. (2019). Assessment Of Trends In The Application Of Digital Marketing, Scientific Journal Of Polonia University, 33(2), 28-35.

Leung, K. H., & Mo, D. Y. (2019, December). A fuzzy-AHP approach for strategic evaluation and selection of digital marketing tools. In 2019 IEEE international conference on industrial engineering and engineering management (IEEM) (pp. 1422-1426). IEEE.

OECD. (2018). Achieving Inclusive Growth In The Face of Digital Transformation and The Future of Work. OECD

Royle, J., & Laing, A. (2014). The digital marketing skills gap: Developing a Digital Marketer Model for the communication industries. International Journal of Information Management, 34(2), 65-73.

Zare, S., & Vilys, M. (2019). Digital marketing strategy formation for pharmaceutical companies.

Bibliometric Analysis of Studies on the Concept of Digital Marketing Strategy with VOSviewer

Hamit Can, Meltem Okur Dinçsoy, Venelin Terziev

1. Introduction

Radical changes have begun to occur with the full integration of technology into social and institutional life. Many issues that we can evaluate within certain conventional patterns and standards have been forced to develop with the combination of technology and the internet. Institutions that do not integrate digital marketing applications that combine traditional marketing methods with the possibilities of technology into their own structures and do not use digital marketing in their interactions with consumers, it is very difficult to compete with their competitors in today's information, communication and technology age. Digital marketing applications, which provide the opportunity to "meet" the consumer in a much shorter time, at very low costs and within an instant interaction, can also be considered as an area where creativity and innovation are 'consumed' very quickly. For this reason, digital marketing strategies, which require the implementation of constantly renewed and creative works, by taking into account the personality traits and behavioral patterns of the target audience, reveal the necessity of creating a 'composition' that will use all the multimedia features provided by the new media.

Although the word revolution is used quite haphazardly today, if a revolution is to be mentioned in the field of technology or the digital world, it should be said that the Internet is the leading actor of this revolution. The Internet, which can also be considered as the most important invention of the last century, has become the trigger of many innovations and changes by increasing its usage area and speed every passing day, especially since the beginning of the 21st century. This new revolutionary process, which can be gathered under the title of new media and communication technologies and in which the Internet is at the center, has started a period that completely revised the entire system after the transition from traditional methods to modern methods in the marketing world. Digital marketing is an approach that can be seen as adding a "virtual" component to traditional marketing methods, and offers many advantages to businesses with its own differences. This new method has also transformed the communication processes with the target audience. In general, it can be defined as a method carried out with digital connections and where all marketing activities are carried out in a digital environment. Digital marketing can be explained as the application of traditional marketing methods on digital platforms, but it offers much greater advantages when compared to traditional methods. First of all, digital marketing, which provides serious economic savings, enables growth with features such as instant interaction with the target audience, constant updating, innovation and rapid adaptation.

In recent decades, ICT (Information and Communication Technologies) has seen a significant development and has an increasing impact on economic and social activities in the world (Okur Dinçsoy, 2008). ICT has also played an important role in economic growth for developed and developing countries (Okur Dinçsoy, 2009). Countries in East Asia, one of the most important geographical regions based on ICT, have been quite dynamic in recent years. Turkey has a great potential as a rapidly developing country and a growing ICT market for foreign market players in the near future; however, it needs to create its own strong and effective world-class companies to use ICT as a better development tool (Okur Dinçsoy, 2010). When the ICT and economic development of Japan and South Korea are compared and the lessons to be learned for Turkey are examined, it is seen that Japan, South Korea and Turkey started with their historical telecommunications history. These countries show similarities in the development of the telecommunications sector throughout history, including the privatization of the sector. However, a significant difference has emerged due to the use of technologies in these countries and the production of new technologies by companies worldwide. ICT developments have strong relationships with the socio-economic development of these countries. Therefore, the study focuses on (i) economic development indicators, (ii) ICT indicators and (iii) Principal Component Analysis. The aim of the findings is to find applicable policies for Türkiye (Okur Dinçsoy, 2009).

It should not be overlooked that studies on digital marketing strategies can also create an impact in different areas. For example, renewable energy production and consumption have a triggering effect on the components related to the energy sector (Korkmaz and Can, 2018; Dinçsoy and Can,

2023). In this context, the use of digital marketing strategies in the energy sector can increase efficiency in this area. The increase in efficiency in the use of technologies such as digitalization, artificial intelligence, etc. in various fields can also create positive effects in different areas (Can et al., 2020). Possible economic development can also affect property rights and government integrity and economic freedom, which are thought to be related in the long term (Dinçsoy et al., 2024).

In this study, it is aimed to create a resource from which studies on digital marketing strategies can be used in detail.

2. Findings

The findings obtained in the study are given under this heading.

2.1. Co-authorship of Authors

According to the co-authorship analysis of the authors, a network map was created by determining the criteria of at least 1 publications and at least 1 citations to identify the most connected and collaborating authors. According to the analysis made among the names with the highest links, 134 items, 1 cluster, 91 links are seen to be combined in a single cluster. Of the 16 most linked authors in the cluster, Damianos P. Sakas (19), the other 15 authors have a total link strength of 13. It is also seen that the most cited authors (Jose Ramon Saura with 208 citations, the other 4 authors Cheng Luo, Fang Qin, G. Alan Wang, Min Zhang with 153 citations) are not the most connected authors. The authors who produced the most works were found as follows: Damianos P. Sakas (7 documents), Jose Ramon Saura (4 documents), and Dimitrios P. Reklitis (4 documents)).

When the figure above is examined, it is seen that publications in this field are concentrated in 2023.

In the figure above, it is seen that the authors who have worked in this field generally concentrate on yellow tones. It would be useful to examine the works of these authors with this yellow intensity in research in these fields.

2.2. Citation of Authors

In order to determine the citation networks, a network map was created for the author citation analysis with the criteria of at least 1 publication and at

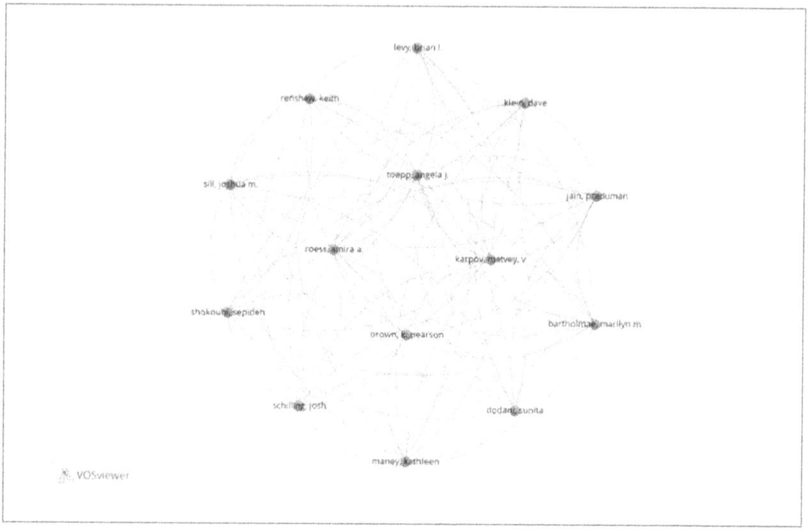

Figure 1: Co-Author Links Showing Collaboration Between Authors (Network Visulization)

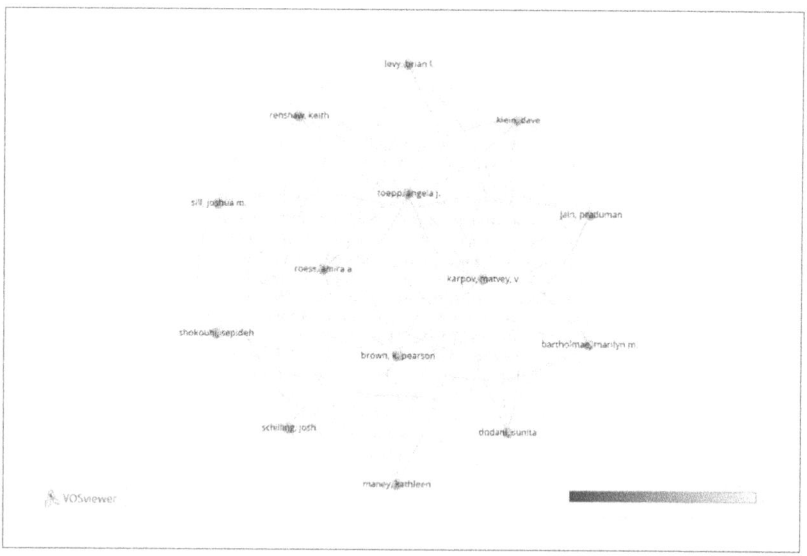

Figure 2: Co-Author Links Showing Collaboration Between Authors (Overlay Visulization)

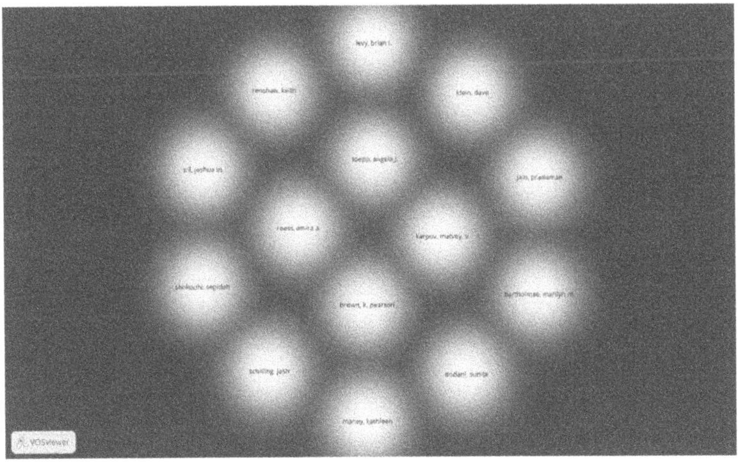

Figure 3: Co-Author Links Showing Collaboration Between Authors (Density Visulization)

least 1 citation. In the analysis conducted on 51 items that were seen to be connected to each other, a total of 6 clusters, 113 links were detected. The most cited authors were Jose Ramon Saura with 208 citations, Cheng Luo, Fang Qin and G. Alan Wang with 153 citations. Jose Ramon Saura is also seen as the most linked author (20 total link strength), Domingo Ribeiro Soriano (17 total link strength), Katherine Smith (15 total link strength).

2.3. Citation of Countries

In order to create a network map regarding the citations received by the publications according to their countries of origin, an analysis was conducted on 26 items that were related to each other within the scope of the criterion that at least 1 pubication was published and a country received 1 citation. 9 clusters, 41 links and 55 total link strengths were identified. The countries with the most citations were Spain (427 citations), USA (376 citations), and England (353 citations). In terms of total link strength, USA (22), Spain (20), England (13) were in the top three. In terms of the number of documents, the ranking was as follows: USA (20 documents), Spain (20 documents) and China (19 documents).

Figure 4: Authors' Citation Links

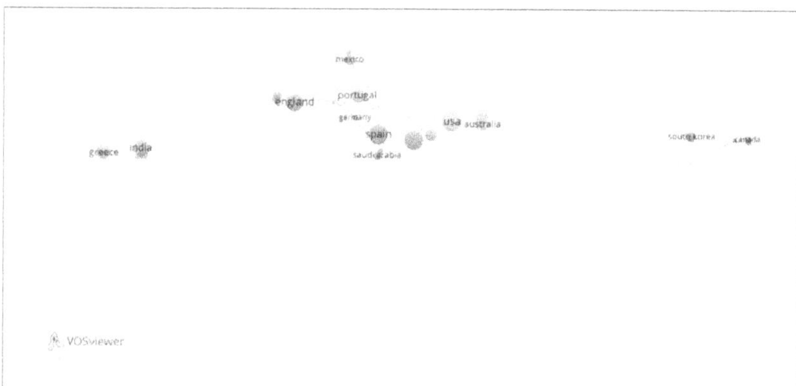

Figure 5: Citation Links of Countries

2.4. Citation of Organizations

In order to create a network map of inter-institutional citations, an analysis was conducted on 39 items that were related to each other within the scope of the criterion that an institution should publish at least 1 work and receive 1 citation. Rey Juan Carlos University (10 documents), Agricultural University of Athens (7 documents), University of Seville (4 documents) were represented by documents, the address institutions of the most cited publications were Rey Juan Carlos University (362 citations), Tianjin University (153 citations) and Virginia Tech (153 citations). A total of 8 clusters, 82 links and a total link strength of 84 were identified.

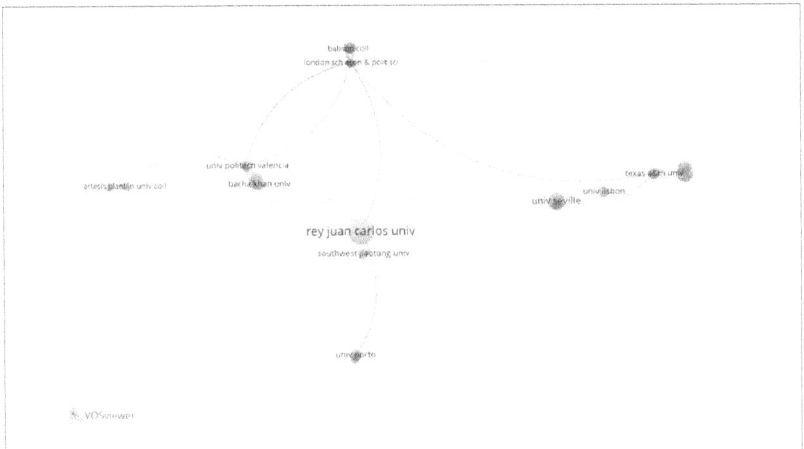

Figure 6: Citation Links of Organizations

2.5. Co-occurence of All Keywords

As a result of the analysis conducted with 44 observation units that were seen at least 3 times and had relationships between them, a total of 8 clusters, 140 links and 221 total link strengths were detected. When looking at the most frequently used keywords in publications related to Digital Markting Strategy, the most common ones are digital marketing with 81 repetitions, Social Media 21 with 21 repetitions, Marketing with 15 repetitions, Digital Marketing Strategy with 14 repetitions, and Big Data with 9 repetitions. The strongest expressions in terms of total link strength were digital marketing, big data, and social media.

In addition, the figure shows which topics the topic of digital marketing strategy is worked on and associated with (big data, social media, web analytics, marketing, strategy, e-commerce, artifical inteligence, sustainability).

We see how the keywords are distributed. Similar ones are shown in the same color.

When looking at the figure above, generally digital marketinf and digital marketing strategy are the most studied topics. The concepts between yellow and blue density are transition concepts. These concepts provide

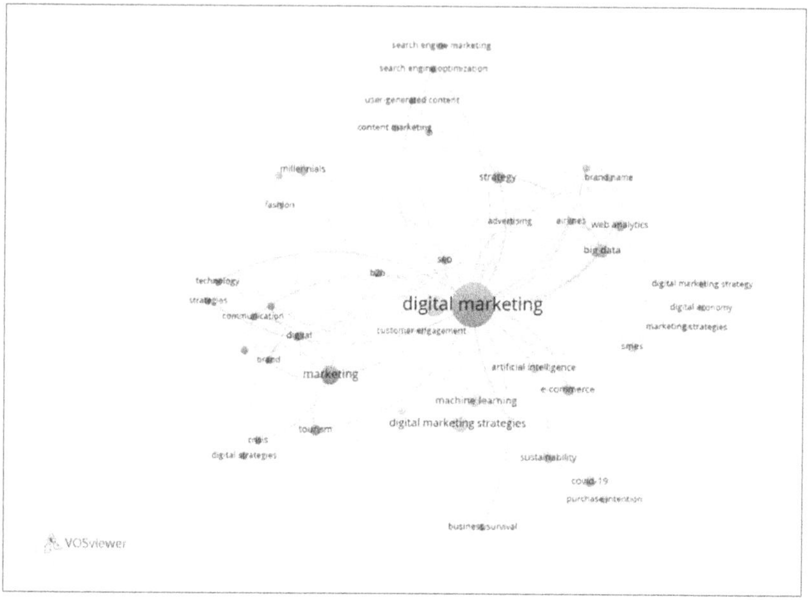

Figure 7: Most Frequently Used Keyword Links (Network Visulization)

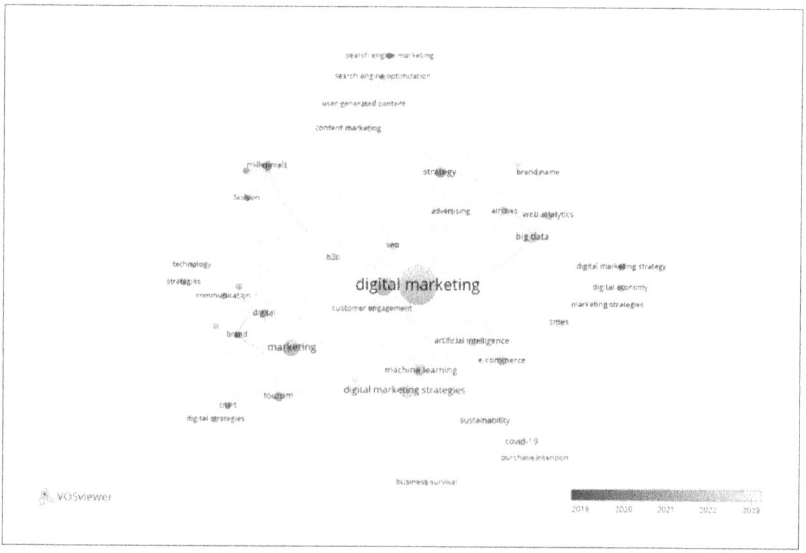

Figure 8: Most Frequently Used Keyword Links (Overlay Visulization)

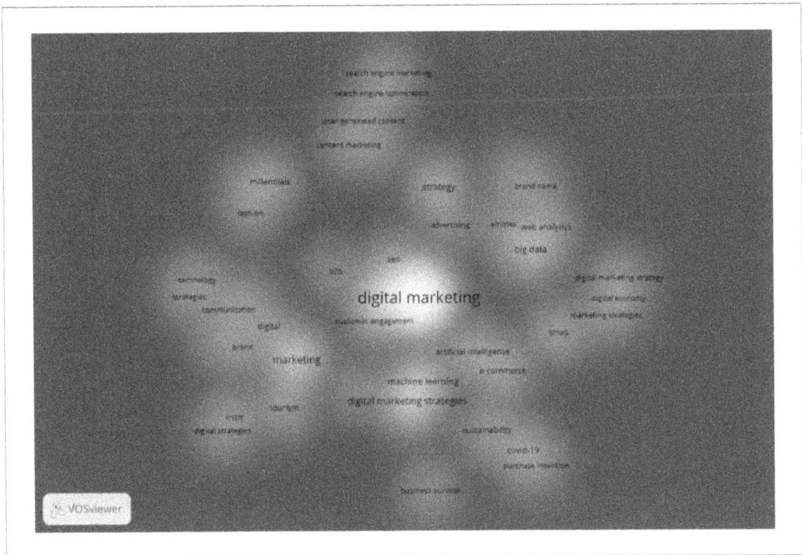

Figure 9: Most Frequently Used Keyword Links (Density Visulization)

information about which concepts can be used when addressing the topic you want to study.

2.6. Bibliographic Coupling of Documents

Bibliographic match refers to the situation of citing a common work cited by two independent sources. According to the analysis conducted with 96 items selected with the criterion of having at least 1 citation and having a connection between them, 10 clusters, 624 links and 963 total link strength were obtained. The publications with the highest bibliographic matches were Ramon Saura (2021) with 170 citations, Zhang (2020) with 153 citations and de pelsrnacker (2018) with 144 citations. The documents with the highest total link strength were deb (2024) with 69 total link strength, Barbosa (2024a) with 64 total link strength and Sakas (2022) with 61 total link strength.

2.7. Bibliographic Coupling of Authors

According to the analysis conducted with 311 items selected with the criteria of having at least 1 publication and 1 citation and having connections between

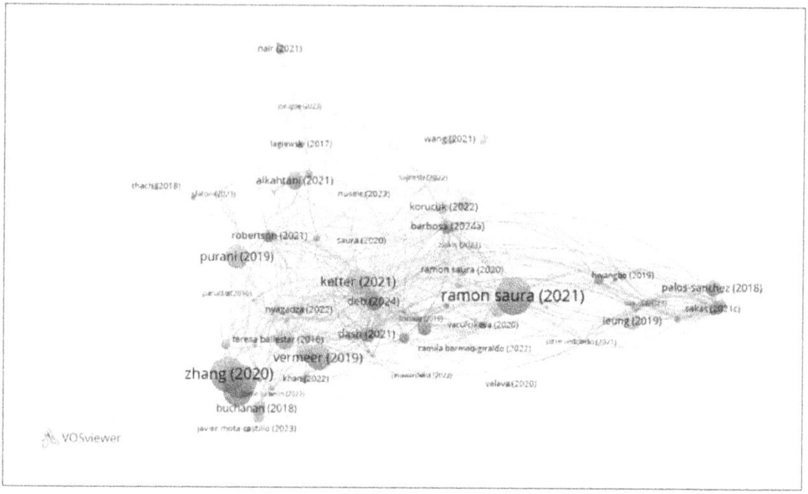

Figure 10: Bibliographic Coupling Links of Documents

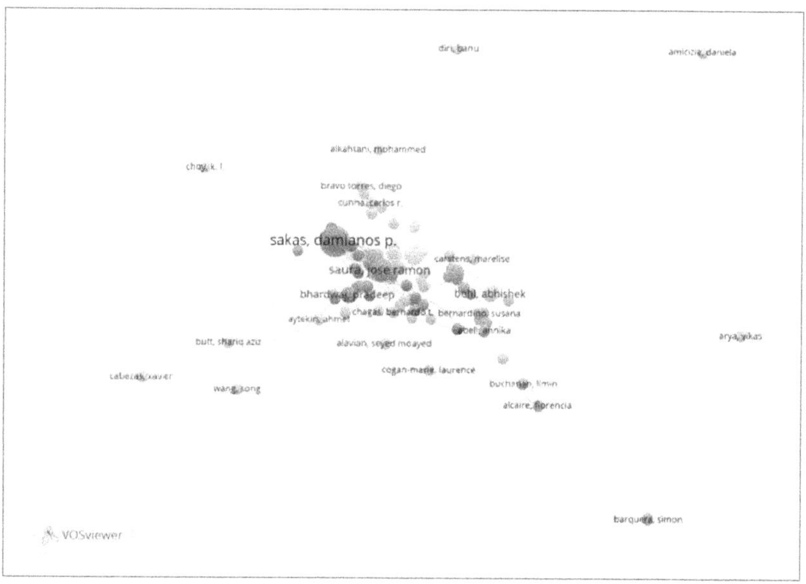

Figure 11: Bibliographic Coupling of Authors

them, 27 clusters, 7812 links and 54956 total link strength were obtained. The authors with the highest number of bibliographic matches were Jose Ramon Saura with 208 citations (695 total link strength), Cheng Luo with 153 citations (371 total link strength) and Fang Qin with 153 citations (371 total link strength).

2.8. Co-citation of Co-authors

Different sources cited in a publication are called co-citations. By selecting a minimum of 10 citations, a total of 5 clusters, 142 links and 630 total link strengths were identified based on the analysis conducted on 21 items. The authors with the most co-citations were identified as J. R. Saura (50), D. Chaffey (35) and P. Kotler (31).

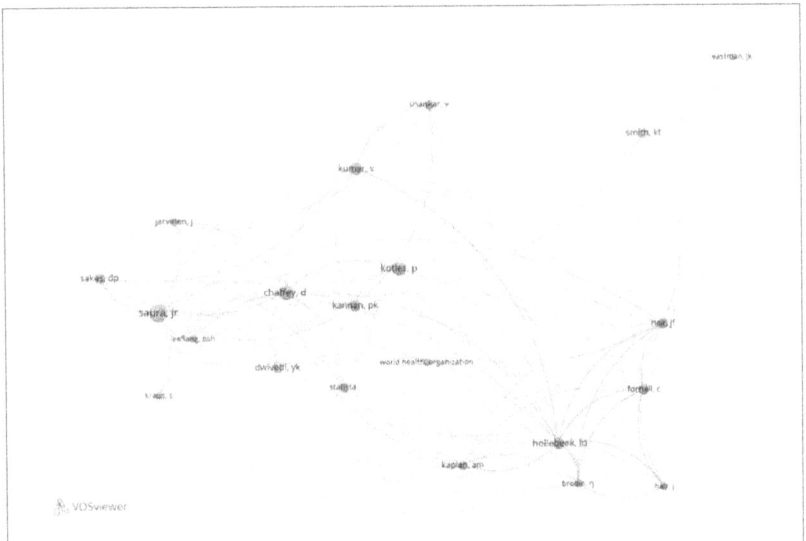

Figure 12: Co-citation of Co-authors

3. Conclusion

In this study, the summary of the studies conducted on the concept of digital marketing strategy is presented. It is thought that the results obtained will lead to studies on the same and similar subjects. It is very important to understand the possible effects of digital marketing strategies and the building blocks underlying the implementation of digital marketing strategies in the development of strategies. The quantitative table that will be presented to those interested in the subject by a series of statistics obtained as a result of this bibliometric analysis clearly shows the points that need to be emphasized.

The general summary of the results obtained can be presented as follows:

The unit of analysis is the bibliometric data of different types of works scanned in the Web of Science database and published between 2011 and 2024. When the distribution of 193 documents published on digital marketing strategy by publication years is examined, it is seen that the highest density was in 2023 (38 documents), 2024 (34 documents), 2020 (32 documents) and 2021 (32 documents); Jose Ramon Saura (7 documents), Damianos Sakas (7 documents), Nikolaos Giannakopoulos (5 documents) were the names that produced the most documents; The publication types were mostly article (147), Proceeding Paper (37), Review Article (8) and Early Access (7); In terms of research areas, it was determined that studies were published in the fields of Business (46), Managment (36), Computer Science Information Systems (21), Environmental Studies (14), Environmental Sciences (13), Green Sustainable Science Technology (13); when the distribution of publications by country was examined, it was determined that the leadership was with publishers from the Spain (20), USA (20), China 19 and England (17); the studies were mostly published in English (175), Spanish (13) and Portugese (4); the majority of publications were scanned in the Emerging Sources Citation Index (ESCI) (80), Social Sciences Citation Index (SSCI) (55) and Science Citation Index Expanded (SCI-EXPANDED) (40) indexes. When we look at the most common ones are digital marketing with 81 repetitions, Social Media 21 with 21 repetitions, Marketing with 15 repetitions, Digital Marketing Strategy with 14 repetitions, and Big Data with 9 repetitions. The strongest expressions in terms of total link strength were digital marketing, big data, and social media.

In an environment where artificial intelligence is on the rise and humanity feeds on the data it produces on the internet, studies on the spread of artificial intelligence and digital marketing strategies are also valuable. The effectiveness and effects of existing social awareness strategies are among the issues that need to be examined. The importance of training in this direction is great in the development of digital marketing strategies. With technological developments, virtual learning can be shown as a learning style that facilitates access to information for people with different learning and perception styles in terms of education quality and information accessibility. The trend towards Massive Open Online Course systems facilitates access to information (Can and Terziev, 2017), and can contribute to the development of strategic marketing strategies.

The critical limitations of the study are the inclusion of studies listed in the WOS Core Collection in the scope of the analysis, the exclusion of databases such as TÜBİTAK Ulakbim and YÖK Thesis Archive in Turkey, and Scopus and Pubmed in the international arena, and other sources that are not in online circulation.

References

Can, H., Minkovska, D., & Stoyanova, L. (2020, October). Estimation of Energy Performance Classes of Concrete Structures with Artificial Intelligence Models. In 2020 III International Conference on High Technology for Sustainable Development (HiTech) (pp. 1-3). IEEE. DOI: 10.1109/HiTech51434.2020.9364003

Can, H., & Terziev, V. (2016). The relationship economic growth and information technologies. Retrieved from SSRN: https://ssrn.com/abstract=3383899 or http://dx.doi.org/10.2139/ssrn.3383899.

Can, H., & Terziev, V. (2017). Massive Open Online Courses: Motivation and Success of Learners. Available at SSRN 3143988. http://dx.doi.org/10.2139/ssrn.3143988.

Okur Dincsoy, M. (2008). A Statistical Analysis of ICT Developments and Regional GDP per capita Convergence in Major East Asian Countries. 岡山大学大学院社会文化科学研究科紀要, 26(1), 125-143.

Okur Dincsoy, M. (2009). Can ICT Economically Catalyze a Regional GDP Per Capita Convergence ?– A Case Study of Major East Asian Countries–. 北東アジア経済研究, 7(1), 45-64.

Okur Dincsoy, M. (2009). A comparative Study of Japan and the ROK on ICT and Economic Development: Lessons for Turkey. 岡山大学大学院社会文化科学研究科紀要, 28, 123-141.

Okur Dincsoy, M. (2010). ICT Experience in East Asia and Modelling for Turkey. ProQuest LLC.

Okur Dinçsoy, M. & Can, H. (2023). The Relationship of Renewable Energy Generation, Renewable Energy Consumption, and Economic Growth: The Case of Türkiye.

Okur Dinçsoy, M. & H. Can (Eds.). (2023). Optimizing Energy Efficiency During a Global Energy Crisis (pp. 65-74). IGI Global. https://doi.org/10.4018/979-8-3693-0400-6.ch005

Okur Dinçsoy, Meltem. and Can, Hamit and Dinçsoy, Enver Erdinç and Terziev, Venelin. (2024). The Impact of Property Rights and Government Integrity on the Economic Freedom: The Case of the European Region, the BRICS Countries, and the USA (February 16, 2024). Available at SSRN: https://ssrn.com/abstract=4905470.

Korkmaz, Ö., & Can, H. (2018). Yenilenebilir Enerji, Fosil Enerji ve Ekonomik Büyüme İlişkisi: Rusya, Çin ve ABD Örneği. In İzmir International Congress on Economics and Administrative Sciences (IZCEAS) (No. 2018, pp. 2953-2966). İzmir International Congress on Economics and Administrative Sciences (IZCEAS).

Zhang, X., Xu, Y. Y., & Ma, L. (2023). Information Technology Investment and Digital Transformation: The Roles of Digital Transformation Strategy and Top Management. Business Process Management Journal, 29(2), 528-549. DOI: 10.1108/BPMJ-06-2022-0254.

An Innovative Approach to the Bulgarian School

Venelin Terziev, Marin Georgiev, Simeon Simeonov

1. Introduction

The meaning of innovation is when it is tied to the economic growth of the society, and the improvement of the standard of living. Innovation creates competition, and competition is the basis of progress. Innovation and education are the engines for successful development and progress. At first glance, innovation in education is not directly related to economic growth. Very often the implementation of an innovation is met with resistance. This action requires additional investment of time, additional efforts, and additional funds and the result is not always positive. This is the main obstacle to innovation in the school, and not only there. An important task is to motivate the team to implement the innovation, and to provide the necessary material and expert base to ensure success.

2. Innovations in education

Innovation is the practical implementation of ideas that result in the introduction of new goods or services, or improvement in offering goods or services (Schumpeter, 1983). ISO TC 279 in the standard ISO 56000:2020 defines innovation as "a new or changed entity, realizing or redistributing value" (ISO, 2020a). Others have different definitions; a common element in the definitions is a focus on newness, improvement, and spread of ideas or technologies.

Innovation often takes place through the development of more effective products, processes, services, technologies, artworks (Lijster, ed., 2018), or business models that innovators make available to markets, governments, and society.

Innovation is related to, but not the same as, invention (Bhasin, 2012a): Innovation is more apt to involve the practical implementation of an invention (i.e. new/improved ability) to make a meaningful impact in a market or society (Morgan, 2015a), and not all innovations require a new invention (Schumpeter, 1939).

Technical innovation often manifests itself via the engineering process when the problem being solved is of a technical or scientific nature. The opposite of innovation is exnovation.

Surveys of the literature on innovation have found a variety of definitions. In 2009, Baregheh et al. found around 60 definitions in different scientific papers, while a 2014 survey found over 40 (Edison et al., 2013a). Based on their survey, Baragheh et al. attempted to formulate a multidisciplinary definition and arrived at the following: "Innovation is the multi-stage process whereby organizations transform ideas into new/improved products, service or processes, to advance, compete and differentiate themselves successfully in their marketplace" (Baregheh et al., 2009a).

In a study of how the software industry considers innovation, the following definition given by Crossan and Apaydin was considered to be the most complete. Crossan and Apaydin built on the definition given in the Organisation for Economic Co-operation and Development (OECD) Oslo Manual (Edison et al., 2013a): Innovation is the production or adoption, assimilation, and exploitation of a value-added novelty in economic and social spheres; renewal and enlargement of products, services, and markets; development of new methods of production; and the establishment of new management systems. It is both a process and an outcome.

American sociologist Everett Rogers, defined it as follows: "An idea, practice, or object that is perceived as new by an individual or other unit of adoption" (Rogers, 2003).

According to Alan Altshuler and Robert D. Behn, innovation includes original invention and creative use. These writers define innovation as generation, admission, and realization of new ideas, products, services, and processes (Innovation in American Government: Challenges, Opportunities, and Dilemmas, 1997).

Two main dimensions of innovation are the degree of novelty (i.e. whether an innovation is new to the firm, new to the market, new to the industry, or new to the world) and kind of innovation (i.e. whether it is process or product-service system innovation) (Edison et al., 2013a). Organizational researchers have also distinguished innovation separately from creativity, by providing an updated definition of these two related constructs:

Workplace creativity concerns the cognitive and behavioral processes applied when attempting to generate novel ideas. Workplace innovation concerns the processes applied when attempting to implement new ideas. Specifically, innovation involves some combination of problem/opportunity identification, the introduction, adoption, or modification of new ideas germane to organizational needs, the promotion of these ideas, and the practical implementation of these ideas (Hughes et al., 2018).

Peter Drucker wrote: Innovation is the specific function of entrepreneurship, whether in an existing business, a public service institution, or a new venture started by a lone individual in the family kitchen. It is how the entrepreneur either creates new wealth-producing resources or endows existing resources with enhanced potential for creating wealth (Drucker, 2002a).

In general, innovation is distinguished from creativity by its emphasis on the implementation of creative ideas in an economic setting. Amabile and Pratt in 2016, drawing on the literature, distinguish between creativity ("the production of novel and useful ideas by an individual or small group of individuals working together") and innovation ("the successful implementation of creative ideas within an organization") (Amabile & Pratt, 2016).

In 1957 the economist Robert Solow was able to demonstrate that economic growth had two components. The first component could be attributed to growth in production including wage labour and capital. The second component was found to be productivity. Ever since, economic historians have tried to explain the process of innovation itself, rather than assuming that technological inventions and technological progress result in productivity growth (Dudley, 2012b).

The concept of innovation emerged after the Second World War, mostly thanks to the works of Joseph Schumpeter (1883–1950) who described the economic effects of innovation processes as Constructive destruction. Today, consistent neo-Schumpeterian scholars see innovation not as neutral or apolitical processes (Jasanoff & Kim, 2015b; Papaioannou, 2020b). Rather, innovation can be seen as a socially constructed process. Therefore, its conception depends on the political and societal context in which innovation is taking place (Robra et al., 2023a). According to Shannon Walsh, "innovation today is best understood as innovation under capital" (Walsh, 2023b). This means that the current hegemonic purpose for innovation is capital valorization and profit maximization, exemplified by the appropriation of knowledge (e.g., through patenting), the widespread practice of Planned obsolescence (incl. lack of repairability by design), and the Jevons paradox, that describes negative consequences of eco-efficiency as energy-reducing effects tend to trigger mechanisms leading to energy-increasing effects (Lange et al., 2020c).

3. The technology of innovative schools in Bulgaria

Innovative schools are a model for building a new educational paradigm, through which students will improve their educational results and increase critical thinking and creativity through innovative educational processes, teaching methods, school leadership, and learning strategies.

To be defined as innovative, the school must prove that by introducing innovative elements, by developing a new way the educational content, curricula, and programs, increase the quality of education, i.e. innovative schools have more freedom in applying new, modern, innovative methods of teaching the learning material.

From the point of view of educational management, we can consider the school as a company, where the final product is a built personality. In the entire process of education and upbringing from the child to the completed young man (girl), we form certain knowledge, skills, and competencies, i.e. a personality is formed with a certain creative and constantly critical thinking.

The Bulgarian education system has not yet reached the level of change. Traditional reproductive education still dominates. Knowledge is taught that students must learn and then reproduce. This suggests that innovations in school occur under the pressure of ongoing processes.

However, with the adoption of the new Law on School and Preschool Education in 2016, the stereotype is gradually breaking. An opportunity is given to the idea-oriented, functional education-seeking teachers to come forward. Accompanying documents to the law Ordinance No. 9 of August 19, 2016, for the institutions in the preschool and school education system; Section II of Ordinance No. 5 of November 30, 2015, on general education, Ordinance No. 4 of November 30, 2015, on the curriculum, Ordinance No. 10 of September 1, 2016, on the organization of activities in school education enable schools to switched to a new way of development or these are different types of innovative solutions. An opportunity is given to create innovative schools that will become a model of the modern school. A school where students will develop the competencies necessary for their social adaptation, develop critical thinking, and create thinking leaders.

For a school to be defined as innovative, it must undertake purposeful planned change. It is necessary to introduce innovative practices that can be implemented both in the form of an educational product and in the organization of the educational process. And this introduction must be done following certain principles.

In order to be defined as such, a Bulgarian school must meet certain characteristics. Some of the most important characteristics of an innovative school are presented without claiming that the list is exhaustive:

- The pedagogical specialist is above all a partner in the educational process;
- Pedagogical specialists use modern pedagogical techniques in their direct work;
- Takes into account the individuality of each student, his needs and seeks the best solution for adaptation in the modern social environment.
- Educates in a spirit of criticality and creativity;
- Changes the learning environment by making it as close as possible to the real world (moved classroom, flipped classroom, etc.)
- Removes boundaries between subjects by stimulating students to make causal connections between them;
- Actively involves parents and the public in the process of upbringing and education.

However, our task is not to give grades on which school is innovative and which is not. The task facing education in Bulgaria is to create conditions for schools to be innovative, if not all, for the most part. No framework can be created in which to place innovative schools. This would mean predetermining their creative capabilities. An example model of an innovative school (Fig. 1).

4. Innovative schools: learning and teaching in the digital era

The European Parliament has published a report on "Innovative Schools, Teacher & Learning in the Digital Era". The report analyses new ways of

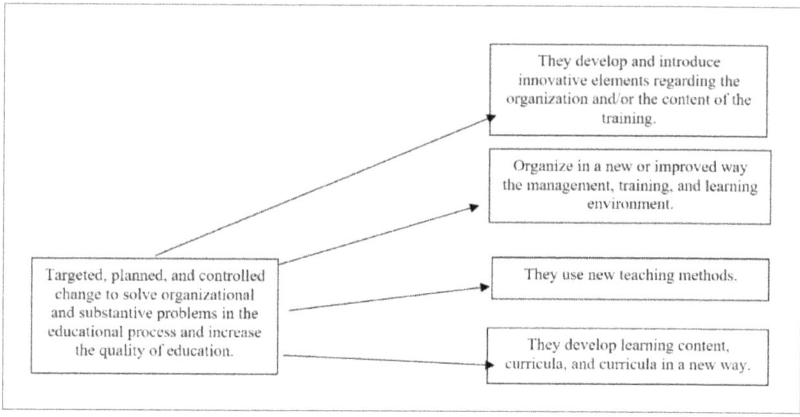

Figure 1: Model of an innovative school

social-digital participation and argues that schools need to adapt to new technologies. It evaluates new practices of knowledge creation, asks how to implement new technologies in schools, and assesses what pedagogic creations are required from teachers.

People who are born after 1980 are often called digital natives, although the term is critically analysed, the authors argue that education systems need to recognise that young people use ICT in everyday life. Schools, teachers and education authorities need to accept this and implement new teaching practices. Pupils need to be prepared for the challenges of the 21st century, such as the digitalisation of the working and private life. Hence it is necessary to teach them a responsible use of ICT, which enables them "to regulate their own use of mobile devices inside and outside of schools."

According to the report, a teacher is required to give "strategic guidance" to pupils, as teachers have an "understanding of the long term objective of learning". "Technical innovations are not necessarily pedagogical innovations," which means that teachers have to face the challenge to accompany pupils in their learning process and to sort out techniques that are not useful. To enable teachers to do this, the report proposes to improve teacher training. ETUCE highlights that the challenges to address these topics cannot be solved by teachers alone. The digital revolution relays additional responsibility to everyone involved in the education system.

4.1. Change is Driven by People, Not by Technology

Although it seems as if everyday lives are different "because" of certain technologies, the reality is that everyday lives are different because people have chosen to use those technologies. Technologies do not, of their own accord, predetermine social or organizational change (Markus & Robey, 1998; Orlikowski & Barley, 2001). Rather, technologies provide occasions for people to experiment and attempt to reconcile present conditions with understandings about the past. In the context of schooling, successful technology use is thus influenced by the norms, expectations, and personal experiences of the users (i.e., educators and students) (Cho & Wayman, 2014a; Ertmer, 2005a). Viewed through this lens, it becomes evident that many "technology problems" might actually be "people problems." For example, the problem of successful engagement in OERs might involve issues of motivation, sense of investment, and the ability to selfregulate one's learning. Similarly, a successful 1:1 program might depend also upon issues of having enough staff to support technology use, teacher's understandings about how to integrate technology into instruction, and student's choices about when (and when not) to use a particular device. The effective use of computer data systems might also depend upon issues involving teachers' knowledge about assessment and instruction, confidence in the data at hand, and local cues from leaders about how and why data ought to be used.

Altogether, these "people problems" highlight the importance of conversation, talk, and training to technology adoption (Ertmer, 2005a; Leonardi, 2009b). Rather than expect OERs to produce learning in and of themselves, people might need to be trained and supported in getting the most out of their online experiences. Similarly, teachers might need increased time to explore and opportunities to collaborate around new technologies. Engaging in such activities helps teachers to innovate new teaching and apply new knowledge (Bredeson, 2002b; Putnam & Borko, 2000). Unfortunately, teachers in Europe may vary greatly when it comes to time and opportunities to connect with colleagues (OECD, 2014b). Accordingly, future investments in technology might benefit from similar investments in helping people to understand and envision how to get the most out of the tools at hand.

4.2. The importance of media and multimedia resources

The value of the focus technologies described in this brief is premised on the capacity for technologies to deliver information to learners or to teachers. For example, OERs and 1:1 initiatives assume that users will find value in text, audio, and video materials. Similarly, computer data systems do not simply provide educators with raw data about students. Rather, data is analyzed and displayed via some form of visualization, such as a color- coded graph, matrix, or map of learning objectives. It is important to realize, however, that not all media or presentations of information carry the same value for recipients. Different forms of media may communicate with varying degrees of richness (Carlson & Zmud, 1999; Daft & Lengel, 1986).

Thus, it might be important to question whether particular media are suited to the challenge. For example, people who attempt to learn via video might pay more attention to the likability of the presenters, rather than to the content of the knowledge presented (Ferran & Watts, 2008). Similarly, the design and aesthetics of graphs or other visualizations influence how well people comprehend the information presented (Purchase, 2002c). In other words, people are not simply passive recipients of media. Instead, people must work to interpret and to make sense of the information before them. Consequently, one next step may involve designing and refining what users experience when attempting to learn using computers. Some content might be best shared using one form of media (e.g., text, audio, video), while at the knowledge might best be shared using several at once. Further, the experience of these media should be personalized and interactive. These measures could include the use of quizzes, simulations, online discussion, or face-to-face conversations. For example, a student in a traditional classroom attempting to learn via technology might be asked to reproduce knowledge, apply it, or reflect about it with other learners. Similarly, a non-traditional student, such as an early school leaver attempting to regain credits, might have similar experiences through an online environment. A teacher attempting to learn about students' performance might be asked to summarize, make predictions, or converse with other educators about the data.

4.3. The assumption of networked communications

The value of the technologies in this brief is also premised on the availability of satellite- based or Internet communications. The promise of OERs is to connect people to the information they need, whenever they need it. Digital devices provide students with points of access to information. Computer data systems can ensure that student data flows from school to school, grade to grade, and teacher to teacher. Although it might seem obvious that geographically remote areas might benefit fromincreased communications infrastructure, it is also important to bear in mind that many students living in poverty face a similar digital divide. These students may see their peers interacting with digital worlds, but themselves have neither devices nor plans for accessing such worlds themselves. Thus, addressing inequities in education is a matter both of geography and of socioeconomics. The potential of OERs is limited if learners must hunt, beg, or borrow for Internet access. Similarly, 1:1 computing might contribute to a few classroom lessons, but the potential value of devices drops when students cannot bring them home or cannot communicate with outside worlds. Further, the observation of trends in student data and the ability of teachers to pick up where others have left off is predicated on local privacy policies and interoperability of data systems. Actions to address these challenges are unique to each technology in question. They range from creating publically available Internet access, to increasing the centralization of data systems, to addressing concerns about privacy and security.

4.4. What might stay the same?

This report addresses questions about the role of technology in supporting educational change. In considering such issues, it is easy to become wrapped up in exuberance around the promises of technology. This exuberance, however, leads to blind spots regarding whether technologies are actually effective at helping students learn (Brooks, 2011a; Cho & Wayman, 2015c). As much as the digital era might seem inescapable today, it is still a relatively new and fresh even in the arc of human progress (Turkle, 2011b). Now is the time for careful reflection about the place of technology in schools. On one hand, some technological innovations might be misused or used to the detriment of student learning. Email provides an example from our everyday lives. Despite promises that email would free up our time, it has actually become a source of increased stress and lost time. Similarly, schools in the United States wrestle with narrow definitions of student learning that in turn lead to shallow and questionable uses of computer data systems (Booher-Jennings, 2005b; Cho

& Wayman, 2014a). On the same note, the increased use of Internet-capable digital devices raises questions about student distraction (Hatakka et al., 2013b), teacher and student privacy (Peck & Mullen, 2008), and the adverse effects of screen time (Pagani et al., 2010; Uhls et al., 2014b).

Future research will be important in determining productive and counterproductive approaches to technology use. Evaluations are needed, not only to examine the most effective designs for OERs, 1:1 initiatives, and computer data systems, but also regarding how they might compare to more traditional educational methods. Under what conditions do such technologies make a difference? Under what conditions are conventional methods still best? Finally, there are some conversations that research might support, but ultimately be unable to answer. For example, what is the definition of a successful student? Do conventional methods promote any social values, qualities, or skills worth preserving? How is responsible, ethical technology use to be promoted outside of the school walls?

5. Conclusion

An innovation makes sense when it is economically justified and helps to raise the standard of living. An indicator of the development of a society is the level of education and inclusion of different social communities. In this way, innovation and education go in the same direction (Terziev & Bogdanova, 2019).

The Bulgarian education system, and the school in particular, cannot yet meet the requirements of the ongoing social processes. The dynamics of the development of social relations and new social requirements are a challenge for education. Changes in the educational environment are much slower and follow certain historical patterns. Transformations in societies are dynamic and require much faster changes that are not accompanied only by upgrading existing educational techniques and technologies. All these undertakings require a thorough scientific approach, which should be accompanied by an accurate analysis of ongoing social processes).

References

Schumpeter, J.A., (1983). The theory of economic development: an inquiry into profits, capital, credit, interest, and the business cycle. Opie, Redvers, Elliott, John E. New Brunswick, New Jersey. ISBN 0-87855-698-2.

"ISO 56000:2020 (EN). Innovation management — Fundamentals and vocabulary". (2020a) ISO. 2020.

Lijster, T., ed. (2018). The Future of the New: Artistic Innovation in Times of Social Acceleration. Arts in society. Valiz. ISBN 978-94-92095-58-9.

Bhasin, K., (2012a). This is the Difference Between "Invention" and "Innovation". Business Insider, https://www.businessinsider.com/this-is-the-difference-between-invention-and-innovation-2012-4, Retrieved November 18, 2024.

Morgan, J., (2015a). What's The Difference Between Invention And Innovation?, Forbes, https://www.forbes.com/sites/jacobmorgan/2015/09/10/whats-the-difference-between-invention-and-innovation/, Retrieved November 18, 2024.

Schumpeter, J.A., (1939). Innovation is possible without anything we should identify as invention, and invention does not necessarily induce innovation, Business Cycles, Vol. 1.

Edison, H., Ali, N.B., & Torkar, R., (2013a). Towards innovation measurement in the software industry. Journal of Systems and Software 86, pp. 1390–1407.

Baregheh, A., Rowley, J., & Sambrook, S. (2009a), Towards a multidisciplinary definition of innovation, Management Decision, Vol. 47 No. 8, pp. 1323-1339. https://doi.org/10.1108/00251740910984578.

Rogers, E.M., (2003). Diffusion of innovations (5th ed.). New York: Free Press. ISBN 0-7432-2209-1.

Innovation in American Government: Challenges, Opportunities, and Dilemmas. (1997). Brookings Inst Pr. 1 June 1997. ISBN 978-0-8157-0358-7.

Hughes, DJ., Lee, A., Tian, A.W., Newman, A., & Legood, A., (2018). Leadership, creativity, and innovation: A critical review and practical recommendations. The Leadership Quarterly. 29 (5): 549–569. doi:10.1016/j.leaqua.2018.03.00.

Drucker, P.F., (2002a). The Discipline of Innovation. Harvard Business Review. Retrieved November 18, 2024.

Amabile, T.M., & Pratt, M.G., (2016). The dynamic componential model of creativity and innovation in organizations: Making progress, making meaning. Research in Organizational Behavior. 36: 157–183. doi:10.1016/j.riob.2016.10.001.

Dudley, L., (2012b). Mothers of Innovation: How Expanding Social Networks Gave Birth to the Industrial Revolution. Cambridge Scholars Publishing. p. 4. ISBN 9781443843126.

Jasanoff, S., & Kim, S-H. (2015b). Dreamscapes of Modernity. University of Chicago Press. ISBN 978-0-226-27652-6, doi:10.7208/chicago/9780226276663.001.0001.

Papaioannou, T., (2020b). Innovation, value-neutrality and the question of politics: unmasking the rhetorical and ideological abuse of evolutionary theory. Journal of Responsible Innovation. 7 (2): 238–255.

Robra, B., Pazaitis, A., Giotitsas, C., & Pansera, M., (2023a). From creative destruction to convivial innovation – A post-growth perspective. Technovation. 125: 102760. ISN 0166-4972, doi: 10.1016/j.technovation.2023.102760.

Walsh, S. (2023b). Marx, subsumption and the critique of innovation. Organization, 30(2), 345-360. https://doi.org/10.1177/13505084211015377.

Lange, S., Pohl, J., & Santarius, T., (2020c). Digitalization and energy consumption. Does ICT reduce energy demand?. Ecological Economics. 176: 106760. Bibcode: 2020 EcoEc. 17606760L. doi: 10.1016/j.ecolecon.2020.106760. ISSN 0921-8009.

Markus, M.L., & Robey, D., (1988). Information technology and organizational change: causal structure in theory and research. Management science, 34(5), 583- 598.

Orlikowski, W.J., & Barley, S.R., (2001). Technology and institutions: What can research on information technology and research on organizations learn from each other? MIS quarterly, 25(2), 145-165.

Cho, V., & Wayman, J. C., (2014a). Districts' efforts for data use and computer data systems: The role of sensemaking in system use and implementation. Teachers College Record, 116(2). http://www.tcrecord.org/library/Abstract.asp?ContentId=17349, Retrieved November 18, 2024.

Ertmer, P.A., (2005a). Teacher pedagogical beliefs: The final frontier in our quest for technology integration? Educational technology research and development, 53(4), 25-39.

Leonardi, P.M., (2009b). Crossing the implementation line: The mutual constitution of technology and organizing across development and use activities. Communication Theory, 19(3), 278-310.

Bredeson, P.V., (2002b). Designs for learning: A new architecture for professional development in schools. Thousand Oaks, CA: Corwin.

Putnam, R.T., & Borko, H., (2000). What do new views of knowledge and thinking have to say about research on teacher learning? Educational Researcher, 29(1), 4–15. http://doi.org/10.2307/1176586.

OECD. (2014). TALIS 2013 results: An international perspective on teaching and learning. Paris: OECD Publishing.

Carlson, J.R., & Zmud, R.W., (1999). Channel expansion theory and the experiential nature of media richness perceptions. Academy of Management Journal, 42(2), 153–170.

Daft, R.L., & Lengel, R.H., (1986). Organizational information requirements, media richness, and structural design. Management Science, 32(5), 554–571.

Ferran, C., & Watts, S., (2008). Videoconferencing in the field: A heuristic processing model. Management Science, 54(9).

Purchase, H. C. (2002c). Metrics for graph drawing aesthetics. Journal of Visual Languages & Computing, 13(5), 501–516. http://doi.org/10.1006/jvlc.2002.0232.

Brooks, C. (2011a). Locating leadership: The blind spot in Alberta's technology policy discourse. Education Policy Analysis Archives, 19(26), http://www.eric.ed.gov/ERICWebPortal/detail?accno=EJ956002, Retrieved November 18, 2024.

Cho, V., & Wayman, J.C., (2015c). Assumptions, strategies, and organization: Central office implementation of computer data systems. Journal of School Leadership, 25(6).

Turkle, S. (2011b). Alone together: Why we expect more from technology and less from each other. New York, NY: Basic Books.

Booher-Jennings, J., (2005b). Below the bubble: "Educational triage" and the Texas accountability system. American Educational Research Journal, 42(2), 231–268.

Hatakka, M., Andersson, A., & Grönlund, Å. (2013b). Students' use of one to one laptops: a capability approach analysis. Information Technology & People, 26(1), 94- 112.

Peck, C.M., & Mullen, C.A., (2008). New media, new voices: A complex school public relations and human resources challenge. Journal of School Public Relations, 29(3), 401–424.

Pagani, L.S., Fitzpatrick, C., Barnett, T.A., & Dubow, E. (2010). Prospective associations between early childhood television exposure and academic, psychosocial, and physical well-being by middle childhood. Archives of Pediatrics & Adolescent Medicine, 164(5), 425–431. http://doi.org/10.1001/archpediatrics.2010.50/.

Uhls, Y.T., Michikyan, M., Morris, J., Garcia, D., Small, G.W., Zgourou, E., & Greenfield, P.M. (2014b). Five days at outdoor education camp without screens improves preteen skills with nonverbal emotion cues. Computers in Human Behavior, 39, 387–392. http://doi.org/10.1016/j.chb.2014.05.036.

Terziev, V., & Bogdanova, M. (2019). The academic capitalism and the new business model of the universities. // Proceedings of ADVED 2019 - 5th International Conference on Advances in Education and Social Sciences, 21-23 October 2019, International Organization Center of Academic Research, Istanbul, Turkey, 2019, pp. 477-484, ISBN: 978-605-82433-7-8.

Research of Social Processes in the Works of Venelin Terziev

Marin Georgiev, Simeon Simeonov

1. Introduction

Social processes are some of the most significant in the development of societies. From the point of view of science, they are difficult to research, study, and analyze, but for people, they are important and significant. This creates certain challenges for scientists who deal with this issue, as well as difficulties in proving their analytical research, judgments, and conclusions.

All these circumstances have placed demands on these researchers to seek a diverse set of opportunities for presenting, proving, and testing research in society. The dynamics of ongoing social processes additionally create difficulties. There are too few scientists who use a large set of instruments, interdisciplinary knowledge, as well as sufficient skills to impose their theses and views. Some of their conclusions are quite bold and sound like an unrealistic forecast for the future development of our societies. Others are not accepted due to the high complexity of these processes and the impossibility of accompanying a specific study or analysis with an appropriate mathematical apparatus. Sometimes the data used has a high degree of relativity and only the high expertise of the authors of these studies helps the process of reaching correct and accurate conclusions in their work.

2. Researching social processes in the works of Professor Venelin Terziev

For example, Professor Marusya Lyubcheva from the University of Burgas, Bulgaria writes the following about one of the seminal works of Professor Venelin Terziev: The book "Policies and Instruments for Social Development" (Terziev, 2019a) managed to keep my interest because my attention was directed to sustainable development all the time. Without sustainable development being the subject of discussion at all, or even mentioned in the texts. Almost a phenomenon but not so unexpected for a person who seeks the projections of sustainable development in practical life, as the author does. It is a well-known fact that social activities/processes are one of the pillars of sustainable development. And this is probably the reason why I found this connection in the book, without it being demonstrated. Assessing even the very title of the book "Policies and Instruments…", it can be said that it sounds like a resonance in a real environment in which the entire social sphere is subject to certain policies that can make it effective, but can also create chaos, from which the entire chain, starting from management and reaching the last person to whom it is directed, can swing in one direction or another. Even with a good set of tools, an unmeasured policy could not be useful.

Why policies? Considering the social system as such, we must undoubtedly take into account that politics is everything. The organization of all elements in the system begins with it and the creation of a service for each member of society ends with it. As a framework in which administrations, priorities, and measures are placed, starting with an analysis of both the state and achievements and comparison with other similar ones, ending with the quality of each service offered.

Why tools? Methodologies and methods are how a policy becomes a reality and acquires its practical dimensions. It should always be borne in mind that the tools can be different and it is good for them to be up-to-date in order to result in efficiency. This is precisely why policies and tools should be considered in synchrony.

Why development? Every action in a country has its social dimension and an emerging perspective of increased well-being for all social groups or individuals. The purpose of the social system is to ensure the quality of life of all citizens, regardless of their education, status, or group affiliation, and to create an environment for social tolerance and perspective. Each subsequent state of the system is a projection of perspectives and development.

Examining policies and tools, the author makes the perfect combination for result-oriented actions as part of sustainable development and part of the sustainability and security of each system. The policy-tools relationship is the key to systematicity and the transformation of theoretical management models into operational schemes through logistic matrices by elements.

This integration is the greatest achievement of Prof. Venelin Terziev's work and it is positioned in each chapter, with the chapters representing certain areas of the country's social system.

The solutions of the individual chapters reflect a sequence along the axis of study of social policy - social economy - social development, and in this relation the formulated social models become real.

Within the framework outlined by the topics of the three chapters, the main problems of social assistance, inequalities, poverty, models of social development, prospects of the social economy, and social enterprises are discussed. At first glance, the third chapter "Continuing vocational training in Bulgaria as a tool for social development" stands slightly detached from the first two topics, but a more in-depth discussion places this emphasis at the center of social development and naturally connects it with the first two. The main reason for this is rooted in the fact that modern social development is validated with new knowledge, skills, and competencies, which are achieved with continuous renewal of the knowledge base. If we are talking about a knowledge-based economy, then it is quite adequate to talk about social activities based on modern knowledge and skills. It is precisely these new knowledge, skills, and competencies that can bring the necessary social security, which the author highlights as an emphasis on social policy and the social economy.

This final announcement of the book makes the relationship development – security – competence certain. This relationship returns to the debate in the first chapter, connecting it to research models and in the second, seeking the security of the social economy.

In other words, the book defines a visual cyclicality with a formal beginning in social development, passing through the modeling of the social economy, and ending with training, which, determined as ongoing, again returns the system to determining a new state in social development.

The book is richly illustrated with factual material that emphasizes rich associative reasoning and the construction of interrelationships that can determine the projections of a strong future social policy with its associated tools.

Prof. Margarita Bogdanova from the Academy of Economics in Svishtov, Bulgaria shares: This is a monographic work by the eminent scientist Prof. Venelin Terziev (Terziev, 2019a). This is a monographic work by an extremely productive researcher who has devoted a large part of his work to topics related to social policy and social assistance. Venelin Terziev is a Doctor of Economic Sciences, Doctor of Sciences (National Security), and Doctor of Sciences in Social Activities. He has held several leading positions in the Ministry of Labor and Social Policy of the Republic of Bulgaria, the Ministry of Culture of the Republic of Bulgaria, and in private business, which determines the practical nature of a large part of his scientific research in the field of economics and management at various hierarchical levels.

This monographic work is aimed at a difficult area to research – social development and the capacity of the administration to provide effective social assistance.

"The topic is particularly relevant both theoretically and practically. Theoretically, because studies and analyses in this area only concern individual aspects of social development problems and often miss the big picture," says Prof. Terziev.

On the other hand, the author has chosen to apply a unified integrated approach that combines structural, normative, functional, and prospective analysis of the object and subject of study. This requires very in-depth knowledge of the system from different perspectives, as well as prospective thinking and a highly prognostic culture, which few researchers possess.

Prof. Terziev does not hide that the topic is also relevant in practical terms due to the complex nature of the social system, which is saturated with numerous contradictions - between individual social groups, between needs and tools for satisfying these needs, between short-term and long-term impacts of policies and regulatory tools, etc.

"These painful discrepancies for society reduce the effect of the functioning of the social system, and therefore scientifically based proposals for their resolution or elimination are more than necessary, relevant and significant," specifies Prof. Terziev.

By considering possible alternatives for action to overcome the contradictions that have arisen, the scientist clearly states his intentions to provide an answer to at least some of the most pressing problems in the object of research. In order to limit the field of study, Prof. Venelin Terziev has chosen as his goal the creation and verification of a scientific theory of an applied nature for social development and the development of adapted scientific-applied models for increasing the effectiveness of social assistance, aimed at the development and improvement of social policy, social enterprises and the training of specialists in social activities, through continuing professional training. Structurally, the work is divided into four separate parts, which are logically justified and closely related to the research tasks. The first part examines and critically analyzes the problems related to modern approaches in the research of social policy and social work. The achievements of the leading authors are extensively analyzed, and new scientific-theoretical statements defining social development and social policy are derived. The good European and global practices in the field of social security and their reflection on the management approaches and the capacity of the relevant administrations in Bulgaria are critically analyzed. On this basis, the principles of social policy are derived. This chapter also enriches and further develops the theory of social work as a process. A retrospective economic analysis of trends in the world and our country is made, and the need for the development of social work is deduced. Key concepts are defined, such as "institutionalization", "identification" and "internationalization of social work". Based on scientific-theoretical and applied analysis, several concepts are enriched, such as "social state", "social security", "social protection", "social benefits", "social services", "social provision", "social insurance" and "social assistance system". The author has analyzed in depth the structure of the social assistance system and the organization of social protection activities for vulnerable groups in Bulgaria. A definition of the profession of "social worker" is introduced, outlining its profile and necessary qualifications. This is an important starting point in the process of providing the social assistance system with competent specialists. The second part is dedicated to the social economy and in particular to social enterprises, which are presented as a model for effective social assistance and social development. The European social model is examined as a universally recognized key tool for achieving sustainable and inclusive growth, following the priorities of the "Europe 2020" Strategy, and now as a vision for "Europe 2030". A very interesting and in-depth analysis of the state and prerequisites for the development of social entrepreneurship in Bulgaria is presented, highlighting regulatory conjunctions and restrictions, sectoral and territorial characteristics, and development trends. The author pays special attention to the typology of social enterprises from the point of view of their goals (including social goals), size, forms of support for risk groups, phases of development, social effects, etc. The proposed typology is a methodological issue of exceptional importance. It is related to the metrics, analysis, and evaluation of social enterprises in order to provide objective, reliable, and relevant information for their regulation with appropriate policies and instruments. Last but not least, the author presents a broad vision of innovations in the field of social enterprises and of policies for their promotion both at the national and regional levels with various financial and non-financial means and instruments. Particularly interesting are the innovative practices presented, such as "positive discrimination", the introduction of the "Social Enterprise Product" brand, etc., which break the established stereotypes in this area and contribute to the imposition of a modern, modern understanding of the phenomenon of social enterprises.

The strategic framework for the development of social entrepreneurship complements the presentation in the second chapter. The relevant European and national strategic and operational documents are indicated. The possibilities for supporting social entrepreneurship in Bulgaria are outlined, not only as financial instruments but also as partnership initiatives, models and various proven good practices for strengthening the institutional capacity of social enterprises, public sector organizations, and the sector as a whole. In support of the defined goal, the third part of the study is dedicated to continuing professional training. A significant contribution of the author is that he enriches the theory of continuing professional training as a tool for social development. The legislative and institutional framework of continuing professional training, trends, factors, and challenges are consistently examined, and also the methodological basis of continuing professional training in the context of lifelong learning. The most adequate forms of continuing professional training in the social sphere are derived and a methodology for the application of continuing professional training based on the concept of "'ifelong learning" is proposed. The fourth part presents the author's ideas regarding the preparation and professional qualification of social work specialists in Bulgaria through continuing professional training. The emanation of labor is the developed model of a system for the preparation and professional qualification of social work specialists in Bulgaria through continuing professional training. The steps for implementing the model are proposed and the expected benefits of its application are outlined. The development uses various theoretical and empirical methods of analysis, adequate to the object and subject of the study, all of which are used correctly and competently. The study is based on a solid empirical database of data from national studies conducted by specialized institutions. As a researcher who works mainly in the field of economics, administration, and management, I am strongly impressed by the fact that the author pays attention to one of the key problems in management - the metrics of the results of the activities of a given system and the related concepts, such as effectiveness and efficiency, especially since they are considered in their social context. The precise solution to the issue of metrics is an extremely challenging task from a research point of view and a basic condition for the validity of the conclusions regarding the relevance of policies and instruments for social development. Perhaps the most important message that V. Terziev sends to the readers is related to improving the sustainability of social policy. This is the leitmotif of the entire work, which is already present in the second chapter - in the analysis and assessment of the prospects for the development of the social economy and social enterprises, but is further developed in the following parts, where the problem of sustainability is also treated as part of the long-term and medium-term strategic impact of social interventions. Without a doubt, the author demonstrates his high erudition both in research and in practice, showing a thorough knowledge of the logic of the processes, of the applicable tools for proving the defined research theses, and of the limitations that shape the framework of the study. It reveals the various aspects of the object of study – social policies and instruments as a basis for development and capacity building for effective social assistance, showing their forms of manifestation, connectivity with other systems, possible transformations, and potential consequences of this. The logical justification of this author's choice is an excellent prerequisite for the creation of a research product with high utility for both the theory and practice of social policy and social assistance. Among the most serious merits of the work is that the author has an established vision for the development of the Bulgarian social model and for the challenges facing its successful implementation in order to bring it into line with the European legal framework and the specifics of the country. I find that the significance of this monographic work goes beyond the framework of what is generally accepted in the field of scientific research and presents the author not only as a serious theorist and practitioner but also as a professional with a responsible attitude to the management of the social system, who continues to be dedicated to the cause of "social development".

Professor Olga Andreeva from Rostov State University of Economics, Russian Federation shares another fundamental work in which Prof. Venelin Terziev is the main co-author "Challenges to active social policies in Bulgaria" (Terziev & Georgiev, 2023a): It should be noted that Prof. Venelin Terziev has a great scientific background on the issues, which allows him to concentrate and summarize the latest results of scientific research.

We believe that the presented monograph is worthy of the attention of the scientific community in terms of the development of theoretical positions on the researched topic, as well as the managerial powers authorized to make decisions in the affected areas. The study will also be useful for a wide range of people interested in the problems of social development in the modern state. He has quite good experience in the research and study of social policies and programs. His main publishing and research work is related to this.

Prof. Venelin Terziev's latest research is related to social transformations, which are of particular interest in dynamically changing social systems. The approach to studying the role of socially dominant leaders in the creation of new social systems, as well as the changes occurring in social systems, is interesting.

Professor Venelin Terziev shares: Personal and collective living in the next political system has exhausted its significance both for those who consume it and for those who observe it from the outside. The inability to self-preserve and react to the changing world is an unambiguous answer that it is seeking its new and completely different transformation. These periods of transformation are usually accompanied by severe and painful transitional states, which are accompanied by many diverse conflicts. No matter how simplistic all this sounds, there is a certain and strong logical, and not only, basis in it - we should not underestimate our historical memory in this direction, which would prove these statements of ours with a high degree of relativity.

The question would be quite immediate - how and what is happening to social reality? The next one is not at all useless - and what is happening to us ourselves? And if the answer to the second question is relatively easier, then to the first it is far more complex, both in essence and in process. We will eventually have to go through periods of active transformations of our entire social system, which will also include a change in political models of existence. If by social system we understand the entire set of relations, it would be practically more justified and more realistic.

The failures and rises of the existing political realities are many and have their essential differences. Comparing and explaining them is important, insofar as this can bring certain benefits in our movement forward, as well as an explanation of the new processes taking place. These processes will carry elements that we know well and will even read and explain well, but also those that will surprise us and will be new with their high sensitivity.

The defective political reality will try to preserve some of its elements, which it will successfully carry over into future periods. This is of course quite uncertain, even unlikely, because these elements existed in a relationship with all the others and even if some of them survive in one form or another, they will have a different relationship with others that are created now.

If we are in a position where the defects in these political realities have already gone through the possibility of being repaired or tamed in that sense of accumulated dissatisfaction in people, then their destruction will occur avalanche-like quickly. The consequences of the defective political reality will be felt with different strengths and to different degrees. This is quite justified because they will be at different distances from the source of these processes. These influences will have a set of fluctuations that will be misunderstood by those participating in them because they are new and unpredictable in nature and consequences.

These processes are highly complex and are almost unpredictable as a final result. Even if we have information and sufficient data about their course, the influence of certain elements cannot be accurately and accurately defined and measured, which will give rise to frequent and unpredictable changes.

The fact that the social system is changing under the pressure of the multitude of social defects is almost visible to everyone and is felt to a certain and varying degree. It is much more interesting how we will manage to get through this long and quite unpredictably difficult period, which we can unambiguously define as a process. We will hardly be able to have such preparedness that would put us in a sufficiently favorable position so that everything happens in a certain acceptability for all participants. Anxiety grows with the constant divergent nature of the signals and with the sequence of emerging social defects in the system.

We know that a system - whatever it may be - must have a certain efficiency, which is also associated with a certain financial significance. Whether those who are trying to be the leading elements in the creation of the new social system have the knowledge and the desire to accept the dependencies that have existed so far is difficult to predict. It is obvious that this system of social efficiency also creates problems in its existence. The problems that can be defined are behavioral. As unacceptable as all this may sound, too often the behavioral patterns of a certain individual have changed a certain social system to such an extent that it has been preserved for a long enough time, without being interested in any effective relationships. It is possible that certain behavioral elements will again significantly influence the already begun process and bring it to a certain stage in which the new realities will have a different meaning.(Terziev, Lyubcheva & Solovev, 2020a; Terziev, 2020b; 2020c).

3. Conclusion

The study of social processes is particularly important at the current stage of social development. The works of Prof. Venelin Terziev published in various scientific and other publications in different languages are particularly significant in this direction. Their knowledge and study are important both for the scientific community and from the point of view of managing social systems (Terziev, 2021a; 2023b; Terziev & Kanev, 2020d; Terziev & Solovev, 2023c).

References

Terziev, V. (2019a). Policies and tools for social development. 2nd ed./ Venelin Terziev, Profi print, Ruse, 2019, 588p., ISBN:978-619-7557-00-8.

Terziev, V., & Georgiev, M. (2023a). Challenges to active social policies in Bulgaria. Gabriell-e-lit, Sofia, Bulgaria, 2023, 357p. ISBN: 978-619-7705-20-1.

Terziev, V., Lyubcheva, M., & Solovev, D. (2020a). The interaction: business-education- investment for development. Proceedings of INTCESS 2020- 7th International Conference on Education and Social Sciences 20-22 January, 2020 - DUBAI (UAE), International Organization Center of Academic Research, Istanbul, Turkey, 2020, pp. 865-869, ISBN:978-605-82433-8-5.

Terziev, V. (2020b). The Bulgarian labor market in a period of extraordinary crisis from the COVID-19 pandemic. 18th RSEP International Economics, Finance & Business Conference – Virtual/Online 26-27 August 2020, Kadir Has University, Istanbul, Turkey, pp.111-115, ISBN:978-605-06961-5-8/September 2020.

Terziev, V. (2020c). Provision of Integrated Employment and Social Assistance Services in Bulgaria. In: Solovev, D. (eds) Smart Technologies and Innovations in Design for Control of Technological Processes and

Objects: Economy and Production. FarEastCon 2018. Smart Innovation, Systems and Technologies, vol 138. Springer, Cham, pp. 24-39, (Print) ISBN978-3-030-15576-6, (Online) ISBN978-3-030-15577-3, https://doi.org/10.1007/978-3-030-15577-3_3.

Terziev, V. (2021a). Management Control as an Effective Instrument in Implementation of the Social Program. In: Bilgin, M.H., Danis, H., Demir, E. (eds) Eurasian Business and Economics Perspectives. Eurasian Studies in Business and Economics, vol 17. Springer, Cham. https://doi.org/10.1007/978-3-030-65147-3_6.

Terziev, V. (2023b). Innovation development of industrial business organizations. In M. Okur Dinçsoy & H. Can (Eds.), Optimizing Energy Efficiency During a Global Energy Crisis (pp. 282-306). IGI Global. https://doi.org/10.4018/979-8-3693-0400-6.ch016.

Terziev, V., & Kanev, D. (2020d). Modern Developments in Behavioral Economics. In: Solovev, D. (eds) Smart Technologies and Innovations in Design for Control of Technological Processes and Objects: Economy and Production. FarEastCon 2018. Smart Innovation, Systems and Technologies, vol 138. Springer, Cham, pp. 10-23, Print ISBN 978-3-030-15576-6, Online ISBN978-3-030-15577-3. https://doi.org/10.1007/978-3-030-15577-3_2.

Terziev, V., & Solovev, D.B. (2023c). Development of the education system in Bulgaria in a period of economic transformations, AIP Conf. Proc. 2910, 020064 (2023), (Online ISSN 1551-7616, Print ISSN 0094-243X), https://doi.org/10.1063/5.0167861.

Sustainable Education and Education for Sustainable Development

Venelin Terziev, Marusya Lyubcheva, Olga Andreeva, Simeon Simeonov

1. Introduction

The world is experiencing serious transformations in almost all spheres – political, economic, social, and ecological. The challenges and transitions we face are unknown and have no analogue in our development so far. The combination of economic and social inequalities in the use of artificial intelligence, through which people discover a new civilization model. All this creates exceptional difficulties in ensuring uniform and standard-compliant transitions that can benefit everyone. Paradoxes arise that open the scissors of differences too much for the future transition to be considered possible at a relatively uniform pace. The concept of sustainable development seeks integration between the three main pillars of global development – economic, social, and ecological. None of the systems defining these three main pillars can ensure sustainability, but their formal integration will also not be successful enough. A moderating environment is needed to ensure their interaction. An environment that creates comprehensibility both within the systems themselves and in their interaction with other systems is needed. The education system is responsible for this interaction. Only education can provide knowledge and skills, as well as form competencies that are necessary for the management of sustainable development and the exploitation of global resources. At the beginning of the emergence of the concept of sustainable development, it was believed that it only applies to environmental protection, gradually it became clear how one-sided this perception is and today no one talks just about the environment. Today, relationships are sought in the general transformational interpenetrating transitions that encompass economic and social aspects in the context of the need for them to ensure environmental protection. The concept of sustainable education is being used, which seeks to prepare people to understand and cope with the complex challenges of the modern world, including to prepare them with the necessary consistency and sustainability of knowledge, skills, and competencies to participate in the process of sustainable development (Nedkova & Atanasova, 2018; Atanasova et al., 2023a; Terziev et al., 2020).

2. Sustainable education or education for sustainable development

2.1. Sustainable education

After the adoption of Agenda 21 and the United Nations Declaration on Sustainable Development, the idea has been implemented in various fields, including the field of education. These documents primarily talk about sustainable education. A concept of sustainable education is being built, which attempts to unite education and the principles of sustainable development, while simultaneously preserving the status of education and its importance for global development. The main focus of the concept is the sustainability and stability of the education system itself as a carrier of specific knowledge and skills, of course in the context of preparing people to deal with the complex challenges of the modern world. The following key aspects are emphasized:

- Integrated approach - sustainable education includes different fields of knowledge, such as ecology, economics, and social sciences, to ensure a comprehensive understanding of the problems;
- Critical thinking - stimulates the development of critical thinking and analysis of information so that learners can make informed decisions.
- Skills Development - providing the skills and knowledge needed to address global challenges;
- Creating informed citizens - applying education to create active and informed citizens who can make informed decisions.

Sustainable development of education is a continuous process of training and building skills, forming life positions and values. At its core lies the complex approach characterizing readiness for action - realization in a life with rapidly changing characteristics, including planning the development and consequences of the steps (actions) taken.

Sustainable education is key to building a better future for each individual and predetermines his participation in a specific direction, regardless of the general and integrated preparation that he receives. The positives for the individual from this participation also become positives for society.

In practice, however, sustainable education is turned inward, and the education system functions for itself. It is necessary to make teaching, the formation of knowledge and skills sustainable, stable, and independent of external factors, to develop and adapt to the conditions, standards, methodology, and methods by which the educational process develops. In this regard, it is necessary to ensure implementation in accordance with the acquired knowledge and skills. The results of the changes in the education systems in the context of the concept of sustainable development remained closed in the system itself. The labour market continued to produce personnel with specific knowledge and skills, without the comprehensiveness that "Agenda 21" provides, i.e. in-depth knowledge in certain scientific fields does not contribute to the inclusion of education as a system moderating the overall process of sustainable development. It is necessary to derive a new model that would encompass not only school education, and higher education, but also training and education in society as a whole, which would put the understanding of sustainable development on a new basis. Sustainable development should be understood as a philosophy and a process of building a sustainable future for all future generations.

2.2. Education for Sustainable Development

Education for sustainable development is a process that corresponds to the transformations of social, ecological, and economic systems provoked by the challenges of the 21st century, such as high technology, climate change, economic inequalities, and social justice. Education for sustainable development is fundamental to understanding the processes of sustainable development and shapes the approaches through which individuals can become part of sustainable development. This is not only for them to find their own fulfillment, but to achieve a result that is commensurate with the trinity of the main pillars of sustainable development and its impact on society.

Sometimes the concepts of sustainable education and education for sustainable development are perceived as analogies, but these are two different concepts (Table 1).

Table 1: Elements of the concepts of sustainable education and education for sustainable development

	Sustainable education	Education for sustainable development
Goals	Prepares learners for implementation in development processes with acquired knowledge and skills	Prepares learners to understand and apply concepts related to sustainable development in various contexts.
Principles	Participation in social development; Integration of knowledge and skills; Sustainability of knowledge and skills over time; Usability and adaptability of skills; Sustainability of methodology and teaching methods; Long-term prosperity; Well-being of future generations.	Awareness of sustainable development; Integration of education in sustainable development; Toolkit for decision-making in favor of sustainable development; Integrated quality of education; Predictability of interactions between elements of sustainable development; Innovation and adequacy with the dynamics of sustainable development.
Focus	On the educational system; On the methodology for forming the knowledge and skills that determine implementation; On the integration of resources.	On the interaction of the education system with sustainable development systems; On education as a tool for sustainable development; On the integrity and synergy of systems.

Source: Authors' elaboration

We are talking about education that is comprehensively related to "Agenda 21" and ensures intelligent connectivity between all elements of sustainable development. In the global plan for sustainable development of the United Nations, education is listed as priority No. 4. This is a more specific concept that emphasizes education as a tool for achieving sustainable development. It focuses on training individuals to address the challenges of sustainable development, such as climate change, social justice, and economic sustainability. Education for sustainable development aims to develop skills and knowledge that allow learners to make informed decisions and act in favor of a sustainable future. This applies not only to their own but also to the future of society.

Sustainable education is a purely educational concept, linearly aimed at training in a certain direction and implementation in a field close to it, while education for sustainable development can be defined as three-dimensional, aimed at preparing individuals for an active role in sustainable development and participation in the transformational interaction of systems. This is a process model that goes beyond purely educational goals, methodologies, and approaches. Education for sustainable development is a comprehensive approach that aims to prepare the younger generation, not only, for the challenges of the modern world, related to environmental protection, social justice, and economic sustainability - elements that determine the existence of social systems as a whole. It is based on the principles of sustainable development and integrates social, economic, and ecological aspects in the educational and extracurricular process. Interactivity, transdisciplinarity, and innovation are key concepts of this education, which some call "education of the future". Those trained in Education for Sustainable Development must play in the field of multifunctionality and be good enough in economics, social problems, and environmental protection. They must be aware of the resources and capabilities of each of these systems individually or in combination, to assess and analyze their mutual influence in order to prevent possible risks that could arise when changing the parameters of any of them. The imposition of the paradigm for Education for Sustainable Development requires a certain amount of time - to understand the processes, analyze the changes, and study the attitudes, and skills for formulating intelligent approaches connecting synergizing systems. In addition, the penetration of digitalization into a significant part of the interactions of these systems requires the inclusion of new elements in educational technologies, not only with a specific perspective for a separate discipline but its integration with the others and with the rest of the world. Education for sustainable development works on the principle that there is no such thing as just mathematics or physics, but rather interrelationships between all sciences that require complexity and common solutions, in which 2+2 does not always equal 4. When technologies, and today also artificial intelligence, determine the direction, education in schools and universities goes beyond the capabilities of a single discipline to provide solutions that new systems need. The basis of Education for sustainable development is divided into two contours: the first contour includes the complex: knowledge-research-innovation; the second contour includes - management, vision, and strategies (these elements are already included in the field of secondary education). The visibly complicated paradigms, provoked by the dynamics of development and the generated problematic challenges, require a change in both thinking and actions. The previous understanding that education accumulates knowledge and skills, forms competencies, and business creates realization, adaptation, and career, gives way to the synergy between the two systems, in which the elements of strategizing, visiona, and career become the main background. The philosophy of sustainable development does not differentiate information and scientific accumulation in a temporal manner and educational degrees but combines and systematizes them as thematic and effective (Table 2).

Table 2: Requirements for Education for Sustainable Development

WHAT	HOW	WHEN	WHERE
So that you know	Form a model of thinking and attitude towards the world	Secondary education Higher education	Education
	Make a connection between your education and life in general	Secondary Education Higher Education Lifelong Learning	Education Lifelong learning
	Adapt to the cyclical transformations in the labour market and education	Secondary Education Higher Education Lifelong Learning	Education Business
So that you can	With professional skills	Secondary education Higher education	Education Business
	With transferable skills	Secondary education Higher education	Education Business

Source: Authors' elaboration

This philosophy includes education and more. The complex of readiness to participate in sustainable development includes research and innovation, competence and entrepreneurship, information security, communication, and digital intelligence. For this preparation, the curriculum system in secondary and higher education is the least suitable.

2.3. Mainstreaming sustainability into all aspects of education and training

Preparing for the future requires rethinking education, modernizing learning, and changing models to create a culture of sustainability that will shape the opportunities for each individual to be a driving force. Making learning for the ecological transition and sustainable development a priority in education and training policies and programmes is the most important part of this change.

How can this all happen?

- By defining the problems orienting learning toward sustainable development and transforming economic, social, and ecological systems;
- By taking action in response to the "Sustainable Development Agenda" in education at all levels of education;
- By developing among learners and teachers the knowledge, skills, and attitudes needed for a greener and more sustainable economy and society at all levels of education;
- By supporting education and training institutions to integrate sustainability into teaching and learning and all aspects of their work;
- By creating a shared understanding of the profound and transformative changes needed in education and training for sustainability and the ecological transition.

Changing the model is a slow process, but the steps it goes through are important in order to fill the entire educational space with the spirit of Education for Sustainable Development - from funding, through equipment and the freedom of learners to be included in the process, to teacher support and a symbiosis between formal and informal learning.

The European Framework of Competences, corresponding to Education for Sustainable Development, includes several main packages:

- Embodying the values of sustainability: valuing sustainability, supporting justice, and promoting nature;
- Embracing the complexity of sustainability: systems thinking, critical thinking, and problem formulation;
- Visualizing a sustainable future: future literacy, adaptability, and inquiry-based thinking;
- Actions for sustainability: political activism, collective activities, and individual initiative.

The dynamism in the transformations of systems puts the updating of the elements of "Agenda 21" on the agenda. A SkillsOVATE study shows that new elements need to be included in the main package of actions of Agenda 21 to take into account these dynamics:

- The digital and green transitions are reshaping European labour markets (mainstreaming sustainability into the green transformation);
- New management schemes are being introduced, focusing on green and digital skills, such as renewable energy and related professions, as well as ecology and green diffusion in professions;
- Rapid digitalisation affects many roles not related to the IT sector, while the willingness to learn is emerging as a prominent skill that is needed.

2.4. Relevance of education for sustainable development to sustainable development

Education for sustainable development should include in its scope of education environmental, social, and economic aspects, considered in interrelation and unity.

- Environmental aspects: understanding ecosystems and their importance; sustainable management of natural resources; problems related to climate change and environmental protection;
- Social aspects: development of social responsibility and activism; support for human rights and equality, understanding of cultural diversity and intercultural communication;
- Economic aspects: foundations of sustainable economic development; understanding of the concept of circular economy; support for innovation and sustainable business practices;
- Interactive and practice-oriented approaches: project-based learning that encourages critical thinking; inclusion of local communities and real cases in the learning process;
- Personal development: promotion of personal commitment and activism in sustainable development; development of problem-solving and decision-making skills.

Education for sustainable development not only informs students about the importance of sustainability but also prepares them to be active participants in its creation, respectively, creating conditions for a better future.

Learning methodologies are essential in the conditions of intercultural and digital interaction. The classroom form of teaching with maximum information saturation should be replaced by approaches that stimulate critical and analytical thinking. What is needed is not the reproduction of certain information, but a creative approach with the generation of ideas, consistent with the level of preparation of the learners. Digital technologies allow the use of own and shared global platforms and applications and tools, such as WWF's EduCare and NASA's Climate Kids, which aim to teach concepts of sustainability and sustainable development. The report of the UNESCO team "Teaching for the Planet" emphasizes that by 2040, more educational programs around the world will adopt a holistic approach focused on emotional, social, and physical well-being, integrating them with traditional academic training to promote a sustainable lifestyle.

The most important skills that are needed for the next generations to be real participants in the processes of sustainable development are transferable and meta-skills. Understanding which skills employers value is key to sustainable development and to overcoming their shortage. The ability to learn is emerging as the most sought-after meta-skill. Employers are increasingly looking for candidates who demonstrate a strong desire to learn and have a clear understanding of how to develop new skills. Other highly sought-after skills include data analysis, digital collaboration, and event and program planning. Two-thirds of non-ICT jobs now require digital skills. Digital skills are becoming almost universal. Data analysis, graphic design, and animation development are in increasing demand, and the importance of green skills such as corporate responsibility, environmental engineering, and green computing is undeniable. The dynamics of transformations of different systems and the demand for new skills pose a serious question about the qualifications of teachers and lecturers, who are responsible for shaping the knowledge, skills, and competencies of young people. Qualification, requalification, as well as changing the training model of lecturers and teachers in universities is a serious challenge for Education for Sustainable Development.

2.5. Learning Models in Education for Sustainable Development

A gradual exit from the comfort zone of today's educational models is necessary. One-way oriented, reproducing information, accumulating purely academic knowledge with little or no practical focus, forming competencies in the classroom instead of in the field. The approaches of Education for Sustainable Development are too different to motivate, guide, challenge, and provoke the mind and thought, on which both the idea and its implementation depend.

The competency model focuses on the overall development of students. It forms a set of competencies that are organized in a common matrix corresponding to the chosen educational model and the types of educational institutions. This model describes all the necessary skills and knowledge to achieve success in a given profession or field.

The Entrepreneurial Model: Focuses on the development of entrepreneurial skills and knowledge in students. It is based on practical training, project work, group work, and active communication. Its goal is to prepare students for a successful career in the dynamic environment of modern business. It forms qualities and skills that fully comply with the requirements of Education for Sustainable Development.

Project-based learning: An innovative pedagogical approach that encourages students to acquire knowledge and skills through participation in projects. It focuses on real-life scenarios, role-playing games, research lessons, robot behavior projects, and assessment. Replacing role-playing games with gamification models would certainly be a suitable option. It engages students through real-life projects and encourages critical thinking and practical skills. It is characterized as an environment that activates learning, as it is focused on learning, not teaching. It relies on the creative energy and provokes the initiative of each student.

2.6. The Reality of Education for Sustainable Development

The educational model applied in Bulgaria is too far from the needs of education for sustainable development. Even though that environmental protection is studied both as an independent subject and in combination with some other disciplines, the philosophy of education for sustainable development is absent from the Bulgarian education system. The information saturation of curricula and textbooks, which provide separated academic knowledge, does not allow students to develop their creative potential, become aware of common problems, connect and evaluate them comprehensively, and form in themselves motives, behavior, and understanding in their entirety. And even with the existing differentiation in education, important skills for the realization of young people are not formed. A study by the Institute for Market Economics (https://ime.bg/) shows that almost no personnel are being prepared for the most sought-after professions in Bulgaria, which are required even without taking into account the concept of Education for Sustainable Development. A survey among secondary school students and university students shows dissatisfaction with the skills that students manage to develop in school.

When asked what the most important skills they need to succeed in the job market are, young people answered: self-confidence and motivation - 20%; financial knowledge - 5%; public speaking - 2%;

flexibility in work - 4%; productivity - 1%; teamwork - 68%; environmental knowledge - 8%; digital technologies - 10%; preparation for university studies and meetings with representatives from different industries - 1%; social realization - 5%; skill - 3%; patience - 1%; - empathy 5%; being able to deal with documents, accounts, etc. - 5%; critical thinking - 10%; sympathy -1%; simple human relationships - 1%; communication - 89%; rhetoric and language - 1%; civic education -1%; leadership - 10%; problem-solving - 4%; emotional intelligence - 1%.

Young people themselves conclude their unpreparedness for life and realization in the labour market.

At the same time, in the applied educational model, there is a great weight of information and data, which are too variable to be reproduced by students, instead of them being taught to analyze and evaluate. Specialties are developed that are not in demand in the labour market or form an insignificant share of it. There is no talk of sustainable development in secondary, even higher education, again knowledge is differentiated by topics, without being connected and even less harmonized and seeking synergy in their interaction. This is the reason for a not-at-all-complicated question for the time in which we live: "What are the main pillars of sustainable development?".

The situation can be improved by using global networks and support provided at the European level through the NextGenerationEU Plan. A much more significant change would occur if education were seen as a strategic resource (not as a service, as many experts believe) and by implementing the following easy-to-implement steps:

- Replace the disciplinary approach with an interdisciplinary one;
- Implement the peer assessment model;
- Reject formal changes at the expense of substantive ones.

In this regard, the names of schools are important, but they do not make a difference (for example: innovative schools). STEM centers are important, but they will not replace human intelligence in school, especially if they are used formally. The overwhelming information saturation will not replace thinking, critical thinking, and creative energy; Examples of good entrepreneurs will not replace the creative potential of young people. Today it is important to give an impulse to education to stay ahead of industry because it is extremely difficult to develop Industry 4.0 with education 2.0, 3.0... The formal raising of the level of education to Education 5.0 is important only as a motivating effect. We must give education those characteristics that, applied in school and outside it, give the young generations security, resilience, and self-confidence that they know the world and can manage processes (Vakleva & Georgieva, 2022a; Grinfild, 2023b; Ivanov, 2010; Bazan, 2022b).

3. Conclusion

Education for Sustainable Development empowers people to cope with change, but it should also empower them to shape change. Innovations in Education for Sustainable Development are closely related to new skills, curricula, teaching methods, and forecasting tools, which should become the main measure of quality education. Implementing the Education for Sustainable Development model is creating a new culture of learning not only in school and university but throughout life. Only then can it be said that human resources have realized their role as a leading force in the processes of sustainable development. There must be a connection between education and reality. The reality is that the world economy is technological, and this should determine the model of the education system and learning models (Terziev & Lyubcheva, 2022c).

References

Nedkova, S., & Atanasova, P. (2018). Study of the effect of implementing an interactive form of education in the discipline "Technical safety and disaster protection", Asen Zlatarov University, Burgas, Bulgaria, Volume XLVII, book 1, 131-134.

Atanasova, P., Nedkova, S., Krasteva, T. (2023a). Development and application of visualization situation models as part of a methodological toolkit for disaster situations and protection, Assen Zlatarov University, Burgas, Bulgaria, Vol. LII, 24-26, ISSN2603-3968.

Terziev, V., Lyubcheva, M., & Solovev, D. (2020). The interaction: business-education-investment for development. Proceedings of INTCESS 2020- 7th International Conference on Education and Social Sciences 20-22 January, 2020 - DUBAI (UAE), International Organization Center of Academic Research, Istanbul, Turkey, 2020, 865-869, ISBN: 978-605-82433-8-5.

Vakleva, Z., & Georgieva, T. (2022a). Educatıon for sustaınable development –practıcal-apply aspects. Азбуки, https://doi.org/10.53656/str2022-3-6-sus.

Grinfild, E. (2023b). The role of education in sustainable development. https://sigmaearth.com/ru/role-of-education-in-sustainable-development/. Retrieved November 27, 2024.

Ivanov, I. (2010). Intercultural education for sustainable development, Innovations in education, 42-57.

Bazan, M. (2022b). Education for sustainable development through active learning methods in primary grades. Author's abstract of a dissertation for the award of the educational and scientific degree "Doctor", 2022.

Terziev, V., & Lyubcheva, M. (2022c). Shared knowledge and changes in the higher education system in Bulgaria. 79th International Scientific Conference on Economic and Social Development – Rabat, 25-26 March, 2022, Economic and Social Development, Cakovec, Croatia, 2022, 228-237, ISSN 1849-7535.

Essential Problems in Implementing Demographic Policies in Bulgaria

Venelin Terziev, Marin Georgiev, Simeon Simeonov

1. Introduction

Social processes in recent years have confronted societies with various challenges, mainly related to the ongoing negative demographic processes. These characteristics are significant for almost all European countries, with indicators deteriorating dramatically in recent years. In countries undergoing active political and economic transformations, these processes have particularly negative fluctuations. The implemented policies fail to improve the situation in this direction and lead to a decrease in the active economic population and, therefore, to serious problems in societies and their development.

The Ministry of Labor and Social Policy in Bulgaria defines the main demographic challenges facing Bulgarian society according to the latest 2021 population census, which are expressed in negative natural growth, deepening territorial disparities in the number of the population, deepening trends in the deterioration of the age structure of the population, decreasing birth rate and aging of the population (Ministry of Labor and Social Policy, 2024a).

Trends for change in the structure and balance of the population in Bulgaria are recorded by the data for the 2021 population census, carried out by the National Statistical Institute of Bulgaria. According to its data, as of September 7, 2021, the population in our country was 6,519,789 people. Over the 10 years between the last two censuses, it decreased by 844,781 people, or by 11.5%. The factors that influence the country's population are natural movement (births and deaths) and external migration. The population decrease as a result of the negative natural increase is - 501 thousand, or 59.3% of the total decrease. The natural increase for all years of the period between the censuses in 2011 and 2021 is negative, with the largest decrease in the population in 2021 (-90,317 people). The remaining 40.7% of the decrease is due to external migration, or this is the number of people who left the country during the period 2011 - 2021 (344 thousand people).

The most significant demographic trend in the development of the population is the aging process. According to NSI data, the negative trends in the change in the age structure of the population continue to deepen. There is an ongoing process of demographic aging, which is expressed in an increase in the absolute number and relative share of the population aged 65 and over. As of September 7, 2021, the population aged 65 and over was 1,532,667, or 23.5% of the country's population. Compared to the previous census in 2011, the population in this age group increased by 171,270, or 12.6%. In 2021, the percentage share of the population over 65 years of age was 23.5% of the total population, while in 2011 it was 18.5%.

The aging of the population over the years leads to an increase in its average age, from 40.4 years in 2001 to 45.2 years at the end of 2022. The average age of the population in Bulgaria is among the highest not only in the European Union but also in the world (Ministry of Labor and Social Policy, 2024a).

The trend in the reproduction of the working-age population is alarming. The reproduction of the working-age population is best characterized by the demographic replacement rate, which shows the ratio between the number of people entering working age (15 - 19 years) and the number of people leaving working age (60 - 64 years). According to data from the 2021 Census, this ratio is 61. For comparison, in 2011, every 100 people leaving the working age were replaced by 70 young people, and in 2001 by 124. The Ministry of Labor and Social Policy leads, coordinates, and controls the implementation of state policy in the field of demographic development, as well as the activity of analyzing, assessing, and forecasting demographic processes in cooperation with other state bodies, social partners, and non-governmental organizations. The Ministry of Labor and Social Policy carries out activities for the organization of coordination and monitoring of demographic policy, which is expressed in maintaining an institutional framework and a national mechanism for policy implementation. Here, the coordination and management of the Interdepartmental Working Group on Demographic Issues is carried out, in which representatives of key state departments, the National Statistical Institute, the National Social Security Institute, the Bulgarian Red Cross, the National Association of Municipalities in the Republic of Bulgaria, and non-governmental organizations participate. Annual monitoring reports are prepared, which integrate information from national statistics, administrative information, and data from sociological surveys. The national mechanism for coordination and monitoring of the implementation of horizontal, inter-institutional, and inter-sectoral demographic policy was improved by establishing a National Council on Demographic Policy under the Council of Ministers.

The priority areas and tasks in the field of demographic policy are formulated in the Updated National Strategy for Demographic Development of the Population in the Republic of Bulgaria (2012 - 2030) and are aimed at achieving the following strategic goal - slowing down the rate of population decline with a tendency to stabilize it in the long term and ensuring high quality of human capital, including people with their health status, education, qualifications, abilities, and skills. An integrated approach is applied to maximize coverage of demographic problems. The main goal of work in the field of demographic policy is to limit the negative impacts of demographic imbalances on public finances and social systems.

Special emphasis on meeting the demographic challenges of population aging is also placed through the National Strategy for Active Living of Older People in Bulgaria (2019-2030). The long-term goal of the Strategy is related to creating conditions for an active and dignified life for older people by ensuring equal opportunities for their full participation in the economic and social life. The Strategy defines four main priorities - Promoting the active life of older people in the field of employment; Promoting the active life of older people in the field of participation in society; Promoting the active life of older people in the field of independent living; Creating capacity and a favorable environment for the active life of older people at the national and regional levels. Two-year implementation plans for the Active Ageing Strategy are being implemented, which provide the operational framework for undertaking and reporting on comprehensive actions and measures in response to the challenges posed by the ageing population.

According to the European Commission's main monitoring mechanism for examining the potential for promoting active ageing, namely the Active Ageing Index, Bulgaria has significant untapped potential for real improvements in the participation of older people in employment, independent living, and social participation in general. More significant efforts are needed at national, regional, and local levels to fully mobilise the valuable potential of older people. According to the EC Active Ageing Index, generating greater capacity and creating a favourable environment for active ageing is a prerequisite for development, especially in the countries of Central and Eastern Europe, including Bulgaria.

2. Main institutions for the implementation of demographic policies

The institutions are as follows (Council of Ministers, 2024b):

2.1. The Council of Ministers of the Republic of Bulgaria – reviews, approves, and adopts regulatory acts relating to the balanced demographic development of the population and the development of the quality of human capital.

2.2. The Ministry of Finance (MoF) has a leading role in the formation of the country's budgetary policy and in maintaining the stability of public finances. The MoF coordinates the programming, management, and monitoring of the implementation of the state budget and the financial assistance provided to the Republic of Bulgaria under the financial instruments of the European Union, taking into account their effect and impact on the balanced demographic development of the population and the development of the quality of human capital.

2.3. The Ministry of Labor and Social Policy is responsible for the development, implementation, monitoring, and reporting of progress in the field of demographic policy. The Ministry manages, organizes, coordinates, monitors, and reports on the implementation of the state demographic policy, given that the aging of the population has the strongest impact and impact on the state and profile of the labor market, the stability of the pension system, the system of social assistance and care, the policy for families and children, and equal opportunities for all. In partnership and jointly with other state bodies, the Ministry of Labor and Social Policy develops regulators and mechanisms for improving the country's demographic indicators and human capital development indicators. The Ministry of Labor and Social Policy organizes, coordinates, and participates in the development of annual National Plans for Demographic Development and monitors their implementation; participates in the development of financial estimates and forecasts for an active policy in the field of demographic development; maintains a System of indicators and metrics for monitoring the implementation of the National Strategy for Demographic Development; coordinates the work of the Interdepartmental Working Group for Demographic Development; coordinates the country's participation in European demographic initiatives; prepares an annual report to the Council of Ministers on the implementation of the demographic strategy; is responsible for the ongoing coverage of new guidelines for the development of demographic policy, proposed by European Union institutions and by authoritative international centers and institutes with competences in the field of demographic development of the population.

2.4. The Ministry of Health has a leading role in implementing programs and measures for health promotion, prevention of socially significant diseases leading to high mortality - general, child, maternal, and premature and permanent disability of people; improving the health of women of childbearing age; creating conditions for improving the health status of the population and prolonging the life of women and men in good health, including by ensuring food safety; developing programs to reduce child and maternal mortality; preventing the spread of HIV/AIDS and diseases of the reproductive system among adolescents and young people; developing measures aimed at restoring and strengthening the school health care system; investing in the development of medical personnel and introducing high technologies in health care. By fulfilling these functions, the Ministry contributes to improving the demographic balance of the population; reducing the negative natural increase, and developing the quality of human capital.

2.5. The Ministry of Education and Science and the Ministry of Youth and Sports have a leading role in implementing those elements of the demographic development strategy that are related to education and training, including: limiting the dropout of children and adolescents from the education system; adult literacy and lifelong learning; acquiring necessary and higher qualifications and additional skills; determining the future needs for a workforce with the necessary qualifications and directing the capabilities of the education system towards the training of specialists, following the needs of the economy and business; introducing a master's degree in demography or other appropriate specialized forms of training in demography in higher education, to meet the needs of the administration for the implementation of the demographic policy. By performing these functions, they contribute to the development of the quality of human capital; increasing the mobility and competitiveness of the workforce on the labor market; reducing the negative social effects of disruptions in the reproduction of the workforce caused by the aging of the population and the long-term decline in the birth rate.

2.6. The Ministry of Culture has a leading role in creating conditions for the intellectual and spiritual cohesion of society and for the development of an individual, family, and public culture of knowledge, determining the way of life of the population in the 21st century. The Ministry of Culture contributes to reducing regional differences in the population's access to achievements and works of art and culture, including through the support and introduction of new and innovative functions of community centers throughout the country. By performing these functions, the Ministry contributes to the development of the quality of human capital; assists in increasing the mobility and competitiveness of the workforce on the labor market; reduces the negative social effects of disruptions in the reproduction of the workforce, caused by the aging of the population and the long-term decline in the birth rate.

2.7. The Ministry of Regional Development and Public Works has a leading role in implementing activities related to overcoming regional differences and territorial imbalances, caused by unfavorable demographic trends in the development of the population and giving rise to such; implements the state housing policy taking into account the needs of the aging society; manages the management of the state building stock in settlements with a decreasing population; implements methodological guidance, coordination and control over the development, improvement, normal functioning and use of the civil registration and administrative service system. MRDPW allocates the largest investment potential in the country and is thus an important domestic investor with a flexible dislocation of the sites taking into account the needs for balanced demographic development of the population.

2.8. The Ministry of Economy and Industry, the Ministry of Energy, and the Ministry of Tourism have a leading role in improving the living standards of the population and increasing the quality of human capital by encouraging investments, especially investments in high technologies and the development of small and medium-sized businesses. They have a leading role in achieving balanced socio-economic development of the regions in the country, and thus also for the balanced demographic territorial development of the population. They contribute to increasing the competitiveness of the workforce and the country's economy by maintaining a clear connection between the needs of business and the economy with the education system to achieve better coordination between the demand and supply of labor. They contribute to the development of a knowledge economy; they create conditions for the development of social entrepreneurship, for the provision of services for the elderly, and for sectors of the economy with the potential for opening new jobs, adequate to the capabilities of the available potential workforce.

2.9. The Ministry of Environment and Water has a leading role in protecting the environment and limiting pollution of land, water, and air that is harmful to human health from various sources. By performing these functions, the Ministry contributes to improving the health status of the population, prolonging people's lives in good health, and developing the quality of human capital.

2.10. The Ministry of Agriculture and Food has a leading role related to the development of rural regions and the control of food of plant and animal origin, raw materials, animal by-products and products derived from them, and specific plant products, by monitoring compliance with food requirements, measures and conditions to ensure their hygiene and safety for human health and the environment. By performing these functions, the Ministry contributes to overcoming the differences in living conditions between the city and the countryside; to the economic and demographic renewal of rural regions; to overcoming territorial disparities and geographic demographic imbalances; to improving the health status of the population.
2.11. The Ministry of Justice has responsibilities regarding the normative regulation of relations in the Bulgarian family through the Family Code; organizes the implementation of the procedures related to Bulgarian citizenship and the adoption of Bulgarian citizens by foreigners, and performs functions under the Convention on the Protection of Children and Cooperation in the Field of Intercountry Adoption (ratified by a law adopted by the XXXIX National Assembly on January 31, 2002, State Gazette, No. 78 of 2002). By performing its functions, the Ministry contributes to creating conditions for balanced demographic development of the population, respect for human rights, and the development of the quality of human capital.
2.12. The Ministry of Foreign Affairs protects the rights and interests of Bulgarian citizens abroad; protects the rights and freedoms of persons belonging to Bulgarian communities abroad, in accordance with international legal norms in this area and with the interests of the country. By performing these functions, the Ministry of Internal Affairs contributes to the observance of human rights and the development of the quality of human capital.
2.13. The Ministry of Internal Affairs plays a key role in reducing road mortality, limiting the negative social effects of cases of human trafficking, domestic violence, prostitution, drug distribution, and reducing crime among minors and juveniles. By performing these

functions, it contributes to reducing mortality and attacks on people's lives and health, observing human rights, and developing the quality of human capital.

2.14. The Ministry of Youth and Sports plays a leading role in developing forms of mass sports and sports for all ages, intending to maintain good physical and health status of the population. By performing these functions, it also contributes to improving the quality of human capital.

2.15. The Ministry of Transport and Communications assists in overcoming regional and territorial disparities by ensuring equal access of the population to convenient transport and advanced information and communication technologies. By performing these functions, it contributes to the even territorial distribution of the population, to the normalization of internal migration flows, the improvement of the standard of living and quality of life, thereby influencing the demographic behavior of the population.

2.16. The National Health Insurance Fund has a leading role in ensuring equal access of the population to health services, thereby contributing to improving the general health and reproductive status, prolonging people's lives in good health, and increasing the quality of human capital.

2.17. The National Statistical Institute performs a leading methodological and coordination role in the collection and processing of statistical information and in the development of forecasts and comparative analyses for the demographic development of the population. Another essential function of the National Statistical Institute is the dissemination of information on demographic events and processes. National Social Security Institute - is responsible for the development of short-term, medium-term, and long-term actuarial estimates and forecasts for maintaining the financial stability of the pension system. It maintains an administrative statistical database on the state and development of social security relations in the country.

2.18. The National Association of Municipalities in Bulgaria assists in the development of regional and/or municipal demographic strategies depending on the regional specificities of the demographic development of the population and in connection with the general philosophy, strategic goal, priorities, directions, and tasks of the National Strategy for Demographic Development of the Population. The Association creates conditions for the development of public-private partnerships for the active and coordinated participation of authorities, citizens, and businesses in the implementation of demographic policy.

2.19. State Agency for Bulgarians Abroad (has a leading role in creating conditions for maintaining the integrity and involvement in social processes in the country of Bulgarian communities living outside Bulgaria.

2.20. General Labor Inspectorate exercises specialized control over compliance with the Law on Healthy and Safe Working Conditions, thereby contributing to the reduction of occupational accidents leading to death or permanent damage to health and disability. In this way, the Inspectorate contributes to protecting the health of the population and creates favorable conditions for extending working life in good health.

3. Population number and structures

As of December 31, 2023, the population of Bulgaria was 6 445 481 persons, representing 1.4% of the EU population . Compared to 2022, the country's population decreases by 2 229 persons or by 0.03% (Petkova et al., 2023a).

Male population was 3 097 698 (48.1%) and female - 3 347 783 (51.9%), or 1 000 males corresponded to 1 081 females. Males prevail among the population, aged up to 55 years. The number and share of females in the total population have increased among the elderly (Petkova et al., 2023a).

By the end of 2023, the number of persons aged 65 and over was 1 530 909, or 23.8% of the country's population. Compared to 2022, the share of the population aged 65 and over increases by 0.3 percentage points (Fig. 1) (Petkova et al., 2023a).

The share of females aged 65 and over is 27.7%, compared to 19.5% of males. The difference is due to the higher mortality among the male population and consequently - lower life expectancy (Petkova et al., 2023a).

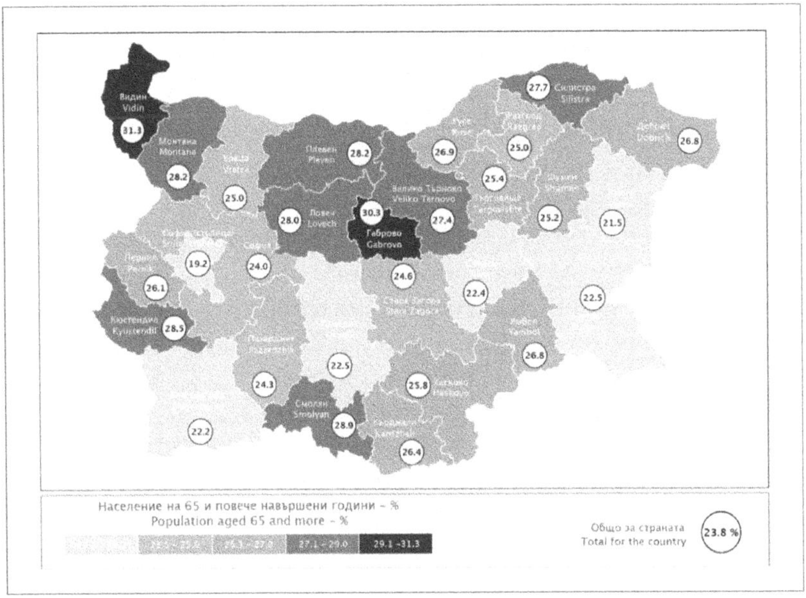

Figure 1: Share of population aged 65 and over by district as of 31.12.2023
Source: National Statistical Institute, Bulgaria

The share of persons aged 65 and over is highest in districts Vidin (31.3%), Gabrovo (30.3%) and Smolyan (28.9%). In 22 districts, the share of people aged 65 and over is higher than the country's average. The lowest is the share of the elderly population in districts Sofia (Sofia city) - 19.2%, Varna - 21.5% and Blagoevgrad - 22.2% (Petkova et al., 2023a).

The share of the population aged 65 and over for EU-27 is 21.3%. The highest is the share of the elderly population in Italy (24.0%), followed by Portugal (24.0%). In seventeen EU member states, including Bulgaria, the share of the elderly is above 20.0% (Petkova et al., 2023a).

As of 31.12.2023, children up to 15 years of age in the country are 911 025, or 14.1% of the total population number (Petkova et al., 2023a).

The share of the population under 15 years of age is highest in districts Sliven - 18.9%, Yambol - 15.2% and Burgas - 14.9% of the district population. As a total, in 17 districts the share of children up to 15 years is lower than the country's average. The lowest is the share registered in districts Smolyan - 10.6%, Vidin - 11.5% and Gabrovo - 11.7% (Petkova et al., 2023a).

The share of the youngest EU-27 population in the beginning of 2022 is 14.9%. The lowest shares are observed in Italy - 12.4%, Portugal - 12.9% and Malta - 12.7%, and the highest - in Ireland - 19.3%, Sweden - 17.4% and France - 17.3% (Petkova et al., 2023a).

As of 31.12.2023, the age dependency ratio1 in the country was 61.0%, or to each person in "dependent" ages (under 15 and over 65 years) corresponded less than two persons in 'independent' age. The ratio in urban areas is 57.6%, and in rural - 71.3%. As a total, in all districts, the age dependency ratio is over 50.0%. The lowest is the ratio in districts Sofia (Sofia city)-51.5%, and the highest is in Vidin (74.8%), Gabrovo and Yambol - 72.3% each (Petkova et al., 2023a).

The population ageing over the years lead to an increase of the population mean age. It has increased from 40.6 years in 2002 to 45.2 years at the end of 2023. The mean age of the population is 44.4 years in urban areas, compared to 47.5 years in rural areas (Petkova et al., 2023a).

The number of population and relative share of population under, at and over working age changes. The last two are influenced not only by the population ageing, but also by legislative changes1 concerning the retirement age.

In 2023, at working age were women up to completion of 62 years and men up to completion of 64 years and 6 months.

The number of the population at working age as of 31.12.2023 is 3 769 thousand persons, or 58.5% of the total population, of which males are 1 971 thousand and females - 1 798 thousand persons. By the end of 2023, the number of the population over working age was 1 698 thousand persons, or 26.3%, and under working age were 977 thousand persons, or 15.2% of the country's population (Petkova et al., 2023a).

The reproduction of the population at working age is characterized by the coefficient of demographic replacement, showing the ratio between the number of persons entering working age (15 - 19 years) and the number of persons exiting it (60 - 64 years). As of 31.12.2023, the coefficient of demographic replacement was 69 (Petkova et al., 2023a).

Most favourable was the value of the indicator in districts Sliven - 92, Sofia (Sofia city) - 87 and Varna -79. The lowest was the ratio in districts Smolyan - 44, Kardhzali - 47 and Silistra where 100 persons exiting working age are replaced by 53 persons entering it (Petkova et al., 2023a).

4. Analysis of the Updated National Strategy for Demographic Development of the Population in the Republic of Bulgaria (2012 – 2030)

The Updated National Strategy for Demographic Development of the Population in the Republic of Bulgaria (2012 – 2030) has formed 12 main directions (Council of Ministers, 2024b).

In connection with slowing down negative demographic processes and reducing the number of the population, activities have been formulated in the following directions:

- Promoting the birth rate by creating an environment favorable for the raising and upbringing of children;
- Improving the reproductive health of the population and preventing sterility;
- Improving the general demographic awareness and sexual and reproductive culture of the population;
- Improving the general health of the population and reducing total, premature, infant, and maternal mortality;
- Developing an adequate migration and immigration policy;
- Significantly reducing the number of emigrating young people of reproductive age.

In order to overcome the negative consequences of population aging and improve the qualitative characteristics of human capital, activities have been formulated in the following areas:

- Adoption of a comprehensive intersectoral approach for the active and productive life of older people in good health. Adaptation of social systems to demographic changes and population aging - labor market, pension system, social assistance and care, healthcare, education, culture, etc.;
- Development of solidarity between generations;
- Increasing the general educational, spiritual, and cultural level, qualifications, abilities, and skills of the population of all age groups.

In connection with achieving social cohesion and creating equal opportunities for a full social and productive life for all social groups, activities have been formulated in the following areas:

- Creating conditions for equal opportunities for a full social and productive life for all social groups.

In connection with limiting the disparities in the territorial distribution of the population and depopulation in some regions and villages, activities have been formulated in the following areas:

Limiting the disparities in the territorial distribution of the population and depopulation in some regions and villages.

In connection with adapting and synchronizing the regulatory framework with public needs for balanced demographic development of the population and development of the quality of human capital, activities have been formulated in the following areas:

Introducing a mandatory assessment of the impact on the demographic development of the population and the quality of human capital of each new, amended, or supplemented regulatory act of the state.

The demographic development strategy sets the following main priorities:

- Slowing down negative demographic processes and the reduction of the population;
- Overcoming the negative consequences of population aging and improving the qualitative characteristics of human capital;
- Achieving social cohesion and creating equal opportunities for a full social and productive life for all social groups;
- Limiting the disparities in the territorial distribution of the population and depopulation in some regions and villages;
- Adapting and synchronizing the regulatory framework with public needs for balanced demographic development of the population and the development of the quality of human capital.

The implementation of the first priority is carried out through the implementation of a set of measures and means to promote the birth rate, increase the average life expectancy, reduce infant and premature mortality, establish the two-child family model, create prerequisites for reversing migration processes and strengthening repatriation processes among the Bulgarian diaspora. The implementation of this priority is expressed in specific quantitative indicators, established in world practice as measures of the general demographic situation of the population in individual countries.

The implementation of the second priority includes the undertaking and implementation of measures to meet the challenges posed by the aging of the population. The measures are aimed at overcoming the negative consequences of the deepening of unfavorable age changes, such as the reduction and aging of the working-age population; increasing the burden on the social security system and the state budget. The measures contribute to increasing the requirements for the quality and expanding the scope of health and social services for the elderly. Providing greater opportunities for education and formal and informal learning as a basis for professional realization in the labor market and a means of developing human resources in the process of lifelong learning, as well as implementing a consistent policy to promote the labor activity of older people.

The implementation of the third priority provides for measures and mechanisms to create equal opportunities for the realization of the desired productive and reproductive behavior and equal access to all information, health, education, and other services related to demographic development for all social groups. The main components of the policies for achieving social cohesion in society are ensuring conditions for the full integration of vulnerable groups (children at risk, social groups at risk, people with disabilities, etc.) strengthening solidarity between generations, and to developing, and maintaining equality between generations.

The fourth priority is aimed at achieving a more even territorial distribution of the population and at approximating the socio-economic conditions and quality of life between individual regions, as well as between the city and the countryside. Efforts and measures will be aimed at slowing down the processes of depopulation taking place in border regions and a number of villages; optimizing the concentration of the population in the capital and some larger regional centers, and optimizing the natural and environmental living environment. The implementation of this priority is inextricably linked to the strengthening of the role of regional policy and the linking of socio-economic development plans with the goals and objectives of the demographic strategy.

The implementation of the fifth priority provides for the introduction of an assessment of the impact on the demographic development of the population and the quality of human capital of each adopted regulatory act of the state.

The full implementation of the priorities of the country's demographic development by 2030 is possible in the conditions of macroeconomic stability, sustainable economic growth, increasing economic activity, employment, and incomes of the population. The proposed measures and actions for demographic development are considered an element of the general concept of sustainable development, according to which the population, the environment, and the economy are mutually conditioned and are in continuous interaction. It can be expected that future favorable changes in the environment will lead to favorable changes in the reproductive processes of the population.

5. Conclusion

The planned activities on the priorities and the relevant directions have not yet yielded positive results. The trends of demographic indicators in Bulgaria are negative. This creates a set of challenges for the institutions that implement policies in this area. It is necessary to take the appropriate corrective actions that will lead to positive change. All this is related to a detailed and comprehensive analysis of the current situation, which will create prerequisites for making correct and correct decisions (Terziev, 2023b; Georgiev & Terziev, 2023c).

References

Ministry of Labor and Social Policy. (2024a). https://www.mlsp.government.bg/, Retrieved 27 December 2024.

Council of Ministers. (2024b). https://www.strategy.bg/strategicdocuments/View.aspx?lang=bg-BG&Id=778, Retrieved 27 December 2024.

Petkova, K., Karlezhova, N., Popcheva, D., Ilieva, S., Shehebar-Daneva, M. (2023a). Population and demographic processes 2023. National statistical institute, 2023, ISSN 1313-1915.

Terziev, V.K. (2023b). Innovation Development of Industrial Business Organizations. In M. Okur Dinçsoy & H. Can (Eds.), Optimizing Energy Efficiency During a Global Energy Crisis (pp. 282-306). IGI Global. https://doi.org/10.4018/979-8-3693-0400-6.ch016.

Georgiev, M.P. & Terziev, V.K. (2023c). The Labor Market Policies and Social Development in Bulgaria. In M. Okur Dinçsoy & H. Can (Eds.), Optimizing Energy Efficiency During a Global Energy Crisis (pp. 239-281). IGI Global Scientific Publishing. https://doi.org/10.4018/979-8-3693-0400-6.ch015.

Changes in the Labour Market in Bulgaria in a Period of Social, Economic and Political Transformations

Venelin Terziev, Marin Georgiev, Simeon Simeonov

1. Introduction

The processes of political and economic transformations at the end of the 20th century caused a series of crises that significantly changed the social structures of a number of countries, as they led to the collapse of the Union of Soviet Socialist Republics. Political transformations last a certain period, which from a historical point of view is too short. The significance of these transformations has particular social implications. These social consequences are experienced to one degree or another by all countries of the socialist camp. The main political and economic ties cease to exist and this leads to the occurrence of severe crises in the economies of these countries. Strong fluctuations in economies lead to social insecurity and the occurrence of phenomena such as mass unemployment and others, which are not characteristic and unknown in the planned mode of functioning of the national economy. All these circumstances make the local communities look for short-term but effective solutions to solve the severe crisis. This all leads to the implementation of not quite popular measures to protect national economies and even more severe consequences for people.

2. The transition in Bulgaria

The Bulgarian transition to democracy and market economy is the general name of the historical, political, and economic processes for the establishment of democracy in Bulgaria in the years after the November Plenum of the Central Committee of the Bulgarian Communist Party in 1989. Often, for brevity, it is simply called "The Transition" or "The Bulgarian Transition".

Some authors place the beginning of the transition on November 10, 1989, when a plenum of the Central Committee of the Bulgarian Communist

Party was held and Todor Zhivkov was deposed. According to others, it was January 19, 1990, when Article 1 of the Constitution of the People's Republic of Bulgaria was repealed for the leadership role of the BKP in the state (Dimitrova & Georgiev, 2019a).

There is also a lack of official agreement on whether this transition is complete and what its stages are (Discussion on the Bulgarian transition, 2003). According to some authors (Kalinova et al., 2010), the first stage was the change of power (from 1989-90 until the convocation of the VII Great National Assembly), followed by the periods 1991-1996, 1997-2001, 2001-2006, and for the end of the transition is considered the admission of Bulgaria to the European Union. The previous totalitarian system with the universal dominance of the Bulgarian Communist Party has been successfully replaced by a system of political pluralism. From 1990 to 2007, 12 governments were replaced with the participation of a large number of political parties. A new constitution and numerous laws were adopted. Membership in the European Union and NATO was achieved. The Bulgarian economy is moving from a state-centralized planning system to a market economy based on private ownership. Deep social changes are taking place in society.

According to Ivan Kostov's opinion from 2019: "it will end when the rule of law is established in Bulgaria. When there are strong institutions that are able to deal with corruption, oligarchy, organized crime, and abuse of monopoly position. And above all, when Bulgarian citizens become true defenders of democracy in their homeland". Interview for media portal "Slaveykov Square" (Dimitrova & Georgiev, 2019a).

Bulgaria's economy is planned. The economic structure in 1989 (according to modern data) includes the following sectors: 59.4% industry (with developed mechanical engineering, electrical engineering, and electronics), 29.7% services, and 12.9% agriculture. However, foreign trade is mainly with the countries of the Council for Mutual Economic Assistance (75%), of which 55% is with the Union of Soviet Socialist Republics, although in the 1980s the import of raw materials and materials from Western countries grew. Until the beginning of the 80s, the trade balance was positive, but in 1985, the trade balance was already negative with a deficit of about 1 billion dollars (Hristov, 2007). By the end of the 1980s, Bulgaria entered an economic crisis related not only to a chronic shortage of convertible currency but also to commodity deficits, which naturally led to rising inflation. The external debt has been growing at a dizzying pace since the mid-1980s, already in 1987 it exceeded the Gross Domestic Product (Danov, 2014a) and at the end of 1988 it reached 10.7 billion dollars (Avramov, 2008) and attempts to obtain external credits failed (Lakov, 2014b) and the country entered a Debt Crisis that lasted from 1987 to 1994 (Ivanov, 2009). At a meeting with the Ministry of the Interior on November 25, 1989, Petar Mladenov described the situation in the economy as very difficult (Secretly, 1989). The economic growth figures were incorrect and from 1983 to 1988 the economic situation was getting worse every year. After the collapse of the Union of Soviet Socialist Republics and the market of the Council for Mutual Economic Assistance (1989 – 1992), the Bulgarian economy turned out to be uncompetitive with other markets (Foundation "Institute for Market Economy", 2004; National assembly, 1990).

With the election of Mikhail Gorbachev as General Secretary of the Central Committee of the Communist Party of the Soviet Union in 1985, "Perestroika" began in the Union of Soviet Socialist Republics - economic reforms to raise the standard of living. It exerts a great influence in the countries of the socialist camp and especially in the Eastern European ones. It is accompanied by "Glasnost" - after many years of restriction of freedom of speech, people are allowed to freely express their opinion, independent media appear, and hundreds of books are published, which remain unpublished due to the presence of censorship. The opinions of the dissidents and the intelligentsia are beginning to be heard more and more. These changes marked the beginning of the collapse of the socialist system in Eastern Europe.

3. The social environment

The social environment turns out to be most sensitive during this period. The consequences that occur in the labor market are so palpably acute that they cannot be compared to any other period, except the periods of the First and Second World Wars. Bulgarian society is facing deep trials that lead to acute social problems. The planned economy practically ceases to function and this leads to the suspension of the activity of industrial enterprises, and some sectors cease to function altogether. All economic ties have been terminated, with only a certain volume of the service sector existing.

The consequences are close to a national catastrophe, with labor markets being the most sensitive. The primary labor market, which exists in new political and economic realities, is unable to cope with the growing number of persons of working age. Mass layoffs are commonplace during this period. In Bulgaria, the absolute number of persons who are dismissed by an economic entity is defined as a mass reduction of the workforce. In some regions of the country, unemployment rates are close to the entire economically active population, which creates deep social inequalities and problems. Governments are forced to look for quick decisions to contain the social tensions that are growing enormously (Photo 1-8) (КАПИТАЛ, 2024a).

The discontent of certain communities is taken to the streets and squares, organizing hundreds of demonstrations and strikes. The country begins a complex of problems, such as high inflation and the inability to regularly service its external debt. Certain periods of this period of social transformations, it was accompanied by problems related to feeding the population due to an insufficient amount of necessities. This necessitates the introduction

Figure 1. "Bulgaria is practically bankrupt and the government of Andrei Lukanov, who ruled for months after 1989, had to impose a moratorium on foreign debt payments."

Source: КАПИТАЛ

Figure 2. "In the second half of 1990, the crisis of public finances entered a much more visible phase: inflation and soaring prices (as far as they were liberalized), empty shops and queues, and growing unemployment."

Source: КАПИТАЛ

Figure 3. "People are in the squares or queues for oil and milk."
Source: КАПИТАЛ

Figure 4. "A coupon system for basic foods and fuels was introduced on August 20, 1990, by the decision of Andrey Lukanov's resigned government."

Source: КАПИТАЛ

Figure 5. "In 1996-1997, 17 banks went bankrupt. The financial system is in collapse, which began with the closure in May 1996 of one of the giants of the time, using a political umbrella - First Private Bank, lists of credit millionaires, and decades-old lawsuits."

Source: КАПИТАЛ

Figure 6. "In 1996-1997, the BNB issued new banknotes every month with an increasingly large denomination due to the sharp devaluation of the lev."

Source: КАПИТАЛ

Figure 7. "Under the government of Zhan Videnov in Bulgaria, an acute grain crisis occurred, leading to a lack of traditional grains and products. People are forced to queue for kilometers. The reason for the situation is a bunch of wrong decisions over the years - a poorly functioning agricultural sector, bad harvest, and uncontrolled export of grain in the same year. However, Videnov's office first denies the problem, and then, in a controversial transaction, imports grain at a much higher than market price."

Source: КАПИТАЛ

Figure 8. "January 1997. Wages are $7 and pensions are $4. "Mass bankruptcies, widespread poverty. And a crisis - total and complex. First financial. It gave birth to economics. The two caused social, and the three together – political", recalls Muravey Radev, finance minister in Ivan Kostov's office, in a text for "Factor.bg".

Source: КАПИТАЛ

of a coupon system, which until now was known only for the period of the war years.

Employment services begin to register more and more unemployed persons, and they become a center for communication on employment mediation. The specialists who are engaged in this activity are not sufficiently prepared, because this process has existed until now under a planned mode of employment. The number of vacancies is smaller than the number of those who could fill them. The number of unemployed persons with high qualifications and enough work experience is such that the natural market principle hardly succeeds in calming the local labor markets (Table 1-2) (Eurostat - European Commission, 2024b).

Table 1. Employment and activity by sex and age - annual data (20-64 years), b- break in time series; d- definition differs

TIME	2014	2015	2016	2017	2018	2019	2020	2021	2022	2023
BULGARIA	64,4	66,5	67,0	70,6	71,7	74,3	72,7	73,2	75,9 b	76,2
Czechia	73,5	74,8	76,7	78,5	79,9	80,3	79,7	80,0	81,3	81,7
Denmark	74,7	75,4	76,0 b	76,6 b	77,5	78,3	77,8	79,0	80,1	79,8 b
Germany	76,7	76,9	77,6	78,2	78,9	79,6	78,2 b	79,4	80,6	81,1
Estonia	75,0	76,7	77,0	79,2	79,7	80,5	79,1	79,3	81,9	82,1
Ireland	68,1	69,8	71,3	72,9	74,0	75,0	72,1	74,9 b	78,2	79,1
Greece	53,1	54,8	55,9	57,4	59,0	60,8	58,3	62,6	66,3	67,4
Spain	59,9	62,0	63,9	65,5	67,0	68,0	65,7	67,5 b	69,3 d	70,5 d
France	70,0	70,3	70,7	71,3	72,0	72,3	72,1	73,2 d	74,0 d	74,4 d
Croatia	59,2	60,6	61,4	63,6	65,2	66,7	66,9	68,2	69,7	70,7 b
Italy	59,5	60,2	61,4	62,3	63,0 b	63,5	61,9	62,7	64,8	66,3
Cyprus	67,6	67,9	68,7	70,8	73,9	75,7	74,9	75,9	77,9	78,9
Latvia	70,6	72,5	73,0	74,6	76,8	77,3	76,9	75,3	77,0	77,5
Lithuania	71,8	73,3	75,2	76,0	77,8	78,2	76,7	77,4	79,0	78,5
Luxembourg	72,1	70,9 b	70,7	71,5	72,1	72,8	72,1	74,1	74,8	74,8
Hungary	68,7	70,9	73,7	75,4	76,7	77,6	77,5	78,8	80,2	80,7
Malta	67,9	69,0	71,1	73,0	74,9	75,6	76,0	77,8	80,1	81,7
Netherlands	76,3	77,2	77,9	78,9	80,0	81,0	80,8	81,7	82,9	83,5
Austria	74,2	74,3	74,8	75,4	76,2	76,8	74,8	75,6	77,3	77,2
Poland	64,9	66,3	68,2	70,0	71,4	72,6 b	72,8	75,5	76,7	77,9

Table 1. *Continued*

TIME	2014	2015	2016	2017	2018	2019	2020	2021	2022	2023
Portugal	66,1	67,9	69,5	72,5	74,7	75,5	74,2	75,5	77,1	78,2
Romania	58,0	59,2	60,3	62,7	63,9	65,1	65,2	67,1	68,5	68,7
Slovenia	67,3	68,6	69,5	72,9	74,9	75,9	74,8	76,1	77,9	77,5
Slovakia	67,8	69,6	71,8	73,2	74,5	75,6	74,6	74,6	76,7	77,5
Finland	72,2	71,8	72,4	73,2	75,3	76,2	75,5	76,8	78,4	78,2
Sweden	79,6	80,1	80,8	81,4	82,0	81,7	80,2	80,4	82,0	82,6
Iceland	84,9	86,5	87,8	87,6	86,5	85,9	82,3 b	81,4	84,8	85,3
Norway	80,1	79,7	79,4	79,2	80,0	80,2	79,7	80,0	80,9	80,4
Switzerland	81,1	81,7	82,0	82,1	82,5	82,9	82,5	81,8	81,9	83,0
Bosnia and Herzegovina	:	:	:	:	:	:	:	52,6	53,9	55,9
Montenegro	55,6	56,7	57,1	58,2	59,8	60,8	55,2	:	:	:
North Macedonia	51,3	51,9	53,3	54,8	56,1	59,2	59,1	:	:	:
Serbia	53,5	54,7	57,6	60,0	61,6	63,6	64,3	66,7	69,3	69,6 b
Türkiye	53,2 b	53,9	54,4	55,3	55,6	53,8	51,0	53,9 b	56,5	57,3

Source: Eurostat - European Commission

Table 2. Employment and activity by sex and age - annual data (20-64 years), b- break in time series; d- definition differs

TIME	2023-10	2023-11	2023-12	2024-01	2024-02	2024-03	2024-04	2024-05	2024-06	2024-07
BULGARIA	4,1	4,2	4,4	4,9	5,0	5,1	5,0	4,7	4,5	:
Czechia	2,9	2,3	2,8	3,2	2,7	3,1	2,7	2,6	2,8	:
Denmark	6,1 b	5,9	5,7	6,3	6,2	5,5	5,6	5,4	5,3	:
Germany	3,2	3,1	2,9	3,2	3,6	3,5	3,2	3,6	3,4	:
Estonia	6,1	6,3	6,9	7,7	7,8	7,7	7,6	7,6	7,5	:
Ireland	4,2	4,1	4,3	4,2	4,0	4,2	4,4	4,5	4,8	5,2
Greece	10,2	10,8	10,5	12,6	12,6	11,2	10,9	10,4	8,2	:
Spain	11,9	11,7	11,7	12,3	12,4	12,2	11,6	11,2	11,0	:
France	7,7	7,7	7,7	7,8	7,6	7,3	6,9	6,9	6,9	:
Croatia	6,0	6,1	6,2	6,3	6,1	5,8	5,1	4,6	4,4	:
Italy	8,1	7,6	7,0	7,6	8,1	7,4	6,8	6,5	6,8	:
Cyprus	4,7	6,5	6,6	6,7	6,1	5,2	4,0	3,6	4,4	:
Latvia	6,6	6,8	7,1	7,2	7,3	7,2	6,9	6,6	6,5	:
Lithuania	6,7	7,3	8,5	8,4	8,1	8,1	7,3	7,1	7,7	:
Luxembourg	5,6	5,8	5,9	5,9	5,9	5,6	5,5	5,4	5,3	:
Hungary	4,1	4,2	4,2	4,5	4,6	4,4	4,4	4,3	4,2	:
Malta	2,9	2,8	2,8	2,9	2,9	3,0	3,1	3,3	3,2	:
Netherlands	3,6	3,4	3,3	3,8	3,9	3,7	3,6	3,5	3,7	3,5
Austria	4,8	4,7	5,4	5,5	5,5	5,4	4,6	5,1	4,9	:

Table 2. *Continued*

TIME	2023-10	2023-11	2023-12	2024-01	2024-02	2024-03	2024-04	2024-05	2024-06	2024-07
Poland	3,0	3,1	3,1	3,2	3,2	3,1	2,9	2,8	2,7	:
Portugal	6,8	6,7	6,7	6,8	6,9	6,6	6,4	6,2	6,4	:
Romania	5,7	5,8	6,0	5,5	5,2	5,1	5,1	5,2	5,3	:
Slovenia	3,5	3,3	3,3	3,6	3,5	3,3	3,2	3,1	3,0	:
Slovakia	5,7	5,6	5,6	5,7	5,6	5,5	5,4	5,4	5,4	:
Finland	6,8	6,8	7,1	8,3	7,8	9,0	9,2	10,2	8,3	7,9
Sweden	7,4	7,1	7,7	8,5	8,5	9,2	8,9	8,7	9,4	:
Iceland	3,1	2,8	3,8	4,5	3,6	:	:	:	:	:
Norway	3,6	3,7	3,3	4,5	3,5	4,2	4,3	4,2	4,3	:
Switzerland	4,0	3,8	4,0	4,2	4,3	4,3	:	:	:	:
Türkiye	8,2	8,8	8,9	9,8	9,2	8,8	8,4	7,7	:	:

Source: Eurostat - European Commission

There are also transformations in the Bulgarian army, which is changing from conscription to mercenary military service. Its strategic goals have been changed and its composition has been drastically reduced, leaving only 1/3 of the previously employed persons. The socialization of persons who have specific skills and habits is almost impossible and a process of retraining is necessary so that these unemployed persons have a chance to find a new job.

A significant problem is also the young people who at that moment are completing their higher education. They are without any professional experience and getting them a job in the primary labor market is almost impossible.

The whole complex of problems creates a primary importance for society, and this necessitates taking measures to quell social discontent and provide time to solve multifaceted problems.

The definition of the target groups is of particular importance, which also determines the measures that will be taken. Determining an adequate policy regarding the risk groups in the labor market is important from the point of view of determining what the relevant measures should be aimed at.

The following groups of unemployed persons are defined:

- unemployed young people up to 29 years of age without work experience in the acquired specialty;
- unemployed persons over 55 years of age;
- unemployed with primary, primary, and lower education;
- unemployed without professional qualification;
- unemployed persons with permanent disabilities;
- persons benefiting from temporary protection with registration at the labor office.
- Long-term unemployed persons - those who have been unemployed for more than 12 (twelve) months.

Each group of the defined groups is treated differently with respect to the subgroups within it. People from these groups are included in training, programs, and measures, according to the Law on Unemployment Protection and Employment Promotion in force at that time.

Special attention to this period of crisis is given to the passive policy of the labor market. Different groups of unemployed persons who receive social assistance in the form of cash compensation are defined. A methodology for determining the amount has been determined, which is based on the amount of the remuneration received so far, and the period of receipt is determined by the years of work experience. The minimum period for receiving monetary compensation is 4 (four) months, and the maximum period is 12 (twelve) months. For persons who have no work experience in the last period, the minimum wage established for the country is defined as the base. Those who have just completed their higher education also receive social assistance.

The most widespread measure that is applied is related to the engagement of unemployed persons in general useful activities, which are related to cleaning the spaces in cities and villages, landscaping, or guarding public buildings. These programs are temporary employment programs that provide minimum benefits to participants for different periods, the longest period being 12 (twelve) months.

Another alternative is employment companies, which are essentially commercial companies. The German model of their creation is used. They only employ unemployed persons who are registered with the employment services. The remuneration of these unemployed persons is financed from the state budget.

In areas with a mixed population, a literacy program is implemented for all unemployed persons who do not speak the official language, and they can also participate in various qualification courses. The program has the following name "Literacy, qualification and employment".

The regulated measures implemented during this period are related to providing employers with the amount of insurance payments on the wages of employed unemployed persons. Employers, however, undertake an obligation to commit them to a longer period of work, which would provide them with the possibility of permanent employment.

Calming labor markets is becoming difficult as more and more unemployed people leave their previous jobs. This process of severe fluctuations continued until the end of the last century. Governments have repeatedly been forced to resort to temporary employment measures and increases in cash benefits and welfare benefits.

All these processes are characteristic of all countries of the post-socialist space and have been going on for about twenty years.

At a much later stage, actions and programs are undertaken to ensure the stimulation of employment by creating Employment Action Plans. These plans envisage and implement a whole complex of programs and measures to respond to the demands and changes of the labor markets. Disparities in local labor markets are still observed, resulting from the severe and prolonged changes of the transition from a planned to a market economy (Terziev, 2023a; Georgiev & Terziev, 2023b; Terziev, 2020; 2019b; 2019c; Georgiev & Solovev, 2024c; 2024d).

4. Conclusion

Political transformations are always accompanied by economic transformations. All this has a serious impact on social processes. The social environment is most sensitive at this stage. Labor markets are experiencing significant fluctuations, with unemployment levels becoming high and unable to be regulated by the natural mechanisms of a market economy. There is a dominance of the primary employment market, which is provided through financial instruments from state budgets or other attracted resources. In practice, the state becomes the main employer, which can be allowed to distort local labor markets. Drastic deviations from real processes are obtained, which leads to incorrect analysis and wrong conclusions. All these manifestations are a fact and can be observed in almost all countries that are making a political and economic transition. The dynamic development of the processes does not allow for an adequate and precise analysis, and decisions are made due to the necessity. This leads to a temporary suppression or deterrence of social tension but does not contribute to solving the crises that have arisen. Even though various social technologies and mechanisms have been developed in this direction, their implementation at the local level is not easy and requires their adaptation.

References

Dimitrova, D., & Georgiev, E.L. (2019a). "Ivan Kostov, I am absolutely free", İnterview with Ivan Kostov. Slaveykov Square. April 18, 2019, Retrieved 09 December 2024.

Discussion on the Bulgarian transition. (2003). Media Times Review, 2003.

Kalinova, E. et al. (2010). The Bulgarian transitions 1939 – 2010. Sofia, Paradigma, 2010, pp. 239 – 395, ISBN 978-954-326-034-8.

Hristov, H. (2007). The Secret Bankruptcies of Communism. Ciela, 2007, p. 269, ISBN 978-954-280-162-7.

Danov, R. (2014a). The Bulgarian liberations. The lost lessons. Sofia, 2014, p. 412, ISBN 978-954-389-274-7.

Avramov, R. (2008). Money and de/stabilization in Bulgaria 1948 – 1989. Sofia, Siela, 2008, p. 220, ISBN 978-954-28-0339-3.

Lakov, K. (2014b). The transition that didn't go as planned. Sofia, 2014, ISBN 978-954-8624-38-1.

Ivanov, M. (2009). The Economy of Communist Bulgaria (1963 – 1989). Znepolski, Ivaylo (ed.). History of the People's Republic of Bulgaria: Regime and Society. Sofia, "Siela Soft and Publishing", 2009, pp. 326 – 332, ISBN 978-954-28-0588-5.

Secretly! (1989). Speech of the General Secretary of the Central Committee of the BKP and Chairman of the State Council of the NRB Petar Mladenov at the meeting with the Ministry of Internal Affairs, which took place on 25.11.1989, p.105, http://www.desehistory.com/2013/10/25111989.html. Retrieved 27 December 2024.

Foundation "Institute for Market Economy". (2004). Collective. Anatomy of transition. Economic policy in Bulgaria from 1989 to 2004 through the eyes of the Institute for Market Economy, Ciela, 2004, p. 22, ISBN 9546496901.

National assembly. (1990). Transcript of the Second Session of the 9th National Assembly of March 29, 1990, p. 6.

КАПИТАЛ, (2024a). https://www.capital.bg/multimedia/fotogalerii/2023/03/07/4455859_fotogaleriia_golemite_krizi/. Retrieved 20 December 2024.

Eurostat - European Commission, (2024b). https://ec.europa.eu/eurostat. Retrieved 28 December 2024.

Terziev, V. K. (2023a). Innovation Development of Industrial Business Organizations. In M. Okur Dinçsoy & H. Can (Eds.), Optimizing Energy Efficiency During a Global Energy Crisis (pp. 282-306). IGI Global. https://doi.org/10.4018/979-8-3693-0400-6.ch016.

Georgiev, M. P. & Terziev, V. K. (2023b). The Labor Market Policies and Social Development in Bulgaria. In M. Okur Dinçsoy & H. Can (Eds.), Optimizing Energy Efficiency During a Global Energy Crisis (pp. 239-281). IGI Global. https://doi.org/10.4018/979-8-3693-0400-6.ch015.

Terziev, V. (2020). The Bulgarian labor market in a period of extraordinary crisis from the COVID-19 pandemic. // 18th RSEP International Economics, Finance & Business Conference – Virtual/Online 26-27 August 2020, Kadir Has University, Istanbul, Turkey, pp.111-115, ISBN: 978-605-06961-5-8/September 2020.

Terziev, V. (2019b). Theoretical basis of development of labor market and social policy in the Republic of Bulgaria. // INTCESS 2019- 6th International Conference on Education and Social Sciences, 4-6 February, 2019, Dubai, International Organization Center of Academic Research, Istanbul, Turkey, pp. 715-726, ISBN: 978-605-82433-5-4.

Terziev, V. (2019c). Social policy and labor market development in Bulgarian transition period. // INTCESS 2019- 6th International Conference on Education and Social Sciences, 4-6 February, 2019, Dubai, International Organization Center of Academic Research, Istanbul, Turkey, pp. 703-714, ISBN: 978-605-82433-5-4.

Georgiev, M., Solovev, D. (2024c). Applications of the Balanced Scorecard concept in relation to social development. // 107th International Scientific Conference on Economic and Social Development – Economic and Social Survival in Global Changes – Zagreb, 16-17 February, 2024, Economic and Social Development (Book of Proceedings), Cakovec, Croatia, 2024, pp.73-82, ISSN 1849-7535.

Georgiev, M., Solovev, D. (2024d). Evolution of the concept of the balanced Scorecard. // 107th International Scientific Conference on Economic and Social Development – Economic and Social Survival in Global Changes – Zagreb, 16-17 February, 2024, Economic and Social Development (Book of Proceedings), Cakovec, Croatia, 2024, pp.83-93, ISSN 1849-7535.

Vocational Education in Bulgaria – Status and Opportunities

Venelin Terziev, Marusya Lyubcheva, Marin Georgiev, Simeon Simeonov

1. Introduction

The discussion about the fate of vocational education is continuous, but in many cases fruitless as far as its adaptation to the modern demands of the economy and the dynamically changing business environment is concerned. If this were not the case, today there would be no shortage of professions, we would not wait for the last drops of state-organized professional education to be drained, to move in leaps and bounds towards the "modern", and much more popular among candidates, professional fields and thus empting of content important for the economic base areas. Its complexity, caused by the necessity to combine the general and professional parts, often causes a set of inconsistencies, which requires continuous adaptation and transitions that ensure not only its functioning, but the functioning of our entire economy. Professionalism in vocational education requires an arrangement of the mission, goals, factors and tools in an appropriate format that can ensure the even development of each business and each single economic direction.

2. Professionalism in vocational education

For too long, vocational education was left to itself, or rather to the "free market", which not only did not regulate it, but also created certain disparities that are very difficult to overcome and last for a long period of time. From the point of view of meeting the needs of skilled workers, this single market did not give Bulgarian economy a chance and today this is already a serious problem - there is a lack of specialists in basic professional fields, specialists with secondary education as well as such with higher education. It was not enough to change the laws, to change the names, to organize recognition of diplomas, to decide on dual education (a forgotten old thing that had already existed in Bulgaria). It was necessary to arrange the system according to clear and precise criteria, to produce specialists in the needed-by-the-economy professions and to make it flexible to easily adapt to the rapidly developing technological processes and the changing business environment. Economy needs education, and education needs economy - not only of its orientations, but of its investments, too. In fact, the people in the education sector did not know exactly what specialists the economy needed; there was nobody to tell them. And they produced specialists according to their internal educational logic, namely – they produced staff in the disciplines and specialities for which they had teachers and/or a material base. In the meantime, there appeared exotic specialties, hardly needed by anyone, but they kept the status quo. Data from evaluations of education quality have long been commented by society. We talk a lot and at length about external assessment, about the content of curricula, about textbooks, we listen to extensive explanations from experts, parents, citizens, but in fact we rarely comment on the fact that it is increasingly difficult to find a handyman to repair our defective kitchen sink, a handyman to replace the tiles in the bathroom, an electrician to fix our outdated electric wiring (Terziev, 2022a; 2022b; Terziev & Lyubcheva, 2022c; 2023).

Without undervaluing the role of education for personal development and independent growth, it is important to provide the economy in its most general dimensions with skilled staff in the needed professional directions.

Change is more than necessary, but change that is subject to principles and rules serving both sides in this process –business as well as education. In fact, serving the state. Even the available strategies do not do enough if implemented sporadically or partially. The strategic agenda of professional education requires the creation of an environment in which any supporting and sustaining business system will develop, including the educational one. There have always existed regulations, but what is needed today is a new reviewing of them, precise criteria, assessment of compliances to fulfil the functions and role they are intended for.

3. The factors of professionalism

Every element in the system of professional education leaves its mark and to some extent affects the quality of specialists with certain qualification. The factors determining the preparation of skilled workers for the sphere of economy fall under the general framework of factors for the development of education, and for this reason it is impossible to completely separate professional education from other types of education. It is an art to make a combination that allows parallelism, enough possible transitions, input and output to match the dynamics of life and technological development. The organizational factors are determinants of the quality of education, insofar as they determine the overall infrastructure and the professional factors related to capacity, quality and professionalization, and there must be found the most precise elements responsible for vocational education (Terziev & Lyubcheva, 2022c; 2023).

3.1. Organizational factors

3.1.1. Legislation

Legislation with an educational field of applicability and that with an economic field of applicability.

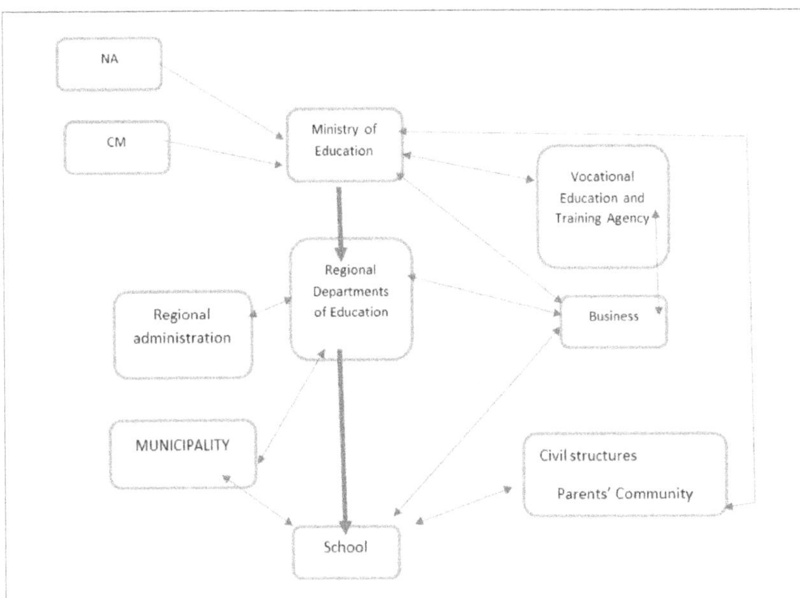

Figure 1: Organizational infrastructure of vocational education
Source: Authors' elaboration

The variety of laws, especially the by-laws, the need to combine the different fields of application of the laws so that they can serve the common goals, the mechanisms for legislation implementation and control are an essential part of the management process in education. The possibility to manage qualitatively and effectively through laws is determined not by the number of laws or their changing but by their skilful codification, not by the number of sub-normative documents, but by their content and quality. The instability of the legislative base, the introduction of foreign practices without the necessary base in our country, as well as the implementation of legislation, is a challenge (Terziev & Lyubcheva, 2022c; 2023).

3.1.2 Organizational Infrastructure

The organizational infrastructure of vocational education is part of the general framework (Fig. 1). The main institution responsible for the organization of the entire educational process, for the creation and implementation of legislation in the system is the Ministry of Education and Science. The role of all other institutions that are connected with and have responsibility for education is also essential. A well-organized and hierarchical structure through which legislation is implemented and education is managed is also important - especially in the area of vocational education, where the number of interested institutions is greater. An essential issue in this structure is the distribution of responsibilities, which is not always the best and does not always consider different interests in the best way.

The target institutions with responsibilities in vocational education – the National Agency for Vocational Education and Training, Regional Administrations, Municipal Administrations, employer organizations and business structures – have a serious but insufficiently regulated place in the system and this is probably one of the reasons for the existing inconsistencies and deficits.

3.1.3. Institutional Interaction

The entire process of management of education depends on the level of this interaction. Even in the presence of a formally good infrastructure, good legislation, institutional interaction (non-interaction) determines the quality of the educational process from the highest to the lowest level. Even a cursory glance at the structure shows how significant is not only the interaction, but the agreement between the institutions, which is often intertwined with different political commitments or with the claims of certain civil groups not always reflecting public opinion. The necessary degree of freedom of each institution must be conformed to that of all others, and only a well-organized mechanism of interaction can lead to a success of the system. Naturally, the institutional interaction is laid down in the legislation, but sometimes it is impossible to overcome the division or the emerging deficits. For example, the interaction between business and vocational education is difficult and very slow to make its way, a deficit that can be easily overcome by strengthening the role of the National Agency for Vocational Education and Training, rethinking the role of the Regional Departments of Education of the Ministry of Education and Science, the regional and local authorities in determining the professional directions in accordance with the priorities of the regional economy. It is a challenge for a Regional Department of Education, for example, to work with only one professional education expert in a rather heterogeneous environment of professional fields. Except for the purely administrative and formal role in approving the admission plan, nothing highly professional can happen. Professional areas of education are often determined by the internal logic of educational institutions, their "enthusiasm" to look for intersections with some employer or other type of business organization, the competence of the regional councils that approve (most often quite formally) the admission plan in the professional education.

3.2. Professional Factors

3.2.1. Institutional Capacity

This factor includes three main elements - managerial, administrative and professional capacity

Institutional capacity gives an answer to the question "to what extent does the professionalism in the management and implementation of the educational process meet the requirements of today - intelligent growth, Industry 4.0, transition to the digital age?" Perhaps this is the question of the questions. Regardless of modernity, to which everyone rushes with great pleasure, leaving out at that those areas that carried and carry the prestige of the normal economic support in the development of any economic entity. Even if we make all schools STEM and innovative, they should have majors supporting core operational activities, and they themselves should be up-to-date, but not red-booked.

3.2.2. Teaching Capacity and Quality

Perhaps the easiest question is the assessment of the capacity of the teaching staff. However, it should be added that it still depends not only on the personal capacity of the teachers, but also on the material base, the textbook fund, the costs of maintaining the systems in vocational education, etc. Even if a professor enters a vocational high school, theory alone will not solve the issue of capacity and quality.

3.2.3. Professionalization

It is determined according to the strategy for economic development, but often the implementation and realization remain far from the strategic guidelines. The list of professions for vocational education and training and the standards for acquiring professional qualifications are essential elements that determine whether the skilled workers "produced" as a result of the thus organized system are sufficient and how qualified they are. The combination of the National Qualifications Framework with the List of Vocational Education and Training Professions, as well as with the standards, is an important part of forming the overall picture.

The applying of the framework programs (A-E) ensures a balance between general education, common and specific professional knowledge. Several trends have a serious impact on the imbalance of professional education - on the one hand, the trend for increase of the number of higher education graduates makes the number of those starting work immediately after finishing secondary education constantly decreasing; on the other hand, there are the negative demographic trends, and on the third, there is the fact that Bulgaria is one of the countries in which the share of early school leavers and the number of young people who neither study nor work is too high. This could be a reserve for vocational education, but it requires a professional approach to each group, as well as an appropriate model by which these young people can be involved in the educational process. This would mean a transformation that connects the labour-market trends on the one hand, and on the other, updating the professional directions, aligning them with the forecasts for the economic development of the country, as well as expanding the scope of professional guidance and orientation of young people for career development (Terziev & Lyubcheva, 2022c; 2023).

4. Qualified staff – professionalism and compliance

Undoubtedly, the responsibility for providing qualified staff for each professional direction falls on professional education - secondary professional and higher. Each professional field and each profession needs qualified workers who must meet their requirements and standards, if there are such. It is in determining the correspondence between demand and supply, i.e. between the demands of the economy and the response of vocational education, that professionalism in management of vocational education fits. Part of the solution to the problem are the Framework Programs (Framework Program A - E) and Standards developed by the Ministry of Education and Science - a necessary but not sufficient condition, especially for some professional areas and especially considering the rapid changes occurring in the industry. The variable parameters in professional areas and professions are a fact – today's professions may not exist tomorrow, just as some professions from earlier times already appear as exotic or are completely absent from the labour market. At the same time, we have a red list of deficit professions. The difficulty comes from the fact that each professional direction needs a serious defining of concrete specialities, as they are often the key to the development of the respective direction. Many of the questions raised above can be solved by better implementation of legislation, better interaction between institutions, better quality control. If quality control in general education is a public problem, then the quality of professional education has not become such at all. It is important to evaluate the processes of the labour market and, more precisely, with regard to the level of qualifications. Professional education "produces" specialists of 1 to 3 qualification degrees. The number of skilled workers with 4th qualification degree is very small. The participation of professional colleges in the formation of the country's workforce is a challenge. A non-exhaustive reference shows that 4th degree is planned for some fields in the spheres of tourism, cosmetics, medicine and especially in military science. What would be the motive to create a professional college, which is a serious investment, when with one postgraduate program at any university one can easily get a certificate providing a 4-degree qualification? (Terziev, 2022a; 2022b; Terziev & Lyubcheva, 2022c; 2023).

We have to answer many questions in order to overcome the challenges and deficits and to give freedom to professional education, but such a freedom that guarantees servicing the economy and providing jobs for the specialists.

There can be defined several sets of questions, namely (Terziev & Lyubcheva, 2022c; 2023):

- Is the List of Professions adequate to the state and prospects for the development of the economy and is the economy provided with the necessary skilled personnel in terms of quality and type?
- Do the protected professional specialties sufficiently protect the development of certain professional areas needed by the state (51 protected professional specialties for academic year 2021/2022)?
- Is the procedure for opening new occupations adequate?
- Do the standards in the education system ensure the achievement of the necessary knowledge, skills and competences with which each individual can realize his full potential and be useful for both themselves and the society. And is there a reliable standard for every profession?
- Is the analysis made to show what skilled workers are needed for the development of the Bulgarian economy reliable enough to have the whole professionalization arranged on the right basis and to ensure the relevant qualification levels, (The List of specialties in professions in which there is an expected shortage of specialists on the labor market for academic year 2021/2022 – 77)?
- Is there a need for a change in the ratios between first to fourth qualification degrees in the different professional fields?

5. Main challenges facing vocational education in Bulgaria

5.1. Recent policy changes

There is a blurring of the boundaries between general education and vocational education and training. Just as many graduates of general education programmes immediately start working (e.g. in administration), up to 90% of students in some vocational education and training programmes (e.g. in economics) continue their education in higher education immediately after graduation. The latest educational reform provides for profiled education in the upper secondary stage of general education, with each student being able to choose profiled subjects (e.g. mathematics or foreign languages). In some cases, instead of profiled training, combined and secondary schools can provide vocational training (Cedefop, 2018).

The Vocational Education and Training Act (1999) regulates the organisation, management and financing of vocational education, and training. The amendments to the Vocational Education and Training Act of 2014 concern:

- widening access to VET through validation of non-formal or informal learning conducted by vocational education and training providers;
- better matching of competencies acquired through vocational education and training with labour market demand;
- strengthening the quality assurance process by training providers;
- providing learners with the opportunity to accumulate credits necessary for acquiring a professional qualification in a given profession. Credits can be transferred between professional qualifications within the same professional field;
- restructuring of the state educational standards for acquiring professional qualifications through units of learning outcomes and assessment criteria;
- introducing a dual system of training, which since 2015 combines training in a school and a real work environment. Dual training is based on the partnership between vocational education and training providers and employers;
- introduction of mandatory requirements for providers of vocational education and training to create an internal quality assurance system that would guarantee the compliance of the services provided with the expectations and needs of society.

The 2016 amendments bring the Vocational Education and Training Act into line with the Pre-school and School Education Act and provide additional opportunities for acquiring professional qualifications in relation to the new structure of secondary education (two upper secondary stages). They also aim to improve the quality of vocational education and training by changing the ratio between theoretical and practical training in favour of practical training, including training in a real work environment. As a result of the amendments to the Vocational Education and Training Act, the Labour Code (1986) was also amended in 2014 to regulate the (dual training system) as a type of apprenticeship. Challenges remain in terms of insufficient funding, weak cooperation with business, the increasing number of early leavers from education and training, as well as the lack of a coherent system for assessing the quality of vocational education and training. To address these challenges, in 2017 The Ministry of Education and Science approved a Concept for the Development of Vocational Education and Training in Bulgaria. The draft Concept has been discussed with social partners (employers' organizations, employers, local government bodies, trade unions, and educational institutions) within a series of regional meetings (Cedefop, 2018).

5.2. Main challenges and opportunities for development

The Law on Vocational Education and Training has been amended several times since its adoption in 1999. Many key concepts, such as quality assurance, work-based learning, validation of non-formal and informal learning, and the implementation of a credit system, have now been fully or partially implemented.

The main challenges can be defined in the following areas (Cedefop, 2018):

- reducing the number of early leavers from the education and training system (generally higher in vocational education and training than in general secondary education);
- wider provision of dual vocational education and training (dual training is still mainly implemented within the framework of various projects);
- improving the professional qualifications of teachers/trainers (aging of the teaching staff). The Law on Pre-school and School Education (2015) introduces reforms in primary and secondary education, including vocational education and training, which are oriented towards overcoming these challenges, but it is still too early to assess the achieved results (Cedefop, 2018).

5.3. Incentives for learners

Students in the vocational education and training system in Bulgaria can receive financial incentives, just like students in general education.

5.3.1. Social benefits/scholarships

Students in the vocational education and training system can receive scholarships (Cedefop, 2018):

- Scholarships for success are awarded to students with high academic achievements;
- Social benefits support access to education and prevent early drop-out of disadvantaged students from the VET system, such as students with special educational needs or orphans.

The scholarships are awarded monthly and range from 5% to 15% of the minimum wage established for the country. Trainees in work-based learning (dual training system) receive a monthly salary from the company in which they are trained based on the contract concluded between them. Students in the secondary vocational education system can participate in projects under the European Social Fund for student internships, where they can also receive an additional scholarship (Cedefop, 2018).

5.3.2 Vouchers for adults

The terms and conditions for providing training vouchers for employed and unemployed persons, co-financed by the European Social Fund, are defined. The different types of training, target groups, and requirements for training providers are regulated. One person (employed or unemployed) is entitled to only one voucher for key competencies and one for vocational education and training during the implementation of the program (Cedefop, 2018).

5.3.3 Reduction when using public transport

All students in the secondary vocational education system are entitled to a reduction when using public transport, including train and urban public transport. The reduction may be up to 60%, the decision being made by the relevant municipality.

5.4 Incentives for businesses

5.4.1 Exemption from value-added tax

According to the Value Added Tax Act, vocational education and training services and training for the acquisition of key competencies provided by vocational education and training institutions, including licensed vocational training centres, are exempt from value-added tax (Cedefop, 2018).

5.4.2 Financial support for the provision of work-based training (dual training system)

The Employment Promotion Act provides financial support for employers who provide a job for work-based training to unemployed persons. The state budget covers the costs of remuneration, social and health insurance of persons employed under this incentive measure for a period of up to 36 months. The costs of the training institution that provides the person's training, as well as the costs of providing a mentor, are also covered (Cedefop, 2018).

5.5 Guidance and Counseling

Guidance and counseling of unemployed and employed persons is well developed. Career guidance services for job seekers (employed and unemployed persons) are provided by the Directorates of the Labour Office of the National Employment Agency and include (Cedefop, 2018):

- career counseling (individual and in groups) to assist in the selection of appropriate professional qualifications and training providers; information on the main characteristics of professions (requirements, demand, and trends) and relevant vocational education and training programs (providers, forms of training, admission requirements, diplomas).

Within the educational system, specialized career guidance services are offered mainly through the career guidance centers at the regional level, established with funding from the European Social Fund. The project results are expected to be implemented at a systemic level.

6. Conclusion

Probably, the answer to many of the questions raised should be sought in the field of higher education, but it should always be taken into account what the risk of retraining for certain activities and positions may be. This requires a refinement of the entire toolkit of vocational education, especially since modern industrial development got primarily interested in training specialists in the digital field, and subsequently led to continued shortages in many other zones (Terziev & Lyubcheva, 2022c; 2023).

References

Terziev, V. (2022a). Higher education system and labour market policies in Bulgaria in COVID-19 crisis and post-crisis periods, Internauka Publishing House, Kiev, 2022, 168 p., ISBN 978-611-01-2645-8.

Terziev, V. (2022b). COVID-19 pandemics and its impact on Bulgarian universities in the context of the new challenges to social system and labour market policies, Internauka Publishing House, Kiev, 2022, 138 p., ISBN 978-611-01-2647-2.

Terziev, V., & Lyubcheva, M. (2022c). Vocational education - professionalism, compliance, challenges. Proceedings of ADVED 2022- 8th International Conference on Advances in Education, Istanbul, Turkey10-12 October 2022, International Organization Center of Academic Research, Istanbul, Turkey, 2022, pp. 69-75, ISBN: 978-605-06286-8-5.

Terziev, V., & Lyubcheva, M. (2023). Vocational education - professionalism, compliance, challenges. IJAEDU- International E-Journal of Advances in Education, Vol. VIII, Issue 24, December 2022, International Organization Center of Academic Research, Istanbul, Turkey, 2023, pp. 225-230, (INT) e-ISSN: 2411-182. https://doi.org/10.18768/ijaedu.1198780.

Cedefop. (2018). Vocational education and training in Bulgaria: a brief overview. Luxembourg: Publications Office. (Print) ISBN 978-92-896-2659-0, (PDF) ISBN 978-92-896-2661-3. doi: 10.2801/728903.

A Theoretical Approach to Sustainability in Business

Lukas Vartiak, Jana Majerova

1. Introduction

Every business, regardless of its subject matter, strives to achieve success. Many businesses understand success as profit. Profit is the basic principle for which businesses are established, but looking at how profit is achieved is also necessary.

Since businesses today find themselves in a challenging competitive struggle, they seek ways to emerge victorious. The basis for victory is to reach customers, which can only be achieved by differentiating themselves from the competition. Differentiation does not consist only in offering a unique product. A business must be focused on customer needs and, at the same time, must look at its surroundings to be profitable. This is the only way to achieve sustainability in business.

A simplified guide for every business is its focus on achieving quality in products, its internal processes, and external relations.

This chapter summarizes the essential theoretical foundations for achieving sustainability in business by examining and assessing the concepts of critical success factors, business excellence, and corporate social responsibility.

2. Critical Success Factors

Success factors were introduced by D. R. Daniel in 1961. He was led to this by discussing the problem of insufficient information among business management on setting goals, formulating strategies, making decisions and measuring results concerning goals. Daniel (1961) states that the planning process in a business should be based on information focused on success factors. He defines them as "factors that determine success and at the same time represent key tasks that must be fulfilled for the business to succeed." D. R. Daniel's work was followed up by John F. Rockart, who introduced the concept of critical success factors in 1979. Rockart (1979) defines Critical Success Factors as "a way of helping to identify the information needs of the business management staff." Rockart himself (1981) describes Critical Success Factors in several ways:

- key areas of the business activities in which it is essential to achieve the desired results;
- key areas where things must work appropriately for a business to thrive;
- factors that are critical to the success of a business;
- key areas of activity that management should pay constant attention to;
- business managers should focus on a relatively small number of essential facts.

Bruno and Leidecker (1984) define Critical Success Factors as "those characteristics, conditions, or variables that, if properly maintained or managed, can significantly impact the success of a business in a given industry."

On the other hand, Hartley (2009) described in 1986 two directions that businesses follow in their quest for success: in addition to following different variants of business success factors, there were also recommendations from successful managers who, thanks to their accomplishments, can convince practically oriented business managers better than management theories.

Pinto and Slevin (1987) consider Critical Success Factors as "factors that, if properly addressed, substantially improve the chances of success for a business." According to a simplified definition by Leidecker and Bruno (1987), Critical Success Factors should be considered as "variables that can influence the success of a business in creating a position in a given industry." Recognizing and classifying these variables can help a business identify the characteristics and scope of resources that must be available to focus on primary objectives. Arce and Flynn (1997) state that it is possible to distinguish between internal and external critical success factors. Internal ones are related to actions taken within the business and are linked to problems within business management's reach.

In contrast, external Critical Success Factors are related to events outside the business and may not be controlled exclusively by business management. The oldest model of Critical Success Factors is Leavitt's diamond. It was proposed by Harold J. Leavitt in 1973. It is a concept used in the change management field. Critical Success Factors include structure, managerial roles, people, and technology (Management Mania, 2015).

According to Leavitt, this concept is about factors that interact and must be aligned. Leavitt's diamond is often called the components model for implementing change and has helped start the trend of critical success factor models (Management Mania, 2015).

2.1. McKinsey 7-S

According to Peters, Waterman and Phillips (1982), the McKinsey 7-S model is based on effective organizational change. "Effective organizational change is not just a matter of structure, although structure is important. It is not as simple as the interactions between strategy and structure, although strategy is also key." The principle of the 7-S is that effective organizational change is the relationship between structure, strategy, management system, knowledge/experience, management style, people and overarching goals.

The idea behind the 7-S is based on the assertion that the effectiveness of a business results from the interaction of several factors. Why pay attention to only one or two and ignore the others? The 7-S elements are defined as follows (Hittmár, 2006):

- structure – definition of the elements of the considered organizational system and the links between them;
- strategy – definition and arrangement of elements ensuring the set goals of the enterprise development and the appropriate trajectory of their achievement, located in space and time;
- management system – rational fulfilment of managerial functions, the essence of which are the procedure, methods and techniques for evaluating the knowledge, experience and abilities of the personnel;
- knowledge/experience – intellectual wealth of the human resources of the enterprise, which represents a successful prerequisite for fulfilling the set goals;
- management style – how managers manage human resources in the enterprise;
- personnel – people who fulfil their mission in the organizational structure and, at the same time, form the collective and the internal corporate culture;
- superior goals – basic orientation and values that the enterprise collective has adopted and strives to fulfil.

2.2. Chung's Critical Success Factors

According to Chung (1986), Critical Success Factors (CSF) identify a business as an open system in which inputs are transformed into outputs through the performance of tasks performed by people in the system.

The concept focuses managers' attention on those aspects of their work that are of fundamental importance to them. It uses the analogy of the Pareto rule, according to which about 80% of the consequences of their actions are the result of decisions made by only 20% of the factors that affect the business. The remaining 80% of the factors cause only 20% of the consequences. Therefore, it is necessary to take into account only those factors that have a significant impact when making decisions (Vodáček & Vodáčková, 2004). Chung's systemic view of the business helps to identify three main Critical Success Factors in its actions (Hittmár, 2006):

- Strategy – a business management tool that expresses and defines a set of business development goals in space and time and establishes an appropriate way to achieve them. The emphasis is placed mainly on change management.
- Operating system – a method of economical use of available enterprise resources, the transformation of which creates valuable results. The emphasis is placed mainly on the use of information systems.
- Human resources – personnel with the required qualifications and professional qualities and serve as the long-term operating potential of the business. The emphasis is placed on the continuous improvement of the qualification of human resources.

2.3. Eight recommendations for an exceptional business

Another breakthrough in recommendations for business success occurred when the well-known pair of authors Peters and Waterman moved the vision of a successful business to excellence in the form of Eight recommendations for an exceptional business. When defining an excellent business, the authors based their work on empirical research on successful businesses in the USA. The basis was that if a business cannot solve a certain problem, it must look at its success (Szabo & Jankelová, 2006). Peters and Waterman used their practical experience from the consulting business McKinsey, thanks to which they selected 62 from a large set of businesses that were considered successful in the long term. The analysis was conducted based on six characteristics chosen of success: growth in assets, growth in common shares, increase in average market value and receivables, average return on total capital, average return on share, average return on sales (Vodáček & Dvořák, 1990). The authors summarized the form of an exceptional business in eight recommendations (Peters & Waterman, 2001):

- Motivation to act, striving to make an impression – there must be a free flow of information and open communication in the business because this makes the business more flexible and able to act faster and make the necessary changes. Management needs to get out of the office and communicate with people in the business, thus motivating small groups or individuals to solve problems quickly.
- Closer to the customer – it is necessary to acquire new customers, but it is necessary not to forget about existing customers. An exceptional business is focused on the customer, mainly by providing quality, service and reliability. High quality and reliability of products make the customer satisfied; because of the perfect service, the customer will return.
- Autonomy and entrepreneurship – a flexible business that supports the creative process will be successful in the long term. An exceptional business must support internal competition and be able to tolerate failure.
- Productivity through people – if employees are treated with dignity and respect, the primary source of productivity growth is created.
- Promoting the practical side, focusing on values – an exceptional business strives to have values formed within it. The correct values and their clear expression will help define the business. The values of the business need to be determined in comparison with the vision of today's modern businesses.
- Loyalty to its field – diversification is good, but a business that branches close to its primary area will be more successful.
- Simple form, organizationally effective number of employees – an appropriate business size can ensure complexity. Still, it is necessary to make the information understandable for dozens, hundreds or even thousands of people working at all levels of the organizational structure.

- Simultaneous loose-tight characteristics are the coexistence of centralized management of the business and individual autonomy. A loose-tight business can strictly control its operations while supporting innovations originating from the ranks of employees.

3. Business Excellence

In theory and practice, one can encounter different views on defining the concept of Business Excellence, which have evolved over the years. The idea of business excellence began to take shape in the late 1970s in the USA when Tom J. Peters and Robert H. Waterman began to study successful American businesses that achieved success thanks to exceptional practices. The concept of Business Excellence itself originated in the early 1980s. The first definition can be considered the description of Corporate Excellence according to Peters and Waterman (1982): "Corporate Excellence is the result of the exceptional efforts of ordinary employees in exceptional situations, which result in sustainable financial performance of the business and above-average employee performance."

Just as the USA lagged behind Japan in Business Excellence, Europe lagged behind the USA. Business Excellence was introduced in Europe in 1992 when the European Foundation for Quality Management (EFQM) introduced the EFQM Excellence Model based on TQM principles (EFQM, 1992).

Also, in the 1990s, Robert Heller began to study exceptional European businesses, following the example of Peters and Waterman. The result of his research was the identification of ten interconnected stages of business recovery leading to the achievement of a state of Business Excellence (Heller, 1997):

- Delegating leadership without losing control or direction,
- Managing radical change throughout the entire business system,
- Reshaping the corporate culture for long-term success,
- Shaping authority,
- Using new approaches to central management,
- Maintaining competitive advantage,
- Achieving continuous renewal,
- Managing motivators,
- Applying teamwork,
- Improving quality in all activities of the business.

"Business Excellence represents the systematic use of quality management principles and tools in business management." The goal is to improve the performance of processes based on customer satisfaction and value for stakeholders such as owners, management, suppliers, and government agencies (Ritchie & Dale, 2000).

"Business Excellence seeks to improve performance in every aspect of the business to increase its overall performance." Specific tools and techniques can be implemented to improve almost any existing process in the business, whether its output is a product or a service (Saunders & Mann, 2007).

According to Ionica and Baleanu (2010), business excellence means achieving exceptional results in strategic business practices and in achieving the performance required by stakeholders, as assessed based on specific Business Excellence models supporting a challenging path to excellence.

Mann (2011) describes the concept of Business Excellence as "a dynamic system for managing a business aimed at increasing competitiveness and productivity." Using it, businesses can identify strengths and opportunities and, based on this, adapt the management system, thereby helping to create an environment for sustainable improvement.

According to the EFQM definition, Business Excellence represents "excellent practices in business management and achieving results, based on a set of eight core principles," which are (EFQM, 2013):

- creating added value for customers,
- sustainable development,
- developing business capabilities,
- combining creativity and innovation,
- leading with vision, inspiration and integrity,
- management agility,
- success through people and their talent,
- sustaining excellent results.

An agency of the Ministry of Trade and Industry in Singapore which aims to help Singaporean businesses grow, Business Excellence is defined as "adopting a holistic approach to strengthening management systems and processes in an enterprise for growth and improved productivity." The Business Excellence concept helps businesses achieve excellence by assessing and improving their performance (SPRING Singapore, 2014).

4. Corporate Social Responsibility

The concept of Corporate Social Responsibility (CSR) emerged gradually, and its formation is linked to the change in orientation of mainly Anglo-American businesses. Already in the 1920s, large American businesses began to take measures to support their employees (establishing pension funds, life insurance, reducing working hours and increasing wages) and support the local community (building schools, libraries, hospitals and contributing to charity). Businesses with significant problems mostly showed such behavior and thus created the public opinion they desired (Porvazník et al., 2008). The first definition of CSR began in the 1950s when Bowen (1953) defined CSR as "the commitment of business people to pursue decisions or carry out activities that are desirable in terms of the goals and values of our society." His ideas were followed by Davis and Blomstrom (1966), who defined CSR as "the commitment of individuals to consider the impact of their decisions and actions on the entire social system." In the 1960s and 1970s, the prevailing view was that those with more power also had more responsibility, gradually shifting the emphasis from the manager's personality to the entire enterprise. Society thus automatically began to expect that influential enterprises would participate in solving social problems, regardless of whether they caused them or not. The view that a business should not only focus on its own goals but should voluntarily accept responsibility for the state of society and contribute to its improvement is still prevalent today (Porvazník et al., 2008).

The concept of CSR has brought a change in the thinking of businesses. They have understood that they depend on a healthy and well-functioning society if they want to be successful. Therefore, they try to create shared value, i.e. "by incorporating social issues into their main business strategies, they create benefits for society while strengthening their long-term competitiveness" (Bockstette & Stamp, 2012).

Conclusion

In conclusion, achieving sustainability and long-term success in business requires a multi-faceted approach that integrates Critical Success Factors, Business Excellence, and corporate social responsibility. By focusing on the essential components that drive success, such as strategy, organizational structure, innovation, and human resources, businesses can create resilient frameworks for growth and adaptability. The principles of Business Excellence highlight the need for continuous improvement, stakeholder value creation, and customer satisfaction. Simultaneously, embracing corporate social responsibility fosters a harmonious relationship between businesses and society, ensuring ethical practices and shared value creation. The evolving landscape of competitive markets demands that businesses not only strive for profit but also adapt to external challenges and contribute positively to their communities. Sustainable business practices rooted in quality, innovation, and social responsibility ultimately form the foundation for enduring success and resilience in a dynamic global economy.

Acknowledgement

The chapter was undertaken as a part of the research project VEGA 1/0551/24.

References

Arce, E. & Flynn, D. (1997). A Case Tool to Support Critical Success Factors Analysis in IT Planning and Requirements Determination. *Information and Software Technology*, 39(5), 311-321.

Bockstette, V. & Stamp, M. (2012). *Vytváření sdílené hodnoty: Průvodce novou firemní (r)evolucí.* Sedlčany: Tiskárna MACÍK.

Bowen, H. R. (1953). *Social Responsibilities of the Businessman*. New York: Harper and Row.

Bruno, A. & Leidecker, J. (1984). Identifying and Using Critical Success Factors. *Long Range Planning*, 17(1), 23-32.

Chung, K. H. (1986). *Management: critical success factors*. Boston: Allyn and Bacon.

Daniel, D. R. (1961). Management Information Crisis. *Harvard Business Review*, 39(5), 111-116.

Davis, K. & Blomstrom, R. L. (1966). *Business and Its Environment*. Columbus, OH: McGraw-Hill.

EFQM. (1992). *EFQM Excellence Model*. Bruxelles: EFQM.

EFQM. (2013). *An Overview of the EFQM Excellence Model*. Brussels: EFQM.

Hartley, R. F. (2009). *Marketing mistakes and successes*. Hoboken: John Wiley & Sons. ISBN 978-

Heller, R. (1997). *In Search of European Excellence: The 10 Key Strategies of Europe's Top Companies*. London: Harper & Collins.

Hittmár, Š. (2006). *Manažment*. Žilina: EDIS.

Ionica, A. & Baleanu, V. (2010). TQM and Business Excellence. *Annals of the University of Petroșani, Economics*, 10(4), 125-134.

Management Mania. (2015). *Leavittův diamant* [online]. Avaliable at: https://managementmania.com/cs/leavittuv-diamant

Mann, R. (2011). *Impact of Business Excellence/Quality Awards on Enterprises.* Tokyo: Asian Productivity Organization.

Peters, T. J. & Waterman, R. H. (1982). *In Search of Excellence: Lessons from America's Best-Run Companies.* New York: Harper & Row.

Peters, T. J. & Waterman, R. H. (2001). *Hledání dokonalosti.* Praha: Pragma.

Pinto, J. K. & Slevin, D. P. (1987). Critical Success Factors in Effective Project implementation. In Cleland, D. I. & William, R. K. (1997). *Project Management Handbook.* West Essex: John Wiley & Sons.

Porvazník, J. et al. (2008). *Spoločenská zodpovednosť organizácií – Corporate Social Responsibility.* Bratislava: Ekonóm.

Ritchie, L. & Dale, B. G. (2000). Self-assessment using the business excellence model: A study of practice and process. *International Journal of Production Economics*, 66(3), 241-254.

Rockart, J. F. (1979). Chief Executives Define Their Own Data Needs. *Harvard Business Review*, 81-92.

Rockart, J. F. & Bullen, C. V. (1981). *Primer on Critical Success Factors.* Cambridge, MA: Center for Information Systems Research, Massachusetts Institute of Technology.

Saunders, M. & Mann, R. (2007). *Business Excellence Tools: The tools used by companies at different stages of Business Excellence maturity.* Palmerston North: Centre for Organisational Excellence Research.

SPRING Singapore. (2014). *Business Excellence Framework.* Singapore: SPRING Singapore.

Szabo, Ľ. & Jankelová, N. (2006). *Faktory úspešnosti agrárnych podnikov v Slovenskej republike.* Bratislava: Ekonóm.

Vodáček, L. & Dvořák, V. (1990). *Management v USA.* Praha: Institut řízení.

Vodáček, L. & Vodáčková, O. (2004). *Malé a střední podniky: konkurence a aliance v Evropské unii.* Praha: Management press.

Comparison of Digital Skills, Interactive Methods and Digital Literacy between Full-Time and Part Time Students: Impact on the Quality of Education and Professional Development

Dijana Vuković, Tanja Grmuša, Neven Marđetko

1. Introduction

The changes in education that we have been witnessing for several years have significantly accelerated after the COVID-19 pandemic and the urgent relocation of teaching to a virtual environment. This is one of the greatest challenges and experiments of modern education, which has redefined the role of teachers and students, and the direct consequence of which is accelerated digitalization, greater use of digital tools (Marchisio et al., 2023) and the shifting of the physical and institutional boundaries of universities with the aim of further integration into society (Bygstad et al., 2022: 1). In addition to quality, the issue of online teaching also requires concern for the well-being of students (Grmuša, 2024) and ensuring conditions of equality in the digital environment, which is also the path to sustainable education (Gunder & Gay, 2023). However, implementing such interventions must be by higher education standards and the fundamental principles of the quality assurance system (Mohamed Hashim et al. 2022: 3175, 3176). This has shown the need for teachers to gain additional knowledge and strengthen their digital skills, which includes: 1) understanding the concept of online learning and 2) strengthening teachers' equipment to better adapt to the online environment (Barbour & Hodges, 2023: 240), which implies continuous reliance on innovation. The implementation of digital tools in teaching and the achievement of set learning outcomes are often challenged by the insufficient financial framework of HEIs, so teachers cope by looking for free alternative solutions such as LMS (Munundanyi & Woodley, 2021: 98).

Driven by the extraordinary threat of the Covid-19 pandemic, the EU is striving to ensure better digital preparedness of European citizens, in terms of resilience, accessibility, high quality, and inclusiveness" (https://www.consilium.

europa.eu/hr/press/press-releases/2023/11/23/digital-skills-and-competences-and-successful-digital-education-and-training-fit-for-the-digital-era/, 27. 12. 2024). The Digital Decade Plan by 2030 aims to ensure that 80% of the population has basic digital skills. In this context, the following documents have been prepared to ensure digital preparedness, but also to strengthen digital competencies: Digital Education Action Plan 2021-2027, The European Pillar of Social Rights, European Skills Agenda, 2030 Digital Compass (Fleaca et. al. 2022: 1236). Accordingly, the national legislation was adjusted by adopting the Digital Croatia Strategy for the period until 2032 (https://narodne-novine.nn.hr/clanci/sluzbeni/2023_01_2_17.html 28122024, 27. 12. 2024), which is based on four strategic goals:„ the digital transition of the economy, digitalization of public administration, development of broadband electronic communication networks, and strengthening digital competences and digital jobs." Changes in the modern business environment prompted by the development of new technologies require constant verification and upgrading of knowledge to ensure competitiveness, therefore the need for employees who have developed digital skills and who are digitally competent is growing.

2. Digital transformation of education

The process of digital transformation is dominantly focused on the inclusion of new technologies in the production process to influence the final product and its outcome, and this includes continuous interaction between all members of the organization and the existing business model. Digital transformation in the educational context means the application of advanced methods to fulfill the educational mission (Alenezi, 2021: 2) to the changing needs of users or students. Just as in other areas of activity, if HEIs want to remain relevant in the market they must listen to the needs of users, and this often means understanding the new set of skills needed for the new age and a holistic approach to education. Explaining the need for digital transformation in higher education, Alenezi states that in reformed programs we often advocate critical thinking, but we do not ensure the contextualization of this term, that is, its actual application in curricula (2021: 5). The dimensions of digital transformation such as digital educational tools, curricula, digital literacy, technical and instructional framework, institutional conditions should also be taken into account (Alenezi, 2021: 6). Digital transformation in education does not only refer to technical and technological aspects but also includes cultural differences, but also mental barriers in the context of understanding the gap and resistance between different generations (Bucăța et al. 2022). Gkrimpizi et al. remind us that this topic causes divided opinions in the public – and while some question the way HEIs work by relying on technology and improving the teaching process, others see the excessive use of technology as dubious, morally unfounded, and even harmful (Selwyn, 2022 according to Gkrimpizi et. al., 2024: 2). The digital transformation of HEIs does not only refer to the issue of the alignment of internal processes, but also to those behind them that reflect organizational capabilities such as agility and flexibility (Parker, 2020 according to Gkrimpizi et. al., 2024: 2), but also question the transformative power of leadership (Burić et al., 2021). Castro Benavides et al. (2022) state that the process of digital transformation of education in the literature most often includes the following elements: infrastructure, employees (teaching and non-teaching staff), management, processes (teaching and non-teaching), curricula, information and marketing (Castro Benavides et al. 2020 according to Castro Benavides et al., 2022: 3). The digital transformation of education encompasses a multidisciplinary and multilevel approach that includes the following dimensions: organizational, technological and social perspectives. Relying on a holistic approach in the implementation of the digital transformation of education is becoming imperative, and this is precisely what is missing in the strategic plans of most HEIs (Castro Benavides, 2020; Kučina Softić et al. 2022).

Leal Filho et al. (2023) state that digital transformation is now seen as an opportunity for sustainable development in some HEIs after the devastating effects of the pandemic. The results of the analysis carried out by Fernández et al. (2023) showed that most of the analyzed universities when it comes to initiatives for digital transformation, are focused on ensuring quality and competitive education. Furthermore, when it comes to the use of technology to achieve this goal, they rely on advanced analytics, the cloud, and various forms of artificial intelligence (Gunder et al., 2023; McDermott et al. 2023), which shows greater potential for shaping and changing the student experience. The perception of digital transformation at HEIs and expectations include: a) revenue growth and b) productivity growth, c) generating value through d) innovative practices and strengthening brand strength and reputation (Matt et al., 2015; Shaughnessy, 2018 according to Mohamed Hashim, 2022: 3180). This allows universities to manage a complex strategy that includes a digital component. However, the results still show that most universities are only at the beginning of digital maturity since only one in four universities has a digital strategy (Fernández et al., 2023: 12352). It is also necessary to highlight the barriers to the successful implementation of digital transformation in HEIs, and they can be divided into, environmental, strategic, organizational, technological, human, and cultural" (2023: 12352). Environmental barriers include budget constraints and the regulatory framework, while strategic barriers include the lack of strategic planning, a holistic approach, an action plan, and institutional policies. Organizational barriers relate to the lack of organizational agility, a narrow view of investments, and a lack of coordination between departments. At the same time, technological barriers include the lack of IT infrastructure, the issue of integrating digital technology into the education system, security and privacy risks, data fragmentation, and third-party systems. Furthermore, human barriers (issues of skills and human resources) include the lack of digital literacy, the lack of leaders to implement changes, the lack of time due to overloaded teaching staff, and inadequate support from the IT department. Finally, cultural barriers manifest themselves through resistance to change, fear of risk, attitudes, and beliefs, and conservative/bureaucratic culture (Gkrimpizi et al. 2023).

3. Review of previous research

The use of digital tools in teaching, but also learning and teaching, can make the content being taught more interesting. At the same time, teachers who use digital tools can increase their popularity and the popularity of the subject (Dancsa et al., 2023: 290). The use of digital tools helps to ensure a student-centered approach, and applications such as Zoom and MS Teams have proven to be extremely effective in this context, despite the varying responses of institutions (Collins & Porras, 1996). The use of digital tools should also be viewed in the context of strengthening teacher competencies and fulfilling the given learning outcomes of the course. In the use of digital tools in education, those based on the principles of gamification have recently attracted particular attention. They are,, educational materials that combine game elements to achieve a didactic effect" (Dancsa et al. 2023: 91).

Such educational materials can be highly motivating since they support the growth and progress of the individual (as in video games), and also contribute to the strengthening of multiskills. Gamification in education, for example, of entrepreneurs, is positively associated with students' entrepreneurial intentions and decisions to pursue this profession (De Melo et al., 2023). It is a new and innovative way of teaching that requires the active participation of students, and encourages their engagement (Ranchhod et al. 2014 according to Isabelle, 2020), satisfaction with the course (He et al., 2023), stimulates curiosity (Wong Mee Mee et al. 2020), and helps them acquire basic entrepreneurial skills (Grivokostopolou et al., 2019). Also, relying on the principle of gamification strengthens teachers' motivation to use a new approach to learning and teaching (Benteá and Vlad, 2021: 43), but also contributes to the development of digital skills and digital literacy in general among students. Babić warns that digital skills were primarily observed through technical and technological knowledge, but today they encompass a wider scope, „ from basic to operational skills" (2021: 61). Speaking about digital competence and digital skills, the author warns about the conceptual overlap with different dimensions of digital literacy: IT, information and communication and media literacy (Ala-Mutka, 2011: 31 according to Babić, 2021: 62). Pavić & Černja Rajter have a similar opinion, warning that the digital gap has narrowed in the meantime about age, socio-demographic status, and education, but that differences in the digital literacy of users are still present (2024: 157). They add that the concepts of skills and competencies have different meanings: skills require less„ specialized knowledge to achieve goals", while competencies are a broader concept that includes a combination of knowledge, attitudes, and skills (Rychen I Tiana, 2004 according to Halász I Michel, 2011: 2011 according to Pavić & Černja Rajter, 2024: 161). Furthermore, they believe that the issue of digital divides and the digital divide has generally moved away from the perception of the technical aspects of using technology, and today predominantly relates to the level of digital literacy of users (2024: 165).

4. Research results

The research results represent key findings obtained from the analysis of data collected to test the hypotheses set. The main objective of this research was to examine the connection between education, entrepreneurship and digital technologies, with a special focus on determining the impact of educational programs and digital tools on the development of entrepreneurial competencies and business outcomes. The research tested hypotheses related to:

- the impact of formal education on the development of digital skills of entrepreneurs.
- the role of digital technologies in improving the curriculum of entrepreneurial education.
- the connection between the use of digital platforms for lifelong learning and the adaptability of entrepreneurs to changes in the market.

Data analysis was conducted by combining quantitative and qualitative methods to provide a comprehensive insight into the researched relationships. Statistical tools were used to test hypotheses, while additional insights were obtained by analyzing the participants' open-ended responses. The results were structured to correspond to the hypotheses, allowing for their confirmation or rejection, and providing insight into broader implications for theory and practice. The research results are presented in detail below, including key findings, statistical indicators, and data interpretation, to clearly understand the impact of education and digital technologies on entrepreneurial activities.

Hypothesis H1: Full-time students have a higher level of developed digital skills in the context of managing technical problems and security in the online environment compared to part-time students.

Hypothesis H2: Part-time students recognize the value of interactive methods in education to a greater extent for acquiring new skills compared to full-time students.

Hypothesis H3: Digital literacy significantly contributes to the quality of education, but its perception and impact on professional development differ between full-time and part-time students.

The sample was constructed to reflect the proportional representation of full-time and part-time students at universities and polytechnics. According to available data, universities have a higher number of full-time students compared to part-time students, while at business polytechnics the share of part-time students is somewhat higher, thus adjusting the distribution to the specificities of these educational institutions. The sample structure of 1,280 students was distributed between university studies and business polytechnic studies. When it comes to university studies, 768 respondents responded to the survey questionnaire, of which 512 were full-time students or 40%, while 256 respondents made up a sample of 20% and had the status of part-time students. At Business Polytechnics, 512 students completed the survey, of which 320 were full-time students, or 30%, and 192 were part-time students or 15%. Among the respondents, students of both sexes are equally represented, with a slight predominance of female participants. This is in line with general trends in higher education, where women are often more numerous, especially in certain disciplines such as social sciences and humanities. Female respondents made up 55% of the sample or 704 students, while male respondents made up 45% of the sample or 576 students. The female majority in the sample and a significant share of younger students reflect the general characteristics of the student population, while the presence of older students and part-time students contributes to diversity and allows for a more detailed analysis of trends in higher education. Such a sample provides a solid basis for concluding the educational and entrepreneurial characteristics of the student population in the Republic of Croatia.

Table 1. Development of digital skills considering the status of a student.

	N=832	% Regular	N=448	% part-time	p
Adoption and development of digital skills					
Adopting digital skills increases competitiveness in the labor market.	832	100	448	100	-
Developed digital skills enable faster adaptation to technological changes and new tools.	784	94.23	408	91.07	0.812
The adoption of digital skills encourages innovation and creativity in business.	766	92.07	406	90.62	0.706
Developed digital skills increase productivity and efficiency in everyday work.	791	95,07	416	92.85	0.470
Digital skills enable greater collaboration on a global scale and access to new markets.	297	35.70	160	35.71	1.000

Table 1. *Continued*

	N=832	% Regular	N=448	% part-time	p
Developed digital skills contribute to better time management and balance between professional and personal life.	782	93.99	412	91.96	0.512
Development of digital literacy					
Having digital literacy makes it easier to understand and use digital tools and platforms.	816	98.07	439	97.99	0.794
Digital literacy enables better navigation in the online environment and management of personal data.	624	75.00	237	53.12	0.001
Developed digital literacy increases the ability to solve technical problems on the Internet and in digital tools.	339	40.74	125	27.90	0.002
Enhanced digital literacy contributes to greater security and privacy protection on the Internet.	691	80.16	340	75.89	0.245
Digital literacy enables better analysis and use of information available on the Internet for decision-making.	250	30.05	160	35.71	0.383
Developed digital literacy helps in more effective use of digital tools for education and professional development.	399	47.96	356	45.52	<0.001
Increased interactivity and engagement by learning new skills					
Increased interactivity in learning helps to acquire new skills faster.	507	60.94	336	75.00	0.021
Using digital tools increases engagement and motivation to learn new skills.	226	27.16	255	56.62	0.019
Interactive education methods enable deeper understanding and better application of new skills.	316	37.98	153	34.15	0.827
Digital tools enable greater personalization in the process of acquiring new skills, which increases student engagement.	317	38.10	394	87.94	<0.001
Increased interactivity in learning enables easier adaptation to market changes and new business challenges.	616	74.0488	395	88.17	0.008

Table 1. *Continued*

	N=832	% Regular	N=448	% part-time	p
Introducing gamification into education increases engagement and facilitates the acquisition of new entrepreneurial skills.	266	31.97	319	71.20	<0.001
Improving the quality of education					
Digital tools significantly improve the quality of education by providing students with access to up-to-date and relevant information.	782	93.99	439	98.00	0.047
The increased use of digital tools contributes to greater flexibility in learning and better adaptation of educational content to student needs.	699	84.01	417	93.08	0.022
The use of digital technologies allows for greater access to educational resources, thereby improving the overall quality of education.	458	55.05	220	49.11	0.334
The digitalization of education improves opportunities for interactive learning, which increases the quality of the educational experience.	594	71.40	342	76.34	0.520
The use of digital tools allows teachers and professors to better monitor student progress, thereby improving the quality of the educational process.	474	56.97	331	73.88	0.011
Improving the quality of education with digital technologies allows students to be better prepared for the labor market through the development of practical skills.	349	41.45	340	75.89	0.835
Global connectivity and collaboration					
Digital technologies allow students and professors to have easier access to global educational resources, thereby improving international cooperation.	71	8.53	38	8.53	1.000
Global connectivity through digital platforms allows students and academic experts to exchange knowledge and experiences from different parts of the world.	624	75.00	353	78,89	0.001

Table 1. *Continued*

	N=832	% Regular	N=448	% part-time	p
Digital collaboration between institutions enables the creation of joint educational programs and projects that enable the spread of global knowledge.	374	44.95	215	47.99	0.730
The use of digital technologies facilitates collaboration between students of different nationalities and cultures, thereby contributing to global educational integration.	624	75.00	359	80.13	0.936
Digital connectivity enables students to participate in global projects and research, which increases international collaboration and networking.	540	64.90	306	68.30	0.771
Global connectivity through digital tools increases opportunities for employment and career development through access to international networks and opportunities.	540	64.90	287	64.90	1.000
Greater social inclusion					
Digital technologies enable easier access to education for people with disabilities or special needs.	432	51.92	256	57.14	0.364
The application of digital tools in education reduces geographical and social barriers, enabling more equal access to learning.	565	67.90	371	82.81	0.008
Digital platforms encourage the participation of socially disadvantaged groups in educational processes, providing them with equal development opportunities.	698	83.89	416	92.86	0.022
The use of digital technologies in education encourages the exchange of experiences among students from different cultural and social backgrounds.	707	84.98	409	91.29	0.213
Online education programs enable greater inclusion of older people or working individuals who want to further their education.	499	60	366	75	0.018

Table 1. *Continued*

	N=832	% Regular	N=448	% part-time	p
Digital tools enable marginalized groups to participate equally in educational and professional opportunities.	599	75.00	358	79.91	0.395
Increasing responsibility and independence					
The use of digital tools in education encourages students to take responsibility for their own learning.	707	84.97	408	91.07	0.213
Independent management of digital resources contributes to the development of students' organizational skills.	594	71.40	342	76.34	0.520
Digital technologies allow students to independently explore and expand their knowledge outside the framework of traditional teaching methods.	474	56.97	328	73.21	0.011
Regular use of digital platforms to track learning progress encourages greater responsibility in students.	624	75.00	242	54.02	0.001
Digital self-learning tools help students become more independent in solving problems and making decisions.	649	78.00	265	59.15	0.002
Using digital learning platforms requires students to regularly monitor their own progress and adjust their learning strategies.	791	95,07	416	92.85	0.047

Source: author's work.

The results of this study, based on a sample of 832 full-time and 448 part-time participants, provide an in-depth insight into the perception and impact of digital skills, literacy, and interactivity in the process of education and professional development. The data analysis highlights several key points about the development of digital competencies, their impact on the labor market, and adaptation to technological changes. The results show almost unanimous agreement among participants that the acquisition of digital skills increases competitiveness in the labor market (100%). This statement reflects the universal importance of digital competencies in modern business. Part-time and full-time students also agree that developed digital skills enable faster adaptation to technological changes (94.23% and 91.07%), with slight differences between groups that are not statistically significant ($p=0.812$). Furthermore, the majority of participants recognize the connection between digital skills and innovation (92.07% full-time; 90.62% part-time), although the difference between groups is again not significant ($p=0.706$). An interesting finding is the perception of digital skills in the context of global collaboration, where only 35.7% of full-time and 35.71% of part-time students recognized this advantage. This result opens up space for further improvement of awareness of the global opportunities offered by digitalization. Possession of digital literacy was assessed as a key factor for understanding and using digital tools (98.07% full-time; 97.99% part-time). This result confirms that digital literacy plays a fundamental role in modern education.

Digital technologies play a significant role in reducing social and geographical barriers. The use of digital tools enables more equal access to education, which is supported by 67.9% of full-time and 82.81% of part-time students ($p=0.008$). In addition, 83.89% of full-time and 92.86% of part-time respondents agree that digital platforms encourage the participation of socially disadvantaged groups in educational processes ($p=0.022$). These results indicate the potential of digital technologies for improving social inclusion, with the need to further develop tools for inclusive education. One of the most important contributions of digital technologies is to encourage student responsibility and independence. Regular use of digital platforms to monitor progress was recognized as a key factor by 75% of full-time and 54.02% of part-time participants ($p=0.001$). Furthermore, 78% of full-time and 59.15% of part-time students believe that digital tools help develop independence in learning ($p=0.002$). These results emphasize the need for additional education and support in the use of digital technologies to increase their effectiveness with outstanding students.

Increased interactivity and engagement in acquiring new skills ranked first with the highest average ($M = 18.02$), indicating its key role in the educational process, especially in fostering motivation and effective knowledge acquisition. Adoption and development of digital skills ranked second ($M = 17.73$), confirming that these skills have high value for the labor market and adaptation to technological changes. The development of digital literacy stands out as the third most important aspect ($M = 15.84$), indicating the

Table 2. Ranking of categories of skills and competence acquisition in education according to the significance of each element in contributing to the quality of the educational process and student development.

	M (SD)	Rank
Adoption and development of digital skills	17.73 (3.27)	2
Development of digital literacy	15.84 (4.16)	3
Increased interactivity and engagement when learning new skills	18.02 (4.79)	1
Improving the quality of education	9.42 (2.66)	5
Global connectivity and collaboration	6.94 (2.05)	7
Greater social inclusion	14.13 (4.49)	4
Increased responsibility and independence	8.46 (2.78)	6

Source: author's work.

need to strengthen competencies for using digital tools and protecting privacy online. Greater social inclusion ranked fourth with an average of 14.13, emphasizing the importance of digital tools in enabling access to education for marginalized groups. Improving the quality of education ranked lower ($M = 9.42$), despite the importance of digital technologies for flexibility and adaptation of educational content to students' needs. Increasing responsibility and autonomy ranked sixth ($M = 8.46$), indicating room for further development of this aspect in education. Global connection and cooperation received the lowest rank ($M = 6.94$), which suggests the need for greater promotion of international cooperation and networking in the educational process.

The research results presented in Table 3. reveal how full-time and part-time students perceive the importance of different aspects of acquiring skills and competencies in education. Key differences and similarities between these two groups were analyzed according to their contribution to the quality of the educational process and student development. The first category, the acquisition and development of digital skills, showed a significant difference between full-time and part-time students. Part-time students ($M = 18.45$, $SD = 3.06$) value this aspect significantly more than full-time students ($M = 15.65$, $SD = 3.01$), which was confirmed by a statistically significant result ($p < 0.001$). This can be attributed to the fact that part-time students are often employed or exposed to professional environments in which digital competence is essential for success. On the other hand, digital literacy development had a higher average score among full-time students ($M = 18.83$, $SD = 3.13$)

Table 3. Method of acquiring skills and competencies in education according to the significance of each element in contributing to the quality of education and the process in student development, considering the status of study.

	Regular M (SD)	Part-time M (SD)	p*
Adoption and development of digital skills	15.65 (3.01)	18.45 (3.06)	<0.001
Development of digital literacy	18.83 (3.13)	16.47 (4.67)	0.293
Increased interactivity and engagement when learning new skills	17.00 (2.58)	18.09 (4.91)	0.665
Improving the quality of education	9.22 (2.31)	9.49 (2.79)	0.617
Global connectivity and collaboration	6.76 (.96)	7.00 (2.34)	0.841
Greater social inclusion	12.00 (1.63)	16.00 (5.42)	0.084
Increased responsibility and independence	8.46 (2.95)	8.46 (2.76)	0.995

Source: author's work.

compared to part-time students ($M = 16.47$, $SD = 4.67$), but the difference was not statistically significant ($p = 0.293$). This suggests that full-time students often use digital tools in an educational context, while part-time students may already have a basic level of digital literacy acquired outside the education system. Regarding increased interactivity and engagement in acquiring new skills, both groups of students showed similar average scores (full-time: $M = 17.00$, $SD = 2.58$; part-time: $M = 18.09$, $SD = 4.91$), with the difference not being statistically significant ($p = 0.665$).

5. Conclusion

The research results confirm the key role of digital technologies in improving education but also highlight differences in perceptions and experiences between full-time and part-time students. Although most participants recognize the benefits of digital tools in terms of interactivity, quality of education, and social inclusion, some areas require additional attention, such as global connectivity and increased accountability. Further efforts should be focused on adapting digital technologies to the different needs of students, thereby ensuring a more inclusive and efficient education system.

References

Alenezi, M. (2021). Deep Dive into Digital Transformation in Higher Education Institutions. *Education Sciences*, 11(12), 770. https://doi.org/10.3390/educsci11120770

Babić, A. (2021). Digitalne vještine kao perspektiva razvoja gospodarstva i važan čimbenik digitalne transformacije. *Ekonomski pregled*, 72 (1): pp. 59-87, https://doi.org/10.32910/ep.72.1.3

Banek Zorica, M. (2022). DIGITOOLS PROJECT - USERS PERSPECTIVE ON THE CURRENT STATE OF DIGITAL EDUCATION // *Towards Smart and Inclusive Learning Ecosystem* / Duart, Joseph M ; Trepule, Elena (ur.). Talin: Digital Learning Europe (EDEN), 2022. pp. 31-38.

Barbour, M., & Hodges, C. (2023). Digital Teacher Education for a Better Future: Recommendations for Teacher Preparation for an Online Environment 2023 Ubiquity Proceedings, 3(1): pp. 240-248. DOI: https://doi.org/10.5334/uproc.92

Bucăța, G., Popescu, F. V., Tileaga, C. (2022). Digital Transformation of Higher Education System, International conference *KNOWLEDGE-BASED ORGANIZATION* 28(1): pp. 158-168, https://doi.org/10.2478/kbo-2022-0025

Brusić, T., Babić, S., Orehovački, T. (2017). Važnost razvoja informatičke pismenosti budućih poduzetnika za primjenu cloud usluga u poslovanju kao podloge za bolju konkurentnost na tržištu rada. *Obrazovanje za poduzetništvo - E4E : znanstveno stručni časopis o obrazovanju za poduzetništvo*. 7 (2): pp. 67-81.

Burić, I., Parmać Kovačić, M., Huić, A. (2021). Transformacijsko vodstvo i kvaliteta poučavanja tijekom pandemije COVID-19: moderirana medijacijska analiza. *Društvena istraživanja: časopis za opća društvena pitanja*, 30 (2): pp. 181-202.

Bygstad, B., Øvrelid, E., Ludvigsen, S., Dæhlen, M. (2022). From dual digitalization to digital learning space: Exploring the digital transformation of higher education, *Computers & Education*, Volume 182, 104463, https://doi.org/10.1016/j.compedu.2022.104463

Castro Benavides, L.M., Tamayo Arias, J.A., Burgos, D. and Martens, A. (2022). Measuring digital transformation in higher education institutions – content validity instrument, *Applied Computing and Informatics*, Vol. ahead-of-print No. ahead-of-print. https://doi.org/10.1108/ACI-03-2022-0069

Castro Benavides, L. M. Tamayo Arias, J. A., Arango Serna, M. D., Branch Bedoya, J. W., & Burgos, D. (2020). Digital Transformation in Higher Education Institutions: A Systematic Literature Review. *Sensors*, 20(11), 3291. https://doi.org/10.3390/s20113291

Collins, J. C. & Porras, J. I. (1996). Building your company's vision. *Harvard Business Review*, 74(5): 65.

Dancsa, Daniel, Štempeľová, Iveta, Takáč Ondrej & Annuš, Norbert (2023). Digital tools in education. *International Journal of Advanced Natural Sciences and Engineering Researches* 7 (4): pp. 289-294.

Elidjen, Hidayat, D. Abdurachman, E. (2022). The roles of gamification, knowledge creation, and entrepreneurial orientation towards firm performance, *International Journal of Innovation Studies*, 6(4): pp. 229-237, https://doi.org/10.1016/j.ijis.2022.07.002

Fernández A, Gómez B, Binjaku K, Meçe EK. (2023). Digital transformation initiatives in higher education institutions: A multivocal literature review. *Educ Inf Technol (Dordr).* Mar 9:1-32. https://doi.org/10.1007/s10639-022-11544-0

Gkrimpizi, T., Peristeras, V., & Magnisalis, I. (2024). Defining the Meaning and Scope of Digital Transformation in Higher Education Institutions. *Administrative Sciences*, 14(3), 48. https://doi.org/10.3390/admsci14030048

Gkrimpizi, T., Peristeras, V., & Magnisalis, I. (2023). Classification of Barriers to Digital Transformation in Higher Education Institutions: Systematic Literature *Review. Education Sciences*, 13(7), 746. https://doi.org/10.3390/educsci13070746

Golenko, D., Martinović, I., Badurina B. (2024). Stavovi i mišljenja studenata Odsjeka za informacijske znanosti Filozofskog fakulteta u Osijeku o vlastitim digitalnim vještinama i ulozi visokoškolske knjižnice u digitalnom opismenjivanju. *Vjesnik bibliotekara Hrvatske*, 67 (3): pp. 25-52., https://doi.org/10.30754/vbh.67.3.1302

Grivokostopoulou, F., Kovas, K., & Perikos, I. 201). Examining the Impact of a Gamified Entrepreneurship Education Framework in Higher Education. Sustainability, 11(20), 5623. https://doi.org/10.3390/su11205623

Grmuša, T. (2024). Student Well-Being as an Important Indicator of Quality Assuramce. *Studies – Business – Society: present and future insights (8)*, 1 (IX): pp. 66-78. https://doi.org/10.52320/svv.v1iIX

Gunder, A., Del Casino Jnr, V., Vito, M., & Dickson, R. (2023). Empowering AI: Recontextualizing Our Pedagogical Impact Through Supportive Uses of Machine Learning *Ubiquity Proceedings*, 3(1): pp. 156-161. https://doi.org/10.5334/uproc.81

Gunder, A., & Gay, K. Centering Equity and Quality in Online, Blended, and Digital Learning (2023). *Ubiquity Proceedings*, 3(1): pp. 345-350. https://doi.org/10.5334/uproc.107

He, Z., Liu, Y., Wang, X., Li, R., & Lv, N. (2023). Gamified Entrepreneurship Courses Motivate College Students' Satisfaction: An Integrated Flow Framework. *Sage Open*, 13(2). https://doi.org/10.1177/21582440231177029

https://www.consilium.europa.eu/hr/press/press-releases/2023/11/23/digital-skills-and-competences-and-successful-digital-education-and-training-fit-for-the-digital-era/ 27. 12 .2024.

Isabelle, D.A. (2020). Gamification of Entrepreneurship Education. Decision Sciences *Journal of Innovative Education*, 18: pp. 203-223. https://doi.org/10.1111/dsji.12203

Katić, M. (2022). Digitalne kompetencije knjižničnih djelatnika Gradske knjižnice "Ivan Goran Kovačić"

Karlovac, *Vjesnik bibliotekara Hrvatske*, 65 (2): 227-245.

Katić, M., Pikić Jugović, A., Holcer, D. (2024). Samoprocjena razine digitalnih kompetencija i korištenje digitalnih tehnologija među narodnim knjižničarima u Hrvatskoj. *Vjesnik bibliotekara Hrvatske*, 67 (3): pp. 1-23., https://doi.org/10.30754/vbh.67.3.1279

Katulić, A., Barbarić, A. (2021). Važnost pismenosti iz privatnosti u prevladavanju digitalnog jaza s naglaskom na ulogu knjižnica, *Bosniaca: časopis Nacionalne i univerzitetske biblioteke Bosne i Hercegovine*, 26 (26): pp. 9-27., https://doi.org/10.37083/bosn.2021.26.9

Krasavina, A. (2024). *Croatia - National Digital Decade Strategic Roadmap*, Posted 27 July 2024 https://digital-skills-jobs.europa.eu/en/actions/national-initiatives/national-strategies/croatia-national-digital-decade-strategic-roadmap 27. 12. 2024.

Strategija digitalne Hrvatske za razdoblje do 2032. godine, https://narodne-novine.nn.hr/clanci/sluzbeni/2023_01_2_17.html 27. 12. 2024.

Kučina Softić, S. Odak, M.; Lasić Lazić, J. (2022). Digital transformation - New Approaches and Challenges in Education // *MIPRO 2022 45th Jubilee International Convention Proceedings* / Skala, Karol (ur.). Rijeka: Hrvatska udruga za informacijsku i komunikacijsku tehnologiju, elektroniku i mikroelektroniku - MIPRO, 2022. pp. 813-817 doi:10.23919/MIPRO55190.2022.9803435

Leal Filho, W., Lange Salvia, A., Beynaghi, A., Fritzen, B., Ulisses, A., Avila, L. V., Shulla, K., Claudio R. P. Vasconcelos, Moggi, S., Mifsud, M., Anholon, R., Rampasso, I. S., Kozlova, V., Iliško, D., Skouloudis, A. & Nikolaou, I. (2023). Digital transformation and sustainable development in higher education in a post-pandemic world. *International Journal of Sustainable Development & World Ecology*, 31(1): pp. 108–123. https://doi.org/10.1080/13504509.2023.2237933

Marchisio, M., Roman, F., Sacchet, M., & Spinello, E. (2023). Students' Digital Competencies in Remote and Online Higher Education in the Security and Defence Field. *Ubiquity Proceedings*, 3(1): pp. 452-457. DOI: https://doi.org/10.5334/uproc.122

McDermott, G., Byrne, A., McLaughlin, R., O'Connor, N., & Griselain, S. (2023). Exploring the Use of Immersive Technologies to Enhance the Student Experience. *Ubiquity Proceedings*, 3(1): pp. 283-288. DOI: https://doi.org/10.5334/uproc.98

Melo, F. L. N. B. de, Soares, A. M. J., Sampaio, L. M. B., & Oliveira, R. L.-de-. (2022). The impact of gamification on entrepreneurial Intention in a Brazilian technical business school. *Brazilian Administration Review*, 20(1), e210033. https://doi.org/10.1590/1807-7692bar2023210033

Mohamed Hashim, M., Tlemsani, I. & Matthews, R. Higher education strategy in digital transformation. *Educ Inf Technol* 27, 3171–3195 (2022). https://doi.org/10.1007/s10639-021-10739-1

Mucundanyi G. & Woodley, X. (2021). Exploring Free Digital Tools in Education. *International Journal of Education and Development using Information and Communication Technology* (IJEDICT), 17 (2): pp. 96-103.

Müller, M. & Aleksa Varga, M. (2020). Digitalne kompetencije učitelja i suradnika na visokim obrazovnim ustanovama Republike Hrvatske. *Informatologia*, 53 (1-2): pp. 8-23. https://doi.org/10.32914/i.53.1-2.2

Pavić, D. & Černja, Rajter, I. (2024). Motivacijski i okolišni čimbenici digitalnih vještina, kompetencija i pismenosti. *Marsonia: časopis za društvena i humanistička istraživanja.* 3(1): pp. 157-172.

Vlad, C. (2021). *Gamification – An Innovative Teaching Method*. Galaţi: Galati University Press.

Wong Mee Mee, R., Shahdan, T., Shahrom T.; Ismail, M. R.; Ghani, K. A. Pek, L. S., Von, W. L., Woo, A.; Rao, Y. S. (2020). Role of Gamification in Classroom Teaching: Pre-Service Teachers' View *International Journal of Evaluation and Research in Education*, 9 (3): pp. 684-690.

Fostering Self-Directed Learning Skills using the Termi App

Yael Livneh, Yael Dubinsky

1. Introduction

Following years of dedicating intellectual, emotional, and financial resources to their academic pursuits, higher education graduates frequently encounter challenges when endeavoring to integrate into the labor market. Numerous nations face the disconcerting phenomenon of prolonged unemployment among higher education graduates. In the United States, the unemployment rate for individuals holding degrees stood at 17.2%, 15.5%, and 14.9% for respective fiscal years 2019–20, 2020–21, and 2021–22 (Ministry of Labor and Employment, 2023).

In the contemporary labor market, a paradox has emerged: a notable prevalence of graduate unemployment juxtaposed against a fervent pursuit of talents by employers. This incongruity is fundamentally rooted in the suboptimal state of graduate work readiness (GWR; Winterton & Turner, 2019). GWR is defined as the extent to which graduates possess attributes and attitudes that prepare them for success in the working world (Caballero & Walker, 2010). The extent to which graduates are ready for work is viewed as indicative of potential job performance, success or promotion, and career advancement (Verma et al., 2019).

The conventional definition of GRW embodies a supply-side perspective, emphasizing competence with a focus on the individual (Winterton & Turner, 2019). It alludes to the extent to which graduates possess certain skills, knowledge, and attributes that contribute to their employability and enable them to be ready for and successful in the work environment (Verma et al., 2019).

Two main challenges have been addressed in research concerning GWR. The first is the identity of the person responsible for developing GWR. Because GWR is related to individual attributes, there has been a tendency of "blaming the victim," meaning viewing graduates as accountable for their employability. This idea is in line with the self-management career approach (Verma et al., 2019). Insufficient GWR in connection with unemployment yields manifold repercussions for graduates, universities, employers, and governments. Consequently, scholars of a recent review (Winterton & Turner, 2019) advocated for a "triple helix" framework, suggesting a collective responsibility among multiple stakeholders in preparing graduates for work. These stakeholders are governments and state agencies, employers, and educational institutions. Each stakeholder, alongside the graduate, is urged to engage proactively in fostering GWR (Winterton & Turner, 2019).

The second challenge involves the attributes needed to develop GWR. Various models and scales describe the needed skills for GWR (Coetzee, 2014; OECD, 2019; Verma et al., 2019; Wilson et al., 2017), among which learning is most mentioned. The OECD Learning Compass 2030 model distinguishes among three types of skills: cognitive and meta-cognitive skills, which include critical thinking, creative thinking, learning to learn, and self-regulation; social and emotional skills, which include empathy, self-efficacy, responsibility and collaboration; and practical and physical skills, which include using new information and communication technology devices (OECD, 2019). Self-directed learning (SDL) is considered a central learning skill that emphasizes the role of motivation and determination of learners during their efforts to achieve their goals (Nadi et al., 2011). Graduates with SDL skills are better prepared as employees in the dynamic labor market (Francom, 2010).

The Israeli higher education milieu and contemporaneous labor market are considered a unique context. Trilingualism has emerged as the prevailing standard, with students and employees speaking Hebrew or Arabic as their native language. Teaching is conducted in Hebrew, yet there is a strong demand for proficiency in English across all disciplines and among employees, especially those in global firms (Kheimets & Epstein, 2005). In previous work (Livneh & Dubinsky, 2023), we developed and evaluated a mobile application named Termi to cope with trilingual environments in higher education. The Termi app assists students by enabling a smooth transition among terms in three languages—Hebrew, English, and Arabic—according to user choice.

The goal of the present case study, which was conducted during a learning program in a higher education institute in Israel, was to map SDL skills regarding their alignment with the concepts and features of the Termi app. Further, based on this map, we assessed how using the Termi app relates to and enables the development of SDL principles to adhere to GWR challenges. In the following, we provide background in Section 2 concerning SDL and the Termi app. In Section 3, we present the case study methodology. In Section 4, we present the findings and discussion. We conclude in Section 5.

2. Background

In this section, we provide the background for this work, mainly addressing the SDL concept and the Termi app that we developed.

2.1. Self-Directed Learning

Learning can be placed on a continuum, ranging from teacher- or other-oriented at one end to self-directed at the other end. According to Knowles' (1975) definition, SDL is "a process in which individuals take the initiative, with or without the help from others, in diagnosing their learning needs, formulating goals, identifying human and material resources, choosing and implementing appropriate learning strategies, and evaluating learning outcomes" (p. 85).

SDL skills increase adaptivity for high-frequency career and job changes (Loyens et al., 2008). Students who have the opportunity to develop SDL skills during their education and learned how to be proactive and self-directed learners may be lifelong learners (Boyer et al., 2014) and better prepared as employees for the dynamic labor market. They are better able to anticipate their organization's needs, tailor their learning to meet their unique learning styles, and acquire the necessary skills, knowledge, and abilities to create value for their customers, employers, and organizations (Artis & Harris, 2007). Thus, SDL skills are among the most important skills that higher formal education can foster among students (Francom, 2010).

The literature has revealed four main prescriptive principles for fostering SDL skills among students in formal education: (a) match the level of SDL required in learning activities to student readiness; (b) progress from teacher to student SDL over time; (c) support the acquisition of subject-matter knowledge and SDR skills together; and (d) have students practice SDL in the context of learning tasks (Francom, 2010). These principles should be considered by higher education institutes to foster SDL among graduates and improve GWR (Francom, 2010). SDL is expressed in our context in a trilingual setting—namely, Hebrew, Arabic, and English—alongside the capacity to shift among them, holding the potential to augment graduate employability. This proficiency is particularly valuable for facilitating effective communication, especially in global enterprises. Additionally, SDL encourages the acquisition of the meta-cognitive skill of lifelong learning (Loyens et al., 2008).

2.2. Termi App

The Termi app is an innovative mobile application that assists students in trilingual environments in higher education (Livneh & Dubinsky, 2023). The main feature of the Termi app is the smooth transition among terms in three languages, Hebrew, English, and Arabic, according to user choice. The following is a description of Termi's main features.

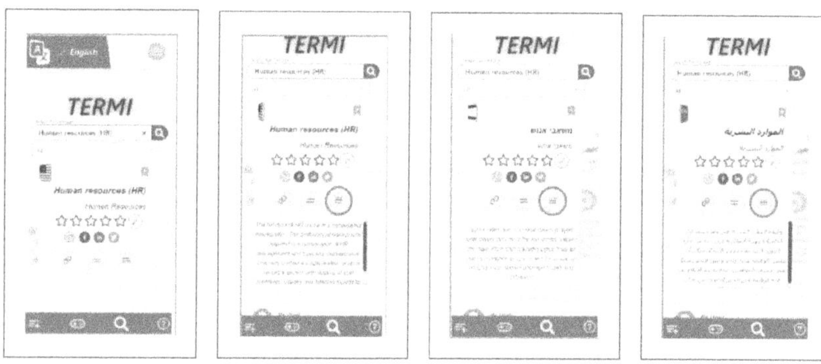

Figure 1. Termi Search, Results, and Smooth Transition among Languages

2.2.1. Search for a Term

The search term feature allows users to find information quickly and easily. The user types the desired term in one of the three languages and the results are displayed, providing brief and extended interpretations and a link to additional external resources. The depth of interpretation is according to the user's preference. The smooth transition among the three languages happens using a swipe gesture. The first panel in Figure 1 shows the text box for the search option. The other three panels show the search results that can be browsed using the swipe gesture in English, Hebrew, and Arabic, respectively.

2.2.2. Share a Term

Users can add new terms to the Termi database in any of the three languages. Once the user has entered the information, it is sent for review and approval by a content expert in the relevant discipline. If the information is approved, it is added to the Termi database for all users.

2.2.3. Learning through Games

Users can play games to learn new concepts and improve their understanding. In Termi, games are used to learn terms in the three languages. Two games offered in the current version are TransMe, which asks for the right translation using the three languages according to user choice, and Hangman, in which the user identifies a word in the chosen language by guessing letters, using the location of guessed letters in each language as clues. Game screenshots are presented in Livneh and Dubinsky (2023).

2.2.4. Personalization, Feedback, and Self-Evaluation

Users receive immediate feedback for each game session and can track their achievements and ranking via a dashboard. Moreover, the app collects data about contributions to the content and overall use patterns (see Figure 2). The data are used to shape the next personal recommendations of Termi. For example, based on the user's previous activity, the app can recommend specific game sessions and new content that are tailored to the user's interests and skill level.

Figure 2. Termi Dashboard of Game Scores, Personal Ranking, and Activity Pattern

3. Methodology

This research was conducted according to the case study method, a popular approach described by Walsham (1995). Data were collected from students using the Termi app while learning the discipline of human resources management (HRM). We used a qualitative analysis method based on content analysis, which involves systematically coding the data and identifying patterns. In the following, we briefly describe the research setting.

3.1. Participants and Data Collection

Data were collected through evaluation of the Termi app with a target population of 148 students from two courses in the HRM Academic Department at the Kinneret Academic College on the Sea of Galilee in Israel. The evaluation and data collection included a sample of 63 second-year students. Most students spoke Hebrew as their native tongue ($n = 47$), followed by Arabic ($n = 14$) and English ($n = 2$). Students were asked to use the app and complete an online questionnaire.

3.2. Pilots

Two pilots were conducted, one in May to June 2023 (Livneh & Dubinsky, 2023) and the second in June 2024. During this time, students were asked but not obligated to complete four tasks in the app for 10% of their grade. The first task enabled users to explore the app's features and functionality. The second suggested searching for terms (brief, extended, and link searching) in their native language and other freely chosen languages, with the goal of identifying at least three favorite terms. The third task was using all games, playing at least five rounds per game, changing the game language, and tracking personal achievements in each game over time. The fourth task

Table 1. SDL Questionnaire Items

Category	Question
Academic studies	Can the app help you succeed as a student? • If you answered yes, how can the app help you succeed as a student? In what situations can you use it? • If you answered no, why won't the app help you succeed as a student?
Working market	Can the Termi app help you get a job in the field of human resources? • If you answered yes, how can the app help you succeed in getting a job? In what situations can you use it to get a job? • If you answered no, why won't the app help you succeed in getting a job?
Skill development	Can using the app contribute to the development of such skills? • If you answered yes, specify what skills can be developed with the help of the app. • If you answered no, specify why the app won't help you develop skills

involved adding at least one new term in any language. The last task was to provide feedback on their experience and attitudes regarding the Termi app via an online questionnaire.

3.3. Questionnaire

We used a 22-question online survey in which students were asked to rate the Termi features and answer open-ended questions. In Table 1, we present three questions relevant to SDL, focusing on how students viewed Termi-based learning for their academic success, entering the working market, and developing skills.

4. Findings and Discussion

Table 2 presents the data collected regarding the three categories: academic studies, working market, and skill development. Participant answers are presented by most to least mentioned.

A high percentage (90%) of users affirmed Termi's usefulness regarding success in exams, deeper learning, accessibility of external resources, self-monitoring knowledge. However, 10% preferred alternative ways of learning. Regarding engagement in the working market, 84% described Termi as a tool that can help users stay updated on relevant terminology, refresh their knowledge before interviews, and improve workplace communication with HRM terminology. Some (16%) noted it doesn't replace practical experience. Self-directed growth received positive feedback from 65% of the users, focus on promoting continuous self-monitoring and self-learning and facilitating effective workplace communication, especially in English for global firms.

Our goal was to map SDL skills regarding their alignment with the concepts and features of the Termi app. Further, based on this map, we assessed how using the Termi app related to and enabled development of SDL principles in addressing GWR challenges. We assessed students' SDL skills when using Termi, aimed at eliminating language barriers when learning the terminology of a discipline. We assessed the app in two ways: (a) by evaluating SDL skills in light of Termi use and (b) by tracking users' feedback related to SDL skills.

We suggest that using the Termi app can be considered an SDL experience, based on the Knowles' (1975) SDL definition and encompassing eight key

Table 2. User Feedback Regarding the Termi App

Categories	Response	Users' answers*
Academic studies	Yes: 90%	Success in exams, deeper learning, accessibility to external resources, self-monitoring knowledge
	No: 10%	Preferring frontal teaching, using alternative learning resources
Working market	Yes: 84%	Being updated with newest terms (after graduating), learning updates before interviews, communicating with acceptable HRM terminology in workplace
	No: 16%	Terminology cannot replace practical experience
Skill development	Yes: 65%	Self-monitored learning, accessibility of continuous learning, communication (in workplace, especially English in global firms), self-learning
	No: 35%	Missing practical experience, skills are developed by practical experience

*Most to least mentioned.

elements according to Boyer et al. (2014): (a) it is a process (b) that is initiated by the individual, (c) which may or may not involve the help of others, (d) to identify their learning needs, (e) develop learning goals from these needs, (f) find the necessary resources to attain these goals, (g) select and implement the proper learning strategies to meet their goals, and (h) determine how to measure learning outcomes.

Termi affords a process of learning with various learning activities that can be used continuously during academic studies and later during a career as an employee (this relates to Element A). In our case study, the first learning initiative for using Termi was encouraged but not obligated by others, such as the teacher (Element C). It also offers a self-learning initiative with high accessibility; it can be used anywhere, anytime, through a mobile phone (Element B). Terni users can self-diagnose their learning needs by tracking their game achievements and personal ranking. They can define needs in their native language or two others (Element D). Users can set goals regarding their scores in games and personal ranking compared to other users (Element F). Termi users have access to built-in resources for self-searching and opportunities to use external resources from the internet. The users choose which resources to use and in which language (Element G). Termi users can self-direct their learning strategy by choosing to learn via games or by searching for terms and choosing the depth of learning when searching

(Element G). For the last SDL component, evaluating learning outcomes, Termi provides immediate feedback in each trial and final scores in each game. Moreover, users can graphically track their performance over time in each game and their performance ranking (Element H). Table 3 provides a map of the Termi App per Knowles' SDL elements, demonstrating that Termi highly aligned with these elements.

Table 3. Map of SDL Elements and the Value of the Termi Experience

SDL Component	Main Observation
It is a process	Termi affords a process of learning with various learning activities that can be used continuously
That is initiated by the individual	Termi offers a self-learning initiative with high accessibility; it can be using anywhere any time via mobile phone
Which may or may not involve the help of others	The first learning initiative for using Termi was encouraged (but not obligated) by others (e.g., teacher)
To identify their learning needs	Terni users can track their game achievements and choose the language
Develop learning goals from these needs	Users can set goals regarding their scores in games and personal ranking compared to other users
Find the necessary resources to attain these goals	Termi users have access to built-in resources and opportunities to use external resources
Select and implement the proper learning strategies to meet their goals	Termi users can choose to learn via games or choose the depth of learning when searching for a term
Determine how to measure learning outcomes	Termi provides immediate feedback in each trial and final scores in each game; users can graphically track their performance over time in each game and their performance ranking

We used these principles for fostering students' SDL skills in formal education as mentioned by Francom (2010) to assess the value of the Termi app. As shown in Table 4, Termi aligns with these principles. Termi enables students to practice SDL in the context of learning tasks using HRM terms as part of learning tasks in the HRM academic program, awarding students with 10% of the course grade. Termi provides HRM terms that match the professional level of Termi users. Termi enables students to add terms, thus creating a new body of knowledge, especially regarding contemporary terms and slang. This creates progress from teacher- to student-directed learning over time.

Table 4. Map of Principles for Fostering Students' SDL Skills and the Value of the Termi Experience

Principles of Fostering SDL Skills	Main Observation
Match the level of SDL required in learning activities to student readiness	HRM terms that match the professional level of Termi users (late second year and beginning of third year in bachelor's program)
Progress from teacher to student direction of learning over time	Students create new terminology that is approved by experts and shared with all other students
Support the acquisition of subject-matter knowledge and SDL skills together	We combined the use of the Termi app with traditional learning
Have students practice SDL in the context of learning tasks	Academic learning tasks refer students to use the terminology of HRM as part of the Termi app activities; completing them accounted for 10% of the students' final course grade

An alternative way of assessing the Termi app's ability to foster students' SDL skills is by tracking the students' feedback through self-report questionnaires. Students reported that Termi added value to their education in various ways: ensuring better academic success through the possibility of deeper SDL; providing access to relevant internal and external resources; and encouraging self-monitoring of knowledge. Self-regulating learning depth, choosing resources, and self-monitoring represent SDL principles (Francom, 2010). The second contribution of Termi relates to fostering GWR by being updated with the newest terms and refreshing knowledge before interviews. The users reported self-learning processes. When asked about skills that can be developed through the use of Termi, students reported the opportunity to develop SDL skills, self-monitored learning, and access to continuous and lifelong learning; all these skills relate to "learn how to learn" skills and are relevant to GWR (Francom, 2010).

By using Termi in higher education, students have the potential to foster SDL. It is important to mention that Termi users also reported that the app had weaknesses, including missing practical experience, which is demanded by employers for GWR (Winterton & Turner, 2019).

5. Conclusion

We presented a case in which using Termi, which enables switching among HRM terms in English, Hebrew, and Arabic, fostered SDL skills. By enhancing SDL skills, Termi may contribute to graduates' success in academic studies, entry into the labor market, and developing skills—all three of which are relevant for GWR. However, it doesn't offer practical experience. We are in the process of expanding Termi, with a focus on conducting a comprehensive analysis of users' recorded behaviors and corresponding attitudes.

References

Artis, A. B., & Harris, E. G. (2007). Self-directed learning and sales force performance: An integrated framework. *Journal of Personal Selling and Sales Management*, *27*(1), 9–24.

Boyer, S. L., Edmondson, D. R., Artis, A. B., & Fleming, D. (2014). Self-directed learning: A tool for lifelong learning. *Journal of Marketing Education*, *36*(1), 20–32.

Caballero, C. L., & Walker, A. (2010). Work readiness in graduate recruitment and selection: A review of current assessment methods. *Journal of Teaching and Learning for Graduate Employability*, *1*(1), 6–25.

Coetzee, M. (2014). Measuring student graduateness: Reliability and construct validity of the Graduate Skills and Attributes Scale. *Higher Education Research & Development*, *33*(5), 887–902.

Francom, G. M. (2010). Teach me how to learn: Principles for fostering students' self-directed learning skills. *International Journal of Self-Directed Learning*, 7(1), 29–44.

Kheimets, N. G., & Epstein, A. D. (2005). Languages of higher education in contemporary Israel. *Journal of Educational Administration and History*, *37*(1), 55–70.

Knowles, M. S. (1975). *Self-directed learning: A guide for learners and teachers.* Prentice Hall.

Livneh, Y., & Dubinsky, Y. (2023). *Termi app to cope with trilingualism in higher education: A case study* [Paper]. International Conference on Teaching, Education, and New Learning Technologies, New York, NY.

Loyens, S. M. M., Magda, J., & Rikers, R. M. J. P. (2008). Self-directed learning in problem-based learning and its relationships with self-regulated learning. *Educational Psychology Review*, *20*, 411–427.

Ministry of Labour and Employment. (2023, March 20). *Unemployment rate of graduate degree holders shows a declining trend as per the annual PLFS reports*. https://pib.gov.in/PressReleaseIframePage.aspx?PRID=1908966

Nadi, M. A., Gordanshekan, M., & Golparvar, M. (2011). Effect of critical thinking, problem solving and metacognitive on student self-directed learning. *Research in Curriculum Planning*, *8*(1–2).

OECD. (2019). *Conceptual learning framework: Skills for 2030*. https://www.oecd.org/education/2030-project/teaching-and-learning/learning/skills/Skills_for_2030_concept_note.pdf

Verma, P., Kumar, S., & Nankervis, A. (2019). Work-readiness integrated competence model: Conceptualization and scale development. *Education + Training*, *61*(5), 568–589.

Walsham, G. (1995). Interpretive case studies in IS research: Nature and method. *European Journal of Information Systems*, *4*(2), 74–81.

Wilson, C., Lennox, P., Brown, M., & Hughes, G. (2017). How to develop creative capacity for the fourth industrial revolution: Creativity and employability in higher education. In F. Reisman (Ed.), *Creativity, innovation and wellbeing* (pp. 241–273). KIE Conference Publications.

Winterton, J., & Turner, J. J. (2019). Preparing graduates for work readiness: An overview and agenda. *Education + Training*, *61*(5), 536–551.

Measuring Personality Characteristics in a Technological Process

Sabina Nedkova, Plamena Atansova

1. Introduction

The personality characteristics directly influence the way a person works, by building the prism through which his skills, knowledge and experience are manifested in the context of his specific duties in a work environment, as a worker or manager, part of a large or small team or working individually. Working in a technological environment brings specific characteristics (physical and chemical parameters) that make it extremely sensitive to human behavior in the context of technical safety and health at work and require the assessment of personal characteristics to be part of the analysis and management of technological risk. The present study examines the personal characteristics of twenty-nine, Bulgarian male workers, with working experience from three to twenty-three years, working on a technological plant with medium to high levels of risk, related to specific chemical hazards and physical factors (pressure and temperature). Their personality characteristics are assessed in relation with their working experience, job satisfaction and their opinion on the level of the technological complexity of their working duties, to see if there are any correlations, between their personalities and the technological environment, which could influence the technological risk management in a positive way (Nedkova & Atanasova, 2020a; Terziev, 2020b; 2023a).

2. Experiment, used methods and instruments

For the purpose of the present study was used a self-assesed paper survey, based on Oliver John's questionnaire for determining personality characteristics according to the five-factor analysis of personality (Big Five Inventory), adapted for Bulgarian respondents. The survey consists of 45 questions, based on the way a respondent defines hisself as "a person who" ... Q1 is talkative; Q2. ...looks for faults in others; Q3. ...does his job responsibly; Q4. ...is depressed, often gets into a bad mood; Q5. ...reacts in an original way in a situation; Q6. ...is reserved towards new things; Q7. ...helps others and is not selfish; Q8. ...can sometimes be careless; Q9. ...is not tense or stressed, reacts well to pressure; Q10. ...is curious; Q11. ...is full of energy; Q12. ...can start a fight or quarrel with others; Q13. ...is a reliable worker; Q14. ...is often emotionally tense; Q15. ...thinks everything, thoroughly; Q16. ...does everything with enthusiasm; Q17. ...has an attitude of forgiving others rather than taking offense; Q18. ...is disorganized; Q19. ...worries a lot about all sorts of things; Q20. ...has a wide imagination; Q21. ..is rather quiet; Q22. ...can generally be trusted; Q23. ...has a tendency to laziness; Q24. ...is emotionally stable, cannot be easily upset; Q25. ...is inventive; Q26. ...is straightforward in dealing with others; Q27. ...can be cold and reserved; Q28. ...continues to work until the task is completed; Q29. ...can be gloomy; Q30. ...has artistic or aesthetic interests (qualities); Q31. ...is sometimes depressed and shy; Q32. ..is attentive and kind to everyone; Q33. ...does everything efficiently (brings everything he starts to a successful end); Q34. ...remains calm in tense situations; Q35 preffers routine, ordinary tasks..., Q36. ...likes to go out, to be among people, is sociable; Q37. ...can sometimes be rude to others; Q38. ...makes plans and follows them point by point; Q39. ...gets nervous easily; Q40. ...likes to break down ideas he hears through his own vision, doesn't trust them blindly; Q41. ...has few artistic interests; Q42. ...likes to work in a team; Q43. ...is easily distracted; Q44. ...has interests and knowledge in literature, the arts and music; Q45. ...is politically more liberal than conservative. There are also added three specifying questions SQ1 "Do you like your job"- describing the job satisfaction, SQ2 - "How long is your working experience in the technological plant" and SQ3 "Do you think that your job is technologically complexed/ you work in a technologically complexed environment"? The structure of the survey is following its original form of likert scale for scaling the answers in which, the respondents specify their level of agreement or disagreement on a symmetric agree-disagree scale for questions from 1 to 45 and the range describe the intensity of their self-assessed acceptance of the statement in the question as true for themselves. The answers were coded at the scale 1-2, where: 1 -100 % negative; 1,25 – 75 % negative; 1,5 – 50/50; 1,75 – 75% positive and 2-100% positive. The answers were grouped acording the five traits they assess, which for the Five-factor inventory are: Neuroticism (N): a tendency to experience nervousness, tension, anxiety, emotional instability, hostility and sadness; Extraversion (E): energetic approach to the outside world, sociability, self-confidence and positive emotionality; Openness to experience (O): describes the breadth, depth, originality and complexity of mental and concretely acquired from practical activities experience; Ability to understand/agree (A): The quality describing interpersonal relationships - compassion, altruism, antagonism and Conscientiousness (C): Stability, organization and motivation of behavior aimed at achieving specific goals and socially directed impulse control. Some of the questions require reverse scoring, because, they are formulated in a way that reflects low levels of a particular trait, even though a high score would indicate a strong presence of that trait, for their coding was used the formula reversed score =3 – original score (original score of 1,75, would be transfered in reverse scoring as 3-1,75=1,25). The questions were grouped into five groups, relevant to the five main traits in Five Factor analysis model, and assined with the relevant code, where the reversed questions were marked with "r", by the authors: Group Neuroticism (N) - Q4/N1, Q9/N2r, Q14/N3, Q18/N4, Q19/N5, Q23/N6, Q34/N7r, Q39/N8, Q34/N9; Group Extraversion (E)- Q1/E1, Q6/E2r, Q11/E3, Q21/E4r, Q27/E5r, Q29/E6r, Q31/E7r, Q36/E8, Q42/E9; Group Openness to experience (O): Q5/O1, Q10/O2, Q20/O3, Q25/O4, Q30/O5, Q35/O6r, Q40/O7, Q41/O8r, Q44/O9; Group Ability to understand/agree (A)- Q2/A1r, Q7/A2, Q12/A3r, Q17/A4, Q25/A5, Q26/A6, Q32/A7, Q37/A8r, Q45/A9;Group Conscientiousness (C) – Q3/C1, Q8/C2r, Q13/C3, Q15/C4, Q16/C5, Q22/C6, Q28/C7, Q33/C8, Q38/C9. The survey data were analyzed with SPSS (John & Srivastava, 1999; John et al., 2008; John et al., 1991a; Burns & Bush, 2008; Barrick & Mount, 1993).

3. Results

Reliability Analysis, describing the internal consistency or the items in each trait, has a value of α=0665, which indicated a good level of internal consistency.

Computing the trait scores for every trait, created a new variable, describing the score for every trait by averaging the responses to the nine questions in each trait group for each of the respondents, the correlation between the results, grouped in five trait score groups, relevant to the values of Openess to experience, Neurotism, Extraversion, Ability to understand/

Table 1. Average trait scores for every trait based on the nine questions in its group

Correlations

		Score_O	Score_N	Score_E	Score_A	Score_C
Score_O	Pearson correlation	1	-0.399*	0.485**	0.290	0.543**
	Sig. (2-tailed)		0.032	0.008	0.127	0.002
	N	29	29	29	29	29
Score_N	Pearson Correlation	-0.399*	1	-0.397*	-0.654**	-0.540**
	Sig. (2-tailed)	0.032		0.033	0.000	0.002
	N	29	29	29	29	29
Score_E	Pearson Correlation	0.485**	-0.397*	1	0.453*	0.408*
	Sig. (2-tailed)	0.008	0.033		0.014	0.028
	N	29	29	29	29	29
Score_A	Pearson Correlation	0.290	-0.654**	0.453*	1	0.513**
	Sig. (2-tailed)	0.127	0.000	0.014		0.004
	N	29	29	29	29	29
Score_C	Pearson Correlation	0.543**	-0.540**	0.408*	0.513**	1
	Sig. (2-tailed)	0.002	0.002	0.028	0.004	
	N	29	29	29	29	29

*. Correlation is significant at the 0.05 level (2-tailed).
**. Correlation is significant at the 0.01 level (2-tailed).

agree, Conscientiousness, as Score_O, Score_N, Score_E, Score A, Score C, shown in Table 1. It is seen that the correlation among four of the traits is positive and comparatively significient, with correlation coefficients ranging from 0.29 to 0.53, excluding the Neurotism trait where is observed a negative correlation ($r=-0.399$, $p<0.05$), relevant to the assessment of this trait, which value closer to the maximium of its scale is interpreted as a negative feature. The strongest correlation can be found between the traits Openness with Conscientiousness ($r=0.543$, $p<0.01$), which proves their positive connection and can be explained with their close baselines related with learning from experience and applying this knowledge responsibly in the job duties, followed by the second strongest relation between the Openess and Extraversion, related with the wider acceptance to the knowledge coming from the others, which an extrovert person is willing to implement in his direct behavior.

The descriptive statistics analysis confirms these results, by the distribution of mean values for Score_O - 1.585, Score_N-1.279, Score_E-1.694, Score_A-1.723 and Score_C -1.760, by which is seen, that the highest and most significantly positive trait is the Conscientiousness.

The Multivariate Analysis of Variance (MANOVA) is applied to assess the effects of independent variables on multiple dependent variables of five trait scores simultaneously. This analysis was apllied for assessing three independent

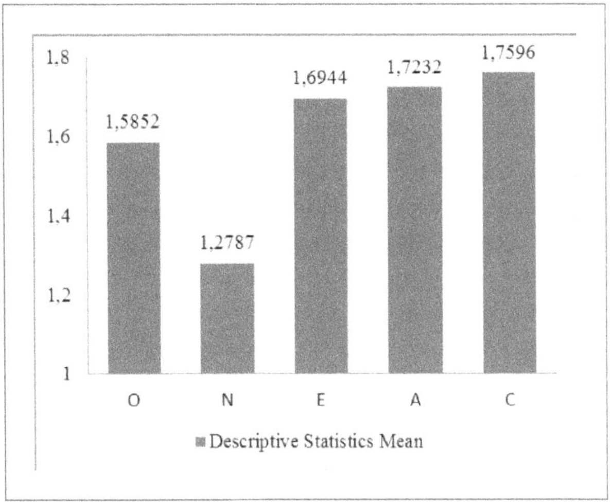

Figure 1: Mean values of the five traits for twenty-nine Bulgarian workers in a technological plant

variables – the years of the working experience SQ1, the satisfaction from the job SQ2 and the assessed level of technological complexity in the working environment from the respondets SQ3. For the first two independent variables assesed - the years of working experience and the job satisfaction the analysis of this data showed that neither working years ($p = 0.335$) nor job satisfaction ($p = 0.221$) demonstrated a significant influence on the dependent variables analyzed in the MANOVA at the usual significance level of 0.05. and based on that can be presumed, that the differences in working years and stated job satisfaction levels is not leading to meaningful changes in personality profile. On the other hand for the assessed level of technological complexity in the working environment MANOVA revealed a significant multivariate effect for score_openness, ($F(3, N) = 5.554$, $p = 0.005$), and even higher for score_conscientiousness, ($F(3, N) = 11.894$, $p = 0.001$). This result can be interpreted with the relavance between the responsible attitute to work duties, as well as the way the job tasks are performed with the technolopgical complexity of the environment in which the respondets are working, relevant to the traits Conscientiousness (C) and Openess to experience (O) (Tett et al., 1991b; Piedmont & Weinstein, 1994; Gellatly & Irving, 2001).

3. Conclusion

The person is the major part of a working environment. His participation through professional, personal and behavioral characteristics can determine a technological system as more or less reliable. In a technological process, the potential dangers for the realization of a risky situation are brought by some main elements - technogenic, technological and human factors, as well as by a number of external elements determining their overall functioning, in which the human factor is also present, as organizational, managerial, etc. and in each of them the person has a dominant role as reason for realization of risk. Assessment of his personality is a way to adapt the working environment and his direct operational activities to his personal characteristic, because in the implementation of a specific critical situation, human errors are not so much due to incompetence, poor motivation or negligence, but rather are the result of the overall work situation, in which the professional and personal characteristics of the person play an important role. Insufficient attention to human reliability, through personal characteristic' assessment places the security of the technological systems at risk and does not allow finding the connection with the economic dimension of this parameter in order to assess the need for preventive activities that would increase human reliability and minimize the likelihood of error. Our research summarized the average personality in the examined technological plant, based on five factor traits as conscient people, agreeable and extrovert, open to new experince and learning and less neurous, described by the mean values of the traits, as shown in Figure 1 (Terziev & Kanev, 2020c; Georgiev & Terziev, 2023b; Terziev, Solovev, 2023c; 2020d; Terziev et al., 2021a; 2021b; Dolganova et al., 2020d).

References

Nedkova, S., & Atanasova, P. (2020a). Assessment of the personality of people, working in technological systems, with Eysenck Personality Questionnaire, Science Conference of Ruse University, Bulgaria, volume 59, book 10.1., p.20-25.

Terziev, V. (2020b). Provision of Integrated Employment and Social Assistance Services in Bulgaria. In: Solovev, D. (eds) Smart Technologies and Innovations in Design for Control of Technological Processes and Objects: Economy and Production. FarEastCon 2018. Smart Innovation, Systems and Technologies, vol 138. Springer, Cham, pp. 24-39, (Print)

ISBN978-3-030-15576-6, (Online) ISBN978-3-030-15577-3, https://doi.org/10.1007/978-3-030-15577-3_3.

Terziev, V.K. (2023a). Innovation Development of Industrial Business Organizations. In M. Okur Dinçsoy & H. Can (Eds.), Optimizing Energy Efficiency During a Global Energy Crisis (pp. 282-306). IGI Global. https://doi.org/10.4018/979-8-3693-0400-6.ch016.

John, O.P., & Srivastava, S. (1999). The Big Five trait taxonomy: History, measurement, and theoretical perspectives. In L. A. Pervin, & O. P. John (Eds.), Handbook of personality: Theory and research (pp. 102-138). New York: Guilford Press.

John, O.P, Naumann, L.P., & Soto, C.J. (2008) Paradıgm shift to the integrative big-five trait taxonomy: History, measurement and conceptual issues. In: John OP, Robins RW, Pervin LA, editors, Handbook of personality: Theory and research, Guilford Press. 114-158.

John, O.P, Donahue, E.M, & Kentle, R.L. (1991a) The big five invertory versions 4a and 54 Berkeley, CA: University of California, Berkeley, Institute of Personality and Social research.

Burns, A.C., & Bush, R.F. (2008). Basic Marketing Research *(Second ed.). New Jersey: Pearson Education. pp.* 245. ISBN 978-0-13-205958-9.

Barrick, M. & Mount, M. (1993). Autonomy as a Moderator of the Relationships Between the Big Five Personality Dimensions and Job Performance. *Journal of Applied Psychology,*Vol. 78. No. 1. pp. 111-118, ISSN 0021-9010

Tett, R., Jackson, D., & Rothstein, M. (1991b). Personality Measures as Predictors of Job Performance: A Meta-Analytic Review. *Personnel Psychology,* Vol. 44. pp. 703-742, ISSN 0031

Piedmont, R., & Weinstein, H. (1994). Predicting Supervisor Rating of Job Performance Using the NEO Personality Inventory. *Journal of Psychology,* Vol. 128. pp. 255-265, ISSN 128255-2655826

Gellatly, I., & Irving, P. (2001). Personality, Autonomy, and Contextual Performance ofManagers. *Human Performance,*Vol. 14 No.3, pp. 231-245, ISSN 0895-9285

Terziev, V., & Kanev, D. (2020c). Modern Developments in Behavioral Economics. In: Solovev, D. (eds) Smart Technologies and Innovations in Design for Control of Technological Processes and Objects: Economy and Production. FarEastCon 2018. Smart Innovation, Systems and Technologies, vol 138. Springer, Cham, pp. 10-23, Print ISBN 978-3-030-15576-6, Online ISBN978-3-030-15577-3. https://doi.org/10.1007/978-3-030-15577-3_2.

Georgiev, M.P., & Terziev, V.K. (2023b). The Labor Market Policies and Social Development in Bulgaria. In M. Okur Dinçsoy & H. Can (Eds.), Optimizing Energy Efficiency During a Global Energy Crisis (pp. 239-281). IGI Global. https://doi.org/10.4018/979-8-3693-0400-6.ch015.

Terziev, V., Solovev, D.B. (2023c). Development of the education system in Bulgaria in a period of economic transformations, AIP Conf. Proc. 2910, 020064 (2023), (Online ISSN 1551-7616, Print ISSN 0094-243X), https://doi.org/10.1063/5.0167861.

Terziev, V., Solovev, D.B. (2020d). Psychological Characteristics of Cadets from the Military Schools as Subjects of Educational Activity. In: Solovev, D.B., Savaley, V.V., Bekker, A.T., Petukhov, V.I. (eds) Proceeding of the International Science and Technology Conference "FarEastCon 2019". Smart Innovation, Systems and Technologies, vol 172. Springer, Singapore, pp 1025–1038, Print ISBN978-981-15-2243-7, Online ISBN978-981-15-2244-4, https://doi.org/10.1007/978-981-15-2244-4_99.

Terziev, V., Georgiev, M., Solovev, D.B. (2021a). Revolution or Evolution is the Inevitable Change in Bulgaria. In: Solovev, D.B., Savaley, V.V., Bekker, A.T., Petukhov, V.I. (eds) Proceeding of the International Science and Technology Conference "FarEastCon 2020". Smart Innovation, Systems and Technologies, vol 227. Springer, Singapore, pp 1159–1164, Online ISBN978-981-16-0953-4, Print ISBN978-981-16-0952-7, https://doi.org/10.1007/978-981-16-0953-4_109.

Terziev, V., Georgiev, M., Solovev, D.B. (2021b). National Employment Plan in Bulgaria and Opportunities for Change as a Result of COVID-19. In: Solovev, D.B., Savaley, V.V., Bekker, A.T., Petukhov, V.I. (eds) Proceeding of the International Science and Technology Conference "FarEastCon 2020". Smart Innovation, Systems and Technologies, vol 227. Springer, Singapore, pp 1165–1176, Online ISBN978-981-16-0953-4, Print ISBN978-981-16-0952-7. https://doi.org/10.1007/978-981-16-0953-4_110.

Dolganova, Y., Istomina, N., Zaborovskaya, A., & Terziev, V. (2020d). State financial resources as a tool for managing sustainable development of territories, E3S Web Conf., 208 (2020) 08015, (eISSN: 2267-1242), DOI: https://doi.org/10.1051/e3sconf/202020808015.

The Impact of Monetary Policy on Vietnam's Circular Economy Transition: Mediating Roles of Financial Institutions

Ngoc-Tien Hoang, Nguyen-Quynh-Nhu Ngo,
Tarlan Ahmadov and Wolfgang Gerstlberger

1. Introduction

The concept of a circular economy has gained significant traction in recent years as a sustainable alternative to the traditional linear economic model (Kirchherr et al., 2017). The transition to a circular economy is particularly crucial for developing and emerging economies like Vietnam, where rapid economic growth has led to increased resource consumption and waste generation (Hai et al., 2020). In Vietnam, the shift towards a circular economy has been officially incorporated into national policy through the Law on Natural Resources and Environment (2020), which came into effect on January 1, 2022. However, the successful implementation of a circular economy model requires not only policy frameworks but also supportive economic conditions and financial mechanisms.

Monetary policy, as a key macroeconomic tool, plays a crucial role in shaping these economic conditions. Bindseil and Fotia (2021) define monetary policy as the set of actions taken by a central bank to manage the money supply and interest rates to achieve specific economic objectives. In the context of Vietnam, the State Bank of Vietnam (SBV) is responsible for implementing monetary policy through various tools, including refinancing, interest rates, exchange rates, reserve requirements, and open market operations (Law on the State Bank of Vietnam, 2010).

The relationship between monetary policy and economic development has been extensively studied (John et al., 2019; Mehar, 2022). However, research on the specific impact of monetary policy on the transition to a circular economy is limited. This gap in the literature presents a significant problem, as policymakers and financial institutions lack a comprehensive understanding of how monetary policy decisions may influence the adoption of circular economy principles and practices.

The main research problem addressed in this study is the lack of empirical evidence on the impact of monetary policy on the transition to a circular economy, particularly in the context of developing countries like Vietnam. This gap in knowledge hinders the development of effective policies and financial mechanisms to support the circular economy transition.

To address this problem, the study seeks to:

- Examine the impact of different monetary policy scenarios (expansionary, contractionary, and stable) on the transition to a circular economy in Vietnam.
- Investigate the mediating roles of commercial banks and non-bank credit institutions in the relationship between monetary policy and the circular economy transition.

This research is particularly timely and relevant given Vietnam's recent policy initiatives towards a circular economy and the growing global emphasis on sustainable development. By investigating the complex relationships between monetary policy, financial institutions, and the circular economy transition, this study aims to contribute to the nascent body of literature on circular economy transitions in developing countries.

2. Literature Background and Hypothesis Development

The relationship between monetary policy and economic development has been extensively studied. John et al. (2019) and Mehar (2022) have examined the impact of monetary policy on economic growth, while Karahan and Bayır (2022) have studied its effects on other economic and financial activities. Research by Chinedu and Ezekwe (2021) has focused on the impact of monetary policy on financial intermediaries.

In the context of Vietnam, several studies have examined the circular economy transition. Nam and Hanh (2019), Schneider et al. (2017), and Tran and Nguyen (2023) have offered policy recommendations for the Vietnamese government to expedite the shift from a linear to a circular economy. These studies have highlighted the importance of flexible financial, monetary, and credit policies in fostering green growth and a circular economy.

However, there remains a significant gap in the literature regarding the specific impact of monetary policy on the transition to a circular economy, particularly in the context of developing countries like Vietnam. This study aims to address this gap by examining how different monetary policy scenarios affect Vietnam's transition to a circular economy, with a focus on the mediating roles of commercial banks and non-bank credit institutions.

Expansionary monetary policy, characterized by lower interest rates and increased money supply, can potentially stimulate investment in circular economy initiatives. This leads to our first hypothesis, supported by research from Nguyen et al. (2017) and Nguyen et al. (2022), who found that expansionary monetary policy generally benefits commercial banks (similarly, for non-bank credit institutions) by increasing lending activity and revenue from loan fees and interest income:

H1: The expansionary monetary policy of the State Bank of Vietnam has a positive impact on the operation of commercial banks.
H2: The expansionary monetary policy of the State Bank of Vietnam has a positive impact on the operation of non-bank credit institutions.

This hypothesis is based on the expectation that lower interest rates and increased money supply would enhance the ability of non-bank credit institutions to provide financial services and support circular economy initiatives (Ozili, 2021). Regarding the direct impact of expansionary monetary policy, research from Hussein and Hamdan (2020), who suggest that expansionary monetary policy can facilitate investment in sustainable practices and circular economy projects:

H3: The expansionary monetary policy of the State Bank of Vietnam has a positive impact on Vietnam's transition to a circular economy.

Conversely, contractionary monetary policy, characterized by higher interest rates and reduced money supply, may have different effects. Based on the expectation that higher interest rates may reduce lending activity and increase credit risk (Harun et al., 2005):

H4: The contractionary monetary policy of the State Bank of Vietnam has a negative impact on the operation of commercial banks.
H5: The contractionary monetary policy of the State Bank of Vietnam has a negative impact on the operation of non-bank credit institutions.

This hypothesis reflects the potential challenges faced by non-bank credit institutions in a higher interest rate environment (Chinedu and Ezekwe, 2021). Regarding the direct impact of contractionary monetary policy on the circular economy transition:

> H6: The contractionary monetary policy of the State Bank of Vietnam has a negative impact on Vietnam's transition to a circular economy.

This hypothesis is based on the expectation that higher interest rates may discourage investment in circular economy initiatives (Hussein and Hamdan, 2020). Stable monetary policy, characterized by consistent interest rates and controlled money supply, may provide a more predictable environment for economic actors. For commercial banks:

> H7: The stable monetary policy of the State Bank of Vietnam has a positive impact on the operations of commercial banks.

This hypothesis is supported by research from Nguyen et al. (2021), who suggest that a stable monetary environment allows banks to better plan their operations and manage risks. Similarly, for non-bank credit institutions:

> H8: The stable monetary policy of the State Bank of Vietnam has a positive impact on the operations of non-bank credit institutions.

This hypothesis reflects the potential benefits of a stable monetary environment for non-bank credit institutions in terms of planning and risk management (Nguyen et al., 2021). Regarding the direct impact of stable monetary policy on the circular economy transition:

> H9: The stable monetary policy of the State Bank of Vietnam has a positive impact on Vietnam's transition to a circular economy.

This hypothesis is based on the expectation that a stable monetary environment may provide a favourable context for long-term investments in circular economy initiatives (Hussein and Hamdan, 2020). The role of financial institutions in facilitating the transition to a circular economy is crucial. Research from Zhelyazkova (2020), who highlight the potential of banks to support sustainable practices through targeted lending and financial products.

H10: The operations of commercial banks have a positive impact on Vietnam's transition to a circular economy.
H11: The operations of non-bank credit institutions have a positive impact on Vietnam's transition to a circular economy.

This hypothesis reflects the potential of non-bank credit institutions to provide alternative funding sources for circular economy projects (Ozili, 2021).

The proposed hypotheses form a comprehensive framework for examining the complex relationships between monetary policy, financial institutions, and the transition to a circular economy in Vietnam. This framework acknowledges the potential direct effects of monetary policy on the circular economy transition, as well as the mediating roles of commercial banks and non-bank credit institutions.

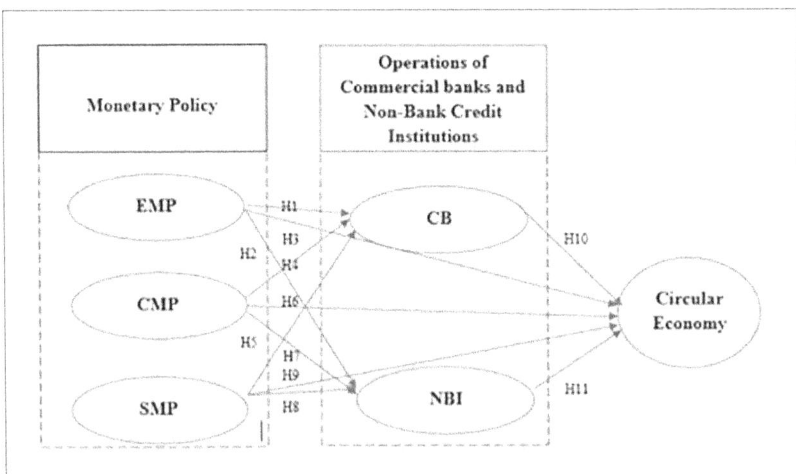

Figure 1. Hypothesized model
Sources: Authors' research results

The research model incorporates three scenarios of monetary policy (expansionary, contractionary, and stable) and examines their impacts on two types of financial institutions (commercial banks and non-bank credit institutions) and the circular economy transition. The hypothesized model is shown in Figure 1 along with the relationships between the relevant variables of interest.

3. Research design and methodology

This study employs a quantitative research approach to examine the impact of monetary policy on Vietnam's transition to a circular economy. Specifically, the study employs PLS-SEM as the primary analytical method, using SmartPLS 4 software. This choice is based on PLS-SEM's suitability for exploratory research, its ability to handle complex models with multiple constructs, and its robustness with non-normal data (Hair et al., 2019). The measurement model is assessed using indicators such as VIF values, outer weights, outer loadings, R-square, and Q-square values. The structural model is evaluated using path coefficients obtained through bootstrapping with 5,000 bootstrap samples. Indirect effects are also analysed to examine potential mediating relationships. Hypothesis testing is conducted by examining the statistical significance of the path coefficients in the structural model.

3.1 Sample and data collection

The study's sample consists of experts with knowledge and experience in economics, finance, and banking in Vietnam. A survey questionnaire was developed using a 5-point Likert scale, ranging from 1 (strongly disagree) to 5 (strongly agree). The data collection process occurred from February 21, 2023, to April 20, 2023. Initially, the survey was sent to 30 experts with master's degrees or higher and over 10 years of working experience at the State Bank of Vietnam, commercial banks, and universities in Vietnam. Based on their feedback and evaluation, the research team refined and finalized the survey questionnaire.

Using a judgment sampling method, the finalized survey was then distributed to a broader group of experts. In total, 450 survey questionnaires were sent out, resulting in 330 responses. After filtering out unqualified responses, the final sample consisted of 321 valid responses. The sample demographics reveal a high level of expertise among respondents: 49.7% of respondents hold postgraduate degrees, while the remainder are university graduates.

Regarding professional experience, 70.5% of respondents have over 10 years of experience in finance, banking, or economics, with the remaining 29.5% having less than 10 years of experience.

3.2 Measures of constructs

The research model comprises four main constructs: Monetary Policy (MP), Commercial Banks (CB), Non-Bank Credit Institutions (NBI), and Circular Economy (CE). Each construct is measured using multiple indicators, reflecting various aspects of these complex concepts.

Monetary Policy (MP) is measured using five indicators based on the tools outlined in the Law on the State Bank of Vietnam (2010): Refinancing (MP1), Interest Rate (MP2), Exchange Rates (MP3), Reserve Requirement (MP4), and Open Market Operations (MP5).

The study examines three scenarios of monetary policy: Expansionary Monetary Policy (EMP), Contractionary Monetary Policy (CMP), and Stable Monetary Policy (SMP).

Commercial Banks (CB) operations are measured using three indicators based on the Law on Credit Institutions (2010): Deposit Taking (CB1), Credit Extension (CB2), and Provision of Payment Services (CB3).

Non-Bank Credit Institutions (NBI) operations are similarly measured using three indicators: Deposit Taking (NBI1), Credit Extension (NBI2), and Non-Bank Services Provision (NBI3).

The Circular Economy (CE) construct is measured using four indicators based on the Law on Environmental Protection (2020) and relevant literature: Enterprises (CE1), Individuals (CE2), Government Agencies (CE3), and Civil Society Organizations (CE4).

4. Results and Discussion

The results reveal complex relationships between different monetary policy scenarios and their effects on financial institutions and the circular economy transition. The measurement model assessment demonstrates the reliability and validity of the constructs used in this study. All items show statistically significant weights ($p \leq 0.05$) and account for the variation in their respective constructs (Benitez et al., 2020) (Tab 1). The VIF readings below 3 indicate no collinearity issues in the model (Hair et al., 2019). The outer loadings of all items are larger than 0.50 and statistically significant, confirming the relevance of indicators with non-significant weights (Tab 2).

Table 1. VIF and outer weights of the measurement model.

Construct	Item	VIF	Outer weights	p-value
CB	CB1	1.943	0.476	0.000
	CB2	1.777	0.207	0.022
	CB3	1.734	0.473	0.000
CE	CE1	1.539	0.495	0.000
	CE2	1.539	0.624	0.000
CMP	CMP1	1.752	0.286	0.007
	CMP2	1.594	0.344	0.000
	CMP4	1.56	0.278	0.003
	CMP5	1.49	0.383	0.000
EMP	EMP1	1.435	0.346	0.000
	EMP4	1.323	0.355	0.000
	EMP5	1.449	0.543	0.000
NBI	NBI1	1.609	0.563	0.000
	NBI2	1.612	0.41	0.000
	NBI3	1.587	0.211	0.013
SMP	SMP1	1.694	0.336	0.000
	SMP3	1.829	0.28	0.002
	SMP4	1.767	0.243	0.010
	SMP5	1.765	0.368	0.000

The R-square values for commercial banks (CB), circular economy (CE), and non-bank credit institutions (NBI) are moderately high (0.483, 0.37, and 0.539, respectively), indicating that the model explains a substantial portion of the variance in these constructs. The Q-square values for CB, CE, and NBI (0.449, 0.226, and 0.503, respectively) suggest medium to high prediction accuracy of the PLS path model, aligning with the recommendations of Hair et al. (2019) for assessing model fit in PLS-SEM (Tab 3).

The path coefficient analysis reveals intriguing patterns in the relationships between monetary policy, financial institutions, and the circular economy transition. Contrary to expectations, contractionary monetary policy shows a positive impact on the transition to a circular economy (correlation coefficient: 0.158**) (Tab 4), while stable and expansionary monetary policies have smaller, non-significant effects. This finding challenges the conventional wisdom that

Table 2. Outer loadings.

	CB	CE	CMP	EMP	NBI	SMP
CB1	0.893					
CB2	0.767					
CB3	0.879					
CE1		0.864				
CE2		0.917				
CMP1			0.785			
CMP2			0.773			
CMP4			0.748			
CMP5			0.788			
EMP1				0.768		
EMP4				0.736		
EMP5				0.87		
NBI1					0.899	
NBI2					0.829	
NBI3					0.731	
SMP1						0.814
SMP3						0.811
SMP4						0.785
SMP5						0.838

Table 3. R square and Q square of the measurement model.

Construct	Item	Q^2predict	Q^2 (=1-SSE/SSO)	R-square
	CB1	0.388		
CB	CB2	0.267	0.449	0.483
	CB3	0.32		
CE	CE1	0.206	0.226	0.37
	CE2	0.161		
	NBI1	0.399		
NBI	NBI2	0.338	0.503	0.539
	NBI3	0.312		

expansionary policies are more conducive to sustainable development initiatives. It aligns with the research of Huang et al. (2022), who found a similar relationship between contractionary policy and reduced CO2 emissions.

The positive effect of contractionary monetary policy on the circular economy transition could be explained by several factors. Higher interest rates may

Table 4. Path coefficients for the research model

Links	Original sample (O)	Sample mean (M)	Standard deviation (STDEV)	T statistics (|O/STDEV|)	P values
CB -> CE	0.295	0.299	0.076	3.909	0.000
CMP -> CB	0.139	0.152	0.084	1.663	0.006
CMP -> CE	0.158	0.155	0.070	2.250	0.024
CMP -> NBI	0.173	0.181	0.089	1.954	0.001
EMP -> CB	0.115	0.111	0.068	1.691	0.001
EMP -> CE	-0.028	-0.026	0.083	0.341	0.733
EMP -> NBI	0.258	0.257	0.076	3.415	0.001
NBI -> CE	0.299	0.297	0.086	3.466	0.001
SMP -> CB	0.511	0.509	0.072	7.100	0.000
SMP -> CE	-0.035	-0.034	0.084	0.419	0.675
SMP -> NBI	0.402	0.403	0.076	5.275	0.000

encourage more efficient resource use and innovation in sustainable practices, as businesses seek to reduce costs and improve competitiveness. This aligns with the findings of Inglesi-Lotz and Ajmi (2021), who observed that higher costs prompted domestic businesses to explore alternative energy sources. Additionally, reduced consumption levels resulting from tighter monetary policy may lead to lower waste generation and longer product life cycles, key principles of the circular economy (Kirchherr et al., 2017).

All three types of monetary policy (contractionary, expansionary, and stable) show positive and significant impacts on the operations of both commercial banks and non-bank credit institutions. This suggests that financial institutions in Vietnam have developed adaptive strategies to thrive under various monetary policy scenarios. The strongest positive effect is observed for stable monetary policy on commercial banks (0.511***), supporting the findings of Nguyen et al. (2021) that a stable monetary environment allows banks to better plan their operations and manage risks.

The significant and strong correlations between commercial banks (CB), non-bank credit institutions (NBI), and the circular economy (CE) (0.295*** and 0.299*** respectively) highlight the crucial role of financial institutions in facilitating the transition to a circular economy. This aligns with the research of Zhelyazkova (2020), who emphasized the potential of banks to support sustainable practices through targeted lending and financial products.

The indirect effects analysis reveals the mediating roles of commercial banks and non-bank credit institutions in the relationship between monetary policy and the circular economy transition. Positive indirect effects are observed for stable monetary policy through both CB and NBI (0.151*** and 0.120*** respectively), and for expansionary monetary policy through NBI (0.077***) (Tab 5). These findings underscore the importance of financial intermediaries in translating monetary policy into tangible impacts on the circular economy transition, supporting the arguments of Ozili (2021) regarding the potential of non-bank credit institutions to provide alternative funding sources for circular economy projects.

Table 5. Indirect effects for the research model.

Links	Original sample (O)	Sample mean (M)	Standard deviation (STDEV)	T statistics (|O/STDEV|)	P values
EMP -> CB -> CE	0.034	0.033	0.022	1.519	0.129
SMP -> CB -> CE	0.151	0.153	0.045	3.353	0.001
EMP -> NBI -> CE	0.077	0.074	0.027	2.809	0.005
SMP -> NBI -> CE	0.120	0.121	0.044	2.717	0.007
CMP -> NBI -> CE	0.052	0.055	0.033	1.557	0.119
CMP -> CB -> CE	0.041	0.046	0.029	1.427	0.154

Interestingly, no significant mediating effects were found for contractionary monetary policy through financial institutions. This suggests that the positive direct effect of contractionary policy on the circular economy transition may operate through other channels, such as changes in consumer behaviour or business practices, rather than through financial intermediation.

The structural model assessment confirms the statistical significance of most hypothesized relationships, with the exception of H3, H4, H5, H6, and H9. The goodness-of-fit indices (SRMR = 0.035, d_ULS = 0.353, d_G = 0.171, and NFI = 0.92) demonstrate that the structural model fits the data well, providing confidence in the overall findings (Tab 6).

Table 6. Results of structural model testing

Hypothesis	Relationship	Proposed effects	SRW	Results
H1	EMP -> CB	Positive	0.115***	Supported
H2	EMP -> NBI	Positive	0.258***	Supported
H3	EMP -> CE	Positive	-0.028ns	Not Supported
H4	CMP -> CB	Negative	0.139**	Not Supported
H5	CMP -> NBI	Negative	0.173***	Not Supported
H6	CMP -> CE	Negative	0.158**	Not Supported
H7	SMP -> CB	Positive	0.511***	Supported
H8	SMP -> NBI	Positive	0.402***	Supported
H9	SMP -> CE	Positive	-0.035ns	Not Supported
H10a	EMP -> CB -> CE	Mediating	0.034ns	Supported, but not significant
H10b	CMP -> CB -> CE	Mediating	0.041ns	Supported, but not significant
H10c	SMP -> CB -> CE	Mediating	0.151***	Supported
H11a	EMP -> NBI -> CE	Mediating	0.077***	Supported
H11b	CMP -> NBI -> CE	Mediating	0.052ns	Supported, but not significant
H11c	SMP -> NBI -> CE	Mediating	0.120**	Supported

5. Conclusion

This study examined the impact of monetary policy on Vietnam's transition to a circular economy, focusing on the mediating roles of commercial banks and non-bank credit institutions. The findings reveal complex relationships between different monetary policy scenarios and their effects on financial institutions and the circular economy transition. Notably, contractionary monetary policy showed a positive impact on the transition to a circular economy, while stable and expansionary policies had smaller, non-significant effects. The study also highlighted the significant mediating roles of financial institutions in translating monetary policy into tangible impacts on the circular economy transition.

5.1 Theoretical Implications:

The positive impact of contractionary monetary policy on the circular economy transition challenges conventional wisdom and suggests that tighter monetary conditions may actually foster sustainability efforts. This aligns with research by Huang et al. (2022), who found that contractionary policy can lead to reduced CO2 emissions. The mechanism behind this effect may involve encouraging more efficient resource use and spurring innovative sustainable practices as businesses and consumers adapt to a more constrained economic environment. For instance, higher interest rates may incentivize companies to invest in resource-efficient technologies and circular business models to reduce costs and maintain competitiveness (Inglesi-Lotz and Ajmi, 2021). The strong positive effects of stable monetary policy on financial institutions underscore the importance of maintaining a predictable economic environment to support long-term investment in circular economy initiatives. This finding is consistent with research by Nguyen et al. (2021), who emphasize that a stable monetary environment allows banks to better plan their operations and manage risks associated with long-term sustainability projects.

5.2 Managerial Implications:

The findings have managerial implications for policymakers and financial institutions in Vietnam. Policymakers should balance the benefits of contractionary policies with the need for stability to create an optimal environment for circular economy investments. This may require developing more sophisticated, adaptive policy frameworks. Targeted policies are needed to enhance financial institutions' capacity to support the circular economy transition. This could include incentivizing green financial products tailored to circular economy projects, such as preferential lending rates or longer repayment periods for certified initiatives. Finally, the government could explore blended finance mechanisms to de-risk circular economy investments, particularly in nascent sectors or for innovative technologies. This approach, combining public and private capital, could help overcome initial barriers and catalyse private sector participation.

Acknowledgments

This work was supported by the Estonian Ministry of Education and Research through the Centre of Excellence in Circular Economy for Strategic Minerals and Carbon Resources (01.01.2024–31.12.2030, TK228).

References

Benitez, J., Henseler, J., Castillo, A., & Schuberth, F. (2020). How to perform and report an impactful analysis using partial least squares: Guidelines for confirmatory and explanatory IS research. Information & management, 57(2).

Bindseil, U., & Fotia, A. (2021). Introduction to central banking (p. 128). Springer Nature.

Chinedu, U. A., & Ezekwe, U. C. (2021). Impact of Monetary Policy on Commercial Banks' Supply of Agriculture Credit in Nigeria. International Journal of Research, 7(21).

Hai, H. T., Quang, N. D., Thang, N. T., & Nam, N. H. (2020). Circular economy in Vietnam. Circular economy: Global perspective, 423-452.

Hair, J. F., Risher, J. J., Sarstedt, M., & Ringle, C. M. (2019). When to use and how to report the results of PLS-SEM. European business review, 31(1), 2-24.

Harun, S. M., Hassan, M. K., & Zaher, T. S. (2005). Effect of monetary policy on commercial banks across different business conditions. Multinational Finance Journal, 9(1/2), 99-128.

Huang, W., Saydaliev, H. B., Iqbal, W., & Irfan, M. (2022). Measuring the impact of economic policies on Co2 emissions: ways to achieve green economic recovery in the post-COVID-19 era. Climate Change Economics, 13(03).

Hussein, S. A., & Hamdan, A. A. (2020). The role of fiscal and monetary policy in stimulating Circular Economy in Iraq. Aestimum, 125-145.

Inglesi-Lotz, R., & Ajmi, A. N. (2021). The impact of electricity prices and supply on attracting FDI to South Africa. Environmental Science and Pollution Research, 28(22), 28444-28455.

John, E. I. (2019). Effect of macroeconomic variables on stock market performance in Nigeria. Journal of Economics, Management and Trade, 22(6), 1-14.

Karahan, Ö., & Bayır, M. (2022). The effects of monetary policies on foreign direct investment inflows in emerging economies: some policy implications for post-COVID-19. Future Business Journal, 8(1), 39.

Kirchherr, J., Reike, D., & Hekkert, M. (2017). Conceptualizing the circular economy: An analysis of 114 definitions. Resources, conservation and recycling, 127, 221-232.

Mehar, M. A. (2022). Role of monetary policy in economic growth and development: from theory to empirical evidence. Asian Journal of Economics and Banking, 7(1), 99-120.

Nguyen, H. H., Nguyen, T. P., & Tram Tran, A. N. (2022). Impacts of monetary policy transmission on bank performance and risk in the Vietnamese market: Does the Covid-19 pandemic matter?. Cogent Business & Management, 9(1).

Nguyen, H. N., & Nguyen, T. H. (2019). Implementing Circular Economy: International experience and policy implications for Vietnam. VNU Journal of Economics and Business, 35(4).

Nguyen, T. N., Vu, N. H., & Le, H. T. (2017). Impacts of monetary policy on commercial banks' profits: The case of Vietnam. Asian Social Science, 13(8).

Ozili, P. K. (2021). Circular economy, banks, and other financial institutions: what's in it for them?. Circular Economy and Sustainability, 1(3), 787-798.

Schneider, P., Anh, L. H., Wagner, J., Reichenbach, J., & Hebner, A. (2017). Solid waste management in Ho Chi Minh City, Vietnam: moving towards a circular economy?. Sustainability, 9(2).

Tran, C. C., & Nguyen, G. T. H. (2023). The Road to Circular Economy in Vietnam: The Policy Review of Vietnam Green Growth Strategy. In Conference on Contemporary Economic Issues in Asian Countries (pp. 263-280). Singapore: Springer Nature Singapore.

Trung, D., & Quynh, T. N. (2021). Impacts of monetary policy on stability of commercial banks–evidence from Vietnam. International Journal of Management, 10(4), 92-103.

Zhelyazkova, V. (2020). The Role of Banks for the Transition to Circular Economy. In Circular Economy-Recent Advances, New Perspectives and Applications. IntechOpen.

Balance Means Sustainability. We have to Get It

Alexandru Trifu

1. Introduction : Defining the present issue

It is an opportunity, from the beginning, to reveal the meaning of the terms we are dealing in this paper.Generally speaking, *balance* means that the two sides presented/involved are the same that make them equal. *Equilibrium*, on the other hand, means that a process stopped at a certain point or level.In our present case, the analysis is about understanding the term of ***Balance***, *both in the private life (family, households) and work activities*. Furthermore, *both at Microeconomic and Macroeconomic level*.Thus, we are focusing on social and economic life, not on the processes from the perspective of physics, chemistry, biology or other exact sciences.

We consider that another outstanding aspect which must be revealed in this matter regards the economic theory of Leon Walras, French mathematician and economist, important representative of the Marginalism, Mathematics line (1834-1910). More precisely, he is one of the founders of the Lausanne School of Economics.The core idea is the *Theory of Equilibrium*, in fact known as *Walras' Law*, with focus on the outstanding comparison with *the communicating vessels action.*

What is the content and meaning? The Law states that the existence of excess supply in one market must be matched by excess demand in another market so that both factors *are balanced out* (our emphasis) (Kenton, 2023). Thus, an excess demand oversupply for a good is balanced by an excess existing supply overdemand for another good. Finally, the markets have to be in a state of balance, in equilibrium. Beyond the belief of that period in the existence of an "invisible hand action", the action of an open economy means that in the situation of excess demand, the invisible hand, in fact the interactions between Demand and Supply from the market, will raise the prices; when there is excess supply, the same actions will lower prices for consumers to drive markets into a state of balance. From this historical example of Economic Thinking, we should keep in mind the idea of *balance, equilibrium*, but not for all markets or activities. *Balance* is considered an even distribution of weight, enabling someone or something to remain upright and steady (see Justin Timmer, 2018).

Sustainability is also linked, by some authors (Agrogiannis & Agrogiannis, 2015), to *CSR (Corporate Social Responsibility)*, a very important aspect nowadays, leading to the necessity of an even action/care, mainly between the entity/business and the society. Companies, firms are part of the society. This concept, in the light of our paper, needs to express their willingness and intention to return to the society a part of the created added value. These authors underline this idea in the title of their work: *A Critical Review and Evaluation of the Lean Concept and* ***the Corporate Social Responsibility/ Sustainability*** (our emphasis)

Last but not least, we add another aspect that supports this idea of the necessity to act, to develop in even situations, with no discrepancies: *bipolarity*. Mainly at macro and global level, it's about a minimum of two centres of power, even asymmetric ones, whose activities, even if they are in opposition in some respects, converge to a so-called *modus in rebus*, a beneficial line/issue for all the entities involved (Kupchan, 2022). This situation is preferable to the single power centre, or to multiple power centres, which which are not capable to decisively influence the situations. Sustainability is considered a continuous movement towards innovation, progress, by accumulating experiences and abilities (mckinsey.com). To close the circle of understanding the problem, we may say that technology continues to evolve at an unprecedented velocity, while businesses must navigate the delicate balance between stability and innovation in order to achieve optimal performance. This artful balancing act requires a strategic approach to ensure that organizations can stay competitive, meet customer demands, and drive growth (Andersen & MoldStud Research Team, 2024).

2. Methodology

We used qualitative research, mainly based on analyses, data, and forecasts regarding the trends and challenges which may occur. Adding the opinions of various persons, such as academicians, specialists, students and MAs, the range becomes wider, offering the opportunity to foresee the development of countries and the development of the world.

We could have situations where, having a lot of data, the opinions of the leaders/entrepreneurs may mislead the due course of an economy. For example, we refer to the economy of Germany which, at World Economic Forum in Davos in January 2024, it was considered that only take a good cup of coffee is sufficient to recover and to "take off". Looking at the data of the Germany economic indicators, it seemed to be only a matter of time that "the engine of Europe" to recover and to be the support of the future entire EU development. However, reaching the end of 2024, reality reveals great trouble for this economy: the danger of Recession and the problem of the workforce, combined with problem of migration.

Therefore, we consider that a thorough analysis and filtering of the data and information received is required. The opinions of the specialists all over the world are also welcome, even required (because the inter-connections are very sensitive and fast), in order to understand what is happening, and much more, which are the possibilities/lines of action to ensure sustainable development in these troubled times.

3. Towards implementing balanced situations

The analysis is based mainly on the HR factor of production, including also entrepreneurs, the generational structure of the people within firms/corporations, because this complex factor of production is determinant both in households management and businesses management and well functioning. It is a desideratum of the living systems to get a balanced status. More precisely, in human activities, balance has to happen between the household/family environment and the work activities. The magic duplex nowadays is *Work-Life Balance* and the imperative need to achieve it. That's why we often see titles such as *Work-Life Balance* in the News. Also, starting from Adam Smith's idea of building a business based on the entrepreneur's egoism and their desire for more profit, the mechanisms of an open market, mainly the "game" between Demand and Supply, and Competition, reach a flattening of the profit and a balanced situation under the conditions of a non-zero-sum game.

We are advocating here for a complete balance. We believe in the achievement of balance, both at micro and macro level. We observe that everything is in motion and solid scaffolding is needed to go forward. We've presented in the first part of this paper the situation of the German economy. It is not in a thriving situation, but the low development contributes to uncertainty amongst the other EU economies. The last data/information shows that the second EU economy, France pursues Germany in this lack of performance. The manufacturing sector remains in decline in October after production and exports fell at the fastest pace since 2024 (Caciuleanu, 2024). Therefore, the French economy is in a real dive and, we see that is needed for quick and robust measures, through economic policies (political decisions-makers in charge) for a balance between the two major economies of the European Union and the other economies, in order to sustain the European economic and social construction, now, when the challenges are very strong, including geo-strategic ones. It is mandatory to go stop this decline, to recover the situation, especially since the gap with US is significant. (EU economy is quite behind the US).

In the first part of the paper, we mentioned a research paper which describes the marketing and psychological term of Lean linked to *Corporate Social Responsibility/Sustainability*. Lean is still a basic method that analyses the relationships with customers. It is also linked to the action of change and modernisation within firms/corporations (Agrogiannis & Agrogiannis, 2015). In our opinion, it is a method that strengthens the relationships between the firm and its customers and ensures sustainability for the business, as well as satisfaction for the clients. This process of lean means, in its essence, achieving performance and value using some inhibitors, the most important being the first one, *waste*: losing everything is undesirable.

For example, we want to present the stages of implementing this concept/method by pursuing 5 (five) decisive stages (see also Melton, 2005):

1. Stage 1 = *collecting the data* for the respective process or action, seeking the elements which don't add value (that is, waste);
2. Stage 2 = *analysing the data*, using cross-functional teams for the diagnosis, but mainly for the undesirable effects of the ongoing processes;
3. Stage 3 = *designing* ***the change***, which means that a new process can be designed, without the founded waste and with the corrections made;
4. Stage 4 = *making* ***the change,*** that is the new ideas were introduced in the processes, and put in place in such a manner that the team (s) operating the process have the knowledge and ability to monitor the *sustainability of the change* (our emphasis);
5. Stage 5 = ***Measuring the benefits***, meaning to observe the results of the new process, as well as the resulting benefits, on an ongoing basis.

This situation presented above underlines the dominant/hriving trend to progress, changes and benefits or satisfaction.

Another business example of the necessity of considering a balance in the activity is represented either by the Balance of Profit & Losses, an indicator of the solidity and solvability of a firm, or the general Balancing of Profit, People & Customer Experience (see the method presented above). And, also as an implementation, we suggest the use of a powerful tool for any firm/corporation: *The Balanced Scorecard*. This one involves the financial traditional metrics, but adding three new domains/perspectives of evaluation: *Customers, Internal Processes, Organisational Capacity* (www.intrafocus.com/2024/).

The Balanced Scorecard offers a holistic view of the organisational performance, helping businesses align activities with strategic goals. *It's like a well-balanced diet for business* (our emphasis)—sustainable and geared towards medium-term health.

Thus, we consider that the normal, logic and reasonable relationship is the following one:

Balanced activities, balanced decisions/communicating vessels →→
→→ *Sustainability and progress*

The above-presented relationship is possible and is functioning only using as main element *the human factor of production*. And, as a consequence, we have to deal with generational workforce, or generational people preparing to become qualified and skilled workforce, within Higher Education. The next level of our analysis is that of considering the generations at work (and in their spare time). And analysing the principles, ideas and thoughts of the respective generations towards the achievement of the goals of their lives in society and at work.

The focus is on 2 (two) generations: the Millennials and Gen Z, or Zers. In this respect, we'll combine the situation of Higher Education (including my experience) with a survey performed by Deloitte[2] in 2024 about the intentions of the Millennials and Gen Z.

---

2 Deloitte is part of the famous Big 4 in Accounting and Financial Consultancy which ensure a specific market of more than 1 billion euro in 2023. The other 3 (three) being EY (Ernst & Young), PricewaterhouseCoopers (PwC) and KPMG (Klynveld Peat Marwick Goerdeler).

A first remark and difference between the 2 (two) generations is that of the importance of the aspects under analysis. The Millennials consider family, friends and work as being approximately equal, but ahead of any other considerations, such as cultural activities and events, volunteering and so on. On the other hand, Gen Z consider activities such as reading (and the last surveys prove this thing), seeing performances are approximately near the work field as importance (Deloitte Insights2Action, 2024).

Continuing the analysis done by Deloitte, we can observe that approximately 2/3 of both - Gen Z (64 %) and Millennials (66 %) are working for organisations which called back the employees, in either full or part-time capacity.

The situation is presented below under the form of a semi-SWOT Analysis, including the positive impact (that is Strengthen points) and the negative impact (that is Weaknesses). Flexibility is the key-name of the actual trend regarding work within entities.

And, based on this trend, but also on the conceptions of both generations (mostly of the Gen Z), they would like employers to create more part-time jobs, as well as job-sharing options, and to ensure that employees who work part-time have comparable career advancement opportunities to full-time employees. Why these requirements? Because they are looking for *a sound balance* between the home/family environment and the work/office job/tasks. Both generations (Millennials and Gen Z) are very focused on maintaining a positive level of work-life balance. This balance is determining the health

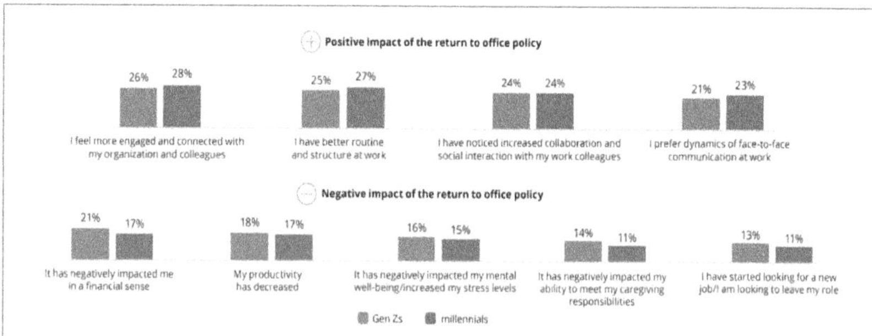

Figure 1. Gen Zs, millennials seek new level for work-life balance

Source : www.action.deloitte.com/insight/3970/ retrieved October 10, 2024.

of mind, health in general and it is a base for getting wealth and, why not?, happiness. This is a milestone for them in choosing the employer and one of the most important traits of the co-workers, or people in general.

In the spirit of this paper, regarding the business environment and the aspirations towards achieving balance within firms/corporations, it is necessary to underline the major role of Generation Y as current performant CEOs, working to implement a good team and work behaviour, especially with Millennials. Employers and teachers from Higher Education expect their staff/students to achieve more and better results, to their benefit and to the benefit of the firm (Wedgood, 2022). And, achieving this balance, that is a sound background, increases the possibilities to improve performance, productivity and innovation.

Thus, Generation Y, with their knowledge, skills, work attitude, career aspirations, and ultimately their knowledge of new technologies, will define the next generation of CEOs in the workplace (Raymond, 2024). This task will be fulfilled especially by the inter-penetration with the characteristics of the Millennials (Marsh, 2018).

In this approach, the lines of actions for Gen Y, crossing the ones of the Millennials, regard the following aspects:

1. **Team-oriented vision,** strengthen by **encouraging cross-generational collaboration,** considered the most important action, leading to balance within firms and thus to achieving the required goals and profit;
2. **Thriving for experiences and technology integration;**
3. ***Promoting work-life integration***, strengthen by ***living a meaningful life towards happiness.***

We consider that this basis of human structure is able to ensure the well-functioning of the firm/corporation. A very significant graphic representation of people' ranking environments, which circulates on WhatsApp, presents the evolution of these environments (in %) during approx. 100 years, from the 1930s until 2024.

If at first the family environment was leading with over 25 percent, followed by the circle of friends, today the online environment is leading with 60% (work and life), the circle of friends is on the second place with about 13 % and on the third place we have the co-workers environment, with about 8 %.

Achieving a healthy work-life balance involves allocating time and energy appropriately between work, family, friends, personal interests, and self-care. It means finding a sustainable rhythm that allows you to excel in your career while also enjoying a fulfilling personal life (see Hreha, 2023). Work-life unit analyzed has the first term work of course, because first of all it is needed to act in a job, in a work, earning money and other advantages and, on this ground, it is possible to sustain the house/family and to get the desired results.

4. Conclusions

From individuals, households, to companies/firms/organisations and nations, we are striving towards balance across all levels. Only through balance we can exist and live as long as we can. Balance is the key to our existence and the support and gate towards the future. By encouraging students, MAs, respectively people/working staff, to ensure or to seek balance between work and life, we will ensure efficiency within the organisations/ higher education institutions.

Achieving balance and sustainability resides mainly in the psychological background: a good mental health-care, which provides general body health, and which can finally lead to happiness and trust in future action. This situation is similar to the following known expression from the urban folklore (and not only): "people feel different when they have an important amount of money in their pockets". Achieving a healthy work-life balance will help you to live a more fulfilled life. Maintaining this balance is an ongoing process that requires self-awareness, communication, and adaptability – but the rewards are well worth the effort, both for all parts involved in, and for the performance of the firm. Therefore, we have to work and fight hard for these achievements. Life must be lived now, with continuous movement and dedication.

References

Agrogiannis, Serafim & Agrogiannis, Christos (2015) *A Critical Review and Evaluation of the Lean Concept and Corporate Social Responsibility/Sustainability*, KTH Royal Institute of Technology, Industrial Engineering and Management, Stockholm, www.cdn.chools.in/LEAN_PDF/ retrieved October 16, 2024.

Andersen, Gary & MoldStud Research Team (2024) *Balancing Stability and Innovation in Site Reliability Engineering*, www.moldstud.com/articles/ retrieved October 15, 2024.

Căciuleanu, Călin (November 4) *A new European power is in dive after Germany* (the original title is in Romanian), www.ziare.com/industrie/ retrieved November 5, 2024.

Hreha, Jason (2023) *Work-Life Balance: Why It's Important And How To Achieve It*, www.personatalent.com/productivity/ retrieved October 29, 2024.

Kenton, Will (2023) *Walras' Law: Definition, History, and View on Supply and Demand*, www.investopedia.com/terms/w/ retrieved October 6, 2024.

Kupchan, Cliff (2022) *Bipolarity is Back: Why It Matters*, The Washington Quarterly, www.eurasiagroup.net/live-post/ retrieved October 1st, 2024.

Marsh, Emily (2018) *The 5 personality traits of Millennials in the workplace*, www.t-three.com/thinking-space/blog/ retrieved October 26, 2024.

Melton, T. (2005) *The Benefits of Lean Factoring: What Lean Thinking Has to Offer the Process Industries*, Chemical Engineering Research and Design, 83, pp. 662-673, https://doi.org/10.1205/cherd.04351, www.mimesolutions.com/PDFs/ retrieved October 28, 2024.

Raymond, Andy (2024) *Nurturing Millennial Leadership as the Next CEO's*, Redline Executive, www.redlineexecutive.com/content-hub/ retrieved October 18, 2024.

Timmer, Justin (2018) *Why balance is key of our existence*, blog, www.justin-timmer.com/ retrieved October 10, 2024.

Wedgood, Joe (2022) *The Importance of Work-Life Balance*, The Happiness Index, www.thehappinessindex.com/blog/ retrieved October 30, 2024.

*** (2024) *Balanced Scorecard Four Perspectives*, www.intrafocus.com/2024/06/ retrieved November 2nd, 2024.

*** (2024) *Gen Zs, millennials seek new level for work-life balance*, Deloitte Insights2Action, www.action.deloitte.com/insight/3970/ retrieved October 10, 2024.

*** *Beyond How to Know*, McKinsey Sustainability, www.mckinsey.com/capabilities/sustainability/ retrieved October 17, 2024.

Integration Opportunities between Hemis and Uzasbo Platforms in Digital Transformation

Turayeva Gulizahro, Khamdamov Shoh-Jakhon, Urazmatov Jonibek, Otabekov Javdod, Mukhammadiyeva Nafisa, Chorshanbayev Umurzak, Yusupov Zulunjon, Zaripov Azamat

1. Introduction

The integration of the HEMIS (Higher Education Management Information System) and UzAsbo (Uzbekistan Information and Accounting Management System) digital platforms offers users numerous advantages, particularly in streamlining processes and enhancing efficiency in education and financial management. HEMIS is an information system designed to manage higher education processes, while UzAsbo, developed by the Information Technology Center of the Ministry of Finance of the Republic of Uzbekistan, automates accounting and reporting for budgetary organizations. The integration of these two systems enables real-time data exchange, improving the correlation between academic processes and financial reporting (Hemis et al., 2024).

This integration provides users with centralized access to essential information, fostering collaboration between educational institutions and budgetary organizations while delivering more user-friendly services. For example, it facilitates the automation of educational processes and financial operations, simplifying tasks such as creating, approving, and monitoring invoices. Additionally, budgetary organizations can automatically retrieve information about employees' educational background, including details about their completed higher education institutions, directly within the system. This not only saves time and resources but also enhances operational efficiency (Law of the Republic of Uzbekistan, n.d., p. 3).

In accordance with the Law of the Republic of Uzbekistan on Accounting, adopted on (1996), state authorities, government agencies, legal entities registered in Uzbekistan, and their branches or representative offices, whether located domestically or abroad, are considered accounting subjects. Their accounting processes cover core and current assets, liabilities, equity, reserves, income, expenses, profits, and losses, all of which are managed and reported through the UzAsbo digital platform A budgetary organization refers to a ministry, state committee, agency, or public organization funded primarily through state budget allocations to fulfill their designated tasks. Recent reforms in the budgetary system have increased the demand for highly qualified specialists capable of implementing international standards in accounting and financial management. Despite this, budgetary organizations face significant staff turnover, often due to insufficient qualifications among personnel. To address this issue, the integration of the HEMIS and UzAsbo systems could provide a robust solution by offering detailed insights into employees' qualifications and educational backgrounds.

The ongoing reforms in Uzbekistan's budgetary system emphasize the importance of managerial accounting, the professional qualifications of personnel, and the growing demand for skilled specialists. These reforms, aligned with international standards, have established a legal foundation for organizing and maintaining accounting records within budgetary organizations. Efficient management of accounting systems ensures the targeted and effective utilization of funds, as well as informed decision-making regarding assets and liabilities. By organizing accounting practices, budgetary organizations can monitor the allocation and sources of funds, forming accurate financial and managerial reports in compliance with established regulations.

2. Literature Review

The origins of accounting trace back to ancient history. The foundational principles of double-entry bookkeeping in commercial enterprises were comprehensively articulated by the renowned Italian mathematician Luca Pacioli (1959) in his seminal work Summa de Arithmetica, Geometria, Proportioni et Proportionalita (Everything About Arithmetic, Geometry, Proportions, and Proportionality). Additionally, the works of I.A. Maslova and B.G. Maslov, particularly Tractatus Particularis de Computis et Scripturis (A Treatise on Accounts and Records), provided detailed insights into the practical application of bookkeeping principles (Maslova & Maslov, 2006). Azamat Abdukarimovich Ostonokulov's book Budget Organizations Formation and Improving Accounting analyzes the role of the UzAsbo system in streamlining accounting processes (Ostonokulov, 2020). 6. Xudoyarov & Komilov

(2022) in his article increasing Automation of Accounting, highlights the automation features of the UzAsbo system and its contribution to modern financial management. Similarly, work of the Bell (1971) on the Hybrid Events Monitoring Instrument (HEMI) explores computer-based monitoring and data analysis capabilities within the HEMIS system.

The textbook Accounting Principles by Mukhametov et al. (2023) proposes leveraging the UzAsbo platform for recording accounting operations in budgetary organizations. Furthermore, our article Opportunities to Use Financial Services – 1C Program discusses contemporary approaches to management accounting and their applications in modern financial systems (Turayeva et al.,2022; Turayeva 2023).

The integration of AI technologies within these platforms can enhance customer experience through personalized recommendations and AI-powered customer support. This includes the use of chatbots for instant customer service and predictive analytics to anticipate customer needs (Salimov et al., 2023; Mamatkulov et al., 2023). Automation of routine tasks through AI can free up human resources to focus on more complex customer interactions, thereby improving operational efficiency. This includes automating data analysis and customer segmentation to provide more targeted services (Mamadiyorov et al., 2023).

Utilizing big data and machine learning, these platforms can provide deep insights into consumer behavior, allowing businesses to offer more engaging and personalized shopping experiences. This includes real-time data analysis for more accurate marketing campaigns and improved customer loyalty (Makhmudov et al., 2023; Kurbonov et al., 2023). The integration of augmented reality (AR) and virtual reality (VR) can offer immersive shopping experiences, enhancing customer engagement and satisfaction. These technologies can be used to visualize products in a real-world context, thereby improving the decision-making process for customers (Khamdamov et al., 2024; Bobakulov et al., 2024).

While the integration of Hemis and Uzasbo platforms offers numerous benefits, it is important to consider potential challenges such as data privacy concerns and the high costs associated with implementing advanced technologies. Businesses must ensure robust data security measures and consider the financial implications of such integrations. Additionally, maintaining a balance between automation and human interaction is crucial to preserving the personal touch in customer service (Bobamuratova et al., 2019; Bobamuratov et al., 2020).

According to data from the Ministry of Finance of the Republic of Uzbekistan, over 26,000 budgetary organizations currently utilize the UzAsbo software suite, which was introduced in 2011 to facilitate accounting processes in budgetary organizations. This widespread adoption underscores the system's critical role in automating financial and managerial accounting.

3. Data and Methodology

The Ministry of Finance of the Republic of Uzbekistan launched the "UzASBO" software suite in 2011 to manage the accounting processes of budgetary organizations. This system was developed in compliance with the requirements of the Guidelines on Accounting in Budgetary Organizations, registered with the Ministry of Justice of the Republic of Uzbekistan on December 22, 2010, under registration number 2169. Notably, UzASBO was one of the first software solutions in the country built on web-based technology. The software is provided free of charge, and as of today, it is utilized by over 26,000 organizations nationwide (See fig.1).

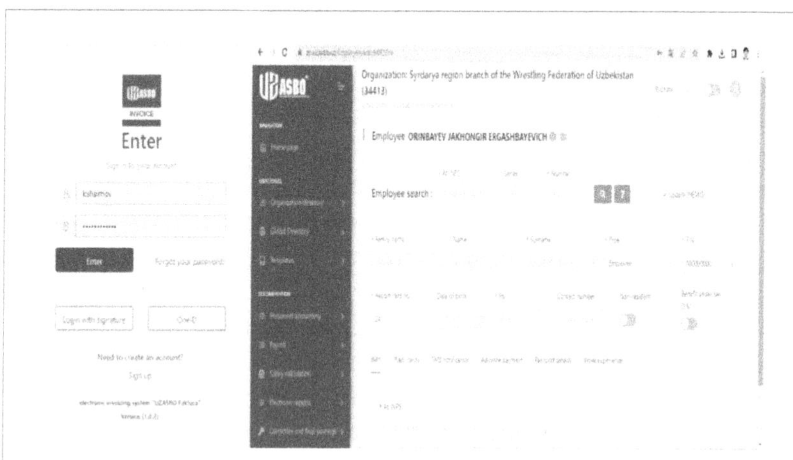

Figure 1. Launching the USASBO Mode and the Recruitment Programme.

The operational framework of UzASBO (Figure 1) is designed specifically for the accounting practices of budgetary organizations. It ensures a structured and efficient workflow that aligns with the intended purposes of budgetary accounting. In this system, various stakeholders, including accountants, financial managers, treasurers, and other users, interact under the "Enterprise Mode," optimizing financial management and reporting processes.

Employees' higher education institutions must be registered within the HEMIS system, which contains detailed information about the accreditation status and academic programs of each institution. Additionally, a specialized module within the UzASBO software suite has been developed to calculate salaries and equivalent payments for employees of budgetary organizations.

Currently, budgetary organizations submit salary and related payment expenses electronically to the relevant institutions. When assigning employees to the system, their educational credentials are automatically displayed in the UzASBO platform. This integration highlights the advancing digitalization of the economy, reflecting the increasing sophistication and efficiency of Uzbekistan's financial and administrative systems.

4. Results and Discussion

The UzAsbo platform is designed to manage the digital invoicing system in Uzbekistan, aimed at simplifying economic processes through the automation of B2G, B2B, and B2C transactions. It also contributes to enhancing collaboration between the public and private sectors during the digital transformation process. In 2012, a specialized module was developed within the UzAsbo system to calculate salaries and equivalent payments for employees of budgetary organizations. The integration of this system with the Hemis platform introduces several innovations.

The Hemis platform automates the core activities of higher education institutions, providing electronic educational services to administrative staff, professors, and students. It acts as an information bridge between higher education institutions and the Ministry of Higher and Secondary Special Education, supporting the digitalization of management systems. Developed by Daminova et al (2022) the Hemis platform has a comprehensive set of interfaces for integrating various systems, allowing users to monitor and manage real-time data from multiple sources.

A mobile application for students has been developed to manage higher education processes using the Hemis platform. Through this application, students can access various educational-related information, including, ranking notebooks, transcripts, academic performance indicators, control schedules and electronic resources for subjects.

Additionally, graduating students can download their diploma and supplementary diploma documents through the Hemis system. This development reduces the reliance on human intervention in the educational process and facilitates easier access to necessary documents. Furthermore, it allows staff and students to download required files at their convenience and from any location. The UzAsbo platform, designed for accounting and reporting in budgetary organizations, ensures that all operations, indicators, and norms—such as hourly wage rates—are regularly updated in accordance with current legislation. The Hemis system, which manages higher education processes, includes modules for "Administrative Management," "Educational Processes," "Scientific Activities," and "Financial Management."As the digital economy evolves, accounting software is advancing, offering more conveniences and opportunities. Innovations are being continuously integrated into the employee recruitment module, further enhancing the platform's capabilities.

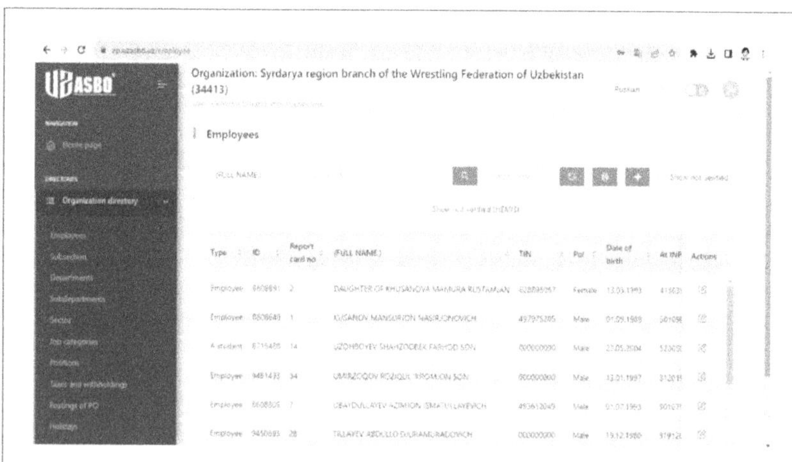

Figure 2. Employee Assignment Process in the UzASBO System

In particular, in the process of attaching an employee to the programme 'UzASBO', when budgetary enterprises hire employees, now under the sign the representation of where the previous education of the employee was received is attached to the programme. It is essential that an employee's higher education specialization is displayed in the HEMIS system. This ensures that the employee's position aligns with the required qualifications and meets the necessary competency standards. Specifically, when hiring employees for budgetary organizations, the process of assigning an employee to the UzASBO system now includes an integration feature, allowing the system to display the institution where the employee completed their education. Previously, this feature was not available in the UzASBO system.

Currently, budget organizations have the capability to electronically obtain statements of their personal treasury accounts from the UzASBO software suite. Additionally, the software allows payment orders to be submitted to treasury authorities and financial reports to higher-level organizations and finance agencies, all with a digital signature, nsuring that these documents are fully verified and submitted in electronic format.

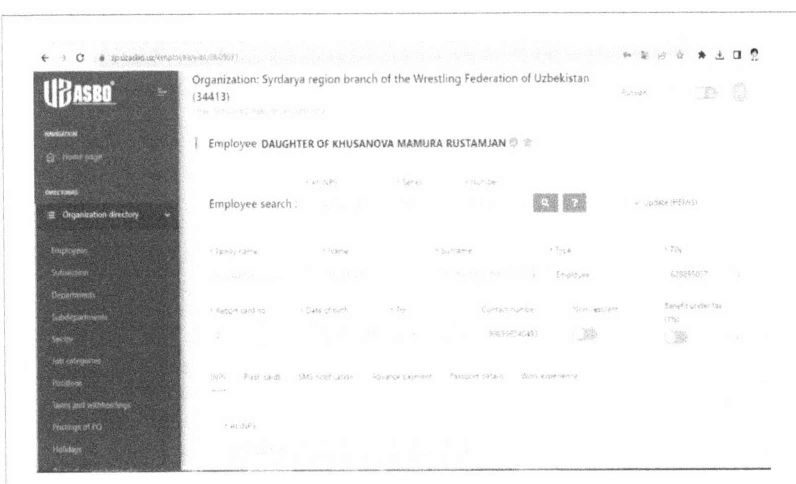

Figure 3. Linking the UzASBO System with the HEMIS Platform to Verify Employees' Previous Education.

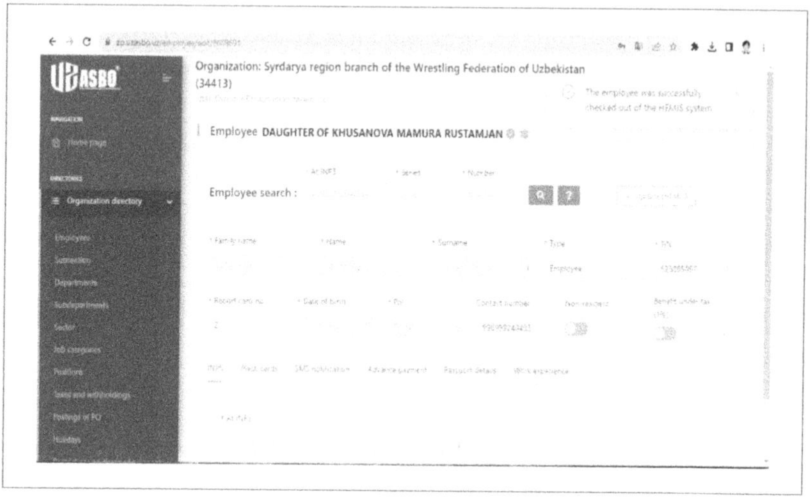

Figure 4: Successful verification of an employee on the HEMIS programme in the UZASBO department.

When verifying an employee's higher education degree and specialization in the HEMIS system, this information is integrated and displayed in the

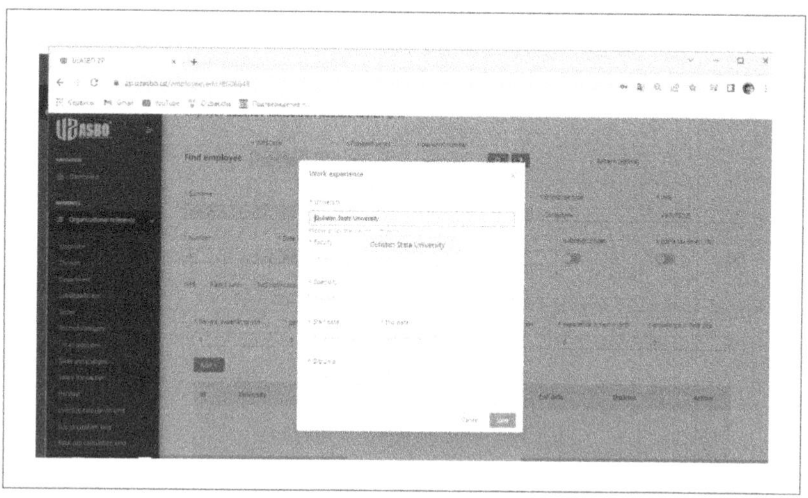

Figure 5. Verification of Employee's Higher Education Degree in the UzASBO System Using HEMIS.

UzASBO system. If the employee's education is validated in HEMIS, it serves as the primary document confirming their qualifications and experience.

The integration of the HEMIS and UzASBO platforms enables the creation of new innovative digital solutions. This contributes to the development of the digital economy and provides users with the opportunity to apply modern technologies. In our view, when verifying an employee's higher education and specialization through the HEMIS system in the UzASBO platform, it holds significant importance. This process plays a key role in enhancing employees' qualifications and ensuring their productivity in the workplace.

5. Conclusion

HEMIS is an Information System for managing higher education processes. This system includes modules for "Administrative Management," "Educational Process," "Scientific Activities," and "Financial Management." The integration of the HEMIS system with other programs brings various innovations. By automating the core activities of higher education institutions, the HEMIS system provides electronic educational services to administrative staff, professors, and students. The HEMIS information system is an information bridge between higher education institutions and the Ministry of Higher and Secondary Special Education and plays a decisive role in the digitization of the management system. In particular, when budget organizations hire employees, the process of attaching an employee to the UzASBO system now includes the possibility to indicate where they completed their previous education under the cap symbol. This system was not previously available in the UzASBO program. Moreover, employees can now download their diplomas and appendices electronically, which is a clear indicator of the rapid growth of digitization in management systems.

The integration between the UzASBO and HEMIS programs is of great importance in determining employees' qualifications and educational levels. To further enhance this process, the following suggestions and recommendations can be made:

Database Updates and Expansion: It is essential to regularly update and maintain the list of higher education institutions registered in the HEMIS system, along with their accreditation status.

Streamlining the Verification Process: Implementing an automated data exchange system between the UzASBO and HEMIS programs would facilitate quick and efficient verification of employees' higher education degrees.

Education and Professional Development Programs: Organizing post-graduate training courses for employees to support their professional growth.

Monitoring and Evaluation: Regularly assessing employees' educational levels and work performance based on the data retrieved from the HEMIS system will improve the overall efficiency of the system.

By implementing the above suggestions and recommendations, the process of verifying employees' educational qualifications through the HEMIS system in the UzASBO program can be made more effective. This will contribute to the improvement of employees' qualifications and educational levels, thereby enhancing their productivity in the workplace.

References

Bell, T. E. (1971). HEMI (Hybrid Events Monitoring Instrument): Performance analysis goals and measurement tools. Report prepared for NASA and the USAF. RAND Project R-584-NASA/PR.

Bobakulov, T., Alimardonov, I., Ishnazarov, A., Salikhodjaeva, U., & Kurbonova, N. N. (2024). Strategies for macroeconomic stability: Financial insights from Uzbekistan's economic policies. Innovations and Contemporary Trends in Business & Economics, 377–390.

Bobamuratova, D. T., Boymuradov, S. A., Polvanov, R. B., Ibragimov, D. D., & Kayumov, I. N. (2019). A complex approach to the health improvement of patients with jaw fractures, with introduction of adequate nutrition, therapeutic physical exercise and comprehensive oral hygiene. International Journal of Pharmaceutical Research, 11(3), 1224–1237.

Bobomuratov, T. A., Rasulov, S. K., Dzhurayeva, Z. A., Samadov, A. A., & Kuliyev, O. A. (2020). Nutritional support with products of fruit origin in prevention of micronutrients deficiency in the "mother-child" system. International Journal of Pharmaceutical Research, 12(4), 450–456.

Daminova, K. M., Gafforova, S., & Sayfutdinova, N. (2022). Evaluation of prodromal stage biomarkers in Parkinson's disease and their role in disease progression using modern digital technologies. In Proceedings of the 6th

International Conference on Future Networks & Distributed Systems (pp. 408–411).

Hemis, M., Bettahar, A., Singh, C. B., Bruneau, D., & Jayas, D. S. (2009). An experimental study of wheat drying in thin layer and mathematical simulation of a fixed-bed convective dryer. Drying Technology, 27(10), 1142-1151.

Khamdamov, S.-J. R., Usmanov, A. S., Sayfullayev, S. N., Xamitova, M. S., & Adkhamjonov, S. B. (2024). The influence of the main rate of the central bank on GDP growth in Uzbekistan and the transition to international financial reporting. Advanced Series in Management, 33A, 107–112.

Kurbonov, K., Makhmudov, S., Mamadiyorov, Z., Samadov, A., & Djalilov, F. (2023). The impact of digital technologies on economic growth in the example of Central Asian and European countries. ACM International Conference Proceeding Series, 403–409.

Law of the Republic of Uzbekistan No. 279-I dated 30.08.1996 on Accounting

Law of the Republic of Uzbekistan. (n.d.). On the Budget System, Article 3.

Makhmudov, S., Khamdamov, S.-J., Karlibaeva, R., Khujamurodov, A., & Imomov, K. (2023). The impact of digital technologies on the labor market of Uzbekistan. ACM International Conference Proceeding Series, 260–267.

Mamadiyorov, Z., Sultanova, N., Makhmudov, S., Mirpulatova, L., & Jumayev, A. (2023). The impact of digitalization on microfinance services in Uzbekistan. ACM International Conference Proceeding Series, 453–463.

Mamatkulov, B., Khamdamov, S.-J., Togayniyazov, S., Quldoshev, Q., & Qarshiev, D. (2023). Predicting future living standards in Uzbekistan: Utilizing econometric analysis. ACM International Conference Proceeding Series, 425–431.

Maslova, I. A., & Maslov, B. G. (2006). History of Accounting. Accounting in Budgetary and Non-Profit Organizations, 19.

Mukhametov, A., Abduvohidov, A., Berdiyev, G., & Turayeva, G. (2023). Accounting. Tashkent: World of Economics.

Ostonokulov, A. A. (2020). Budget Organizations Formation and Improving Accounting. International Journal of Advanced Science and Technology, 29(8s), 11–16.

Pacioli, L. (1959). Summa de arithmetica, geometria, proportioni e proportionalitá: Distinctio IX-Tractatus XI (tractatus de computis et scripturis). (No Title).

Salimov, B., Kholikova, R., Khamdamov, S.-J., Nosirova, N., & Akhmedova, D. (2023). Strategies for integrating digitalization in leveraging regional economic and scientific expertise for the innovative growth of small and medium enterprises. ACM International Conference Proceeding Series, 483–490.

Turayeva, G. (2023). The significance of sustainability of grain production in the consumer basket. E3S Web of Conferences, 420, 01019.

Turayeva, G., Mukhametov, A., Abduvohidov, A., & Berdiyev, G. (2022). Opportunities to use financial services – "1 C PROGRAM." In Proceedings of the 6th International Conference on Future Networks & Distributed Systems (pp. 556–561).

Xudoyarov, R., & Komilov, H. I. (2022). Increasing automation of accounting documentation. Journal of Academic Research and Trends in Educational Sciences, 1(12), 294–303. Retrieved from http://www.ijournal.uz/index.php/jartes/article/view/389.

The Resilience and Transformation of the Tourism Industry: An Empirical Review

Stavros G. Efthimiou

1. Introduction

More importantly, tourism brings together the interests of people from various parts of the world. Tourism encourages economic development and is also a way of interchanging cultures. The industry is one of the fastest-growing sectors in the world and has considerable contributions it makes to gross domestic products, employs labors in large numbers, and encourages understanding between cultures(Cheer, & Lew, 2017). Unfortunately, this sprawling growth has, on another side, made tourism rather easily targetable and prone to crises-everything from natural calamities to political uprising, and the more recent COVID-19 pandemic that saw travel crippled at an unprecedented scale and exposed the very basic fragility and resilience of this sector.

The pandemic was thus a critical juncture in tourism, where stakeholders were forced to confront some of the longer-term vulnerabilities while also accelerating the uptake of transformative technologies and sustainable practices. Conventionally, the industry has shown its resilience by adapting to global shocks, but the protracted nature of the COVID-19 crisis indeed required deeper structural transformation. This transformation has also been witnessed across various other dimensions: innovation in the digital environment, sustainable development of tourism, and crisis management strategy coupled with organizational resilience(Lin et al., 2024). Indeed, most destinations in the world show clear signs of paths to recovery through embracing technology, integrating models of sustainable tourism development, and resilience against the risk of future disruptions. In this respect, digital transformation has been a valuable enabler for rapid adaptation of the tourism operator. It has opened new models toward virtual engagement, personalized services, and operational efficiency. Technologies like artificial intelligence, mobile applications, and virtual reality reshape customer experience and thus allow industries to stay in contact with consumers even in times of travel restrictions(Sharma et al., 2024). Meanwhile, the pandemic increased awareness of the need for sustainable tourism that minimizes environmental impacts while promoting responsible travel. This turn toward sustainability is not solely a reaction to environmental concerns but reflects a shift in consumer values that give precedence to ethics and responsible choices regarding tourism. Today, resilience in tourism has evolved from merely recovery to a proactive attitude toward enterprise survival through adaptability, innovation, and cross-industry collaboration(Sharma et al., 2024;Lin et al., 2024). The following article debates internal and external strategies of resilience development-from organizational adaptability to supportive or hindering policies-and shares important lessons on how industry has learned to regrow and prosper in times of turbulence. The research applies both case studies and resilience frameworks for an in-depth analysis of the key factors that account for the ability of tourism to adapt and change. The sector reaches a fork in the road, being challenged by restoring the dual demands of traveler confidence while building out a more resilient and sustainable model for the future. This article adds to the body of knowledge on tourism resilience and transformation by providing an all-encompassing platform on innovations, policies, and practices reshaping the sector considering unprecedented global disruptions. This paper, through both theoretical and real-life examples, compiles ways in which tourism is changing roles in a world increasingly demanding adaptability, sustainability, and resilience.

2. Digital Transformation as a Resilience Strategy

In this regard, digital transformation has become a major cornerstone of resilience in the tourism industry and, most recently, a response to the challenges posed by the COVID-19 pandemic. Forcing tourism operators to be innovative, digital technologies rapidly became key instruments necessary for keeping up with consumers, operation management, and support for business continuity amidst travel restrictions and social distancing(Mihalic, 2024;Barykin et al., 2021).

2.1 The Role of Digital Platforms and Virtual Experiences

Accordingly, digital platforms change the tourist's interaction with destinations insofar as travelers have increased capabilities to explore, engage, and virtually "visit" places when physical travel cannot be managed. For example, VR and AR have been adopted by museums, cultural sites, and natural attractions for immersive experiences that can be offered online(Gutierriz et al., 2023). These virtual offerings keep the travelers engaged in periods of restricted movement and further create new revenue opportunities by reaching a wider global audience who may not contemplate physical travel in the near future (Richards, 2020;Lew et al., 2020). Equally important are the mobile applications, which have turned into a source of necessary information for tourists, an avenue for easy booking, and customized tours. Indeed, digital means like these provide for modern consumer needs for convenience and customization, allowing travelers to become increasingly independent in cities they visit and with more confidence. By integrating AI-driven recommendation systems, sites like booking websites and travel apps will offer more personalized experiences, increasing customer satisfaction and loyalty (Higham & Miller, 2018).

2.2 Data Analytics and Customer Insights

Big data and analytics have enabled tourism enterprises to understand and respond to the changing behavior of consumers. From customer data, businesses can anticipate trends and needs and cater for services that would exactly meet the changing preferences of travelers(Sharma et al., 2024). Data analytics tools yield information on anything from peak travel times to preferences in experiences, allowing operators to refine their offering for an enhanced visitor experience. Analytics on customer feedback and behavior, for instance, will permit dynamic pricing of the company's offerings, effective marketing campaigns, and resource allocation consistent with maximizing resilience(Pappas et al., 2023; Barykin et al., 2021).

2.3 Blockchain Technology and Enhanced Security

Yet another innovation is blockchain technology, which furthers resilience on this point. It addresses two major problems: security and transparency of transactions. While digital transactions continue to grow, so do the concerns regarding data privacy and integrity in transactions. That has made blockchain a very enticing solution. It offers secure, decentralized transactions that could foster more trust among consumers. For example, the blockchain-based travel insurance and ticketing platforms have empowered travelers to book and pay in a way that is very secure and verifiable. That is quite reassuring during uncertain times(Higham & Miller, 2018).

2.4 Challenges to Digital Transformation in Tourism

On the other hand, adopting digital transformation in tourism has also brought some challenges. This could be infrastructural, especially in quite remote or underdeveloped areas where such digital progress may not have taken root, and specific digital literacy among regions and demographic groups equally affects the level at which some consumers and operators can engage in the potential of such digital solutions. Another important concern is data privacy: for businesses collecting and processing high-volume volumes of customer data, the way ahead passes through strict protection legislation as well as keeping the trust of the customers. Overcoming these bottlenecks will be important to any successful, inclusive digital transformation that benefits all the stakeholders(Barykin et al., 2021;Lew et al., 2020).

2.5 Case Studies in Digital Resilience

Different destinations and companies have already shown that digital transformation is an effective strategy for resilience. For instance, with the COVID-19 pandemic, many tour operators and destination management organizations shifted onto virtual tour platforms able to offer real-time, live experiences with local guides as a means of sustaining interest and supporting local economies(Sharma et al., 2024). In Germany, the region of Franconia had to adjust its business models to add in digital touchpoints for tourists, letting them have safe but engaging travel despite restrictions on travel (Pappas et al., 2023). These examples illustrate how digital innovation not only supports immediate recovery but also contributes to long-term resilience by enabling flexibility and responsiveness to future disruptions.

3. Impact of COVID-19 as a Catalyst for Change

The COVID-19 pandemic has been the moment of truth for the tourism sector, being not only a crisis but also a strong catalyst for transformation. The sudden arrival caused global lockdowns, bringing tourism activity to an abrupt standstill and driving losses of unprecedented nature. According to estimates, during the high point of the pandemic in 2020, international tourist arrivals collapsed by as much as 98%, down from forecasts-underlining once more the vulnerability of this industry to external shocks(Chen, 2022;Kyriakakis & Tzirakis, 2020). While the immediate impact was serious, COVID-19 also exposed some structural weaknesses in traditional models of tourism, especially in those depending on large numbers of international visitors, crowded tourist attractions, and revenues from seasonal activities(Efthimiou, 2024).

3.1 Acceleration of Digital and Remote Services

COVID-19 accelerated this need for digital solutions that allow tourism businesses to operate during restricted conditions. That is, the offering of services remotely, virtual tours being carried out, customer service online, and booking platforms online will be of paramount importance for sustaining engagement with customers(Lin et al., 2024). Virtual tour formats were an example for many tour operators, enabling the provision of immersion into the experiences and maintaining brand visibility to keep consumer interest. The shift showed that digital solutions were not about adapting to the crisis; rather, they proved to be some of the long-term resiliency strategies which could extend the market reach beyond traditional boundaries (Pappas et al., 2023;Lew et al., 2020).

3.2 Shifts in Consumer Preferences and Travel Patterns

The pandemic replaced old consumer priorities with new ones: health, safety, and flexibility. Many consumers now avoid traditional high-density tourist areas in favor of less crowded or local or nature-based destinations(Orindaru et al., 2021). In addition, demand for flexible booking policies that permit last-minute changes has shot up. This suggests that tourism companies must be able to offer flexible services. This has forced the industry to reimagine how it will engage with travelers on health and hygiene and personal, low-touch experiences (Kyriakakis & Tzirakis, 2020; Lew et al., 2020).

3.3 Government Policies and Support Mechanisms

In response to the pandemic, many different governments implemented support mechanisms that would enable the tourism industry to survive the crisis. Examples of policy intervention include financial aid packages, wage subsidies, and targeted support for small and medium-scale enterprises in tourism. For regions whose economies depend so much on tourism, such as Greece and Thailand, their governments have also increased campaigns on domestic tourism, replacing lost international visitors and boosting hometown economies. These interventions underlined the importance of a proactive policy framework for tourism resilience and called for government-business collaboration in times of crisis (Chen, 2022;Kyriakakis & Tzirakis, 2020).

3.4 Innovation in Crisis Management

Thus, the pandemic made sure that effective tourism crisis management had to be in place. Many organizations put into practice an effective crisis management plan involving contingency strategy, flexible workforce arrangements, and agile marketing campaigns. In addition, hospitality businesses developed rapid-response protocols to immediately adjust business operations with a view to sustaining cash flow and preserving employee welfare(Vinh et al., 2022). For example, some hotels granted packages on staycations for the locals or even changed their areas to workstations for those working from home, tapping into new market needs while sustaining their revenue flows. This ability to innovate with speed during the crisis gave further impetus to the importance of organizational agility and the importance of enterprise continuously developing capabilities in crisis management(Pappas et al., 2023; Richards, 2020).

4. The Role of Transformational Leadership and Workforce Resilience

In such a dynamic and crisis-prone industry as tourism, strong leadership is the most critical issue that can adapt to any kind of situation. The transformational type of leadership, which has been characterized by vision, aptitude for adaptation, and the capacity to motivate teams, has become fundamental in leading through crises and developing a resilient tourism workforce(Orindaru et al., 2021). The COVID-19 pandemic has underlined the need for leaders who could rapidly adjust to an ever-changing context, while making critical decisions with uncertainty surrounding them and creating supportive conditions for staff who had been facing exceptional challenges(Vinh et al., 2022).

4.1 Transformational Leadership in Times of Crisis

Transformational leaders in the tourism industry instill confidence and commitment in the people of an organization to see them through times of crisis. Unlike the traditional commanding leadership style, transformational leadership concerns itself with long-term vision and shared goals, teams empowered for innovation and adaptability. During the pandemic, leaders who had this kind of approach often guided their organizations through hardship with purpose and inclusion. It means that hospitality and tourism management leaders adopted flexibility policies, encouraged innovation during service delivery, and communicated openly to instill confidence among team members (Maslova et al., 2020;Richards, 2020). A turning-point activity source characterizing the role of transformational leadership is in identifying crises as opportunities. Disruptions, therefore, create greater chances for leaders to turn out and apply proactive strategies that prepare their teams for a future challenge. It is this mindset that transforms organizations from a reactive to an anticipatory approach with continuous upgrading of their resilience in the face of changing industry requirements and a potential crisis(Pappas et al., 2023;Gutierriz et al., 2023).

4.2 Building Workforce Resilience

Resilient organizations need resilient workforces. Tourism is a labour-intensive industry with frontline workers catering to customers and playing a vital role in determining the quality of the experience. In the pandemic situation, all these employees of the tourism industry underwent immense stress and uncertainty regarding job insecurity, health concerns, putting up with new safety protocols, and operational changes. The process, therefore, should be approached through training, support systems, and policies that focus on the wellbeing of employees to build a resilient workforce(Lew et al., 2020).

4.3 Role of Organizational Culture in Supporting Resilience

The culture of an organization intrinsically plays a major role in workforce resiliency. In this respect, a culture that promotes collaboration, innovation, and adaptability would significantly impact how the tourism organization responds to the crisis(Orindaru et al., 2021). For instance, firms that optimize knowledge sharing and employee feedback are well-placed to exploit the gains of insights that could improve the quality of the response during crises and services. An inclusive culture, which takes care of employees and their contributions, helps individuals to be involved and committed-a prelude to resilience during times of difficulty(Barykin et al., 2021;Maslova et al., 2020). Successful implementation suggests that a resilient organization will always be communicative from inside, with transparent leadership and flexible policy to the point where employees can feel supported even in quite uncertain conditions. It is by making an investment in such supportive cultures that tourism businesses get loyal workforces, agile, and creative responses to change.

4.4 Innovative Workforce Management Practices

The work-from-home and hybrid model has been one huge transition in response to the pandemic, which influences every other policy on workforce management across various industries, inclusive of tourism. While tourism by nature requires physical interaction, many organizations have embraced hybrid models where physical presence may not be necessary(Vinh et al., 2022). Remote options, flexible schedules, and virtual training also opened new avenues for support without sacrificing productivity. Apart from working remotely, the ups and downs of demand have seen some organizations pursue flexible staffing models. For example, seasonal and gig work arrangements mean that tourism companies can ramp up during peaks or an unexpected change in demand. This has its own set of financial benefits for employers and employees-to give companies a chance to minimize fixed labor costs and, in turn, give employees greater autonomy and flexibility(Richards, 2020).

4.5 The Importance of Leadership Development Programs

The training and development of leadership cadres are very instrumental in building a pipeline of future leaders that will help the organization maintain resilience. Investment in training and mentorship helps tourism organizations build leaders who can manage crises and drive innovation(Gutierriz et al., 2023). Several successful organizations operate leadership training programs focused on crisis management, empathy, and communication skills-very critical to leading such a complex, evolving industry as tourism. Programs such as these also include adaptive strategies on how to approach scenario planning and decision-making under uncertainty. This will better position the future leaders of an organization to respond with aplomb when confronted with unexpected setbacks. Instilling such capabilities ensures that leadership becomes well entrenched within the organization and helps to contribute toward its resilience in the longer term(Higham & Miller, 2018;Maslova et al., 2020).

5. Revisiting Business Models for Enhanced Resilience

The crises that have plagued tourism of late have imposed an expanding need for adaptability from businesses, to become something different from what they have always been. Indeed, many players within tourism-like hotels, tour operators, and DMOs-have been rethinking strategies in a bid to ensure these actors are more resilient to future disruptions and changes in consumer preferences(Pongtanalert & Assarut, 2022). This section looks at evolving business models in tourism, discussing diversification, localization, and the development of adaptive frameworks which allow the long-term build-up of resilience.

5.1 Diversification of Revenue Streams

Recent crises within tourism have imposed an increasing demand for businesses to agilely turn themselves into something other than what they have been. The players in tourism-hotels, tour operators, and DMOs-have, in fact, been recalibrating their strategies with an appetite to better position the actors for enhanced resiliency against future disruptions and shifts in consumer preferences. This chapter discusses evolving business models in tourism that involve diversification, localization, and development of adaptive frameworks that enable the long-term build-up of resilience(Kyriakakis & Tzirakis, 2020;Barykin et al., 2021). Diversification also involves creating non-traditional services that will complement the core business. An example might be when a hotel contracts with local wellness providers to develop special retreats in wellness or may work with nearby cultural sites to offer special tours. By developing diversified offerings, tourism businesses can appeal to disparate market segments, decrease dependence on a specific demographic of traveler, and enjoy more predictable year-round revenues(Higham & Miller, 2018;Maslova et al., 2020).

5.2 Emphasis on Localized and Community-Based Tourism

However, as global travel continues to open and close their tides, local tourism has gained momentum as one of the resilient models. It is for this reason that destinations and business enterprises are increasingly diverting attention to initiatives in local tourism that attract residents and domestic travelers(-Gutierriz et al., 2023). Another model is community-based tourism, which blends culture, traditions, and landscapes of the locals into the visitor experience and thus creates economic benefits in the local communities while providing an authentic experience to visitors. By developing close links with local stakeholders, tourism businesses can play their full part in regional development and establish tourism products less susceptible to disruption in travel(Richards, 2020; Lew et al., 2020). Meanwhile, local tourism has become prominent among the resilient models, since travel restrictions around the world have seesawed in an unending process. Many destinations and private sector businesses have shifted their attention to local tourism initiatives that attract residents and domestic travelers(Sharma et al., 2024). This is community-based tourism, where local culture, traditions, and landscapes are threaded into the tourist experience, hence assuring economic benefits to the local communities while offering a comprehensive authentic experience for visitors. By developing close relationships with regional stakeholders, tourism businesses are helping create a more regional focus of development and a tourism product less subject to disruption when international travel is disrupted(Barykin et al., 2021).

5.3 Flexible Pricing and Service Structures

Variable demand has made flexible price and service models increasingly important. Varied pricing models include dynamic pricing according to demand and seasonal adjustments, enabling operators to entice customers in off-peak periods and maximizing revenues when demand is high (Pongtanalert & Assarut, 2022). Several operators implemented flexible booking policies, such as free cancellations or postponements, considering the situation of travelers with uncertainties regarding health restrictions or plans for travel (Richards, 2020). All these flexible approaches extend into service offerings, too. For instance, hotels might offer anything from short staycations to extended-stay options, affording visitors choices that suit their changing needs. Airlines and tour operators also moved toward more flexible loyalty programs and refund policies to earn the trust and loyalty of customers in uncertain times. This agility in pricing and services allows for business responses to ever-changing market conditions with added value aimed at attracting an even bigger audience(Pappas et al., 2023;Lew et al., 2020).

5.4 Adoption of Agile Business Frameworks

First, the concept of "agility" has permeated the tourism sector, considering that businesses feel the urgent need to adapt to crises. An agile business framework promotes speed toward any change due to the flexible planning of iterative development and decentralized decision-making(Pongtanalert & Assarut, 2022). In this regard, tourism companies could make a quick turn toward adjusting their marketing strategies, reallocate resources, or develop and launch new products to meet the needs that have just cropped up(Gutierriz et al., 2023). For example, some tour operators have innovated their operations and shifted their focus to small-group and private tours; not only do these operations meet current health concerns, but they also cater to the higher demand for personalized experiences that characterize travelers nowadays. Similarly, agile frameworks enable faster rollouts of new digital solutions, such as virtual tours, enhancements in online booking, and contactless services, that have become imperative in the post-COVID-19 world. By embracing agility in their operations, tourism businesses can respond effectively to challenges or opportunities as they arise(Maslova et al., 2020;Barykin et al., 2021).

5.5 Collaboration and Strategic Partnerships

Strategic partnerships or collaborations work in many tourism businesses, as their usage tried to expand services or obtain resources. It thus allows tourism businesses to create alternative services by sharing resources and reaching a bigger market in collaboration with other organizations in tourism and non-tourism companies(Gutierriz et al., 2023). For instance, some hotels have been able to partner with digital platforms to enable virtual experiences among its guests, while others have been creating special packages of tourism combined with local companies in food, culture, and hospitality. Furthermore, collaborations build resilience by enabling businesses to draw on the strengths of others, reduce operational expenses, and share market intelligence. For example, in regions adopting "destination resilience" strategies, tourism businesses, public agencies, and other sectors collaborate on joint recovery plans, pool marketing resources, and communicate support for others through economic hard times. This greatly strengthens the whole ecosystem, developing resilience and adaptability against future disruptions (Lew et al., 2020).

6. Conclusion

Equally promising, the path of resilience and transformation for tourism has its challenges. Recent global disruptions have forced industry to review traditional models, adapt to rapidly changing circumstances, and realign its practices to wider goals of sustainability and inclusivity. The tourism sector is now moving toward a more robust and adaptive future with appropriate inclusions of digital innovation, sustainable practices, and proactive crisis preparedness(Sharma et al., 2024; Gutierriz et al., 2023). This paper has discussed critical factors that make the tourism industry resilient-from transformational leadership to flexibility in business models and from obstacles to pervasive transformation. In conclusion, lessons learnt from recent crises have underlined the imperative for an inclusive collaborative approach, where actors across the tourism ecosystem come together with one end in mind: to craft an industry that will be ready to prosper in a rapidly changing world. Although these challenges range from financial constraints to regulatory hurdles, strategies of resiliency adopted by enlightened tourism businesses and destinations provide a guidepost for success(Sharma et al., 2024). It is only through continuous innovation, building strong relationships, and alignment with sustainable development goals that the tourism sector can recover from recent adverse impacts and even reinvent itself in ways that yield positive impacts for travelers, communities, and the natural environment alike. Ahead, the way is clearer-continuous commitment to flexibility, cooperation, and responsible growth. Guided by such tenets, tourism would be strategically placed to cope with the uncertainties of the future and to make full contribution to global resilience, sustainability, and social welfare. Finally, for future studies research directions would be the comparative recording and presentation of the adaptation of the tourism sector to various shocks as well as the changes in tourists' choices due to the new forms of tourism that have resulted from the whole transformation of the tourism sector and the economy development.

References

Barykin, S. E., De la Poza, E., Khalid, B., Kapustina, I. V., Kalinina, O. V., & Iqbal, K. M. (2021). Tourism Industry: Digital Transformation. In B. Khan, M. Kuofie, & S. Suman (Eds.), *Handbook of Research on Future Opportunities for Technology Management Education* (pp. 414-434). IGI Global Scientific Publishing. https://doi.org/10.4018/978-1-7998-8327-2.ch025

Chen, T.-S. (2022). The Transformation Opportunity of Tour ism after COVID-19. *Theoretical Economics Letters*, 12, 916-923. https://doi.org/10.4236/tel.2022.123049

Cheer, J. & Lew, A. (2017). Sustainable tourism development: Towards resilience in tourism. *Interaction*. 45, 10-15.

Efthimiou, S. (2024) The Adaptation of Tourism Industry and COVID-19. *Theoretical Economics Letters*, 14, 2081-2094. https://doi.org/10.4236/tel.2024.146103

Gutierriz, I., Ferreira, J. J., & Fernandes, P. O. (2023). Digital transformation and the new combinations in tourism: A systematic literature review. *Tourism and Hospitality Research*, *0*(0). https://doi.org/10.1177/14673584231198414

Higham, J., & Miller, G. (2017). Transforming societies and transforming tourism: sustainable tourism in times of change. *Journal of Sustainable Tourism*, *26*(1), 1–8. https://doi.org/10.1080/09669582.2018.1407519

Kyriakakis, A., & Tzirakis, D. (2020). Tourism in the post Covid-19 era: An opportunity for expansion of the tourism season; The case of Crete. *HAPSc Policy Briefs Series*, 1(1), 227–237. https://doi.org/10.12681/hapscpbs.24970

Lew, A. A., Cheer, J. M., Haywood, M., Brouder, P., & Salazar, N. B. (2020). Visions of travel and tourism after the global COVID-19 transformation of 2020. *Tourism Geographies*, *22*(3), 455–466. https://doi.org/10.1080/14616688.2020.1770326

Lin, CY., Li, C., Mahmood, S., Guo, F., & Qian, Z. (2024). Integrating Culture and Tourism: A Resilient Scale for Digital Transformation Innovation. *J Knowl Econ*. https://doi.org/10.1007/s13132-024-01753-y

Maslova, T., Pletneva, N., Althonayan, A., & Tarasova, E., & Krasnov, A. (2020). Transformation of consumer behavior in the tourism industry in the conditions of digital economy. *IOP Conference Series: Materials Science and Engineering*. 940. 012070. 10.1088/1757-899X/940/1/012070.

Mihalic, T. (2024). Trends in Sustainable Tourism Paradigm: Resilience and Adaptation. *Sustainability*, *16*(17), 7838. https://doi.org/10.3390/su16177838

Orindaru, A., Popescu, M. -F., Alexoaei, A. P., Caescu, S. -C., Florescu, M. S., & Orzan, A. -O. (2021). Tourism in a Post-COVID-19 Era: Sustainable Strategies for Industry's Recovery. *Sustainability*, *13*(12), 6781. https://doi.org/10.3390/su13126781

Pappas, N., Michopoulou, E., & Farmaki, A. (2023). Tourism Innovation and Resilience during Uncertainty. *Tourism Planning & Development*, *20*(2), 135–137. https://doi.org/10.1080/21568316.2023.2176647

Pongtanalert, K., & Assarut, N. (2022). Entrepreneur Mindset, Social Capital and Adaptive Capacity for Tourism SME Resilience and Transformation during the COVID-19 Pandemic. *Sustainability*, *14*(19), 12675. https://doi.org/10.3390/su141912675

Richards, G. (2020). Tourism in challenging times: Resilience or creativity? *Tourism Today*, 19, 8-15.

Sharma, S., Dogra, J., & Khan, S. (2024). Destination resilience and transformations in the tourism sector: new tendencies in destination development and management. *Tourism & Management Studies*, *20*(4), 17-26. https://doi.org/10.18089/tms.20240402

Vinh, N. Q., Hien, L. M., & Do, Q. H. (2022). The Relationship between Transformation Leadership, Job Satisfaction and Employee Motivation in the Tourism Industry. *Administrative Sciences*, *12*(4), 161. https://doi.org/10.3390/admsci12040161

List of Contributers

Lothar Huschbeck, Danubius University Slovak Republic

Torsten Huschbeck, University of Economics in Bratislava Dolnozemská cesta 1, 852 35 Bratislava, Slovakia

Kerstin Knees, European Institute of Management, Malta

Yuliia Fedorova, Comenius University Bratislava, Slovakia; N.V. Karazin Kharkiv National University, Kharkiv, Ukraine,

Maija Zakrizevska-Belogrudova, RISEBA University of Applied Sciences, Faculty of Business and Economic, Latvia

Anna Pilková, Comenius University Bratislava, Slovakia

Juraj Mikuš, Comenius University Bratislava, Slovakia

Constantinos Challoumis, N.K.U.A. (National and Kapodistrian University of Athens), Athens, Greece

Bruna Costa, ISCAP, Polytechnic of Porto, Porto, Portugal

Humberto Nuno Rito Ribeiro, GOVCOPP, ESTGA, University of Aveiro, Portugal

Amélia Cristina Ferreira da Silva, CEOS.PP, Polytechnic of Porto, Porto, Portugal

Albertina Paula Monteiro, CEOS.PP, Polytechnic of Porto, Porto, Portugal

Anabela Martins da Silva, University of Minho, School of Economics and Management, Braga, Portugal

Ione Aparecida Silva Cruz, State University of Feira de Santana, Feira de Santana, Brasil

Augusto Simões, GOVCOPP, University of Aveiro, Portugal

Ubaldo Comite, Giustino Fortunato University, Benevento, Italy

Alba M. Gallo, Giustino Fortunato University, Italy

Maria Carmela Serluca, Giustino Fortunato University, Benevento, Italy

Eveny Ciurleo, University of Calabria, Cosenza, Italy

Pedro Fernandes da Anunciação, Setúbal Polytechnic University, Setúbal, Portugal

Cláudia Ramião, Setúbal Polytechnic University, Setúbal, Portugal

Francisco José Videira Cachatra, Setúbal Polytechnic University, Setúbal, Portugal

Mariana dos Santos Miranda, Setúbal Polytechnic University, Setúbal, Portugal

Francisco Joaquim Madeira Esteves, Setúbal Polytechnic University, Setúbal, Portugal

José Luís Riço Bucho de Matos, Setúbal Polytechnic University, Setúbal, Portugal

Hélder Miguel da Graça Alexandre, Setúbal Polytechnic University, Setúbal, Portugal

Cátia Susana Claro Chasqueira, INDEG-ISCTE, Executive Education, Lisboa, Portugal

Fernando Miguel do Couto Gonçalves, Setúbal Polytechnic University, Setúbal, Portugal

Antonio Juan Briones Peñalver, Polytechnic University of Cartagena, Cartagena, Spain

Israel Seriki Akinadewo, University of Ilesa, Department of Accounting, Ilesa, Osun State, Nigeria

Oluyinka Isaiah Oluwagbade, Afe Babalola University, Department of Accounting, Ado-Ekiti, Ekiti State, Nigeria

Jeremiah Oreoluwa Akinadewo, Afe Babalola University, Department of Accounting, Ado-Ekiti, Ekiti State, Nigeria.

Temitayo Oluwatimilehin Abe, Afe Babalola University, Department of Accounting, Ado-Ekiti, Ekiti State, Nigeria

Omobolanle Ogundele, University of Johannesburg, Department of Commercial Accounting, South Africa

Ifeoluwa Mary Adebiyi, Afe Babalola University, Department of Accounting, Ado-Ekiti, Ekiti State, Nigeria

Dildora Karimova, Institute of Macroeconomic and Regional Studies (IMRS), Tashkent, Uzbekistan

Diydor Berdiklichev, Institute for the Development of Social Protection, Tashkent, Uzbekistan

Dostonbek Djalilov, Institute of Macroeconomic and Regional Studies (IMRS), Tashkent, Uzbekistan

Margarita Bogdanova, Tsenov Academy of Economics, Svishtov, Bulgaria

Evelina Parashkevova, Tsenov Academy of Economics, Svishtov, Bulgaria

Marusya Smokova, Tsenov Academy of Economics, Svishtov, Bulgaria

Mariela Stoyanova, Tsenov Academy of Economics, Svishtov, Bulgaria

Nikolay Ninov, Tsenov Academy of Economics, Svishtov, Bulgaria

Farah Hamila, Montpellier Research on Management MRM (University of Montpellier, France) and University of Tunis, Higher Institute of Management of Tunis, GEF2A-Lab, Le Bardo (Tunisia)

Ouidad Yousfi, Montpellier Research on Management MRM (University of Montpellier, France)

Olga Andreeva, Rostov State University of Economics, Rostov-on-Don, Russia

Venelin Terziev, Black Sea Institute, Bourgas, Bulgaria

Marin Marinov, Georgi Benkovski Bulgarian Air Force Academy, Dolna Mitropolia, Bulgaria

Marin Georgiev, Black Sea Institute, Bourgas, Bulgaria

Simeon Simeonov, University Hospital Kaneff, Rousse, Bulgaria

Hamit Can, Trakya University, Edirne, Türkiye

Meltem Okur Dinçsoy, Trakya University, Edirne, Türkiye

Marusya Lyubcheva, Black Sea Institute, Bourgas, Bulgaria

Lukas Vartiak, Comenius University in Bratislava, Bratislava, Slovakia

Jana Majerova, AMBIS University, Prague, Czechia

Dijana Vuković, University of North, Varaždin, Croatia

Tanja Grmuša, Zagreb School of Business, Zagreb, Croatia

Neven Mađetko, Doctorate Paneuropean Studies, Eisenstadt, Austria

Yael Livneh, Kinneret Academic College on the Sea of Galilee, Israel

Yael Dubinsky, Kinneret Academic College on the Sea of Galilee, Israel

Sabina Nedkova, Prof. d-r Asen Zlatarov University, Burgas, Bulgaria

Plamena Atansova, Prof. d-r Asen Zlatarov University, Burgas, Bulgaria

Ngoc-Tien Hoang, Duy Tan University, Da Nang City, Vietnam

Nguyen-Quynh-Nhu Ngo, Ton Duc Thang University, Ho Chi Minh City, Vietnam

Tarlan Ahmadov, Tallinn University of Technology, Tallinn, Estonia

Wolfgang Gerstlberger, Tallinn University of Technology, Tallinn, Estonia

Alexandru Trifu, "Petre Andrei" University of Iasi, Romania

Turayeva Gulizahro, Gulistan State University, Guliston, Uzbekistan

Khamdamov Shoh-Jakhon, Mamun University, Khiva city, Uzbekistan, Alfraganus University, Tashkent, Uzbekistan Tashkent State University of Economics, Uzbekistan,

Urazmatov Jonibek, Gulistan State University, Guliston, Uzbekistan

Otabekov Javdod, Gulistan State University, Guliston, Uzbekistan

Mukhammadiyeva Nafisa, Tashkent State University of Economics, Uzbekistan

Chorshanbayev Umurzak, Gulistan State University, Guliston, Uzbekistan

Yusupov Zulunjon, Tashkent State Agrarian University, Uzbekistan

Zaripov Azamat, Gulistan State University, Guliston, Uzbekistan

Stavros G. Efthimiou, University of Piraeus, Greece

www.ingramcontent.com/pod-product-compliance
Ingram Content Group UK Ltd.
Pitfield, Milton Keynes, MK11 3LW, UK
UKHW021847100926
8556IPUK00020B/1102

9 783631 935934